NATIVE
AMERICANS
IN EARLY PHOTOGRAPHS

NATIVE AMERICANS
IN EARLY PHOTOGRAPHS

TOM ROBOTHAM

THUNDER BAY
P·R·E·S·S

Published by
Thunder Bay Press
5880 Oberlin Drive, Suite 400
San Diego, California 92121

Produced by
Brompton Books Corporation
15 Sherwood Place
Greenwich, Connecticut 06830

Native Americans in early photographs / [compiled by] Tom
Robotham.
     p.   cm.
   ISBN 1-57145-008-4 : $14.98
     1. Indians of North America—Portraits.   2. Indians of
North America—Pictorial works.   I. Robotham, Tom.
E89.N39   1994
970.004'97—dc20   94-12504
                                             CIP

Printed in China

Page 1:
Crying to the Spirits
Edward S. Curtis
The Library of Congress

Page 2:
Little Big Mouth and Lodge, 1867-74
William S. Soule
*Smithsonian Institution National Anthropological Archives,
Bureau of American Ethnology Collection*

Right:
**Panoramic View of Buffalo Bill and His Indians
on the Beach in Front of the Cliff House, San
Francisco, California** (detail), n.d.
Photographer unknown
*National Museum of the American Indian,
Smithsonian Institution*

Contents

Introduction 6

The Early Years 18

Cultural Transitions 40

Sunset of a Dying Race 80

List of Photographs 112

INTRODUCTION

Europeans and white Americans since Columbus's time have been fascinated by Native Americans. Columbus himself wrote that the "Indios" he encountered were "so tractable and peaceable that . . . there is not in the world a better nation. They love their neighbors as themselves, and their discourse is ever sweet and gentle, and accompanied with a smile." The kindness and generosity of the natives did not, however, deter Columbus from enslaving them or from initiating policies that would ultimately result in genocide. But even as the subsequent expansion of white America decimated Native American tribes, many whites remained intrigued with their exotic ways and "primitive" nature.

It wasn't long before this intense curiosity sparked a demand for pictures and written descriptions of the natives. By the middle of the seventeenth century, narratives of captivity among Indians had become extremely popular. Indeed, according to literary historian Richard VanDer Beets, first editions of these narratives are now quite rare because they were "literally read to pieces." English artists, meanwhile, had begun to paint pictures of Native Americans as early as the sixteenth century. Many of these paintings, such as the famous portrait of Pocahontas wearing English clothing as a sign of her "civilized" status, were done in England during visits by Indians.

Artists continued to paint pictures of Native Americans throughout the eighteenth century. Some of the images painted during this period reflected the romantic notion of the "Noble Red Man," while others depicted Indians as treacherous savages. Either way, however, they were indicative of white America's continuing tendency to mythologize the people whose continent they shared.

In the early decades of the nineteenth century, this tendency began to change. Increasingly, as settlers rolled back the frontier and forced tribesmen from their homelands, educated whites desired a deeper understanding of Native American culture. And, ironically, the more white America established its dominance over the native population, the more this curiosity grew. By 1813, when the great Shawnee leader Tecumseh was killed and Indian resistance to white settlement in the Midwest was effectively eliminated, this quest for understanding began to take on a sense of urgency.

"In the room of fear," observed a New York minister in 1819, "should now arise a sentiment of pity. The red men are melting, to borrow the expressive metaphor of one of their most celebrated warriors – 'like snow before the sun'; and we should be anxious, before it is too late, to copy the evanescent features of their character, and to perpetuate them on the page of history."

Among those who shared the minister's view was Colonel

Thomas L. McKenney. Serving under four presidents as the Government's chief liaison with Indian tribes, McKenney was instrumental in bringing Indian peace delegations to Washington. Although these efforts did little to improve the plight of Native Americans, they did facilitate the creation of an Indian archive, a collection of items "relating to our aborigines. . . ." In 1821, when a group of Midwestern chiefs visited Washington for a series of treaty negotiations, McKenney commissioned the artist Charles Bird King to paint their portraits. Over the next two decades, King continued to paint Indian delegations to Washington. But beginning in 1832, his efforts were overshadowed by those of George Catlin.

Like McKenney and others, Catlin was motivated by an acute desire to depict "the living manners, customs, and character of an interesting race of people, who are rapidly passing away from the face of the earth . . . [and] who have no historians or biographers of their own to portray with fidelity their native looks and history." Catlin, moreover, wanted white

Left:
Two Young Girls, Laguna Pueblo, New Mexico, 1902
Dr. Philip M. Jones
Phoebe Hearst Museum of Anthropology, University of California, Berkeley

Above:
Keokuk on Horseback, 1835
George Catlin
Oil on canvas mounted on aluminum
National Museum of American Art, Smithsonian Institution

Right:
Three Yankton Dakota, 1857
Julian Vannerson and Samuel Cohner of the James E. McClees Studio
Smithsonian Institution, National Anthropological Archives

Americans to look at Indians anew – to forget the stories they had heard of "Indian barbarities" and rid themselves of "deadly prejudices . . . against this most unfortunate and most abused part of the race of his fellow man."

With this mission in mind, Catlin embarked in 1832 on a 2,000-mile journey up the Missouri River. During the trip, he encountered the Lakota, Blackfoot, Ojibwa, and Crow. Over the next five years he visited the Sauk and Fox, Winnebago, Seminole, and many other tribes, and by 1837, he had done more than 500 oils as well as countless drawings.

Throughout the middle decades of the century numerous artists followed in Catlin's footsteps in search of whatever "wild" Indians still remained beyond the frontier. And while few of these men were as dedicated or open-minded as Catlin had been, they managed to create a plethora of images to satisfy white America's curiosity.

Meanwhile, a new science of image-making was taking the world by storm. In 1839, six years after Catlin's first journey up the Missouri River, the Frenchman Louis Jacques Mande

Daguerre had announced a process whereby an image could be captured on a silver-coated copper plate. Like all new inventions, the daguerreotype had its drawbacks. For one thing, exposure times ran anywhere from 8 to 30 minutes. As a result, capturing any kind of image was difficult, and creating photographs that truly reflected everyday life was virtually impossible. In spite of these problems, the invention of photography astounded the American public, and people quickly recognized its potential.

With the introduction of the wet-plate process in 1851, pioneers of the art form began to develop that potential. Taking photographs remained an expensive, cumbersome, and time-consuming process for many years afterward. But early photographers somehow managed to overcome the problems, and images of interesting subjects – including Indians – soon began to multiply.

Ironically, as new images of Native Americans spread across the land, the Native American population continued to decline. Between 1822 and 1842, the so-called Five Civilized

Left:
Indian Encampment, Shoshone Village, 1860
Albert Bierstadt
Oil on millboard, 24 × 19¾"
The New-York Historical Society, New York City

Right:
Shoshone Warrior, 1859
Albert Bierstadt
Stereograph
The Kansas State Historical Society, Topeka, Kansas

Tribes of the East had been herded from their homes in the Southeast to Indian Territory west of the Mississippi. The winter of 1838-39 had been especially tragic, as the Cherokee were forced to march westward on what came to be known as the Trail of Tears. Before their journey was over, nearly 25 percent of the group had died.

Over the next two decades, the Indians of the Far West also felt the full impact of white civilization as discoveries of gold in California and Colorado encouraged hordes of adventurers to stake claims on Native American lands. In the process, the natives were cut off from food sources, exposed to deadly diseases their immune systems could not fight, and killed in battles. Thus in California alone, the Native American population declined from 150,000 before the first gold rush to 35,000 in 1860.

Realizing that the spread of white civilization could not be stopped, many Indian leaders agreed to treaty negotiations in Washington. Most of the earliest photographs of Native Americans were taken during these delegation visits.

The first systematic effort to photograph Native Americans, as Paula Richardson Fleming and Judith Luskey have noted in their book *The North American Indians in Early Photographs* (1986), was made during 1858 when approximately 90 delegates from 13 tribes traveled to Washington, D.C. Most of the photographs were individual portraits taken by Julian Vannerson and Samuel Cohner of the James E. McClees Studio. McClees quickly promoted these images as another important attempt to preserve a dying culture.

"To the student of our history, as additions to libraries and historical collections, and as mementoes of the race of red men, now rapidly fading away, this series is of great value and interest," wrote McClees.

In addition to the work of McClees and his associates, Mathew Brady, operating out of a new Washington studio managed by Alexander Gardner, took a number of group portraits of the visiting Native Americans.

During the early 1860s, some photographers also traveled west of the Mississippi in search of Indian subjects. Joel Emmons Whitney, for instance, took numerous photographs of Sioux warriors after they had been imprisoned at Fort Snelling, Minnesota, for their role in the 1862 Sioux uprising.

Another photographer of frontier Indians during this period was the painter Albert Bierstadt. Traveling into the Rockies with a road-improvement expedition in 1859, Bierstadt gathered a wealth of material for the massive landscape paintings that would soon make him famous. In addition to sketches, this material included a series of stereographs – two photographic images of a single scene that were mounted in a device called a stereoscope to create the illusion of three dimensions. Many of these photographs featured Indians or Indian-related subjects, foreshadowing Bierstadt's lifelong interest in Native American culture.

The efforts of men like Bierstadt and Whitney notwithstanding, most of the important photography during the early 1860s took place on the battlefields and in the campgrounds of the Civil War. Indeed, these battlefields and encampments served as training grounds for many photographers who would later travel to the frontier and achieve significant recognition for their pictures of Indians. Moreover, as historian Lee Clark Mitchell has noted in his book *Witnesses to a Vanishing America: The Nineteenth-Century Response* (1982), wartime improvements transformed the camera into an efficient and reliable instrument. Thus when the war ended, efforts to photograph the Indian resumed with more fervor than ever.

In 1867, numerous Native American delegations again traveled to Washington, and several leading photographers were on hand to record the historic occasion. Gardner, who had taken some of the finest pictures of the Civil War, was

Left:
Alexander Gardner (left) with
his horse-drawn photographic
supply wagon while traveling
west to photograph Native
Americans in their homelands.
(*The Bettmann Archive, New
York*)

Below:
**Indian Village Near Fort
Laramie**, 1868
Alexander Gardner
The Missouri Historical Society

among those who photographed this new round of treaty negotiations, and he again demonstrated his superior skills. As
Fleming has noted, his group portraits were posed to record the
most significant aspects of each occasion. In many cases, therefore, they are of greater historical interest than the individual
portraits taken by Vannerson and others.

Gardner, moreover, was not content to wait for Indians to
come to Washington. In 1868, he secured the job as Government photographer for another round of treaty negotiations –
this time at Fort Laramie, Wyoming. He returned with a number of important photographs documenting meetings with the
Cheyenne, Arapaho, and Oglala Dakota tribes.

Other post-war photographers were even more adventurous.
Indeed, some of the most interesting photographs taken in the
late 1860s and 1870s were shot by photographers who had
traveled to the frontier – either privately or with government
surveys – in an effort to capture images of Indians in their
homelands. Three of the most important survey photographers
of this period were Timothy O'Sullivan, William Henry Jackson, and John K. Hillers.

O'Sullivan, who had apprenticed under Mathew Brady and
later worked for Alexander Gardner, was the chief photographer on two post-war surveys. The first, which began in
1867 under the direction of geologist Clarence King, afforded
O'Sullivan excellent opportunities to explore Nevada and
Utah. But it was with the second survey, which started four
years later under the leadership of Army Lieutenant George
Montague Wheeler, that O'Sullivan took his most important

photographs. The year 1873 was especially productive, as O'Sullivan encountered numerous Apache, Hopi, Zuni, and Navaho tribesmen. By 1875, he had produced more than 2,500 prints.

John K. Hillers, meanwhile, was doing equally extensive work with the Powell Survey, led by Illinois geologist John Wesley Powell. After serving in the Civil War, Powell began exploring the mountains of Colorado in search of areas of geological interest. In the process, he came in contact with many Utes and became interested in their culture. When presented with the opportunity to lead a Government-sponsored geological survey, Powell saw it as a chance to pursue that interest.

Hillers initially joined Powell as boatsman for a trip down the Colorado River in 1869, but after apprenticing under Powell's original photographer, E. O. Beaman, he became the survey's principal photographer in 1872. By the time the survey ended in 1879, he had taken some 3,000 images.

Another important post-war survey was that of Ferdinand Vandeveer Hayden, which began in 1870 and included William Henry Jackson as its chief photographer. Jackson, who was born in 1843, worked for a short time as a freelance photographer in Nebraska following the war, and it was there that he first photographed Native Americans. By 1877, having worked with the Hayden survey and on his own, he had compiled an extensive catalogue.

While Hillers, Jackson, and O'Sullivan were traveling with the surveys, other photographers went west on their own. William Soule, for example, had opened a studio in Pennsylvania shortly after the war. But when it burned down a year or so later, he departed for Fort Dodge and quickly began taking pictures of Indians in the region.

Another important frontier photographer was William S. Prettyman, a Delaware native who traveled west in 1879. After serving for a short time as an apprentice to Kansas photo-

grapher I. H. Bonsall, Prettyman opened his studio, and for the next 20 years he photographed numerous tribes on the Southern Plains and in Indian Territory.

The collection of photographs amassed by all of these men is impressive when taken at face value, but it is all the more noteworthy when we consider the difficulties they had to overcome. Not the least of these difficulties was a lack of cooperation on the part of some of their subjects.

Jackson recalled how, during one stay among Uncompahgre Utes at the Pine Agency in Colorado, none of the Indians would pose. "Nor would they permit me to use my camera from a distance," he wrote. "When I set up my tripod on a commanding elevation to take a panoramic picture of the whole village, three or four Indians detailed to get in my way. As I attempted to focus, one of them would snatch the cloth from my head, or toss a blanket over the camera. . . .

"After three or four days of organized opposition I gave up. I had got a few really superb negatives, and I could foresee only mounting trouble if I persisted."

Top: An engraving of Charles M. Bell photographing Ponca and Sioux delegates, September 10, 1881; from *Leslie's Illustrated Weekly.* (*Smithsonian Institution, National Anthropological Archives*)

Left:
Sauk and Fox in Front of Elm Bark Lodge, 1880s
William S. Prettyman
Smithsonian Institution, National Anthropological Archives

Toward the end of his stay, Jackson wrote, "a chief who rejoiced in the name of Billy visited me . . . to give me friendly warning: this country, regardless of treaties and boundaries, was owned by his people; it would be dangerous for us to proceed farther with my strange box of bad medicine; hunters who had destroyed their game had died; other men who had dug in the ground and took away their gold had also died; it would be better for me and my companions to return at once the way we had come."

The Utes' reaction was not unusual. Some Indians called photographers "Shadow Catchers," believing that photographs captured part of the subject's spirit. But fear of photography was by no means universal among Indians. John Mix Stanley, the official artist and photographer on an 1853 railroad-survey expedition, had an experience quite different from the one Jackson described. According to Isaac I. Stevens, the survey leader, the Blackfoot tribesmen photographed by Stanley were "delighted and astonished to see their likeness produced by direct action of the sun. They worship the sun, and they [believed] Mr. Stanley was inspired by their divinity, and thus became in their eyes a great medicine man." (Unfortunately, none of Stanley's photographs survived.)

As time went on, other Native Americans came to see photography as a means of documenting their plight. Un-

fortunately, many photographers of the late 1800s were not interested in straight documentation. White Americans wanted to see Indians as they imagined them to be, not as they actually were. Thus Hillers and other photographers sometimes posed and dressed subjects in a certain way in order to heighten the viewer's sense of romance. That the Indians they encountered were often far removed from the wild tribesmen of American mythology did not seem to bother the image-makers. Moreover, while photographers often selected subjects based on ethnographic value, they were at other times motivated by commercial considerations.

Not all photographs of the late nineteenth century were sentimental delusions, however. Some photographers staunchly resisted the trend toward romanticism in favor of a documentary approach. As a result, they captured on film a wide range of images, from ritual dances to harsh scenes of reservation life. The latter scenes were not, perhaps, what white Americans wanted to see, but they reflected the physical reality of Indian life.

Indian reservations, in a general sense, had been around for some time, but after the Civil War they were located on smaller, more remote desert or semi-desert tracts. Throughout the 1870s and early 1880s, meanwhile, professional hunters slaughtered an estimated 30 million head of buffalo, leaving the Plains Indians without a major source of food and clothing. Adding insult to injury, the white hunters often took nothing more than the tongues and the hides, leaving the carcasses to rot in the sun. The tribesmen, who used every part of the animal for food, clothing, and other purposes, were horrified.

Initially, when they were sent to reservations, Indians tried to retain a sense of their traditional life in a variety of ways. Some, for instance, insisted on being given live government cattle instead of meat so they could preserve the ritual of the hunt despite the decimation of the buffalo herds. Thomas J. Morgan, Commissioner of Indian Affairs in the late 1800s, eventually put an end to such imitation-hunts because he felt they were unsanitary and served to "nourish brutal instincts." Increasingly, whites forced Indians to give up all sorts of traditional practices on the premise that they encouraged savagery.

The emergence of schools designed to teach Indian children the ways of white culture reflected this belief. Established at the urging of a small but dedicated group of white Christians who called themselves "Friends of the Indian," the schools initially appeared to be successful. Photographs, often taken by the teachers themselves, reinforced this impression by showing Native American children wearing neatly pressed uniforms and working diligently at some "civilized" task. Ultimately, however, whites had to acknowledge that the experiments in education had failed. The failure was due, in large part, to the fact that Indians simply did not want to become part of white culture. Indeed, when looking at these photographs today, one is struck by the sadness in the children's eyes.

A related attempt to assimilate Native Americans into white culture was made in 1887 when Congress passed the Dawes Severalty Act, also known as the General Allotment Act. The legislation converted all Indian tribal lands to private property, under the assumption that adherence to the "communistic" ways of tribal culture was preventing the Indian from becoming "civilized." Each Indian family was allotted 160 acres, while individuals were granted 80 acres. But the act had two stipulations. First, the Government would hold each allotment in trust for 25 years to give Indians time to learn to protect their property from shrewd whites who might try to take it away. Second, since the allotments, in total, did not equal the total acreage controlled by Indians at the time, all "surplus" lands were opened up for white settlement. Consequently, while the act was ostensibly passed for the good of the Native Americans, it resulted in even more land being taken away from them.

Left:
Indians Killing and Cutting Up a Steer, 1868
Alexander Gardner
The Missouri Historical Society

Below:
A Group of Omaha Boys, Carlisle Indian School, Pennsylvania, c. 1880
J. N. Choate
The National Archives

Gathering up the Dead at the Battle Field at Wounded Knee S.D.
Copyrighted by the North Western PhotoCo
Jan 18 1891 Chadron Neb

While Native Americans held some 138 million acres in 1887, they had less than 78 million by 1900, and by 1934, when the act was reversed and tribes were again recognized, their land holdings had dwindled to 48 million acres.

The Government's unrelenting attempts to destroy Native American culture and its unwillingness to ensure decent living conditions on reservations brought a variety of responses from tribal groups in the last decades of the nineteenth century. Some fled to Mexico or Canada, while others tried to adjust to reservation life as best they could. Increasingly, however, the Army reacted violently to even the smallest signs of protest. Such was the case in December 1890 at Wounded Knee Creek in South Dakota.

The trouble began in the late fall when the cult of the Ghost Dance spread rapidly across Sioux reservations. The cult was wholly non-violent, but whites who witnessed its ritual dance were nonetheless terrified, and they moved quickly to arrest those believed to be responsible for the "disturbances."

In late December, after Sitting Bull was killed during a confrontation with soldiers, the Army moved to arrest Big Foot, another alleged instigator. Upon learning of Sitting Bull's death, Big Foot and his band of Minneconjou departed for the Pine Ridge Reservation, hoping to find safety in the camp of the great chief Red Cloud. Before he could get there, however, the Army intercepted him.

Big Foot, who was quite ill, immediately raised a white flag. Unfortunately, as the soldiers attempted to disarm the Indians, a shot rang out, and within seconds the soldiers began gunning down the Indians indiscriminately. When it was over, some 300 men, women, and children had been killed.

The first photographer to arrive at Wounded Knee Creek after the massacre was George Trager. His photographs, including the frequently reproduced picture of Big Foot's corpse lying in the snow, were widely distributed. Other photographers arrived afterward to document the horror.

As vivid as they were, however, these photographs could not convey the true significance of the tragedy at Wounded Knee: the days of Indian resistance to white settlement had come to an end. Indeed, that same year, the U.S. Census had declared that the American frontier no longer existed. Whites had settled in every region of the United States. The Native American population in the continental United States, meanwhile, had dropped to just 228,000 from a high of one to several million in pre-Columbian times. (Some estimates put the number at 1 million, others as high as 10 million.)

The final subjugation of the Native American gave rise to new feelings of ambivalence, guilt, and regret among many white Americans, and much of the photography that followed was as highly romanticized as some earlier paintings had been. One exception to this trend was the work of A. C. Vroman. In his diary, Vroman expresses deep respect for the Hopi tribesmen that he photographed as well as a sense of awe at the beauty of their costumes and rituals. As Susan Sontag has noted in her book *On Photography* (1977), however, his photographs are "unexpressive, uncondescending, [and] unsentimental." They are, in other words, true visual documents.

Other late nineteenth and early twentieth century photographers, the most notable of whom is Frederick I. Monsen, took a similar approach. But the style that ultimately prevailed among photographers of Indians during this period was that

Left:
Gathering the Dead at Wounded Knee, January 1, 1891
George Trager
Smithsonian Institution, National Anthropological Archives

Right: "The Club," San Juan Capistrano, California, 1900 (left to right) H. E. Hoopes, G. J. Kuhrts, A. C. Vroman (seated), H. I. Chatfield, unidentified. (*Seaver Center for Western History Research, Natural History Museum of Los Angeles County*)

Below:
Cañon de Chelly, 1904
Adam Clark Vroman
Platinum print
Amon Carter Museum, Fort Worth, Texas

15

Wanamaker elaborated on this point: "In undertaking these expeditions to the North American Indian, the sole desire has been to perpetuate the life story of the First Americans and to strengthen in their hearts the feeling of allegiance and friendship for their country."

Curtis, however, went even further. Indeed, not since Catlin had any one white man committed himself so thoroughly to the visual documentation of Native American culture. During the last decade of the nineteenth century, Curtis enjoyed considerable success as a photographer specializing in portraits of Seattle's social elite. The year 1900, however, would mark the beginning of his lifelong intense interest in the American Indian. Curtis's interest was piqued when George Bird Grinnell, a leading conservationist, invited Curtis to join him on a trip through Blackfoot country. The trip, according to Curtis's daughter, was the "pivotal experience" of his life. Indeed, the trip did not simply spark an interest in the Blackfoot. Curtis resolved in the aftermath of the journey to photograph all the Indian tribes west of the Mississippi.

Seven years later, Curtis published the first volume of a 20-volume photographic collection. In the introduction, he lamented the passing of Native American culture, just as so many of his predecessors had.

"The great changes in practically every phase of the Indian's life," he wrote, "have been such that had the time for collecting much of the material been delayed, it would have been lost forever. The passing of every old man or woman means the passing of some tradition, some knowledge of sacred rites possessed by no other; consequently the information that is to be gathered for the benefit of future generations . . . must be collected at once or the opportunity will be lost for all time."

By 1905, Curtis had achieved national recognition for what one critic called his "remarkable artistic and historical work." Among his admirers was President Theodore Roosevelt, who helped convince J. P. Morgan to underwrite the publication of Curtis's photographs. As a result, Curtis's reputation as America's premier photographer of Native Americans was secured.

In spite of Curtis's expressed desire to gather information for future generations, the photographs of this remarkable artist are not what they appear to be. By his own admission, Curtis attempted to depict Indians as they "moved about before [they] ever saw a paleface." To achieve this goal, he often posed his subjects in costumes that he thought were appropriate and in settings that seemed to him to represent days gone by.

Given the "artistic liberties" taken by Curtis, Dixon and many of their predecessors, it is sometimes difficult to look uncynically at early photographs of Native Americans. Indeed, even when there was no apparent tampering on the part of the photographer, one cannot help but feel uncomfortable with the notion, suggested by many of the photographs, that the subjects were exotic curiosities rather than men and women deserving of respect on their own terms.

On the other hand, it is clear that many photographers did

Above:
The Last Outpost, 1908-17
Joseph Kossuth Dixon
Smithsonian Institution, National Anthropological Archives

which is best exemplified by two photographers: Joseph Kossuth Dixon, and Edward Sheriff Curtis.

Dixon, who traveled between 1908 and 1913 with expeditions sponsored by department store heir Rodman Wanamaker, is especially important because he helped popularize sentiments about "the vanishing race" with a book published under that title. As Crawford R. Buell notes in his introduction to the 1973 edition of the book, Dixon's photography reflected a widespread tendency to "glamorize the Indian" out of desire to make "atonement for past injustices."

approach their subjects with respect. Curtis's dedication, in spite of all his faults, was especially remarkable. As Lee Clark Mitchell has noted, no painter or photographer before or after – Catlin included – collected such a wealth of ethnological information.

In the late 1800s, and even into the early decades of the twentieth century, such information was not easy to come by. Indeed, all photographers of Native Americans faced a daunting task, since the technology was invented at a time when unrestricted tribal life had all but faded into history. Because of this unfortunate timing, at least one historian has argued that early photographs of American Indians constitute "a visual record of a harassed, defeated, and degraded people." This is true, of course, but it is only a partial description. Many of the pictures reflect not only tragedy, but also triumph – the triumph of tribesmen who clung tenaciously to rituals, customs, and a sense of honor, in spite of all the changes they were forced to endure; and the triumph of those photographers who recognized this tenacity and integrity and went to great lengths to preserve it on film.

Below:
Three Chiefs, Piegan, 1900
Edward S. Curtis
The Library of Congress

Right: Edward S. Curtis in 1906. (*Special Collections Division, University of Washington Libraries, Seattle, Washington*)

THE EARLY YEARS

The earliest photographs of Native Americans sometimes disappoint modern viewers. We hope to get from them a sense of the vitality of nineteenth-century Indian culture, and instead we are struck by how stiff and unnatural the subjects look. Indeed, some of these photographs, like A. Zeno Shindler's 1867 image of Yankton Dakota delegates in a war-dance pose, seem almost absurdly at odds with the realities of Native American life.

The stiffness of these early images, of course, reflects the considerable technological limitations faced by early photographers. Exposure times were so slow, in fact, that portrait subjects often had to wear braces to help them keep still. Obviously, under such circumstances, photographs of a more expressive nature were not a possibility.

Given these limitations, it is remarkable that these mid-nineteenth century photographs hold any appeal for modern viewers, beyond their value as historical artifacts. But upon close inspection, the emotional power of these photographs does emerge.

The photographs of Thomas M. Easterly, who was among the first to work with Indian subjects, are good examples of how early photographers worked within the confines of the technology to produce portraits of subtle intensity. Easterly, a native of Vermont, moved to Missouri in the 1840s and began taking daguerreotypes of Sauk and Fox tribesmen in the region. Among the images that have been preserved from this period is the widely reproduced portrait of chief Keokuk, which was probably taken in 1847 in Illinois.

A decade earlier, both George Catlin and Charles Bird King had painted the chief's portrait. "Keokuk is, in all respects, a magnificent savage," wrote James Hall in the text accompanying the published lithograph of King's painting. "Bold, enterprising, and impulsive, he is also politic, and possesses an intimate knowledge of human nature." King's and Catlin's portraits both reflect this romantic impression. Easterly's daguerreotype, by contrast, is pure documentation. It evokes a profound sense of sadness, not because Easterly imposed his view upon the subject but simply because the camera lets us stare into the chief's expressive eyes.

Keokuk was originally chief of the Fox, a tribe that had remained at peace with whites throughout Andrew Jackson's campaign against the Indians. When the Sauk chief Black Hawk declared war on whites in 1832, the uprising was quickly suppressed and Jackson recognized Keokuk as chief of a united Sauk and Fox tribe. Subsequently, Jackson forced the tribe to relocate from Wisconsin to Iowa, and finally to Kansas. Keokuk remained on peaceful terms with whites until his death in 1848. Easterly, meanwhile, continued operating out of various studios in the St. Louis area until his death in 1882.

While Easterly was building his photography business in St. Louis in the 1850s, many of the century's most important photographers were beginning to do the same thing back east. Among the most important photographers of this group were James Earle McClees, Samuel Cohner, Julian Vannerson, and Marcus Aurelius Root, all of whom worked in Philadelphia.

In 1852, when a delegation of 19 Arapaho, Cheyenne, and Sioux traveled east for a visit with President Millard Fillmore and other white leaders, photographers seized the opportunity to record history in the making. Unfortunately, many of the photographs taken during this period cannot be credited to individual photographers with any degree of certainty. Nonetheless, it is safe to say that McClees and his fellow Philadelphians were involved in this endeavor.

A visit by a much larger delegation five years later marked the first systematic effort to photograph Indians, as Paula Richardson Fleming and Judith Luskey have noted in their book *The North American Indians in Early Photographs*. Among the most interesting images of this period is a portrait of the Mdewakanton Dakota leader Little Crow, taken in Washington by Vannerson and Cohner under the auspices of the McClees studio.

Like many other tribal leaders, Little Crow worked hard to maintain peace with the United States government. As Dee Brown noted in *Bury My Heart at Wounded Knee*, he even joined the Episcopal Church, built a house and started a farm after his visit to Washington. But by 1862, he was beginning to feel disillusioned. These feelings intensified when, in July of that year, thousands of Santee Sioux, including the Mdewakantons, waited in vain for money to which they were entitled under the terms of a treaty that Little Crow had signed.

In spite of his anger, Little Crow initially tried to calm his more militant followers. Some of the braves interpreted these efforts as a sign of cowardice, but the chief, as his son recalled later, insisted that the white man simply could not be beaten. The whites are "like locusts," Little Crow is reported to have said. "Kill one, two, ten, and ten times ten will come to kill you."

Little Crow was, of course, correct. Nonetheless, the chief eventually gave in to the cries for war and ordered an attack on the government agency that was responsible for the Indians in the area. When it was all over, 20 whites had been killed and the government warehouses had been emptied. During the following weeks, the warriors attacked several other white strongholds, including nearby Fort Ridgely, and in the process killed hundreds of people. But by late fall, the Santees had been defeated. During subsequent trials, more than 300 Santees

Sioux Delegation on Visit to President Johnson, 1867
Alexander Gardner
The Missouri Historical Society

were found guilty of participating in the uprising and were sentenced to death. President Lincoln later commuted most of these sentences, but the day after Christmas, 1862, 38 Santees were hanged.

Little Crow avoided the trial altogether, having escaped to Canada with a small band of followers. The following July, however, he returned to Minnesota in an effort to obtain some horses and was shot by bounty hunters. His son later learned that his scalp and skull had been put on display in St. Paul.

Six months after Little Crow's death, two other Santee leaders, Shakopee and Medicine Bottle, were also captured. For the next year they were held prisoner at Fort Snelling, Minnesota, but in November 1865, they were finally executed for their part in the ill-fated rebellion.

During their term of imprisonment in 1864, Joel Emmons Whitney photographed both Medicine Bottle and Shakopee. Whitney, a native of Maine, had gone to Minnesota in 1850 and learned photography under Alexander Hesler. His highly expressive portraits of the participants in the Sioux revolt are certainly among the finest of the period. In many ways they evoke the sense of melancholy that Edward Curtis would later try to convey. The difference was that Whitney's photographs were pure historical documents, whereas Curtis's were attempts to recreate the past. (See Chapter 3).

The horrors of the Sioux uprising were, of course, largely overshadowed for most whites by the Civil War. But when the war ended, the U.S. government renewed efforts to deal with the problem of white-Indian relations. In 1867, another wave of Native American delegates arrived in Washington, and a number of major photographers were on hand to record the meetings. Among them was A. Zeno Shindler.

Shindler, a native of Bulgaria, had studied painting in France before coming to America sometime before 1850. It is not known exactly when he took up photography, but by 1867 he was established enough to take over the management of McClees's Washington gallery. (McClees had actually sold the gallery several years earlier.) Shindler remained in Washington for most of the rest of his life, although he spent five years in New York and Philadelphia during the 1870s. He is also reported to have taken a trip west sometime during this period, although according to Paula Richardson Fleming, this report has never been substantiated. In any event, no frontier photographs have been attributed to him.

A more skilled photographer of the period was Alexander Gardner. Indeed, taking into account his extraordinary work during the Civil War and his later work on the frontier, it is safe to say that Gardner ranks among the greatest photographers of the nineteenth century.

What is most striking about Gardner's work is its range. Some of the studio portraits he took during the 1867 delegation visits are not significantly different from those taken by Shindler or any number of other photographers. But Gardner appears to have given more thought to composition than many of his contemporaries. His group portrait of a Sioux delegation with President Johnson at the White House is particularly striking. Moreover, in the years following the delegation visit, Gardner traveled west to capture images of Indians on their homelands.

Among the fascinating pictures taken during this period was his shot of an Oglala Sioux named Young Man, Even Whose Horses Are Feared, smoking a "peace" pipe during a treaty negotiation (see page 30). As Paula Richardson Fleming noted in *An Enduring Interest: The Photographs of Alexander Gardner*, this is the only known image of the pipe-smoking ritual.

Gardner returned to Washington after the Fort Laramie trip, and in 1872 he became the leading photographer of delegations. Ironically, although the government a year earlier had stopped negotiating treaties, 1872 would be an important year for delegation visits. Red Cloud, the Oglala Sioux chief, was among the most prominent delegates. "I want to be better acquainted with [the white man] and have a talk about many things," he said.

Several months after Red Cloud's visit, a Brule Dakota delegation led by Spotted Tail arrived in Washington, and Gardner took a number of important photographs of the group. His portrait of the chief's wife, taken during this visit, is among his finest studio works. Gardner photographed other delegations in 1873, but from 1874 until his death in 1882 he spent most of his time on other activities.

While Gardner was photographing delegations in Washington, another important photographer, William Soule, was hired by the U.S. Army to document the construction of Fort Sill, Oklahoma. The fort was deep inside Indian territory and thus afforded Soule an unusual opportunity to photograph the Kiowa, Arapaho, Apache, Cheyenne, and other tribes.

Meanwhile the careers of Timothy O'Sullivan and William H. Jackson were also beginning to peak. Their professional fortunes would be tied in large part to the Government's scientific surveys of the West.

As noted in the introduction, most of O'Sullivan's important work was done in the Southwest while he was traveling with the Wheeler survey between 1871 and 1875. The work was not only difficult, but also dangerous. Indeed, in November of 1871, several of O'Sullivan's companions were killed by Apaches as they were traveling by stagecoach to California. In spite of the danger, however, O'Sullivan managed that year to take hundreds of photographs of Mohave, Apache, Paiute, and Shoshone tribesmen. The two Mohave braves in the picture on page 38 were probably his guides.

In 1873, Wheeler appointed O'Sullivan "executive in charge of the main party," and it was during this period that he photographed numerous scenes of life among the Navahos near Fort Defiance, Arizona.

A decade earlier, the Navahos' life had been disrupted when Army troops under Colonel Christopher "Kit" Carson raided Canyon de Chelly, the tribe's traditional homeland in northeastern Arizona, and forced them to relocate to the Bosque Redondo Reservation in New Mexico. A new treaty in 1868, however, had allowed them to return to Arizona.

When O'Sullivan arrived, he found that he was able to photograph the Navahos engaged in a variety of traditional activities. One image, for example, shows a Navaho woman working a horizontal loom – a weaving method that was unique to the tribe.

While O'Sullivan was exploring the Southwest in 1871, Jackson was traveling farther to the north with the Hayden Survey. Among the Indians he encountered that summer was a family of the Bannock sheep-eater tribe in southern Idaho. Jackson later reported that the family agreed to have their picture taken in exchange for a small quantity of sugar and coffee.

The photograph of the Bannock family reflects their struggle for survival. Their primary food source, the bighorn sheep, was in short supply in the 1870s, and the Bannocks were, as a result, forced to wander about the region in search of sustenance. Many other tribes shared such an existence, of course, but few photographers captured the essence of that existence as well as Jackson did.

The Wheeler and Hayden surveys continued until 1879, as did the Powell Survey, which helped launch the career of John K. Hillers (see Chapter 2). But opportunities to photograph traditional Native American ways of life were rapidly disappearing. Increasingly, as Indians were forced to adopt the ways of whites, photographers faced new challenges. The various ways in which they responded to these challenges reflects the ways in which white America in general regarded the Native American in the last quarter of the nineteenth century.

Right:
Longhorn, a Sauk and Fox, c. 1846
Thomas Easterly
Smithsonian Institution, National Anthropological Archives

Left:
Keokuk, 1847
Thomas Easterly
Smithsonian Institution, National Anthropological Archives

Three Cheyenne Indians, White Antelope, Alights on a Cloud, and Little Chief, 1851-52
Probably by Marcus Aurelius Root or James E. McClees in Philadelphia
Smithsonian Institution, National Anthropological Archives

Above:
Little Six, Also Known as Shakopee, 1858
Julian Vannerson and Samuel Cohner of the
McClees Studio
*Smithsonian Institution, National Anthropological
Archives*

Left:
Petalesharo of Skidi Pawnee, 1858
McClees Studio
*Smithsonian Institution, National Anthropological
Archives*

**Cheyenne and Kiowa Delegates in the White House
Conservatory**, 1863
Photographer unknown
Smithsonian Institution, National Anthropological Archives

Medicine Bottle at Fort Snelling Prison, 1864
Joel Emmons Whitney
Smithsonian Institution, National Anthropological Archives

Above:
Yankton Dakota Delegates in Pose from War Dance, 1867
A. Zeno Shindler
Smithsonian Institution, National Anthropological Archives

Below:
Pawnee Men Before Earth Lodge, 1868-69
William Henry Jackson
Museum of New Mexico

Below:
Pawnee Men Before Earth Lodge, 1868-69
William Henry Jackson
Museum of New Mexico

**Young Man, Even Whose Horses Are Feared, Smoking Council
Pipe During Oglala Dakota Treaty Meeting at Fort Laramie,
Wyoming,** 1868
Alexander Gardner
Smithsonian Institution, National Anthropological Archives

Short Bull of the Sioux, n.d.
Photographer unknown
The National Archives

A Bannock Family in Medicine Lodge Creek, Idaho, 1871
William Henry Jackson
Smithsonian Institution, National Anthropological Archives

Wife of Spotted Tail, 1872
Alexander Gardner
Smithsonian Institution, National Anthropological Archives

Right:
Powder Face, War Chief of the Arapahoe, 1868-74
William S. Soule
Museum of New Mexico

Left:
Navahos with Horizontal Loom, 1873
Timothy O'Sullivan
Smithsonian Institution, National Anthropological Archives

Apache Desert Hunters Using Bows and Arrows, 1870s-1880s
Photographer unknown
Smithsonian Institution, National Anthropological Archives

Left:
Two Mohave Braves, 1871
Timothy O'Sullivan
The National Archives

Manuelito, Navaho War Chief, 1874
Photographer unknown
Smithsonian Institution, National Anthropological Archives

Cultural Transitions

The photographs of Native Americans taken during the last two decades of the nineteenth century reflect a culture in transition. Indians have been struggling with cultural change, of course, ever since their first encounter with whites. But whereas the earlier photographs tended to reflect these changes in very subtle ways, many of the images taken in the 1880s and 1890s clearly reveal the impact of white society.

One of the most interesting photographs of this period is a panoramic view of William F. "Buffalo Bill" Cody and the Indians who participated in his Wild West shows. Launched in 1883, the shows captivated audiences with colorful parades, exciting races, and elaborate reenactments of stagecoach robberies and Custer's Last Stand.

From a modern perspective, it seems curious that Indians were willing participants in these gaudy displays. But at a time when many tribes were barely managing to survive, opportunities to make money could not be taken lightly. Sitting Bull himself agreed to join the show in 1885, in exchange for $50 a week, a $125 bonus, and exclusive rights to the sale of his portraits and autographs, although he refused to participate in mock battles.

While most whites enjoyed these shows immensely, self-proclaimed Indian rights advocates were adamantly opposed to them. As one advocate put it, the shows "teach the Indian that what the white man really wants of him is amusement furnished by exhibitions of picturesque barbarism, not the acquisition of those sober, unpicturesque but absolutely necessary qualities which alone can make him equal to the battle of life. . . . "

In reality, many white Americans regarded the prospect of the Indians' cultural assimilation with profound ambivalence. Certainly most whites thought Native American culture was inferior to European-American culture. Nonetheless, many whites tended to romanticize the Indian. Their romantic attitudes toward Indian culture was expressed not just in their support of Wild West shows but in more serious endeavors to document traditional ways of life.

One photographer who recorded such traditional-looking subject matter in the early 1880s was John K. Hillers. As noted in the introduction, Hillers had established himself as a leading photographer of Native Americans while traveling with the Powell Survey. In 1879, Powell became the first director of the newly established Bureau of Ethnology, and he hired Hillers to be the bureau's staff photographer.

Under the auspices of the bureau, Powell organized an expedition to study the Indians of New Mexico, and by August Hillers was busy photographing the Hopi and Zuni pueblos. He returned to the Southwest again in 1880, and, with the help of Frank Cushing, a young naturalist who had gained the trust of the Zuni people, he was able to photograph many places and activities that would have been off limits to most whites.

While few photographers of the 1880s had the opportunities that Hillers had, he was not the only one to capture images of traditional Native American culture during this period. Ben Wittick, for example, took numerous photographs of Navahos and other tribes from his independent studio in Albuquerque between 1881 and 1884.

Another important independent photographer active during the early 1880s was A. Frank Randall. Working mainly in Arizona, Randall concentrated on the Apaches in the years leading up to Geronimo's surrender.

The Apaches had waged fierce guerrilla warfare against the U.S. Army for years, but in September 1872, the legendary tribal leader Cochise reached a peace accord with General Oliver O. Howard. When Cochise died two years later, however, younger Apache leaders, including Geronimo, resumed the guerrilla attacks. By 1880, when all other major tribes had surrendered to government control, Geronimo had become the principal warrior chief of the Apaches.

Geronimo's chief pursuer during this period was General George "Grey Wolf" Crook. In May 1883, Crook finally caught up with his adversary and convinced him to surrender. After spending two years on the San Carlos reservation, however, Geronimo fled once again, and it took Crook nearly a year to negotiate another surrender.

Camillus S. Fly, an Arizona photographer, was on hand to record the second meeting between the two leaders in March 1886. At one point, according to witness John Gregory Bourke, Fly "cooly asked Geronimo and the warriors with him to change positions, and turn their heads or faces, to improve the negative."

Crook was subsequently forced to resign after Geronimo broke the accord. By September, however, Crook's replacement, General Nelson Miles, captured Geronimo for the last time. Shortly thereafter, he was taken by train to Fort Marion, Florida. During the journey, he and a number of other Apache prisoners were photographed by A. J. McDonald of New Orleans.

Another Indian leader who attracted a following because of his disdain for treaties and reservation life was Sitting Bull, chief of the Hunkpapa Teton Sioux. During the 1860s, the principal leader of the Teton Sioux had been Red Cloud. But when the older chief signed the Fort Laramie treaty in 1868 and agreed to live on a reservation, his influence began to diminish, and Sitting Bull's dominance grew. In 1873, one of the major events of Indian-white relations was foreshadowed when Sitting Bull skirmished with a lieutenant-colonel named

George Armstrong Custer. Three years later, the Battle of Little Big Horn would turn both men into legends.

Following his victory at Little Big Horn, Sitting Bull fled to Canada, but in 1881 he returned to the United States and surrendered. Although he was initially imprisoned at Fort Randall, he was eventually permitted to live on the Standing Rock Reservation, and it is likely that this is where David F. Barry photographed him in the mid-1880s.

A native of New York state, Barry moved with his family to Wisconsin in 1861 and soon afterward met the photographer O. S. Goff. By 1878, he was managing Goff's studio, and the following year he took complete control of it. Throughout the 1880s, Barry took countless images of the Indians of the Northern Plains, and he developed a special interest in the Battle of Little Big Horn. His photographs of Sitting Bull are noteworthy for their simplicity.

Panoramic View of Buffalo Bill and His Indians on the Beach in Front of the Cliff House, San Francisco, California, n.d.
Photographer unknown
National Museum of the American Indian, Smithsonian Institution

Not long after Barry photographed him, Sitting Bull was killed as Indian police were attempting to arrest him. The government had grown angry with the Hunkpapa chief because of his support of what they viewed as a subversive phenomenon – the cult of the Ghost Dance.

The Ghost Dance cult took on many variations, but its basic premise was that a messiah had predicted the ultimate demise of whites and the restoration of the land as it was prior to Euro-

41

**Masked "Mud Heads" Prepared to Dance, Zuni Pueblo,
New Mexico**, 1879
John K. Hillers
The National Archives

pean settlement. The ritual's exotic nature naturally attracted photographers.

To George E. Trager, a Chadron, Nebraska, photographer, the commercial potential of the Ghost Dance was irresistible. He is reported to have made several trips to the Pine Ridge Reservation where Ghost Dance activities were concentrated,

although it is unclear whether he actually did make money from the photographs he took there. In any case, his efforts to capture images of the Ghost Dance were overshadowed by his own subsequent coup: Trager was the first to arrive on the scene after the massacre at Wounded Knee.

Trager's photographs were widely distributed, according to Fleming and Luskey, but his success was short-lived, and by 1892 he had apparently given up photography altogether. Other photographers, meanwhile, followed in Trager's footsteps, including John C. H. Grabill, who had been operating in Dakota Territory since 1886. In the long run, however, Trager's images were the ones that were generally associated with the tragedy.

The massacre at Wounded Knee was so psychologically devastating to Indians throughout the region that many people assumed it had put an end to the Ghost Dance. The cult had emerged, however, as an expression of hope against all odds, and the slaughter in South Dakota only heightened the need for such a ritual.

In an effort to understand the power behind the Ghost Dance, the government sent anthropologist James Mooney to investigate it. "The Indians are dancing the ghost dance day and night," Mooney wrote shortly after his arrival. "They are bringing out costumes not worn in years. . . . " Mooney was so swept up in the phenomenon that he continued to study it for the government and on his own for the next two years. In the process, he took a number of photographs of the dance as well as the only known image of Wovoka, the founder of the cult.

Activities such as the Ghost Dance, while fascinating to many white Americans, only strengthened the resolve of Christian reformers who were trying to teach "civilized" behavior to the Indians. Among the photographers who documented this effort was Jesse Hastings Bratley.

As a teacher at various Indian schools between 1893 and 1903, Bratley was in a unique position to document the assimilation efforts. The photographs he took at the Rosebud Reservation in South Dakota between 1895 and 1899 are especially noteworthy, but he also did important work at the Havasupai Reservation in Arizona.

While photographs by Bratley and others initially appeared to provide evidence of successful assimilation, enthusiasm for the schools waned as white America came to realize that these images were delusions. Indian children were indeed wearing uniforms and working diligently at assigned tasks, but ultimately they could not fully embrace white culture. As a result, they were caught in a kind of cultural void.

Over the next few decades, they would struggle to survive in this void. Some tribal groups clung to traditional ways of life, while others had no choice but to rely on meager government rations. Katherine T. Dodge's photograph of Apaches awaiting rations at the San Carlos Reservation is a poignant illustration of the latter. Such photographs made it increasingly clear to sensitive white Americans that the triumph of Manifest Destiny had its dark side.

Hopi Dance Rock and Kiva, Walpi Pueblo, Arizona, 1879
John K. Hillers
Smithsonian Institution, National Anthropological Archives

Approach to Pueblo Acoma, c. 1883
Ben Wittick
Museum of New Mexico

Left:
Hopi Woman Dressing Her Husband's Hair, 1880-82
John K. Hillers
Museum of New Mexico

Hopi Woman Dressing Hair of Unmarried Girl, c. 1900
Henry Peabody
The National Archives

Left:
Governor Ahftche of San Felipe Pueblo, Drilling Hole in Tortoise Shell, 1880
John K. Hillers
Smithsonian Institution, National Anthropological Archives

Navaho Man Hammering Silver, Another Using a Bow Drill, and a Child with Bellows in Front of a Hogan, 1892
James Mooney
Smithsonian Institution, National Anthropological Archives

Crow Woman Decorating Staked and Stretched Buffalo Hides,
Montana, n.d.
From Charles Rau Collection
National Museum of the American Indian, Smithsonian Institution

Navaho Silversmith With Examples of His Work and Tools,
c. 1880
Ben Wittick
The National Archives

Right:

Two Apache Babies in Cradles, Arizona, before 1884
A. Frank Randall
Phoebe Hearst Museum of Anthropology, University of California, Berkeley

Nachez (Son of Cochise), Chief of Chiricahua Apaches, and His Wife, 1882
From Williamson Collection
The Arizona Historical Society Library

Left:
Red Cloud of the Oglala Dakota, 1880
Charles M. Bell
Smithsonian Institution, National Anthropological Archives

An Apache Princess, Granddaughter of Cochise, c. 1886
Ben Wittick
The National Archives

Flathead Delegation, 1884

Left:
Flathead Delegation of Six and an Interpreter, 1884
Charles M. Bell
The National Archives

Council Between General George Crook and Geronimo, 1886
Camillus S. Fly
Smithsonian Institution, National Anthropological Archives

Left:
Geronimo, 1887
Ben Wittick
The National Archives

Marianetta, Wife of Geronimo, n.d.
Photographer unknown
National Museum of the American Indian, Smithsonian Institution

Apache Prisoners, 1886
A. J. McDonald
The National Archives

Left:
Sitting Bull of the Hunkpapa Sioux, n.d.
David F. Barry
National Museum of the American Indian, Smithsonian Institution

Sitting Bull's House and Family, n.d.
David F. Barry
National Museum of the American Indian, Smithsonian Institution

No. 3609. "VILLA OF BRULE."
The great hostile Indian Camp on River Brule
near Pine Ridge, S. D.
Photo. and copyright by Grabill, 1891,
Deadwood, S. D.

Camp of the Brule Sioux, Near Pine Ridge, South Dakota, 1891
John C. H. Grabill
National Museum of the American Indian, Smithsonian Institution

Right:
"Typical Home," Pine Ridge Reservation, South Dakota, 1891
John C. H. Grabill
National Museum of the American Indian, Smithsonian Institution

Part of the Ghost Dance, c. 1893
James Mooney
Smithsonian Institution, National Anthropological Archives

Big Foot's Corpse at Wounded Knee, January 1, 1891
George Trager
Smithsonian Institution, National Anthropological Archives

**Dakota Girls Sewing at Indian Day School, Rosebud
Reservation, South Dakota,** 1897
Jesse Hastings Bratley
Smithsonian Institution, National Anthropological Archives

Group of Students at Havasupai Reservation, c. 1900
Jesse Hastings Bratley
Smithsonian Institution, National Anthropological Archives

Group of Seneca, Cattaraugus Reservation, New York, 1900
Joseph Keppler
National Museum of the American Indian, Smithsonian Institution

Above:
Apaches Awaiting Rations at San Carlos, Arizona, 1899
Katherine T. Dodge
Smithsonian Institution, National Anthropological Archives

Below:
Salish Woman Smoking Salmon, British Columbia, n.d.
Photographer unknown
National Museum of the American Indian, Smithsonian Institution

Beginning of White Deerskin Dance, Hupa Tribe, California,
1890-97
A. W. Ericson
Smithsonian Institution, National Anthropological Archives

**Gable-Roofed House and Totem Pole, Bellacoola Village,
British Columbia**, before 1901
Photographer unknown
Smithsonian Institution, National Anthropological Archives

Kwakiutl Village, Hope Island, British Columbia, 1899
Photographer unknown
*Phoebe Hearst Museum of Anthropology, University of California,
Berkeley*

Sunset of a Dying Race

When photography was developed in the mid-nineteenth century, people assumed that the camera accurately reflected reality. And often, it did. But as time went on, photographers of Native Americans increasingly looked for ways to "enhance" their images, either by adding costumes and props, posing subjects in particular ways, or "sandwiching" negatives for the purposes of adding dramatic backdrops.

After the turn of the century, this tendency toward embellishment was taken to new heights. Men like Edward Sheriff Curtis and Joseph Kossuth Dixon began to regard photography as an "art-science," and they unabashedly strove to capture the spiritual essence of the Indian rather than current, purely physical realities.

"The camera, the brush, and the chisel have made us familiar with [the Indian's] plumed and hairy chest," wrote Dixon in the 1913 edition of *The Vanishing American*, "but what of the deep fountains of his inner life? What riotous impulses, or communion with the Great Mystery, carved his face of bronze?" He went on to note that few scientists or artists had been able to shed light on these mysteries because "the inner Indian shrine is crossed by only a favored few."

Dixon counted himself among those favored few, as did his contemporary Edward Curtis. And like Dixon, Curtis believed his work revealed more spiritual depth than that of previous photographers.

"[T]he photographs are each an illustration of an Indian character or of some vital phase in his existence," Curtis wrote in the introduction to his book, *The North American Indian*. He added that in seeking "subjects of aesthetic character" he was not "neglecting the homelier phases of aboriginal life." But, in an effort to convey the Indian's true nature, he did indeed ignore the "homely" aspects.

Not all photographers of Native Americans in the early twentieth century produced such idealized images. M.R. Harrington, for example, traveled extensively in the East during the first two decades of the century and documented the gritty reality of contemporary life among the Seminoles and other tribes. Similar efforts were made by Alanson B. Skinner, DeCost Smith, and Joseph Keppler. But it is clear that the romanticized images of Curtis and Dixon, rather than Harrington's more journalistic photographs, reflected white America's sentiments about the "vanishing race."

As noted in the introduction, Curtis's early professional success was as a society photographer in Seattle. His love of the outdoors often brought him in contact with local Indian villages, and he occasionally photographed them.

Curtis's interest in Native Americans was heightened during an expedition to Alaska in 1899 with Dr. C. Hart Merriam, chief of the United States Biological Survey, and Dr. George Bird Grinnell, an editor and authority on Plains Indians. Although Curtis took numerous landscape photographs during the trip, it was Merriam who took most of the photographs featuring natives.

The year after the Alaskan expedition, Curtis began taking more photographs of Native Americans. The best of these images earned him two first prizes from the National Photographic Convention. It was not until 1904, however, that Curtis began seriously contemplating his own "comprehensive and permanent record of all the important tribes of the United States that still retain to a considerable degree their primitive traditions and customs."

For the next two years, Curtis sought support for his massive undertaking, and he was largely successful in this effort. Ultimately, President Theodore Roosevelt himself took an interest in the project. But even more important than Roosevelt's support was that of J.P. Morgan. Curtis had approached the railroad magnate in 1906 with the idea of producing 20 volumes of ethnological text and illustrative photographs as well as 20 companion portfolios, each containing 35 large prints. Morgan was initially reluctant to offer his support, but after seeing the impressive body of work Curtis had already compiled, he decided to finance the project. It was the beginning of a 24-year effort that would eventually destroy his marriage, seriously endanger his health, and wipe out his finances. But Curtis's determination allowed him ultimately to complete the project: the last volume was published in 1930 when Curtis was 62 years old.

Curtis began work on the first volume in June of 1906, and his routine that year established the general pattern he would follow for the better part of two decades. The first five weeks were devoted to a general study of the culture of the Western Apache, and the remainder of the summer was spent actually taking photographs. The following fall was devoted to writing and preparing material for publication.

Volume one focused on the Navaho as well as the Apache, and Curtis was especially impressed with the tribe's crafts. A Navaho woman, he wrote, may not "write books, paint pictures, or deliver ringing addresses . . . but when, after months of labor, she finishes a blanket, her pride in her work is well justified."

This was no superficial observation. On the contrary, Curtis's comments were rooted in his extremely thorough study of the language and customs of the various tribes he visited. Nowhere was this dedication more evident than in his approach to Indian ceremonies. Not content to be a mere observer, Curtis would attempt to become part of the culture he

Lodge Interior – Piegan
Edward S. Curtis
The Library of Congress

was photographing. After repeated visits with the Hopis, for instance, he was finally able to convince the tribal priests to initiate him into the Snake Order so that he could actually take part in the sacred Snake Dance, a spectacular late-summer ritual that lasts nine days.

Curtis made comparable efforts to understand the rituals of other tribes, and such photographs as "Placating the Spirit of a Slain Eagle" reveal his empathy with the subjects.

While Curtis left no stone unturned in his research, however, he was quite selective in what he chose to publish. Any evidence of the impact of white society on Native American culture was generally removed. One picture of the interior of a Piegan lodge, for instance, shows a clock sitting on the ground. As Christopher M. Lyman has noted in *The Vanishing Race and Other Illusions* (1982), Curtis eliminated the clock through retouching before including a different exposure of this scene in *The North American Indian*.

By manipulating his images in this way, many scholars have argued, Curtis reinforced widely embraced stereotypes which survive to this day. But as Lyman notes, Curtis must be credited with artistic, if not scientific, integrity. Indeed, his entire body of work expresses a remarkably forceful and cohesive vision – one that is equivalent to a work of fine literary fiction. And fiction, after all, sometimes conveys a deeper truth than "fact."

Dixon, as already noted, took much the same approach, as the photographs in his book *The Vanishing Race* indicate. Published in 1913, the book was a report of the second of three expeditions sponsored by Rodman Wanamaker. The first, which traveled to Montana's Valley of the Little Big Horn in 1908, was undertaken primarily for the purposes of filming the movie *Hiawatha*, but Dixon took numerous still photographs as well. The second, in 1909, focused on the same region, but the objective was far different. This time, with an endorsement from President William Howard Taft, the members of the expedition would organize a council of Indian chiefs to record their recollections and attitudes in words and pictures.

Among those who participated in what came to be called "The Last Great Indian Council" were chiefs Plenty Coups of the Crow Nation, Timbo of the Comanches, John of the Apaches, Running Bird of the Kiowa, Brave Bear of the Southern Cheyenne, Runs-the-Enemy of the Teton Sioux, and Pretty Voice Eagle of the Yankton Sioux.

For the most part, these leaders were as enthusiastic about the council as its white organizers were. "I feel that I am engaging in a great work in helping to make this historic picture of a great Indian council," said Chief Two Moons of the Northern Cheyenne. "I have led the Cheyennes in so many battles, and my life has been so full, that I felt when I came here that I was an old man. [B]ut since meeting the chiefs . . . and recalling my old life for this record, I feel like a young man again. It is a great day for all of us, because there are no more wars between us, and we meet in peace. . . ." The other chiefs made similar remarks at the closing of the council.

The success of his early efforts encouraged Wanamaker to take further steps to pay tribute to the Native American. In May of 1909, he proposed that a national memorial to the Indian be built on the grounds of Fort Wadsworth, Staten Island, near the entrance to New York Harbor. Congress voted to support the proposal, and in February 1913, the groundbreaking ceremonies took place. Unfortunately, World War I interrupted the project and it was never resumed.

As part of the ceremonies at Fort Wadsworth, the 32 Indian chiefs had signed an oath of allegiance to the United States. Several months after the ceremony, Wanamaker organized another expedition to bring a flag from the Fort Wadsworth site to 169 Indian communities, in honor of the Indians' becoming citizens. Since many Indians had been citizens for some time, the third expedition was received less enthusiastically than the second. Wanamaker and Dixon pushed forward with it nonetheless, and in the process added to the visual record of their great undertaking. In all, it is estimated that the Wanamaker expeditions produced approximately 11,000 photographs and 50 miles of movie film.

Looking back on the expeditions, Dixon imagined a time when Native Americans would have disappeared. "The door of the Indian's yesterdays," he wrote in his typically romantic style, "opens to a new world – a world unpeopled with red men, but whose population fills the sky . . . with sad spectre-like memories – with the flutter of unseen eagle pinions."

The irony of this view, of course, is that the Indian race was not vanishing at all. The Native American population had been decimated, to be sure, and it is easy to understand why the dying-race concept caught on in the early years of this century. Yet the descendants of ancient tribes have managed not only to survive, but also to hold on to some semblance of their traditional cultures. Theirs is, to borrow Dixon's words, an "imposing triumph of solitary grandeur sweeping beyond the reach of militant crimes. . . ."

Nez Perce Warriors, 1906
Major Lee Moorhouse
Smithsonian Institution, National Anthropological Archives

Blackfoot in Traditional Costume, Montana, 1903-10
Fred R. Meyer
National Museum of the American Indian, Smithsonian Institution

Right:
Angelic La Moose, Granddaughter of a Flathead Chief, Flathead Reservation, Montana, 1913
H. T. Corey
The National Archives

Left:
Very Old Chippewa Man in Traditional Costume, n.d.
From Fred R. Meyer Collection
National Museum of the American Indian, Smithsonian Institution

Seneca Eagle Dancer, Allegheny Reservation, New York,
c. 1905
M. R. Harrington
National Museum of the American Indian, Smithsonian Institution

Last Family of Potters and Pipe Makers, Pamunkey, Virginia,
1908
M. R. Harrington
National Museum of the American Indian, Smithsonian Institution

Right:
Indians of Santa Clara Pueblo, New Mexico, Making Pottery,
1916
H. T. Corey
The National Archives

X2611-08

Left:
Sioux Maiden
Edward S. Curtis
The Library of Congress

Overlooking the Camp – Piegan
Edward S. Curtis
The Library of Congress

Cayuse Mother and Child
Edward S. Curtis
*Special Collections Division, University of Washington Libraries,
Seattle, Washington*

A Blackfoot Travois
Edward S. Curtis
The Library of Congress

X2759-08

Left:
Ready for the Charge
Edward S. Curtis
The Library of Congress

Start of a War Party
Edward S. Curtis
The Library of Congress

Above:
Coming For the Bride – Qagyuhl
Edward S. Curtis
The Library of Congress

Below:
Kwakiutl Masked Dancers in the Winter Ceremony
Edward S. Curtis
Phoebe Hearst Museum of Anthropology, University of California, Berkeley

Kwakiutl Masked Dancers in the Winter Ceremony
Edward S. Curtis
*Phoebe Hearst Museum of Anthropology, University of California,
Berkeley*

Left:
Placating the Spirit of a Slain Eagle – Assiniboin
Edward S. Curtis
The Library of Congress

Snakes and Antelopes at Oraibi
Edward S. Curtis
The Library of Congress

Buffalo Dance at Hano
Edward S. Curtis
The Library of Congress

A Jicarilla Apache
Edward S. Curtis
Special Collections Division, University of Washington Libraries,
Seattle, Washington

Right:
Chief Joseph – Nez Perce
Edward S. Curtis
The Library of Congress

The Vanishing Race – Navaho
Edward S. Curtis
The Library of Congress

Right:
Praying to the Spirits at Crater Lake – Klamath
Edward S. Curtis
The Library of Congress

Skirting the Skyline, 1908-17
Joseph Kossuth Dixon
Smithsonian Institution, National Anthropological Archives

War Memories, 1908-17
Joseph Kossuth Dixon
Smithsonian Institution, National Anthropological Archives

Right:
Sunset of a Dying Race, 1908-17
Joseph Kossuth Dixon
Smithsonian Institution, National Anthropological Archives

Part Five
**Mathematical Techniques and
Socialist Planning** 399

19 O. Lange (1967)
The Computer and the Market 401

20 V. Nemchinov (1963)
Basic Elements of a Model of Planned Price Formation 406

21 L. V. Kantorovich (1959)
*Mathematical Formulation of the Problem of
Optimal Planning* 435

22 A. L. Veinshtein (1966)
Notes on Optimal Planning 469

23 J. Kornai (1965)
*Mathematical Programming as a Tool of
Socialist Economic Planning* 475

Part Six
The Chinese Model 489

24 Jack Gray
*The Chinese Model: Some Characteristics of Maoist
Policies for Social Change and Economic Growth* 491

Further Reading 511

Acknowledgements 516

Author Index 517

Subject Index 521

Introduction

In the customary division of the world into three parts – the West, the Socialist bloc and the Third World – the socialist countries[1] represent over one-third of the world's population and industrial output. Despite wide differences in the economic institutions of these countries and their respective stages of development, fairly similar patterns of economic organization have emerged. The main common features are:

1. *Public ownership of the means of production.* This takes the form of state, cooperative or collective ownership, and by no means implies social – as opposed to élitist – control. It need not be *total* ownership, and a relatively small private sector can exist in minor sectors of the economy; but there are strict limits on the ability to command labour other than one's own. The banking system and foreign trade are also nationalized.

2. *Centralized control of the rate of accumulation and the principles guiding the directions of economic growth.*

3. *The existence of a market for consumption goods* (though not necessarily of 'consumer sovereignty') *and for labour. Collective consumption* is of the order of 10–15 per cent of national income, all the rest of consumption goods are exchanged in the market, wages are paid and transactions take place in cash. The market for production goods, in so far as it exists, is separated to greater or lesser extent from the market for consumption goods.

4. *Prices, price limits or price fixing criteria, for all goods sold by the state are decided by the planning authorities; prices cannot change spontaneously.*

The main *economic* differences between these countries and between their stages of development depend on the degree of central control over the functioning of the economy, and are concerned with the decision-making agencies and their relations, the

1. Albania, Bulgaria, Czechoslovakia, East Germany, Hungary, Poland, Rumania, the Soviet Union, Yugoslavia; The People's Republic of China, North Korea, Mongolia, North Vietnam; Cuba.

use of money and value (as opposed to physical) indicators, the relative scope of plans and markets and the nature of incentives and of methods of plan implementation.

The functioning of a socialist economy deserves to be the object of a separate study because of the adoption of concepts and national accounting conventions[2] different from those prevailing in western economic theory and practice, and because of the important differences with respect to the agents taking economic decisions; the decisional parameters and the way they are determined; and the decision-making criteria. These differences can be investigated by means of standard methods of economic analysis.

Rosa Luxemburg wrote that 'the realization of socialism will be the end of Economics as a science'. This prediction was wrong – a large body of literature has now accumulated on the functioning of the socialist economy.

The reader will find in the pages that follow a selection which is necessarily very incomplete. The editors freely admit that some of the omissions will be hard to defend. Where, someone will say, are Kautsky, Trotsky, Sweezy? Why are there no Yugoslavs or Czechs? On the anti-socialist side why no Böhm-Bawerk, Hayek, Robbins? Our defence must be that any selection is in some respect a subjective one, and our criterion has been not eminence but representativeness, in respect of aspects of socialist thought in particular times and places. Thus obviously we do not think that Kosygin, or the editors themselves, constitute intellectual peaks of socialism. They have been included because we believe that they enlighten the reader on matters of significance in the given context.

We begin with a series of quotations from socialist classics (Reading 1). Brief excerpts from Marx and Engels, whose works are presumably widely accessible, illustrate the more general features of the two stages of communism: socialism, the 'lower phase' in which all the countries mentioned above can be said to

2. Socialist conventions of national economic accounting define among others, *national income* excluding 'non-material services' (e.g. public administration, education, entertainment, health and the use of durable assets for consumption purposes such as houses and hotels). Some 'material services' (e.g. goods transport, laundries, restaurants, trade) are however included. See: *United Nations – ECE* (1959) also reprinted in: Parker–Harcourt (1969).

be, and communism, the 'higher phase'. The quotations from Lenin reflect his thoughts on the eve of the seizure of power, a period in which he tended to underestimate the importance of specifically economic problems. Perhaps overimpressed by the centralization of the German war economy, he imagined that the proletariat once in power would have to cope mainly with technological and accountancy questions. It is noteworthy that even at this period Lenin was no syndicalist, treating as nonsensical the view that railways should be controlled by railwaymen and tanneries by tanners. He certainly cannot be represented as a supporter of theories of workers' self-management. The bitter experience of war communism led him to attach great importance to markets, prices and trade in his last years of political life.

A generation of communists was brought up on Bukharin and Preobrazhensky's essay *The ABC of Communism*, written during the civil war. This represents an extreme position but one that was then held by the majority of party intellectuals, who espoused a moneyless economy and a direct leap into socialism. Bukharin also wrote the important *Economics of the Transition Period*, which expressed similar views. He anticipated the imminent withering away of economics under socialism: there would be no room for markets and prices when goods are allocated consciously by society. Lenin did not go quite so far as this. By 1921 the New Economic Policy was adopted, this being a compromise between market forces and the peasantry. The state kept hold of the 'commanding heights' of the economy (large-scale industry, banking, foreign trade) while permitting private enterprise in industry and trade and basing its relations with the peasantry on purchase and sale.

Also included in the selection is an extract from Stalin. Stalin wrote little on economics (as distinct from economic policy), and so we have quoted from one of his very last writings, 'Economic Problems of Socialism in the USSR', though this may seem chronologically incongruous.

Anti-socialist literature is represented by two classical essays. The remarkable early work by Barone (Reading 2) stands the test of time. Its author did not idealize capitalism, and the problems which he identified were all real problems, which must still be taken seriously by anyone interested in the economics of socialism.

Mises, in his powerful attack, (Reading 3) tends to spoil his case by the implicit assumption that capitalism and optimum resource allocation go together, that the theoretical model is realizable in the real world. He also seems to imply that a socialist economy could not function at all, which is plainly not the case. In a valuable piece, which we unfortunately found ourselves unable to include here, Robbins assumed that while a socialist economy could function, its efficient functioning would require the solution of millions of simultaneous equations, which would plainly be impracticable.

Lange in his famous 1938 essay (Reading 4) found an answer: trial and error, socialist *tâtonnement*, using the market. He denied that market relations were alien to socialist economics. He envisaged their being used by the Central Planning Board. His model was intended above all as a formal refutation of Mises and Robbins. He in no way concerned himself either with growth or with motivation (why should either the planners or the managers operate in the manner required?). Lange was right to remind us that many Marxist socialists accepted the necessity of money, exchange and of markets during a transition period of unknown duration.

Part Two is concerned with accumulation and growth. Maurice Dobb's essay (Reading 5) fills the gap left by Lange and other participants to the debate in the field of the dynamics of socialism; it stresses that the state 'creates' its own profits by its own investment and discusses the role of prices (including the interest rate) in investment planning. The extracts from Preobrazhensky (Reading 6) highlight the problems *actually* faced by Lenin's successors. They viewed the New Economic Policy in different ways. Bukharin became the chief protagonist of caution and of an alliance with the peasantry, which meant a modest rate of capital investment. He sharply criticized Trotsky for demanding faster growth rates and action against the richer peasants. Preobrazhensky sided with Trotsky. His 'New Economics', from which the extract is taken, was not just an exercise in economic theory but also a blow in the factional struggle. When he wrote about primitive socialist accumulation he was advocating a more rapid transfer of resources from the private (principally peasant) sector to the state sector. The implied challenge to the then dominant official policy led him into spirited polemics with Bukharin, who was at that time backed by Stalin. The argument also concerned the possibility of building socialism in one country. Preobrazhensky's consciousness of the problems of accumulation in backward Russia led him, as it led Trotsky, to deny that it was possible. The Stalin–Bukharin majority accused them of defeatism and asserted that socialism could be built. In due course Stalin split with his ally and launched his revolution from above, with rapid industrialization and forcible collectivization. Both Bukharin and Preobrazhensky perished in the great purges, as did many other economists, politicians, generals, writers.

The second part also includes Domar's essay (Reading 7) on the work of a pioneer Marxist growth theorist, Feldman. An officer of Gosplan, Feldman was given the task of preparing the theoretical framework for a general plan, extending over a period of ten to twenty years, to be drafted by Gosplan alongside the first five-year plan. Starting from Marx's schemes of expanded reproduction, Feldman built a two-sector model of acceleration of economic growth. This expresses the foundations of the Soviet strategy for economic growth until the mid-1950s, based on priority for heavy industry and production goods; the same strategy was passively followed by the other socialist countries of Eastern Europe after the war. (Domar performed a service to the profession by dragging Feldman out of the obscurity to which he was so unjustly consigned by his fellow countrymen. Feldman spent many years in exile in the far North and died in Moscow as recently as 1958, though writing nothing after 1930). Conversely, the contribution by Brus and Laski (Reading 8) inspired by Kalecki's work and by the Polish experience, stresses the conflict between current consumption and growth, and the factors limiting economic growth, anticipating the more recent trend of giving priority to consumption rather than to production goods.

The third part, which deals with planning techniques, is largely self explanatory. Kalecki's outline (Reading 9) of a method for constructing a perspective plan is based mainly on the Polish experience in the preparation of the 1961–75 long-run plan but can be taken as a generalization of the planning procedures used in most socialist countries. Montias (Reading 10) describes the method of material balances, budget-type accounts for the main inputs of the economy, and relates the procedure followed in their preparation with the more modern and sophisticated input–output techniques. The contribution by Kalecki and Rakowski (Reading 11) on the choice of production techniques in investment projects contains an original approach to the problem which, beside having theoretical interest, was immediately embodied in the official instructions of the Polish Planning Commission. Joan Robinson's essay (Reading 12) deals with the general problems of consumption planning, and Garvy's contribution (Reading 13) is devoted to the role of money and the planning of monetary flows in the management of the socialist economy.

Part Four is devoted to reforms. The centralization model inherited from the Stalin period may perhaps have suited a country with Russia's traditions, in which a powerful post-revolutionary government was engaged in rapid industrialization and social transformation. The efficacy of the system has come to be questioned throughout Eastern Europe, including Russia itself. Can it operate with tolerable efficiency in a modern industrial society under normal conditions? The first challenge to economic Stalinism came from Yugoslavia in the early fifties, and then in Poland in 1956. Increasingly Soviet reformers began to be heard in the years that followed, and the chorus swelled with voices from Hungary and Czechoslovakia. We include Liberman's *Pravda* article (Reading 14) though his role and influence have been overrated in the West, and the reader will see that he had no coherent alternative model to propound. Kosygin's speech of 1965 (Reading 15) appears, partly as an authoritative statement of intention, partly as a sample of the language in which official thinking is expressed. However, even the cautious proposals of 1965 have been only partially implemented; investment planning, in particular, has been lagging behind in the schedule of reforms, though the Czechoslovak-planned changes in this field, analysed in Nuti's paper, (Reading 17) indicate significant trends. Things are very different both in theory and practice in Hungary, and the contrast is highlighted in Nove's contribution. Kosygin himself, speaking to the 24th Congress in April 1971, said quite clearly: 'the dominant and decisive (principle) is directive planning', and commodity–money relations are to be subordinated to the exigencies and logic of central control.

Part Five, which deals with mathematical techniques, is intimately linked with reform. Thus Nemchinov (Reading 20), Novozhilov (Reading 18) and Kantorovich (Reading 21) were all feeling their way towards an economic reform based on programming techniques and the computer. The economy's constraints (i.e. the amounts of initial resources: land, labour, machines, inventories, foreign currency), technology and the planners' preferences (assumed to be known, consistent and complete, and easily translatable into mathematical form) determine, by means of programming techniques, the optimal plan and a set of shadow (dual) prices to go with it, that could conceivably be used to decentralize economic decisions in a market-less economy. Much space had to be devoted to reconciling the new ideas, and their implication for pricing, with Marxist value theory. The resultant jargon may seem clumsy or unnecessary to some, yet the point at issue is a very important one; does Marxist value theory inhibit the effective use of prices and valuations? If a good is relatively scarce, then its use for any purpose ought surely to be affected by knowledge of opportunities forgone, a fact that would be reflected in its price in any computer programme. The theory of equilibrium prices is inapplicable to a situation of disequilibrium. If the best use of capital or land is achieved by levying a differential charge for their use, why should this be un-Marxist? It is incomes for landlords and capitalists which are contrary to doctrine, not a monetary recognition of the shortage of good land or the most modern machines. Thus argue the reformers. The three men mentioned above jointly received the Lenin Prize for their works, yet at present it is their critics who seem to be in the ascendancy, and few of their proposals are being implemented. Of course, some of these proposals raise severe practical difficulties. One has only to refer to Novozhilov's article, in which the author shows himself to be conscious of the limitations of his prices in the context of investment decisions, and to Veinshtein's pessimism on the feasibility of the task. However, the main source of opposition must surely come from those who oppose the 'socialist market' implication of the doctrine of the mathematical reformers.

Mathematical thinking has been developing rapidly also outside the USSR, and Lange (Reading 19) and Kornai (Reading 23) are included as examples of such thinking. The latter's ideas on multi-level planning are an important contribution to the possible solution of what has been described as 'the accursed problem of large numbers'. It is impossible to handle at the centre of the vast amount of information required for a fully disaggregated rational plan. Indeed, one Soviet academician claimed that it would take a computer several thousand years to do it. This academician could be said to be restating Robbins's old objection, and indeed emphasizing that it is not removable by the invention of the computer, if it were imagined that a single body of central planners would take all necessary decisions. No one knows better than the mathematicians that this is utterly impracticable. This is why, in feeling their way towards a multi-level structure of decision making, they favour the use of market relations as an irreplaceable basis for resource allocation in the context of micro-economics.

This whole approach has given rise to opposition among some socialists. They regard it as revisionist, and perhaps even a stage in the process of restoring capitalism. A very different approach has manifested itself in Cuba, and certainly Chinese ideas at the height of the Cultural Revolution belong to quite another world. Gray's essay discusses the specific features of Maoist economic theory and policies. There is no doubt that these have a great significance for the future of the economics of socialism.

References

PARKER, R. H., and HARCOURT, G. C. (1969), *Readings in the Concept and Measurement of Income*.

UNITED NATIONS-ECE (1959), 'A note on some aspects of national accounting methodology in Eastern Europe and the Soviet Union', *Economic Bulletin for Europe*, no. 11.

Part One
The Socialist Economy

Marx and Engels had no detailed blueprint for the socialist
economy. Some of their statements on the essential features of a
socialist economy – abolition of private property, principles of
distribution, the difference between socialism and communism,
division of labour, the economic plan – are included here. More
detailed features of an actual socialist economy emerged in the
Soviet practice: the problems of transition to socialism, the
organization of planning, accounting and control, money and
banking, exchange and distribution were discussed soon after
the October Revolution. A sample of contributions to this
discussion is given here by excerpts from Lenin, Bukharin and
Preobrazhensky. Stalin's later pronouncement is representative
of the economic orthodoxy and dogmas of the Stalinist era
(readers should be warned that when Stalin, and Eastern
European economists in general, refer to the applicability of the
'law of value' in a socialist economy they do not refer to the
Marxian labour theory of value, but to the role of 'commodity–
money relations', i.e. the role of purchase and sale as against
directive plans). More recent developments in socialist theory
and practice are included in Part Four (especially Readings 14
and 15 respectively by Liberman and Kosygin): they are
representative of the 1960s and of the current process of economic
reform. For an outline of the Chinese alternative model, see
Reading 24.

The question of the functioning of a socialist economy soon
became the object of study by bourgeois economists. Barone's
essay is a significant contribution because it shows that the task
of the Minister of Production in a collectivist state is feasible in
theory (though the equations of the equilibrium are not soluble

a priori, on paper) and, at the same time, that the Minister would have to use the same categories and instruments as in a capitalist economy: the solution of his task would be equivalent – *mutatis mutandis* – to the operation of a perfectly competitive capitalist economy. This answers, before they are even raised, some of the questions Mises asked later about the rationality of a socialist economy. Mises had other comments on the actual practicability of a rationally managed socialist economy, and this is why we reproduce most of his essay. Out of the discussion that developed on this subject in Western literature in the thirties (with important contributions by Dickinson, Dobb, von Hayek, Lange, Lerner, Robbins, Taylor and others) we include most of Lange's classic essay because it is addressed directly to Mises's challenge, it develops the argument from where Barone left off, and it can be compared with the later development of Lange's theory of the socialist economy (see Reading 19).

1 Selected Quotations from Marxist Sources

1.1 K. Marx and F. Engels,
The Communist Manifesto, 1873

The distinguishing feature of communism is not the abolition of property generally, but the abolition of bourgeois property. But modern bourgeois private property is the final and most complete expression of the system of producing and appropriating products that is based on class antagonisms, on the exploitation of the many by the few.

In this sense, the theory of the communists may be summed up in the single sentence: abolition of private property.

We communists have been reproached with the desire of abolishing the right of personally acquiring property as the fruit of a man's own labour, which property is alleged to be the ground work of all personal freedom, activity and independence.

Hard-won, self-acquired, self-earned property! Do you mean the property of the petty artisan and of the small peasant, a form of property that preceded the bourgeois form? There is no need to abolish that; the development of industry has to a great extent already destroyed it, and is still destroying it daily.

Or do you mean modern bourgeois private property?

But does wage labour create any property for the labourer? Not a bit. It creates capital, i.e. that kind of property which exploits wage labour, and which cannot increase except upon condition of begetting a new supply of wage labour for fresh exploitation. Property, in its present form, is based on the antagonism of capital and wage labour. Let us examine both sides of this antagonism.

To be a capitalist is to have not only a purely personal but a social *status* in production. Capital is a collective product, and only by the united action of many members, nay, in the last resort, only by the united action of all members of society, can it be set in motion.

Capital is, therefore, not a personal, it is a social power.

When, therefore, capital is converted into common property, into the property of all members of society, personal property is not thereby transformed into social property. It is only the social character of the property that is changed. It loses its class character.

Let us now take wage labour.

The average price of wage labour is the minimum wage, i.e., that quantum of the means of subsistence which is absolutely requisite to keep the labourer in bare existence as a labourer. What, therefore, the wage-labourer appropriates by means of his labour, merely suffices to prolong and reproduce a bare existence. We by no means intend to abolish this personal appropriation of the products of labour, an appropriation that is made for the maintenance and reproduction of human life, and that leaves no surplus wherewith to command the labour of others. All that we want to do away with is the miserable character of this appropriation, under which the labourer lives merely to increase capital, and is allowed to live only in so far as the interest of the ruling class requires it.

In bourgeois society, living labour is but a means to increase accumulated labour. In communist society, accumulated labour is but a means to widen, to enrich, to promote the existence of the labourer.

In bourgeois society, therefore, the past dominates the present; in communist society, the present dominates the past. In bourgeois society capital is independent and has individuality, while the living person is dependent and has no individuality.

And the abolition of this state of things is called by the bourgeois, abolition of individuality and freedom! And rightly so. The abolition of bourgeois individuality, bourgeois independence, and bourgeois freedom is undoubtedly aimed at.

By freedom is meant, under the present bourgeois conditions of production, free trade, free selling and buying.

But if selling and buying disappears, free selling and buying disappears also. This talk about free selling and buying, and all the other 'brave words' of our bourgeoisie about freedom in general, have a meaning, if any, only in contrast with restricted selling and buying, with the fettered traders of the Middle Ages, but have no meaning when opposed to the communistic abolition of buying and selling, of the bourgeois conditions of production, and of the bourgeoisie itself.

You are horrified at our intending to do away with private property. But in your existing society, private property is already done away with for nine-tenths of the population; its existence for the few is solely due to its non-existence in the hands of those nine-tenths. You reproach us, therefore, with intending to do away with a form of property the necessary condition for whose existence is the non-existence of any property for the immense majority of society.

In one word, you reproach us with intending to do away with your property. Precisely so; that is just what we intend.

From the moment when labour can no longer be converted into capital, money, or rent, into a social power capable of being monopolized, i.e. from the moment when individual property can no longer be transformed into bourgeois property, into capital, from that moment, you say, individuality vanishes.

You must, therefore, confess that by 'individual' you mean no other person than the bourgeois, than the middle-class owner of property. This person must, indeed, be swept out of the way, and made impossible.

Communism deprives no man of the power to appropriate the products of society; all that it does is to deprive him of the power to subjugate the labour of others by means of such appropriation.

It has been objected that upon the abolition of private property all work will cease, and universal laziness will overtake us.

According to this, bourgeois society ought long ago to have gone to the dogs through sheer idleness; for those of its members who work, acquire nothing, and those who acquire anything, do not work. The whole of this objection is but another expression of the tautology: that there can no longer be any wage labour when there is no longer any capital.

1.2 K. Marx, *Critique of the Gotha Programme, 1891*

Within the cooperative society based on common ownership of the means of production, the producers do not exchange their products; just as little does the labour employed on the products appear here *as the value* of these products, as a material quality possessed by them, since now, in contrast to capitalist society, individual labour no longer exists in an indirect fashion but directly as a component part of the total labour. The phrase 'proceeds of labour', objectionable also today on account of its ambiguity, thus loses all meaning.

What we have to deal with here is a communist society, not as it has *developed* on its own foundations, but, on the contrary, just as it *emerges* from capitalist society; which is, therefore, in every respect, economically, morally and intellectually, still stamped with the birth-marks of the old society from whose womb it comes. Accordingly, the individual producer receives back from society – after the deductions have been made – exactly what he gives to it. What he has given to it is his individual quantum of labour. For example, the social working day consists of the sum of the individual hours of work; the individual labour time of the individual producer is the part of the social working day contributed by him, his share in it. He receives a certificate from society that he has furnished such and such an amount of labour (after deducting his labour for the common funds), and with this certificate he draws from the social stock of means of consumption as much as costs the same amount of labour. The same amount of labour which he has given to society in one form he receives back in another.

Here obviously the same principle prevails as that which regulates the exchange of commodities, as far as this is exchange of equal values. Content and form are changed, because under the altered circumstances no one can give anything except his labour, and because, on the other hand, nothing can pass to the ownership of individuals except individual means of consumption. But, as far as the distribution of the latter among the individual producers is concerned, the same principle prevails as in the exchange of commodity-equivalents: a given amount of labour in one form is exchanged for an equal amount of labour in another form.

Hence, *equal right* here is still in principle – *bourgeois right*, although principle and practice are no longer at loggerheads, while the exchange of equivalents in commodity exchange only exists *on the average* and not in the individual case.

In spite of this advance, this *equal right* is still constantly stigmatized by a bourgeois limitation. The right of the producers is *proportional* to the labour they supply; the equality consists in the fact that measurement is made with an *equal standard*, labour.

But one man is superior to another physically or mentally and so supplies more labour in the same time, or can labour for a longer time; and labour, to serve as a measure, must be defined by its duration or intensity, otherwise it ceases to be a standard of measurement. This *equal* right is an unequal right for unequal labour. It recognizes no class differences, because everyone is only a worker like everyone else; but it tacitly recognizes unequal individual endowment and thus productive capacity as natural privileges. *It is, therefore, a right of inequality, in its content, like every right.*

Right by its very nature can consist only in the application of an equal standard; but unequal individuals (and they would not be different individuals if they were not unequal) are measurable only by an equal standard in so far as they are brought under an equal point of view, are taken from one *definite* side only, for instance, in the present case, are regarded *only as workers* and nothing more is seen in them, everything else being ignored. Further, one worker is married, another not; one has more children than another, and so on and so forth. Thus, with an equal performance of labour, and hence an equal share in the social consumption fund, one will in fact receive more than another, one will be richer than another, and so on. To avoid all these defects, right would have to be unequal rather than equal.

But these defects are inevitable in the first phase of communist society as it is when it has just emerged, after prolonged birth-pangs, from capitalist society. Right can never be higher than the economic structure of society and its cultural development conditioned thereby.

In a higher phase of communist society, after the enslaving subordination of the individual to the division of labour, and with it also the antithesis between mental and physical labour, has vanished, after labour has become not only a livelihood but life's prime want, after the productive forces have also increased with the all-round development of the individual, and all the springs of cooperative wealth flow more abundantly – only then can the narrow horizon of bourgeois right be crossed in its entirety and society inscribe on its banners: From each according to his abilities, to each according to his needs!

1.3 F. Engels, *Anti-Dühring*

In making itself the master of all the means of production to use them in accordance with a social plan, society puts an end to the former subjection of men to their own means of production. It goes without saying that society cannot free itself unless every individual is freed. The old mode of production must therefore be revolutionized from top to bottom, and in particular the former division of labour must disappear. Its place must be taken by an organization of production in which, on the one hand, no individual can throw on the shoulders of others his share in productive labour, this natural condition of human existence; and in which, on the other hand, productive labour, instead of being a means of subjugating men, will become a means of their emancipation, by offering each individual the opportunity to develop all his faculties, physical and mental, in all directions and exercise them to the full – in which, therefore, productive labour will become a pleasure instead of being a burden.

Today this is no longer a fantasy, no longer a pious wish. With the present development of the productive forces, the increase in production that will follow from the very fact of the socialization of the productive forces, coupled with the abolition of the barriers and disturbances, and of the waste of products and means of production, resulting from the capitalist mode of production, will suffice, with everybody doing his share of work, to reduce the time required for labour to a point which, measured by our present conceptions, will be small indeed.

Nor is the abolition of the old division of labour a demand which could only be carried through to the detriment of the productivity of labour. On the contrary. Thanks to modern industry it has become a condition of production itself.

1.4 K. Marx, *Economic and Philosophic Manuscripts of 1844*

Communism as the *positive* transcendence of *private property*, as *human self-estrangement*, and therefore as the real *appropriation of the human* essence by and for man; communism therefore as the complete return of man to himself as a *social* (i.e. human) being – a return become conscious, and accomplished within the entire wealth of previous development. This communism, as fully developed naturalism, equals humanism, and as fully developed humanism equals naturalism: it is the *genuine* resolution of the conflict between man and nature and between man and man – the true resolution of the strife between existence and essence, between objectification and self-confirmation, between freedom and necessity, between the individual and the species. Communism is the riddle of history solved, and it knows itself to be this solution.

1.5 V. I. Lenin, *From the Destruction of the Old Social System to the Creation of the New*

Communist labour in the narrower and stricter sense of the term is labour performed gratis for the benefit of society, labour performed not as a definite duty, not for the purpose of obtaining a right to certain products, not according to previously established and legally fixed quotas, but voluntary labour, irrespective of quotas; it is labour performed without expectation of reward, without reward as a condition, labour performed because it has become a habit to work for the common good, and because of a conscious realization (that has become a habit) of the necessity of working for the common good – labour as the requirement of a healthy organism.

1.6 V. I. Lenin, *The Tax in Kind*

Socialism is inconceivable without large-scale capitalist engineering based on the latest discoveries of modern science. It is inconceivable without planned state organization which keeps tens of millions of people to the strictest observance of a unified standard in production and distribution.

1.7 V. I. Lenin, *The Eighth All-Russia Congress of Soviets*

Communism is Soviet power plus the electrification of the whole country. Otherwise the country will remain a small-peasant country, and we must clearly realize that. We are weaker than capitalism, not only on the world scale, but also within the country. That is common knowledge. We have realized it, and we shall see to it that the economic basis is transformed from a small-peasant basis into a large-scale industrial basis. Only when the country has been electrified, and industry, agriculture and transport have been placed on the technical basis of modern large-scale industry, only then shall we be fully victorious.

1.8 V. I. Lenin, *Session of the All-Russia C.E.C., 29 April 1918*

And when I express my dissent to those people who claim to be socialists and who promise the workers they shall enjoy as much as they like and whatever they like, I say that communism presupposes a productivity of labour that we do not have at present. Our productivity is too low, that is a fact. Capitalism leaves us as a heritage, especially in a backward country, a host of customs through which all state property, all public property, is regarded as something that may be maliciously spoilt. The psychology of the petty-bourgeois mass is felt at every step, and the struggle in this sphere is a very difficult one. Only the organized proletariat can endure everything. I wrote: 'Until the higher phase of communism arrives, the socialists demand the strictest control by society and by the state'.

1.9 V. I. Lenin, *The State and Revolution*

Accounting and control – that is *mainly* what is needed for the 'smooth working', for the proper functioning, of the *first phase* of communist society. *All* citizens are transformed into hired employees of the state, which consists of the armed workers. *All* citizens become employees and workers of a *single* country-wide state 'syndicate'. All that is required is that they should work equally, do their proper share of work, and get equal pay. The accounting and control necessary for this have been *simplified* by capitalism to the utmost and reduced to the extraordinarily simple operations – which any literate person can perform – of supervising and recording, knowledge of the four rules of arithmetic, and issuing appropriate receipts.[1]

When the *majority* of the people begin independently and everywhere to keep such accounts and exercise such control over the capitalists (now converted into employees) and over the intellectual gentry who preserve their capitalist habits, this control will really become universal, general and popular; and there will be no getting away from it, there will be 'nowhere to go'.

The whole of society will have become a single office and a single factory, with equality of labour and pay.

But this 'factory' discipline, which the proletariat, after defeating the capitalists, after overthrowing the exploiters, will extend to the whole of society, is by no means our ideal, or our ultimate goal. It is only a necessary *step* for thoroughly cleaning society of all the infamies and abominations of capitalist exploitation, *and for further* progress. . . .

For when *all* have learned to administer and actually do independently administer social production, independently keep accounts and exercise control over the parasites, the sons of the wealthy, the swindlers and other 'guardians of capitalist traditions', the escape from this popular accounting and control will inevitably become so incredibly difficult, such a rare exception, and will probably be accompanied by such swift and severe punishment (for the armed workers are practical men and not sentimental intellectuals, and they will scarcely allow anyone to trifle with them), that the *necessity* of observing the simple, fundamental rules of the community will very soon become a *habit*.

Then the door will be thrown wide open for the transition from the first phase of communist society to its higher phase, and with it to the complete withering away of the state.

1. When the more important functions of the state are reduced to such accounting and control by the workers themselves, it will cease to be a 'political state' and 'public functions will lose their political character and become mere administrative functions. . . .'

1.10 V. I. Lenin, *The State and Revolution*

Abolishing the bureaucracy at once, everywhere and completely, is out of the question. It is a utopia. But to *smash* the old bureaucratic machine at once and to begin immediately to construct a new one that will make possible the gradual abolition of all bureaucracy – this is *not* a utopia, it is the experience of the Commune, the direct and immediate task of the revolutionary proletariat.

Capitalism simplifies the functions of 'state' administration; it makes it possible to cast 'bossing' aside and to confine the whole matter to the organization of the proletarians (as the ruling class), which will hire 'workers, foremen and accountants' in the name of the whole of society.

We are not utopians, we do not 'dream' of dispensing *at once* with all administration, with all subordination. These anarchist dreams, based upon incomprehension of the tasks of the proletarian dictatorship, are totally alien to Marxism, and, as a matter of fact, serve only to postpone the socialist revolution until people are different. No, we want the socialist revolution with people as they are now, with people who cannot dispense with subordination, control and 'foremen and accountants'.

The subordination, however, must be to the armed vanguard of all the exploited and working people, i.e. to the proletariat. A beginning can and must be made at once, overnight, to replace the specific 'bossing' of state officials by the simple functions of 'foremen and accountants', functions which are already fully within the ability of the average town dweller and can well be performed for 'workmen's wages'.

We, the workers, shall organize large-scale production on the basis of what capitalism has already created, relying on our own experience as workers, establishing strict, iron discipline backed up by the state power of the armed workers. We shall reduce the role of state officials to that of simply carrying out our instructions as responsible, revocable, modestly paid 'foremen and accountants' (of course, with the aid of technicians of all sorts, types and degrees). This is *our* proletarian task, this is what we can and must *start* with in accomplishing the proletarian revolution. Such a beginning, on the basis of large-scale production, will of itself lead to the gradual 'withering away' of all bureaucracy, to the gradual creation of an order – an order without inverted commas, an order bearing no similarity to wage-slavery – an order under which the functions of control and accounting, becoming more and more simple, will be performed by each in turn, will then become a habit and will finally die out as the *special* functions of a special section of the population.

1.11 V. I. Lenin, *The State and Revolution*

A witty German Social-Democrat of the seventies of the last century called the *postal service* an example of the socialist economic system. This is very true. At present the postal service is a business organized on the lines of a state-*capitalist* monopoly. Imperialism is gradually transforming all trusts into organizations of a similar type, in which, standing over the 'common' people, who are overworked and starved, one has the same bourgeois bureaucracy. But the mechanism of social management is here already to hand. Once we have overthrown the capitalists, crushed the resistance of these exploiters with the iron hand of the armed workers, and smashed the bureaucratic machine of the modern state, we shall have a splendidly equipped mechanism, freed from the 'parasite', a mechanism which can very well be set going by the united workers themselves, who will hire technicians, foremen and accountants, and pay them *all*, as indeed *all* 'state' officials in general, workmen's wages. Here is a concrete, practical task which can immediately be fulfilled in relation to all trusts, a task whose fulfilment will rid the working people of exploitation, a task which takes account of what the Commune had already begun to practise (particularly in building up the state).

To organize the *whole* economy on the lines of the postal service so that the technicians, foremen and accountants, as well as *all* officials, shall receive salaries no higher than 'a workman's wage', all under the control and leadership of the armed proletariat – this is our immediate aim. This is the state and this is the economic foundation we need. This is what will bring about the abolition of parliamentarism and the preservation of representative institutions. This is what will rid the labouring classes of the bourgeoisie's prostitution of these institutions.

1.12 V. I. Lenin, *The Impending Catastrophe and How to Combat It*

All a government would have had to do, if its name of revolutionary-democratic government were not merely a joke, would have been to decree, in the very first week of its existence, the adoption of the principal measures of control. . . .

These principal measures are:

1. Amalgamation of all banks into a single bank, and state control over its operations, or nationalization of the banks.

2. Nationalization of the syndicates, i.e. the largest, monopolistic capitalist associations (sugar, oil, coal, iron and steel, and other syndicates).

3. Abolition of commercial secrecy.

4. Compulsory syndication (i.e. compulsory amalgamation into associations) of industrialists, merchants and employers generally.

5. Compulsory organization of the population into consumers' societies, or encouragement of such organization, and the exercise of control over it. . . .

The banks, as we know, are centres of modern economic life, the principal nerve centres of the whole capitalist economic system. To talk about 'regulating economic life' and yet evade the question of the nationalization of the banks means either betraying the most profound ignorance or deceiving the 'common people' by florid words and grandiloquent promises with the deliberate intention of not fulfilling these promises. . . .

Only by nationalizing the banks *can* the state *put itself in a position* to know where and how, whence and when, millions and billions of roubles flow. And only control over the banks, over the centre, over the pivot and chief mechanism of capitalist circulation, would make it possible to organize real and not fictitious control over all economic life, over the production and distribution of staple goods, and organize that 'regulation of economic life' which otherwise is inevitably doomed to remain a ministerial phrase designed to fool the common people. Only control over banking operations, provided they were concentrated in a single state bank, would make it possible, if certain other easily-practicable measures were adopted, to organize the effective collection of income tax in such a way as to prevent the concealment of property and incomes; for at present the income tax is very largely a fiction.

1.13 V. I. Lenin, *Can the Bolsheviks Retain State Power?*

Capitalism has created an accounting *apparatus* in the shape of the banks, syndicates, postal service, consumers' societies, and office employees' unions. *Without big banks socialism would be impossible.*

The big banks *are* the 'state apparatus' which we *need* to bring about socialism, and which we *take ready-made* from capitalism; our task here is merely to *lop off* what *capitalistically mutilates* this excellent apparatus, to make it *even bigger*, even more democratic, even more comprehensive. Quantity will be transformed into quality. A single State Bank, the biggest of the big, with branches in every rural district, in every factory, will constitute as much as nine-tenths of the *socialist* apparatus. This will be country-wide *book-keeping*, country-wide *accounting* of the production and distribution of goods, this will be, so to speak, something in the nature of the *skeleton* of socialist society.

We can 'lay hold of' and 'set in motion' this 'state apparatus' (which is not fully a state apparatus under capitalism, but which will be so with us, under socialism) at one stroke, by a single decree, because the actual work of book-keeping, control, registering, accounting and counting is performed by *employees*, the majority of whom themselves lead a proletarian or semi-proletarian existence. . . .

The conversion of the bank, syndicate, commercial, etc., etc., rank-and-file employees into state employees is quite feasible both technically (thanks to the preliminary work performed for us by capitalism, including finance capitalism) and politically, provided the *Soviets* exercise control and supervision.

1.14 N. I. Bukharin and E. Preobrazhensky, *The ABC of Communism*

Characteristics of the communist system
Production under communism

It is evident that the new society must be much more solidly constructed than capitalism. As soon as the fundamental contradictions of capitalism have destroyed the capitalist system, upon the ruins of that system there must arise a new society which will be free from the contradictions of the old. That is to say, the communist method of production must present the following characteristics: In the first place it must be an *organized* society; it must be free from anarchy of production, from competition between individual entrepreneurs, from wars and crises. In the second place it must be a *classless* society, not a society in which the two halves are at eternal enmity one with the other; it must not be a society in which one class exploits the other. Now a society in which there are no classes, and in which production is organized, can only be *a society of comrades*, *a communist society based upon labour*.

Let us examine this society more closely.

The basis of communist society must be the social ownership of the means of production and exchange. Machinery, locomotives, steamships, factory buildings, warehouses, grain elevators, mines, telegraphs and telephones, the land, sheep, horses and cattle, must all be at the disposal of society. All these means of production must be under the control of society as a whole, and not as at present under the control of individual capitalists or capitalist combines. What do we mean by 'society as a whole'? We mean that ownership and control is not the privilege of a class but of all the persons who make up society. In these circumstances society will be transformed into a huge working organization for cooperative production. There will then be neither disintegration of production nor anarchy of production. In such a social order, production will be organized. No longer will one enterprise compete with another; the factories, workshops, mines, and other productive institutions will all be subdivisions, as it were, of one vast people's workshop, which will embrace the entire national economy of production. It is obvious that so comprehensive an organization presupposes a general plan of production. If all the factories and workshops together with the whole of agricultural production are combined to form an immense cooperative enterprise, it is obvious that everything must be precisely calculated. We must know in advance how much labour to assign to the various branches of industry; what products are required and how much of each it is necessary to produce; how and where machines must be provided. These and similar details must be thought out beforehand, with approximate accuracy at least; and the work must be guided in conformity with our calculations. This is how the organization of communist production will be effected. Without a general plan, without a general directive system, and without careful calculation and book-keeping, there can be no organization. But in the communist social order, there is such a plan.

Mere organization does not, however, suffice. The essence of the matter lies in this, that the organization shall be a cooperative organization of *all* the members of society. The communist system, in addition to effecting organization, is further distinguished by the fact that *it puts an end to exploitation*, that *it abolishes the division of society into classes*. We might conceive the organization of production as being effected in the following manner: a small group of capitalists, a capitalist combine, controls everything; production has been organized, so that capitalist no longer competes with capitalist; conjointly they extract surplus value from the workers, who have been practically reduced to slavery. Here we have organization, but we also have the exploitation of one class by another. Here there is a joint ownership of the means of production, but it is joint ownership by one class, an exploiting class. This is something very different from communism, although it is characterized by the organization of production. Such an organization of society would have removed only one of the fundamental contradictions, the anarchy of production. But it would have strengthened the other fundamental contradiction of capitalism, the division of society into two warring halves; the class war would be intensified. Such a society would be organized along one line only; on another line, that of class structure, it would still be rent asunder. Communist society does not merely organize production; in addition, it frees people from oppression by others. It is organized throughout.

The cooperative character of communist production is likewise displayed in every detail of organization. Under communism, for example, there will not be permanent managers of factories, nor will there be persons who do one and the same kind of work throughout their lives. Under capitalism, if a man is a bootmaker, he spends his whole life in making boots (the cobbler sticks to his last); if he is a pastrycook, he spends all his life baking cakes; if he is the manager of a factory, he spends his days in issuing orders and in administrative work; if he is a mere labourer, his whole life is spent in obeying orders. Nothing of this sort happens in communist society. Under communism people receive a many-sided culture, and find themselves at home in various branches of production: today I work in an administrative capacity, I reckon up how many felt boots or how many French rolls must be produced in the following month; tomorrow I shall be working in a soap-factory, next month perhaps in a steam-laundry, and the month after in an electric power station. This will be possible when all the members of society have been suitably educated.

Distribution in the communist system

The communist method of production presupposes in addition that production is not for the market, but for use. Under communism, it is no longer the individual manufacturer or the individual peasant who produces; the work of production is effected by the gigantic cooperative as a whole. In consequence of this change, we no longer have *commodities*, but only *products*. These products are not exchanged one for another; they are neither bought nor sold. They are simply stored in the communal warehouses, and are subsequently delivered to those who need them. In such conditions, money will no longer be required. 'How can that be?' some of you will ask. 'In that case one person will get too much and another too little. What sense is there in such a method of distribution?' The answer is as follows. At first, doubtless, and perhaps for twenty or thirty years, it will be necessary to have various regulations. Maybe certain products will only be supplied to those persons who have a special entry in their work-book or on their work-card. Subsequently, when communist society has been consolidated and fully developed, no such regulations will be needed. There will be an ample quantity of all products, our present wounds will long since have been healed, and everyone will be able to get just as much as he needs. 'But will not people find it to their interest to take more than they need?' Certainly not. Today, for example, no one thinks it worth while when he wants one seat in a tram, to take three tickets and keep two places empty. It will be just the same in the case of all products. A person will take from the communal storehouse precisely as much as he needs, no more. No one will have any interest in taking more than he wants in order to sell the surplus to others, since all these others can satisfy their needs whenever they please. Money will then have no value. Our meaning is that at the outset, in the first days of communist society, products will probably be distributed in accordance with the amount of work done by the applicant; at a later stage, however, they will simply be supplied according to the needs of the comrades.

It has often been contended that in the future society everyone will have the right to the full product of his labour. 'What you have made by your labour, that you will receive.' This is false. It would never be possible to realize it fully. Why not? For this reason, that if everyone were to receive the full product of his labour, there would never be any possibility of developing, expanding, and improving production. Part of the work done must always be devoted to the development and improvement of production. If we had to consume and to use up everything we have produced, then we could never produce machines, for these cannot be eaten or worn. But it is obvious that the bettering of life will go hand in hand with the extension and improvement of machinery. It is plain that more and more machines must continually be produced. Now this implies that part of the labour which has been incorporated in the machines will not be returned to the person who has done the work. It implies that no one can ever receive the full product of his labour. But nothing of the kind is necessary. With the aid of good machinery, production will be so arranged that all needs will be satisfied.

To sum up, at the outset products will be distributed *in proportion to the work done* (which does not mean that the worker will receive 'the full product of his labour'); subsequently, products will be distributed *according to need*, for there will be an abundance of everything.

Administration in the communist system

In a communist society there will be no classes. But if there will be no classes, this implies that *in communist society there will likewise be no State*. We have previously seen that the State is a class organization of the rulers. The State is always directed by one class against the other. A bourgeois State is directed against the proletariat, whereas a proletarian State is directed against the bourgeoisie. In the communist social order there are neither landlords, nor capitalists, nor wage workers; there are simply people – comrades. If there are no classes, then there is no class war, and there are no class organizations. Consequently the State has ceased to exist. Since there is no class war, the State has become superfluous. There is no one to be held in restraint, and there is no one to impose restraint.

But how, they will ask us, can this vast organization be set in motion without any administration? Who is going to work out the plans for social production? Who will distribute labour power? Who is going to keep account of social income and expenditure? In a word, who is going to supervise the whole affair?

It is not difficult to answer these questions. The main direction will be entrusted to various kinds of book-keeping offices or statistical bureaux. There, from day to day, account will be kept of production and all its needs; there also it will be decided whither workers must be sent, whence they must be taken, and how much work there is to be done. And inasmuch as, from childhood onwards, all will have been accustomed to social labour, and since all will understand that this work is necessary and that life goes easier when everything is done according to a prearranged plan and when the social order is like a well-oiled machine, all will work in accordance with the indications of these statistical bureaux. There will be no need for special ministers of State, for police and prisons, for laws and decrees – nothing of the sort. Just as in an orchestra all the performers watch the conductor's baton and act accordingly, so here all will consult the statistical reports and will direct their work accordingly.

The State, therefore, has ceased to exist. There are no groups and there is no class standing above all other classes. Moreover, in these statistical bureaux one person will work today, another tomorrow. The bureaucracy, the permanent officialdom, will disappear. The State will die out.

Manifestly this will only happen in the fully developed and strongly established communist system, after the complete and definitive victory of the proletariat; nor will it follow immediately upon that victory. For a long time yet, the working class will have to fight against all its enemies, and in especial against the relics of the past, such as sloth, slackness, criminality, pride. All these will have to be stamped out. Two or three generations of persons will have to grow up under the new conditions before the need will pass for laws and punishments and for the use of repressive measures by the workers' State. Not until then will all the vestiges of the capitalist past disappear. Though in the intervening period the existence of the workers' State is indispensable, subsequently, in the fully developed communist system, when the vestiges of capitalism are extinct, the proletarian State authority will also pass away. The proletariat itself will become mingled with all the other strata of the population, for everyone will by degrees come to participate in the common labour. Within a few decades there will be quite a new world, with new people and new customs.

Money and the dying-out of the monetary system

Communist society will know nothing of money. Every worker will produce goods for the general welfare. He will not receive any certificate to the effect that he has delivered the product to society; he will receive no money, that is to say. In like manner, he will pay no money to society when he receives whatever he requires from the common store. A very different state of affairs prevails in socialist society, which is inevitable as an intermediate stage between capitalism and communism. Here money is needed, for it has a part to play in commodity economy. If I, as a bootmaker, need a coat, I change my wares, the boots that I make, into money. Money is a commodity by means of which I can procure any other commodity I may please, and by means of which in the given case I can procure the particular thing I want, namely a coat. Every producer of commodities acts in the same way. In socialist society, this commodity economy will to some extent persist.

Let us suppose that the resistance of the bourgeoisie has been overcome, and that those who formerly constituted the ruling class have now become workers. But the peasants still remain. They do not work for the general account of society. Every peasant will endeavour to sell his surplus product to the State, to exchange it for the industrial products he needs for his own use. The peasant will remain a producer of commodities. That he may settle accounts with his neighbours and with the State, he will still need money; just as the State will need money in order to settle accounts with all those members of society who have not yet become members of the general productive commune. Still more is it impossible to abolish money immediately, when private trade still continues to a considerable extent, and when the Soviet Power is not yet in a position to replace private trade entirely by socialist distribution. Finally, it would be disadvantageous to abolish money altogether so long as the issue of paper money is a substitute for taxation, so long as it helps the proletarian State to cope with the exceedingly difficult conditions now prevailing.

Socialism, however, is communism in course of construction; it is incomplete communism. In proportion as the work of upbuilding communism is successfully effected, the need for money will disappear. In due time the State will probably be compelled to put an end to the expiring monetary circulation. This will be of especial importance in order to bring about the final disappearance of the laggards of the bourgeois classes who with hoarded money will continue to consume values created by the workers in a society which has proclaimed: 'He who does not work, neither shall he eat.'

Thus, from the very outset of the socialist revolution, money begins to lose its significance. All the nationalized undertakings, just like the single enterprise of a wealthy owner (for the owner of the unified enterprises is now the proletarian State), will have a common counting-house, and will have no need of money for reciprocal purchases and sales. By degrees a moneyless system of account-keeping will come to prevail. Thanks to this, money will no longer have anything to do with one great sphere of the national economy. As far as the peasants are concerned, in their case likewise money will cease by degrees to have any importance, and the direct exchange of commodities will come to the front once more. Even in private trade among the peasants, money will pass into the background, and the buyer will find himself able to procure corn only in exchange for products in kind, such as clothing, household utensils, furniture, etc. The gradual disappearance of money will likewise be promoted by the extensive issue of paper money by the State, in association with the great restriction in the exchange of commodities dependent upon the disorganization of industry. The increasing depreciation of the currency is, essentially, an expression of the annulment of monetary values.

But the most forcible blow to the monetary system will be delivered by the introduction of budget-books and by the payment of the workers in kind. In the work-book will be entered how much the holder has done, and this will mean how much the State owes him. In accordance with the entries in his book, the worker will receive products from the consumers' stores. In such a system it will be impossible for those who do no work to procure goods for money. But the method can only be realized when the State has been able to concentrate into its own hands such a quantity of articles of consumption as is requisite for the supply of all the working members of socialist society. It will be impossible to carry it out until our disorganized industrial system has been reconstructed and expanded.

Speaking generally, the process of abolishing monetary circulation takes the following form today. First of all, money is expelled from the domain of product-exchange as far as the nationalized undertakings are concerned (factories, railways, soviet farms, etc.). Money likewise disappears from the domain of account-keeping between the State and the workers of the socialist State (that is, as far as concerns account-keeping between the Soviet Power on the one hand, and the employees and the workers in soviet undertakings on the other). Furthermore, money becomes superfluous in so far as the direct exchange of goods is effected between the State and the small producers (the peasants and the home workers). Even within the realm of small-scale industry, the direct exchange of goods will tend to replace the use of money; but it may be that money will not completely disappear until small-scale industry itself disappears.

1.15 **J. Stalin,** *Remarks on Economic Questions*
Connected with the November 1951 Discussion on the
Character of Economic Laws under Socialism

Some comrades deny the objective character of laws of science, and of the laws of political economy under socialism in particular. They deny that the laws of political economy reflect law-governed processes which take place independently of the will of man. They believe that in view of the specific role assigned to the Soviet state by history, the Soviet state and its leaders can abolish existing laws of political economy and can 'form', 'create', new laws.

These comrades are profoundly mistaken. It is evident that they confuse laws of science, which reflect objective processes in nature or society, processes which take place independently of the will of man, with the laws which are issued by governments, which are made by the will of man, and which have only juridical validity. But they must not be confused.

Marxism regards laws of science – whether they be laws of natural science or laws of political economy – as the reflection of objective processes which take place independently of the will of man. Man may discover these laws, get to know them, study them, reckon with them in his activities and utilize them in the interests of society, but he cannot change or abolish them. Still less can he form or create new laws of science.

Does this mean, for instance, that the results of the action of the laws of nature, the results of the action of the forces of nature, are in general inavertible, that the destructive action of the forces of nature always and everywhere proceeds with an elemental and inexorable power that does not yield to the influence of man? No, it does not. Leaving aside astronomical, geological and other similar processes, which, even if he has come to know the laws of their development, man really is powerless to influence, in many other cases man is very far from powerless, in the sense of being able to influence the processes of nature. In all such cases, having come to know the laws of nature, reckoning with them and relying on them, and intelligently applying and utilizing them, man can restrict their sphere of action, and can impart a different direction to the destructive forces of nature and convert them to the use of society.

Here, too, the laws of economic development, as in the case of natural science, are objective laws, reflecting processes of economic development which take place independently of the will of man. Man may discover these laws, get to know them and, relying upon them, utilize them in the interests of society, impart a different direction to the destructive action of some of the laws, restrict their sphere of action, and allow fuller scope to other laws that are forcing their way to the forefront; but he cannot destroy them or create new economic laws.

One of the distinguishing features of political economy is that its laws, unlike those of natural science, are impermanent, that they, or at least the majority of them, operate for a definite historical period, after which they give place to new laws. However, these laws are not abolished, but lose their validity owing to the new economic conditions and depart from the scene in order to give place to new laws, laws which are not created by the will of man, but which arise from the new economic conditions.

It is said that economic laws are elemental in character, that their action is inavertible and that society is powerless against them. That is not true. That means making a fetish of laws, and oneself the slave of laws. It has been demonstrated that society is not powerless against laws, that, having come to know economic laws and relying upon them, society can restrict their sphere of action, utilize them in the interests of society and 'harness' them, just as in the case of the forces of nature and their laws.

The economic law that the relations of production must necessarily conform with the character of the productive forces has long been forcing its way to the forefront in the capitalist countries. If it has failed so far to force its way into the open, it is because it is encountering the most powerful resistance on the part of obsolescent forces of society. Here we have another distinguishing feature of economic laws. Unlike the laws of natural science, where the discovery and application of a new law proceeds more or less smoothly, the discovery and application of a new law in the economic field, affecting as it does the interests of obsolescent forces of society, meets with the most powerful resistance on their part. A force, a social force, capable of overcoming this resistance, is therefore necessary. In our country, such a force was the alliance of the working class and the peasantry, who represented the overwhelming majority of society. There is no such force yet in other, capitalist countries. This explains the secret why the Soviet government was able to smash the old forces of society, and why in our country the economic law that the relations of production must necessarily conform with the character of the productive forces received full scope.

It is said that the necessity for balanced (proportionate) development of the national economy in our country enables the Soviet government to abolish existing economic laws and to create new ones. That is absolutely untrue. Our yearly and five-yearly plans must not be confused with the objective economic law of balanced, proportionate development of the national economy. The law of balanced development of the national economy arose in opposition to the law of competition and anarchy of production under capitalism. It arose from the socialization of the means of production, after the law of competition and anarchy of production had lost its validity. It became operative because a socialist economy can be conducted only on the basis of the economic law of balanced development of the national economy. That means that the law of balanced development of the national economy makes it *possible* for our planning bodies to plan social production correctly. But *possibility* must not be confused with *actuality*. They are two different things. In order to turn the possibility into actuality, it is necessary to study this economic law, to master it, to learn to apply it with full understanding, and to compile such plans as fully reflect the requirements of this law. It cannot be said that our yearly and five-yearly plans fully reflect the requirements of this economic law.

It is said that some of the economic laws operating in our country under socialism, including the law of value, have been 'transformed', or even 'radically transformed', on the basis of planned economy. That is likewise untrue. Laws cannot be 'transformed', still less 'radically' transformed. If they can be transformed, then they can be abolished and replaced by other laws. The thesis that laws can be 'transformed' is a relic of the incorrect formula that laws can be 'abolished' or 'formed'. Although the formula that economic laws can be transformed has already been current in our country for a long time, it must be abandoned for the sake of accuracy. The sphere of action of this or that economic law may be restricted, its destructive action – that is, of course, if it is liable to be destructive – may be averted, but it cannot be 'transformed' or 'abolished'.

Consequently, when we speak of 'subjugating' natural forces or economic forces, of 'dominating' them, etc., this does not mean that man can 'abolish' or 'form' scientific laws. On the contrary, it only means that man can discover laws, get to know them and master them, learn to apply them with full understanding, utilize them in the interests of society, and thus subjugate them, secure mastery over them.

Hence, the laws of political economy under socialism are objective laws, which reflect the fact that the processes of economic life are law-governed and take place independently of our will. People who deny this precept are in point of fact denying science, and by denying science they are denying all possibility of prognostication – and, consequently, are denying the possibility of directing economic activity.

Commodity production under socialism

Certain comrades affirm that the Party acted wrongly in preserving commodity production after it had assumed power and nationalized the means of production in our country. They consider that the Party should have banished commodity production there and then.

It is said that commodity production must lead, is bound to lead, to capitalism all the same, under all conditions. That is not true. Not always and not under all conditions! Commodity production must not be identified with capitalist production. They are two different things. Capitalist production is the highest form of commodity production. Commodity production leads to capitalism only *if* there is private ownership of the means of production, *if* labour power appears in the market as a commodity which can be bought by the capitalist and exploited by him in the process of production, and *if*, consequently, the system of exploitation of wage-workers by capitalists exists in the country. Capitalist production begins when the means of production are concentrated in private hands, and when the workers are bereft of means of production and are compelled to sell their labour power as a commodity. Without this there is no such thing as capitalist production.

Well, and what if the conditions for the conversion of commodity production into capitalist production do not exist, if the means of production are no longer private but socialist property, if the system of wage labour no longer exists and labour power is no longer a commodity, and if the system of exploitation has long been abolished – can it be considered then that commodity production will lead to capitalism all the same? No, it cannot. Yet ours is precisely such a society, a society where private ownership of the means of production, the system of wage labour and the system of exploitation have long ceased to exist.

Commodity production must not be regarded as something sufficient unto itself, something independent of the surrounding economic conditions. Commodity production is older than capitalist production. It existed in slave-owning society, and served it, but did not lead to capitalism. It existed in feudal society and served it, yet, although it prepared some of the conditions for capitalist production, it did not lead to capitalism. Why then, one asks, cannot commodity production similarly serve our socialist society for a certain period without leading to capitalism, bearing in mind that in our country commodity production is not so boundless and all-embracing as it is under capitalist conditions, being confined within strict bounds thanks to such decisive economic conditions as social ownership of the means of production, the abolition of the system of wage labour, and the elimination of the system of exploitation?

It is said that, since the domination of social ownership of the means of production has been established in our country, and the system of wage labour and exploitation has been abolished, commodity production has lost all meaning and should therefore be done away with.

That is also untrue. Today there are two basic forms of socialist production in our country: state, or publicly-owned production, and collective-farm production, which cannot be said to be publicly owned. In the state enterprises, the means of production and the product of production are public property. In the collective farm, although the means of production (land, machines) do belong to the state, the product of production is the property of the different collective farms, since the labour, as well as the seed, is their own, while the land, which has been turned over to the collective farms in perpetual tenure, is used by them virtually as their own property, in spite of the fact that they cannot sell, buy, lease or mortgage it.

The effect of this is that the state disposes only of the product of the state enterprises, while the product of the collective farms, being their property, is disposed of only by them. But the collective farms are unwilling to alienate their products except in the form of commodities, in exchange for which they desire to receive the commodities they need. At present the collective farms will not recognize any other economic relation with the town except *the commodity relation – exchange through purchase and sale*. Because of this, commodity production and trade are as much a necessity with us today as they were, say, thirty years ago, when Lenin spoke of the necessity of developing trade to the utmost.

Of course when instead of the two basic production sectors, the state sector and the collective-farm sector, there will be only one all-embracing production sector, with the right to dispose of all the consumer goods produced in the country, commodity circulation, with its 'money economy', will disappear, as being an unnecessary element in the national economy. But so long as this is not the case, so long as the two basic production sectors remain, commodity production and commodity circulation must remain in force, as a necessary and very useful element in our system of national economy. How the formation of a single and united sector will come about, whether simply by the absorption of the collective-farm sector by the state sector – which is hardly likely (because that would be looked upon as the expropriation of the collective farms) – or by the setting up of a single *national* economic body (comprising representatives of state industry and of the collective farms), with the right at first to keep account of all the consumer product in the country, and eventually also to distribute it, by way, say, of products-exchange – is a special question which requires separate discussion.

Consequently, *our* commodity production is not of the ordinary type, but is a special kind of commodity production, commodity production without capitalists, which is concerned mainly with the goods of associated socialist producers (the state, the collective farms, the cooperatives), the sphere of action of which is confined to items of personal consumption, which obviously cannot possibly develop into capitalist production, and which, together with its 'money economy', is designed to serve the development and consolidation of socialist production.

Absolutely mistaken, therefore, are those comrades who allege that, since socialist society has not abolished commodity forms of production, we are bound to have the reappearance of all the economic categories characteristic of capitalism: labour power as a commodity, surplus value, capital, capitalist profit, the average rate of profit, etc. These comrades confuse commodity production with capitalist production, and believe that once there is commodity production there must also be capitalist production. They do not realize that our commodity production radically differs from commodity production under capitalism.

The law of value under socialism

It is sometimes asked whether the law of value exists and operates in our country, under the socialist system.

Yes, it does exist and does operate. Wherever commodities and commodity production exist, there the law of value must also exist.

In our country, the sphere of operation of the law of value extends, first of all, to commodity circulation, to the exchange of commodities through purchase and sale, the exchange, chiefly, of articles of personal consumption. Here, in this sphere, the law of value preserves, within certain limits, of course, the function of a regulator.

But the operation of the law of value is not confined to the sphere of commodity circulation. It also extends to production. True, the law of value has no regulating function in our socialist production, but it nevertheless influences production, and this fact cannot be ignored when directing production. As a matter of fact, consumer goods, which are needed to compensate the labour power expended in the process of production, are produced and realized in our country as commodities coming under the operation of the law of value. It is precisely here that the law of value exercises its influence on production. In this connection, such things as cost accounting and profitableness, production costs, prices, etc., are of actual importance in our enterprises. Consequently, our enterprises cannot, and must not, function without taking the law of value into account.

Is this a good thing? It is not a bad thing. Under present conditions, it really is not a bad thing, since it trains our business executives to conduct production on rational lines and disciplines them. It is not a bad thing because it teaches our executives to count production magnitudes, to count them accurately, and also to calculate the real things in production precisely, and not to talk nonsense about 'approximate figures', spun out of thin air. It is not a bad thing because it teaches our executives to look for, to find and to utilize hidden reserves latent in production, and not to trample them underfoot. It is not a bad thing because it teaches our executives systematically to improve methods of production, to lower production costs, to practise cost accounting, and to make their enterprises pay. It is a good practical school which accelerates the development of our executive personnel and their growth into genuine leaders of socialist production at the present stage of development.

The trouble is not that production in our country is influenced by the law of value. The trouble is that our business executives and planners, with few exceptions, are poorly acquainted with the operations of the law of value, do not study them, and are unable to take account of them in their computations. This, in fact, explains the confusion that still reigns in the sphere of price-fixing policy. Here is one of many examples. Some time ago it was decided to adjust the prices of cotton and grain in the interest of cotton growing, to establish more accurate prices for grain sold to the cotton growers, and to raise the prices of cotton delivered to the state. Our business executives and planners submitted a proposal on this score which could not but astound the members of the Central Committee, since it suggested fixing the price of a ton of grain at practically the same level as a ton of cotton, and, moreover, the price of a ton of grain was taken as equivalent to that of a ton of baked bread. In reply to the remarks of members of the Central Committee that the price of a ton of bread must be higher than that of a ton of grain, because of the additional expense of milling and baking, and that cotton was generally much dearer than grain, as was also borne out by their world market prices, the authors of the proposal could find nothing coherent to say. The Central Committee was therefore obliged to take the matter into its own hands and to lower the prices of grain and raise the prices of cotton. What would have happened if the proposal of these comrades had received legal force? We should have ruined the cotton growers and would have found ourselves without cotton.

But does this mean that the operation of the law of value has as much scope with us as it has under capitalism, and that it is the regulator of production in our country too? No, it does not. Actually, the sphere of operation of the law of value under our economic system is strictly limited and placed within definite bounds. It has already been said that the sphere of operation of commodity production is restricted and placed within definite bounds by our system. The same must be said of the sphere of operation of the law of value. Undoubtedly, the fact that private ownership of the means of production does not exist, and that the means of production both in town and country are socialized, cannot but restrict the sphere of operation of the law of value and the extent of its influence on production.

In this same direction operates the law of balanced (proportionate) development of the national economy, which has superseded the law of competition and anarchy of production.

In this same direction, too, operate our yearly and five-yearly plans and our economic policy generally, which are based on the requirements of the law of balanced development of the national economy.

The effect of all this, taken together, is that the sphere of operation of the law of value in our country is strictly limited, and that the law of value cannot under our system function as the regulator of production.

This, indeed, explains the 'striking' fact that whereas in our country the law of value, in spite of the steady and rapid expansion of our socialist production, does not lead to crises of overproduction, in the capitalist countries this same law, whose sphere of operation is very wide under capitalism, does lead, in spite of the low rate of expansion of production, to periodical crises of overproduction.

It is said that the law of value is a permanent law, binding upon all periods of historical development, and that if it does lose its function as a regulator of exchange relations in the second phase of communist society, it retains at this phase of development its function as a regulator of the relations between the various branches of production, as a regulator of the distribution of labour among them.

That is quite untrue. Value, like the law of value, is a historical category connected with the existence of commodity production. With the disappearance of commodity production, value and its forms and the law of value also disappear.

In the second phase of communist society, the amount of labour expended on the production of goods, will be measured not in a roundabout way, not through value and its forms, as is the case under commodity production, but directly and immediately – by the amount of time, the number of hours, expended on the production of goods. As to the distribution of labour, its distribution among the branches of production will be regulated not by the law of value, which will have ceased to function by that time, but by the growth of society's demand for goods. It will be a society in which production will be regulated by the requirements of society, and computation of the requirements of society will acquire paramount importance for the planning bodies.

Totally incorrect, too, is the assertion that under our present economic system, in the first phase of development of communist society, the law of value regulates the 'proportions' of labour distributed among the various branches of production.

If this were true, it would be incomprehensible why our light industries, which are the most profitable, are not being developed to the utmost, and why they are not given preference over our heavy industries, which are often less profitable, and sometimes altogether unprofitable.

If this were true, it would be incomprehensible why a number of our heavy industry plants which are still unprofitable and where the labour of the worker does not yield the 'proper returns', are not closed down, and why new light industry plants, which would certainly be profitable and where the labour of the workers might yield 'bigger returns', are not opened.

If this were true, it would be incomprehensible why workers are not transferred from plants that are less profitable, but very necessary to our national economy, to plants which are more profitable – in accordance with the law of value, which supposedly regulates the 'proportions' of labour distributed among the branches of production.

Obviously, if we were to follow the lead of these comrades, we should have to cease giving primacy to the production of means of production in favour of the production of articles of consumption. And what would be the effect of ceasing to give primacy to the production of means of production? The effect would be to destroy the possibility of the continuous expansion of our national economy because *the national economy cannot be continuously expanded without giving primacy to the production of means of production.*

These comrades forget that the law of value can be a regulator of production only under capitalism, with its private ownership of the means of production, and competition, anarchy of production, and crises of overproduction. They forget that in our country the sphere of operation of the law of value is limited by the social ownership of the means of production, and by the law of balanced development of the national economy, and is consequently also limited by our yearly and five-yearly plans, which are an approximate reflection of the requirements of this law.

Some comrades draw the conclusion from this that the law of balanced development of the national economy and economic planning annul the principle of profitableness of production. That is quite untrue. It is just the other way round. If profitableness is considered not from the standpoint of individual plants or industries, and not over a period of one year, but from the standpoint of the entire national economy and over a period of, say, ten or fifteen years, which is the only correct approach to the question, then the temporary and unstable profitableness of some plants or industries is beneath all comparison with that higher form of stable and permanent profitableness which we get from the operation of the law of balanced development of the national economy and from economic planning, which save us from periodical economic crises destructive to the national economy and causing tremendous material damage to society, and which ensure a continuous and high rate of expansion of our national economy.

In brief, there can be no doubt that under our present socialist conditions of production, the law of value cannot be a 'regulator of the proportions' of labour distributed among the various branches of production.

References

BUKHARIN, E., and PREOBRAZHENSKY, E. (1920), *The ABC of Communism*, Moscow; London, 1922.

ENGELS, F. (1878), *Anti-Dühring*, London, pp. 403–4.

LENIN, V. I., *Collected Works*, Moscow.

MARX, K. (1891), *Critique of the Gotha Programme*. English edition 1933.

MARX, K., and ENGELS, F. (1872), *The Communist Manifesto*. English edition 1888.

MARX, K. (1959), *Economic and Philosophic Manuscripts of 1844*, Moscow. English edition, p. 102.

2 E. Barone

The Ministry of Production in the Collectivist State

Excerpt from E. Barone, 'The ministry of production in the collectivist
state', in F. A. von Hayek (ed.), *Collectivist Economic Planning*,
Routledge & Kegan Paul, 1935, pp. 247–90. Originally published in Italian
in *Il Giornale degli Economisti*, 1908.

The individualist régime

1. *The data and the unknown quantities.* The data are: the quantity
of capital (including free capital) possessed by each individual;
the *relations*, in a given state of technique, between the quantity
produced and the factors of production; and the *tastes* of the
various individuals. On these last we will make no pre-supposition,
no preliminary inquiry, limiting ourselves simply to assuming the
fact that at every given series of prices of products and productive
services, every single individual portions out the income from his
services between consumption and saving in a certain manner
(into the motives of which we will not inquire) by which, at a
given series of prices, the individual makes certain demands and
certain offers. These quantities demanded and offered vary when
the series of prices vary.

Thus we disengage ourselves from every metaphysical or
subtle conception of utility and of the functions of indifference,
and rely solely on the authenticity of a fact.[1]

2. Let us represent among the data the quantities of the different
kinds of capital possessed by single individuals. Let the different
kinds of capital be S, T,... to n terms. The total quantities of
these existing in the group will be Q_s, Q_t,... Among these n
kinds of capital there is also working capital, and also the kinds
H, K,... (to n terms) of new capital in process of construction.

Let the technical coefficients be a_s, a_t,..., b_s, b_t..., indicating,

---

1. In my elementary treatise, 'Principi di economia politica' (Biblioteca
del *Giornale degli Economisti*), I used the conception of utility, because it
seemed to me the simplest and clearest method to explain to the beginner
some of the most notable results of the new theories. This treatise will be
referred to in future by the short name 'Principi'.

respectively, the quantity of services S, T... necessary for the manufacture of every unit of A, B... which are the various kinds of products, m in number.

For the present we will not count the technical coefficients among the unknown; let us suppose them given, temporarily. We shall see afterwards that they are determined by the condition of minimum cost of production.

The unknowns are set out in the following table:

Table 1

	Quantity	Number of unknowns
Products		
Quantity demanded and produced	R_a, R_b,	m
with cost of production	π_a, π_b,	m
and prices	1, P_b,	$m - 1$
Existing capital		
Quantity of their services directly consumed[2]	R_s, R_t,	n
prices of services	P_s, P_t,	n
New capital		
Quantity manufactured	R_h, R_k,	n'
with cost of production	Π_h, Π_k,	n'
Total excess of income over consumption, expressed in numerical terms[3]	E	1

There are altogether $3m + 2n + 2n'$ unknowns.

The question now is to see if there is an equal number of independent equations.

3. *Equations expressing the Rs and E as functions of prices.* Let us begin with individual budgets. It is convenient to suppose – it is a simple book-keeping artifice, so to speak – that each individual sells the services of all his capital and re-purchases afterwards the part he consumes directly. For example, A, for eight hours of work of a particular kind which he supplies, receives a certain

2. Thence the quantities $Q_s - R_s$, $Q_t - R_t$ ... are devoted to the manufacture of new capital and of final products.

3. This excess serves for the manufacture of new capital and the constitution of new working capital.

remuneration at an hourly rate. It is a matter of indifference whether we enter A's receipts as the proceeds of eight hours' labour, or as the proceeds of twenty-four hours' labour less expenditure of sixteen hours consumed by leisure. The latter method helps to make easier the comprehension of certain maxims of which we shall speak later. Naturally we shall not use this artifice when we deal with the case of services being monopolized by an individual or a group.

The individual then, selling at prices $p_s, p_t...$ the quantities $q_s, q_t...$ of the services of capital of which he disposes, devotes the proceeds to certain products $r_a, r_b...$ and certain services $r_s, r_t...$ which he consumes, saving e.

The individual, then, within the limits of the equation

$$p_a r_a + p_b r_b + ...p_s r_s + p_t r_t + ... + e = p_s q_s + p_t q_t + ...,$$

which the economic society in which he lives imposes, after having sold all his services, reserves a part of his receipts for saving.

We shall not inquire into the criteria on which this distribution is made. It is a *fact*, and here we confine ourselves to formulating it; and to showing that if the series of prices were different, he would demand final products and consumable services in different amounts and would save a different amount.

Hence each of these quantities demanded (and likewise the amount of the individual's savings) depend on the entire series of prices, according to certain functions which it is not necessary to define here. By saying that the individual rs and e are functions, intricate though they be, of all prices, we are only stating a *fact* of universal experience. And that is enough.

Given, then, a series of prices, the rs and e are determinate; and consequently the Rs and E are determinate as functions of prices. Note that each one of these $m+n+1$ quantities is a function of *all* the $m+n-1$ prices of products and services.

4. *The equations of the equilibrium.* Beside $m+n+1$, which express the Rs and E in functions of all the prices of final goods and services, the following relationships can be established.

The first system of equations expresses the physical necessities of production: the total of the services of existing capital must suffice for final goods and services and for the manufacture of new capital, including new working capital:

$$Q_s = R_s + a_s R_a + b_s R_b + \ldots + h_s R_h + k_s R_k + \ldots,$$
$$Q_t = R_t + a_t R_a + b_t R_b + \ldots + h_t R_h + k_t R_k + \ldots. \qquad \mathbf{1}$$

There are n of these equations.

Then we have an equation, which says that the excess of incomes over consumption is used in the manufacture of new capital:

$$E = \Pi_h R_h + \Pi_k R_k + \ldots. \qquad \mathbf{2}$$

Another system of equations gives the cost of production of final goods and new capital as functions of prices of productive services:

$$\pi_a = a_s p_s + a_t p_t + \ldots \qquad \Pi_h = h_s p_s + h_t p_t + \ldots$$
$$\pi_b = b_s p_s + b_t p_t + \ldots \qquad \Pi_k = k_s p_s + k_t p_t + \ldots \qquad \mathbf{3}$$
$$\vdots \qquad \vdots \qquad \vdots \qquad\qquad \vdots \qquad \vdots \qquad \vdots$$

They are $m + n'$ in number.

Lastly, another system expresses one of the characteristics of free competition that the price of final products and of services of new capital equal their cost of production:

$$1 = \pi_a \qquad p_h = \Pi_h \cdot p_e$$
$$p_b = \pi_b \qquad p_k = \Pi_k \cdot p_e \qquad \mathbf{4}$$

There are $m + n' - 1$ of these equations, because among the varieties of new capital is new working capital, the price of which is p_e.

For new capital the condition of the price of the services being equal to the cost of production means that the net rate of yield of new capital is equal everywhere to the interest p_e on free capital (included among the ps of the various services).

5. Counting the number of the equations of the four systems and adding the $m + n + 1$ relations which express the Rs and E in functions of all prices, we find in all $3m + 2n + 2n' + 1$ equations. These exceed by 1 the number of the unknowns; but, as it is easy to see, one of the equations is the result of the others. In fact, summing up on the one hand the equalities of the individual formulae, we arrive at

$$R_a + p_b R_b + \ldots + p_s R_s + p_t R_t + \ldots + E = p_s Q_s + p_t Q_t + \ldots,$$

which is the same result as is obtained by adding together, on the other hand, those of system 1 after having multiplied by $p_s, p_t,...$ and taking account of 2, 3 and 4.

Thus we have the same number of equations as of unknowns. The entire economic system is thus determinate. [There follows an analysis of the competitive equilibrium in the individualist régime.]

The collectivist régime

6. *The statement of the problem.* Some resources remain the property of the individuals (e.g. that which they devote to personal uses): let them be $M, N,...$ to l terms. Let the resources which become the collective property of the state (e.g. fixed capital and land capital) be $S, T,...$ to $n-l$ terms.

The Ministry of Production has to solve the problem of combining these individual and collective services in order to procure the *maximum welfare* for its people. We shall see in what precise sense this vague formula can be understood. The Ministry has studied the very complex problem and has solved it, on the basis of a certain formula of distribution which has been established by the community, on certain ethical and social criteria, with which we do not propose to concern ourselves directly. Such a formula of distribution we suppose (we shall deal with the wherefore later) may be embodied in a certain law, according to which is distributed between the members of the community, what in the old régime was the *yield* of resources now appropriated by the State and what was the profit from various enterprises now administered directly by the State (i.e. socialized). We shall see later whether *all* this *income* can be effectively distributed among the community.

7. If the exposition of the solution of the problem were to follow step by step the route followed in the inquiry, it would be long and confusing.

Therefore, with a view to brevity and clarity of exposition, we shall first enunciate the conditions in which the Ministry is faced with the task of solving the problem. We shall see how in such conditions, and with the criterion of the maximum collective welfare, it succeeds in determining the equilibrium perfectly, with as many equations as unknowns.

Later we shall return to the conditions which it has imposed on itself and we shall show how, if the conditions were different, scientific collectivism would break down either because the problem was indeterminate (the number of conditions insufficient to determine the equilibrium), or because the problem is not only practically but also logically insoluble (the number of equations exceeding the number of quantities to be determined), or, indeed, even when the number of conditions equals the unknowns and the equilibrium is therefore determinate, because the maximum of collective welfare obtainable in this equilibrium would be less than that necessary to provide the distribution formulated.

Hence it is preferable for it to plan production in its own way, and if it still wishes to correct the distribution it should work directly on the formula of distribution, varying certain co-efficients γ which we shall define later, rather than directing production on lines inconsistent with the fundamentals of its own arrangement.

Hence the reader must expect that the conditions which we have posited here will be discussed later (Sections **15–22**), after the solution of the problem, when a comparison will be made between those conditions and others which could have been posited.

8. Here are the conditions in which the Ministry of Production faces the problem:

1. There is no money. There are *products* of a certain work of a given kind. There are no *prices*: but the Ministry maintains, for no other purpose than the social accounts, some method of determining ratios of *equivalence* between the various services and between the various products and between products and services.

2. On the basis of these equivalents[4] the individuals themselves bring their *products* to the *socialized shops* to obtain consumable goods or to obtain from the social administration permission to use some resources of which the State is the proprietor.

The Ministry also maintains ratios of equivalence between the services of socialized resources and other goods, because it is

4. We will discuss later if and when it is convenient, in the interests of the community, to establish different equivalences for the same goods according to the various categories of the individuals.

agreed (we shall state the reasons later) that it would be a grave social loss to cancel arbitrarily the equivalences of these socialized resources. Let 1, $\lambda_b,\ldots,\ \lambda_m, \lambda_n,\ldots,\ \lambda_s, \lambda_t\ldots$ be the equivalences determined upon.

3. The members of the community can enjoy the benefit of the quantity $Q_s\lambda_s + Q_t\lambda_t + \ldots$ which we will call x (remember that $Q_s, Q_t\ldots$ are the quantities of collectively-owned resources) either by an *indirect* distribution, the equivalents of the products being reduced, or by a *direct* distribution, that is giving to the members a *supplement* (to income) which is a quota of x.

The Ministry of Production has agreed that, generally, from the point of view of the greatest collective welfare, the *direct* distribution is preferable to the *indirect*.

The same cannot always be said for certain economic quantities which appear in the collectivist equilibrium and which are analogous to the *profits* of the old régime. We shall discuss them later.

4. Being obliged to proceed with the system of *direct* distribution of x, the Ministry has decided, in agreement with the people, to try a certain system of distribution of x as a supplement to incomes. To each individual belongs γx. The γ could be different for every individual or different for different groups or arranged in such other ways as are possible. We shall discuss these different arrangements afterwards. For now and throughout the greater part of our discussion, let us suppose that γ is determined and differs from one individual to another. It is clear that $\Sigma \gamma = 1$.

5. As for saving, the Ministry, although the people do not wish to hear the words 'saving' and 'interest', still ought to arrange things so that all its productive services are not directly consumed or employed in the production of goods for consumption. Capital, or if we do not wish to speak of capital, the *means of production*, is used up and unless something is substituted for it, it will be necessary to reserve a part of the productive services for the manufacture of it.

But that is not all. The Ministry knows that if it devotes an *adequate* portion of productive services to this manufacture of the *means of production* it will in the future assure a still greater benefit to its people. The Ministry therefore requires some saving to be done. If it is left to individuals to save as much as they like (they then being obliged to lend the savings freely to the State), the amount of saving may not be sufficient to provide for the manufacture of that quantity of new capital which will be considered of maximum social advantage. It could impose a greater saving on individuals; but what if these are not content and prefer a greater present consumption to a greater one in the future? It could deduct from x, before proceeding to the direct distribution of it, that amount which it thinks appropriate for the manufacture of new capital; but it is agreed (we shall see later, in the sequel, the reason for this) that by such a method it would attain a collective maximum *less* than that which is possible by adopting the following method: let it choose at random a rate of *premium* for *deferred consumption*; let it then see how much saving on the basis of this premium its people put freely at its disposition. Then let it find out if with this sum of saving it is possible to manufacture such a quantity of new capital that it will be able, in the future, to put at the disposition of the people a quantity of products and consumable services so great that it can really give them the promised premium for deferred consumption. And by trial and error, raising and reducing the promised premium, it will eventually make its promise in terms which can be realized. By such a method it could provide for their greater future welfare without disturbing their freewill and without interfering with that distribution which each one makes of the *income* he receives for his work, between his present and future needs.

It could, if it wished – and nothing prevents it – prohibit the savers from lending their savings to others and oblige them to lend them to the State so that the production of some goods would be the monopoly of the Government. In the collectivist régime, the Ministry of Production orders the use of individual saving to be sold *only* to the Government.

6. In distributing his earnings, which he receives in exchange for his services – according to the established equivalents of the Ministry – and that amount which he receives as a supplement to distribution (x), between consumption of various kinds and saving the individual is left free to choose, according to his own pleasure.

The Ministry of Production, after mature reflection, imposes these same conditions on itself in striving to provide the maximum collective welfare. Consequently it ought to order production so as to obtain the maximum benefit for its people with the services of which the State disposes and those of which the individuals dispose. These have the freedom, in ordering their own individual economies, to make the choice they believe most convenient, consistent with the equation

$$r_a + \lambda_b\, r_b + \ldots + \lambda_s\, r_s + \lambda_t\, r_t + \ldots + e = \lambda_m\, q_m + \lambda_n\, q_n + \ldots + \gamma x.$$

9. *The collective maximum.* The Ministry of Production commences with the adoption of the technical coefficients which happen to exist at the time (but which satisfy their technical equations). It does not for the present preoccupy itself with the economic variability of these coefficients. It fixes, moreover, at random, a series of Rs which, however, accord with the physical necessities of production (that is system 1 of section **8**). It is absolutely essential that, having chosen the technical coefficients, whatever afterwards may be the system of production which it wishes to follow, the quantity of productive services available must always be precisely that which is necessary to provide for services which are consumed directly and for the manufacture of products and of new capital.

Let it give now, a *random* series of equivalents and the modifications which may be necessary in order that these technical conditions of production (system 1) may be satisfied. It is understood that there is not a *single* system of equivalents which satisfies these conditions. If indeed, it, announced at random $m+n-1$ equivalents of products and productive services, each of its people will make, as we say, a schedule. The individual schedules will give, for the series of equivalents selected by chance, the individual rs and e, whence are derived the totals Rs and E. But as system 1 gives a number of relations between these Rs and the E, less than the number of equivalents, which are $m+n-1$, the system of equivalents satisfying system 1 will admit an infinite number of solutions. Then the Ministry decides on one among those which satisfy system 1 as a starting-point. It will then make adjustments in such a way as to attain the end of the maximum collective welfare.

10. What concrete and unequivocal significance must be attached to this very vague expression 'maximum collective welfare'?

If the Ministry corrects one of the equivalents consistently with 1, the individual will make a new choice, which will be more or less advantageous than the preceding choice according as

$$\Delta r_a + \lambda_b \, \Delta r_b + \ldots + \lambda_s \, \Delta r_s + \lambda_t \, \Delta r_t + \ldots + \Delta e$$

which we call $\Delta\theta$, is positive or negative (14) according to which, we will say, for the sake of brevity, the individual will be *higher* or *lower*.

The meaning of the *collective maximum* would be patent if, by successive attempts, the Ministry could arrive at such a series of equivalents that every further modification of it would place *all* individuals lower. *But such a series of equivalents does not exist; it is useless to try to find it.* It would be necessary to find such a series of equivalents, that by modifying one of them by a very small quantity, the $\Delta\theta$ for each individual would be reduced to zero. And that is *impossible*; since, as we shall now see, the sole condition for reducing to zero not the individual $\Delta\theta$s but their sum $\Sigma \, \Delta\theta$,[5] implies as many conditions as are sufficient to determine completely all the equivalents.

We must bear in mind the possibility that, by making use of the great freedom with which the individual γs can be varied (subject to the sole condition that $\Sigma \gamma = 1$), we can obtain a series of γs and of such equivalents that not only $\Sigma \, \Delta\theta$ is zero but all individual $\Delta\theta$s are zero also. We will show in an appropriate place that this is impossible.

11. What does the reduction of $\Sigma \, \Delta\theta$ signify? To eliminate

$$\Delta R_a + \lambda_b \, \Delta R_b + \ldots + \lambda_s \, \Delta R_s + \lambda_t \, \Delta R_t + \ldots + \Delta E$$

means that every other series of equivalents, different from that which accords with this condition, would make that sum negative. That is to say, either it causes a decline in the welfare of all or, if some decline while others are raised, the gain of the latter is less than the loss of the former. (So that, even taking all their gain from those who gained in the change, reducing them to their

---

5. Which does not mean eliminating every *individual* $\Delta\theta$, for the individuals may not be *identically* provided with the resources and have *identical* tastes.

former position, to give it completely to those who lost, the latter would always remain in a worse situation than their preceding one, without the situation of the others being improved.) Since it is absurd to attempt to resolve the *impossible* problem of finding such a series of equivalents that every further alteration would produce a reduction of welfare for everyone, we will consider that the sole criterion of maximum welfare which the Ministry of Production can use is $\Sigma \, \Delta\theta = 0$.

12. *How the equilibrium is determined.* $\Sigma \, \Delta\theta$ can be put in the form

$$\Delta R_a + \lambda_b \, \Delta R_b + \ldots + \lambda_s \, \Delta R_s + \lambda_t \, \Delta R_t + \ldots + \Delta_h \, \Delta R_h + \Delta_k \, \Delta R_k \ldots$$

calling $\Delta_h, \Delta_k \ldots$ the quantities of saving necessary for the manufacture of a unit of $H, K, \ldots$.

Let us remember that in the first approximate solution the Ministry of Production had assumed a series of technical coefficients at *random* (though satisfying their technical equations) and one of such possible series of equivalents and of Rs as will satisfy system 1.

Now it is necessary to correct this series of quantities so long as successive corrections always give a positive $\Sigma \, \Delta\theta$, and stop at that point at which further corrections give a zero increment, a sign that the maximum is attained and that further modifications would give rise to a decline in welfare.

13. The technical coefficients are not changed at first: this task is reserved for later.

Keeping an eye on the system 1 of the physical necessities of production which must always be satisfied:

(*a*) R_b is increased by ΔR_b, the necessary services being taken from those directly consumed. Then $\Sigma \, \Delta\theta$ is constituted by the increment $\lambda_b \, \Delta R_b$ in the product *less* the diminution

$$(\lambda_s \, b_s + \lambda_t \, b_t + \ldots) \, \Delta R_b,$$

in the consumable services. Therefore in these changes the Ministry ought to stop when the total increment is zero, which can never happen except when

$$\lambda_b = \lambda_s \, b_s + \lambda_t \, b_t + \ldots. \qquad\qquad \text{A1}$$

For the purpose of verification, and because thereby the significance of this argument will appear still more clear, let us begin by considering a situation in which the equivalent of B (which is afterwards the *price*, under another name, expressed in terms of that special kind of work which is called the *goods*) is greater than the cost of production. In such a case, the Ministry of Production, in the interests of the community, agrees to increase R_b and to decrease the consumable services, because by manufacturing more of R_b, the addition being ΔR_b, there is for $\Sigma \Delta \theta$ on the one hand the increase $\lambda_b \Delta R_b$, by the increase in B, and on the other hand the diminution $(\lambda_s b_s + \lambda_t b_t + ...) \Delta R_b$, by the diminution in consumable services. The net result of this is evidently advantageous because, by hypothesis, λ_b exceeds $\lambda_s b_s + \lambda_t b_t + ...$ The maximum will be achieved only when there is no more advantage to be gained by such adjustments, which is when $\lambda_b = \lambda_s b_s + \lambda_t b_t + ...$

(*b*) Increase one of the new productive resources H by ΔR_h, taking the services necessary from those directly consumed. Then for $\Sigma \Delta \theta$ there will be on the one hand the increase $\Delta_h \Delta R_h$ and on the other the decrease

$$(\lambda_s h_s + \lambda_t h_t + ...) \Delta R_h;$$

and hence, with the same reasoning as before, we arrive at the condition

$$\Delta_h = \lambda_s h_s + \lambda_t h_t + ... \hspace{3cm} \text{A2}$$

(*c*) Now let us proceed to the savings. The Ministry disposes of a quantity of saving

$$E = \Delta_h R_h + \Delta_k R_k + ... + R_e,$$

with which it must increase as much as is possible the total quantity of services available for subsequent production. It will approach this maximum, by transferring new capital from one use to another, until, $\lambda_h \lambda_k ... \lambda_e$ being the equivalents of the services of the new kinds of capital[6] $\lambda_h R_h + \lambda_k R_k + ... + \lambda_e R_e$ reaches the maximum.

This condition of the maximum is only satisfied, evidently, when

6. λ_e is the *premium* for deferring for one unit of time consumption of one unit of saving.

$$\frac{\lambda_h}{\Delta_h} = \frac{\lambda_k}{\Delta_k} = \dots = \lambda_e. \qquad \text{A3}$$

(*d*) Now we proceed to the technical coefficients. The Ministry, in the first approximate solution, had chosen them in such a way that they should simply satisfy their technical equations. But we know that some of them are variables, in the sense that some can be diminished while in others there is a compensating increase. Let S and T be the services for which in the manufacture of B these variations can be made. Then, per unit of B, more of S and less of T will be employed as far as is advantageous from the point of view of the collective maximum. The $\Sigma \; \Delta \theta$ is constituted, with regard to the consumable services, by an addition $\lambda_t \; R_b \; \Delta b_t$ and a diminution $\lambda_s \; R_b \; \Delta b_s$. Therefore the variation is zero if

$$\lambda_s \; \Delta b_s + \lambda_t \; \Delta b_t = 0$$

which is one of the conditions of the λ_t minimum when the *economic* variability of the technical coefficients is considered.

14. Taking account of what we have just said on the technical coefficients and glancing at the relations a, β, γ of section **13**, it is immediately evident:

1. That the system is perfectly determined: there are as many equations as unknowns.

2. That the Ministry of Production in this perfecting of its first approximate and indeterminate solution (the sole criterion of perfection being the maximum collective welfare) comes to the conclusion that production should be so organized that (with the systems of technical coefficients, of the λs and Rs) *the cost of production may be minimized* and that the *equivalents for the products* and *for the additions to capital may be such as will correspond to their respective costs of production.*

3. That the system of the equations of the collectivist equilibrium is no other than that of the free competition.

Which only means that with equal resources (the quantities Q) the economic quantities of the collectivist equilibrium (λ, R, etc.) will be the same as those in the individualist equilibrium; and that is due to the presence of that *supplementary term γx* in the individual equations of the collectivist régime, which does not occur in the individual equations of the individualist régime.

15. *The distribution of x.* Now is the time to discuss the conditions (section **8**) which the Ministry has considered as the basis of its problem.

There are five problems concerned here: the distribution of services possessed by the State; saving and the creation of new capital; the distribution of the profits from the undertakings; multiple prices; and the supplements to income x. Let us discuss them in order.

If the productive resources $S, T \dots (n-l$ in number) are the property of the State, there are two different ways of enabling the community to reap the benefit of this collective property: either that which we have assumed as one of the conditions in the solution of the problem of the collectivist equilibrium (that is, the *direct* division of x, giving to each individual a supplement to his income γx); or that of reducing to zero, in the cost of production, the equivalent of the services of resources which are the property of the State, and taking as the equivalent of each product (the λ, which is subsequently the *price*) the cost of the direct personal services which are required for its production. When the product is made with others, this cost is found by dividing the total cost in personal services by the entire quantity produced.

16. This system of indirect distribution, coupled with the reduction of the equivalents of the services of collective property to zero, is, at bottom, Marx's theory of value.

Those people who have criticized Marx have justly directed attention to the fact that such a system would be far from achieving the result, 'to each person the entire product of his labour', which is asserted to be connected therewith, because it is evident that a certain quantity of work of a given kind would be rewarded by a greater or smaller quantity of a certain product, according to the quantity and quality of the State-property with which it is employed. Hence the distribution of the product, made by such a system, is very far from realizing the formula of 'the whole produce'. But showing that this formula is not realized does not mean that indirect distribution is shown to be unsuitable. With more effect is it remarked that even when some resources are collective property the State can do no less than fix a price for their services, since there would otherwise be an enormous waste of these, with a consequent destruction of wealth. These services would be used in a large measure, not for further production, but as consumable services, and of those employed productively there might easily be an excess in one kind of production, which excess would be more useful socially in another industry in which there was a deficiency of resources.

This is the correct and fundamental argument against indirect distribution and in favour of direct distribution: the impossibility of obtaining a maximum as high as that which could be achieved with the latter method.

17. Of such a truth we can give, in a few words, a more general and 'synthetic' demonstration which can be applied equally to all those systems which propose to reduce to zero the equivalents of all or some of the services of those resources which become collective property.

To wish that the $n-l$ quantities $\lambda_s, \lambda_t \ldots$ may be equal to zero, is to introduce into the general system of equilibrium, which we have seen *entirely* determined, $n-l$ new equations. Hence either there is an impossible problem (the number of equations greater than the number of unknowns), or, to make it at least logically possible, it is necessary to exclude from the system $n-l$ of the equations which are already there. And as this exclusion cannot be done by taking the equations of the Rs from system 1, because they express the physical necessities of production which any economic order whatever must necessarily respect; then to make the problem possible, it would be necessary to exclude as many equations as those which express the minimum costs or the equality of prices and costs. This means that it is necessary to exclude as many equations from those which express the obtaining of that certain maximum; exclusions by virtue of which it certainly could only obtain a lower maximum. The Ministry of Production, instead of rising to the limit, would be forced to stop half-way.

Hence one can affirm that the better way for the Ministry of Production to provide for the welfare of its subjects, is not that of indirect distribution (i.e. the reduction to zero of the λs of the services of collective property), but that of *direct* distribution of supplements to income.

18. The collectivists persist in defending themselves, by expounding, with subtle and laborious interpretations, certain propositions which are either contrary to facts or do not bear a penetrating analysis. They do not appear to think that, if they are to remain collectivists, they must now cast off these gross errors which they derived from a nebulous vision of the phenomenon and from a muddled idea of the mutual dependence of economic quantities.

Of course their attitude in this respect is reminiscent of the reluctance with which the dogmas of a religion are discussed, especially when the latter has great propaganda value.

In addition there is a consideration of great moment in a collectivist régime: that is, that indirect distribution is rigid and does not permit certain ethical and social criteria to be observed with all that liberty which is realized (by giving opportunity values to the γs) by direct distribution.

19. *Saving and the creation of new capital.* For the discussion of the condition which the Ministry has imposed on itself concerning saving and the creation of new capital it will be enough for us to make:

1. A brief observation on what we should call the productivity of capital.

2. A comparison between the method followed by the Ministry of Production and another which it would be possible to follow, by deducting from x, before distributing it, that part which is necessary for the manufacture of new capital. Here it will be easy to show that by this second method it would realize a lower collective maximum than that which it can secure with the system preferred.

20. As for the first point, it is necessary to understand well that whether some capital is the property of individuals or whether it is collective property, does not upset the technical fact, that by once subtracting a part of the disposable productive services from the production of consumption goods, and then to produce new capital (new *means of production*, if that term is preferred), there is secured for always an increase of production greater than the *amortization* of capital.

Let us express this conception, which is the crux of the matter, with greater precision.

With the quantities $R_s + R_s'$ and $R_t + R_t'$ of the services S and T it may be possible for us to manufacture the quantity $R_b + R_b'$ of the product B. We are speaking of a given unit of time, e.g. one year. In this unit of time we may sacrifice the consumption R_b' and with the services R_s' and R_t' we may manufacture instead some capital R_k. And let us call ε the fraction of R_k which it is necessary to manufacture every year in order to maintain the quantity intact (amortization).

In the next unit of time, and so in continuation, with the same services $R_s + R_s'$ and $R_t + R_t'$ along with R_k, after having taken away from those services the part which is necessary for the reintegration of R_k, we could have, instead of the product $R_b + R_b'$ which we obtained formerly, a quantity of product which we shall call $\bar{R}_b$, which is obviously given by these equations:

$$R_s + R_s' = b_s \bar{R}_b + \varepsilon k_s R_k$$
$$R_t + R_t' = b_t \bar{R}_b + \varepsilon k_t R_k$$
$$R_k = b_k \bar{R}_b.$$

It often happens technically – and the most obvious experience shows it – that with the choice of an appropriate method $\bar{R}_b > R_b + R_b'$; thus this is the criterion on which the decision, whether to manufacture capital or not, is based. That condition is necessary though not always sufficient. Then with the sacrifice of R_b' once made, there is an everlasting additional product $\bar{R}_b - (R_b + R_b')$. Hence there is the possibility of a premium on deferred consumption of $\dfrac{\bar{R}_b - (R_b + R_b')}{R_b'}$ for every unit of B subtracted from present consumption. It is precisely this purely *objective* technical fact, which does not depend in the slightest on whether the capital is individual property or collective property, which gives the Ministry the means to promise a premium on deferred consumption to those who are willing to provide it with savings for the construction of the new means of production. In substance, these people promise not to present a part of their earnings at the general shops to obtain goods, but to deposit it (though it continues to be their property) with the Ministry. The Ministry is thereby enabled to manufacture, with the total available services, a smaller quantity of final products and to set aside a part of the same services for the manufacture of new means of production. These new means of production will then be available to it in successive periods of production. It is precisely this *objective* fact which is the origin of what may be called the *economic productivity* of savings employed in production even in the collectivist régime.

21. Now we pass to another point: is it advantageous that the Ministry of Production, instead of having recourse to individual saving and promising (in order to secure a sufficient quantity of it) a premium on deferred consumption to those individuals who supply it, should, before distributing x, deduct that part of it which is considered necessary for the creation of new capital?

The criterion is, and must be, always the same: the greatest welfare for society.

Let us leave aside the consideration that by the second method the Ministry would take no account of the wishes of its subjects, who might prefer a greater γx today to a smaller future increment; and let us also leave aside the consideration that the Ministry would by such a method be without any means of determining the most advantageous quantity of new capital to create. We will confine ourselves here to viewing the case exclusively from the point of view of the collective maximum.

Then, in order to manufacture by this second method the same quantities of new capital R_h, R_k... the Ministry distributes to the community an amount reduced by E. But each individual, even without the promise of a premium for deferred consumption, and simply for the provision of future needs, might for his own advantage decide not to consume all his *earnings*, but to save a certain amount. Hence there is a certain sum of individual saving, which we will call E_i to distinguish it from the quantity E which the Ministry, by reducing x, uses for the manufacture of new capital.

E_i is the sum of all the e_is which result from the individual equations, which now become like this:

$$r_a + \lambda_b\, r_b + \ldots + \lambda_s\, r_s + \lambda_t\, r_t + \ldots + e_i = q_m\, \lambda_m + q_n\, \lambda_n + \ldots + \gamma(x - E).$$

Or for the community:

$$R_a + \lambda_b\, R_b + \ldots + \lambda_s\, R_s + \lambda_t\, R_t + \ldots + E_i + E$$
$$= Q_m\, \lambda_m + Q_n\, \lambda_n + \ldots + Q_s\, \lambda_s + Q_t\, \lambda_t + \ldots.$$

That is to say, that with this second method (i.e. the method of the Ministry deducting from x the quantity E necessary for the manufacture of new capital, before distributing x among the people) the whole body of individuals is forced to limit the sum of goods and services consumed *more* than they did with the other system, with the prospect of a future increase of products and services *no greater* than that which the other system offers. Therefore evidently, in the interests of the maximum welfare of the community, the former method is preferable to the latter.

This conclusion will be more readily understood, if it is realized that this second method (which is not to be preferred) does not use, for increasing goods and services in the future, that sum of money which various individuals still save even without the promise of a premium for deferred consumption.

22. The effects of distribution on production would vary with the different methods by which x is distributed.

We have already noted (**14**) how the complete resemblance between the equations of free competition and the equations of the collectivist equilibrium, established with the idea of obtain-in the maximum collective benefit, only means that there being in the group the same quantities of capital in one case as in the other, the appropriation alone being different, the economic quantities of the equilibrium will be equal to those of the other, there still being in both cases equations expressing the conditions of minimum cost and of prices equal to costs; that is precisely on account of that supplement added to the income of each individual. The distribution, which is made of that x in one way or another according to the various values which are given to the γs, influences diversely these economic quantities. The study of these diverse influences gives rise to interesting speculations, one of the most remarkable (though not unexpected) results being that there would be a sharp rise in the premium for deferred consumption – which is the parallel to *interest* on saving in the old régime – which according to most superficial collectivist doctrines would be abolished. Precisely the opposite is the case!

23. *The equations of the equilibrium insoluble* a priori. For the solution of the problem it is not enough that the Ministry of Production has arrived at tracing out for itself the system of equations of the equilibrium best adapted for obtaining the collective maximum in the well-known sense (to which we need not return). It is necessary to solve the equations afterwards. And that is the problem.

Many of the writers who have criticized collectivism have hesitated to use as evidence the practical difficulties in establishing on paper the various equivalents; but it seems they have not perceived what really are the difficulties – or more frankly, the impossibility – of solving such equations *a priori*.

24. If, for a moment, we assume that the economic variability of the technical coefficients may be neglected and we take account of their technical variability only, it is not impossible to solve on paper the equations of the equilibrium. It would be a tremendous – a gigantic – work (work therefore taken from the productive services): but it is not an *impossibility*.

It is conceivable, in fact, that with a vast organization for this work it would be possible to collect the individual schedules for every given series of the various equivalents, including the premium for deferred consumption. Hence it is not inconceivable that with these schedules collected – always supposing the technical coefficients known are invariable – it would be possible by a paper calculation to find a series of equivalents, which would satisfy the equations expressing the physical necessities of production and the equalization of costs of production and the equivalents, which become the *prices*. There is no analytical difficulty about it: it is a problem of very simple linear equations. The difficulty arises rather from the very great number of individuals and goods of which we must take account; but it is not inconceivable that, with still more arduous work, such difficulty could be overcome.

25. But it is frankly *inconceivable* that the *economic* determination of the technical coefficients can be made *a priori*, in such a way as to satisfy the condition of the minimum cost of production which is an essential condition for obtaining that maximum to which we have referred. This *economic* variability of the technical coefficients is certainly neglected by the collectivists; but that it is one of the most important sides of the question Pareto has already very clearly shown in one of his many ingenious contributions to the science.

The determination of the coefficients economically most advantageous can only be done in an *experimental* way: and not on a *small scale*, as could be done in a laboratory, but with experiments on a *very large scale*, because often the advantage of the variation has its origin precisely in a new and greater dimension of the undertaking. Experiments may be successful in the sense that they may lead to a lower cost combination of factors; or they may be unsuccessful, in which case that particular organization may not be copied and repeated and others will be preferred, which *experimentally* have given a better result.

The Ministry of Production could not do without these experiments for the determination of the *economically* most advantageous technical coefficients if it would realize the condition of the minimum cost of production which is *essential* for the attainment of the maximum collective welfare.

It is on this account that the equations of the equilibrium with the maximum collective welfare are not soluble *a priori*, on paper.

26. Some collectivist writers, bewailing the continual destruction of firms (those with higher costs) by free competition, think that the creation of enterprises to be destroyed later can be avoided, and hope that with *organized* production it is possible to avoid the dissipation and destruction of wealth which such *experiments* involve, and which they believe to be the peculiar property of 'anarchist' production. Thereby these writers simply show that they have no clear idea of what production really is, and that they are not even disposed to probe a little deeper into the problem which will concern the Ministry which will be established for the purpose in the Collectivist State.

We repeat, that if the Ministry will not remain bound by the traditional technical coefficients, which would produce a destruction of wealth in another sense – in the sense that the greater wealth which could have been realized will not be realized – it has no other means of determining *a priori* the technical coefficients most advantageous economically, and must *of necessity* resort to experiments on a large scale in order to decide *afterwards* which are the most appropriate organizations, which it is advantageous to maintain in existence and to enlarge to obtain the collective maximum more easily, and which, on the other hand, it is best to discard as failures.

27. *Conclusions.* From what we have seen and demonstrated hitherto, it is obvious how fantastic those doctrines are which imagine that production in the collectivist régime would be ordered in a manner substantially different from that of 'anarchist' production.

If the Ministry of Production proposes to obtain the collective maximum – which it obviously must, whatever law of distribution may be adopted – all the economic categories of the old régime must reappear, though maybe with other names: prices, salaries, interest, rent, profit, saving, etc. Not only that; but always provided that it wishes to obtain that maximum with the services of which the individuals and the community dispose, the same two fundamental conditions which characterize free competition reappear, and the maximum is more nearly attained the more perfectly they are realized. We refer, of course, to the conditions of minimum cost of production and the equalization of price to cost of production.

28. This conclusion could have been reached, at first sight, by a 'synthetic' argument; but it could not have acquired the value of a demonstrated truth, without the phenomenon being subjected to a minute quantitative analysis, as has been done in the preceding pages. The argument would be this: to hand over some capital to the State and afterwards to distribute the yield thereof among the individuals, according to a certain law, whatever it is, is like starting from a situation in the individualist régime, in which the individuals, besides having their own capital, may be possessors of certain quotas of capital of which the State has become the controller, quotas corresponding to that same law of distribution which we supposed adopted.

In such a situation what are the technical coefficients and what is the system of equivalents which allow the attainment of the maximum? Those which give the equalization of price to cost of production and the minimum cost of production!

29. That supplement to income distributed among the individuals – whatever may be the system of distribution – does not augment, as we have seen, the consumption of products and consumable services of the group, by the total *income* which in the old régime the possessors of capital received and which is appropriated by the State in the new régime, even when this appropriation takes place without some promise of compensation to the expropriated owners. When there is no intention of restricting saving and the creation of new capital to narrower limits than in the old régime (to this we shall return in a moment) the total consumption of products and of consumable services can be scarcely different from what it was before.

Hence, given that there is no wish to check the creation of new capital in the new régime, the distribution of consumable goods and services among the people must inevitably be restricted within the limits of what in the old régime the possessors of the capital, which is now socialized, consumed, not the whole of what they received as income. Besides this, account must be taken of the necessary remuneration of the army of officials whose services would be devoted not to production but to the laborious and colossal centralization work of the Ministry (assuming the practical possibility of such a system).

30. If it were so desired, it would be possible to augment consumption, at the expense, however, of the formation of new resources, but of *all* the new resources, even at the expense of the birth-rate. To promise increased welfare and to propose to 'organize' production and to preach about free love in the new régime is simply ridiculous nonsense. If the State does not wish the collective maximum to decrease rapidly in time, the accumulation of capital must be regulated according to the birth-rate; or, conversely, the latter must be restricted within the limits set by the former.

3 L. von Mises

Economic Calculation in the Socialist Commonwealth

Excerpts from L. von Mises, 'Economic calculation in the socialist
commonwealth' in F. A. von Hayek (ed.) *Collectivist Economic Planning*,
Routledge & Kegan Paul, 1935, pp. 89–130. Originally published in
German in the *Archiv für Sozialwissenschaften 1920*.

The distribution of consumption-goods in the socialist commonwealth

Under socialism all the means of production are the property of
the community. It is the community alone which can dispose of
them and which determines their use in production. It goes without saying that the community will only be in a position to
employ its powers of disposal through the setting up of a special
body for the purpose. The structure of this body and the question
of how it will articulate and represent the communal will is for us
of subsidiary importance. One may assume that this last will
depend upon the choice of personnel, and in cases where the
power is not vested in a dictatorship, upon the majority vote of
the members of the corporation.

The owner of production-goods, who has manufactured
consumption-goods and thus becomes their owner, now has the
choice of either consuming them himself or of having them consumed by others. But where the community becomes the owner of
consumption-goods, which it has acquired in production, such a
choice will no longer obtain. It cannot itself consume; it has
perforce to allow others to do so. Who is to do the consuming
and what is to be consumed by each is the crux of the problem
of socialist distribution.

It is characteristic of socialism that the distribution of consumption-goods must be independent of the question of production
and of its economic conditions. It is irreconcilable with the nature
of the communal ownership of production-goods that it should
rely even for a part of its distribution upon the economic im-
putation of the yield to the particular factors of production. It is
logically absurd to speak of the worker's enjoying the 'full yield'

of his work, and then to subject to a separate distribution the shares of the material factors of production. For, as we shall show, it lies in the very nature of socialist production that the shares of the particular factors of production in the national dividend cannot be ascertained, and that it is impossible in fact to gauge the relationship between expenditure and income.

What basis will be chosen for the distribution of consumption-goods among the individual comrades is for us a consideration of more or less secondary importance. Whether they will be apportioned according to individual needs, so that he gets most who needs most, or whether the superior man is to receive more than the inferior, or whether a strictly equal distribution is envisaged as the ideal, or whether service to the State is to be the criterion, is immaterial to the fact that, in any event, the portions will be meted out by the State.

Let us assume the simple proposition that distribution will be determined upon the principle that the State treats all its members alike; it is not difficult to conceive of a number of peculiarities such as age, sex, health, occupation, etc., according to which what each receives will be graded. Each comrade receives a bundle of coupons, redeemable within a certain period against a definite quantity of certain specified goods. And so he can eat several times a day, find permanent lodgings, occasional amusements and a new suit every now and again. Whether such provision for these needs is ample or not, will depend on the productivity of social labour.

Moreover, it is not necessary that every man should consume the whole of his portion. He may let some of it perish without consuming it; he may give it away in presents; he may even in so far as the nature of the goods permits, hoard it for future use. He can, however, also exchange some of them. The beer-tippler will gladly dispose of non-alcoholic drinks allotted to him, if he can get more beer in exchange, whilst the teetotaller will be ready to give up his portion of drink if he can get other goods for it. The art-lover will be willing to dispose of his cinema tickets in order the more often to hear good music; the philistine will be quite prepared to give up the tickets which admit him to art exhibitions in return for opportunities for pleasure he more readily understands. They will all welcome exchanges. But the material of these exchanges will always be consumption-goods. Production-goods in a socialist commonwealth are exclusively communal; they are an inalienable property of the community, and thus *res extra commercium*.

The principle of exchange can thus operate freely in a socialist state within the narrow limits permitted. It need not always develop in the form of direct exchanges. The same grounds which have always existed for the building up of indirect exchange will continue in a socialist state, to place advantages in the way of those who indulge in it. It follows that the socialist state will thus also afford room for the use of a universal medium of exchange – that is, of money. Its role will be fundamentally the same in a socialist as in a competitive society; in both it serves as the universal medium of exchange. Yet the significance of money in a society where the means of production are State controlled will be different from that which attaches to it in one where they are privately owned. It will be, in fact, incomparably narrower, since the material available for exchange will be narrower, inasmuch as it will be confined to consumption-goods. Moreover, just because no production-good will ever become the object of exchange, it will be impossible to determine its monetary value. Money could never fill in a socialist state the role it fills in a competitive society in determining the value of production-goods. Calculation in terms of money will here be impossible.

The nature of economic calculation

One may anticipate the nature of the future socialist society. There will be hundreds and thousands of factories in operation. Very few of these will be producing wares ready for use; in the majority of cases what will be manufactured will be unfinished goods and production-goods. All these concerns will be inter-related. Every good will go through a whole series of stages before it is ready for use. In the ceaseless toil and moil of this process, however, the administration will be without any means of testing their bearings. It will never be able to determine whether a given good has not been kept for a superfluous length of time in the necessary processes of production, or whether work and material have not been wasted in its completion. How will it be able to decide whether this or that method of production is the more profitable? At best it will only be able to compare the quality and quantity of the consumable end-product produced, but will in the rarest cases be in a position to compare the expenses entailed in production. It will know, or think it knows, the ends to be achieved by economic organization, and will have to regulate its activities accordingly, i.e. it will have to attain those ends with the least expense. It will have to make its computations with a view to finding the cheapest way. This computation will naturally have to be a value-computation. It is eminently clear, and requires no further proof, that it cannot be of a technical character, and that it cannot be based upon the objective use-value of goods and services.

Now, in the economic system of private ownership of the means of production, the system of computation by value is necessarily employed by each independent member of society. Everybody participates in its emergence in a double way: on the one hand as a consumer and on the other as a producer. As a consumer he establishes a scale of valuation for goods ready for use and consumption. As a producer he puts goods of a higher order into such use as produces the greatest return. In this way all goods of a higher order receive a position in the scale of valuations in accordance with the immediate state of social conditions of production and of social needs. Through the interplay of these two processes of valuation, means will be afforded for governing both consumption and production by the economic principle throughout. Every graded system of pricing proceeds from the fact that men always and ever harmonize their own requirements with their estimation of economic facts.

All this is necessarily absent from a socialist state. The administration may know exactly what goods are most urgently needed. But in so doing, it has only found what is, in fact, but one of the two necessary prerequisites for economic calculation. In the nature of the case it must, however, dispense with the other – the valuation of the means of production. It may establish the value attained by the totality of the means of production; this is obviously identical with that of all the needs thereby satisfied. It may also be able to calculate the value of any means of production by calculating the consequence of its withdrawal in relation to the satisfaction of needs. Yet it cannot reduce this value to the uniform expression of a money price, as can a competitive economy, wherein all prices can be referred back to a common expression in terms of money. In a socialist commonwealth which, whilst it need not of necessity dispense with money altogether, yet finds it impossible to use money as an expression of the price of the factors of production (including labour), money can play no role in economic calculation.[1]

Picture the building of a new railroad. Should it be built at all, and if so, which out of a number of conceivable roads should be built? In a competitive and monetary economy, this question would be answered by monetary calculation. The new road will render less expensive the transport of some goods, and it may be possible to calculate whether this reduction of expense transcends that involved in the building and upkeep of the next line. That can only be calculated in money. It is not possible to attain the desired end merely by counterbalancing the various physical expenses and physical savings. Where one cannot express hours of labour, iron, coal, all kinds of building material, machines and other things necessary for the construction and upkeep of the railroad in a common unit it is not possible to make calculations at all. The drawing up of bills on an economic basis is only possible where all the goods concerned can be referred back to money. Admittedly, monetary calculation has its inconveniences and serious defects, but we have certainly nothing better to put in its place and for the practical purposes of life monetary calculation as it exists under a sound monetary system always suffices. Were we to dispense with it, any economic system of calculation would become absolutely impossible.

The socialist society would know how to look after itself. It would issue an edict and decide for or against the projected building. Yet this decision would depend at best upon vague estimates; it would never be based upon the foundation of an exact calculation of value.

The static state can dispense with economic calculation. For

1. This fact is also recognized by Neurath (1919, pp. 216 et seq.). He advances the view that every complete administrative economy is, in the final analysis, a natural economy. 'Socialization', he says, 'is thus the pursuit of natural economy.' Neurath merely overlooks the insuperable difficulties that would have to develop with economic calculation in the socialist commonwealth.

here the same events in economic life are ever recurring; and if we assume that the first disposition of the static socialist economy follows on the basis of the final state of the competitive economy, we might at all events conceive of a socialist production system which is rationally controlled from an economic point of view. But this is only conceptually possible. For the moment, we leave aside the fact that a static state is impossible in real life, as our economic data are forever changing, so that the static nature of economic activity is only a theoretical assumption corresponding to no real state of affairs, however necessary it may be for our thinking and for the perfection of our knowledge of economics. Even so, we must assume that the transition to socialism must, as a consequence of the levelling out of the differences in income and the resultant readjustments in consumption, and therefore production, change all economic data in such a way that a connecting link with the final state of affairs in the previously existing competitive economy becomes impossible. But then we have the spectacle of a socialist economic order floundering in the ocean of possible and conceivable economic combinations without the compass of economic calculation.

Thus in the socialist commonwealth every economic change becomes an undertaking whose success can be neither appraised in advance nor later retrospectively determined. There is only groping in the dark. Socialism is the abolition of rational economy.

Economic calculation in the socialist commonwealth

Are we really dealing with the necessary consequences of common ownership of the means of production? Is there no way in which some kind of economic calculation might be tied up with a socialist system?

In every great enterprise, each particular business or branch of business is to some extent independent in its accounting. It reckons the labour and material against each other, and it is always possible for each individual group to strike a particular balance and to approach the economic results of its activities from an accounting point of view. We can thus ascertain with what success each particular section has laboured, and accordingly draw conclusions about the reorganization, curtailment, abandonment, or expansion of existing groups and about the institution of new ones. Admittedly, some mistakes are inevitable in such a calculation. They arise partly from the difficulties consequent upon an allocation of general expenses. Yet other mistakes arise from the necessity of calculating with what are not from many points of view rigorously ascertainable data, e.g. when in the ascertainment of the profitability of a certain method of procedure we compute the amortization of the machines used on the assumption of a given duration for their usefulness. Still, all such mistakes can be confined within certain narrow limits, so that they do not disturb the net result of the calculation. What remains of uncertainty comes into the calculation of the uncertainty of future conditions, which is an inevitable concomitant of the dynamic nature of economic life.

It seems tempting to try to construct by analogy a separate estimation of the particular production groups in the socialist state also. But it is quite impossible. For each separate calculation of the particular branches of one and the same enterprise depends exclusively on the fact that it is precisely in market dealings that market prices to be taken as the bases of calculation are formed for all kinds of goods and labour employed. Where there is no free market, there is no pricing mechanism; without a pricing mechanism, there is no economic calculation.

We might conceive of a situation in which exchange between particular branches of business is permitted, so as to obtain the mechanism of exchange relations (prices) and thus create a basis for economic calculation even in the socialist commonwealth. Within the framework of a uniform economy not knowing private ownership of the means of production, individual labour groups are constituted independent and authoritative disposers, which have indeed to behave in accordance with the directions of the supreme economic council, but which nevertheless assign each other material goods and services only against a payment, which would have to be made in the general medium of exchange. It is roughly in this way that we conceive of the organization of the socialist running of business when we nowadays talk of complete socialization and the like. But we have still not come to the crucial point. Exchange relations between production-goods can only be established on the basis of private ownership of the means of production. When the 'coal syndicate' provides the 'iron syndicate' with coal, no price can be formed, except when both syndicates are the owners of the means of production employed in their business. This would not be socialization but workers' capitalism and syndicalism.

The matter is indeed very simple for those socialist theorists who rely on the labour theory of value.

As soon as society takes possession of the means of production and applies them to production in their directly socialized form, each individual's labour, however different its specific utility may be, becomes *a priori* and directly social labour. The amount of social labour invested in a product need not then be established indirectly; daily experience immediately tells us how much is necessary on an average. Society can simply calculate how many hours of labour are invested in a steam engine, a quarter of last harvest's wheat, and a 100 yards of linen of given quality. . . . To be sure, society will also have to know how much labour is needed to produce any consumption-good. It will have to arrange its production plan according to its means of production, to which labour especially belongs. The utility yielded by the various consumption-goods, weighted against each other and against the amount of labour required to produce them, will ultimately determine the plan. People will make everything simple without the mediation of the notorious 'value' (Engels, 1878, p. 335).

Here it is not our task once more to advance critical objections against the labour theory of value. In this connection they can only interest us in so far as they are relevant to an assessment of the applicability of labour in the value computations of a socialist community.

On a first impression, calculation in terms of labour also takes into consideration the natural non-human conditions of production. The law of diminishing returns is already allowed for in the concept of socially necessary average labour-time to the extent that its operation is due to the variety of the natural conditions of production. If the demand for a commodity increases and worse natural resources must be exploited, then the average socially necessary labour-time required for the production of a unit increases too. If more favourable natural resources are discovered, the amount of socially necessary labour diminishes (Marx, 1867). The consideration of the natural condition of production suffices only in so far as it is reflected in the amount of labour socially necessary. But it is in this respect that valuation in terms of labour fails. It leaves the employment of material factors of production out of account. Let the amount of socially necessary labour-time required for the production of each of the commodities P and Q be ten hours. Further, in addition to labour the production of both P and Q requires the raw material a, a unit of which is produced by an hour's socially necessary labour; two units of a and eight hours' labour are used in the production of P, and one unit of a and nine hours' labour in the production of Q. In terms of labour P and Q are equivalent, but in value terms P is more valuable than Q. The former is false, and only the latter corresponds to the nature and purpose of calculation. True, this surplus, by which according to value calculation P is more valuable than Q, this material substratum 'is given by nature without any addition from man' (Marx, 1867, p. 12). Still, the fact that it is only present in such quantities that it becomes an object of economizing, must be taken into account in some form or other in value-calculation.

The second defect in calculation in terms of labour is the ignoring of the different qualities of labour. To Marx all human labour is economically of the same kind, as it is always 'the productive expenditure of human brain, brawn, nerve and hand' (Marx, 1867, p. 13).

Skilled labour counts only as intensified, or rather multiplied, simple labour, so that a smaller quantity of skilled labour is equal to a larger quantity of simple labour. Experience shows that skilled labour can always be reduced in this way to the terms of simple labour. No matter that a commodity be the product of the most highly skilled labour, its value can be equated with that of the product of simple labour, so that it represents merely a definite amount of simple labour.

Böhm-Bawerk is not far wrong when he calls this argument 'a theoretical juggle of almost stupefying naïveté' (Böhm-Bawerk, 1890, p. 384). To judge Marx's view we need not ask if it is possible to discover a single uniform physiological measure of all human labour, whether it be physical or 'mental'. For it is certain that there exist among men varying degrees of capacity and dexterity, which cause the products and services of labour to have varying qualities. What must be conclusive in deciding the question whether reckoning in terms of labour is applicable or not, is whether it is or is not possible to bring different kinds of labour under a common denominator without the mediation of the economic subject's valuation of their products. The proof Marx attempts to give is not successful. Experience indeed shows that goods are consumed under exchange relations without regard of the fact of their being produced by simple or complex labour. But this would only be a proof that given amounts of simple labour are directly made equal to given amounts of complex labour, if it were shown that labour is the source of exchange value. This not only is not demonstrated, but is what Marx is trying to demonstrate by means of these very arguments.

No more is it a proof of this homogeneity that rates of substitution between simple and complex labour are manifested in the wage rate in an exchange economy – a fact to which Marx does not allude in this context. This equalizing process is a result of market transactions and not its antecedent. Calculation in terms of labour would have to set up an arbitrary proportion for the substitution of complex by simple labour, which excludes its employment for purposes of economic administration.

It was long supposed that the labour theory of value was indispensable to socialism, so that the demand for the nationalization of the means of production should have an ethical basis. Today we know this for the error it is. Although the majority of socialist supporters have thus employed this misconception, and although Marx, however much he fundamentally took another point of view, was not altogether free from it, it is clear that the political call for the introduction of socialized production neither requires nor can obtain the support of the labour theory of value on the one hand, and that on the other those people holding different views on the nature and origin of economic value can be socialists according to their sentiments. Yet the labour theory of value is inherently necessary for the supporters of socialist production in a sense other than that usually intended. In the main socialist production might only appear rationally realizable, if it provided an objectively recognizable unit of value, which would permit of economic calculation in an economy where neither money nor exchange were present. And only labour can conceivably be considered as such.

The most recent socialist doctrines and the problem of economic calculation

Since recent events helped socialist parties to obtain power in Russia, Hungary, Germany and Austria, and have thus made the execution of a socialist nationalization programme a topical issue, Marxist writers have themselves begun to deal more closely with the problems of the regulation of the socialist commonwealth. But even now they still cautiously avoid the crucial question, leaving it to be tackled by the despised 'Utopians'. They themselves prefer to confine their attention to what is to be done in the immediate future; they are for ever drawing up programmes of the path to socialism and not of socialism itself. The only possible conclusion from all these writings is that they are not even conscious of the larger problem of economic calculation in a socialist society.

To Otto Bauer the nationalization of the banks appears the final and decisive step in the carrying through of the socialist nationalization programme. If all banks are nationalized and amalgamated into a single central bank, then its administrative board becomes 'the supreme economic authority, the chief administrative organ of the whole economy. Only by nationalization of the banks does society obtain the power to regulate its labour according to a plan, and to distribute its resources rationally among the various branches of production, so as to adapt them to the nation's needs' (Bauer, 1919, p. 26). He is not discussing the monetary arrangements which will prevail in the socialist commonwealth after the completion of the nationalization of the banks. Like other Marxists he is trying to show how simply and obviously the future socialist order of society will evolve from the conditions prevailing in a developed capitalist economy. 'It suffices to transfer to the nation's representatives the power now exercised by bank shareholders through the Administrative Boards they elect,' (Bauer, 1919, p. 25) in order to socialize the banks and thus to lay the last brick on the edifice of socialism. Bauer leaves his readers completely ignorant of the fact that the nature of the banks is entirely changed in the process of nationalization and amalgamation into one central bank. Once the banks merge into a single bank, their essence is wholly transformed; they are then in a position to issue credit without any limitation (von Mises, 1912, p. 474). In this fashion the monetary system as we know it today disappears of itself. When in addition the single central bank is nationalized in a society, which is otherwise already completely socialized, market dealings disappear and all exchange transactions are abolished. At the same time the Bank ceases to be a bank, its specific functions are extinguished, for there is no longer any place for it in such a society. It may be that the name 'Bank' is retained, that the Supreme Economic Council of the socialist community is called the Board of Directors of the Bank, and that they hold their meetings in a building formerly occupied by a bank. But it is no longer a bank, it fulfils none of those functions which a bank fulfils in an economic system resting on the private ownership of the means of production and the use of a general medium of exchange – money. It no longer distributes any credit, for a socialist society makes credit of necessity impossible. Bauer himself does not tell us what a bank is, but he begins his chapter on the nationalization of the banks with the sentence: 'All disposable capital flows into a common pool in the banks' (Bauer, 1919, p. 24). As a Marxist must he not raise the question of what the banks' activities will be after the abolition of capitalism?

All other writers who have grappled with the problems of the organization of the socialist commonwealth are guilty of similar confusions. They do not realize that the bases of economic calculation are removed by the exclusion of exchange and the pricing mechanism, and that something must be substituted in its place, if all economy is not to be abolished and a hopeless chaos is not to result. People believe that socialist institutions might evolve without further ado from those of a capitalist economy. This is not at all the case. And it becomes all the more grotesque when we talk of banks, bank management, etc. in a socialist commonwealth.

Reference to the conditions that have developed in Russia and Hungary under Soviet rule proves nothing. What we have there is nothing but a picture of the destruction of an existing order of social production, for which a closed peasant household economy has been substituted. All branches of production depending on social division of labour are in a state of entire dissolution. What is happening under the rule of Lenin and Trotsky is merely destruction and annihilation. Whether, as the liberals hold, socialism must inevitably draw these consequences in its train, or whether, as the socialists retort, this is only a result of the fact that the Soviet Republic is attacked from without, is a question of no interest to us in this context. All that has to be established is the fact that the Soviet socialist commonwealth has not even begun to discuss the problem of economic calculation, nor has it any cause to do so. For where things are still produced for the market in Soviet Russia in spite of governmental prohibitions, they are valued in terms of money, for there exists to that extent private ownership of the means of production, and goods are sold against money. Even the Government cannot deny the necessity, which it confirms by increasing the amount of money in circulation, of retaining a monetary system for at least the transition period.

That the essence of the problem to be faced has not yet come to light in Soviet Russia, Lenin's statements in his essay on *Die nächsten Aufgaben der Sowjetmacht* best show. In the dictator's deliberations there ever recurs the thought that the immediate and most pressing task of Russian Communism is 'the organization of book-keeping and control of those concerns, in which the capitalists have already been expropriated, and of all other economic concerns' (Lenin, 1918, pp. 12 and 22). Even so Lenin is far from realizing that an entirely new problem is here involved which it is impossible to solve with the conceptual instruments of 'bourgeois' culture. Like a real politician, he does not bother with issues beyond his nose. He still finds himself surrounded by monetary transactions, and does not notice that with progressive socialization money also necessarily loses its function as the medium of exchange in general use, to the extent that private property and with it exchange disappear. The implication of Lenin's reflections is that he would like to re-introduce into Soviet business 'bourgeois' book-keeping carried on on a monetary basis. Therefore he also desires to restore 'bourgeois experts' to a state of grace (Lenin, 1918, p. 15). For the rest Lenin is as little aware as Bauer of the fact that in a socialist commonwealth the functions of the bank are unthinkable in their existing sense. He wishes to go farther with the 'nationalization of the banks' and to proceed 'to a transformation of the banks into the nodal point of social book-keeping under socialism' (Lenin, 1918, pp. 21 and 26; cf. Bukharin, 1918, p. 27).

Lenin's ideas on the socialist economic system, to which he is striving to lead his people, are generally obscure.

'The socialist state', he says 'can only arise as a net of producing and consuming communes, which conscientiously record their production and consumption, go about their labour economically, uninterruptedly raise their labour productivity and thus attain the possibility of lowering the working day to seven or six hours or even lower' (Lenin, 1918, p. 24). 'Every factory, every village appears as a production and consumption commune having the right and obligation to apply the general Soviet legislation in its own way ('in its own way' not in the sense of its violation but in the sense of the variety of its forms of realization), and to solve in its own way the problem of calculating the production and distribution of products.' (Lenin, 1918, p. 32).

The chief communes must and will serve the most backward ones as educators, teachers, and stimulating leaders. The successes of the chief communes must be broadcast in all their details in order to provide a good example. The communes 'showing good business results' should be immediately rewarded 'by a curtailment of the working day and with an increase in wages, and by allowing more attention to be paid to cultural and aesthetic goods and values (Lenin, 1918, p. 33).

We can infer that Lenin's ideal is a state of society in which the means of production are not the property of a few districts, municipalities, or even of the workers in the concern, but the whole community. His ideal is socialist and not syndicalist. This need not be specially stressed for a Marxist such as Lenin. It is not extraordinary of Lenin the theorist, but of Lenin the statesman, who is the leader of the syndicalist and smallholding peasant Russian revolution. However, at the moment we are engaged with the writer Lenin and may consider his ideals separately, without letting ourselves be disturbed by the picture of sober reality. According to Lenin the theorist, every large agricultural and industrial concern is a member of the great commonwealth of labour. Those who are active in this commonwealth have the right of self-government; they exercise a profound influence on the direction of production and again on the distribution of the goods they are assigned for consumption. Still labour is the property of the whole society, and as its product belongs to society also, it therefore disposes of its distribution. How, we must now ask, is calculation in the economy carried on in a socialist commonwealth which is so organized? Lenin gives us a most inadequate answer by referring us back to statistics. We must

bring statistics to the masses, make it popular, so that the active population will gradually learn by themselves to understand and realize how much and what kind of work must be done, how much and what kind of recreation should be taken, so that the comparison of the economy's industrial results in the case of individual communes becomes the object of general interest and education (Lenin, 1918, p. 33).

From these scanty allusions it is impossible to infer what Lenin understands by statistics and whether he is thinking of monetary or *in natura* computation. In any case, we must refer back to what we have said about the impossibility of learning the money prices of production-goods in a socialist commonwealth and about the difficulties standing in the way of *in natura* valuation.[2] Statistics would only be applicable to economic calculation if it could go beyond the *in natura* calculation, whose ill-suitedness for this purpose we have demonstrated. It is naturally impossible where no exchange relations are formed between goods in the process of trade.

Conclusion

It must follow from what we have been able to establish in our previous arguments that the protagonists of a socialist system of production claim preference for it on the ground of greater rationality as against an economy so constituted as to depend on private ownership of the means of production. We have no need to consider this opinion within the framework of the present essay, in so far as it falls back on the assertion that rational economic activity necessarily cannot be perfect, because certain forces are operative which hinder its pursuance. In this connection we may only pay attention to the economic and technical reason for this opinion. There hovers before the holders of this tenet a

2. Neurath, too (cf. 1919, pp. 212), imputes great importance to statistics for the setting up of the socialist economic plan.

muddled conception of technical rationality, which stands in antithesis to economic rationality, on which also they are not very clear. They are wont to overlook the fact that 'all technical rationality of production is identical with a low level of specific expenditure in the processes of production' (Gottl, 1914, p. 220). They overlook the fact that technical calculation is not enough to realize the 'degree of general and teleological expediency' (Gottl, 1914, p. 219) of an event; that it can only grade individual events according to their significance; but that it can never guide us in those judgments which are demanded by the economic complex as a whole. Only because of the fact that technical considerations can be based on profitability can we overcome the difficulty arising from the complexity of the relations between the mighty system of present-day production on the one hand and demand and the efficiency of enterprises and economic units on the other; and can we gain the complete picture of the situation in its totality, which rational economic activity requires (Gottl, 1914, p. 225).

These theories are dominated by a confused conception of the primacy of objective use-value. In fact, so far as economic administration is concerned, objective use-value can only acquire significance for the economy through the influence it derives from subjective use-value on the formation of the exchange-relations of economic goods. A second confused idea is inexplicably involved – the observer's personal judgment of the utility of goods as opposed to the judgments of the people participating in economic transactions. If anyone finds it 'irrational' to spend as much as is expended in society on smoking, drinking and similar enjoyments, then doubtless he is right from the point of view of his own personal scale of values. But in so judging, he is ignoring the fact that economy is a means, and that, without prejudice to the rational considerations influencing its pattern, the scale of ultimate ends is a matter for conation and not for cognition.

The knowledge of the fact that rational economic activity is impossible in a socialist commonwealth cannot, of course, be used as an argument either for or against socialism. Whoever is prepared himself to enter upon socialism on ethical grounds on the supposition that the provision of goods of a lower order for human beings under a system of a common ownership of the means of production is diminished, or whoever is guided by ascetic ideals in his desire for socialism, will not allow himself to be influenced in his endeavours by what we have said. Still less will those 'culture' socialists be deterred who, like Muckle, expect from socialism primarily 'the dissolution of the most frightful of all barbarisms – capitalist rationality'[3] (Muckle, n.d., p. 213). But he who expects a rational economic system from socialism will be forced to re-examine his views.

References

BAUER, O. (1919), *Der Weg zum Socialismus*, Vienna.

BÖHM-BAWERK, E. VON (1890), *Capital and Interest*, London.

BUKHARIN, N. I. (1918), *Das Programm der Kommunisten*, Zurich.

ENGELS, F. (1878), *Anti-Dühring*, English edition, London 1934.

GOTTL-OTTLILIENFELD (1914), *Wirtschaft u. Technik* (Grundriss d. Sozialokonomik, Section 2, Tubingen, 1914).

LENIN, V. I. (1918), *Die nächsten Aufgaben der Sowjetmacht*, Berlin.

MARX, K. (1867), *Capital* (trans. E. & C. Paul).

VON MISES, L. (1912), *Theorie des Geldes u. der Umlaufsmittel*, Munich and Leipzig.

MUCKLE, (n.d.), *Das Kulturideal des Socialismus*.

NEURATH, O. (1919), *Durch die Kriegswirtschaft zur Naturalwirtschaft*, Munich.

3. Cf. Muckle. On the other hand, Muckle demands the 'highest degree of rationalization of economic life in order to curtail hours of labour, and to permit man to withdraw to an island where he can listen to the melody of his being.'

4 O. Lange

On the Economic Theory of Socialism

Excerpt from O. Lange and F. Taylor, *On the Economic Theory of Socialism*, University of Minnesota Press, 1938, pp. 72–98. Originally published in a slightly different form in *Review of Economic Studies*, vol. 3, 1936–7.

The trial and error procedure in a socialist economy

In order to discuss the method of allocating resources in a socialist economy we have to state what kind of socialist society we have in mind. The fact of public ownership of the means of production does not in itself determine the system of distributing consumers' goods and of allocating people to various occupations, nor the principles guiding the production of commodities. Let us now assume that freedom of choice in consumption and freedom of choice of occupation are maintained and that the preferences of consumers, as expressed by their demand prices, are the guiding criteria in production and in the allocation of resources. Later we shall pass to the study of a more centralized socialist system.[1]

In the socialist system as described we have a genuine market (in the institutional sense of the word) for consumers' goods and for the services of labor. But there is no market for capital goods and productive resources outside of labor.[2] The prices of capital goods and productive resources outside of labor are thus prices

---

1. In pre-first world war literature the terms 'Socialism' and 'Collectivism' were used to designate a socialist system as described above and the word 'Communism' was used to denote more centralized systems. The classical definition of socialism (and of collectivism) was that of a system which socializes production alone, while communism was defined as socializing both production and consumption. At the present time these words have become political terms with special connotations.

2. To simplify the problem we assume that all means of production are public property. Needless to say, in any actual socialist community there must be a large number of means of production privately owned (e.g. by farmers, artisans, and small-scale entrepreneurs). But this does not introduce any new theoretical problem.

in the generalized sense, i.e. mere indices of alternatives available, fixed for accounting purposes. Let us see how economic equilibrium is determined in such a system. Just as in a competitive individualist régime, the determination of equilibrium consists of two parts.

1. On the basis of *given* indices of alternatives (which are market prices in the case of consumers' goods and the services of labor and accounting prices in all other cases) both the individuals participating in the economic system as consumers and as owners of the services of labor and the managers of production and of the ultimate resources outside of labor (i.e. of capital and of natural resources) make decisions according to certain principles. These managers are assumed to be public officials.

2. The prices (whether market or accounting) are determined by the condition that the quantity of each commodity demanded is equal to the quantity supplied. The conditions determining the decisions under 1 form the *subjective*, while that under 2 is the *objective*, equilibrium condition.

3. Finally, we have also a condition 3, expressing the social organization of the economic system. As the productive resources outside of labor are public property, the incomes of the consumers are divorced from the ownership of those resources and the form of condition 3 (social organization) is determined by the *principles of income formation adopted*.

The possibility of determining condition 3 in different ways gives to a socialist society considerable freedom in matters of distribution of income. But the necessity of maintaining freedom in the choice of occupation limits the arbitrary use of this freedom, for there must be some connection between the income of a consumer and the services of labor performed by him. It seems, therefore, convenient to regard the income of consumers as composed of two parts: one part being the receipts for the labor services performed and the other part being a social dividend constituting the individual's share in the income derived from the capital and the natural resources owned by society. We assume that the distribution of the social dividend is based on certain principles, reserving the content of those principles for later discussion. Thus condition 3 is determinate and determines the incomes of the consumers in terms of prices of the services of labor and social dividend, which, in turn, may be regarded as determined by the total yield of capital and of the natural resources and by the principles adopted in distributing this yield.[3]

Condition 1. Let us consider the subjective equilibrium condition in a socialist economy:

1. Freedom of choice in consumption being assumed,[4] this part of the subjective equilibrium condition of a competitive market applies also to the market for consumers' goods in a socialist economy. The incomes of the consumers and the prices of consumers' goods being given, the demand for consumers' goods is determined.

2. The decisions of the managers of production are no longer guided by the aim of maximizing profit. Instead, certain rules are imposed on them by the Central Planning Board which aim at satisfying consumers' preferences in the best way possible. These rules determine the combination of factors of production and the scale of output.

One rule must impose the choice of the combination of factors which minimizes the average cost of production. This rule leads to the factors being combined in such proportion that the marginal productivity of that amount of each factor which is worth a unit of money is the same for all factors. This rule is addressed to whoever makes decisions involving the problem of the optimum combination of factors, i.e. to managers responsible for running

3. In formulating condition 3 capital accumulation has to be taken into account. Capital accumulation may be done either 'corporately' by deducting a certain part of the national income before the social dividend is distributed, or it may be left to the savings of individuals, or both methods may be combined. But 'corporate' accumulation must certainly be the dominant form of capital formation in a socialist economy.

4. Of course there may be also a sector of socialized consumption the cost of which is met by taxation. Such a sector exists also in capitalist society and comprises the provision not only of collective wants, in Cassel's sense, but also of other wants whose social importance is too great to be left to the free choice of individuals (for instance, free hospital service and free education). But this problem does not represent any theoretical difficulty and we may disregard it.

existing plants and to those engaged in building new plants. A second rule determines the scale of output by stating that output has to be fixed so that marginal cost is equal to the price of the product. This rule is addressed to two kinds of persons. First of all, it is addressed to the managers of plants and thus determines the scale of output of each plant and, together with the first rule, its demand for factors of production. The first rule, to whomever addressed, and the second rule when addressed to the managers of plants perform the same function that in a competitive system is carried out by the private producer's aiming to maximize his profit, when the prices of factors and of the product are independent of the amount of each factor used by him and of his scale of output.

The total output of an industry has yet to be determined. This is done by addressing the second rule also to the managers of a whole industry (e.g. to the directors of the National Coal Trust) as a principle to guide them in deciding whether an industry ought to be expanded (by building new plants or enlarging old ones) or contracted (by not replacing plants which are wearing out). Thus each industry has to produce exactly as much of a commodity as can be sold or 'accounted for' to other industries at a price which equals the marginal cost incurred *by the industry* in producing this amount. The marginal cost incurred by an industry is the cost to that industry (not to a particular plant) of doing whatever is necessary to produce an additional unit of output, the optimum combination of factors being used. This may include the cost of building new plants or enlarging old ones.[5]

Addressed to the managers of an industry, the second rule performs the function which under free competition is carried out by the free entry of firms into an industry or their exodus from it:

5. Since in practice such marginal cost is not a continuous function of output we have to compare the cost of each additional *indivisible input* with the receipts expected from the additional output thus secured. For instance, in a railway system as long as there are unused carriages the cost of putting them into use has to be compared with the additional receipts which may be obtained by doing so. When all the carriages available are used up to capacity, the cost of building and running additional carriages (and locomotives) has to be compared with the additional receipts expected to arise from such action. Finally, the question of building new tracks is decided upon the same principle. Cf. Lerner (1937, pp. 263–7).

i.e. it determines the output of an industry.[6] The second rule, however, has to be carried out irrespective of whether average cost is covered or not, even if it should involve plants or whole industries in losses.

Both rules can be put in the form of the simple request to use always the method of production (i.e. combination of factors) which minimizes average cost and to produce as much of each service or commodity as will equalize marginal cost and the price of the product, this request being addressed to whoever is responsible for the particular decision to be taken. Thus the output of each plant and industry and the total demand for factors of production by each industry are determined. To enable the managers of production to follow these rules the prices of the factors and of the products must, of course, be given. In the case of consumers' goods and services of labor they are determined on a market; in all other cases they are fixed by the Central Planning Board. Those prices being given, the supply of products and the demand for factors are determined.

The reasons for adopting the two rules mentioned are obvious. Since prices are indices of terms on which alternatives are offered, that method of production which will minimize average cost will also minimize the alternatives sacrificed. Thus the first rule means simply that each commodity must be produced with a minimum sacrifice of alternatives. The second rule is a necessary consequence of following consumers' preferences. It means that the marginal significance of each preference which is satisfied has to be equal to the marginal significance of the alternative preferences the satisfaction of which is sacrificed. If the second rule was not

6. The result, however, of following this rule coincides with the result obtained under free competition only in the case of constant returns to the industry (i.e. a homogeneous production function of the first degree). In this case marginal cost incurred by the industry equals average cost. In all other cases the results diverge, for under free competition the output of an industry is such that average cost equals the price of the product, while according to our rule it is marginal cost (incurred by the industry) that ought to be equal to the price. This difference results in profits being made by the industries whose marginal cost exceeds average cost, whereas the industries in which the opposite is the case incur losses. These profits and losses correspond to the taxes and bounties proposed by Professor Pigou in order to bring about under free competition the equality of private and social marginal net product. See Pigou (1929, pp. 223–7).

observed certain lower preferences would be satisfied while preferences higher up on the scale would be left unsatisfied.

3. Freedom of choice of occupation being assumed, laborers offer their services to the industry or occupation paying the highest wages. For the publicly owned capital and natural resources a price has to be fixed by the Central Planning Board with the provision that these resources can be directed only to industries which are able to 'pay', or rather to 'account for', this price. This is a consequence of following the consumers' preferences. The prices of the services of the ultimate productive resources being given, their distribution between the different industries is also determined.

Condition 2. The subjective equilibrium condition can be carried out only when prices are *given*. This is also true of the decisions of the managers of production and of the productive resources in public ownership. Only when prices are given can the combination of factors which minimizes average cost, the output which equalizes marginal cost and the price of the product, and the best allocation of the ultimate productive resources be determined. But if there is no market (in the institutional sense of the word) for capital goods or for the ultimate productive resources outside of labor, can their prices be determined objectively? Must not the prices fixed by the Central Planning Board necessarily be quite arbitrary? If so, their arbitrary character would deprive them of any economic significance as indices of the terms on which alternatives are offered. This is, indeed, the opinion of Professor Mises (see von Hayek, 1935, pp. 88, 183–4). And the view is shared by G. D. H. Cole, who says (1936, pp. 88, 183–4):

A planless economy, in which each entrepreneur takes his decisions apart from the rest, obviously confronts each entrepreneur with a broadly given structure of costs, represented by the current level of wages, rent, and interest. . . . In a planned socialist economy there can be no objective structure of costs. Costs can be imputed to any desired extent. . . . But these imputed costs are not objective, but *fiat* costs determined by the public policy of the State.

This view, however, is easily refuted by recalling the very elements of price theory.

Why is there an objective price structure in a competitive market? Because, as a result of the parametric function of prices, there is generally only *one* set of prices which satisfies the objective equilibrium condition, i.e. equalizes demand and supply of each commodity. The same objective price structure can be obtained in a socialist economy if the *parametric function of prices* is retained. On a competitive market the parametric function of prices results from the number of competing individuals being too large to enable any one to influence prices by his own action. In a socialist economy, production and ownership of the productive resources outside of labor being centralized, the managers certainly can and do influence prices by their decisions. Therefore, the parametric function of prices must be imposed on them by the Central Planning Board as an *accounting rule*. All accounting has to be done *as if* prices were independent of the decisions taken. For purposes of accounting, prices must be treated as constant, as they are treated by entrepreneurs in a competitive market.

The technique of attaining this end is very simple: the Central Planning Board has to fix prices and see to it that all managers of plants, industries, and resources do their accounting on the basis of the prices fixed by the Central Planning Board, and not tolerate any use of other accounting. Once the parametric function of prices is adopted as an accounting rule, the price structure is established by the objective equilibrium condition. For each set of prices and consumers' incomes a definite amount of each commodity is supplied and demanded.

Condition 3 determines the incomes of the consumers by the prices of the services of ultimate productive resources and the principles adopted for the distribution of the social dividend. With those principles given, prices alone are the variables determining the demand and supply of commodities.

The condition that the quantity demanded and supplied has to be equal for each commodity serves to select the equilibrium prices which alone assure the compatibility of all decisions taken. *Any price different from the equilibrium price would show at the end of the accounting period a surplus or a shortage of the commodity in question.* Thus the accounting prices in a socialist economy, far from being arbitrary, have quite the same objective character as the market prices in a régime of competition. Any mistake made by the Central Planning Board in fixing prices would announce itself in a very objective way – by a physical shortage or surplus of the quantity of the commodity or resources in question – and would have to be corrected in order to keep production running smoothly. As there is generally only one set of prices which satisfies the objective equilibrium condition, both the prices of products and costs[7] are uniquely determined.[8]

Our study of the determination of equilibrium prices in a socialist economy has shown that the process of price determination is quite analogous to that in a competitive market. The Central Planning Board performs the functions of the market. It establishes the rules for combining factors of production and choosing the scale of output of a plant, for determining the output of an industry, for the allocation of resources, and for the parametric use of prices in accounting. Finally, it fixes the prices so as to balance the quantity supplied and demanded of each commodity. It follows that a substitution of planning for the functions of the market is quite possible and workable.

Two problems deserve some special attention. The first relates to the determination of the best distribution of the social dividend. Freedom of choice of occupation assumed, the distribution of the social dividend may affect the amount of services of labor offered to different industries. If certain occupations received a larger social dividend than others, labor would be diverted into

7. Hayek maintains that it would be impossible to determine the value of durable instruments of production because, in consequence of changes, 'the value of most of the more durable instruments of production has little or no connection with the costs which have been incurred in their production' (1935, p. 227). It is quite true that the value of such durable instruments is essentially a capitalized quasi-rent and therefore can be determined only after the price which will be obtained for the product is known (cf. ibid., p. 228). But there is no reason why the price of the product should be any less determinate in a socialist economy than on a competitive market. The managers of the industrial plant in question have simply to take the price fixed by the Central Planning Board as the basis of their calculation. The Central Planning Board would fix this price so as to satisfy the objective equilibrium condition, just as a competitive market does.

8. However, in certain cases there may be a multiple solution.

the occupations receiving a larger dividend. Therefore, the distribution of the social dividend must be such as not to interfere with the optimum distribution of labor services between the different industries and occupations. The optimum distribution is that which makes the differences of the value of the marginal product of the services of labor in different industries and occupations equal to the differences in the marginal disutility[9] of working in those industries or occupations.[10] This distribution of the services of labor arises automatically whenever wages are the only source of income. *Therefore, the social dividend must be distributed so as to have no influence whatever on the choice of occupation.* The social dividend paid to an individual must be entirely independent of his choice of occupation. For instance, it can be divided equally per head of population, or distributed according to age or size of family or any other principle which does not affect the choice of occupation.

The other problem is the determination of the rate of interest. We have to distinguish between a short-period and a long-period solution of the problem. For the former the amount of capital is regarded as constant, and the rate of interest is simply determined by the condition that the demand for capital is equal to the amount available. When the rate of interest is set too low the socialized banking system would be unable to meet the demand of industries for capital; when the interest rate is set too high there would be a surplus of capital available for investment. However, in the long period the amount of capital can be increased by

9. It is only the *relative* disutility of different occupations that counts. The absolute disutility may be zero or even negative. By putting leisure, safety, agreeableness of work, etc., into the preference scales, all labor costs may be expressed as opportunity costs. If such a device is adopted each industry or occupation may be regarded as producing a joint product: the commodity or service in question *and* leisure, safety, agreeableness of work, etc. The services of labor have to be allocated so that the value of this marginal *joint* product is the same in all industries and occupations.

10. If the total amount of labor performed is not limited by legislation or custom regulating the hours of work, etc., the value of the marginal product of the services of labor in each occupation has to be *equal* to the marginal disutility. If any limitational factors are used, it is the marginal *net* product of the services of labor (obtained by deducting from the marginal product the marginal expenditure for the limitational factors) which has to satisfy the condition in the text.

accumulation. If the accumulation of capital is performed 'corporately' before distributing the social dividend to the individuals, the rate of accumulation can be determined by the Central Planning Board *arbitrarily*. The Central Planning Board will probably aim at accumulating enough to make the marginal *net* productivity of capital zero,[11] this aim being never attained because of technical progress (new labor-saving devices), increase of population, the discovery of new natural resources, and, possibly, because of the shift of demand toward commodities produced by more capital-intensive methods.[12] But the rate, i.e. the *speed*, at which accumulation progresses is arbitrary.

The arbitrariness of the rate of capital accumulation 'corporately' performed means simply that the decision regarding the rate of accumulation reflects how the Central Planning Board, and not the consumers, evaluate the optimum time-shape of the income stream. One may argue, of course, that this involves a diminution of consumers' welfare. This difficulty could be overcome only by leaving all accumulation to the saving of individuals.[13] But this is scarcely compatible with the organization of a socialist society.[14] Discussion of this point is postponed to a later part of this essay.

Having treated the theoretical determination of economic equilibrium in a socialist society, let us see how equilibrium can be determined by a method of *trial and error* similar to that in a competitive market. This method of trial and error is based on the *parametric function of prices*. Let the Central Planning Board start with a given set of prices chosen *at random*. All decisions of the managers of production and of the productive resources in

11. Wicksell (1934, p. 241).

12. These changes, however, if very frequent, may act also in the opposite direction and diminish the marginal *net* productivity of capital because of the risk of obsolescence due to them. This is pointed out by Lerner (1936, p. 72).

13. This method has been advocated by Barone (see von Hayek, 1935, pp. 278–9).

14. Of course, the consumers remain free to save as much as they want out of the income which is actually paid out to them, and the socialized banks could pay interest on savings. As a matter of fact, in order to prevent hoarding they would have to do so. But *this* rate of interest would not have any necessary connection with the marginal *net* productivity of capital. It would be quite arbitrary.

public ownership and also all decisions of individuals as consumers and as suppliers of labor are made on the basis of these prices. As a result of these decisions the quantity demanded and supplied of each commodity is determined. If the quantity demanded of a commodity is not equal to the quantity supplied, the price of that commodity has to be changed. It has to be raised if demand exceeds supply and lowered if the reverse is the case. Thus the Central Planning Board fixes a new set of prices which serves as a basis for new decisions, and which results in a new set of quantities demanded and supplied. Through this process of trial and error equilibrium prices are finally determined. Actually the process of trial and error would, of course, proceed on the basis of the prices *historically given*. Relatively small adjustments of those prices would constantly be made, and there would be no necessity of building up an entirely new price system.

This process of trial and error has been excellently described by the late Professor Fred M. Taylor. He assumes that the administrators of the socialist economy would assign provisional values to the factors of production (as well as to all other commodities). He continues (1929):

If, in regulating productive processes, the authorities were actually using for any particular factor a valuation which was too high or too low, that would soon disclose itself in unmistakable ways. Thus, supposing that, in the case of a particular factor, the valuation . . . was too high, that fact would inevitably lead the authorities to be unduly economical in the use of that factor; and this conduct, in turn, would make the amount of that factor which was available for the current production period larger than the amount which was consumed during that period. In other words, too high a valuation of any factor would cause the stock of that factor to show a surplus at the end of the productive period.

Similarly, too low a valuation would cause a deficit in the stock of that factor. 'Surplus or deficit – one or the other of these would result from every wrong valuation of a factor' (Taylor, 1929). By a set of successive trials the right accounting prices of the factors are found.

Thus the accounting prices in a socialist economy can be

determined by the same process of trial and error by which prices on a competitive market are determined. To determine the prices the Central Planning Board does not need to have 'complete lists of the different quantities of all commodities which would be bought at any possible combination of prices of the different commodities which might be available'. (See von Hayek, 1935, p. 211.) Neither would the Central Planning Board have to solve hundreds of thousands (as Professor Hayek expects, 1935, p. 212) or millions (as Professor Robbins thinks (1934, p. 151) of equations. The only 'equations' which would have to be 'solved' would be those of the consumers and the managers of production. These are exactly the same 'equations' which are 'solved' in the present economic system and the persons who do the 'solving' are the same also. Consumers 'solve' them by spending their income so as to get out of it the maximum total utility; and the managers of production 'solve' them by finding the combination of factors that minimizes average cost and the scale of output that equalizes marginal cost and the price of the product. They 'solve' them by a method of trial and error, making (or imagining) small variations *at the margin*, as Marshall used to say, and watching what effect those variations have either on the total utility or on the cost of production. And only a few of them have been graduated in higher mathematics. Professor Hayek and Professor Robbins themselves 'solve' at least hundreds of equations daily, for instance, in buying a newspaper or in deciding to take a meal in a restaurant, and presumably they do not use determinants or Jacobians for that purpose. And each entrepreneur who hires or discharges a worker, or who buys a bale of cotton, 'solves equations' too. Exactly the same kind and number of 'equations', no less and no more, have to be 'solved' in a socialist as in a capitalist economy, and exactly the same persons, the consumers and managers of production plants, have to 'solve' them.

To establish the prices which serve the persons 'solving equations' as parameters no mathematics is needed either. Neither is there needed any knowledge of the demand and supply functions. The right prices are simply found out by watching the quantities demanded and the quantities supplied and by raising the price of a commodity or service whenever there is an excess of demand over supply and lowering it whenever the reverse is the case, until, by trial and error, the price is found at which demand and supply are in balance.

As we have seen, there is not the slightest reason why a trial and error procedure, similar to that in a competitive market, could not work in a socialist economy to determine the accounting prices of capital goods and of the productive resources in public ownership. Indeed, it seems that this trial and error procedure would, or at least could, work *much better* in a socialist economy than it does in a competitive market. For the Central Planning Board has a much wider knowledge of what is going on in the whole economic system than any private entrepreneur can ever have, and, consequently, may be able to reach the right equilibrium prices by a *much shorter* series of successive trials than a competitive market actually does.[15] The argument that in a socialist economy the accounting prices of capital goods and of productive resources in public ownership cannot be determined objectively, either because this is theoretically impossible, or because there is no adequate trial and error procedure available, cannot be maintained. In 1911 Professor Taussig classified the argument that 'goods could not be valued' among the objections to socialism that are 'of little weight' (Taussig, 1911, pp. xvi, 456–7). After all the discussions since that time, no reason can be found to change this opinion.

15. In reducing the number of trials necessary a knowledge of the demand and supply schedules derived from statistics, on which Dickinson wants to base the pricing of goods in a socialist economy, may be of great service, but such knowledge, although *useful*, is *not necessary* in finding out the equilibrium prices. However, if the Central Planning Board proceeds in fixing prices purely by trial and error and the managers of production adhere strictly to treating the prices fixed as constant, in certain branches of production the fluctuations described by the cobweb theorem might appear also in a socialist economy. In such cases the Planning Board would have, in order to avoid such fluctuations, deliberately to use anticipations as to the influence of variations of output on the price of the product, and vice versa (i.e. a knowledge of demand and supply schedules) in fixing the accounting prices. Such deliberate use of demand and supply schedules is useful in all other cases, too, for it serves to shorten the series of trials and thus avoids unnecessary waste.

The general applicability of the trial and error method

The procedure of trial and error described is also applicable to a socialist system where freedom of choice in consumption and freedom of choice of occupation are non-existent and where the allocation of resources, instead of being directed by the preferences of consumers, is directed by the aims and valuations of the bureaucracy in charge of the administration of the economic system. In such a system the Central Planning Board decides which commodities are to be produced and in what quantities, the consumers' goods produced being distributed to the citizens by rationing and the various occupations being filled by assignment. In such a system also rational economic accounting is possible, only that the accounting reflects the preferences of the bureaucrats in the Central Planning Board, instead of those of the consumers. The Central Planning Board has to fix a scale of preferences which serves as the basis of valuation of consumers' goods.

The construction of such a preference scale is by no means a practical impossibility. The consumer on a competitive market is never in doubt as to what to choose if only the prices of the commodities are given, though he certainly would find it impossible to write down the mathematical formula of his utility (or rather preference) function. Similarly, the Central Planning Board does not need to have an elaborate formula of its preferences. By simple judgment it would assign, for instance, to a hat the valuation of ten monetary units when 100,000 hats are produced monthly, and a valuation of eight monetary units to a hat when 150,000 hats per month are produced.

The preference scale of the Central Planning Board being given, the prices, which in this case are *all* accounting prices, are determined in exactly the same way as before. The Central Planning Board has to impose on the managers and builders of plants the rule that factors of production should be combined so as to minimize the average cost of production. For each plant and each industry the rule must be adopted to produce exactly as much of a commodity as can be 'accounted for' at a price equalling marginal cost; and on the managers of ultimate productive resources the rule must be imposed to direct these resources only to the industries which can 'account for' the price fixed by the Central Planning Board. The last two rules were formerly consequences of following the preferences of the consumers, now they are consequences of keeping to the preference scale fixed by the Central Planning Board. They are thus rules which make the decisions of the managers of production and of productive resources consistent with the aims set by the Central Planning Board. In other words, they are rules of internal *consistency* of the planned economy. The rule to choose the combination of factors that minimizes average cost secures *efficiency* in carrying out the plan.

Finally, the Central Planning Board has to impose the parametric function of the accounting prices fixed by itself and to fix them so as to balance the quantity supplied and the quantity demanded for each commodity. The price fixing can be done by trial and error, exactly as in the case studied above; the equilibrium prices thus fixed have a definite objective meaning. The prices are 'planned' in so far as the preference scale is fixed by the Central Planning Board; but once the scale is fixed, they are quite determinate. Any price different from the equilibrium price would leave at the end of the accounting period a surplus or a shortage of the commodity in question and thus impair the smooth running of the production process. The use of the right accounting prices is vital to avoid disturbances in the *physical* course of production and those prices are far from being arbitrary.

The determinateness of the accounting prices holds, however, only if all discrepancies between demand and supply of a commodity are met by an appropriate change of its price. Thus, outside of the distribution of consumers' goods to the citizens, rationing has to be excluded as a method of equalizing supply and demand. If rationing is used for this purpose the prices become arbitrary. But it is interesting to observe that, even if rationing is used, there is, within limits, a tendency to produce the same quantities of commodities as would have been produced if all adjustments between demand and supply were made exclusively by price fixing. If, for instance, the accounting price has been set too low, there is an excess of demand over supply. The Central Planning Board would have to interfere in such a case and order the industry producing the commodity in question to increase its output while ordering the industries using this commodity as a factor of production to be more economical in its use.[16]

Thus the method of rationing leads, by a very rough approximation, to the point where fixing the equilibrium price would have led. But if rationing becomes a general procedure the rules enumerated above cease to be reliable indices of the consistency between the decisions of the managers of production and the aims established by the plan. The consistency of those decisions with the plan can be, instead, measured by fixing quotas of output and comparing them with the actual achievement (as is done in the Soviet Union). But there is no way of measuring the *efficiency* in carrying out the plan without a system of accounting prices which satisfies the objective equilibrium condition, for the rule to produce at the minimum average cost has no significance with regard to the aims of the plan unless prices represent the relative scarcity of the factors of production.[17]

16. Let DD' and SS' be the demand and the supply curves respectively. BQ is the equilibrium price and OB the equilibrium quantity. If the price is set at AP the quantity OA is forthcoming while OC is demanded. As a result of the intervention of the Planning Board the quantity produced will be set somewhere between OA and OC.

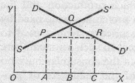

Figure 1

17. There exists, however, a special case where prices are not needed to carry out the plan efficiently. This is the case of constant coefficients of production. If all factors of production are limitational there is no economic problem in finding out the best combination of factors. The combination of factors of production is imposed by the technological exigencies of production. But there remains the problem of determining the optimum scale of output and for this purpose the prices of the factors of production are needed. But if the amount required of all factors of production is simply proportional either to the quantity of the product (if the limitational factors are of the first kind) or to the quantity of another factor used (if the limitational factors are of the second kind) – this is Pareto's case of constant coefficients of production – marginal cost is independent of the scale of output. The problem of choosing the optimum scale of output is thus ruled out

By demonstrating the economic consistency and workability of a socialist economy with free choice neither in consumption nor in occupation, but directed rather by a preference scale imposed by the bureaucrats in the Central Planning Board, we do not mean, of course, to recommend such a system. Lerner (1934, pp. 51–61) has sufficiently shown the undemocratic character of such a system and its incompatibility with the ideals of the socialist movement. Such a system would scarcely be tolerated by any civilized people. A distribution of consumers' goods by rationing was possible in the Soviet Union at a time when the standard of living was at a physiological minimum and an increase of the ration of any food, clothing, or housing accommodation was welcome, no matter what it was. But as soon as the national income increased sufficiently, rationing was given up, to be replaced to a large extent by a market for consumers' goods. And, outside of certain exceptions, there has always been freedom of choice of occupation in the Soviet Union. A distribution of consumers' goods by rationing is quite unimaginable in the countries of Western Europe or in the United States.

But freedom of choice in consumption does not imply that production is actually guided by the choices of the consumers. One may well imagine a system in which production and the allocation of resources are guided by a preference scale fixed by the Central Planning Board while the price system is used to distribute the consumers' goods produced. In such a system there is freedom of choice in consumption, but the consumers have no influence whatever on the decisions of the managers of pro-

---

too. In the particular case under consideration, where all coefficients of production are constant, no prices and no cost accounting whatever are needed. Efficiency in production is maintained merely by technological considerations of avoiding waste of materials, etc. It seems that those who deny the necessity of an adequate price system in a socialist economy have this case in mind. If the quotas of consumers' goods to be produced are given, all further problems of planning production are purely technological and no price system or cost accounting is needed. But we need not say how extremely unrealistic is the assumption that all coefficients of production are constant. The very fact that in the Soviet Union such great stress is laid on cost accounting shows how far from reality this special case is removed. But if cost accounting is to fulfill its purpose of securing efficiency in carrying out the plan, the accounting prices cannot be arbitrary.

duction and of the productive resources.[18] There would be two sets of prices of consumers' goods. One would be the market prices at which the goods are sold to the consumers; the other, the accounting prices derived from the preference scale fixed by the Central Planning Board. The latter set of prices would be those on the basis of which the managers of production would make their decisions.

However, it does not seem very probable that such a system would be tolerated by the citizens of a socialist community. The dual system of prices of consumers' goods would reveal to the people that the bureaucrats in the Central Planning Board allocate the community's productive resources according to a preference scale different from that of the citizens. The existence of a dual price system of consumers' goods could scarcely be concealed from the people, especially if there existed an institution (like the Workers' and Peasants' Inspection in the Soviet Union[19]) giving to the rank and file citizen the right to pry into the book-keeping and into the management of the community's resources.

Thus the accounting prices of consumers' goods would be permitted to deviate from the market prices only in exceptional cases in which there is general agreement that such deviation is in the interest of social welfare. For instance, it might be agreed upon that the consumption of whisky ought to be discouraged, while the reading of the works of Karl Marx or of the Bible (or of both, as certainly would be the case in an Anglo-Saxon community) ought to be encouraged, and the prices of those things would be fixed accordingly. But such things do happen also in a capitalist society. If the bureaucrats want successfully to impose a preference scale of their own for the guidance of production, they have to camouflage the inconsistency of their preference scale with that of the citizens by resorting to rationing in the sphere of

18. Of course, there remains the possibility of influence through political channels, but there is no regular economic mechanism through which the consumers automatically influence the direction of production. Zassenhaus has suggested a very interesting theoretical formulation of the influence through political channels, analogous to the economic theory of choice. See Zassenhaus (1934, p. 511).

19. This institution was abolished in June 1934, and replaced by the Commission of Soviet Control. A part of its functions has been taken over by the trade-unions. See Webb, S. and B. (1935, pp. 99, 474–8).

producers' goods and of resources.[20] Thus a socialist community which has been able to impose the principle that rationing must be excluded, and price fixing used as the only method of balancing quantities demanded and quantities supplied, may be fairly confident that it will be able to ensure that the Central Planning Board follows the preferences of the consumers.

20. It seems that the great extent to which rationing was used in the Soviet Union was partly due to the necessity of concealing the share of the national income going to the bureaucracy but mainly to the failure properly to understand and utilize the price mechanism. Its continuance after the civil war and reconstruction is a symptom of the bureaucratic degeneration of the Soviet economy.

References

BARONE, E. (1908), *The Ministry of Production in the Collectivist State*, translated from the Italian in F. A. von Hayek, (1935) *Collectivist Economic Planning*, Routledge & Kegan Paul.

COLE, G. D. H. (1936), *Economic Planning*, New York.

LERNER, A. P. (1934), 'Economic theory and socialist economy', *Rev. econ. Stud*.

LERNER, A. P. (1936), 'A note on socialist economics', *Rev. econ. Stud*., vol 4, pp. 72–76.

LERNER, A. P. (1937), 'Statics and dynamics in socialist economics', *Econ. J*., vol. 47, pp. 263–7.

PIGOU, A. C. (1929), *The Economics of Welfare*, Macmillan. 3rd edn.

ROBBINS, L. C. (1934), *The Great Depression*, Macmillan.

TAUSSIG, F. W. (1911), *Principles of Economics*, vol. 2, Macmillan.

TAYLOR, F. M. (1929), 'The guidance of production in a socialist state', *Amer. econ. Rev*., vol. 19, pp. 1–8.

VON HAYEK, F. A. (ed.) (1935), *Collectivist Economic Planning*, Routledge & Kegan Paul.

WEBB, B. and S. (1935), *Soviet Communism*, vol. 1, London.

WICKSELL, K. (1934), 'Professor Cassell's system of economics', reprinted in L. Robbins (ed.) *Lectures on Political Economy*, vol. 1, Routledge & Kegan Paul.

ZASSENHAUS, H. (1934), 'Uber die otonomische Theorie der Planwirtschaft', *Zeitschrift für Nationalökonomie*, Bd 5.

Part Two
Accumulation and Economic Growth

Contrary to widespread belief, Marx did *not* confine his vision of the realization of socialism to the most advanced capitalist countries; he only postulated that a level of capitalist development would have to be reached, sufficient for the creation of an industrial proletariat. The fact that the 'weakest link' of the system turned out to be a relatively underdeveloped country vastly damaged by war put a strong emphasis on accumulation and growth, first to reconstruct the economy, then to engage the economy in a race with the advanced capitalist countries, with an aim to reach and overcome these countries and realize the 'higher' stage of communism. The emphasis on accumulation and growth therefore played a crucial role in the shaping of the first instance of a socialist economy.

Dobb's essay is an important contribution to the general theory of investment under socialism (and under capitalism as well): he points out the relation between wages, prices and accumulation policy and discusses the use of interest rates in short and long term planning. When, however, accumulation policy was discussed in the 1920s in the Soviet Union more specific problems had to be tackled. Preobrazhensky considers the problems of an economy in transition to socialism, especially the financing of 'primitive' socialist accumulation, i.e. capital accumulation within the state sector of a mixed economy (as opposed to capital accumulation in the whole economy where public and private sector still coexist under a socialist régime). The methods he suggests for channelling the surplus produced in the private sector to the State sector have all been widely used to finance socialist industrialization in the Soviet Union and the other socialist countries: these are the manipulation of the terms of trade between the two sectors, and deliberately inflationary policies. Fel'dman formalized the main features of the Soviet investment strategy in a two-sector model of acceleration of growth, given here in the more modern presentation by Domar. The assumptions of the model – capital equipment as the limiting factor, plentiful labour, a closed economy, technical rigidities – correspond closely to the Soviet conditions in the period between the Wars, and Fel'dman seems to vindicate the principle 'priority for heavy industry' that characterized socialist investment policy. However, this policy continued to be implemented when the fundamental assumptions of the model ceased to be satisfied – when reserves of labour had long been exhausted, with international trade and balance of payments problems – and was imitated by other socialist countries whose economic reality did not correspond to these assumptions. The Polish economic school, under the guidance of Kalecki, were the first to reformulate the theory of socialist accumulation to take the new conditions into account. The paper by Brus and Laski is one of the earlier contributions to this change and emphasize the limits set by objective conditions to planned acceleration of growth. This change of emphasis has been an important element in the background to the economic reforms (See Part Four, especially Reading 15).

5 M. H. Dobb

A Note on Saving and Investment in a Socialist Economy

Excerpts from M. H. Dobb, 'A note on saving and investment in a socialist economy', *Economic Journal*, 1939; reprinted in M. H. Dobb, *On Economic Theory and Socialism*, Routledge & Kegan Paul, 1955, pp. 41–55.

The purpose of this Note is to point out certain considerations concerning the equilibrium of the system as a whole which seem to have been overlooked in recent discussions of the working of a socialist economy: in particular, to suggest that a rate of interest cannot *simpliciter* provide a stabilizing mechanism in such an economy, and that the principle of equating price with marginal cost (as enunciated by several writers) may well run counter to the maintenance of full employment, and in certain circumstances will be impossible of application.

Hitherto discussion of a socialist economy has been pre-occupied with the problem of the allocation of a given quantity of resources between various uses, and little or no attention has been given to problems connected with the rate of investment and its relation to the level of wages and the price level of consumption goods, or to the conditions adequate to ensure the full employment of resources. To solve the problem of ideal allocation a number of writers – I refer particularly to Lange, Lerner and Hall – have agreed in proposing that decisions as to output and investment in a socialist economy should be ruled by the following principles. *First*, all prices, whether in the case of finished goods or of factors of production (in some cases these may be no more than 'accounting prices', as suggested by Lange), shall be fixed by a process of trial and error until an 'equilibrium price' is found at which the current supply is equal to the demand. If the commodity or factor in question is in surplus supply (e.g. if unsold stocks are accumulating) the price will be lowered; if it is in deficit-supply, the price will be raised. *Secondly*, decisions as to output and investment shall be taken by each industry on the basis of carrying the utilization of resources to the point where marginal cost is equated to price: the output of each plant presumably being extended to the point where the short-period (or prime) cost of additional output is equal to the value of that output, and new investment in the industry being undertaken if, and only if, the additional output resulting from the investment, when valued at current prices, equals or exceeds its long-period cost, including the current interest-charge on the capital involved in the construction of the new equipment.[1] The advantage of this mechanism that its sponsors appear to have in mind is that it would facilitate a considerable decentralization of investment and output decisions. The central planning authority need decide only the *total* amount[2] to be invested in any period: the direction and the form of the investment, and *a fortiori* the output of existing

1. Lange (1938, pp. 75–6, 78, 79) postulates that all managers of industries and plants must be ordered first to choose 'the combination of factors which minimizes the average cost of production', secondly 'to produce as much of each service or commodity as will equalize marginal cost and the price of the product'. With regard to capital he states that 'a price has to be fixed by the Central Planning Board with the provision that these resources can be directed only to industries which are able to "pay", or rather "account for" this price'. Lerner (1937, p. 257) has suggested that instructions should be issued 'that the use of every factor is to be extended up to the point where the marginal physical product multiplied by its price is equal to the price of the factor. . . . This value, which has to be equated to the price of the product, we shall call the marginal cost. . . . The guiding principle that we seek is none other than the equation of price to marginal cost'. Hall (1937, pp. 92, 119, 129) has written: 'If the rate of interest has been chosen correctly, the total expansions should balance the total contractions . . . if there is a general tendency to expand, the rate must be raised in order to turn some of the apparent profits into losses, and *vice versa*.' 'The aim of the Ministry (of Production) is to equate prices and marginal costs, which is done by varying the amounts of the various goods. . . . Every unit, if properly conducted, will extend its operations to the point where the marginal cost equals the price which is received'. Pigou (1937, pp. 112, 115, 129) has assumed that an accounting price for capital (as for other factors) can be arrived at that 'will exactly clear the market, without shortage or surplus, of that part of money income that is on offer for net investment', but that each industry is told to adjust its production so that 'aggregate costs are equal to aggregate sales proceeds' and its 'average accounting cost is a minimum'.

2. I do not recall that it has anywhere been stated how this total is to be valued. As will later appear, it will be a matter of considerable importance whether the total is expressed in terms of wage-units or of the value of final output.

plants, could be left to the managements of the various industries to determine according to the second of the above rules. All that the central planning authority would need to do, having decided the total investment for the system as a whole, would be to adjust the aggregate demand for capital to that supply by appropriate shifts of an interest rate.

Closer inspection reveals the danger that a system controlled in this way may inherit two of the principal vices of capitalism. With a price-mechanism of this kind in operation, the only way of precluding a large measure of chronic unemployment may be to maintain the rate of investment at a given, 'arbitrary' level, which may be quite different from the level that would be dictated by other considerations. Moreover, it is not difficult to show that, unless some stabilizing mechanism is introduced, in addition to or as a substitute for this pricing-mechanism, a socialist economy may inherit the instability of capitalism in an even more pronounced form. Perhaps it is a lingering habit of thinking of the 'demand for capital' in terms of the marginal productivity of a given *stock* of capital that is responsible for the apparent readiness to conceive of the rate of interest as a simple mechanism for controlling the rate of investment – to imagine that the 'demand for capital' is a sufficiently stable quantity for the supply and demand for capital to be easily equated by means of appropriate adaptations of an interest-rate. As soon, however, as it is realized that the 'demand for capital' is a function, *inter alia*, of the current *rate of investment*, and that (for reasons to be explained below) this demand will vary directly, and not inversely, with the rate of investment, *ceteris paribus*, the existence of a powerful *de*-stabilizing influence inherent in this relationship becomes apparent. In other words, the so-called schedule of the marginal efficiency of capital is *not* independent of the rate of investment. If the rate of investment is increased (or decreased), so will be the inducement to invest; and the situation will be one of unstable equilibrium, where the tendency to a Wicksellian cumulative movement, with increased investment 'creating its own draught', can hardly be controlled efficiently by a trial-and-error process of searching for an equilibrium-price for capital. If, moreover, an attempt is made to adhere to the rule of equating price and marginal cost, the volume of output from existing plant, and hence employment, will be determined by the relation between the price level of finished goods and money wages, and this relation is also (and for the same reason) a function of the rate of invest-ment. If, therefore, the rate of investment upon which the State happens to have decided is a relatively low one, unemployment may be impossible to avoid, since to intensify the utilization of existing plant by employing more labour per unit of equipment would cause marginal prime cost to exceed price.[3] On the other hand, if a condition of full employment has already been attained, it will be *impossible* both to increase the rate of investment and at the same time to maintain an equality between price and cost, even between price and short-period marginal cost.[4]

To eludicate the reason for these statements let us examine the working of such a mechanism as is proposed by Lange and Lerner and Hall, in a simplified situation and in their own terms. To make the task of analysis easier we will start from the following assumptions. (*a*) We will assume both that the only form of personal income consists of wages,[5] and that wage-earners spend the whole of their income in a given period on consumption goods – that their saving is zero. (*b*) We will assume that prime costs of current output consist exclusively of wages (this is plausible if we imagine that each industry is vertically integrated, and that pro-duction in each plant embraces all processes from extraction from the soil to a finished product). We may further assume that each industry undertakes the repair and maintenance of its own plant, employing permanent repair workers as well as process-workers, and counts the wages of the former in its prime or operating costs. (*c*) We will assume that land is a free good and is not priced, so that the only element in total cost other than wages consists of the accounting-price of capital, as currently fixed by the State Bank or Investment Board or Central Planning Council. (*d*) We will assume that there is technical homogeneity between

3. This, of course, is to assume that output is at the level at which short-period costs are *rising*.

4. Cf. below, p. 119 footnote 7.

5. This implies that there is no subsidy to consumption in the shape of a money-grant to individuals, i.e. no form of 'social dividend in money'. It is also implied, for the present, that the State levies no taxation, either direct or indirect, on wage earners.

various industries to the extent of making the ratio of capital to labour approximately uniform in the mall. (*e*) We will assume that the amount of reserve productive-capacity that exists, at the outset, in the industries producing consumption-goods is small (i.e. short-period costs have a rising tendency).

It will be obvious that there follows from assumptions (*a*) and (*b*) the corollary which can be expressed by saying that:

$$C = W \text{ and } P = \varphi W$$

where C represents the value of output of consumption goods, W represents the total wage-bill of the country, P represents total profits of industry, and φ the proportion of the total wage-bill which is expended by the State in new constructional work (i.e. φW is the rate of investment).

It will be convenient to distinguish four classes of decisions that the management of industry will have to take.

1. Given a plant of a particular type and size, how much labour to employ in that plant and how much output to obtain from it? This we will call the intensity of utilization of a given plant by labour. If the second of the above rules is observed (controlling output in such a way as to attempt to equate price and marginal cost), this will depend on the price of output, the level of wages and the extent to which marginal operating cost (MOC) rises as the intensity of utilization of the plant is increased. The difference between the price of output and the average operating cost (AOC) multiplied by the output will represent the profit of that plant.

2. What should be the *size* of each plant? (This is, of course, a decision that will arise only as existing plant wears out, or the construction of new ones is under consideration.) This will be determined by the average *total* cost (ATC) of production in plants of different sizes (including in this the cost of constructing the plant *plus* the accounting-price of the capital involved), according to the rule that, where the plants in the industry are numerous, that size of plant should be chosen which makes ATC a minimum.[6] This can be expressed by Lerner's envelope

6. The contradiction between this and Lerner's principle that the size of plant should be chosen which equates MTC and the demand-price (*Economic Journal*, June 1937) is only apparent. Lerner's principle comes into play where the plants in an industry are sufficiently few to make impossible

U-curve, where the envelope curve represents the ATC under plants of different sizes, and the smaller curves tangential to it represent the cost of producing with a plant of a *given* size.

3. What should be the *number* of plants in an industry? This will generally depend on the profit that each plant is making, as defined under 1. If the profit-rate (i.e. the ratio of profit to the value of the plant when valued at reconstruction-cost) being earned by a typical plant in an industry is greater than the accounting-price of capital, then presumably the number of plants will generally be increased, and *vice versa*. (But there may be exceptions to this rule where economies are to be gained from enlarging the size of the whole industry, or conversely dis-economies; and these economies or diseconomies may make expansion or contraction desirable even when the profit-rate is equal to the accounting-price of capital.)

4. Which of a variety of technical types of plant (irrespective of their size) to choose to construct? These types will differ, not only in that operating costs under each type of plant will be different, but also in their costs of construction and maintenance. Taking these factors into account, a choice will be made according to a similar rule as in cases of class 3. It will follow that if the accounting-price of capital is low, plant-types which have a relatively high cost of construction, compared to the economies of operating costs that they promise, will be preferred to a greater extent than when the accounting-price is high. Changes of this class represent Hawtrey's 'deepening process', as distinct from his 'widening process'.

Let us suppose that the State, in order to stimulate an increase of investment, lowers its accounting-price for capital. There will then be a tendency for changes under 3 and 4 to take place. The increased constructional activity will involve either a transfer of labour from making consumption goods to construction jobs (in which case it will necessarily involve some lowering of the in-tensity of utilization of plant in the consumption trades), or else the absorption of previously unemployed labour into construction work. The net effect will be a rise in the price of consumption

---

such a nice adjustment of their *number* as to enable them all to be of optimum size and at the same time to be operated at 'normal' capacity.

goods (measured either in money or in wage-units);[7] since, as we have seen above, P, which $= C-(W-\varphi W)$, varies with the rate of investment. In other words, if the demand, depending on the total wage-bill, rises relatively to the supply of consumption goods, as will be the consequence of increased investment, the consumption price-level must rise relatively to the wage-level. At a later stage, it is true, as the new plants come into existence, the output of consumption goods will increase and their price will tend to fall again. But for the time being while the investment is taking place, the price level of finished output will inevitably rise, and with it the profits of industry. This rise will, indeed, measure the community's 'saving'; the profits of industry corresponding to the rate of investment, so that from a budgetary point of view the State investment programme will be self-financing, creating exactly the amount of profit necessary to finance the investment.[8]

But this very rise of price, by increasing profits, has increased the 'demand for capital', and hence raised the equilibrium-price of capital *above the level at which it originally stood*. If the State

7. If there is full employment there will be the difficulty that the rise of price will encourage an increase of output in the consumption trades at the same time as there is an increased demand for labour for construction work. In this case there *must* be some mechanism such as a tax on output of the consumption trades to bridge the gap between MOC and price, and thereby prevent an expansion of output, or even curtail output, so as to release labour for construction work. If, however, there is a reserve of unemployed labour, this difficulty does not arise, and increased investment can occur together with increased output and employment in the consumption trades (MOC and the higher price being equated by an expansion of output, provided that short-period costs are rising for increases of output).

It is to be noted that even if the effect of the increased demand for workers was to raise wages, this would not alter the fact that profits would be raised in step with increased investment. If wages rose, the price of consumption goods would rise correspondingly higher. Similarly, if the increased investment resulted, not in a transfer of labour, but in the employment of some new reserve of labour, the price of consumption goods would be raised by the expenditure of an enhanced total of wages.

8. The amount by which the 'employment multiplier' exceeds unity will here depend simply on the gradient of the (rising) short-period cost-curves in existing plants; since this gradient determines the 'shift to profit' as demand increases. But whatever this gradient, equilibrium on the above assumptions requires that output in these plants should be increased to the point where marginal cost has risen sufficiently (relatively to average cost) to yield an aggregate of profit that is equal to the amount of investment.

delays the raising of its accounting-price (after the initial lowering of it), the inducement to expand constructional activity will not only persist, but will grow cumulatively greater. If, on the other hand, after initially lowering its rate to stimulate investment, it is too quick to raise it again as a check on the inflationary tendency, it may find itself in future in the position where its power to influence investment by a change in its accounting price is seriously blunted, since industrial managers will never expect such a change in price to last beyond a brief interval, and will take it as heralding an *opposite* change in the near future. In other words, the difficulty which today exists in influencing long-term investment through changes in the short-term rate may reappear, and reappear in an accentuated form.[9]

These results will not appear strange to those familiar with the proposition that 'saving equals investment'. Where the State is the investor, its investment decisions will determine and create the communal 'saving' necessary to finance it, as will be the case when investment is done by private entrepreneurs. But when all (or nearly all) personal incomes are spent, this saving must partake of the nature of so-called 'forced saving': the significant

9. It will follow that the 'true' accounting-price for capital will be at its lowest when, for any reason, a zero rate of net investment prevails. Profits in this case will be zero, since with a zero rate of investment equilibrium can only be achieved when the price-level of output = AOC of output; wages being, *ex definitione*, the only source of demand for final output, and operating costs consisting solely of wages. It might seem to follow that, since profits are zero, the 'true' accounting-price must also be zero. But this is not the case; since a zero accounting-price for capital might stimulate changes of class 4 above (changes in the technical type of plant), owing to the economy of operating costs that the new type of plant could yield; and to maintain a zero rate of net investment the accounting-price would have to be high enough to offset the advantage of any such change. (It will be clear that this corresponds to the marginal productivity of the existing *stock* of capital in traditional capital theory. It will only be zero when changes of class 4 above have proceeded sufficiently far to reach what has been called the point of 'capital saturation': Dobb (1937) and Lange (1938). On the other hand, if the rule applicable to case 3 above were to be rigidly applied in the sense of reducing the number of plants in an industry if the profit rate was less than the price of capital, any positive accounting-price for capital would cause changes of this type in the course of time, and the position would be inherently unstable. There would, however, be some level of this accounting-price at which presumably the rate at which changes of type 4 were occurring exactly balanced the rate at which opposite changes of type 3

effect of the investment will be, not to enhance the money incomes of individuals, but the income of the State in the shape of industrial profits. The notion that the State 'creates' its own profits by its own investment is, of course, analogous to the contention of Kalecki (1937) that, on similar assumptions, capitalists' spending 'creates' capitalists' profits (see also van Dorp (1937)). If, therefore, changes in the price of output, and in the profits to which these give rise, are allowed to influence the investment decisions of industry, a cumulative tendency will be latent in any acceleration or deceleration of investment during the short period (i.e. until the number or the type of plants has had time to be affected, and so influence sufficiently the *rate* of profit in an opposite direction to that in which *total* profit has previously moved).

This characteristic of the situation is more marked in a Socialist economy (unless its investment is centrally planned) because, in so far as wages are the only form of personal income and little or nothing is 'saved' out of wages, the demand for finished output is identified with the short-period cost of output unless State expenditure is taking place. In a capitalist society other incomes than wages exist, and to the extent that expenditure from these incomes (measured in real terms) tends to alter inversely with the price of finished output, a stabilizing element is introduced; and it is on some such assumption as this that traditional writers seem to have relied when they have pictured the system as tending towards stable equilibrium, and in particular have treated variations in money wages as an equilibrating influence.

It will further be seen to follow that in this situation, if the rules suggested by Lange and others are adhered to, the amount of

---

were taking place; and in this sense what could be defined as zero net investment for the economy as a whole could prevail, even though changes inside the total of existing capital equipment were occurring. It is further to be noted that, if the rule of equating MOC to price is to be observed, the intensive utilization of existing plant will have to be restricted to a point where AOC = MOC, i.e. to a point below that where operating costs begin to rise as output from the plant expands. But this condition can only be fulfilled, either at the expense of some unemployment of existing labour, or else if the number (or size) of plants in each industry has been increased up to the point which corresponds to (and therefore implies the previous existence of) a zero accounting-price for capital.

employment will be determined by the rate of investment, given the amount and type of plant already in existence; since the rate of investment, determining as it does the ratio of the price level of consumption goods to money wages, determines the level of output and hence the employment capacity of existing plant in the consumption trades. If, therefore, it is desired to maintain full employment, the rate of investment cannot be fixed at the will of the planning authority, except by departing from the rule of equating price with MOC. That the State should be under the compulsion in any given situation to maintain a given rate of investment, irrespective of other considerations, as the only alternative to unemployment, on the one hand, or to acute labour shortage, on the other hand, is clearly irrational.[10]

These results do not, of course, follow if we drop our assumption that wages are the only form of personal income and imagine that each individual, over and above his wages, receives a 'social dividend' issued directly by the State.[11] But it is not merely the

10. Only when 'capital saturation' has already been achieved is full employment consistent with a zero rate of net investment on the above assumptions. As the amount of plant and its productivity is increased by successive additions to the stock of capital-equipment, the profit rate yielded to each industrial plant (and the intensity of utilization of the plant required to yield this profit) by a given rate of investment will fall. Whether the total amount of labour required to operate the total plant in existence tends to increase or decrease will depend upon whether changes of type 3 are proceeding faster than changes of type 4 in a labour-saving direction, i.e. on the relative rate of changes in the 'widening' process and changes in the 'deepening' process. If no investment were taking place, the capacity of industry to employ labour would be uniquely given by the amount of plant in existence and its productivity, i.e. by the employment-giving capacity of existing plant (given the above rule of equating MOC to price).

11. As Lange himself suggests where he refers to part of income being paid in this way. Dickinson has also hinted at something of the same kind. But these writers apparently regard this as an optional, and not as a *necessary*, arrangement, and the amount of any such income as being 'arbitrary'. Lange, indeed, refers to this dividend as being 'determined by the total yield of capital and natural resources' minus investment. But this seems to be to put the cart before the horse, since it is the size of this dividend *plus* investment that will determine both the profits of State industry (i.e. 'the total yield of capital', presumably) and the level of employment, and unless the dividend is made to fall as investment rises (or *vice versa*) total profits will rise (or fall).

presence of this additional income, but appropriate variations in it, that will exercise a stabilizing influence. If, therefore, the cumulative tendencies latent in the situation are to be counter-acted, this social dividend must be made to vary inversely with the rate of investment; while its absolute amount must be fixed so that, together with the rate of investment, it is able to secure full employment. Again, an excise or turnover tax, varying directly with the rate of investment, could be employed as a stabilizing mechanism. In this case, marginal cost *plus* the tax would presumably be equated to price;[12] and when the rate of investment was increased in a condition of full employment, the inevitable gap between MOC and price would be bridged by the tax, profits in the consumption trades would be prevented from expanding, and output in these trades would be restricted and labour released for transfer to constructional work.[13] Where the rate of invest-ment was relatively high a tax would be the appropriate mech-anism; where the rate of investment was below a certain critical level, a social dividend. Provided that such a mechanism, centrally controlled, was in operation, the kind of pricing system suggested by Lange would not be impracticable.

But it may well seem to many a somewhat strange and cum-brous procedure to have to create a specialized device of variable social dividends or taxes in order to 'neutralize' money sufficiently for a system of accounting-prices to operate smoothly; and one may be tempted to think that it has little to recommend it except as an ingenious proposal for reproducing in a socialist economy the 'ideal capitalism' of economists' imagination. If the absolute level of prices (whether of finished or intermediate products) is irrelevant and the significant consideration is the *comparative* productivity of economic resources, it is not clear why economic decisions could not be as wisely and more simply taken by a direct inspection of these comparative productivities, rather than by an

12. Marginal cost, although no longer equal, would still be *proportional* to price; and this, as Khan (1935) has pointed out, is all that is required to secure the 'ideal' allocation of resources.

13. It seems clear that this is the primary function performed by the very high turnover taxes in USSR under the very high rates of investment of the Five-Year Plans. Without them the symptoms of labour scarcity would grow more acute and the queues and goods shortages of the early 1930s would recur. At the same time, these turnover taxes are used to differentiate between different kinds of consumption goods, e.g. luxuries and necessaries.

elaborate attempt to equate two sets of prices – that of products and of all resources used. The former method would require that all investment decisions (at any rate in their general outline) should be centralized in the hands of the central planning authorities, and only wages (and not the price of capital) included in the calculation of costs. This would mean that control over questions of class 2, 3 and 4 above was centralized: in deciding *how much* of the community's resources to invest the planning authority would simultaneously decide (on the basis of data and advice provided by each industry) how and where investment should take place. For this method there seems to be much more to be said than has generally been admitted. In taking such decisions the planning authority would apply the rule of the maximum directly, instead of through the mediation of an accounting-price for capital: i.e. it would direct each type of resource to that use where its productivity (at the margin), valued in terms of final output, was estimated to be a maximum. Since the decision would be concerned directly with the comparative productivities of different uses (and not with the difference between value of output and an accounting-price) changes in the *absolute* level of price of final output would be irrelevant to the decision, so that the difficulties we have mentioned connected with changes in this level would not arise. The planning authorities would simply have to know which direction was uphill on the productivity slope, and always shift resources uphill until they could climb no further. It has been objected that the centralizing of such investment-decisions might prove unduly cumbersome for them to be wisely taken. But it would, surely, be possible for each industrial management to submit its own draft sectional plan on the basis of precisely the same data as are available to them under Lange's scheme (plans drafted, perhaps on the basis of an accounting-price, or else simply on provisional data about quantity of resources available to that industry),[14] and

14. It is quite possible that Lange's proposal would prove serviceable as part of the technique of planning, even though it ceased to play a role as an automatic regulator of the actual decisions ultimately taken. In other words a preliminary accounting-price might be issued to industrial units as a basis on which to construct the first draft plans, this price being issued simply as a 'feeler' during the process of drafting, but not necessarily playing any decisive role subsequently.

for the central authority to confine itself to subsequent pruning and integration of these draft sectional plans? The difference would be that the process of trial and error and adjustment and readjustment would take place *before* any plans were finally sanctioned and embodied in concrete acts of investment, instead of after.

Would the planning authority, nevertheless, operate ('on paper') with ratios analogous to the traditional concept of a rate of interest, even though it did not *charge* an interest rate even for accounting purposes? In taking decisions of any of types 2, 3 and 4 above, the planning authority would presumably be confronted with data that could be expressed in terms of a ratio of net productivity (after allowing for the cost of depreciation or maintenance as well as ordinary operating costs) to construction cost. If all projects were expressed in terms of such a ratio, a priority list of projects could be drawn up, and the allocation of resources be simply decided by moving down this priority list. Here it is clear that the comparative, and not the absolute, size of these ratios would be the dominant consideration. The important thing would be that an investment use which showed a higher net productivity ratio should always be satisfied before an investment use with a lower net productivity ratio. Thus, decisions of type 2 would be made by giving priority to the construction of that size of plant which yielded the highest net productivity in relation to construction cost. With regard to the choice between changes of types 3 and 4: it would probably happen that some technical methods with a small construction cost figured higher in the list even though their current cost of operation and maintenance was relatively high; and consequently their construction would at first be preferred. As, however, the number of plants of this type was increased, the price of their products would tend to fall, thereby lowering their productivity ratio *proportionately more*[15] than that of technical methods with lower costs of operation and maintenance but higher initial construction costs; and as this occurred the latter would climb in the priority list and investment

15. This for the reason that if x is the product, y the cost of the product, $x - y$ the profit, and a/b the ratio of the new price level to the old, then $\dfrac{(a/b)\,(x - y)}{x - y}$ will be larger, the *smaller* is y.

in the new method would begin. When the new method had come into use, it would then pay to transfer labour previously employed on the repair and maintenance of the old plant to maintenance work on the new, since the net productivity of maintenance work on the latter would now be the greater. In this way the new plant would gradually replace the old; and the process of successive transition to more complicated projects would continue, until the possibilities of economies in operating and maintenance costs by changes of type 4 had been exhausted.[16]

But there is a consideration which is to my mind conclusive in rendering centrally planned investment superior to a decentralized system operating under the control of an accounting price or interest rate. It is that by the former method investment could be more wisely and consistently planned through time, since investment decisions could be taken in the light of fuller knowledge of the data on which the rightness or wrongness of such decisions must depend. This would seem to be so crucial an element in the superiority of a socialist over a capitalist economy as to render it an essential keystone of a planning system. If, on the other hand, questions of plant construction were left to be decided decentrally, according to rule-of-thumb responses to accounting prices, the industrial managers who decided these things would be largely in blinkers with regard to developments elsewhere and to future developments, upon which their decisions ought to depend. It follows from the situation in which they are placed that these managers could not have all the relevant data before them; and this is the crucial difficulty.[17] It is an over-simplification to

16. I have elsewhere suggested that there may be situations where it would be desirable *immediately* to invest in the most productive methods, even where these were relatively slow-yielding and involved a large initial construction cost. The example above is intended to show how the calculation of comparative productivity ratios could take place where more gradual progression from simple to complex technical methods was appropriate.

17. That this is a matter of the objective situation and not of subjective factors (the efficiency of managers and their powers of vision, etc.), does not seem always to have been appreciated; e.g. Pigou (1935, pp. 114–15) and Hutchison (1938, pp. 186–7), where this argument is cited as though it depended on the personal qualities of administrators who take the decisions, and not on their situation.

imagine that all that is necessary, either in a capitalist or a socialist economy, is to know the *present* loan price and the present price of products. Since investment represents a locking up of resources over time, the *future* price of capital and the future price of products would be relevant to any of the decisions of types 2, 3 and 4 referred to above. The capitalist entrepreneur takes his decision on the basis of *expectations* as to the future trend of these factors, and because these expectations are necessarily mere guesses, mistakes and subsequent jerks in development and fluctuations develop. On what is the industrial manager in a socialist economy to base his decision? If on similar guesses, then similar mistakes and jerks and possibly fluctuations (if not quickly corrected) will result. In order to estimate the future trend of interest-rates and the price of his product, he will have to guess not only what the State policy with regard to investment is going to be (of this, as Lange points out, he may have a pretty fair idea), but what the current reaction of industrial managements is going to be to the current interest rate – how much current construction work is being undertaken in the economy at large, and its results. In other words, the future trend will itself be affected by his own decision and that of all his fellow industrialists; and his decision will have to depend, in part, on what he guesses the response of his fellow managers will be, this including a guess as to what *they* will guess *his* decision will be. It seems inconceivable that this guessing-game can be reduced to any simple set of rules. Nor is this something that can be remedied by a grading of the accounting price of capital according to the period of the investment; since the central planning board can, in turn, only fix a long-term rate on the basis of a guess as to what the reaction of industrial managers will be both to it and to current short-term rates, and this reaction will partly depend on guesses as to how this long-term rate is going to *change*. Indeed, it is difficult to see how Lange's accounting price for capital, if it is to be a long-term rate, can be a 'trial and error' rate in any significant sense of the term, since the process of trial and error that is to test it and adjust it necessarily lies in the future, and is itself being influenced by current happenings which, under a régime of decentralized investment decisions, are outside the planning authority's immediate control. It would seem as though the only accounting price for capital that can properly be said to be subject to trial and error, and hence have any tendency to be a 'true rate', is a short-term rate.

Where decisions cannot be quickly revised, as is the case with long-term investment, it would seem to be rational that a series of decisions, each of which affects the others, should be coordinated in a unified decision instead of being separated into a number of autonomous decisions. But even if all questions of investment were decided (or had to be finally sanctioned) centrally, questions of class 1 above (the volume of output from a *given* plant) might still be settled according to Lange's and Lerner's rule; i.e. of equating MOC with price. This would mean that 'short-period' questions could be decentralized; i.e. day-to-day decisions about the intensity of utilization of plant, and as much adaptation to meet unforeseen circumstances as would be possible within a given set of investment-decisions recently taken. But here again some of the difficulties discussed in the first half of this article would obtrude and the wisdom of even this amount of de-centralized autonomy might be questioned. Where there was a reserve of unemployed labour, it would be preferable as we have seen to extend output and employment beyond the point where price = marginal prime cost. On the other hand, in a condition of full employment the problem of acute labour shortage would emerge if the rate of investment were to be increased; and to meet it, control over the output programmes of individual plants would have to revert to the central planning authority, or output be limited by means of an output tax levied on each plant. With sufficient foresight, however, this difficulty could be partly prevented; which is a particular witness to the importance of taking investment decisions in the light of knowledge of future investment trends. The situation just described implies that there are (at the moment) too many plants in each industry. If in the past investment had taken the form of appropriate changes of class 4, instead of changes of class 3 – if there had been an ex-tension of the 'deepening process' faster than the 'widening process' – this situation need not have arisen. To prevent such a situation from *ever* arising would, of course, require a length of vision that is beyond the bounds of reasonable hope. But with a moderate degree of planning ahead its possibility could be considerably reduced.

References

VAN DORP, E. C. (1937), *A Simple Theory of Capital, Wages, Profit or Loss*, London.

DICKINSON, H. D. (1939), *The Economics of Socialism*, Oxford University Press.

DOBB, M. H. (1937), *Political Economy and Capitalism*, Routledge & Kegan Paul.

HAU, R. (1937), *The Economic System in a Socialist State*, London.

KALECKI, M. (1937), 'A theory of the business cycle', *Rev. economic Studies*, vol. 4, pp. 77–97.

KHAN, R. F. (1935), 'Some notes on ideal output', *Economic J.*, vol. XLV.

HUTCHISON, T. W. (1938), *Basic Postulates of Economic Theory*, London.

LANGE, O. (1938), *The Economic Theory of Socialism* (See Reading 4).

LERNER, A. P. (1936), 'A note on socialist economies, *Review of Economic Studies*', February.

LERNER, A. P. (1937), 'Statics and dynamics in socialist economics', *Economic J.*, vol. XLVII.

PIGOU, A. C. (1935), *Economics in Practice*, London.

PIGOU, A. C. (1937), *Socialism and Capitalism*, Macmillan.

6 E. Preobrazhensky

Socialist Primitive Accumulation

Excerpts from E. Preobrazhensky, *The New Economics*,
Clarendon Press, Oxford, 1965, pp. 79–124. Originally published in
Russian, Moscow, 1926.

Primitive accumulation, capitalist and socialist

In order to understand the present phase of development of the
Soviet economy it is extremely helpful to carry out a systematic
comparison between the first steps of socialism and the first steps
of the capitalist mode of production. This comparison is most
instructive and will greatly assist us in our analysis. Both the
similarity and the difference – and the differences are incomparably greater than the similarities – bring out remarkably well the
special features of the Soviet system of economy.

Let us begin with the most important difference, which conditions a number of others.

Capitalist production arises and develops within the womb of
feudal society, or of feudal society which has been half dis-
integrated by commodity economy, many decades before the
bourgeois revolutions. This fully applies to the development of
merchant capital, as the necessary preliminary stage of capitalist
production. It applies also to the first steps of manufacture in
England and to the first steps of capitalist machine industry on
the Continent. Capitalism was able to pass through its period of
primitive accumulation in the age of absolutism in politics and of
simple commodity production and feudal-serfdom relations in
the economic sphere.

Bourgeois revolutions begin after capitalism has gone far in
building up its system in the economic sphere. The bourgeois
revolution is only an episode in the process of bourgeois development, which begins long before the revolution and goes on more
rapidly after it. The socialist system, on the contrary, begins its
chronology with the seizure of power by the proletariat. This
follows from the very essence of the socialist economy as a single

complex which cannot be built up molecularly within the world of capitalism. While merchant capital could develop in the pores of feudal society, while the first capitalist enterprises could function without coming into irreconcilable contradiction with the existing political structure and property-forms (being, on the contrary, as we shall see below, nourished by their juices), the complex of state socialist production can appear only as a result of a breaking through of the old system all along the line, only as a result of social revolution. This fact is of colossal significance for understanding not only the genesis of socialism, but also the entire subsequent process of socialist construction. Conversely, insufficient understanding, or forgetting, of the essential nature of socialism has often led and still leads a number of comrades into a purely philistine, sometimes directly reformist conception of the Soviet economy and its paths of development.

For capitalist accumulation to begin, the following prerequisites were needed:

1. A preliminary accumulation of capital in particular hands to an extent sufficient for the application of a higher technique or of a higher degree of division of labour with the same technique.

2. The presence of a body of wage-workers.

3. A sufficient development of the system of commodity economy in general to serve as the base for capitalist commodity production and accumulation.

Regarding the first of these conditions Marx says:

The basis of the production of commodities can admit of production on a large scale in the capitalist form alone. A certain accumulation of capital in the hands of individual producers of commodities forms therefore the necessary preliminary of the specifically capitalist mode of production. We had, therefore, to assume that this occurs during the transition from handicraft to capitalistic industry. It may be called primitive accumulation—because it is the historic basis instead of the historic result of specifically capitalist production. How it itself originates we need not here inquire as yet. It is enough that it forms the starting point.[1]

The question arises of how matters stand in this connection

1. *Capital*, vol. 1 part I, English Edition, London, 1938, p. 638.

with primitive *socialist* accumulation. Has socialism a pre-history? If so, when does it begin?

As we have seen above, primitive capitalist accumulation could take place on the basis of feudalism, whereas socialist accumulation cannot take place on the basis of capitalism. Consequently, if socialism has a pre-history, this can begin only after the conquest of power by the proletariat. The nationalization of large-scale industry is also the first act of socialist accumulation, that is, the act which concentrates in the hands of the state the minimum resources needed for the organization of socialist leadership of industry. But it is just here that we come up against the other aspect of the question. In socializing large-scale production the proletarian state by that very act changes from the start the system of ownership of the means of production: it adapts the system of ownership to its future steps in the matter of socialist reconstruction of the whole economy. In other words, the working class acquires by revolution only that which capitalism already possessed in the shape of the institution of private property, without any revolution, on the basis of feudalism.[2] Primitive socialist accumulation, as a period of the creation of the material prerequisites for socialist production in the true sense of the word could begin only with the seizure of power and nationalization.

By *socialist* accumulation we mean the addition to the functioning means of production of a surplus product which has been created within the constituted socialist economy and which does not find its way into supplementary distribution among the agents of socialist production and the socialist state, but serves for expanded reproduction. *Primitive socialist* accumulation, on the other hand, means accumulation in the hands of the state of material resources mainly or partly from sources lying outside the complex of state economy. This accumulation must play an extremely important part in a backward peasant country, hastening to a very great extent the arrival of the moment when the technical and scientific reconstruction of the state economy begins and when this economy at last achieves purely economic superiority over capitalism. It is true that in this period accumulation

2. I say nothing here about the limitations on the institution of private property in the feudal period. Fundamentally, private property existed then, in spite of these infringements.

takes place also on the production-base of state economy. In the first place, however, this accumulation also has the character of preliminary accumulation of the means for a really socialist economy and is subordinated to this purpose. Secondly, accumulation of the former kind, that is, at the expense of the non-state milieu, greatly predominates in this period. For this reason we should call this entire stage the period of primitive or preliminary socialist accumulation. This period has its special features and its special laws. The basic law of our Soviet economy, which is now passing through this stage, is called precisely the law of primitive or preliminary socialist accumulation. To this law are subordinated all the basic processes of economic life within the range of the state economy. This law, moreover, changes and partly does away with the law of value and all the laws of commodity and capitalist commodity economy, in so far as they appear or can appear in our system of economy. Consequently, *not only can we speak of primitive socialist accumulation, we can understand nothing of the essence of Soviet economy if we do not discover the central role which is played in this economy by the law of primitive socialist accumulation, which determines, in conflict with the law of value, both the distribution of means of production in the economy and the distribution of labour power, and also the amount of the country's surplus product which is alienated for expanded socialist reproduction.*

Let us now dwell upon the methods of primitive accumulation based mainly on plundering of small-scale production and non-economic pressure upon it, and let us see how matters stand in this connection in the period of primitive socialist accumulation.

As regards colonial plundering, a socialist state, carrying out a policy of equality between nationalities and voluntary entry by them into one kind or another of union of nations, repudiates on principle all the forcible methods of capital in this sphere. This source of primitive accumulation is closed to it from the very start and for ever.

It is quite different in the case of the alienation in favour of socialism of part of the surplus product of all the pre-socialist economic forms. Taxation of the non-socialist forms not only must inevitably take place in the period of primitive socialist accumulation, it must inevitably play a very great, a directly decisive role in peasant countries such as the Soviet Union.

Another source of socialist accumulation can be taxation of private capitalist profit, that is, systematic deductions from capitalist accumulation. The nature of this kind of resource can be various, but, of course, in the last analysis it is here again a matter of accumulation at the expense of the labour of the workers on the one hand and of the peasants on the other. When the state imposes heavy taxes on private capitalist enterprises it is restoring to the fund of socialist accumulation part of the surplus value which would have been received as surplus product by the state if it had, *all other conditions being equal*, been conducting these enterprises itself. Here the capitalists play in relation to the socialist state the same role which was played by the feudal land-lords in relation to the knights of primitive accumulation. In just the same way the taxation of the class of rural kulaks who employ hired labour means in the last analysis accumulation at the expense of the semi-proletarian labour of the countryside. Conversely, in so far as the socialist state taxes traders, buyers-up, capitalists, and kulaks who obtain part of their income from the peasantry who carry on *independent economies* we have here accumulation at the expense of the peasant economy, the persons mentioned constituting, as in the previous case, both accumulators of capitalist accumulation and, from another point of view, the intermediate stage of one of the processes of socialist accumulation.[3]

As regards state loans, which form a very important channel of primitive capitalist accumulation, their role is different in the period of socialist accumulation. Here one must distinguish between two loan systems which differ in principle. Our semi-compulsory loans, such as the first and second lottery loans, belong rather to the category of accumulation from taxation sources, that is, accumulation by methods of non-economic compulsion. It is quite a different matter with credit operations of the type of normal loans, carried out according to the bourgeois system. Such loans, let us say, as the loan from the British capitalists, for thirty years at 7 per cent, cannot be treated directly

3. Below, where the context makes my meaning clear, I speak for brevity's sake of socialist accumulation instead of primitive socialist accumulation.

as sources of socialist accumulation, because the Soviet state will have to pay interest on the loan out of its revenues and thereby will function as an intermediate stage in capitalist accumulation and capitalist exploitation of the working masses of the Soviet Union by the foreign bourgeoisie. But on the other hand these loans can serve as a powerful stimulus to socialist accumulation, contributing thereby a larger percentage to the socialist accumulation fund than they contribute to the capitalist accumulation fund. We touch upon these loans in another connection when we analyse the economic significance of external loans and concessions under the commodity-socialist system of economy.

Before we pass to the form of primitive accumulation on an economic basis we must say more about a source of state revenue, and thereby under the Soviet system a source of primitive accumulation, which more correctly should be grouped with taxes, but which is externally and formally not as a rule so grouped in theoretical economic writing. I mean the issue of paper money. In my pamphlets *Paper Money in the Epoch of the Dictatorship of the Proletariat* and *The Causes of the Fall in the Rate of Exchange of Our Ruble* I showed that the issue of paper money under a system of declining rates of exchange is one of the forms of taxation. Here it is only necessary to note that the issue of paper money is also one of the methods of primitive accumulation. In the corresponding period in the history of the bourgeois system of economy, the issue of paper money did not play the role of an auxiliary factor in capitalist accumulation. Debasement of the coinage, which was committed by the feudal princes and our tsars, and the issue of paper money in the subsequent period constituted taxation by the state of the whole population, including in part taxation of the bourgeoisie's money capital. When the state is at the same time an organ which rules the country and the master of a huge economic complex, issue of paper money directly serves as a channel for socialist accumulation. This accumulation is carried out at the expense either of the incomes of the petty-bourgeois and capitalist elements or of reduced wages of the state's workers and office employees. How substantial this source is may be seen from the fact that from the time the Soviet power was organized until the final introduction of a stable currency the issue of paper money, including losses by the State itself, amounted to about 1,800 million gold rubles. Paper money served as an important financial resource also for the Hungarian Soviet Government during its four-month existence.

Let us now pass to the methods of primitive accumulation of capital by way of economic channels. Here we must distinguish between accumulation which is carried out in production itself, at the expense of the surplus value created in enterprises belonging to the proletariat, and, on the other hand, the exchange of a smaller quantity of labour by one system of economy or one country for a larger quantity of labour furnished by another system of economy or another country.

The difference from the period of primitive capitalist accumulation here consists, first, in the fact that socialist accumulation has to take place at the expense not only of the surplus product of petty production but also of the surplus value of capitalist economic forms. Secondly, the difference here is conditioned by the fact that the state economy of the proletariat arises historically on the back of monopoly capitalism and therefore has at its disposal means of regulating the whole economy and of redistributing the national income economically which were not available to capitalism at the dawn of its history.

Let us begin with railway charges. This powerful lever of economic regulation, which is wholly in the hands of the state power of the USSR, is used very little in the interests of regulation and is not used at all as an instrument of primitive socialist accumulation. A system of favourable charges for certain freights (coal, petrol, salt) serves as a means of redistributing state resources rather than as an indirect way of taxing the non-socialist sector of the economy. Of just as little importance are the small privileges which are accorded to state and cooperative dispatches of freight as compared with private ones. Use of this lever of primitive accumulation is still completely something for the future. Only when transport ceases to be a source of deficit and becomes a profitable undertaking will there become possible a corresponding reconstruction of railway charges, based on the distinction between state and private freights, so as to effect a systematic taxation of private producers and traders, and in this way to cut off part of the profit made by private capital. There is no need to prove that this will be one of those blows at the law of value which make the economy of the period of socialist accumulation a period of gradual change, restricting and partly abolishing this law.[4]

A second powerful lever of primitive accumulation is the monopoly of the banking system. In the period of primitive capitalist accumulation usurious credit was a means whereby the national income was redistributed from the hands of the feudalists into those of the bourgeoisie, which was rising and becoming stronger. Credit as an instrument for mobilizing the free resources of society and distributing them by the channel of expanded reproduction was at that time either non-existent or existed only in embryo. Contrariwise, in the period of preliminary socialist accumulation which the USSR economy is passing through, that is, in its first stages, the state's credit system operates more in the field of redistributing the free resources of the country than in that of redistributing the national income. This may seem untrue, in so far as the interest collected by the banks for loans – if the period of the rapidly falling rate of exchange be left out of account – is very large in comparison with normal capitalist conditions, whereas deposit operations are fairly inconsiderable. But we must not for one moment forget the economic source which really makes possible the *chervonets* issue and the loan operations by the bank out of the sources of this issue. If the bank issues 60 million *chervontsi*, with no variations in the rate of exchange, this means, economically, that by one means or another the country's commodity values to that amount have been placed at the disposal of the State Bank for different periods. If we consider that this 'loan from circulation' is drawn from the state economy and from private economy, proportionally, let us say, to the share of each in the monetary circulation of the country, while the resources of this loan go to financing almost exclusively state and cooperative

4. Here, as in all the following exposition, I speak of the law of value as the spontaneous regulator under the commodity and commodity-capitalist system of production, that is, of the historically-transient *form* assumed in exchange society by the regulation of the economy by labour-expenditure. I do *not* speak of this regulation *in itself*. *This* regulation will exist under planned economy, too, but will be effected in another way, that is, on the basis of direct calculation of labour time.

industry and trade, then we see swiftly passing before our eyes a process of socialist accumulation.

As regards the question of redistributing *the national income* through the agency of the credit system, here the main task still lies in the future. If the State Bank charges a high rate of interest to state enterprises which receive long-term or short-term loans, what we have here is a process, not of accumulation in the state sector, but rather of redistributing resources within the state sector. Redistribution from private economy into the socialist sector can occur directly only when the resources of private economy, accumulated by the banking system through deposits, are redistributed through private economy by means of loans at a higher rate of interest, and the difference between the sums paid into the bank as deposits and the sum received by the bank as loan-interest and other forms of payment for its services goes into the socialist accumulation fund. We have the same situation if state resources are lent at interest as credits to private economy. The latter operation, however, with the general shortage of capital in the country and especially in the state sector itself, while being formally a source of accumulation, is at the present time quite unprofitable, because it is transformed at the present stage into an obvious instrument of capitalist accumulation at the expense of state credit. For this operation can take place only at the expense of the more advantageous operation of advancing credits to state enterprises, because credits to the latter realize not only bank interest but also accumulation of capital in state enterprises on a basis of production. Under these conditions credits to private trade and industry which are capable, let us say, of paying 10 per cent annually to the bank, are less profitable than credits to state industry which, let us assume, are capable of paying the bank 8 per cent on loan capital but themselves obtain from production 15 per cent on this loan capital. In this case the State Bank, as such, would find it more profitable to advance credits to private industry and trade; but from the standpoint of the state complex as a whole and of socialist accumulation in the whole complex, and not only in the State Bank's part of it, this operation is clearly one which incurs loss. This explains the fact that at the present moment the State Bank hardly grants any credits to private trade and industry, in spite of their readiness to pay more than state enterprises, but grants them almost exclusively to the latter. From the standpoint of the tasks of socialist accumulation this policy is the only correct one.

In the future, however, the situation in this field is bound to change, and a moment may come when the granting of credits to private economy may become one of the most important instruments for redistributing the national income in the interests of the state economy and one of the chief economic means of subjecting its regulatory centres to the state economy. The credit system of the USSR can play an especially big role in this connection with the development of long-term agricultural credit, in particular, if we succeed in obtaining large-scale loans abroad and the State Bank functions as distributor of these loans, transfusing foreign resources into the economic organism of the USSR.

From what has been said we thus see that our entire credit policy at the present time is subordinated and cannot but be subordinated to the law of primitive socialist accumulation.

Let us turn now to exchange in the system which exists in the USSR, and more particularly in internal trade. Here we have to distinguish:

1. Exchange within the sector of the state economy itself.
2. Exchange within private economy.
3. Exchange between the state sector and the private sector.

As regards the first division there can, of course, be no positive tasks for socialist accumulation there. The economics of exchange consist in this sphere merely in exchanging economically, in keeping down the costs of the circulation process. These costs are a direct deduction from the surplus product of state economy, and in cases when private middlemen participate in exchange between state enterprises what happens is not only a deduction from the socialist accumulation fund but also an increment to the fund of 'secondary' capitalist accumulation. As the gods of Epicurus had their homes in the pores of the universe, so private middlemen, in the first period of the emergence of the state trusts on to the free market, tried to seat themselves not only in the channels of private trade but also in the nooks and crannies separating one state enterprise from another, and here they collected 'costs of circulation'. Rationalization of state trade means systematic elimination of these leeches of capitalist accumulation from the socialist sector, and it leads not only to a reduction in the circulation costs of the state sector but also to the organization of circulation itself by the state sector's own forces.

As regards the second division, that is exchange within private economy, there, however, socialist accumulation is possible. Of the non-economic method of accumulation from this source, that is, of taxes on trade in the products of the private sector, we have already spoken. Accumulation of the other kind, that is on the basis of trade exchange, is not only possible, it already occurs to some extent now and will doubtless increase in the future.[5] As an example of this kind of accumulation we may take, for example, purchase from the peasants of grain and food products generally by Khleboprodukt[6] and the sale of this produce to private consumers in the urban markets. The merchant's profit obtained in this way is essentially a deduction from the income of the producers who sell to a state organ in order to realize their goods. When the organs of state and cooperative trade realize through private consumers the products not only of peasants but also of artisans, craftsmen and private entrepreneurs, and receive profit from doing so, this part of their profit is one of the sources of socialist accumulation being examined by us. The struggle of state and cooperative trade against private trade in this sector of exchange faces, from the standpoint of socialist accumulation, positive, not negative, tasks. Here accumulation takes place (at present, unfortunately, only on a small scale) out of the fund of one system of economy into that of the other. What is taken from private trade, all other conditions being equal, is acquired, in one way or another, for the fund of the state economy. I say 'all other conditions being equal' because it is possible to adopt a trade policy here which is in the interests, not of socialist accumulation,

5. Increase in railway tariffs on freight belonging to private capital, realized within private economy, belongs to the category of accumulation from this source.

6. All-Russia Joint Stock Company for the Sale of Grain and Agricultural Products.

but of the petty-bourgeois producers, since it aims to reduce the deductions from their incomes. Whether such a policy is expedient depends on which at the given moment is more important for the state economy: cheapening of goods being sold and elimination of private capital, or accumulation in the sphere of circulation. Economically such a policy involves, without doubt, a reduction in the socialist accumulation fund and a present to private production – *a present which is all the more costly for state economy the poorer this economy is in capital and the less convenient it is for it to employ in trade part of that capital which is inadequate for production itself, instead of intensifying the mobilization of the resources of the petty producers themselves in order to develop co-operative trade.* Moreover, at the present stage state trade is carried on in a less businesslike way than private trade, and the current need is for the state trading organizations to reduce their costs at least to the level of private trade. But here it is important for us to pose the whole problem in a theoretically correct way, because it is not a matter of the policy of the passing moment but of understanding the fundamental processes of the entire period of socialist development. We shall see below what tremendous difficulties stand in the way of state trade's competing with private capital and how these difficulties rest upon the basic problems of socialist construction in general. We must mention at this point only that, as a result of the country's extreme poverty in capital, and given the circumstances of a fairly rapid growth of commodity-exchange in the country, merchant's profit attains huge dimensions, which recall the situation in the period of primitive capitalist accumulation. Under these conditions this sector of accumulation is of extreme significance: for the successes of private capital very powerfully hinder the flow of resources from the petty-bourgeois milieu into the socialist accumulation fund and eat up part of the surplus product of the state economy itself.

The third sub-division, that is, exchange between state economy and private economy, is the point where socialist accumulation faces both purely negative tasks, as with exchange within its own circle, and also positive ones, that is, nourishment of the state economy at the expense of the non-socialist milieu. From this angle we must consider the realization of the products of state industry outside the socialist sector separately from the realization of the products of private economy within the state sector.

Let us begin with the first process, that is, the movement of the mass of commodities produced by state industry into the non-socialist milieu. The tasks here, from the standpoint of socialist accumulation, are both negative: to reduce the costs of circulation of the state economy's own organs, that is, in plain words, to trade with the least possible expenditure on the trading apparatus; and to eliminate private trade from the whole of the road which a commodity produced by the trusts has to cover, from the factory to the final link, that is the consumer.

The first of these tasks is a matter of improving the organization within the system of state economy itself. Contrariwise, the second task is of very much greater importance, because it is part of the struggle between two mutually hostile systems for the surplus product of the state economy. Here we find the enemy almost in our own home. We must mention at this point the difference of principle which exists in the mutual relations, on the one hand, between merchant and industrial capital in the epoch of primitive *capitalist* accumulation, and on the other, between private merchant capital and state industry in the epoch of primitive *socialist* accumulation. If in the period of capitalist accumulation merchant capital collects from private productive capital most of the surplus value created in industry, this is only a matter of a different distribution of surplus value *within one and the same system of economy*. What today is accumulated to excess by merchant capital from the surplus value of industrial capital is returned tomorrow to industry; the passing of the excess capital of trade into industry is an uninterrupted process which has gone on from the very beginning of the rise of capitalist production. It is quite a different matter when industry fundamentally belongs to one system and the trading network belongs to another, hostile system, as in the case expounded. Then the accumulation of private merchant capital is a direct and irrevocable deduction from the surplus product created by the workers of state industry. Supposing, let us say, the annual total of the new commodity values created in state industry and passing through commodity circulation, is equal, in terms of the wholesale prices of the trusts, to 1 milliard, and this mass of commodities is sold retail at $1\frac{1}{2}$ milliard, then 500 million is a direct deduction for the benefit of the trading network from the surplus product of industry. If four-fifths of this, or 400 million, is taken by the private trading network, this is a very harmful leak from the source of socialist accumulation, and not only accumulation but even simple reproduction in the system of the state economy. Here we have expropriation by private capital, not of the surplus product of petty production on the basis of which capitalism develops historically and which it never ceases to exploit thereafter, but of the surplus product of socialist industry, a phenomenon hitherto unknown to economic history. The struggle against private capital in this sector is for the state economy a struggle against the wastage of values it has itself created. For the struggle against private capital to move to this particular section is quite correct, as it is quite correct to pass from the solving of easier tasks to the solving of more difficult ones, that is, to the mastering of wholesale and wholesale-and-retail trade in the products of state industry.

Thus, in the matter of mastering the process of exchanging its own products the state economy is solving for itself a task of a negative kind: not to give to private capital what essentially belongs to the socialist sector itself and constitutes its own fund, created on its own production base.

It is quite a different matter with the movement of values from private economy into the state economic sector. Here the struggle of the organs of state trade against private capital is to a considerable extent a struggle for the surplus product of private economy. When, for example, the procurement of raw material for industry on the peasant market is carried out by private capital and the entire road from the producer of the raw material to the trust is barred by private middlemen, the difference between the price paid to the peasant and the trust's selling price is basically a deduction from the income of peasant economy. Contrariwise, if the State organs, say, themselves carry out all the procurement of raw material, everything which is deducted from the income of the peasantry flows into the state economic sector. At the present stage of primitive socialist accumulation the struggle against private capital is both more difficult technically and has less significance than the struggle against the plundering by private capital of the surplus product of the state economy itself. On the other hand success in this latter struggle, that is, ousting of private capital from trade in the products of industry, would undoubtedly intensify the process of transition of private capital into private industry, a process, generally speaking, which is economically advantageous and harmless provided there is a rapid growth in the state economy.

Let us now proceed to price policy in relation to industry. This policy is highly important not only for socialist accumulation but also for the normal course of production in general, even in its unexpanded state; it is of very great importance for peasant economy; it affects, finally, the political relations between the proletariat and the peasantry. We will concern ourselves with it only from the standpoint of primitive socialist accumulation.

The fundamental theoretical question which must be answered here from the very outset is this: is equivalent exchange between the state economy and the non-socialist milieu possible in general? There are three possibilities here:

1. When the state economy receives less value from the non-socialist milieu than it gives. In this case we shall have a steady decomposition of large-scale socialist production and a gradual selling-off of its products below cost. This decomposition can take the form either of a sale below cost of the fixed capital of industry not yet fully restored, with wages at a constant level, or a clearance sale for next to nothing of the labour power of the industrial proletariat, or, finally, both together. In the intial period of NEP we had a number of examples of such a bargain sale of industrial products, which involved selling for a song both the fixed capital and the labour power of the proletariat.[7] The transformation of this price policy into a system would undoubtedly mean a gradual dissipation of large-scale industry and the triumph of petty over large-scale production. . . . This case must not be confused with another, when as a result of price competition there is an increase in depreciation of fixed capital, but in fact restoration

7. A striking example of the same thing, but from capitalist practice, is offered by the price policy of German industry in the period of the falling exchange after the first world war.

of fixed capital does not take place because the appropriate sums recovered are spent either on increased wages or on reserves of raw material, that is, they go to increase circulating capital. Such temporary loans from the fund of fixed capital for other, more urgent needs have played a big part in the life of Soviet industry. This process was inevitable with the extreme poverty of state industry in circulating capital, and often took place even with fairly high prices, not lower than restoration prices.

2. Prices of the products of state industry are so calculated that when there is an exchange of products between this industry and private economy there is an exchange of equivalents, that is neither of the economic systems exploits the other. This situation is in general possible only as a very brief episode. To consider such a situation as normal is to suppose that the socialist system and the system of private commodity production, included in a single national economy, can exist side by side on the basis of complete mutual economic equilibrium. Such equilibrium cannot exist for long, because one system must oust the other. Either decay or development is possible, but not remaining at the same point. Speaking in a certain connexion about capital as a process of movement, Marx wrote: 'Capital as self-expanding value embraces not only class relations, a society of a definite character resting on the existence of labour in the form of wage-labour. It is a movement, a circuit-describing process going through various stages, which itself comprises three different forms of the circuit-describing process. Therefore it can be understood only as motion, not as a thing at rest.'[8] If capital, both in its individual circulation in some enterprise, and also if we take the capitalist system as a whole, in its relation to the pre-capitalist milieu, constitutes motion, in what way can the socialist form in its relation to the pre-socialist milieu be 'a thing at rest'? And what does motion mean in this case? Motion in this case means one of two things: either the capitalist form rapidly erodes the monolithic block of the state economy which was formed by the lava of the October revolution and the civil war, or the socialist form develops at the expense both of its own accumulation and of the non-socialist milieu, which also nourishes it with its juices. If

8. *Capital*, vol. 2, English edition, (Moscow, 1957, p. 105.)

capitalism is motion, socialism is *still more rapid motion*. And what it loses in speed in the period of primitive accumulation, in the sense of development of its technical economic base, owing to extreme poverty in capital, it is *obliged* to make up for by intensified accumulation at the expense of the non-socialist milieu. One of the most important means of this accumulation, beside the methods described above, and another which will be discussed later, is non-equivalent exchange of values with the non-socialist milieu. This exchange with advantage to the socialist form is possible only with an appropriate price policy in relation to the products of state industry.

3. And so we come to the third case, which is not only possible but also inevitable under our conditions, that is a price policy consciously calculated so as to alienate a *certain* part of the surplus product of private economy in all its forms. This policy is possible because the state economy of the proletariat has arisen historically on the basis of monopoly capitalism. The latter, as a result of the ending of free competition, leads to the creation of monopoly prices on the home market for the products of national industry, receives surplus profit through the exploitation of petty production, and thereby prepares the basis for the price policy of the period of primitive socialist accumulation. But the concentration of all the large-scale industry of the country in the hands of a single trust, that is in the hands of the workers' state, increases to an enormous extent the possiblity of carrying out on the basis of monopoly a price policy which will be only another form of taxation of private economy. The obstacles which state economy encounters on this road arise not from inadequate economic power to carry out this policy but from other causes. The greatest of these is the need to combine this policy with a policy of reducing prices, which can be achieved only if the reduction in costs of production goes forward still faster. And this in its turn presupposes the need to re-equip industry as soon as the limits of rationalization of production with the old technique are reached. Another difficulty results from the fact that the state is not a monopolist in all branches of industry. Consequently, price policy must be calculated so that state accumulation does not automatically entail private capitalist accumulation. I

do not mention here the difficulties of a political kind which result from the relations between the working class and the peasantry and often compel us to talk about equivalent exchange, though this is, under socialization of large-scale industry, an even greater utopia than under the rule of monopoly capitalism.

Accumulation by way of an appropriate price policy has advantages over other forms of direct and indirect taxation of petty economy. The most important of these is the extreme facility of collection, not a single kopeck being needed for any special taxation apparatus.

The objection which comes down to this, that taxation on the basis of a definite price policy[9] will affect the wages of the workers and the rural poor is completely futile. It is not the rural poor who are the chief buyers of the products of our industry. Whatever they may lose in this way they can recover from the state in the form of credit, in the form of obligatory accumulation of the fixed capital of their economy, and so on. As regards the workers, this objection is as baseless as the objection to indirect taxes, which are completely transferable to wages. Here is a numerical example: if as a result of an appropriate price policy the working class along with the rest of the population, pays to state industry say 50 millions, the state can easily return this sum to the workers by an increase in wages, while the money received from the bourgeois and petty-bourgeois consumers is not returned to them and goes to swell the socialist accumulation fund.

The fundamental law of primitive socialist accumulation is the mainspring of the entire Soviet state economy. But it is probable that this law is of universal significance, except perhaps for those countries which will be the last to go over to the socialist form of economy. Proceeding from what we have said above, we can formulate this law, or at least that part of it which relates to the redistribution of the material resources of production, in this way.

9. I deliberately avoid saying 'on the basis of an increase in prices', because taxation is not only possible with falling prices but in our circumstances it will take place precisely with falling prices, or, for some periods, with unchanging prices; this is possible because with cheapening in the cost of production of products reduction in prices takes place not to the full extent of this cheapening but to a smaller extent, the difference going into the socialist accumulation fund and toward increases in wages.

The more backward economically, petty-bourgeois, peasant, a particular country is which has gone over to the socialist organization of production, and the smaller the inheritance received by the socialist accumulation fund of the proletariat of this country when the social revolution takes place, by so much the more, in proportion, will socialist accumulation be obliged to rely on alienating part of the surplus product of pre-socialist forms of economy and the smaller will be the relative weight of accumulation on its own production basis, that is, the less will it be nourished by the surplus product of the workers in socialist industry. Conversely, the more developed economically and industrially a country is, in which the social revolution triumphs, and the greater the material inheritance, in the form of highly developed industry and capitalistically organized agriculture, which the proletariat of this country receives from the bourgeoisie on nationalization, by so much the smaller will be the relative weight of pre-capitalist forms in the particular country; and the greater the need for the proletariat of this country to reduce non-equivalent exchange of its products for the products of the former colonies, by so much the more will the centre of gravity of socialist accumulation shift to the production basis of the socialist forms, that is, the more will it rely on the surplus product of its own industry and its own agriculture.[10]

10. This law must of course, undergo certain modifications when there is a transfer of means of production from an advanced socialist country to a backward one.

Reference

MARX, K. (1867), *Capital*, vol. 1, English edition, London, 1938.
MARX, K. (1885), *Capital*, vol. 2, English edition, Moscow, 1957.

7 E. Domar

A Soviet Model of Growth

Excerpts from E. Domar, *Essays in the Theory of Economic Growth*,
© 1957 by Oxford University Press Inc, pp. 223–61. Reprinted by
permission.

I

This essay is based on a remarkable article by the Soviet
economist Fel'dman (1928a and 1928b).[1]

Besides the first five-year plan (undoubtedly familiar to the
reader), the Soviet State Planning Commission was working then
on a so-called General Plan extending over a period of some ten
to twenty years. Fel'dman was instructed to prepare a theoretical
model as a basis for this plan, and his report was embodied (or
possibly summarized) in the article mentioned above. It was followed by two other articles which did not add much to the
original one (Fel'dman 1929a, 1929b). Being concerned with the
theory of long-range planning, Fel'dman could disregard the
immediate and pressing practical problems of his day; this explains the academic and abstract nature of his article, and is also
responsible for its high quality and for its striking naïveté.

At first I intended to translate his original article in full. But it
is long (fifty-three printed pages), involved, and repetitious. He
does not go beyond elementary calculus, and yet his derivations
are hard to follow. There is too much detail. However significant
his achievement is from a historical point of view, his results are
essentially similar and reducible to those since developed in the
West. We shall share his start – the most interesting part of his
model – bypass his derivations, and reconstruct his model in the
simpler manner used in the other essays; and proceed then to
some of the implications of this model for economic development.

1. I am grateful to Gregory Grossman for telling me about this article.
The Library of Congress system is used for the transliteration of all
Russian words.

II

As a good Marxist, Fel'dman starts with Marx's celebrated division of the total output of an economy (W) into Category 1 – Producer goods (raw materials and capital), and Category 2 – Consumer goods, the production of each category expressed as the sum of C (constant capital = depreciation plus raw materials broadly defined), V (variable capital = payrolls), and S (surplus value):

$$C_1 + V_1 + S_1 = W_1$$
$$C_2 + V_2 + S_2 = W_2$$
$$\overline{C + V + S = W.}$$

With certain changes, this scheme would approximate our allocation of output by factor costs (depreciation, wages and salaries, and property income).[2] Fel'dman, however, was not concerned with factor costs; his Marxism was sufficiently flexible to allow him to dismiss this question entirely, and concentrate all his attention on the distribution of currently produced capital goods (a part of the output of Category 1) between the two categories. But first he had to modify Marx's scheme once more by redefining the categories.

Since in Marx's scheme C_2 consists not only of depreciation, but also of raw materials (in the broad sense), presumably all made good by or obtained from Category 1,[3] Category 2 should

2. The major adjustment would consist in eliminating inter-firm purchases within each category from both sides of each equation. On the comparison between Marxist and Keynesian schemes see Tsuru (1942, pp. 365–74); also Tsuru (1954, pp. 320–44).

The Marxian scheme would cause no special difficulties if the Marxists did not try simultaneously to incorporate into it the corresponding allocation of output by expenditures (consumption and investment), a procedure which leads to unnecessary complications even in skillful hands. This is particularly true of problems involving capital accumulation. See chapter 21 of vol. 2 of the *Capital*; also Sweezy (1942) and Tsuru (1942 and 1954); and Preobrazhensky (1931), as examples. Additional difficulties (connected with stocks and flows) arise in computations of the organic composition of capital and of the rate of profit, but we are not concerned with them here. On this see Robinson (1942), ch. 2.

3. In this connection, C_2 really includes replacement rather than depreciation. I wonder if those who use Marx's scheme are aware that in a growing economy replacement and depreciation are not identical.

contain only the final stage of production of consumer goods, that is, retail trade, utilities, services, and the like. A more liberal interpretation would add the last stage of manufacturing, but this is a vague notion: now the consumer buys bread and now flour. In any case, as a starting point for a model of economic development, which to Fel'dman (and to others) meant the expansion of capital goods industries, what use could Marx's scheme be if the bakery was placed in Category 2, while the flour mill remained in Category 1? Surely Category 2 should contain not only the bakery, but also the flour mill, the grain elevator, some transportation, the farm, and so on. Fel'dman's real aim was to place all activities merely sustaining output at the present level in Category 2, while all capacity-increasing ones were located in Category 1. This is an attractive proposal, and not only to a Marxist,[4] but how is it to be carried out in practice? In many countries, a part of expenditures on food, education, public health, and so forth, serves to increase productive capacity. (And wouldn't we also have to allow for depreciation or replacement of human beings?) No wonder that economists usually settle for a less satisfying but more practical division of total output into consumption and investment along more or less traditional lines, and Fel'dman is forced to follow this course as well. So in his final version, Category 1 produces all capital goods for both categories, while all consumer goods, including the corresponding raw materials, are produced in Category 2, the output of each category consisting of its respective final products only.[5]

As a result, the economy is literally split from top to bottom into these two categories. Theoretically, the scheme is still attractive, but it is impossible to give it any but the roughest empirical meaning simply because an economy is not organized in this manner. Many industries produce raw materials, semi-finished goods, and services used by both categories – metals, chemicals, coal, petroleum, transportation, power, and even textiles, to name only a few. Perhaps Fel'dman could claim that in the Russia of his day practically all metals were used in Category 1 only, but what could he say about the rest? Nor would it

4. A similar suggestion was made by Kuznets (1955, pp. 19–106).

5. Similar schemes were suggested by Burchardt (1931, vol. 34, part 2, pp. 525–64 and 1932, vol. 35, part 1, pp. 116–76); by Nurkse (1934–5); and by Lowe (1952 and 1955, pp. 581–634).

help to divide an industry (like coal or transportation) between the two categories, because the respective proportions would by their very nature lack stability. Of course any division of an economy by industries, or even of output between consumption and investment, is difficult and arbitrary, but it is clear that Fel'dman's method creates special difficulties.[6]

The empirical content of his model worried Fel'dman less than its deviation from the standard Marxist scheme. The latter he justified at some length by the difference between his problem and that of Marx (Fel'dman, 1928b, 1929b). As to the former, he was rather inconsistent, now expecting his scheme to be applied with absolute exactness (Fel'dman, 1928a), then admitting that this could not be done 'at the moment, on the basis of materials on hand' (Fel'dman, 1928b), and finally suggesting that the categories need not be separated physically, but only in an accounting sense (Fel'dman, 1929b, p. 105). At the end of his last article (pp. 119–25) he did make an attempt to divide the capital invested in each industry into two parts, one to be used for current production, and the other for increasing the latter, as if agriculture were to produce its own tractors, an exercise which leaves me rather puzzled regarding Fel'dman's understanding of the empirical meaning of his own model.[7]

Should Fel'dman's model be abandoned altogether? This, I believe, would be too extreme a step. Pigou's wage-goods industries, Hayek's stages of production, Marx's standard scheme, Hicks's induced versus autonomous investment, to name only a few, all give rise to models with an elusive empirical content and yet not devoid of interest.[8] It seems to me worth while to

6. This difficulty was recognized by the Soviet economist Ignatov (1932). He tried to solve it by assigning individual industries to the two categories in accordance with the nature of the major part of each industry's production.

7. He computed the expected increments in output of the several industries from 1 April, 1927 to 1 April, 1928 and then multiplied each increment by its respective capital coefficient (actually divided each increment by its capital productivity) to obtain the amount of capital devoted to the increase in output. It is interesting that a report of the Committee on the General Plan based on Fel'dman's model did not use Fel'dman's division of the economy into these two categories.

8. See Pigou (1933); Hayek (1935); Hicks (1950). I should add here that the empirical content of my own models is certainly not beyond reproach.

explore a growth model constructed on a Marxist foundation,[9] even if modified, and to show its relation to a corresponding Keynesian one. For all its empirical shortcomings, Fel'dman's model is not inapplicable, in very broad terms of course, to the Soviet experience, and it may be of use in unravelling a few puzzles in Soviet economic development and in achieving a better understanding of Soviet economic thinking. It also raises some questions regarding economic development in general.[10]

III

Like other growth models, Fel'dman's is based on a number of simplifying assumptions, such as: constant prices (with a five-page justification, 1928a, pp. 146–50); capital as the only limiting factor; absence of lags; a closed economy (except for a short section, 1928b, pp. 165–9); production independent of consumption;[11] absence of government expenditures as a separate category distinct from consumption and investment; absence of bottlenecks; and several others which will come to the surface as we go along. But one important attribute of the model should be indicated now.

The division of the economy between the two categories is complete, in the sense that no existing capital can be transferred from one to another (there being no other limitations on production). Thus the rate of investment is rigidly determined by the capital coefficient and the stock of capital in Category 1. Similarly, the output of consumer goods is determined by the stock of capital and the capital coefficient of Category 2.[12] Hence the division

9. This was suggested by Sweezy (1950). This article was reprinted in Sweezy's collection of essays (1953, pp. 352–62).

10. There is one more difficulty. Investment, all of which is produced by Category 1, presumably contains increments to inventories held by both categories. But this contradicts the assumption that Category 2 produces all its raw materials and finished goods, including such quantities as are added to its inventories. Fel'dman was not aware of this problem. It could be solved by allowing the capital in Category 2 to produce a part of itself. I have not made this adjustment because it is of little importance in comparison with the basic defect of the model.

11. Kovalevskiĭ (1930) did recognize the dependence of labor productivity on consumption.

12. If the productive capacity of Category 1 is so small that it is merely sufficient for replacement of wearing-out capital assets in both categories (a

of total output between consumption and investment at any given moment depends on the relative productive capacities of the two categories, and not on the propensity to save, though the latter can reassert itself by causing an underutilization of the capital stock in one category or another, a waste ruled out in the model. The division of total investment (that is, of output of Category 1) between the two categories is, however, completely flexible. Indeed, the fraction of total investment allocated to Category 1 is the key variable of the model.

We shall now put Fel'dman's work aside, and derive his major results in an easier way.[13] Two separate cases will be considered: 1, Permanent Assets, and 2, Assets Subject to Wear.

Case 1. Permanent Assets[14]

List of Symbols. In order of their appearance.

γ = fraction of total investment allocated to Category 1

I = annual rate of net investment (output of Category 1)

I_1 and I_2 indicate annual rates of net investment allocated to the respective categories, so that $I_1 + I_2 = I$

t = time measured in years

V = marginal capital coefficient for the whole economy

V_1 and V_2 indicate the marginal capital coefficients of the respective categories (not to be confused with Marx's V, p. 150)

C = annual rate of output of consumer goods (not to be confused with Marx's C, p. 150)

Y = annual net rate of output of the whole economy (national income)

a = average propensity to save (ratio of total investment to national income)

---

possible situation in an undeveloped country), then in Fel'dman's model growth can be achieved only by a temporary failure to replace wearing-out assets in Category 2. Whether total output of the economy will show growth during this process will depend on the valuation weights assigned to the outputs of the two categories.

13. A similar model was constructed by Mahalanobis (1953). Mahalanobis was evidently not aware of Fel'dman's work.

14. The permanency of assets is assumed merely to avoid questions related to depreciation and replacement, which are considered in Case 2. Alternatively, this assumption can be removed, and all variables interpreted net of depreciation which is made good continuously.

a' = marginal propensity to save (ratio of the increment in total investment to the increment in national income)

I_0, C_0, and Y_0 indicate the respective initial magnitudes of these variables (when $t = 0$).

By definition of γ,

$$I_1 = \gamma I, \tag{1}$$

and since only I_1 increases the capacity of Category 1,

$$\frac{dI}{dt} = \frac{I_1}{V_1}. \tag{2}$$

Substituting 1 into 2, we obtain

$$\frac{dI}{dt} = \frac{\gamma I}{V_1}, \tag{3}$$

the solution of which is

$$I = I_0 . e^{(\gamma/V_1)t}. \tag{4}$$

To simplify all derivations, we set $I_0 = 1$; then

$$I = e^{(\gamma/V_1)t}; \tag{5}$$

in other words, total investment will grow at a constant exponential rate of γ/V_1.

Again, by definition of γ,

$$I_2 = (1-\gamma)I = (1-\gamma)^{(\gamma/V_1)t}. \tag{6}$$

I_2 being the only source of increased capacity in Category 2,

$$\frac{dC}{dt} = \frac{I_2}{V_2} = \frac{1-\gamma}{V_2} e^{(\gamma/V_1)t} \tag{7}$$

and

$$C = C_0 + \left(\frac{1-\gamma}{\gamma}\right)\frac{V_1}{V_2}[\{e^{(\gamma/V_1)t}\} - 1], \tag{8}$$

$$\frac{dY}{dt} = \frac{dC}{dt} + \frac{dI}{dt} = \frac{e^{(\gamma/V_1)t}}{V_1 V_2}\{V_1 - \gamma(V_1 - V_2)\}, \tag{9}$$

$$Y = I + C = Y_0 + \left[\left(\frac{1-\gamma}{\gamma}\right)\frac{V_1}{V_2} + 1\right][\{e^{(\gamma/V_1)t}\} - 1]. \tag{10}$$

Thus C and Y each represent a sum of a constant and an exponential in t. Their rates of growth will therefore differ from γ/V_1. As time goes on, the exponential will dominate the scene and the rates of growth of C and Y will gradually approach γ/V_1. But this may take quite a long time, unless of course it so happens that

$$C_0 = \frac{1-\gamma}{\gamma} \frac{V_1}{V_2},$$

in which case the constants will vanish and C and Y will grow at the rate of γ/V_1 from the very beginning – not an interesting case from the point of view of this model. Table 1 shows the behaviour of the rates of growth of I, Y, and C over time under given conditions. It is based on the simplifying assumption that $V_1 = V_2$, which will be discussed shortly.

Table 1 A Comparison of the Relative Rates of Growth of I, Y and C over Time for Given a_0, γ and V[15]
$(V_1 = V_2 = 3)$

| | $a_0 = 0.1;$ | $\gamma = 0.3$ | | $a_0 = 0.2;$ | $\gamma = 0.5$ | |
| | Percentage rates of growth of | | | Percentage rates of growth of | | |
t	I	Y	C	I	Y	C
0	10·0	3·3	2·6	16·7	6·7	4·2
1	10·0	3·6	2·8	16·7	7·3	4·7
2	10·0	3·8	3·0	16·7	8·0	5·3
3	10·0	4·0	3·2	16·7	8·7	5·9
4	10·0	4·3	3·4	16·7	9·4	6·6
5	10·0	4·5	3·7	16·7	10·1	7·2
10	10·0	5·8	4·9	16·7	13·0	10·6
20	10·0	7·9	7·2	16·7	15·8	15·1
30	10·0	9·1	8·8	16·7	16·5	16·3
50	10·0	9·9	9·8	16·7	16·7	16·7

15. Based on the expressions

$$\frac{dy/dt}{Y} = \frac{\gamma/V}{(\gamma Y_0 - 1)e^{-(\gamma/V_1)t} + 1},$$

and

$$\frac{dC/dt}{C} = \frac{\gamma/V}{\{\gamma C_0/(1-\gamma) - 1\}e^{-(\gamma/V)t} + 1},$$

derived from **7–10**. In all examples $I_0 = 1$.

The reader familiar with my other essays may wonder now why the rate of growth of investment here differs from the one derived there. The latter was equal to a/V where a indicated both the marginal and the average propensities to save and V was the over-all capital coefficient. To compare the earlier models with Fel'dman's it is necessary to rework their results *without* the assumption that the average propensity to save, a, equals the marginal one, a'. We shall continue to treat a' as a constant, but since $a \neq a'$, a has now become a variable. It can be easily shown that the rate of growth of investment will now be a'/V, while that of income will remain a/V.[16] The expression a'/V is of course the ratio of the marginal propensity to save to the over-all capital coefficient. In Fel'dman's model, however, we have obtained γ/V_1 as the rate of growth of investment, where γ is the fraction of investment allocated to Category 1, and V_1 is the capital coefficient of this category only.

Let us find a' of the present model. From **5** and **9** we obtain

$$a' = \frac{\gamma V_2}{V_1 - \gamma(V_1 - V_2)} = \frac{\gamma}{(V_1/V_2) - \gamma\{(V_1/V_2) - 1\}}. \qquad \mathbf{11}$$

In the special case when $V_1 = V_2$ we obtain the not-quite-expected result that

$$a' = \gamma, \qquad \mathbf{12}$$

that is, Fel'dman's fraction of investment allocated to Category 1 and Keynes's marginal propensity to save become identical.[17] If

16. *The first proposition:* Let $I = b + a'Y$, and hence $\dfrac{dY}{dt} = \dfrac{dI/dt}{a'}$. By definition of V, $dY/dt = I/V$. Substituting this into the previous expression, we obtain $dI/dt = a'I/V$ and $(dI/dt)/I = a'/V$.

The second proposition: The results just obtained give us $(dY/dt)/Y = (dI/dt)/a'Y = a'I/Va'Y = I/YV = a/V$, since $a = I/Y$.

17. The case where $V_1 = V_2$ may appear rather unrealistic because we usually think of Category 1 as heavy industry with high capital coefficients. And yet according to Leontief, the highest capital coefficient (in 1939) $- 7 \cdot 1 -$ was in home renting, a branch of Category 2, while the lowest but one $-0 \cdot 076$ $-$ was in construction, which belongs to Category 1. Other high coefficients were found in petroleum and natural gas, communications, steam railroads, transportation, electric public utilities, etc. $-$ industries belonging to both categories. It should be noted, however, that these coefficients represent the ratios of the stock of capital to productive capacity, and not to value added. Leontief *et al.* (1953, pp. 191, 220–1).

$V_1 > V_2$ then of course $\gamma > a'$. Table 2 shows the magnitudes of the ratio γ/a' for given a' and V_1/V_2. It is interesting that for reasonably small magnitudes of a', γ/a' is close to V_1/V_2. As a' increases, γ/a' moves toward unity from below or above depending upon whether V_1 is smaller or larger than V_2.

Table 2 The Magnitudes of γ/a' for Given Values of a' and V_1/V_2 [18]

V_1/V_2 a'	0·50	0·75	1·00	1·50	2·00
0·05	0·51	0·76	1·00	1·46	1·90
0·10	0·53	0·77	1·00	1·43	1·82
0·20	0·56	0·79	1·00	1·36	1·67
0·50	0·67	0·86	1·00	1·20	1·33
0·75	0·80	0·92	1·00	1·09	1·14
1·00	1·00	1·00	1·00	1·00	1·00

That Fel'dman's γ and Keynes's a' should be so closely related, and even identical when $V_1 = V_2$, may be surprising, but it is merely a reflection of the fact that if a certain fraction of the increment in national income (a') is to be devoted to investment, a corresponding fraction of investment (γ) must be allocated to capital goods industries to make the production of this increment in investment possible.[19] In other words, in a growing economy some capital is used to make more capital. The explicit recog-

18. Based on the expression $\dfrac{\gamma}{a'} = \dfrac{V_1/V_2}{1 + a'\{(V_1/V_2) - 1\}}$ derived from **14**.

19. Perhaps a simple numerical example will help us understand the relation between a' and γ. Let us take $a' = 10$ per cent, and let $V_1 = V_2$. Then if the ratio between C and I is to be maintained at 9 to 1, the new investment must be allocated between the consumer and capital goods industries in the same ratio. On the other hand, if $V_1 = 4$, $V_2 = 2$, the corresponding division of investment will be approximately in the ratio of 1·8 to 8·2.

This relation between a' and γ (though not in these terms) was also pointed out by Robinson (1952, pp. 92–6). She assumed their identity without explaining, however, that the latter depends on the equality of the capital coefficients.

It should be pointed out that this close relation between γ and a' does not of course solve Fel'dman's classification problem.

nition of this fact is, I believe, one of the virtues of Fel'dman's model, though ironically enough its author kept insisting that the final purpose of all production is consumption. In a growing economy this is simply not true.

The relationship between V_1 and V_2 on the one hand and V (the over-all coefficient for the whole economy) on the other is also simple. The rate of growth of investment being independent of the manner in which it is expressed,

$$\frac{\gamma}{V_1} = \frac{a'}{V}. \qquad \qquad 13$$

Solving 11 for γ in terms of a', we have

$$\gamma = \frac{a'V_1}{V_2 + a'(V_1 - V_2)}, \qquad \qquad 14$$

and inserting 14 into 13, we obtain

$$V = a'V_1 + (1 - a')V_2, \qquad \qquad 15$$

that is, V is a weighted average of V_1 and V_2.

Thus development decisions made in terms of a or a' imply corresponding decisions regarding the magnitude of γ, and vice versa.

The average propensity to save (ratio of investment to income) a plays a minor role in Fel'dman's model. It can be computed and it is relevant to many policy decisions (the level of taxation, for instance), but it has no life of its own, so to speak, and is completely determined by the relative productive capacities of the two categories (see above, p. 153), because the underutilization of capital in either category is excluded by the assumed absence of any limits to production other than capital.

Though exaggerating the rigidities of the real world, Fel'dman's model contains an important element of truth: a closed economy without well-developed metal, machinery, and subsidiary industries (the complex of the so-called heavy industries) is unable to produce a sizable quantity of capital goods and thus to invest a high fraction of its income, however high its *potential* saving propensity may be. In Soviet economic thinking the former consideration has been predominant; in our recent literature the ability to save has been emphasized. Perhaps a synthesis, or more correctly, a return to a synthesis, is in order.[20]

Table 3 illustrates the behaviour of a over time under two arbitrarily chosen sets of conditions. In both cases, a_0 is small as compared with γ. As expected, a rises over time and gradually approaches γ, but it remains relatively low for quite some time, in spite of the very high assumed rates of growth of investment given by γ/V_1 (10 to 17 per cent). Thus for some time, a country's *investment* can grow very rapidly even with a low average propensity to save. The latter does, however, determine the rate of growth of *income* as was shown on pp. 155–7, and a low a will of course result in a slowly growing income (see Table 1). But a low a is not incompatible with a high rate of growth of investment for

Table 3 The Behaviour of a over Time for Given a_0, γ and V [21]
$(V_1 = V_2 = 3)$

t	$a_0 = 0\cdot10$ $\gamma = 0\cdot30$	$a_0 = 0\cdot20$ $\gamma = 0\cdot50$
0	0·100	0·20
1	0·107	0·22
2	0·114	0·24
3	0·121	0·26
4	0·128	0·28
5	0·136	0·30
10	0·173	0·39
20	0·236	0·47
30	0·273	0·50
50	0·296	0·50

20. The importance of the relationship between the capacity of capital goods industries and the current propensity to save is recognized by Abramovitz (1952, pp. 155–6) and by Lowe (1955). This relationship was also the cornerstone of the so-called overinvestment business cycle theories, such as Hayek's (1935) and Cassel's (1924).

The inability of undeveloped countries to produce capital goods should not, however, be exaggerated. A good deal of construction can be carried on with fairly primitive methods.

21. Based on the expression $a = \dfrac{\gamma}{(\gamma Y_0 - 1)e^{-(\gamma/V)t} + 1}$ derived from 5 and 10. The reader is reminded that $I_0 = 1$.

a period of time. Here may be found at least a partial explanation of their simultaneous existence in Soviet Russia, as found by Norman Kaplan, a phenomenon which has puzzled some economists, including myself.[22] [Case 2, *Assets subject to wear*, is omitted.]

IV

With capital coefficients being treated as given, the one and only variable which can be varied as an instrument of planning is our γ, the fraction of total investment allocated to Category 1 (capital goods industries). Since Fel'dman's model allows complete intra-category flexibility, γ can vary all the way from zero to one.[23] The optimum size of γ (and it need not be constant) chosen by the planning authorities will depend on what they consider to be the purpose of economic development. This question is about as simple as that regarding the purpose of life itself, and I have no ready answer to either.[24] We are working here with a very limited model, too rigid in some respects and too flexible in others. It can be applied to only a few of the simplest objectives of economic development.

If the purpose of economic development lies in the maximization of investment or of national income (without differentiation between investment and consumption) at a point of time, or of their respective rates of growth, or of integrals over time, γ should be set as high as possible. This is always true for investment, and nearly always for income, the only exception being when V_1 greatly exceeds V_2, and even then for only a short period of time.[25] A high γ does not imply, however, any reduction in

22. See Kaplan (1953) and comments on his paper by Domar, Erlich, and Millikan (1953, pp. 37–100). I may add that my own comments expressed in terms of a *given* average propensity to save hardly helped to clarify the issue.

23. In a model with assets subject to wear, γ, being a fraction of the net investment, can be smaller than zero and larger than one if the wear of the assets in one category or another is not made good. This possibility is excluded in this paper.

24. The theory of profit maximization raises similar questions; see Lutz and Lutz (1951).

25. The derivation is given in the Appendix (not included here). For this exception to hold for income with $\gamma = 0.3$, $V_1 = 3$, and $t = 3$ years, V_1/V_2 must be (approximately) at least 1.8; if $t = 5$ years, V_1/V_2 must not be less

consumption. With capital assets assumed to be permanent, even $\gamma = 1$ would merely freeze consumption at its original level. If assets were subject to wear, consumption would be slowly reduced by failure to replace them. Finally, a transfer of resources from consumption to investment industries would reduce consumption still further. The latter possibility is, however, excluded from Fel'dman's model, and the former – assets subject to wear – is outside the present discussion.

Such an indifference between consumption and investment irrespective of the magnitude of γ (or of a) must be rare even among Soviet planners: after all, consumption standards affect the ability and the incentive of the populace to work and the willingness to obey. Fel'dman, who did not regard labor as a factor limiting production, had no room for such considerations, but he insisted time and again that consumption was the sole purpose of production, the emphasis given to investment in his model being only temporary (Fel'dman, 1928a, pp. 150, 163). He did not specify whether the variable to be maximized should be consumption at a point of time, or its rate of growth, or its integral over time; whether consumption should be discounted or not; and what value, if any, should be attached to the increasing capital stock as such, particularly in Category 1, so important during a war. On the whole, he was most concerned with the (relative) rate of growth of consumption, and desired a high γ with that end in mind. We shall consider here several possibilities: consumption at a point of time, its integral over a period of time, and its (relative) rate of growth; brief remarks will be made about the discount problem and about the value of the capital stock as such.

The examination of the expression 8 quickly reveals that γ has a dual effect on C. As the numerator of the exponent of $e^{(\gamma/V_1)t}$, it is related to C directly; as a member of the expression $(1-\gamma)/\gamma$, inversely. As γ increases, the latter falls very rapidly; thus with $\gamma = 0.1$, $(1-\gamma)/\gamma = 9$; when $\gamma = 0.2$; $(1-\gamma)/\gamma = 4$; a γ of 0.5 brings it down to 1. Over short periods of time C is dominated by $(1-\gamma)/\gamma$ and is therefore depressed by a high γ. As time goes on,

---

than 3·5; with $t = 6$ years, not less than 5·8; when t reaches 8 years, the case becomes impossible. If we examined the integral of Y, rather than Y itself, V_1/V_2 could be somewhat larger.

the exponential $e^{(\gamma/V_1)t}$ will assert itself, and a high γ will eventually produce a large C.

When one variable (γ) has a dual effect on another (C), it is usually possible to find the magnitude of the former maximizing the latter. It can be shown that γ maximizing C *at a given point* of time is given by the expression

$$\gamma = 1 - \frac{1 - e^{-(\gamma/V_1)t}}{(\gamma/V_1)t}, \qquad\qquad \textbf{16}$$

and that this value of γ, being independent of V_2, varies inversely with V_1, and directly with t (it is a direct function of the ratio t/V_1); thus the longer the period in question, the higher the value of γ should be set. All this presupposes a constant γ over time. A variable γ would be a more flexible instrument.[26]

Table 4 The Optimum Magnitude of γ Maximizing C at a Given Point of Time[27]

| $(\gamma/V_1)t$ | γ | t/V_1 | Implied t | | |
			with $V_1 = 3$	with $V_1 = 4$	with $V_1 = 5$
0·01	0·005	2·000	6·00	8·00	10·00
0·02	0·010	2·010	6·03	8·04	10·05
0·03	0·015	2·017	6·05	8·07	10·09
0·04	0·020	2·028	6·08	8·11	10·14
0·05	0·025	2·034	6·10	8·14	10·17
0·10	0·05	2·07	6·20	8·27	10·34
0·20	0·09	2·14	6·41	8·54	10·68
0·30	0·14	2·20	6·61	8·82	11·02
0·40	0·18	2·28	6·83	9·10	11·38
0·50	0·21	2·35	7·04	9·39	11·73
0·75	0·30	2·53	7·59	10·12	12·65
1·00	0·37	2·72	8·15	10·87	13·59
2·00	0·57	3·52	10·57	14·09	17·62

26. See note 31.
27. Based on expression **16**. The correspondence among the several columns is not exact because of rounding.

As far as I know, the expression **16** cannot be solved explicitly for γ. Numerical results can be obtained by the simple device of taking a given value for $(\gamma/V_1)t$, finding the corresponding γ, and dividing the latter into $(\gamma/V_1)t$ to find t/V_1. Table 4 gives the results. It reveals a most unhealthy sensitivity of γ to t/V_1. While t/V_1 ranges from 2·0 to 2·5, γ covers all the distance from practically nothing to 30 per cent. With $V_1 = 3$ and $t = 6$ years, the optimum γ is less than 1 per cent; but if the period is extended to 8 years, γ jumps to 37 per cent. A larger V_1 (such as 4 or 5) makes γ a bit more stable, but not much. Since a planning horizon is a hazy notion at best, even if expressed in terms of one or more five-year plans, the maximization of consumption at some point of time provides no sensible clue to the optimum magnitude of γ.

To explain this mathematical puzzle, Figure 1 presents the actual behaviour of C over time. The lower straight line corresponding to $\gamma = 1$ is horizontal: all investment being allocated

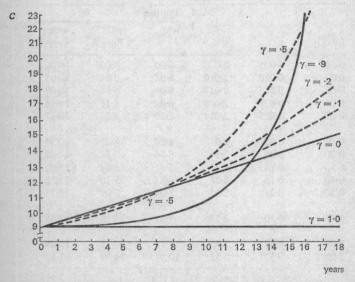

Figure 1 The behaviour of consumption over time for given magnitudes of γ ($V_1 = V_2 = 3$; $C_0 = 9$).

to Category 1, consumption stays at its original level without any increase. This is an extreme and a misleading example, because even a slight reduction in γ (to 90 per cent) results in a rapid growth of C (the solid curve) after a few years. The $\gamma = 0$ straight line is more interesting: here all investment is directed to consumer goods industries (Category 2); hence the capacity of Category 1 remains constant, as does its output, i.e. the total stream of investment. Consequently the capacity of Category 2 increases, but only at a *constant absolute rate*. Its relative rate of growth declines with time.[28]

The dotted curves on Figure 1 correspond to several reasonable magnitudes of γ (10, 20, and 50 per cent), and as expected, the higher the γ, the smaller C is in the early years, and the more rapidly it grows thereafter. These curves are fairly close to each other and to the straight line $\gamma = 0$; they all intersect the latter within a surprisingly narrow period of time, in our case between 6 and 8 years. This explains why the maximization of C gave such an unstable magnitude of γ.

The message conveyed by Figure 1 is fairly clear: if the planning authorities have a short time horizon, they may just as well leave capital goods industries alone and stay on the line $\gamma = 0$. As their horizon expands, a strong effort to develop these industries should be made. Not much is gained by playing with small magnitudes of γ. If reality only corresponded to Fel'dman's model, the presence of so many undeveloped countries would be inexplicable.[29]

28. A linear, but not constant, C given by $\gamma = 0$ is possible only because of the assumed absence of need for replacements. Otherwise, as the capacity of Category 2 expands, so will its replacement needs (though with a lag), and it will be impossible to satisfy them without allocating some investment to Category 1.

These qualifications are outside our present case with permanent assets.

29. The introduction of time lags between investment and the resulting output dilutes this message, but not by much, unless unforeseen bottlenecks arise. Thus a lag of 2 or 3 years would reduce a 3 per cent annual rate of growth to some 2·8 per cent; a rate of growth of 10 per cent would be reduced to 8·4 and 7·9 per cent respectively – all this of course after the expiration of the initial lag period. The latter is not as long as it appears to be at first sight: roughly speaking, the average lag between the investment of resources into a project and its fruition is about one-half as long as the period between the beginning and the completion of the project.

A large fraction of output invested produces such a rapid increase in consumption because a capital coefficient of 3 (without a lag) means a high return on investment in terms of output (but not necessarily in terms of profits). If V_1 rose to 4, the dotted curves would intersect the straight line $\gamma = 0$ in the 8–10 year range; a coefficient of 5 would move the latter to 10–12·7 years. But as these examples show, the range remains quite narrow, so that for any given V_1 the curves intersect the straight line $\gamma = 0$ more or less simultaneously and fairly independently of the magnitude of γ unless the latter becomes very high.[30]

The maximization of consumption at a point of time may not be a satisfactory objective of economic development because it implies an indifference to the behaviour of consumption during the intervening period.[31] To remedy this defect, the integral of C over the whole period should be maximized instead. This approach, however, turns out to be no more helpful in determining the optimum magnitude of γ than the preceding one did. As shown on Figure 2, the dotted ($\gamma = 50$ per cent) curve and the solid ($\gamma = 0$) one – now a quadratic, as an integral of a straight line – are so close together that there is no room for drawing the $\gamma = 10$ and $\gamma = 20$ per cent curves. (Note, however, the difference in scale between the two charts.) If drawn, all these curves would

30. The point of intersection of C with the straight line $\gamma = 0$ (more correctly Lim C) is given by the equation

$$\left(\frac{1-\gamma}{\gamma}\right)\frac{V_1}{V_2}\left(e^{(\gamma/V_1)t}-1\right) = \frac{t}{V_2}. \qquad 17$$

V_2 cancels out and hence does not affect the result. The solution takes the form of

$$\frac{(\gamma/V_1)t}{e^{(\gamma/V_1)t}-1} = 1-\gamma, \qquad 18$$

which cannot be solved for t explicitly; however, we can obtain approximate numerical solutions by first assuming given values for $(\gamma/V_1)t$, computing the left side of the equation which gives $1-\gamma$; then finding the magnitudes of γ and dividing them into $(\gamma/V_1)t$. This gives the value of t/V_1, from which t can be computed for given values of V_1.

It should be made clear that the capital coefficient discussed above in the text is V_1, and not V_2.

31. It is also fairly obvious that a strict adherence to this objective requires not a constant but a variable γ: it should equal zero in the last few years of the period, and by the same reasoning, it should be set high at the beginning. This is essentially a problem in calculus of variation which we shall not try to solve here.

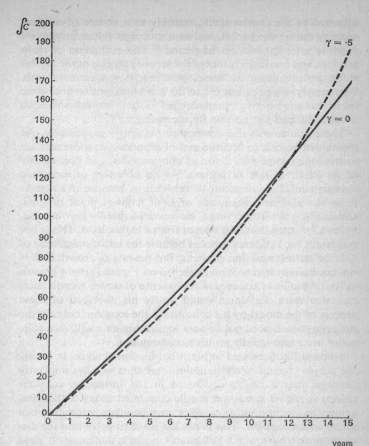

Figure 2 The behaviour of the integral of consumption over time for given magnitudes of γ
($V_2 = V_2 = 3$; $C_0 = 9$).

again intersect the $\gamma = 0$ one in a very narrow range, between 9 and 11 years, though the range itself is further away in time than it was on Figure 1 (6 and 8 years). For a country with a reasonably long time horizon, a high magnitude of γ is still worth while.

This conclusion will become even more forceful if some value is attached to the capital stock, possibly as a source of military security during the period, and as a source of future productive capacity after the end of the period.[32] The evaluation of these services, and particularly that of the security aspects of the capital stock, so important to Soviet planners, is not an easy task. Fortunately, we need not try to do it here, except to note once more that any positive value attached to these services will serve as an additional justification for increasing γ.

These refinements did not bother Fel'dman particularly. As mentioned before, to him the aim of economic development lay in the long-run maximization of consumption, and particularly of its (relative) rate of growth. As an objective of economic development, the latter can be misleading, because it abstracts from the absolute magnitude of C at a given point of time. Obviously, a slowly growing C can exceed a rapidly growing one, at least for some time, if it started from a higher level. This is not important for Fel'dman's model because the initial magnitude of C is the same for all time patterns. But the rate of growth of C is not constant over time, and as shown on Figure 1, rapid growth at the beginning is achieved at the expense of slower growth later, and vice versa. Fel'dman could justify his disregard of these aspects of the model by his concern for the long run only. In the long run, which need not be very long, a higher γ will, as a rule, result in a more rapidly growing consumption.[33]

Nothing has been said so far about time preference. In taking the simple integral of consumption over time we have implicitly assumed that a rouble consumed in the future (in constant prices) is just as good as a rouble consumed today. Otherwise, some adjustment of future roubles must be made before they can all be added together. This is not the place to delve into the discount problem for which Fel'dman's model is unnecessarily rigid and complex. We need not even inquire whether the public, or in

32. Similar reasoning is commonly used in the case of an individual saver whose welfare function is made to consist of the stream of consumption, his stock of wealth at the end of the period (such as his life) which can presumably be converted then into consumption, and possibly a certain satisfaction from pure possession of the (increasing) stock of wealth during the period. The sum of these streams is usually discounted in time, a problem to which we shall turn presently.

33. The larger V_1 is relative to V_2, the weaker this rule is.

our case, the planning authorities, are endowed with the classical impatience to consume, so that confronted with two equally large integrals of consumption they would invariably prefer a declining stream to a constant or an ascending one.[34] In our model the stream of consumption is not constant; it grows (though it should be adjusted for the growth of population), and unless the planning authorities have very queer notions, a rouble of future consumption should be less valuable than that of the present simply because there will be more roubles to consume. Hence future consumption should be discounted before being compared with (or added to) present consumption, but just how this should be done is not obvious.[35]

It certainly makes no sense to discount the stream of consumption and the final stock of capital at what might be the implied rate of interest, because in the context of our model the latter would equal the reciprocal of the capital coefficient (i.e. the average productivity of investment, which equals the marginal), and the integral of such a discounted stream plus the discounted final stock of capital (if we deal with finite periods) will be the same, irrespective of the size of γ.[36] Besides, the rate of discount cannot be a constant. It should vary directly with the rate of growth of consumption and with the proportion of income

34. This question is ably handled by Harrod (1948). Besides Marshall, whom Harrod quotes, the reader is also referred to Fisher (1907). See also Samuelson (1943).

It should be emphasized that the question raised in the text deals not with the preference for present as compared with future *income* – which I would expect most people to have – but with the preference for present over future *consumption*, which may or may not exist.

35. The need for discount arises from the application of the law of diminishing marginal utility to consumption, and not necessarily because of mere passage of time. That a growing stream of consumption should be discounted on these grounds will, I believe, be accepted, and even insisted upon, by most economists. Yet we add individual incomes to obtain a national total without bothering about discount, even though we know quite well that, however difficult interpersonal welfare comparisons are, a small income contains more utility units per dollar, as it were, than a large one does.

36. If the rate of discount is to equal the reciprocal of the capital co-efficient, we must either operate with the over-all coefficient as the weighted average of V_1 and V_2 given by **15**, or assume that $V_1 = V_2$.

The capital coefficients were defined (p. 154) as marginal relative to capital; hence they are average relative to investment.

saved, and thus be a direct function of γ and an inverse function of the capital coefficient. If the planning authorities gave us this function we could compute the optimum magnitude of γ, not necessarily constant in time, which would maximize this or that discounted objective. But the discount function, like a consumer preference map between apples and oranges, is highly subjective, and no amount of theorizing could enable *us* to tell the planning authorities what *their* discount function should be.[37] So having recognized its legitimate existence, we shall leave the discount function alone, perhaps with a face-saving remark that γ should be increased until the marginal rate of discount equals the marginal rate of return – an innocent but not a particularly helpful suggestion.

Fel'dman did not even mention the discount problem. Perhaps he was not aware of it, or thought it smacked of Wall Street. But perhaps he also felt that there was not much he could say about it. His task was to explain to the Soviet planners the basic principles of economic growth and to furnish them with several alternative patterns of development, depending on the magnitudes of γ and of the capital coefficients. It was up to the planners to choose the optimum path, depending on their own objectives, and on their evaluation of existing economic and political conditions and possibilities.[38] Such an evaluation of 'the state of the mind of the masses' was in a sense a search for a discount function, but what exactly would be gained by an attempt to formalize it?

37. This does not imply that the planning authorities should not set some rate of discount of future inputs and outputs to enable their local agents to choose between investment alternatives with different time patterns.

38. He was quite explicit: 'The politician will have to determine which patterns of growth of consumer goods capital and therefore of consumption are acceptable and desirable, and what magnitudes these rates of growth should reach. Technicians and statisticians should indicate what coefficients of effectiveness (the reciprocal of the capital coefficient) can be achieved in what time. Then the social engineer will be able to construct a plan for the development of the national economy.' (1928b, p. 155).

References

ABRAMOVITZ, M. (1952), 'Economics of growth', in B. F. Haley (ed.), *A Survey of Contemporary Economics*, vol. 2, Homewood, Illinois.

BURCHARDT, F. (1931–2), 'Die Schemata des stationären kreislaufs bei Böhm-Bawerk und Marx', *Weltwirtschaftliches Archiv*.

CASSEL, G. (1924), *The Theory of Social Economy*, New York.

DOMAR, E., ERLICH, E., and MILLIKAN, M. (1953), (Comments on Kaplan's paper 'Capital formation and allocation') in A. Bergson (ed.), *Soviet Economic Growth*, Evanston, Illinois.

FEL'DMAN, G. A. (1928a), 'K teorii tempov narodnogo dokhoda', *Planovoe Khoziaĭstvo*, November, pp. 146–70.

FEL'DMAN, G. A. (1928b), 'K teorii tempov narodnogo dokhoda', *Planovoe Khoziaĭstvo*, December, pp. 151–78.

FEL'DMAN, G. A. (1929a), 'O limitakh industrialisatsii', *Planovoe Khoziaĭstvo*, no. 2, February, pp. 184–96.

FEL'DMAN, G. A. (1929b), 'Analitischeskii metod postroeniia perspektivnykh planov', *Planovoe Khoziaĭstvo*, no. 12, pp. 95–127.

FISHER, I. (1907), *The Rate of Interest*, New York.

HARROD, R. F. (1948), *Towards a Dynamic Economics*, Macmillan.

HAYEK, F. A. (1935), *Prices and Production*, Routledge & Kegan Paul, 2nd edn.

HICKS, J. R. (1950), *A Contribution to the Theory of the Trade Cycle*, Oxford.

IGNATOV, B. (1932), 'Balans narodnogo khoziaistva', *Planovoe Khoziaĭstvo*, June, pp. 112–36.

KAPLAN, N. M. (1953), 'Capital formation and allocation', in A. Bergson (ed.), *Soviet Economic Growth*, Evanston, Illinois.

KOVALEVSKII, N. A. (1930), 'K postroeniia generalnogo plana', *Planovoe Khoziaĭstvo*, no. 3, pp. 117–209.

KUZNETS, S. (1955), 'International differences in capital formation and financing', in *Capital Formation and Economic Growth* (A conference of the Universities-National Bureau Committee for Economic Research), Princeton.

LEONTIEF, W., *et al*. (1953), *Studies in the Structure of the American Economy*, Oxford University Press.

LOWE, A. (1952), 'A structural model of production', *Social Research*, vol. 19, pp. 135–76.

LOWE, A. (1955), 'Structural analysis of real capital formation', in *Capital Formation and Economic Growth* (a conference of the Universities-National Bureau Committee for Economic Research), Princeton.

LUTZ, F., and LUTZ, V. (1951), *The Theory of Investment of the Firm*, Princeton.

MAHALANOBIS, P. C. (1953), 'Some observations on the process of growth of national income', *Sankhayā, The Indian Journal of Statistics*, vol. 12, pp. 307–12.

NURKSE, R. (1934–5), 'The schematic representation of the structure of production', *The Review of Economic Studies*, vol. 2, pp. 232–44.

PIGOU, A. C. (1933), *The Theory of Unemployment*, London.
PREOBRAZHENSKY, E. (1931), *Zakat Kapitalizma*, Moscow–Leningrad.
ROBINSON, J. (1942), *An Essay on Marxian Economics*, London.
ROBINSON, J. (1952), *The Rate of Interest and Other Essays*, London.
SAMUELSON, P. A. (1943), 'Dynamics, statics and the stationary state',
    The Review of Economic Statistics, vol. 25, pp. 58–68.
SWEEZY, P. M. (1950), 'In answer to criticisms on *The Theory of
    Capitalist Development*', *The Economic Review*, Hitotsubashi University,
    Tokyo, April, pp. 135–9.
SWEEZY, P. M. (1953), *The Present as History*, New York.
TSURU, S. (1942), 'On reproduction schemes', in Paul M. Sweezy (ed.),
    The Theory of Capitalist Development, New York.
TSURU, S. (1954), 'Keynes versus Marx: the methodology of aggregates',
    in Kenneth K. Kurihara (ed.), *Post-Keynesian Economics*, New Brunswick.

8 W. Brus and K. Laski

Problems in the Theory of Growth under Socialism

Excerpts from W. Brus and K. Laski, 'Problems in the theory of growth under socialism', in E. A. G. Robinson (ed.), *Problems of Economic Development*, Macmillan, 1965, pp. 21–54.

General approach to the factors of growth

Realistic models of growth in a socialist economy take as their starting-point the problems of the dimensions of available factors of growth, and not the problems of aggregate effective demand, emphasizing thus, above all, 'supply' as limiting the size and the growth rate of production.

Factors concerning the 'supply-side' can be dealt with in two ways: first from the point of view of current labour (labour reserves and their increase; level of labour productivity and its changes). Viewed thus the gross national income (Y) is determined by the product of employment (Z) and productivity (W) defined as gross value added per employee:

$$Y = Z \times W. \qquad\qquad 1$$

Secondly, we can approach the same problems from the point of view of stored-up labour (stocks of means of production and their increase; effectiveness of means of production and its changes). Thus the gross national income can be presented as the product of the real productive fixed capital (M) by the effectiveness of this fixed capital (E) defined as gross value added per unit of capital, or

$$Y = M \times E. \qquad\qquad 2$$

This twofold approach to factors determining the national income presents sometimes a temptation to unite the elements of formulae 1 and 2 into one formula. In Poland such attempts are known, based among others on the Cobb-Douglas function. (See for example, Pajestka, 1961. Regarding the concept of the factors of growth see Lissowski, 1960 and Laski, 1960.) However, the use of a Cobb-Douglas type of function is questioned, first of all because of its problematical theoretical quality and the practical difficulty of dividing the increased income into the 'part due' to employment and the 'part due' to the real productive fixed capital (there is an analogous question as to 'ascribing' the increase of labour productivity to the substitution and to the independent technical progress).[1]

The model of growth formulated by Kalecki is most often used in Poland in theoretical studies including those for long-term planning. It will also form a suitable starting-point for our discussions.[2]

On the basis of the methodological assumptions expressed by formula 1, the rate of growth of the national income (r) during the period t is determined in this model as follows:

$$r = \frac{\Delta Y}{Y} = a + \beta \qquad\qquad 3$$

where ΔY is the increment of national income during the period t, i.e. the difference between gross national income at the period t and at the period $t-1$;

Y is gross national income at the period $t-1$;

a is rate of increase in average productive employment at the period t in relation to period $t-1$;

β is rate of increase in average labour-productivity at the period t in relation to period $t-1$.

The product $a.\beta$ is omitted as negligible.

Thus the rate of income growth is the sum of the rate of increase in employment and of the rate of increase in productivity. But both the increase in employment and the increase in productivity assume at the same time a corresponding increase in real

1. Such attempts were made in Poland by Lisikiewicz (1961) and by Knyziak (1960).

2. In the first place the work of Kalecki (1960) should be mentioned. In addition, in preparing this paper we availed ourselves of Professor Kalecki's latest work, *Teoria wzrostu w gospodarce socjalistycznej* ('The theory of growth in a socialist economy', Kalecki, 1970) which is now published. We wish to express our profound gratitude to Professor Kalecki for having kindly allowed us to use this material, as well as for his friendly advice and critical comments. There is no need to stress that the authors are solely responsible for the opinions and formulations contained in this paper.

productive fixed capital and in its effectiveness. Thus the rate of income growth should at the same time be expressed in terms of the methodological assumptions resulting from formula 2:

$$r = \frac{\Delta Y}{Y} = i \times \frac{1}{m} - a + u \qquad\qquad 4$$

where

I is gross productive investment in fixed capital (the increase in inventories omitted for simplicity) at the period $t-1$, put into operation at the period t;

$i = I/Y$ is the rate of investment or the share of gross productive investment in the gross national income at the period $t-1$;

m is investment outlay necessary to obtain an increase in national income by one unit or the ratio $I/\Delta Y'$, where $\Delta Y'$ is the increase in national income due to investment;

a coefficient of the decrease in national income resulting from the actual loss of means of production or the diminution in their effective functioning due to physical depreciation;

u coefficient of the increase of national income resulting from all kinds of improvements raising the effectiveness of the existing real productive fixed capital.

Kalecki stresses the fact that formula 4 cannot be applied in a capitalist economy, as there the coefficient 'u' is not an independent variable and fluctuates greatly (even in terms of $+$ or $-$) as a result of the business cycle. On the other hand in a socialist economy in normal conditions this coefficient is always positive, reflecting the tendency of continued improvement of the existing productive apparatus. It results therefrom that the magnitude $i \times (1/m)$ becomes a strategic factor determining the rate of economic growth. This argument can be reinforced by emphasizing that in a capitalist economy the rate of investment also is not independent of the magnitude 'm', which really determines the rentability of investments (assuming a given distribution of income between profits and wages).

In comparing the formulae 3 and 4 we see that

$$a + \beta = i \times \frac{1}{m} - a + u$$

as is obvious, since the rate of growth in the national income does not change according as we look at it from the point of view of labour or of real productive fixed capital.

The confrontation of these two aspects is important as it enables us to realize some of the interrelations needed to define the optimal rate of growth in given conditions. One of these very simple but useful truths, brought to light by this confrontation, is the necessity to co-ordinate precisely the factors shown on both sides (of the comparative formula) in order to assure the optimal course of the process of growth. It is obvious, of course, that first of all the key magnitude $I/Y = i$ – i.e. the rate of investment – must be properly established.

The degree of complexity of the problem of properly defining the rate of investment depends on the degree of variability of the remaining factors to which the rate of investment should correspond. Were the economy to develop at a stabilized rate r, with a rate of increase in employment perfectly adapted to secure a balance of the labour force (there is no possibility of change unless there should occur a deficit in the labour force or unemployment) and with a constant rate of increase in productivity (also without any possibility of change assuming that the coefficients m, a and u are constant) – in such a simplified case there would have been a single and constant rate of investment fulfilling the postulate of a full utilization of the growth potential.

Thus, to obtain the optimal rate of growth, it would be necessary to do two things only: first, to establish satisfactorily the unequivocally determined rate of investment; secondly, to put into operation a mechanism to ensure the actual attainment of such a rate of investment and its maintenance at the same level. Naturally the word 'only' – especially so far as the second point is concerned – should be written in quotation marks as it is not at all a simple matter. This is shown by the voluminous writings on the problems of the theoretical conditions for bringing an economy on to the trend of stabilized growth that corresponds to the potential possibilities. The importance of the earlier mentioned characteristics of a socialist system – creating, as they do, real premises for the direct establishment of a rate of investment on a national scale that corresponds to the postulated rate of growth – is manifest even with these extremely simplified assumptions.

And yet every step toward reality must mean at the same time a progressive relaxation of the assumptions regarding the invariability of the factors present in the model under consideration. In reality the rate of growth of available labour resources, as well as the rate of productivity, are variable. The coefficients m, a and u have different values at different stages, especially when account is taken of different time-horizons. It follows therefrom that the problem of the optimal course of the process of growth does not, and cannot, consist in putting the economy on to the path of a rate of growth stabilized once and for all – that is in attaining a single postulated rate of investment. A full utilization of the growth potential requires in reality a variable rate of growth, and therefore also a rate of investment that varies at least at certain intervals of time.

This means that the criteria for the evaluation of the conditions, within the given social and economic system, for the optimal process of growth, cannot be limited to the possibility of attaining once and for all a definite rate of investment. These criteria include also the essential factor of flexibility in establishing the rate of investment, a proper relation, that is, of investment to consumption in the national income. And this flexibility must be such that it will not cause a lack of effective aggregate demand in relation to productive capacities and thus will not cause any waste of the real growth potential.

We wish to argue that a socialist planned economy creates – and perhaps it does so especially from this point of view – favourable conditions for a full utilization of the national growth potential. In any case these conditions are more favourable than those created by an economy where the general rate of investments depends on the private 'propensity to invest'.[3]

We will return later to this question in relation to certain particular problems, mostly connected with the variability of the factors of growth. As was said in the introductory paragraph, we will try to base our discussion on the experience of our country and on the reflection of that experience in Polish economic writings.

3. See Brus and Laski (1962).

Acceleration of growth with existing labour reserves

May we begin by rejecting the assumption of stability of a – that is the rate of increase in employment. The rate of growth of the national income (r) existing at the starting period t_o is below the limit set by the labour force (there exists a reserve of population able to work and not yet employed) and therefore it can – or it should, rather, in these conditions – be increased. The assumption of stability in the rate of increase of productivity (β), in as much as β depends on the coefficient m, is meanwhile maintained.

This order in our exposition corresponds to the consecutive order of the conditions that actually prevailed in Poland. At the beginning of industrialization of the country (before 1949) our economy had at its disposal comparatively large reserves of un-employed labour (even taking into consideration the then existing technical and organizational level). They took the form in general of disguised unemployment (agrarian overpopulation) rather than of open unemployment.

The variability of the rate of growth at the period of acceleration

When a' indicates the rate of growth of the labour-force-supply due to the rate of increase of the population with a given ratio of active to total population and $a' > a$, meaning that the rate of increase in employment has been less than the rate of growth of the labour force, so that the growth potential was not fully taken advantage of, this would necessitate a change from the rate $r = a + \beta$ to the rate of $r' = a' + \beta$ (assuming that β remains constant, which is not precisely true even when the coefficient m remains unvariable). A change, however, from the rate r to the rate r' is a very complicated process which cannot follow a uni-form path.[4] Though the gradual increase of r to r' means a formal equalization of the actual and of the potential rate of growth, the absolute increase of employment in this situation is still lower than the absolute increase in labour force. If the above-mentioned conditions were stabilized, then employment would grow by a', but simultaneously unemployment would grow also, at the same rate, a'. Thus to stabilize the rate of growth after n years in the year t_n at the level r' there must be some moment between the

4. See Sadowski (1958 and 1961).

period t_o and the period t_n during which the rate of growth $r'' > r'$, in order to bring the economy on to the new course of growth. Only after a period during which the rate of growth is sufficient both to absorb the whole current increase in labour force and in addition the surplus of labour from the preceding periods, can growth be stabilized at the level r'. We have, therefore, the following course of the process of changing the economy from the rate of growth r to the rate of growth r', corresponding to the rate of increase of labour force a': $r \to r' \to r'' \to r'$ while $r < r' < r''$. In Figure 1 this process is shown diagrammatically.

Until the year t_o the economy grows at the rate r with the rate of investment i. In the year t_m (intermediate between the year t_o and the year t_n), the economy attains for the first time the rate of growth r' with a rate of investment i'. The line AB shows the development between the year t_o and t_m. The line BC shows the development from the year t_m to t_n, when the rate of income growth and the rate of investments must temporarily increase above r' and i' to r'' and i'' in order to secure the elimination of unemployment. In the year t_n the economy returns to the rate of growth r' with the rate of investment i'. This is the rate adapted to the equilibrium balance of the labour force. The change to the new stabilized growth goes through the points $A \to B \to C \to B$.

This analysis of the probable course of the process of absorption of the unutilized labour force and of the elimination of this source of difference between the actual and the potential rates of growth confirms the complexity of this process. The rate of investment must not only increase but even exceed temporarily the long-term optimal level (on given assumption), and decrease again later. It is necessary, therefore, not only to evaluate correctly, organize and finally attain the ultimate ratio aimed at, but also to evaluate correctly, organize and attain the ratios corresponding to the intermediate points. This requires, among other things, even a temporary reversal of the direction of the change in the rate of growth and in the rate of investment.

Acceleration and the dynamics of consumption

The question arises whether the best solution is an immediate setting of the economy on the new course of growth, taking account of the possibility of flexible planned adjustment of the

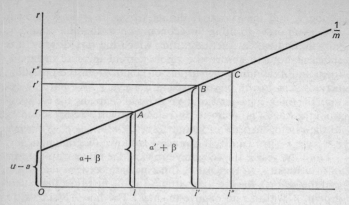

Figure 1 On the horizontal axis is measured the rate of investment (i), on the vertical axis the rate of growth of the national income (r). The coefficient of direction of the straight line is $\frac{1}{m}$, the distance from the origin $u-a$, if we assume that $u-a > 0$

rate of investment, characteristic of a socialist economy. Such a solution is tempting not only because it shortens the complicated period of adjustment, but because it shortens also the period of losses due to the unutilized growth potential, between the years t_o and t_n.

This would have been in practice the best solution if one could assume that the central planning authorities were completely free in defining the rate of investment. But of course such an assumption is inadmissible. And this is not only due to the numerous technical difficulties connected with the structure of the national product (the necessity to increase violently the share of investment goods), but also to the organizational problems of large invest-ment works, the shortage of qualified personnel and the lack of technical knowledge, as well as other considerations.

The basic problem is the degree of freedom in determining the ratio of investment to current consumption in the national in-come. The current consumption (defined as $Y-I$) is the more affected, the lower is the starting-point, defined as the relative value r and i, and also the lower the starting level of consumption per head of population. The lower is the figure r in relation to r'

(and also r''), so, *ceteris paribus*, the larger must be the growth of i. The growth of i diminishes correspondingly the share of consumption in the national income $(1-i)$, and during the period of acceleration it restricts the rate of increase in consumption. The consequences of this restriction are the more onerous the lower is the level of consumption per head of population.

From this point of view of course not only is the rate of acceleration of fundamental importance, but also the length of time in which the economy is to take the new course of growth. The shorter is n, the more violent is the growth of i and the fall of $1-i$, and the slower is the growth of consumption. Thus if we accept even the mildest limiting condition – e.g. that the absolute magnitude of consumption cannot decrease – then it will as a rule be found that the shortest technically possible length of the period n will not be consistent even with this condition. This is still more true if one substitutes the condition that consumption must grow at least at the same rate as the increase of population (so that the consumption per head does not fall), or the alternative condition that average real wages do not decrease.

Let us now consider in detail the problem of acceleration in relation to the dynamics of consumption. It is of great importance to the understanding of certain phenomena that occurred during the first stage of industrialization of Poland. In order to simplify we shall not take into consideration all the intermediary stages of the course between the points $A \rightarrow B \rightarrow C \rightarrow B$.

Before the year t_o the economy grows at the rate r. There is the same rate of growth of consumption, C. This growth is the sum of $a+\beta$, which means that β is not only the rate of growth of labour productivity but also the rate of growth of average real wages. On the other hand population grows by $a' > a$ so that consumption per head grows by $a+\beta-a'$, or slower than labour productivity and average wages β, as $a+\beta-a' < \beta$ when $a' > a$.

By the year t_n the economy will have attained the stabilized rate of growth $r' = a'+\beta$. Total consumption will thenceforth increase at the same rate. Simultaneously the rate of increase in labour productivity and that of average real wages will equal the rate of increase in consumption per head of population, which will amount to $a'+\beta-a' = \beta$.

The final effect is satisfactory. But what happens during the n

years between the year t_o and t_n? Let us assume that the decision to increase the rate of growth was taken in the year t_o. This, assuming one year as period of 'maturing' of investment, leads to a change in the rate of investment in the year t_1, and to a change in the rate of growth of the national income in the year t_2.[5] Essential importance should be attached to the fact, that in the year t_o, when the decision is taken to increase the investment rate in the year t_1, a given rate of investment already exists, resulting from decisions taken in the year t_{-1}. Thus the rate of growth of the national income in the year t_1 and the absolute level of the national income in that year are determined completely independently of the fact whether and to what degree the rate of investment may change. In such conditions, however, any growth of the investment rate does not only mean a reduction of the share of consumption in income – which is always true – but it also means that the level of consumption is absolutely below the level which would have been attained had the acceleration process not been started in the economy concerned.

Let us denote national income, consumption and investments in the year t_o by Y, C and I correspondingly. Were there no acceleration, in the year t_1 these figures would amount respectively to $Y(1+r)$, $C(1+r)$ and $I(1+r)$. If we intend to accelerate growth and establish a share of investment in income amounting to

$$i' = \frac{I(1+r)+\Delta I}{Y(1+r)},$$

then consumption would amount to

$$Y(1+r)-I(1+r)-\Delta I < C(1+r).$$

The rate of increase in consumption in the year t_1 will be therefore smaller than $r = a+\beta$, and it must be smaller if acceleration is to be achieved. (See Sulmicki, 1962, ch. 3, sec. 3.)[6]

5. In practice the gestation period of investment is much longer than one year. This is of the greatest importance to this problem, and especially when the scale of investment expansion is violently changed.

6. Minc (1961, pp. 480–1), employs the notion of the year of equalization more or less in an analogous meaning. But by a 'period of equalization' he means a 'period in which the total consumption in different years at a higher rate of investment becomes equal to total consumption at a lower rate'. Regarding the year of equalization see also Sulmicki (1962, p. 138) and Polaczek (1961).

The extent of the limitation of consumption depends on several factors, but above all on the magnitude ΔI which in turn depends on the difference $r'-r$ with the given coefficient m. If r' is much larger than r, then ΔI must also be large and it must limit relatively strongly the consumption in the year t_1. It depends further on the magnitude r whether this limitation takes the form of a slower growth, a stabilization or an absolute decline. The lower r, the greater the danger of stabilization or even of absolute decline of consumption in conditions in which it is necessary to increase markedly the rate of income growth.

Independently, however, of different possible quantitative changes, the phenomenon of initial losses of consumption in order to raise the economy to a higher growth path of national income and consumption always occurs in the process of acceleration. It is illustrated by Figure 2 (on a logarithmic scale).

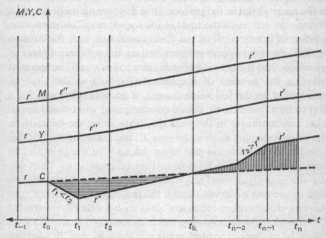

Figure 2

Until the year t_o the economy (national income $= Y$, real productive fixed capital $= M$, consumption $= C$) has been growing at a stable rate $r = a+\beta$ lower than the potential rate of growth $r' = a'+\beta$. In the year t_o the decision is taken to increase the rate of investment in order to adapt it to the available labour force.

In order to simplify let us assume that there has occurred a single increase in the rate of investment to a magnitude sufficient to ensure the absorption of the whole labour surplus (the increase of population and those unemployed in the preceding period). The rate of investment will increase initially up to i'' (corresponding to the rate of growth of fixed capital r''). Assuming, however, that the maturing period of investment is one year, then in the year t_1 national income continues to grow at the rate r. When the rate of investment is increased, this means a decline in the rate of consumption, which in case of drastic changes in proportions may lead even to an absolute fall of consumption. In any case, as it is shown in the diagram, the rate of increase in consumption in the year t_1 is lower than the hypothetical one (that which would occur were there no acceleration, indicated by a broken line). In the year t_2 the rate of growth of national income reaches r'', consumption grows correspondingly at the rate r'', which is higher than the rate r at the initial period. Thus at some moment t_k actual consumption will reach the level of the hypothetical consumption (the point of intersection of the continuous line with the broken one). This moment (year) is described as the moment (year) of equilization, and the period between this moment and the moment of starting the process of acceleration $(t_k - t_o)$ as the time of equalization.[7] In the following period, if growth continues for a period to be at the rate r'', actual consumption will exceed hypothetical consumption. In the year t_{n-2}, foreseeing the exhaustion of the labour surplus during the year t_n, the planning authorities will decide to decrease the rate of investment for the year t_{n-1} to i', corresponding to the long-term rate of growth r'. Thus between the year t_{n-2} and t_{n-1} there will occur a phenomenon inverse to the one observed during the interval of time from t_o to t_1: income grows still at the rate r'', but with a rate of investment $i' < i''$ the increase in consumption is more rapid than r''. From the year t_n, national income, consumption and real productive fixed capital grow at the long-term rate r', which is higher than the initial rate r and corresponds (on the basis of the assumptions we have made) to the potential rate of growth $a' + \beta$. The segment

7. See Pajestka (1961) who describes the problem of reserves of labour force at the initial stage of industrialization from a somewhat different methodological position.

hatched horizontally represents relative losses in consumption (in relation to the hypothetical consumption) during the period $t_o - t_k$, the segment hatched vertically represents the relative gain in the period $t_k - t_n$. During the period after the year t_n, the relative gains are proportionate to the difference between the rates of growth r' and r.

Obviously the process of the acceleration manoeuvre depends on the limiting conditions we have to deal with. If, for instance, an absolute decrease in consumption is inadmissible – which is usually the case in any normal situation – then it is difficult to adopt the variant of a single acceleration of the rate of growth even if there are no technical impediments. The central planning authorities are bound to accept some tolerable consumption in the year t_1, and this will influence the whole further course of the process.

Let us assume that the postulate of stable real wages is the condition limiting the reduction of the rate of increase in consumption. Naturally the rate of growth of national income in the year t_2 will be, in these conditions, lower than r'' and the process of acceleration will extend over a longer time.

It is important to realize the part played in the process by the length of time over which acceleration takes place. At the end of this period the rate of investment must grow from i to i''. If, however, the changes in the rate of investment occur gradually and are spread over a larger number of years, the income becomes higher (than e.g. in the year t_1). Thus the share of consumption in the income, decreased to $1 - i''$, will represent a larger consumption the higher is the income.

A lengthening of the time over which the process of acceleration occurs is necessary to relieve the conflict between the growth of investment and the level of current consumption, as it makes it possible to have a higher rate of investment i'' when income and consumption have also attained an absolutely higher level. This is the problem facing socialist planning, since – except in special cases of an abnormal character – such planning cannot aim exclusively at a maximum shortening of the period of underutilization of the labour reserve (though theoretically it would be most advantageous), but it should aim at what is in the given conditions the best compromise between growth with future consumption and the needs of present consumption. Thus even in this relatively simple case of intention to accelerate the rate of growth because it is below the limit set by the labour force, it is impossible to accept the view, still prevalent here and there in Western literature, that the planning authorities are completely free to push up the rate of investment without regard to actual consumption, which is treated as a residuum. The problem of correct choice from this point of view is even more important in conditions in which the labour force is fully utilized, so that the rate of growth of national income is determined almost wholly by the rate of growth of labour productivity (which will be dealt with below).

The role of non-investment factors

In the light of the above discussion it is clear that the strategy of growth during the period concerned must emphasize the taking advantage of all possibilities of shortening the period of under-absorption of the labour force, just so far as that can be done without damaging the actual consumption. In the first place attention should be paid to whatever opportunities are latent in the fields involved by the coefficients a and u. Thus far we have assumed that these two coefficients are constant. This assumption, however, did not correspond to the actual conditions that prevailed in Poland during the initial stage of industrialization, and it does not correspond either to the actual situation in any country which becomes socialist at an intermediate level of economic development.

Countries at an intermediate stage of development have at their disposal a productive equipment which in conditions of capitalism is not fully utilized owing to lack of effective demand. We have, therefore, at the beginning of industrialization not only an under-utilized labour force but also some under-utilized productive capacity, the mobilization of which does not require any investment outlays. With the expansion of investment the violently growing internal demand can be met in some measure by the elimination of shorter working weeks, the increase of the number of shifts, and similar measures. From the point of view of the national economy this is advantageous in general, even though it is not profitable according to a capitalist calculation from the point of view of the particular enterprise because of the comparatively small increase of production. We have here another example of the importance of the power of macro-economic calculation under socialism to take advantage of an existing growth potential.

An analogous part may be played, for a very short period, indeed, by the reduction of repair and period outlay maintenance (provided it does not decrease immediately output capacity in proportion to the reduction of outlay), and especially by refraining from replacing equipment which is out of date from the economic viewpoint. It is true that this equipment gives a very low return, in many cases not even exceeding the wages of the workers employed. It makes it possible, however, to use productively the surplus labour. Thus we can temporarily increase u and decrease a, increasing the difference $u-a$, which means an increase in the rate of income growth independently of changes in i. This factor is of special importance since, unlike investment, it produces very quick effects merely by increasing income, in which the share of productive investment may be expected to be greatly augmented.

The increase of the difference $u-a$, achieved mainly by employing gradually a larger labour force on already existing equipment, can be considered as an alternative to applying primitive methods of production in order to take advantage of the so-called saving potential existing in incomplete employment. After the Second World War this alternative was rather commonly used in socialist countries.

The influence of the change in the difference $u-a$ on the process of setting the national economy on a new path of growth can be illustrated in Figure 3.

In comparison with the diagram on page 180 we have here an additional straight line at the same inclination $(1/m)$ as the line AC, but at a greater distance from the base of the diagram. This distance is greater by the segment $\Delta(u-a)$, which expresses the average total effect of the increase of u and of the decrease of a during the period (number of years) in which this effect occurs. We assume in this connection, as usually happens in practice, that workers additionally employed as a result of the increase in $\Delta(u-a)$ stay there permanently. In consequence of this effect, the

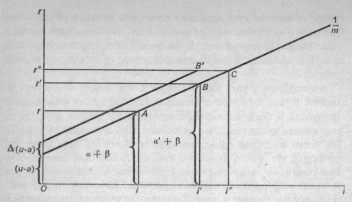

Figure 3

rate of growth r'' is temporarily attained due to the rate of investment i' (point B'). When the temporary effect $\Delta(u-a)$ ceases, at the rate of investment i', we descend to point B on the straight line AC. But if at that moment unemployment is still existing, we must reach point C, that is increase the rate of investment to i'', in order to liquidate unemployment and – according to our previous consideration (page 180) – to come to point B. In view of the fact, however, that some part of unemployed was absorbed by taking advantage of the effect $\Delta(u-a)$, the period of our stay at point C will correspondingly be shorter, which brings, of course, an essential advantage from the point of view of actual consumption. Independently of it, an extremely important advantage consists in the fact too, that the rate of investment grows from i to i' and eventually from i' to i'' when there is an absolutely higher level of income, and thus also at an absolutely higher level of consumption.

It is evident that the problem has been presented here in a schematic way which makes it impossible to consider different possible variants of the course of the process. All this, however, does not alter the fact that taking advantage of the effect $\Delta(u-a)$ facilitates the acceleration of the rate of growth in the most difficult initial phase; thus it weakens the contradictions appearing in the process as compared with those considered earlier. In

Poland this phase played a very essential part especially at the first stage of the Six-Year Plan (1950–55).

Inflationary pressures

Our conclusions should not be regarded as implying that owing to the addition of the temporarily acting factor $\Delta(u-a)$ it is possible to avoid completely any sacrifice involved in the increase of the investment rate. The additional increase of income due to non-investment factors will consist in the first place of capital goods and not of consumption goods. Without previous investment no growth in agricultural production is to be expected, and in the countries concerned agriculture produces the main part of consumption goods. On the other hand labour productivity will grow more slowly when non-investment factors are utilized, than if the labour reserve were absorbed by new equipment. There occurs therefore a notable trend towards the increase of employment to the detriment of the factor of the increase of productivity. If it is not possible here to analyse this problem in detail a few remarks seem to be necessary, especially so that this question may be related to the problem of the appearance of inflationary phenomena in the first stage of socialist industrialization.

The growth of labour productivity, amounting in the initial variant to β, plays an important part in the reduction of strains in consumption caused by the acceleration of growth. It is easiest to represent it by denoting the rate of investment as the function of the level of labour productivity (W) and of real wages (w). We have then

$$i = \frac{I}{Y} = \frac{Z(W-w)}{ZW} = 1 - \frac{w}{W}. \qquad 5$$

It follows therefrom that the rate of investment depends on the ratio of wages to labour productivity, assuming that the whole difference $W-w$ is productively invested.

The increase of i calls for a decrease in the ratio w/W. When productivity grows by β annually, some increase in real wages is compatible with a decrease of the ratio w/W provided that the rate of increase of real wages is lower than β. If, however, a significant increase of i is required, then the increase of real wages must remain far below β. When β is large enough, real wages can grow, or at least not fall, even if their trend is far below β. But if β decreases, then the possibility of real wage increase, which is far less than β, falls also. When $\beta = 0$ or W is constant, any increase of i requires unconditionally the fall of w to a level determined by the postulated magnitude i. Again when β is positive, but relatively low, in general the required magnitude of the rate of investment will not be attained without a certain decrease in real wages. Thus the danger of decrease of real wages is greater when investment is linked with non-investment than when investment alone is imposed (but within definite limits).

But the level of real wages should not be identified with consumption per head. If, when investment alone is imposed unemployment lasts longer, then employment is lower also at the start. With a given consumption fund, wages will be higher the lower is employment. With an additional utilization of non-investment factors $\Delta(u-a)$ employment is higher in the first stage, while unemployment is lower. With the same consumption fund, wages will be lower if employment is higher. This will be the case also, even when the consumption fund is greater, provided that employment is still correspondingly greater. It would seem that this last case was characteristic of the first stage of rapid industrialization in Poland. At that period real wages increased very little and in the years 1951–53 they even decreased markedly. But the increase in employment was so great in comparison with the growth of population that consumption per head grew during the whole of this period. Even a stabilization, not to speak of a decrease, in real wages is a hard nut to crack for a socialist society. On the other hand, when there is a conflict between increase in wages and increase in consumption per head, it is in the general interest of the economy to solve it to the benefit of consumption.

In these conditions the danger of inflation generally arises. It occurs when real wages cannot rise further, while money wages still must rise by a certain percentage even if only because of payment by piece rates (and also because of some elements in the methods of remuneration leading automatically to increases of money wages from time to time). If efficiency grows by β, then money wages grow by β/p, where $p \geqslant 1/(1/p)$ is the coefficient of increase of money wages in relation to the increase in productivity. But since real wages are to stay fixed, then prices and costs of living must rise also by β/p. Naturally this phenomenon operates more acutely if real wages have to decrease at some time, and much less acutely if real wages are able to rise though to a smaller degree than the 'natural' increase in money-wages.

It should be remembered that during the phase of rapid industrialization of a country the growth of average money wages is strongly influenced by rapid changes in the structure of employment arising from the transformation of the general economic structure. Employment increases most rapidly in heavy industry and in building, where relative wages are high, as is necessary to attract labour in the desired direction. The resulting increase of average money wages becomes an inevitable additional factor increasing the inflationary pressure.[8]

The problems of inflationary phenomena in the introductory stage of socialist industrialization deserve consideration in more detail and separately, both from the point of view of the character of these phenomena and their differences from those that arise in a planned economy to determine and to control the proportion between purchasing power and the volume of goods and services available. This would, however, go beyond the province of this paper. We must confine ourselves to emphasizing that the problem of inflationary phenomena under socialism can be understood correctly only as an element in a complex total of a planned process of setting the socialist economy on the path of long-term dynamic equilibrium.

We have considered the problems relating to the process of the acceleration of growth by employing for production unemployed and hitherto surplus labour. On the assumptions made, this means that – as far as the element of employment is concerned – the potential rate of growth is determined, after the completion of this process, by the rate of growth of population and the consequent rate of growth of the supply of manpower. In practice this is not exactly true as there remains the possibility of change of

8. Regarding the relations of real wages, nominal wages and changes of prices see Kucharski (1961, ch. 2). Regarding the problem of inflation in socialist economy see also Fedorowicz (1959) and articles by Sulmicki (1957) and Oyrzanowski (1957) and Mlynarski (1957).

the active participation ratio of the population by drawing into production a certain margin of persons who are not technically unemployed, but who are free to take up some form of activity. The increase of the ratio of active participation renders possible growth at a higher rate, but only so long as there exist conditions favourable to the increase of this ratio. We have here a problem in a certain sense analogous to those considered earlier, because the utilization of this factor of growth requires a corresponding adaptation of the rate of investment. In the interests of brevity we shall not discuss it here, but we wish to make clear that the ratio of participation of the population depends in a great measure on expenditure on social institutions (e.g. crèches and kindergartens which make possible an increase in the participation ratio of women) and in certain other forms (transportation facilities, hostels for workers, etc.).

Thus we touch here on a vast problem of the socio-economic effectiveness of expenditure outlays for the development of the so-called non-productive sector. Besides those mentioned above, the main elements in this field are the expenditure for education and professional training of skilled personnel and for health measures. Again we must note the problem and do not propose to elaborate it. We must stress, however, that this is an extremely important factor in the achievement of a high rate of growth in a socialist economy. The possibility of allocating funds to these purposes directly by the planning authorities according to the criteria of socio-economic productivity – without having to depend on private 'propensity' to meet these needs adequately – is widely adopted in socialist countries, including Poland. This is shown by many indices reaching, and even exceeding, the levels of highly developed capitalist countries, let alone countries at the same level of general development.

Acceleration of growth taking into account technical progress

In the second part of this paper we assumed stability of the rate of growth of labour productivity. We made only passing comments on possible changes of this rate (showing the consequences of increasing the difference $u - a$). We omitted, among other points, the theoretically very interesting problem, which Kalecki has called the 'rejuvenation' of capital stock, that is the increase of the proportion of new capital in the total of all capital. If we raise the rate of increase in employment, a corresponding growth in average labour productivity will follow. It will be higher than β, though the incremental labour productivity of the newly employed grows at a stable rate β. The effect of the 'rejuvenation' of capital stock will naturally disappear gradually as the process advances, but this does not diminish its importance. (See Kalecki, 1970.)

It is clear, therefore, that changes in the rate of increase in employment, and even more so changes in the structure of employment, are bound to influence the dynamics of labour productivity. In spite of this our initial assumption was justified, inasmuch as we wished to eliminate in the first stage of our analysis the basic factor in the increase of labour productivity – that is technical progress, a factor that is fundamentally different in character.

Change in the rate of increase of labour productivity acquires a special importance in conditions when the possibilities of raising the rate of increase in employment are exhausted.

If the rate of employment growth α' cannot be increased, the only way to raise the rate of growth r' is to raise the rate of increase in labour productivity β. We must therefore now proceed to the analysis of this question.

Technical progress and the choice of the rate of growth

The question immediately arises whether the planning authorities have any freedom of choice at all in this field. If we assume that the rate of β attainable at a moment of time is determined unequivocally by technical progress – then there is no such freedom of choice. It seems, however, that such an assumption is an oversimplification. It would correspond to reality only if at every period there were one single method of possible production, and if technical progress would lead to a new method of production, absolutely better than the previous in the sense that in order to attain a given result it is possible to use a smaller volume of labour with the same or smaller investment expenditure.[9]

9. By 'method of production' we mean here the combination of labour expenditure and investment expenditure inescapably necessary to increase national income by one unit (assuming an unchanged structure). In addition

In practice various methods of production co-exist in any given period and thus at any given state of technical knowledge. And technical progress achieved in the course of this period may also lead to new methods of production which are not absolutely better than the previous ones (e.g. requiring less human labour but higher investment expenditure to attain the given effect). It cannot be considered, therefore, that β is uniquely determined.

Variability of the rate of growth during the acceleration period

In view of the co-existence of methods of production embodying different degrees of mechanization (including also degrees of automatization), planning authorities aiming to accelerate the existing rate of growth may decide to raise the degree of mechanization of investment goods. Let us assume that, during the period preceding this decision, the process of growth was stabilized at a fixed rate of growth $r' = a' + \beta$ and continued for at least n years, representing the average period of life of the different constituents of the real productive fixed capital. Included in this assumption is not only the rate of growth of average labour productivity, but also the rate of growth of incremental labour productivity, defined as the ratio of labour productivity attained in completed investments put into operation in the year t_n to labour productivity achieved in investments put into operation in the year t_{n-1}.

Any increase in labour productivity greater than β and any rate of income growth greater than r' will be the result of the above-mentioned decision. But in these circumstances, the coefficient m will increase too. An increase of the coefficient m is inevitable with increasing mechanization and a given state of technical knowledge. Were it possible to increase the rate of growth of labour productivity without any increase of m, there would be no reason to choose methods of production absolutely worse than others co-existing at that time. The increase of the coefficient m

---

we abstract from the possibility of changes in the methods of production consisting in diminishing investment outlays while the volume of human labour remains constant since we are interested here only in technical progress leading to the increase of labour productivity, which is the essence of technical progress.

is the price to be paid for a higher rate of labour productivity resulting from higher mechanization. Let us assume that planning authorities decide on such a single increase of the coefficient m to m'. Let us assume that it will lead to a considerable single growth of incremental labour productivity (in the sense given above) by more than β and in the following years the incremental labour productivity will continue to grow by β. This will in turn lead to the process shown in Figure 4.

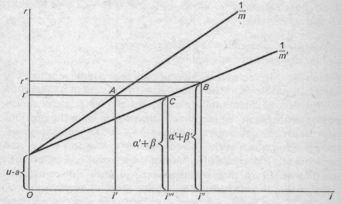

Figure 4

This single increase of the capital coefficient from m to m' is expressed by a lower inclination of the straight line having the direction coefficient $1/m$. We assume that the single increase of incremental labour productivity, achieved by this decision, will imply a rate of average labour productivity amounting to β'. And accordingly the increase will grow for once by $r'' = a' + \beta'$, but as point B indicates this will require an increase in the rate of investment from i' to i''. It will be impossible, however, to keep up this rate of investment with the given assumptions. We have assumed that the realization of investment at the coefficient m' gives a rate of growth of incremental labour productivity amounting still to β. Accordingly the increase of average labour productivity, which for once was β', will decrease and tend to β. It will reach it after n years, during which the entire productive equipment will 'change' into a new capital coefficient m'. Thus during the period of 'change' of the productive equipment we shall have to deal with a decline of the rate of increase of average labour productivity from β' to β, and together with it, a decline of the rate of income growth from r'' to r'. This process will be accompanied by a fall of the investment rate from i'' to i'''. At this rate of investment, the rate of growth will again become $r' = \alpha' + \beta$, but the absolute increment of income will be larger than were they achieved without changing the productive equipment to a new capital coefficient. Thus the whole process follows the line $A \to B \to C$. (See Kalecki, 1960.)

Acceleration connected with technical progress and the dynamics of consumption

Following this line makes the economy face similar, though not identical, problems to those that arise in the case of acceleration of growth consequent on the elimination of a labour surplus. The analogy consists in the fact that in the present as in the previous case the process of acceleration brings as a rule indisputable gains, the price for which is the increase of the investment rate i, and consequently a decrease of $1 - i$ or of the share of consumption in the income. For a time consumption will grow slower as compared with a hypothetical consumption without acceleration (cf. pp. 178–83 and Figure 1 illustrating the problem of the year and period of equalization). The scale of this reduction in the rate of consumption growth cannot be determined theoretically as it depends on the scale of an inevitable increase in the rate of investment. But at the beginning of the period the consumption must be affected and thus one of the elements of the decision to follow the road $A \to B \to C$ will be the balance of losses and gains in consumption. At the start consumption will grow by less than r', but as income later grows by more than r' (momentarily by r''; thenceforward the difference between r'' and r' grows smaller, but until the complete change of productive capacities – that is during the whole period n – income grows at a rate higher than r'), then, apart from the period of the single increase of m, consumption grows too at a rate higher than r'. Thus in time consumption as a rule equals and exceeds the hypothetical level of consumption associated with a rate of growth r'.

Despite this fundamental analogy, there are some essential

differences between the acceleration connected with the liquidation of labour surplus and the acceleration connected with the increase of labour productivity due to the increase of the co-efficient m.

First of all, in the previous case the higher rate of income growth r'' could be maintained for some time, while in the present case the rate of growth rises temporarily to r'' and then falls again. Thus, in the previous case, apart from the starting point when the increase of the rate of investment reaches i'', consumption grows for a time (between the year t_2 and t_{n-2}) at the same rate as the income; in the present case, on the other hand, during the process of extinction, consumption grows more rapidly than income, as the rate of investment declines continually.[10] It would seem then that acceleration due to changing productive equipment to a higher m will be more advantageous to consumption. This is not so, however. In the present case, that is, due to the increase of m, the effect of a given increment of the investment rate (Δi) in the form of the increase of the rate of growth (Δr) is smaller in comparison with the situation when m remains constant. Furthermore, Δr tends to 0, declining in the process of extinction. Thus, although in the period of 'change' of the productive equipment consumption grows more rapidly than income, this growth of consumption is *ceteris paribus* slower in comparison with the growth of consumption during the period of absorption of the labour-surplus. As a result, the time required to reach equality, k, will be longer in the case of acceleration achieved through changing productive equipment into a higher m, than in the case first analysed.

Decisive for consumption in the long run is, however, the fact that, when the acceleration process is complete, in the first case the economy achieved, at a higher rate of investment, a higher rate of long-term growth than it had at the start ($r' > r$); now, due to changing the productive equipment to a higher m, the rate of growth r', identical with the initial rate, will need a higher rate of investment. In both cases, after completing the process of acceleration, the actual level of national income will certainly be higher than the hypothetical one. This need not, however,

10. For simplicity we can assume that r'' and n represent the same magnitudes in both cases.

necessarily be true for consumption. In both cases actual consumption in the year t_n can be lower than the hypothetical one, if the impact of increased investment rate will exceed the effect of the increased rate of growth of income during n years. In other words, in both cases the time of equalization, k, can – but by no means must – be longer than n.

If this ($k > n$) should be the case, the single increase of m would lead to permanent losses in consumption also in the long run. Indeed, taken from a lower basis the same *relative* increments (at the rate r') would represent smaller *absolute* increments in consumption, meaning that the hypothetical level of consumption would never be attained. In eliminating the surplus of labour such a situation cannot occur. In the period after the year t_n consumption grows here at a higher rate ($r' > r$), which means that sooner or later the actual level of consumption must exceed the hypothetical one.

We do not wish to argue that the process under consideration is undesirable from the point of view of consumption. The probability of the time k exceeding n is in general very much smaller than the reverse situation, in which already during the period of change of the productive equipment relative gains in respect of consumption become manifest. And if that is the case, the relative gains will still continue after the end of time n, since they will be calculated on a higher basis.

These two cases reflect in a certain sense two stages of development – one extensive and one intensive (this is, of course, a simplification as in reality they cannot be strictly separated one from the other). Their comparison served the purpose of showing that, from a certain point of view, the second case may cause difficulty. It is important to stress this, since the planning authorities are no longer so bound by compulsions. In considering whether to accelerate growth by utilizing the labour surplus – that is by eliminating unemployment – there is no choice for a socialist state whether 'to accelerate, or not to accelerate'. There is no question regarding the advantage and necessity of utilizing the possibility created by socialism of accelerating the rate of growth. The matters of choice are only the forms and the speed of the process. But in the second case, the very advantage of the acceleration has to be considered. Thus all arguments for and against it must be carefully balanced in order to reduce to a minimum the damaging effects.

In emphasizing the specific difficulties involved in changing the productive equipment into a higher m, it should be remembered at the same time that, after the initial reserves have been exhausted, this is the main means to accelerate the rate of growth, and also that we have then to deal with an economy that is much more mature in all respects, and with an absolutely higher level of consumption. It is thus an economy capable of solving much more complex problems. The experience gained from the second stage of industrialization in Poland fully confirms this view.

Three types of technical progress

Finally, attention should be drawn to the fact that, in evaluating the difficulty of accelerating growth in this way, it must be remembered that an essential part is played by an assumption which is by no means inviolable. We assumed that the single increase of the coefficient m indeed increases labour productivity, but the incremental labour productivity (in the above carefully defined sense) at a new capital coefficient amounting to m' continues to grow by β, as it did with the previous coefficient m. Whether this will be so depends on the type of technical progress, and this cannot be predicted theoretically. It is quite possible that the incremental labour productivity with the capital coefficient m' will not grow by β, but by more than β. If this happened after having changed the productive apparatus into a new degree of capital intensity, the rate of income growth would be stabilized at a level higher than r'. The opposite would occur if the single increase of the capital coefficient should yield an increase of incremental labour productivity lower than β. It is clear, therefore, that the gain from changing the productive equipment to a higher m will be different, *ceteris paribus*, with each of these three possibilities, arising from the type of technical progress in the period concerned: if there is a possibility of securing an incremental labour productivity greater than β there will be clear incentives to increase the capital-intensity; if the possibility of increasing the incremental labour productivity is lower than β, the opposite situation will arise (and this not only in regard to increasing the capital-intensity but even maintaining it); if there is the possibility of securing an incremental labour productivity equalling β, there will be no incentive whatever in either direction. On the basis of such reasoning, Kalecki deduces his criteria differentiating the types of technical progress, defining the first as encouraging capital-intensity, the second as discouraging capital-intensity and the third as neutral.[11] With given preferences, the planning authorities will be the more disposed to apply additional mechanization designed to increase labour productivity and thus to accelerate the rate of growth, the more capital intensive – in the sense given above – is the type of technical progress.

This brief sketch of the problems of adjusting the rate of growth in the light of technical progress seems to confirm the thesis advanced at the beginning of this paper regarding the significance of production-relations in taking advantage of national growth potential and the favourable conditions in this respect created by socialism. The importance is again evident of planned determination of basic macro-economic magnitudes and of possible flexibility in adapting the rate of investment to the varying requirements of the different stages of the development process. Apart from this the problems involved in raising the rate of growth in different conditions of technical progress, bring to light the role of the time-horizon in taking advantage of growth potential. The broad time-horizon of the central planning authorities in a socialist economy renders possible the mobilization of such factors of growth of which otherwise advantage could not be taken. In the light of our discussion above it seems clear, moreover, why it cannot be expected that the premises of strategic decisions concerning development – taken in consideration of long-term and current interests of the society as a whole – will be achieved correctly by the free-working market mechanism. In a socialist economy, decisions of this type are taken outside of the market mechanism, which – as is proved even by the experience of a number of capitalist countries in recent years – is not capable of handling the problems that have been described.

11. See Kalecki (1960). This definition completes the definition of technical progress contained in Kalecki's paper.

Factors limiting the rate of growth

The examination of the problem here presented has, by the nature of things, been at a high level of abstraction. This is of advantage in that it enables us to realize better the relevance of some of the problems to the strategy of growth and to visualize the opportunities created by socialism to apply this strategy. But at the same time there is danger in applying the conclusions of this highly abstract analysis directly to an actual situation of much greater complexity.[12] To do this may result in overlooking some of the inevitable difficulties met in the rapid process of growth under socialism.

We are concerned not only with such obvious issues, as frictions and planning mistakes while the rate of growth is being changed and the sectoral proportions involved are changing too. We are concerned with problems of a more general character. Polish authors have paid a great deal of attention to the study of factors limiting freedom to determine the rate of growth. The theoretical work in this field is undoubtedly a reflection and generalization of practical experience, which showed the complete inadequacy of an approach (in other respects very valuable) to the rate of growth which concentrated exclusively on the general proportions between income, investment and consumption – an approach, that is, from the point of view of the interests of present and future consumption at a very high degree of aggregation. It may seem, for instance, that since there is a certain readiness to suffer some temporary sacrifice in the form of a heavier burden through current investment on current consumption, and since this increased investment makes possible through additional mechanization an acceleration of the rate of increase of labour productivity, there are no obstacles to accepting and achieving a decision to increase the rate of growth of national income. But this is not so. It can be seen that even in this framework the planning authorities are not yet completely sovereign, though there is no question that they dispose of a much wider freedom of choice – the wider the longer is the period of time included into the plan.

12. See Lange's methodologic consideration (1959, pp. 101–8) on this question, among others the importance he attaches to avoiding the error which Whitehead defined as a 'fallacy of misplaced concreteness'.

Kalecki was the first to study these problems and he proved that the difficulties connected with the acceleration of the rate of growth are related above all to foreign trade, and this both directly and indirectly. In countries strongly dependent on imports of investment goods and, especially, of raw materials (most countries, Poland included, belong to this last group), the acceleration of growth implies directly the necessity to increase imports and – with a well-balanced foreign trade – exports. The acceleration of growth of imports may present, and has presented, difficulties both in respect of supply and of outlet. To overcome these difficulties, it may be necessary to make some less profitable exports or even to take measures against imports. Thus the corresponding investment will have a comparatively high capital coefficient. The price to be paid for the acceleration of growth of national income in the face of difficulties in foreign trade will be acceptance by the planning authorities of the need to increase the coefficient m to the extent required to overcome these difficulties. But this is possible only to some degree. In every situation there exists a certain limit imposed by foreign trade which cannot be exceeded; it may be nearer or further from the existing rate of growth, but it will not allow the rate to exceed a certain maximum magnitude.

It should also be borne in mind that foreign trade is the universal remedy for a number of difficulties arising during the acceleration of growth, quite apart from any necessity to increase imports. These difficulties are the familiar 'bottlenecks'. The narrowest, if it concerns an important factor, determines the trend of the whole economy. These 'bottlenecks' may take the form of a shortage of natural resources; of a shortage of highly qualified technical personnel and experienced workers; or of a shortage of personnel in some regions while there is satisfactory balance of supply and demand for the labour force as a whole. They may take the form of delays in planning and completing investment projects in some sectors; of limited production capacity in design of office and building enterprises, and so on. Such difficulties may be, and are, overcome by widening these 'bottlenecks' and by adjusting them to the needs of the national economy rather than by adjusting the economy to them. But it often requires additional investment, for example in geological research, housing-construction, personnel training, mechanization of building and construction work and the like. A specific role may be played by difficulties of accelerating the rate of increase of agricultural production, which is of the greatest importance in maintaining the necessary balance of the economy. (See Herer, 1962.) A rapid acceleration of growth of agricultural production may prove impossible, or on a smaller scale very expensive. Thus in this respect also, the capital coefficient will increase when the rate of growth is raised.

There is no question that the development of cooperation between socialist countries is diminishing foreign trade difficulties, especially when acceleration takes place simultaneously in all or most of the countries concerned. But since 'bottlenecks' occur, none the less, in all socialist countries and since relations between these countries and the non-socialist countries exist and are expanding, the difficulties described above emerge sooner or later when it is attempted to raise the rate of growth above some level (assuming that it is possible to do so from the viewpoint of the growth of manpower and/or labour productivity).

The increase of the capital coefficient involved in overcoming difficulties in foreign trade and in removing 'bottlenecks' plays an essential part in giving effect to decisions concerning the acceleration of growth. This is illustrated in Figure 5.

The planning authority is prepared to introduce some limitation on current consumption and to raise the rate of growth from r_0 to r_1, or pass from point A to point B by increasing the rate of investment from i_0 to i_1. This implies that the capital coefficient grows from m to m'; which increases the average labour productivity from β_0 to β_1. But to attain the rate of growth r_1 difficulties in foreign trade must be overcome and 'bottlenecks' must be removed – the price to be paid for it is the further increase of the capital coefficient to m''. Thus the point B is unattainable and the rate of income growth r_1 is represented by point C with the rate of investment i_2. But though the planning authorities were willing to increase the rate of investment to i_1 as the price of gaining the rate of growth r_1, it is doubtful that they would be willing to make a much greater effort, that is to increase the rate of investment to i_2, to obtain the same result. To simplify the problem we assume that the planning authorities are willing to increase i_0 only up to i_1 – considering for some

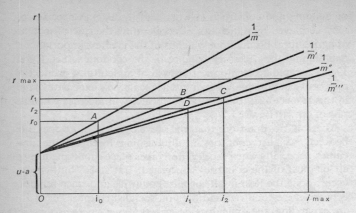

Figure 5

reason that this is the optimum in given conditions – then they
will plan a rate of growth indicated at point D, that is $r_2 < r_1$.
This means that in the event of foreign trade difficulties and
'bottlenecks' appearing, the planning authorities choose a lower
acceleration of the rate of growth rather than the acceleration to
which they would have given priority were there no difficulties or
'bottlenecks'. Finally, on the vertical axis the magnitude r_{max} is
shown, corresponding to the share of investment in the income
i_{max} at the capital coefficient m''' which results in these conditions
and is sufficient to overcome the difficulties mentioned. If the
planning authorities were willing to increase the share of investment in the income higher than i_{max} in order to attain a rate of
growth higher than r_{max}, then this willingness would be faced by
an impassable limit (a deadline) of the maximum magnitude of
acceleration of growth. Thus the real range of choice for the
planning authorities, when r_0 is a rate correlated with the balance
of labour force at a given magnitude β_0, is within the magnitudes
represented by $r_0 - r_{max}$.

Some comments on the relations between
macro- and micro-economic decisions

The transition from abstract generalities of the theory of growth
to the complex conglomerate of practical limitations and inter-

dependencies would require both a study of methods and forms of disaggregation of different elements of economic structure in dynamics and a study of the relation of decisions taken at the highest level to those made at lower levels in the process of the practical application of the selected path of development. We have no space here to discuss fully these complicated problems, so we will confine ourselves to the main trends of Polish economic thought in this field.

In the first place we should mention work designed to improve and develop the techniques of co-ordination calculus and of optimization of the plan. We refer here to the work devoted to the analysis of input-output, both from the theoretical and the technical point of view, and to work on the theory and the technique of programming.[13]

Special effort was made in Poland to study the methods of rational choice of investment variants and foreign trade variants. These studies led to a thorough examination in all their aspects of various economic concepts among which the main role has been played by the concepts of 'terminal pay-off period' and of 'maximal rate of exchange'. The specific virtue of these concepts is that, when calculated from a general economic point of view on the basis of macro-economic relations involved in the process of growth, they fulfil the function of parameters in calculation at lower levels which may be concerned with choice of concrete methods of production in new units or with determining the relative advantages of different kinds of exports and imports.[14] These parameters have made it possible to calculate and take decisions at the lower levels while maintaining the necessary degree of co-ordination with basic general trends determined by the central planning authorities.

We have touched on the problem of relations of the highest central level and the lower levels in a socialist economy. This problem is fundamental from the point of view of growth. Known under the somewhat imprecise terms of centralization and de-

13. First of all the works of Lange should be mentioned (1961a, 1961b). From the numerous publications on these problems we mention as examples, Sulmicki (1959); Porwit (1960); and Sadowski (1960).
14. See Kalecki and Rakowski (1959) and the collective work under Rakowski (1961). And as regards foreign trade Trzeciakowski (1961).

centralization, it became in Poland, especially since 1956, a subject of a great discussion in relation to the so-called model of the functioning of a socialist economy.[15]

The starting-point of this discussion was the thesis that, with the raising of the economy to a higher stage of development, the complexity of economic problems grows also. With it, there is a growing importance of such factors as: the flexibility of adjustment of the structure of supply to the structure of demand (both in production and in consumption); economically justifiable substitution of different forms of expenditures; expansion of different enterprises and sectors related to their economic achievements. It was just from this point of view that excessive centralization was criticized, since this takes the form of concentrating nearly all decisions at the highest level and passing targets and resources to lower echelons only in the form of orders and physical allocations. As a result, the functions of lower echelons (particularly in enterprises) were limited to pure execution of orders only.

The discussion showed that the problem of centralization and decentralization under socialism cannot be considered in terms of centralization or decentralization of *all* economic decisions. It can be considered only in terms of the *division* of centralized and decentralized decisions, with the obvious assumption that the basic macro-economic decisions are centralized. In this connection, the discussion treated broadly the question of the possibility and of the scope for using the market-mechanism within the framework of a planned socialist economy. A lot of space was devoted to the theoretical and practical problems of economic incentives and of prices, as their importance – as macro-economically designed parameters of micro-economic decisions – is growing in proportion to the enlargement of the scope of decentralization.

Beside its direct importance, this 'discussion of the models' was, and still seems to be, of a certain general importance. For it proved, at least in our opinion, that the problem of creating institutional conditions favourable to the full use of potential growth does not disappear once the socialist system is built. Socialism

15. A series of articles *Ekonomisci dyskutuja o prawie wartości* (Economists discuss the law of value), Warsaw, 1957. *Dyskusja o polskim modelu gospodarczym* (Discussion on the polish economic model), Warsaw, 1957, and also Brus (1961).

overcomes a number of fundamental contradictions of the capitalist system; this does not mean, however, that it eliminates all contradictions of every kind, nor that it avoids creating new contradictions arising from the characteristics of the socialist system as such. This implies a necessity for continual search for optimal institutional forms to solve these contradictions, and especially to adapt the functioning system of a socialist economy to the various stages of development, both from a purely economic point of view and a socio-political one. In our opinion this 'discussion of the models' proved also that a socialist socio-economic system provides a possibility of different solutions of the method of functioning of the economy, thus allowing choice of alternatives in this field also, within certain obvious limits.

References

BRUS, W. (1961), *Ogólne problemy funkcjonowaniia gospodarki socjalistycznej* (General Problems of Functioning of Socialist Economy), Warsaw.

BRUS, W., and ŁASKI, K. (1962), 'Istotna treść marksowskiego ujęcia problematyki rozwoju ekonomicznego' (The essential content of Marxian approach to the problems of economic development), *Ekonomista*, no. 4.

FEDOROWICZ, Z. (1959), *Zagadnienia rownowagi monetarnej w gospodarce socjalistycznej* (Problems of Monetary Equilibrium in Socialist Economy), Warsaw.

HERER, W. (1962), *Rolnictwo a rozwoj gospodarki narodowej* (Agriculture and the Development of the National Economy), Warsaw.

KALECKI, M., and RAKOWSKI, M. (1959), 'Ogólnienie wzoru efektywnosci inwestycji' (Generalization of the formula of investment effectivity), *Gospodarka planowa* (Planned Economy), no. 11.

KALECKI, M. (1960), 'Zagadnienia teorii dynamiki gospodarki socjalistycznej' (On problems of the theory of socialist economy dynamics) in the collective work *Zagadnienia ekonomii politycznej socjalizmu* (Problems of the Political Economy of Socialism), Warsaw, 3rd edn.

KALECKI, M. (1963), *Teoria wzrostu w gospodarce socjalistycznej* ('Outline of a theory of growth in a socialist economy'), Warsaw; English edition, 1969, Oxford.

KNYZIAK, Z. (1960), 'Inwestycyjne i pozainwestycyjne czynniki wzrostu produkcji przemysłowej w Polsce w latach 1950–60' (Investment and non-investment factors of growth of industrial production in Poland in 1950–60), *Ekonomista*, no. 5.

KUCHARSKI, M. (1961), *Pieniądz, dochód, proporcje gospodarcze* (Money, Income, Economic Proportions), Warsaw, Library of the School of Planning and Statistics in Warsaw.

LANGE, O. (1959), *Ekonomia Polityczna* (Political Economy), vol. 1, Warsaw; English edition 1963, New York.

LANGE, O. (1961a), 'Model wzrostu gospodarczego' (The model of economic growth); 'Kilka uwag o analizie nakładów i wyników produkcji' (Some remarks on input–output analysis); 'Produkcyjno – techniczne podstawy efektywności inwestycji' (Productive and technical foundations of investment effectivity), included in *Pisma ekonomiczne i społeczne 1930–1960*, Papers in Economics and Sociology, 1930–60, Warsaw; English edition, 1970, London.

LANGE, O. (1961b), *Teoria reprodukcji i akumulacji* (The Theory of Reproduction and Accumulation), Warsaw; English edition, 1969, Warsaw.

ŁASKI, K. (1960), 'Czynniki wzrostu dochodu narodowego w gospodarce socjalistycznej' (Factors of growth of national income in socialist economy), *Ekonomista*, no. 2.

LISIKIEWICZ, J. J. (1961), 'O metodach analizy wpływu postępu technicznego na wydajność pracy w przemyśle' (On methods of analysing the influence of technical progress on labour productivity in industry), *Ekonomista*, no. 4.

LISSOWSKI, W. (1960), *Zastosowanie relacji majątek-praca-produkcja w programowaniu rozwoju przemysłu* (The Application of the Ratio Capital-Labour-Production in Planning the Development of Industry), Warsaw.

MINC, B. (1961), *Ekonomia polityczna socjalizmu* (Political Economy of Socialism), Warsaw, P.W.N.

MŁYNARSKI, F. (1957), 'Walka z niebezpieczenstwem inflacji' (Battle against the danger of inflation), *Myśl Gospodarcza* (Economic Thought) no. 5.

OYRZANOWSKI, B. (1957), 'Walka z niebezpieczenstwem inflacji' (Battle against the danger of inflation), *Myśl Gospodarcza* (Economic Thought), no. 5.

PAJESTKA, J. (1961), *Zatrudnienie inwestycyjne a wzrost gospodarczy* (Employment and Investment in Connection with Economic Growth), Warsaw.

POLACZEK, S. (1961), *Inwestycje w krajach gospodarczo nierozwiniętych i ich wpływ na bilans handlowy* (Investment in Economically Under-Developed Countries and their Influence on the Trade Balance), Warsaw, Library of the School of Planning and Statistics in Warsaw.

PORWIT, K. (1960), 'Wybór ekonomiczny w planie przedsiębiorstwa' (Economic choice in the plan of enterprise), *Ekonomista*, no. 2.

RAKOWSKI, M. (1961), *Efektywnosc inwestycji*, (Investment Effectivity), Warsaw.

SADOWSKI, W. (1958), 'Zmiana stopy wzrostu gospodarczego' (The change in the rate of economic growth), *Ekonomista*, no. 6.

SADOWSKI, W. (1960), *Teoria podejmowania decyzji* (The Theory of Decision Making), Warsaw.

SADOWSKI, W. (1961), 'Przyspieszenie długofalowego wzrostu w gospodarce socjalistycznej' (The acceleration of long-term growth in socialist economy), *Ekonomista*, no. 4.

SULMICKI, P. (1957), 'Pojęcie inflacji w gospodarce socjalistycznej' (The notion of inflation in a socialist economy), *Mysl Gospodarcza* (Economic Thought), no. 5.

SULMICKI, P. (1959), *Przepływy międzygaleziowe* (Input-Output), Warsaw.

SULMICKI, P. (1962), *Proporcje Gospodarcze* (Economic proportions), Warsaw.

TRZECIAKOWSKI, W. (1961), 'Problemy kompleksowego systemu analizy, efektywności bieżącej handlu zagranicznego' (Problems of the complex system of analysing the current effectivity of foreign trade), *Gospodarka planowa* (Planned Economy), nos. 4 and 5.

Part Three
Planning Techniques

The knowledge that – as Barone and Lange have shown
(Readings 2 and 4) – the allocation of resources in a planned
socialist economy is equivalent to the competitive solution of a
general equilibrium system, does not tell the Minister of
Production *how* to obtain that solution in practice, that is, how to
draw and implement the economic Plan, or Plans. Some of the
techniques developed in the course of the experience of socialist
countries are discussed in this section.

Kalecki's paper describes the sequence of steps to be followed
in the construction of a long-run plan to ensure the feasibility and
internal consistency of production targets, given the constraints
set by current consumption requirements, balance of payments
equilibrium, and the availability of labour. One of the most
important steps in drawing the plan is the construction of
'balances' for materials and other inputs; these 'material
balances', as it appears from Montias's paper, have played in the
centralized organization of supply a role similar to that which
could have been played by input-output methods. Since the
mid-1950s input-output methods have also been used, but
material balances are still prepared and both methods appear to
have a role to play in the planning process. Attempts to achieve
overall efficiency – or 'optimality' – as well as consistency of
plans were made with the introduction of mathematical methods,
see Part Five.

Financial balances were also drawn, originally as a way of
organizing and controlling the implementation of plans, then
more recently (see Part Four) as a more flexible instrument of
economic policy. Garvy's essay illustrates the main features of
the traditional monetary system of Soviet type. In that system,

interest rates had no place in investment policy, but the necessity of choosing between alternative investment projects has led to the development of criteria which, if observed, would perform the role of a capital charge. The paper by Kalecki and Rakowski discusses the theoretical foundation of these criteria, and their work is particularly interesting because their suggestions were actually turned into official rules used in Poland throughout the 1960s (now these rules have been changed and replaced by others, closer to the ordinary methods of discounted cash flows, and shadow capital charges have been replaced by actual charges – See Reading 17).

Consumption planning has relied on fairly crude methods of predicting consumption patterns by means of techniques not dissimilar from those used in the West (family budgets, extrapolation of time trends, inventory analysis, etc.). Robinson's paper is devoted to the difficulties of consumption planning and the general problem of 'consumer's sovereignty' under socialism.

9 M. Kalecki

Outline of a Method of Constructing a Perspective Plan

M. Kalecki, 'Outline of a method of constructing a perspective plan', *Teaching Materials*, vol. 8 (1962), pp. 1–15, Szkola Główna Planowania i Statystyky, Warsaw. Presented as a conference paper, United Nations, Geneva, 1963.

I

Although this paper is based on the Polish experience in perspective planning it does not represent the official point of view on the subject. In the construction of the Polish twenty years plan a variety of approaches were used and this happens to be one of them.

As the paper deals to a considerable extent with the problem of choice of the appropriate rate of growth of the national income it is necessary to say a few words about the concept in common use in the socialist countries which differs from that applied in the capitalist ones in that it excludes the production of services. It is true that the so-called material services such as transport, laundry, restaurants and even trade are included. However, the national income does not include the administrative services of the Government, entertainment, education, medical services etc. There are also excluded from the national income the services rendered by such fixed assets as residential houses, hotels etc.

I believe that for the purpose of long-run planning this approach has something to commend itself. It is easier to measure the real value of commodities than that of services. For instance, in the statistics of capitalist countries the real increase in administrative activities is measured by means of an index of employment of the officials (weighted according to the salaries in the base year). No account is, and hardly could be, taken of changes in productivity of labour in this case.

For other reasons it is convenient not to include the residential rent in the national income. The capital coefficient is very high in this case and therefore the application of a general capital coefficient to the national income, in which residential rent is included, is fairly meaningless because the coefficient is very much influenced then by the relative share of residential building in total investment.

Our approach does not mean, of course, that services should be neglected in the long-run planning. They are accounted for by appropriate planning of employment (for instance in the case of the administrative activities of the Government) or by planning of capacities of fixed assets of consumer type (e.g. dwelling space).

In line with the concept of national income used here we distinguish in investment the productive and unproductive investment. By productive investment we mean that destined for the production of goods and material services while other investment, such as construction of dwelling houses, streets, parks etc., is classified as unproductive investment.

Before proceeding with the subject proper it is still necessary to mention that in the Polish national planning no accrual of foreign credits is assumed. Such will be also our assumption in the subsequent discussion. This approach does not differ substantially from assuming an accrual of moderate foreign credits which are fixed beforehand in their amount. On the other hand, the difference between our approach and the assumption that any gap in foreign trade, however large, will be always covered by credits, is of crucial importance. For such an assumption would eliminate altogether the problem of balancing foreign trade which, as we shall see below, emerges as an essential factor in our approach to perspectivic planning.

II

The most important parameter of a long-run plan may be considered the average annual rate of growth of the national income. Thus the selection of the correct variant of the plan is really tantamount to a choice of the appropriate rate of growth of the national income. The Government has the natural tendency to develop the country as fast as possible, i.e. to fix the rate of growth at the highest possible level. There will be, however, a number of limiting factors which have to be taken into consideration here. The most obvious of these is the fact that the higher is the rate of growth the higher the relative share of productive investment in the national income. Indeed, the higher the increment of the national income at its given level the higher the investment which is necessary to achieve this increment (abstracting from utilization of the existing excess capacity). It follows directly that the higher is the ratio of the increment of the national income to its level the higher the ratio of investment to the national income. Now, a higher relative share of productive investment in the national income will affect unfavourably consumption and unproductive investment in the short-run. This tendency obviously cannot be pushed too far because it would create dissatisfaction of the population even though in the long-run the cumulative effect of the high rate of growth contributes to an increase of the standard of living.

In many instances, however, the increase in the relative share of productive investment in the national income which accompanies the increase of the rate of growth is still enhanced by an additional factor. It appears, as will be shown in more detail below, that with the increase of the rate of growth there emerge difficulties in equilibrating the balance of trade. In its effort to achieve this equilibrium the country is forced down the path of investment requiring higher capital outlays in relation to the effect achieved in foreign trade and thus the relative share of productive investment in the national income (which we imagine to be adjusted for deterioration in the terms of trade) will increase *pro tanto* more. It is very likely that at some level of the rate of growth balancing of foreign trade becomes an altogether impossible proposition and in this way there appears an absolute limit to the rate of growth.

Finally, at a sufficiently high rate of growth there may also well emerge a scarcity of labour. This can be overcome by increasing sufficiently the capital outlays in the plan but this will again aggravate the problem of the relative share of investment in the national income.

To sum up: the obstacles to a very high rate of growth in a perspectivic plan are the high capital outlay required both directly and as a result of the difficulties in equilibrating the balance of foreign trade and possibly also of the shortage of labour. In fact the difficulties in foreign trade may make virtually impossible exceeding a certain level of the rate of growth.

III

The first step in the construction of a perspectivic plan is to draw a crude outline of the plan assuming the rate of growth which is high in the light of the past experience of the country in question (or failing such an experience in the light of experience of other countries in similar conditions). We thus choose deliberately a high variant which it may be necessary to scale down already at the stage of preliminary testing.

Next, we have to make some assumption about the capital co-efficient which relates the increment of the national income and productive investment. The value of the capital coefficient will have to be again chosen on the basis of past experience or the experience of other countries taking as much as possible under consideration the peculiar features of the period and the country in question. It is in any case impossible to have here anything but a crude approximation because the capital coefficient depends to a very great extent on the structure of the increment of output which may differ considerably from that in the past or in another country.

Now, having accepted some level of this coefficient for better or for worse we obtain the first approximation to the annual productive investment in the perspectivic plan, say, at its beginning, at its end, and in the middle of the plan. We handle in a similar way the problem of the coefficient relevant to the increase in inventories which enables us to determine this item. By deducting productive investment and the increase in inventories from the national income we determine finally the sum of consumption and unproductive investment.

In order to split this item into two components we have to compare the resulting standard of consumption of goods with the capacity of fixed assets yielding consumer services (e.g. with the *per capita* dwelling space in residential houses). In this way it is possible to arrive at some reasonable decision which, however, would be obviously to a great extent arbitrary.

Already at this stage we may find out that the relative share of productive investment plus the increase in inventories in the national income is so high as to make the plan untenable because the inroads into consumption and unproductive investment would be too formidable in the short-run. However, since the result depends to a great extent on the level of a capital co-efficient which is altogether hypothetical in character – it may be safer even in such a case to pursue the variant somewhat further.

IV

The next step is to establish at least in general lines the industrial structure of the national income. We have split the national income in the plan (i.e. at its beginning, at its end, and in the middle) into four major components: productive investment, increase in inventories, unproductive investment and consumption. If we shall make still some reasonable assumptions about the future structure of consumption which may be based, for instance, on that of the more developed countries taking into consideration the local conditions of the country in question, we may proceed to a crude determination of the industrial structure. This is necessary for two reasons: for carrying out the test of the balance of trade and for obtaining a second approximation to the capital coefficient which would reflect the structure of the increment in output.

Here, however, an important distinction has to be made between two types of industries (including all branches of econ-omic activity as agriculture, transport, etc.). We shall call these two categories supply determined and demand determined in-dustries. By supply determined industries we mean such activities which have a certain ceiling for the long-run rate of growth for technical and organizational reasons, so that even a considerable increase in capital outlay will not be helpful in raising this output at a higher rate. The demand determined industries have no such ceilings, at least for the range of the rates of growth of the national income which come into consideration. Thus the output of such industries can increase in the long run in accordance with demand.

The technological and organizational factors on which, in turn, depend the ceilings of the rate of growth of the supply determined industries are of a very varied nature. Limited natural resources are the simplest and most obvious example.

The time necessary for adaptation of new technological pro-cesses is another factor. The most serious difficulties in the way of introduction of new techniques are probably to be encountered in agriculture, where there is always a certain element of spontaneity in the development of production. Even the amount of artificial fertilizers which can be profitably absorbed by agriculture is to a certain extent dependent on agrotechnical knowledge.

A further factor impeding development may arise from difficulties in recruiting manpower for certain trades (e.g. coal-mining) or in making adequate progress in training of skilled technicians. Of particular importance can be the deficiency of technical and managerial personnel indispensable for construction of new plant, which must be highly qualified and experienced. This is in fact the underlying factor of the adverse effect of the long period of construction on the rate of expansion of a particular industry.

With a given rate of investment in a particular industry, the number of establishments under construction is proportionate to the construction period. If this period is long, and the rate of investment high, the number of 'building sites' is so large that the existing highly qualified and experienced technical and organizational personnel cannot master them. If, in spite of that, the high rate of investment is maintained, the construction period becomes longer still, which results in freezing of capital rather than in accelerating expansion of the industry in question.

V

After this digression let us turn back to the determination of the industrial structure of the national income. Knowing the volume of productive and unproductive investment as well as of the increase in inventories; knowing moreover the volume and structure of consumption it is possible to make a rough estimate of the home demand for the products of the various branches of the national economy. This involves, of course, some knowledge of the technical coefficients of production with allowance for future technical progress and also some decision as to the choice of technological variants (about the latter more will be said at the end of the paper). Now, if the branch in question is a supply industry, it can be ascertained how much of its produce is left for export or how much is necessary to import. In the import requirements there will be also obviously included commodities which cannot be manufactured at home at all. This determination will have to allow for possible home produced substitutes for imported materials.

In this way the first approximation to the total demand for imports will be established. And after deducting from their value that of exports provided out of the surpluses of the supply determined industries it may be found how much is still to be covered by the exports of the demand determined industries. Now, the production of these industries must be fixed in such a way that: firstly, they should cover the home demand for their products; secondly, the total of their contributions to exports should cover the remaining part of import requirements mentioned above. The total of production of all branches of the national economy determined in this way is of necessity equal to the national income. For it covers the demand generated by the four major home components of the national income either directly or by providing for exports which are required in order to cover the remainder of that demand by imports.

At this stage of the argument it may be wondered whether a problem of equilibrium of the balance of trade really exists at all because it follows from above that the imports required are always automatically covered by exports if the total value of production equals the value of the home components of the national income. However, the equilibrium of the balance of trade arrived at in this way may be of no practical significance. It may be virtually impossible to place the exports in the foreign market at a scale corresponding to the export plans set out in a way described above. As a result of the pressure of the supply of the products in question their average prices may fall to such an extent as to make it impossible to achieve the revenue of foreign exchange required for purchasing the necessary imports. Or even if it is possible to achieve this purpose, it will require very high capital outlays in relation to the effect in terms of foreign exchange, and as a result it will aggravate the problem of the relative share of investment in the national income which, as said above, we imagine to be corrected for the deterioration in terms of trade.

If the country bases a part of its plan for foreign trade on long-term agreements, it will be again possible to place in these agreements only limited quantities of goods available for export. It should be noted, however, that long-term agreements have a considerable advantage over 'normal' trade in making at least a part of the plan for foreign trade independent of the changes in the international economic situation.

It is from the point of view of practical implementation that the plan for exports must be examined. If it proves unrealistic it is clear that the rate of growth has to be scaled down. It should be added that the scaling down of the rate of growth, while maintaining unchanged the development of supply determined industries, will contribute considerably to the restoration of the equilibrium in the balance of trade. For this will cause a relatively steep reduction in the demand for imports and possibly also a steep increase in surpluses of the supply determined industries available for export.

If, on the other hand, the plan for foreign trade proves to be fairly realistic, it is still necessary to ascertain the influence of the expansion of exports upon the capital outlays.

VI

Finally, before making an estimate of the necessary investment, the balance of supply of and demand for labour has to be considered. For this purpose a forecast of supply of labour based on demographic considerations has to be made. Moreover, on the basis of the industrial structure of the national income, the demand for labour is to be approximately ascertained allowing for the increase in productivity resulting from technical progress. It should be noticed that in estimating the demand for labour in agriculture the peculiar problems involved are to be taken into consideration. [See Kalecki and Rakowski, 1959, Reading 11 of this volume].

If the comparison between the demand for and the supply of labour leads to the conclusion that at the assumed rate of growth a labour shortage will be imminent, it is necessary to assume in the plan more mechanization and modernization which will, of course, again lead to higher investment outlays. It should be noted that this problem is less likely to arise in underdeveloped countries than that of the difficulties in balancing foreign trade.

VII

Now, having estimated the industrial structure of the national output and also being familiar with the impact that difficulties in foreign trade and possibly also the shortage of labour exercise upon the capital outlays – we can proceed with estimating again the total productive investment. This estimate may differ considerably from the first one made on the basis of a hypothetical capital coefficient. It may occur that even though it is within practical possibilities to achieve the equilibrium in the balance of trade at the assumed rate of growth the relative share of productive investment in the national income at which we arrive may prove intolerable. We have then to reduce somewhat the rate of growth and examine the new variant in the way described above.

The variant finally adopted should be distinguished by the highest possible rate of growth at which there is a realistic possibility of balancing foreign trade and at which the relative share of productive investment plus the increase in inventories in the national income is considered tolerable by the authorities from the point of view of the impact upon consumption and unproductive investment in the short run.

VIII

It has been mentioned above that in the course of ascertaining the demand for products of single industries generated by the home components of national income the problems of choosing between various technological alternatives will be encountered. As an example may be quoted the choice between electrification and dieselization of railways depending on the load of traffic on a given line. In order to settle such problems it is necessary to have a method for comparing the efficiency of two technological alternatives of producing the same final effect. Such methods have been in fact developed in Poland as well as in other socialist countries.

A similar problem arises in connection with various possibilities of earning foreign exchange by means of exports or substituting home production for imports. For the purpose of comparing various alternatives of earning one dollar in foreign trade there may be applied the same method as for comparing technological alternatives for achieving the same final productive effect.

It should be added, however, that the importance of such efficiency calculations for the determination of the structure of exports is reduced by two factors: firstly, the existence of supply determined industries, and secondly, the imperfection of foreign markets. Indeed, it is impossible to concentrate on the most favourable exports because the development of the production of the goods in question may be limited by technical or organizational factors; or because placing these goods in the foreign market is impossible in large quantities without reducing their price which would make invalid the results of calculation of efficiency of investment based on given world prices. In this way the planner who has made the most of the profitable exports must also put up with the less efficient export alternative.

It should be added that the calculation of efficiency should be applied as thoroughly as possible for the purposes mentioned above, and such is the case in Poland and other socialist countries. On the other hand, there is no point in applying them for anything else but the choice of technological alternatives or for the examination of the structure of foreign trade.

The structure of output in a planned economy cannot be determined apart from these two aspects by considerations of efficiency. Indeed, in an economy which would be closed and where only one method of achieving a given final productive effect were available, the calculations of efficiency would be out of place. For, as follows from the above argument, with a given rate of growth of the national income, a given relation between unproductive investment and consumption, and a given structure of consumption – the industrial structure of the output would be fully determined by the technical coefficients of production.

10 J. M. Montias

Planning with Material Balances in Soviet-Type Economies[1]

From J. M. Montias, 'Planning with material balances in Soviet-type economies', *American Economic Review*, December 1959, pp. 963–85.

The material balance is at the core of Soviet planning; it is the most operational (or bureaucratic) of all balances in the sense that all its elements – output orders, import and export quotas, inventory changes and allotments of materials to various consuming groups – hang on administrative decisions.

Until recently so little was known about the practice of central planning in the Soviet Union and in Eastern Europe that material balances and other 'balanced estimates' meshing the supply and demand for commodities and for factors of production were rarely discussed in Western economic literature.[2] But of late Soviet and

1. [Since the above article was written there have been some organizational changes in the Soviet Union. Thus the regional economic councils (*sovnarkhozy*), which were set up in 1957, have been abolished and the industrial Ministries recreated. These Ministries now have important functions in allocating many products, as well as in planning output, though several thousand key products are still allocated by *Gosplan*. The State Committee on Supplies (*Gossnab*) is responsible for operating the supply system and also plays an active role in planning the network of relationships between suppliers and customers. Consequently some of the detailed institutional description is no longer correct. However, the underlying principles of planning by material balances are still as they were when Professor Montias wrote his article. It is true that various reform proposals have been made, and that there has been talk of replacing administrative allocation of inputs by wholesale trade, which would involve purchase and sale untramelled by administrative supply rationing. However, wholesale trade of this type is still exceptional, though some progress has been made in the direction of long-term supply agreements under the *Gossnab* umbrella. Eds.]

2. A notable exception is a recently published book by Hirsch (1957). Useful information on the subject is also to be found in Granick (1954) and Grossman (1955). Levine's highly competent paper (1959) was published while this article was in the press.

Czech publications have become more candid about planning methods actually in use; while of course the Poles and the Hungarians, ever since 1955, have been less reticent than any other members of the Soviet bloc to expose their economic system to public scrutiny.

The structure of planning and of administrative organs differs in these various countries, and it has undergone a substantial reform since 1957 in the Soviet Union itself. Yet the task of elaborating a set of consistent balances presents the same basic problems in every centralized economy despite these differences: regional or industrial organs of the bureaucratic apparatus, whether higher or lower, are called upon to make economic decisions, the coordination of which, in the absence of markets and of flexible price system,[3] must be effected by matching the total demand for every major resource against its available supply at the highest level of planning. This is the role of the USSR *Gosplan* and of the Planning Commissions of the other Soviet bloc countries.[4]

The first section of this paper briefly describes the administrative framework of central planning in Soviet-type economies. In the second, I consider various procedures open to the central planners for approximating perfect consistency in building up a large set of interlocking balances. These theoretical alternatives are then compared with the information available about actual planning methods in the Soviet Union and in the other countries of the Soviet bloc. In the last two sections, the practical limitations of planning by the method of balances are brought out in detail on the basis of recent evidence taken from these economies.

3. Soviet economists are eager to mend their price system to improve economic accounting, but they have no intention at the present time of allowing prices to play a major role in allocating resources. After three years of lively debate, the Poles now seem to have reconciled themselves to the primacy of physical planning.

4. As of 1958, *Gosplan* prepared balances for ferrous and nonferrous metals, fuels, oil products, electric energy, chemicals, lumber and building materials, the main types of machinery and equipment, agricultural raw materials and the chief products of the light and food-processing industries (Karpov, 1958, p. 14).

The administrative framework

Material balances may be drawn up for short-run planning purposes (for a quarter or for a year) or as the foundation for the long-run plans (five years and upwards). The latter, called 'perspective balances', are not so operational as the short-term balances, since the long-term-plan output figures are subject to change and the requirements for materials (the outlay side of the balance) are only round estimates. The long-term plans, however, do mark out the course along which the socialized sector of the economy will travel, and they tend to hold good, barring major changes in policy, as long as no really troublesome obstacles supervene. However, 'shortfalls' due to forecasting errors on the credit or on the debit side of perspective balances may have repercussions on the yearly balances, which can only be 'closed' by cutting the output of certain branches of the economy short of their productive capacity.

The following procedure illustrates how the yearly plans for critical ('funded') products[5] were elaborated in the Soviet Union and in Poland, Czechoslovakia and Hungary before various – and divergent – reforms were put into effect in 1957 and 1958.

Some six to eight months before the beginning of the plan-year, the Planning Commission prepared preliminary balances of essential materials, taking into account the latest production figures as well as forecasts of productive capacity and labor force. Tentative targets ('control figures') based on these balances were handed down to the various industrial ministries, which subdivided them among their Chief Industrial Administrations (*glavki*). Each *glavk* in turn set specific targets for its subordinate enterprises, which were then expected to calculate the material inputs they would require to hit these production targets. The enterprise's material requirements, written up in formal applications (*zaiavki*), were transmitted to its *glavk* and eventually to the procurement organization of its ministry. At

5. 'Funded' products were essential materials (from planned or from above-plan production of socialized enterprises), which could be distributed solely by the Council of Ministers of the USSR. The most widely used raw materials and semifabricates were still funded in 1958.

every echelon, all applications were checked and their approved version consolidated with other applications. Each authority made sure that the material requirements corresponded both with the latest available output figures and with the established 'technical-progressive norms' regulating the maximum permissible expenditure of materials per unit of output.[6]

The ministry finally turned over its procurement plan (covering the material requirements of all its enterprises) to the Council of Ministers and to *Gosplan*. Simultaneously with this process, ministries, with the help of their marketing organizations and of their *glavki*, drafted more detailed production plans, modifying and complementing the control figures they had previously received. These plans were also submitted to *Gosplan*, whose specialized industrial departments were now charged with preparing material balances for funded commodities on the basis of these latest production and procurement data. The process of concurrent adjustment of the supply and demand for each balanced commodity ended with the 'closing' of the material balance – when the sum total of allocations earmarked for the various consuming groups matched the total supply from all sources planned for the year. Before all balances could simultaneously be closed, it was often necessary to go through most of this administrative procedure a number of times, on each occasion the relevant department of *Gosplan* or the ministry being expected to figure out the input requirements of subordinate enterprises from the output targets in the latest 'version' of the yearly plan.[7]

Once all the material balances had been closed and had received approval by the Council of Ministers, each ministry subdivided its global allotment of material inputs among subordinate enterprises (Eidel'man, 1953, p. 8). The latter, within

6. These norms or coefficients of output are fixed by special commissions for each enterprise. They must, in principle, be rigorous enough to guarantee that the enterprise will only maintain itself within their limits by dint of the most stringent economy. See p. 240.

7. In the later stages of planning, the input requirements of new output targets were usually calculated within the Planning Commission itself. (For certain limitations and exceptions to this basic scheme, see below, pp. 238–42.)

their appointed portions, communicated their exact requirements by size, type or make of the material to procurement agencies at various administrative levels. The detailed requirements were eventually transmitted to the marketing organization of the supplying ministry, which supervised the transfer of goods from selling to purchasing enterprises.

In 1957, as part of the reorganization of Soviet planning on territorial principles, most industrial ministries were liquidated and a hundred-odd regional Economic Councils (*Sovnarkhozy*) were charged with the concrete supervision of 18,000 enterprises, accounting for the bulk of industrial output (Koldomasov, 1959). Production and procurement plans instead of shuttling back and forth between *Gosplan* of the USSR and the enterprise along functional-ministerial lines were now made to travel along territorial lines – through the *Gosplan* of each constituent Republic down to the regional Economic Council. Transmission channels are now different but the procedure for building up and controlling procurement plans is still essentially the same as it was prior to the reform (Kaser, 1959).

Some Soviet economists argue that the reorganization will make it easier to coordinate plans from the center: *Gosplan* of the USSR will work on fewer balances (800 to 1000 in all). This reduction will be effected by grouping together many commodities formerly balanced separately. These more aggregated balances are supposed to account for a more complete coverage of industrial production than in the past, when nonfunded commodities were planned by ministries and their output was imperfectly coordinated with the rest (Koldomasov, 1959). In any case, it should now be possible to manipulate a smaller number of balances more flexibly and a more systematic effort can be made to reach over-all consistency.

Theoretical models of administrative planning

Let us first consider theoretically how all the balances can simultaneously be 'closed' with the labor force and resources available, leaving aside for the moment the problem of limited plant capacity.

We assume that the material balances form an interlocking set which can be arranged as an input-output table.[8] Coefficients are now calculated relating the amount of each material input needed for producing a unit of each of the different outputs and ordered as a square matrix, with as many rows and columns as there are balances. Since the balances are all expressed in physical units (e.g., tons of steel, thousands of tractors), the coefficients are 'technological' (e.g., tons of coke per ton of pig iron), unlike the coefficients in a Leontief matrix which express the costs of input necessary to produce a dollar's worth of output.

Let us suppose that certain final demands are communicated by the authorities to the planners for investment goods and construction, defense, consumer goods, exports and reserves. The gross output target for each good necessary to fulfill its quota of final demand plus any amounts required by other industries as inputs can theoretically be calculated by input-output methods.[9] In recent years, the Russians and their more advanced partners (the Poles, the Czechs, the Hungarians and the East Germans) have studied the use of systematic methods of input-output programming, but their attempts to apply these techniques have

8. In input-output terminology, our simplified balances look as follows:
resources   disposals

$$x_i = \sum_{j=1}^{n} a_{ij}x_j + y_i,$$

where x_i is the gross output of the ith commodity, a_{ij} is the technological coefficient showing the amount of x_i required to produce every one of n commodities, and y_i is the final demand for the ith commodity. There are n balances, one for each commodity.

A mathematical appendix to this section of the paper is obtainable from the author.

9. In general, for this to be possible, the matrix formed by subtracting the technology matrix from the identity matrix must have an inverse. It is not certain that such an inverse will always exist, since the technological coefficients are supposed to be drawn, not from the actual performance of the economy, but from engineering data; and it may turn out, by a freak of chance, that the total inputs required to produce a given set of gross outputs with the prescribed technical processes exceed these outputs. The system would then 'eat itself up'; no positive final bill of goods could be produced. It is only when the coefficients are calculated *after* the plan has been fulfilled, that we can be sure that the iteration process will be convergent. We may note in passing that if the technology matrix can be transformed into a Leontief matrix by a suitable change in units, and if every column of these new coefficients adds up to less than one, inversion will be possible. In this case, every product could be produced at zero or positive profit.

hitherto been confined to small-scale (highly aggregated) pilot schemes.[10] Up to now, no system of interlocking balances for the national economic plan has been 'harmonized', or made to 'close' by these methods.

Soviet planners, who apparently believe that an internally consistent plan can be framed by traditional bureaucratic methods, given any feasible initial conditions of final demand or of minimum gross outputs, envisage the use of input-output methods mainly to work out the ultimate effects of different 'variants' in these initial conditions. At present, the method of balances with its successive approximations to reach consistency, involves so cumbersome and time-consuming a procedure that an insufficient number of variants can be investigated, particularly in drafting long-range plans.[11]

But can the method of balances even lead to one consistent plan? The shuttling back and forth of targets, the groping toward a simultaneous 'closing' of the balances, suggests various iterative techniques, which, systematically carried out, would, in effect, invert a matrix made up of the technological coefficients and approximate full consistency in the output plan. Our task now consists in finding the iterative technique which most closely resembles the administrative procedures actually followed in Soviet-type economies.

We start again with our somewhat unrealistic assumption, namely, that the first set of output targets circulated to all industries consists of final demands only. On the basis of these targets, all industries producing end-products calculate their input requirements, which are then summed for the whole economy, and added to the original targets of final demand to yield first estimates of gross output. These estimates make up a second set of targets which again are sent around to the various industries. Input requirements are now revised upward in line with the higher targets. The old summation procedure is then repeated to yield second estimates of gross outputs. It can be

10. Articles which describe some of the basic research being conducted in the Soviet-bloc countries are: for the Soviet Union, Belkin (1957); for Poland, Porwit (1958) and Krzekowska and others (1958); for Czecho-slovakia, Červený and Vácha (1959); for East Germany, Schöhen (1957); and for Hungary, Bródy (1957).

11. Interview material.

shown that every new set of gross-output targets obtained in this manner would come close to the perfectly consistent set of targets that could be calculated by direct matrix inversion.[12]

An immediate improvement in this method suggests itself. Final demands are usually not a good starting point for the first iteration, especially if they represent only a small proportion of total production; therefore, gross-output targets adapted from the five-year plan or adjusted upward from last year's targets may be used, instead, to compute requirements of intermediate products in the first round. If these preliminary targets (the 'control figures' of Soviet practice) are not too far out of line with each other, the first iteration will yield larger, more accurate estimates of the 'correct' (consistent) output targets than by starting with final demand. The successive approximations starting from this arbitrary point should converge toward the same consistent set of gross outputs as before (Evans, 1956, pp. 53–102).

Are there any other shortcuts which would pare down the time required to reach an acceptable approximation? At least three come to mind: aggregation of coefficients, extrapolation toward more exact estimates and more 'efficient' routing of the control figures throughout the administrative system.

1. The principal advantage of aggregation lies in the possibility of restricting the iteration process to a smaller number of planning organs and of speeding up the entire procedure. In Poland,

12. Letting $x_i^{(1)}$ stand for the first estimate of any gross output, we may use the terminology of note 8 to represent the initial phase:

$$x_i^{(1)} = \sum_{j=1}^{n} a_{ij} y_j + y_i. \qquad\qquad 1$$

The second set of targets follows by repeating this procedure. Thus for the ith sector:

$$x_i^{(2)} = \sum_{j=1}^{n} a_{ij} x_j^{(1)} + y_i. \qquad\qquad 2$$

This expression can be expanded by substituting 1 into 2. Each subsequent set of targets can be derived from the preceding set and expanded in the above manner. The iterative technique described here is equivalent to the inversion of a Leontief-type matrix (formed by subtracting the technological coefficients from an identity matrix) by a power series. It is assumed of course that this matrix has an inverse, otherwise iteration will fail to converge toward *any* set of targets (Evans, 1956, p. 63).

for example, it is known that the last stages of planning a yearly program are all carried out within the Planning Commission itself, with the various departments of material balances (e.g., for metallurgy or for light industries) grinding out input requirements on the basis of aggregated coefficients (Porwit, 1958). In this way the material requirements needed to produce the various estimates of the gross output targets can be worked out much more rapidly – though less exactly – than if these estimates had to filter all the way down to the producing plants.

Aggregation entails a loss in accuracy, unless the input-output coefficients of every product in each consolidated group happen to be the same or unless the relative outputs of the individual commodities to be aggregated are expected to remain in exactly the same proportions for all variations in the final program (Malinvaud, 1956, pp. 195–200). American experience with inverting large matrices indicates that the loss of accuracy due to this cause is not so damaging as might at first blush be supposed (Morgenstern and Whitin, 1955). In practice, as we shall see in the next section, the worst losses due to aggregation probably stem from errors and omissions in the aggregation process itself.

2. Extrapolation: if the iteration process converges, then the differences between successive estimates of the gross outputs will tend to fall according to a constant ratio.

Let this ratio be called k. Then the planners could reach forward from, say, the third iteration to an ultimate approximation of the correct values of the gross outputs by computing the increase in the gross output of any good generated by the third iteration (compared to the second), multiplying this increase by the ratio of k to $1-k$, and adding the result to the output of the third iteration for this good (Evans, 1956, p. 74).[13] No such formal methods are used in Soviet planning, although the planners do seem to anticipate feedbacks by using their past experience and their planning 'instinct' to extrapolate the estimates of material requirements on the outlay side of their balances.[14]

13. Experience with the inversion of US input-output matrices has shown that four to five iterations *cum* extrapolation were sufficient to encompass at least 96 per cent of the true value of the gross outputs.

14. Interview material.

3. In this theoretical model of administrative planning, inefficient use has been made of the data generated at each step in the process. All the agencies and firms have computed their material needs from estimates of gross outputs corresponding to the *same* stage in the iteration process. It will usually be more advantageous to start the iteration process with industries producing mainly finished products and work back toward raw materials, making use at each stage of the gross outputs already generated. The advantages of this method are illustrated by the following example.

Let all industries be classified into three groups:

1. Manufactures.
2. Semifabricates.
3. Raw materials.

Suppose that the last two groups drew no inputs from any manufacturing industry, while raw material industries consumed neither manufactured nor semifabricated products. The matrix of input-output coefficients for these three groups would then be free of all 'circular relations' between groups.[15] The Planning Commission might be instructed first to calculate all the internal needs of the manufacturing group, add these needs to the final demand for manufactures and fix gross output targets for this group;[16] then use this target (together with the final demand for the second group) to work out the total needs for semifabricates. And, in the third stage, use both the gross-output targets for groups 1 and 2 to derive the target for group 3. These three steps would be sufficient

15. Letting a_{ij} $(i, j = 1$ to $3)$ stand for an aggregated coefficient relating any two groups, the matrix of these three industries could be arranged as follows:

$$\begin{bmatrix} a_{11} & 0 & 0 \\ a_{21} & a_{22} & 0 \\ a_{31} & a_{32} & a_{33} \end{bmatrix}.$$

A positive value for any coefficient above the diagonal of the matrix means that two or more groups are purchasing inputs from each other ('circular relation').

16. Note that the requirements of any group for its own products (a_{ii}) add a complication. The gross output target for the first group should theoretically equal the final demand for this group divided by $1 - a_{ii}$. But if the a_{ii} were small, the error involved in ignoring their higher powers would be negligible.

to provide the planners with a consistent plan for all three sectors. No further iterations would be necessary. The above procedure, which corresponds formally to the Gauss-Seidel method for finding the inverse of a matrix by iteration, would obviously save much time, provided that the technology matrix lent itself to its employment.

In practice, according to a Soviet economist interviwed, work on the balances starts simultaneously from 'both ends': balances are first prepared for industries turning out mainly finished products and for industries producing mainly raw materials. Inconsistencies come to light somewhere 'in the middle' as balances of intermediate products are reconciled with both raw-material availabilities and final demand requirements. This procedure probably reaps only a fraction of the computational savings of the Gauss-Seidel method.

In order to test roughly the effect of calculating gross outputs from final demands in a few iterations, the *Gauss-Seidel* method was tried out on the Rand Corporation's twenty-sector input-output matrix of the Soviet economy for 1941 (Kaplan *et al.*, 1952), rearranged so as to minimize the total value of above-diagonal elements.[17] In one complete iteration, approximately 84 per cent of the known value of the total of gross outputs was derived from the final bill of goods. Another iteration left 9 per cent unaccounted for. However, certain sectors with a small percentage of final demand to gross outputs – such as coal, peat, ferrous and nonferrous metallurgy – were still underestimated by as much as 30 or 40 per cent. By adjusting for the heavy internal requirements of these sectors,[18] and by limiting the next Gauss-Seidel iteration to just those sectors (using values already obtained for the remaining sectors), all sectors can be brought up to a minimum 85–90 per cent of the correct outputs. In practice, if sufficient reserves and inventories were available, and if the final demand for exports and for low-priority sectors offered a modicum of flexibility, the results might already be held satisfactory for operational purposes.

17. The above-diagonal elements were reduced in a few operations to 2·5 per cent of the sum of gross outputs. These elements could be brought down further by more trial-and-error reshuffling of rows and columns.

18. See note 16 above.

There is a strong presumption that better estimates could be made after two iterations if control figures of gross output were used in the first iteration, since some of the final demands amounted to only a fraction of gross output (e.g. 6 per cent in the coal industry).

In the long run, however, the case for iterative planning is not so strong. As a country develops, its products normally become more fabricated. Fewer products go directly from the mine or from the field to the ultimate consumer. The proportion of final demand in total output may be expected to fall. Once the industrial structure has become more complex, it should take more iterations to reach acceptable estimates of gross output whether we start from final demand or from any arbitrary starting point (Evans, 1956, p. 83). In addition, relations among industries consuming each other's products (directly or indirectly) are more likely to develop with time. Indeed, such industries as chemicals, paper products, ferrous and nonferrous metals, which account for a large share of the circular relations, tend to grow more rapidly than the rest and assume increasing importance in more developed countries (Chenery and Watanabe, 1958). These circular relations will have the effect of slowing down the convergence process for any method of iteration. In so far as the Russian economy conforms to these general trends in development, the Soviet planners are likely to get larger errors than in the past (for a given number of iterations). This in itself may help explain the recent flurry of Soviet interest in the application of formal input-output techniques to planning problems.

Up to this point we have assumed that gross output targets could be systematically derived from a neat bundle of final demands.[19] But it has been suggested by at least one observer of the Soviet economy that certain intermediate products might belong to a higher order of priorities than the end-uses they can generate.[20]

19. The use of 'control figures' as initial estimates of gross outputs, instead of final-demand requirements is only a convenient device to accelerate convergence. In the last analysis final demand still determines gross outputs and not the other way around.

20. In the Soviet Union, according to Gregory Grossman 'production targets for certain key intermediate goods are set by political decision. . . . These are . . . the goods which symbolize military-economic power and

Take for example, the 'leading links' of Soviet planning, sectors of the economy that were given top priority in order to widen bottlenecks in development. The yearly increases in the output or services planned for these sectors were not determined directly by their net contributions to the investment program, to defense or to private consumption; neither did they follow automatically from the nicely calculated requirements of other sectors for their products. The planning of these leading links had a profound impact on the entire program for the year – which may in certain cases have overridden planners' preferences for end-products.

Still this objection cannot be pushed too far: the ultimate decision-makers need not have a sharply etched preference map to tell whether they wish to see more tanks produced or more automobiles, whether they plan more investments in electric power or in dairy production; and the choice of gross-output targets does have a decisive effect on whether tanks or automobiles will be produced this year, and electric light or milk five years hence. The planners must eventually adjust gross-output targets to any strong preferences they may have for end-products. Moreover, as the quality of long-range planning improves and flagrant disproportions in the economy are gradually eliminated, hectic campaigns to build up top-priority sectors 'at all costs' should eventually yield to a more comprehensive approach to planning problems.

Capacity limitations in certain key industries also contradict the basic assumption of one-factor scarcity implicit in our iterative solution of an input-output program. It may actually wreck all our theorizing, for, strictly speaking, no program saddled with both capacity limitations and a limited supply of labor is susceptible of solution by input-output methods; and linear programming, which can handle this type of problem, has no counterpart in the planning of Soviet economies. Fortunately, only one not-too-far-fetched assumption needs to be made to bring us back into charted territory, namely, that the entire capacity of every capacity-limited industry should be used up. This implies that the planners will have to be content with just

independence in the mind of the régime: e.g. coal, petroleum, electric power, steel, etc. . . . ' (Grossman, 1955, p. 102).

those quantities of net output in the capacity-limited industries that will be left over after satisfying the internal requirements of the system and the final demands prescribed for the remaining industries.[21]

Economists of the Polish Planning Commission have recently analysed the problem of finding an input-output solution to such a program, in the belief that, for short-run planning, a 'mixed model' (with capacity limitations) would better answer practical needs than one where output in every industry was determined solely by its supply of material inputs (Porwit and Żurkowski, 1958).

An approximate solution to a mixed program can be found by iteration with even less effort than in the case where no capacity limitations have been allowed for. The planners may proceed as follows: they may calculate by iteration the gross-output requirements of the industries whose output is limited by their supply of material inputs (introducing the gross outputs of the capacity-limited industries only as a source of demand for inputs from the industries under consideration) and, once acceptable estimates of these gross outputs have been ground out, use them to calculate the residual net outputs of the capacity-limited industries. The iteration process can therefore be confined to sectors with a predetermined final demand, while data from the limited-capacity sectors need only be introduced into the balances after all the time-consuming calculations on the remaining sectors have been completed.[22]

21. That this is an assumption and not a necessity can be shown by the following example. Suppose industries A and B were capacity-limited and bought inputs from each other. Then the *net* output of A could be increased slightly by operating B below capacity, thus releasing some of A's intermediate products for final demand, which would otherwise be bought by B from A. This possibility is ruled out in the model that follows.

22. We again use the terminology of notes 7 and 11 for a three-sector model. It is assumed that the output of sector 1 (the capacity-limited industry) cannot exceed x_1. Final demand is known for the remaining sectors (y_2 and y_3). Our unknowns are y_1 (residual final demand in sector 1) and gross outputs x_2 and x_3. We call $x_2^{(1)}$ and $x_3^{(1)}$ our first estimates of x_1 and x_3, equal to $y_2 + a_{21} x_1$ and $y_3 + a_{31} x_1$ respectively. The second estimates of x_1 equal the first estimate plus indirect requirements amounting to $(a_{22} x_2^{(1)} + a_{23} x_3^{(1)})$. This sum expands to $(1 + a_{22})(y_2 + a_{21} x_1) + a_{23}(y_3 + a_{31} x_1)$. Further estimates can be obtained by repeating the same operations. Once

To conclude the foregoing analysis: the method of material balances is not inherently wasteful or theoretically unsound. It *may* lead to full consistency if the iteration process is carried on long enough and if the technical coefficients are accurate. Even if we knew that only one or two iterations were carried out, we still could not be sure that the method would lead to large errors; for the organization of planning and the nature of the technology matrix might be such that substantially correct estimates of gross outputs could be derived by its use.

Finally, attention should be drawn to the essential flexibility of iterative procedures. The technological coefficients need not all be transmitted to the Planning Commission. A 'control figure', or preliminary output target, may be sent to a ministry, to a *glavk* or to a regional Economic Council, depending on how industry is organized and on where it may be convenient to calculate the inputs to hit this target. The working out of input needs at lower echelons saves on the time and expense and on the errors in aggregation involved in bringing all the coefficients together in one place. It is conceivable that these savings might more than offset the increased cost of transmitting input and output estimates back and forth between the center and the peripheries.

A Yugoslav economist and former central planner has pointed out that trial-and-error methods for reaching consistency permit more *ad hoc* adjustments in the coefficients than the mechanical inversion of a matrix (Orthaber, 1956). Suppose, for example, that an increased final demand for aluminum hollowware and agricultural machinery has given rise to larger electric-power requirements than were originally planned. The full extent of the discrepancy has perhaps come to the attention of the planners only in the third 'version' of the program. The extra power must come from inefficient generating capacity with a high coal intake. The average coal-electricity coefficient can now be raised to take these new circumstances into account. And there is no

---

acceptable estimates of the unknown outputs have been reached after k iterations, the residual final demand of the first industry can be obtained as follows:

$$y_1 = (1 - a_{11})x_1 - a_{12}x_2^{(k)} - a_{13}x_3^{(k)},$$

where $x_2^{(k)}$ and $x_3^{(k)}$ are the kth estimates of x_2 and x_3.

need to start the whole programming over again – as long as coal output can be raised to the new required level.

Similarly, if the balances for certain key materials cannot be closed, substitution of other materials in more abundant supply may be enjoined on all producers by the Planning Commission, and corresponding adjustments in the technological matrix and in the production program may be made for further iterations.

The models compared with actual planning methods

In the models of the preceding section, a set of interlocking balances has been posited for all commodities: if aggregation had to be resorted to, it was not supposed to affect the interdependencies linking all the commodities in the system. This assumption will not bear scrutiny: in all the economies under study, a good many of the less important commodities were planned, balanced and distributed at lower administrative levels – sometimes even by the producers themselves, more often by marketing organizations.[23] These plans were poorly integrated, if at all, with the more fundamental balances elaborated in the Planning Commission and approved by the Council of Ministers. Furthermore, at all administrative stages, material requirements were consolidated along 'organizational' lines (by ministries or lower organizations named as 'custodians' of allotted funds) rather than according to the type of output which they would help to produce. Thus, prior to the reorganization of Soviet industry, total coal disposals in *Gosplan* balances were broken down by ministry, not by detailed use. (Only the principal commodities for which coal served as input, such as coke and steel, were typed out under each ministry in the Polish balances.) According to a Soviet statistician, though detailed data are collected from each producing enterprise on its consumption of materials (corresponding to the widest industrial classification in use), 'this extremely valuable material is neither summarized nor pro-

23. In 1954, out of 62 machinery groups or subgroups balanced by the Polish planners, 18 were balanced in the Planning Commission, 14 by the Central Agency for Machine Economy (CZGM); 3 by departments of ministries, 9 by central boards, 4 by procurement organizations, and 14 by marketing organizations (Piklikiewicz, 1954). Some, but not all, of those balances were integrated into summary balances drafted in the Planning Commission.

cessed' (Riabushkin, 1959, p. 368). It is evident, however, that the central planners must have at their disposal aggregated input-output norms for all commodities for which they wish to draw up a consistent plan by successive approximations.

In the opinion of Soviet experts, the organizational makeup of the balances also limits their use as a source of data for input-output programming; considerable expense would have to be incurred to fill the gaps by working up raw data furnished by enterprises.[24]

Summarizing some of these difficulties, the *Gosplan* economist Efimov complains that 'material balances . . . for individual products, not being integrated into a single system, solve only limited problems of intersectoral proportions' (Efimov, 1957, p. 108).[25]

This failure is particularly evident when changes must be made in the last stages of drawing up the year's program. Efimov remarks that, in view of the great expenditure of computational labor needed to rework the material balances, as well as the lack of time for carrying out this work, 'recalculations may be limited in practice to the balances directly affected by the changes.' These he calls 'first-order linkages' (e.g. the adjustment of the steel balance to an increase in the demand for trucks). 'Balances

24. The input-output team of the Polish Planning Commission has found an ingenious way of circumventing this difficulty by combining data based on 'product-organizational' lines (e.g. tons of coal per million zlotys of output of the ministry of the chemical industry) with detailed physical output data supplied by the different ministries and their subordinate agencies (Porwit and Żurkowski, 1958). The Czechs propose to develop a new industrial classification to make up their input-output tables and to collect the requisite data directly from plants for this purpose (Červený and Vácha, 1959).

25. Similar, but more detailed, criticism of the balances is to be found in the work of various Hungarian economists (for example Ausch, 1958). In a 1957 article, another Hungarian economist, Bródy, complained that statistical data available at present are not sufficient to prepare a detailed input-output table for industry as a whole. Differences in nomenclature among the various administrative organs are mostly to blame. No information can be had on 'products that are not easily measurable' (steel castings and forgings, some types of machines etc. . . .). Consequently, 'one is unable to find out what happens to over half of the output of heavy industry' (Bródy, 1957, pp. 138–9). These, and all the other Hungarian references in this paper, were kindly made available to me by Bela Balassa from his forthcoming study on the economy of communist Hungary.

related to the original change by second-order and especially by third- and fourth-order linkages are altered only where the changes are significant' (Efimov, 1957, p. 107).[26]

Nevertheless, if I may judge from the Polish example, a determined effort *is* made to achieve consistency at least for priority sectors, even if the balances have to be closed by cutting down allotments to lower-priority sectors. Two plausible courses of action for resolving basic inconsistencies in the master-plan can be looked into. First, the planners may meet deficits in the balances by calling for a reduction in the input-output coefficients of heavy users of materials in short supply; second, the allocation of materials to consumer-goods industries may function as a buffer which softens the impact of shortages on the other key sectors. Both hypotheses are partially valid but neither holds up under all circumstances.

1. The input-output coefficients the planners work with are already strained. Only a hortatory purpose can be served by decreeing their further reduction:[27] firms will have to make shift with the materials actually dealt out to them; if they exert enough effort toward reducing unit costs, they may still hit their output targets with lower coefficients. But they may just as easily exceed their allowances – especially if the quality of materials rationed out is below standards. This approach will not go far toward eliminating the trouble.

2. The quotas of materials earmarked for household consumption are sometimes cut; but these quotas already tend to be niggardly, since the original bill of consumer goods – low in the planners' priority scale – was already pared down to bare essentials. There is not much more 'play' here than in the producer-goods sector.

26. For further comments of the same nature, see Belkin (1957) and Ausch's remarks on Hungarian planning (1958).

27. In the stormy industrialization period of the early 1930s, systematic overcommitment of resources may well have helped to 'mobilize the masses' toward more strenuous effects to fulfill impossible plans. (Cf. the chapter 'Problem Solving, the Overcommitment of Resources and "Storming"', in Bauer, Inkeles and Kluckhohn, 1956. In the 1950s, the Soviet economic system seems to have moved away from these *Sturm und Drang* methods toward a tighter budgeting of resources. This trend is important in assessing the present Soviet search for more rational planning procedures.

It is interesting to note, in the case of Poland, that, from about the middle of 1954 on, the consumer-goods sector (of key industry) became the least resilient of all – after acting as one of the most elastic buffers in former years: an effort was being made at that time to regain the losses in real wages suffered in the first stages of the six-year plan, and if any element of demand had to 'give' when shortages arose, it was industrial construction and other investment activities rather than any consumer-goods industry.[28]

A minor component of demand to feel the pinch in certain cases is the 'pool' of materials going to producers' cooperatives and to private handicrafts. The beneficiaries of this pool – whether they produce consumer or producer goods – receive harsher treatment at the hands of the planning board than large-scale textile or food-processing plants by reason of their inferior social status and of the marginal nature of their deliveries in the total supply of most goods. It is apparently believed that ups and downs in the output of these dwarf producers (caused by their procurement difficulties) are less damaging than occasional cuts in the production of consumer staples by plants employing thousands of workers.

If exports are an essential ingredient needed for industrial growth – through the imports of raw materials that they make possible – then exports will be the last 'end-use' to be cut. This was apparently the case in Hungary. However, in Poland, exports of raw materials and semifabricates (including coal and rolled zinc) were frequently trimmed when the requirements of domestic industry and transportation could not otherwise be satisfied.[29]

There is no set of rules binding for every time and place to deal

28. This does not imply that the investment budget was greatly reduced – it was actually held at approximately the same absolute level as in former years – but it was thought expedient to maintain a certain level of output of consumer goods as an irreducible minimum, irrespective of the vagaries of planning.

29. In the routine planning of material balances in Poland, the officials of the Planning Commission earmarked for export those quantities of goods that could be drawn off from the pool of domestic allotments 'without prejudice to procurement needs at home.' The quantities exported of many goods ended up as a resultant item, 'left over after other needs had been met' (Rolów, 1956).

with shortages in the balances as they arise: consumer goods, investment projects, exports, or even the defense program may bear the brunt of adjustments, depending on the priorities of the moment.

Obstacles to accurate planning by the method of balances

The routine obstacles that stand in the way of accurate planning by the method of balances may be divided into two groups: 1. Failures in the transmission to higher authorities of information about the production functions of individual producers, and 2. Errors that come to light in the process of fulfilling the plan.

1. The knowledge which planners in *Gosplan* or the equivalent organization have of the relevant input-coefficients may be inaccurate for a number of reasons:

(a) Technical norms are often unrealistic to start with, since they usually assume a quality of material inputs and conditions of repair and maintenance of equipment which are not normally met in practice. They may also hinge on an above-average performance of the workers operating the materials-consuming equipment.

(b) Many norms at the plant level are ignored because the complexities of the production processes and the frequently changing specification of the products render them useless for planning purposes.[30]

(c) Due to rapid technical progress, it is not possible to keep all the norms up to date.

(d) The norms are often poorly aggregated even at the level of the enterprise – there are as many norms of coal utilization as there are furnaces and boilers in a plant (and there may be several plants in the enterprise) – but particularly, prior to the reorganization of Soviet industry, at the level of *glavk*. Only a few of the aggregated norms are systematically built up from their output-weighted components; in a majority of cases the planners make use of 'statistical coefficients' relating inputs to outputs

30. The complex factors bearing on fuel norms and the difficulty of working out usable technical-progressive norms are described in a Czech article by Tadra (1958).

for a group of enterprises in the most recent planning period.[31] (e) The relation between the output of a product and the consumption of materials for repairs and maintenance associated with its production cannot be predicted with accuracy. The quotas of materials earmarked for these uses are liable to a wide margin of error (Savkin, 1956).

(f) The output-mix of an industry is frequently so complex that materials needs can only be gauged in proportion to the gross value of output of the industry or of a group of products rather than for each of the products separately. In the Soviet Union, the material inputs of the construction industry are estimated as so many tons of bricks, cement or lumber per million roubles of construction. This is a highly unreliable method since the material-intensity of different stages of construction varies appreciably. (See Karpov, 1958.) In Polish industry, only about 60–70 per cent of total output could be planned with physical coefficients; for the rest, materials needs were geared to gross output forecasts and were to some extent distorted by the irrational elements in the prices that served as output weights for the individual commodities aggregated.

Breakdowns in the transmission of operational information cause still another source of errors in the balancing process. The correct material quota on the expenditure side of a balance depends not only on the output of its consumers and on their coefficients but also on the inventories of materials and goods in process these consumers may have on hand. Unfortunately, accurate data on these inventories are hard to get, not only for technical reasons – constant fluctuations, poor accounting methods, and the like – but because firms find an advantage in concealing their materials hoards to be able to claim higher rations.[32]

31. The technical difficulties of conveying usable information about production functions to the ministries and to the Planning Commission must be formidable when we consider that a single machine-building factory in the Urals turned over to its superiors 17,000 sheets of 'documentation' relating to its norms and to its actual consumption of materials. (See Gal'perin, 1958.)

32. Devons (1950) reports on the British experience with physical planning of aircraft production during the second world war, offering a vivid sketch of similar statistical deficiencies and of the mistakes they sometimes

The shortcomings of the norms might be alleviated if producing firms had a real voice in planning their inputs. But because firms tend to 'plan upwards' (inflating their requirements in expectation of cuts) and because it takes too much time and trouble to bring every firm into the laborious planning process, the contribution of producers to the drafting of material balances is often perfunctory. This has evidently been the case in Poland since 1954 when 'planning from above', as this short-cut method was termed, began to prevail.[33] In Russia, also, ministries did not always consult their subordinate enterprises in drafting their plans, particularly in industries with a highly diversified output.[34]

2. So many unforeseen contingencies may cause production and consumption plans to go awry in the course of their fulfillment that we can only list the major sources of disturbance.

(a) Changes in the demand for finished products ordered by the authorities during the year: political events – such as war scares – may precipitate short-run revisions in the investment program affecting the make-up of most material balances. If time is too short to elaborate a new consistent set of interlocking balances, then quotas earmarked for one purpose may be preempted for another without adjustment for the consequent indirect effects. This will upset the fulfillment of enterprise plans.[35]

---

occasion. Indeed, a good part of the book might apply to planning in Soviet-type economies.

33. See Stefanski (1955). Before firms were cut off from detailed planning, they had to rework their industrial-financial technical plans as many as ten times a year in response to changes suggested by higher authorities. To reduce excessive 'versionism', the instructions for the 1954 plan called for a maximum of independent planning by the Planning Commission and by the ministries – the first on the basis of the previous year's results, the second on the basis of technical data – with a final reconciliation of all projects in the last stage of planning. (See Zalewski, 1953). This arrangement seems to have been patterned after Soviet practice of the late 1930s. (See Granick, 1954, pp. 64–8.)

34. Eidel'man (1953) writes that 'when ministries prepare their applications for materials without the participation of producing firms, they are subsequently compelled to introduce significant corrections in their applications'. For further details on Russia see Gal'perin (1958, pp. 53–102) and on Czechoslovakia, Hejsek (1956).

35. A Slovak economist, writing in the official organ of the Czechoslovak Planning Board, remarks that 'the effects of foreign trade, changes in the

(b) The time-lag between the drafting of the plans and operational decisions is such that, for the first quarter of the year, most firms operate without any approved plan at all.[36] In the Soviet Union, special 'advances' of funded materials equivalent to the previous year's rate of consumption must be extended to consumers of materials pending receipt of final plans. (See Karpov, 1958.)[37] During this hiatus, there is a minimum of coordination, since with a high, uneven rate of growth in the different sectors of the economy, the structure of the economy's output is constantly undergoing changes which will disturb the balances of last year's plans. Even if the previous year's plans were all perfectly balanced, a projection of these plans into the next year, disregarding the increased capacity and the new needs for end-uses that have come up in the meantime, could hardly be consistent.

(c) Producers frequently fail to notify consumers of production breakdowns and, when their deliveries must be postponed, they present their clients with a *fait accompli*, leaving them no chance to find alternative sources of supply.

(d) Above-plan output, rewarded by bonuses to management, usually necessitates extra consignments of material inputs, which must either be deflected from other consumers (by administrative fiat) or made good by unplanned output somewhere else. Unforeseen increases in materials requirements by priority consumers, from this and from other causes too numerous to mention, call for a myriad of lower-level decisions which may or may not be in harmony with the central plan or, for that matter, with each other.

---

demand of private consumers, technical progress, natural events, and defects in the elaboration of the plan militate against the absolute inflexibility of yearly plans . . .' (Križan, 1956).

36. In Poland, the ministries and the Planning Commission started work on the coordination of the plans as early as May and June of the year preceding the plan year. Most of the work of formulating an internally consistent plan was supposed to be over by mid-September. (See Zalewski, 1953, p. 9.) Yet producers only received concrete directives by the end of the time quarter of the plan year or, in 1953 for instance, as late as May. (See Hatt and Karpiński, 1953.)

37. Polish enterprises operated during the first quarter on the basis of tentative plans submitted to the Central Boards of Industry in the fall of the preceding year – which usually differed substantially from later versions. (See Hatt and Karpiński, 1953.)

(e) Certain industrial consumers are allotted supplies from 'new production' of factories scheduled to be launched during the year. But it is difficult to fix an exact date for the start of full-scale operations in new projects. Consumers are therefore at the mercy of 'bugs' in the production processes of their suppliers. Shortfalls in deliveries will of course upset their own output plans with repercussions in the rest of the economy. This element takes on special significance in the first periods of rapid industrialization when each new plant put into operation may contribute a large proportion of the nation's output of a particular commodity.

What do all these discrepancies amount to? According to *Pravda* (10 August 1955), 31 to 40 per cent of all industrial plants in the Soviet Union failed to fulfil their annual plans between 1951 and 1954.[38] Even if a large number of plants produced over and above their plan, the chances are that differences in the location of the surplus-output plans and in the specifications of their products would make the latter somewhat less than perfectly substitutable for the products in deficient supply.

Disproportions in short-run planning are made good, in so far as possible, by the manipulation of reserves held by the planning board and by other agencies, or by fluctuations in the inventories maintained by producers and consumers. Inventories in the Soviet Union apparently have to be built up to higher levels than in capitalist economies such as the United States. (See Campbell, 1958, pp. 561–5.) But they still are not sufficient to cushion all disturbances in procurement; and production breakdowns due to material shortages remain a perennial source of complaints in all the centralized economies.[39]

Concluding remarks

This paper confines itself to the purely technical aspects of drawing up a consistent set of interlocking balances of material

38. In Czechoslovakia, according to a detailed breakdown for 1957 published in 1958, only 15 per cent of 1,429 enterprises covered in a survey failed to fulfill their production plan. (See Červený, 1958.)

39. These snags in procurement are chiefly responsible for the uneven rate of production in many plants (*nieritmitchnost*), which must slow down during certain periods while they wait for essential parts or materials and then must 'storm' the plan in the last ten days of the month.

resources. We have not related these balance sheets to the composite ('synthetic') balance sheets of money flows which are used, among other purposes, to equilibrate the aggregate supply and demand for consumer goods. Neither have we related *the short-term balances to investment planning or to plant capacity*. We have thus by-passed one essential function of the material balances: the detection of bottlenecks and their eventual elimination by suitable investments (in plant capacity, in equipment, or in the expansion of extractive industries, including geological prospecting).

This technical survey also fails to explore the relation between our limited 'ideal' of Soviet planning (the working out of a perfectly consistent program) and the static model for the efficient allocation of resources. In view of the fact that factor-mixes are endowed with *some* flexibility in many, if not in most, production processes, we might ask how the method of balances and administrative rationing are expected to reach an efficient allocation (where the ratios of marginal physical products of any two factors will be equated in every use). How can the most economical production processes be selected without any more refined knowledge of relative scarcities than the occurrence of surpluses or deficits in trial-balances? Can an effective price system be grafted on physical planning and help to resolve these dilemmas?

It will appear to some readers that these questions need only to be raised in order to be answered.[40] But before we become complacently critical, let us bear in mind that static efficiency is not the be-all and end-all of the art of planning. The Soviet system with all its compulsion and waste is a vehicle for high rates of growth. To some extent, a higher rate of growth than might otherwise be feasible makes up for short-run inefficiencies. These speculative remarks aside, my conclusions are levelled at a lower plane.

Whether or not the method of balances is, at best, inherently wasteful, there is vast room for improvement before this 'best'

40. Eucken (1948) in his illuminating analysis of German wartime planning supplied an unequivocal answer to our questions – 'it cannot be done.' Another West German economist, Hensel (1954, p. 134) argues that surpluses and deficits in the balances do give a sufficiently exact measure of relative scarcities. Hensel's contentions on this point are refuted by Hirsch (1957, pp. 25–6).

can be attained in the economies of the Soviet bloc. It is clear that achievement of the things the planners strive for, such as better technological norms, standardization, faster and more exact materials accounting procedures at the plant level, and more efficient processing of data at intermediate levels, must help to overcome some of the present weaknesses of the planning process.

For the purpose of improving the coordination of the plans, the Soviets may have much to gain from the studies of input-output programming being conducted at present by their own theoreticians. Even if they do not find it practicable to invert a matrix of coefficients with electronic machines within *Gosplan* – possibly because not all the coefficients can be brought together in one place – they may learn from studying their *tableaux économiques* how to devise a scheme of administrative iteration which will invert the matrix without shedding along the way any of the significant interdependences that link together the different sectors of the economy. If, moreover, the Communist planners, by resort to some form of linear programming, can contrive to find more economical input-mixes to achieve their goals, they will be tapping a new potential for increased power and growth.

References

Ausch, S. (1958), 'A népgazdasági mérlegrendszer néhány fobb problémájá' (Some problems of the national economic balance system), *Kozgazdasagi szemle*, no. 6, pp. 561–74.

Bauer, R., Inkeles, A., and Kluckhohn, C. (1956), *How The Soviet System Works*, Cambridge, Mass.

Belkin, V. (1957), 'O primenenii elektronnykh vychistitelnykh mashin v planirovanii i statistike narodnogo khoziaistva' (The application of electronic computers to economic planning and statistics), *Voprosy ekonomiki*, no. 12, pp. 139–48.

Brody, A. (1957), 'A nehézipar néhány fajlagos mutatójának alakulása' (Changes in some quantitative indices of heavy industry), in *A Magyar Tudományos Académia Közgazdaságtudományi Intézétének évkönyve* (Year book of the Economic Institute of the Hungarian Academy of Sciences), Budapest, pp. 134–55.

Campbell, R. W. (1958), 'Soviet and American inventory-output ratios' *Amer. econ. Rev.*, no. 48, pp. 549–65.

Červený, A. (1958), 'K rovnomernosti plnění plánu prumylové výroby (For the balanced fulfilment of the plan for industrial output), *Statistický obzor*, vol. 38, no. 2, pp. 49–52.

ČERVENÝ, A., and VÁCHA, J. (1959), 'Přípravy pro sledování meziodvětvových a mezioborových vztahů' (Preparations for the investigation of interbranch and intersector relations), *Statistický obzor*, vol. 39, no. 8, pp. 337–42.

CHENERY, H. B., and WATANABE, T. (1958), 'International comparisons of the structure of production', *Econometrica*, October, no. 26, pp. 487–521.

DEVONS, E. (1950), *Planning in Practice: Essays in Aircraft Planning in Wartime*, Cambridge, Eng.

EFIMOV, A. N. (1957), *Perestroika upravlenia promyshlennostiu i stroitelstvom v SSSR* (The Reform of the Direction of Industry and Construction in the Soviet Union), Moscow.

EIDEL'MAN, M. R. (1953), *Statistika material'no-teknicheskogo snabzhenia* (Statistics of Material-Technical Procurement), Moscow.

EUCKEN, W. (1948), 'On the theory of the centrally administered economy: An analysis of the German experiment', *Economica*, May and August, no. 15, pp. 79–100 and 173–93.

EVANS, W. D. (1956), 'Input-output computations' in T. Barna (ed.) *The Structural Interdependence of the Economy*, New York and Milan, pp. 53–102.

GAL'PERIN, N. (1958), 'Sovershenstvovanie material'no-tekhnicheskogo snabzhenia i borba protiv mestnicheskikh tendentsii' (The improvement of material-technical supply and the struggle against localistic tendencies), *Voprosy ekonomiki*, no. 7, pp. 43–56.

GRANICK, D. (1954), *Management of the Industrial Firm in the USSR*, New York.

GROSSMAN, G. (1955), 'Suggestions for a theory of Soviet investment planning', in *Investment Criteria and Economic Growth*, Cambridge, Mass., pp. 91–115.

HATT, S., and KARPIŃSKI, A. (1953), 'Doświadczenia z prac nad planami na rok 1953' (Experiences in working out the plans for 1953), *Gospodarka planowa*, vol. 8, no. 11, pp. 29–35.

HEJSEK, J. (1956), 'K zjednodůsení materiálně-technického zásobování' (Toward the simplification of material-technical procurement), *Plánovane hospodařství*, no. 7, pp. 550–9.

HENSEL, K. P. (1954), *Einfuhrung in die Theorie der Zentralverwaltungswirtschaft*, Stuttgart.

HIRSCH, H. (1957), *Mengenplanung und Preisplanung in der Sowjerunion*, Basel and Tübingen.

KAPLAN, N., et al. (1952), *A Tentative Input-Output Table for the USSR 1941 Plan*, Rand RM-924, Santa Monica.

KARPOV, P. (1958), 'Organizatsia i planirovanie material'no-tekhnicheskogo snabzhenia v novykh usloviakh upravleniia promyshlennosti i stroitelstvom' (The organization and planning of material-technical procurement under the new administrative system for industry and construction), *Planovoe khoziaistvo*, no. 7, pp. 11–19.

KASER, M. C. (1959), 'Changes in planning methods during the preparation of the Soviet seven-year-plan', *Soviet Stud.*, April, no. 10, pp. 321–34.

KOLDOMASOV, IU. I. (1959), *Metod material'nykh balansov v planirovanii narodnogo khoziaistva* (The method of material balances in national economic planning), Moscow.

KOLDOMASOV, IU. I. (1959), 'Voprosy organizatsii i planirovaniia material'no-tekhnicheskogo snabzheniia' (Problems in the organization and planning of material-technical supply), *Planovoe khoziaistvo*, no. 4, pp. 54–65.

KREMER, M. (1955), *A szállitási szerződések és a népgazdaság tervezés* (Procurement contracts and national economic planning), Budapest.

KRIŽAN, M. (1956), 'K otazkam zlepsenia a decentralizacie material notechnickeho zasobovania' (Toward the improvement and the decentralization of material-technical procurement), *Plánovane hospodařství*, no. 8, pp. 629–35.

KRZEKOWSKA, E., SZYBISZ, B., and ZIEŃKOWSKI, L. (1958), 'Tablice przepływów międzydziałowych i międzygałęziowych w gospodarce narodowej Polski w 1956 r' (Tables of intersector and interbranch flows in the Polish economy in 1956), *Ekonomista*, no. 1, pp. 98–118.

LEVINE, H. S. (1959), *Comparisons of the United States and Soviet Economies*, Pt. 1. Papers submitted before the Subcommittee on Economic Statistics, Joint Economic Committee, 86th Congress, 1st session citing 'The Centralized Planning of Supply in Soviet Industry" pp. 151–76.

MALINVAUD, E. (1956), 'Aggregation problems in input-output analysis' in T. Barna (ed.) *The Structural Interdependence of the Economy*, New York and Milan, pp. 189–202.

MORGENSTERN, O., and WHITIN, T. (1955), 'Comments' in *Input-Output Analysis: An Appraisal*, Studies in Income and Wealth, no. 18, pp. 128–35.

ORTHABER, A. (1956), 'Pitanje primene sistema tabela "ulaza-izlaza" kod nas' (The problem of adopting the system of input-output tables in our country), *Ekonomist* (Belgrade), no. 2, vol. 9, pp. 191–221.

PIKLIKIEWICZ, H. (1954), 'Metodologia i organizacja bilansowania maszyn i urzadzen' (The methodology and organization of drawing up balances of machines and equipment), *Gospodarka materiatowa*, vol. 6, no. 21, pp. 647–51.

PORWIT, K. (1958), 'Międzygałęziowa koordynacja planu zaopatrzenia' (Interbranch coordination of the supply plan), *Gospodarka materiałowa*, no. 10, vol. 10, pp. 337–44.

PORWIT, K., and ŻURKOWSKI, J. (1958), 'Niektóre specjalne przykłady możliwości zastosowania współczynnikow powiazan międzygałęziowych w planowaniu gospodarczym' (A few special applications of inter-industry coefficients in economy planning), *Prace i materiały zakładu badań ekonomicznych*, no. 14, pp. 1–43.

Riabushkin, T. V. (1959), *Problemy ekonomicheskoi statistiki. Analiz struktury narodnogo khoziaistva i vzaimosviazi ego elementov* (Problems of economic statistics. Analysis of the structure of the national economy and the interrelations of its elements), Moscow.

Rolów, A. (1956), 'Ulepszyć współpracę przy planowaniu i realizacji zadan eksportowych' (To improve the coordination between the planning and the carrying out of export tasks), *Gospodarka planowa*, vol. 11, no. 7, pp. 25–9.

Savkin, A. (1956), 'Zadachi uluchshenia material'no-tekhicheskogo snabzhenia promyshlennosti' (Tasks ahead in the improvement of industrial procurement), *Planovoe khoziaistvo*, no. 1, pp. 60–70.

Schöhen, Hans (1957), 'Die Rohstoffbasis der industrie der DDR' (The raw material basis of the German Democratic Republic), *Materialwirtschaft*, no. 21–4.

Stefański, S. (1955), 'Zasady planowania materiałów podstawowych' (Principles for planning basic materials), *Gospodarka materialowa*, vol. 7, no. 12, pp. 375–9.

Tadra, O. (1958), 'Otázky normování spotřeby paliv a energie' (Tasks in the setting of norms for the consumption of fuels and energy), *Planovane hospodařství*, no. 6–7, pp. 549–52.

Zalewski, K. (1953), 'Uwagi o sposobie opracowania narodowego planu gospodarczego w przemyśle' (Remarks on the manner of elaborating the national economic plan in industry), *Gospodarka planowa*, no. 4, vol. 8, pp. 6–9.

11 M. Kalecki and M. Rakowski

Generalized Formula of the Efficiency of Investment

Excerpt from A. Nove and A. Zauberman (eds.), *Studies on the Theory of Reproduction and Prices*, Warsaw, originally published in Polish in *Gospodarka Planowa*, no. 11, 1959. 1964, pp. 191–201.

Polish and Soviet discussions on methods of calculating the efficiency of investment have shown that some of the greatest difficulties are confronted here in connection with such problems as the 'freeze' of investment resources during the construction period, the different durabilities of plant and the uneven distribution of output and costs over time.

In particular the formula for determination of the efficiency of investment suggested at the June 1959 symposium was rightly criticized for inadequate treatment of these problems.

On the other hand, the suggestions (made at the symposium) to discount investment outlays, outputs and current costs at a rate equal to the average rate of growth of the economy do not solve the problem. They have no theoretical justification; moreover, they dissociate the problem of the reduction of current costs through higher capital outlays from that of the balance of labour force.

The present paper summarizes the results of a further methodological inquiry into the subject. The basic principle adopted is that two investment variants A and B are equally effective if investing by method A or B yields the same final effect in the development of the economy while preserving the equilibrium in the labour-force balance.

The simplest form of the formula for efficiency of investment

Let us consider first a highly simplified model of a national economy in which all the plant are built 'instantaneously' and thus the problem of the 'freeze' of investment resources during the period of construction is avoided. Moreover, let all the plant constructed have the same durability, say of twenty years; we can therefore eliminate the issue of different life-spans of plant operation. Finally, to eliminate from our model the problem of uneven distribution of output and costs over time let us assume that they are constant. Thus, the only remaining problem in this simplified model is the amount of additional investment outlays ΔI, which one is prepared to make in order to reduce the current costs by ΔK or the problem of the upper limit to the recoupment period T. As has been pointed out (see for example Rakowski, 1959) the value T should be chosen so as to maximize the increment in the national income corresponding to a given level of investment. There are numerous possibilities in the Polish economy of cost reduction through replacement or modernization of old equipment or mechanization of single processes at the expense of a moderate investment outlay with the recoupment period of certainly less than six years. Hence reduction of costs at the expense of initial investment outlays with a longer recoupment period would be wasteful. The condition for the choice of the more capital intensive alternative of the two variants yielding the same output may be now represented as

$$I_2 - I_1 \leqslant (K_1 - K_2)T$$

or

$$\frac{I_2}{T} + K_2 \leqslant \frac{I_1}{T} + K_1.$$

In other words, of the two alternatives the more favourable is that with a lower value of

$$E = \frac{I(1/T) + K}{P}. \qquad \textbf{1}$$

This is equivalent to the hitherto used

$$\frac{I + Iqn + Kn}{Pn},$$

where $q = 1/T - 1/n$. However, whereas this expression was considered valid for any life-span of the plant n, expression **1** assumes a standard period n_s (say twenty years). For periods other than the standard one the expression requires modifications discussed in the third section of this paper.

Influence of the 'freeze' of investment outlays in the course of construction

The fact that construction of plant takes appreciable time and the resulting 'freeze' of investment resources have an influence upon the efficiency of investment. It is evident that this influence is proportionate to the magnitude of the 'freeze' of the funds in the course of construction, i.e. to

$$\sum_0^{t_b} i_t(t_b - t),$$

where i_t is the partial outlay made at the time t after construction was started, t_b is the total construction period and $i_t(t_b - t)$ is the 'freeze' of the partial outlay i_t. Let us replace the above by In_z, where I is the total investment outlay and, therefore, is equal to:

$$\sum_0^{t_b} i_t,$$

whereas n_z is the 'freezing period' equal to the volume of the 'freeze' divided by total investment outlay. If investment outlays are evenly distributed over construction time, $n_z = t_b/2$; if they are concentrated at the beginning of construction, $n_z > t_b/2$; if they concentrated at the end of construction, $n_z < t_b/2$.

Let us now consider the impact of the 'freeze' of investment resources in the course of construction[1] on the economy. In our simplified model in which construction of plant is 'instantaneous' resources 'frozen' gradually in the course of construction would be at the disposal of the national economy for an immediate generation of output. Let q_z be the net national product generated per unit of investment resources per annum (the value of q_z will be presently discussed in greater detail). The yield of the partial outlay till the completion of the plant would be $i_t q_z(t_b - t)$. It follows that in our simplified model the total additional yield would be $Iq_z n_z$. In other words, as a result of the 'freeze' the outlay on the plant is – in relation to the simplified model – $I(1 + q_z n_z)$ rather than I. Thus, 1 assumes the form

$$E = \frac{I(1/T)(1 + q_z n_z) + K}{P}. \qquad 2$$

1. The argument that follows is based on the same approach as the paper of Kalecki (1959).

There remains the problem of determination of q_z, i.e. of the net national product yielded annually by a unit of investment outlays which in fact are 'frozen' in the course of construction, but in our simplified model with 'instantaneous construction' are 'harnessed to production'. Let us assume that these outlays yield a national product of an average sectoral pattern and let m stand for the capital–output ratio (this means that in order to obtain one zloty of the annual gross national product an investment of m zlotys is required). Thus gross product yielded by one zloty spent on investment is $1/m$ per annum and, allowing for depreciation of fixed capital at a rate v net national product is $1/m - v$ per annum. It would seem *prima facie* that q_z equals the difference $1/m - v$, but an essential corrective must be still introduced into our argument.

The point is that an increment of national product requires additional employment as well as investment. When the balance of the labour force is in equilibrium some investment outlay must be incurred in order to release elsewhere in the economy the required workers.

Thus, in order to obtain an increment d of the gross national product some investment as a substitute for the labour force necessary in the production of d is required in addition to the direct investment md. Let rd stand for wage cost corresponding to the increment d; assuming an upper limit of the recoupment period T the corresponding investment is Trd. Thus the increment d of the gross national product requires a total investment outlay of $md + Trd$, while the gross national product yielded by one zloty of investment outlay is:

$$\frac{d}{md + Trd} = \frac{1}{m + Tr}.$$

In other words, when the balance of the labour force is in equilibrium the annual net product of one 'unfrozen' investment zloty is

$$\frac{1}{M + Tr} - v$$

rather than $(1/m) - v$.

We thus arrive finally at the following formula:

$$q_z = \frac{1}{m+Tr} - v.$$

Assuming for Poland $m = 2\cdot5$, $T = 6$, $r = 0\cdot5$ and $v = 0\cdot03$ we obtain

$$q_z = \frac{1}{2\cdot5 + 6\cdot0\cdot5} - 0\cdot03 = 15 \text{ per cent.}$$

Modification of the formula for non-standard durability of plant

We have assumed so far that all the plant have the same standard durability n_s. Thus the formulae arrived at cannot be applied when projects of plant of different durabilities are compared. We shall now try to determine the correctives for output and costs which enable us to substitute a project of lifetime n_s for one with durability n.

Let us consider aggregate investment in the plant of a durability of n years. Let us suppose that investment of this type per unit of time grows at a rate a per annum and that the capital output ratio is m.

We assume moreover that m does not change over time. Thus if investment of the type considered maturing in a given year is J, then in the preceding year it was $J/(1+a)$ and $(i-1)$ years back it was $J[1/(1+a)]^{i-1}$. Thus the stock of fixed capital operating in a given year is the sum of investment carried in past n years or:

$$M_n = \sum_{i=1}^{n} J\left(\frac{1}{1+a}\right)^{i-1} = \frac{J\{1-[1/(1+a)]^n\}(1+a)}{a}.$$

Since the capital–output ratio is m the output from this stock of fixed capital is

$$F_n = \frac{M_n}{m} = J\frac{\{1-[1/(1+a)]^{n_s}\}(1+a)}{am}.$$

Let us now determine the output for an identical flow of investment in the plant characterized by the same capital–output ratio m but having a standard durability n_s. We obtain:

$$F_{n_s} = \frac{M_{n_s}}{m} = J\frac{\{1-[1/(1+a)^n]\}(1+a)}{am}.$$

Thus the same flow of investment results in a larger output if the durability of the plant is higher and the advantage from construction of the plant of a durability greater than n is shown by the ratio:

$$\frac{F_n}{F_{n_s}} = \frac{1-[1/(1+a)]^n}{1-[1/(1+a)]^{n_s}} = Z_n > 1.$$

The advantage would be highest in the case of $a = 0$, i.e. in the case of simple reproduction. Then $Z_n = n/n_s$, which means that with a greater durability of the plant and a given flow of investment the output grows in proportion to the durability n. However, under conditions of expanded reproduction, i.e. when the rate of investment increases continuously advantages from a higher durability are considerably reduced since (the smaller) investment volumes of earlier years exert a correspondingly lesser influence on total output.

Indeed if we assume a equal to 7 per cent corresponding to the actual annual rate of growth of productive investment in Poland, we obtain for $n_s = 20$ years the following values of the coefficient Z_n:

n (years)	5	10	15	20	25	30	35	40	∞
Z_n (per cent)	38·6	66·1	86·0	100·0	110·0	117·0	123·0	126·0	131·0

It will be seen that for a life-span twice the standard one, the increase in output is only 26 per cent and for an infinite durability – only 31 per cent. This shows clearly that in an expanding economy a greater durability of plant gives a smaller advantage than in an economy subject to simple reproduction.

Now let us imagine that we replace every plant of a durability of n years and capital–output ratio m by a plant of a standard durability n_s and of a capital–output ratio m/Z_n. Thus, if the capacity of the actual plant is P, the capacity of the imaginary substitute plant is PZ_n. It will be easily seen that in either case, actual or imaginary, to the same flow of investment there corresponds the same flow of output. Indeed the capacity of the actual plant is P and that of the fictitious plant PZ_n. On the other hand the same flow of investment yields in the case where the durability of the plant is n a flow of output Z_n times larger than in the case where the durability is n_s.

Obviously to a higher life time of plant there corresponds a larger flow of costs as well as a larger flow of output. To account for this factor we can follow an analogous line of argument as in the case of output, however, an essential modification must be introduced. Indeed, if the investment flow increases at a rate a per annum the aggregate production costs in the plant completed in a given year increase at a rate c per annum, c being smaller than a owing to technical progress, which reduces continuously production costs per unit of output. The same argument as in the case of output leads to the conclusion that to the same flow of investment there corresponds in the case of a durability higher than n_s aggregate production costs Y_n times higher, Y_n being determined by the formula:

$$Y_n = \frac{G_n}{G_{n_s}} = \frac{1 - [1/(1+c)]^n}{1 - [1/(1+c)]^{n_s}},$$

where G_n and $G_n{}^s$ are the totals of production costs for durabilities n and n_s respectively.

For $n_s = 20$ and $c = 3$ per cent the values of Y_n are as follows:

n (years)	5	10	15	20	25	30	35	40	∞
Y_n (per cent)	31	57	80	100	117	132	145	155	227

Following again the same line of argument as in the case of output, we can demonstrate that production costs in the imaginary substitute plant of standard durability n_s should be Y_n times higher. Thus if the costs in the actual plant of durability are K, then the costs of the imaginary substitute plant of durability n_s are $K Y_n$.

Therefore, if the durability of the plant considered is n years, its output is P, and its current production costs are K, then this project can be replaced by an equivalent of a durability n_s whose investment outlay would be the same, i.e. I, but whose output would be $P Z_n$ and costs $K Y_n$. Thus, the formula for efficiency of investment for the project of the plant of durability n assumes the form:

$$E = \frac{I \cdot (1/T)(1+q_z\,n_z)+KY_n}{PZ_n}.$$

This equation may also be written as

$$E = \frac{I(1/T)(1+q_z\,n_z)(1/Z)_n+K(Y_n/Z_n)}{P}.$$

The higher efficiency of investment in the case where durability of the plant exceeds the standard period is expressed in this equation by $I(1+q_z\,n_z)$ being divided by Z_n. On the other hand multiplication of current costs K by Y_n/Z_n (the value of this fraction is > 1) reduces the efficiency of investment. The latter reflects the loss caused by fixing the level of current costs for a longer period in the more durable plant, which circumscribes the opportunities for taking advantage of technical progress. Which of these two influences prevails depends on relative values of K and $I(1+q_z\,n_z)$. With a given proportion of K and $I(1+q_z\,n_z)$ there will be a certain value of n at which E will reach its minimum, i.e. the efficiency of investment will be at its highest level. Below this optimum n efficiency is lower because the gain in output through a longer period of the operation of the plant is greater than the loss through incurring the relatively high costs by using outmoded equipment. When n is above the optimum the position is reversed. It is clear that in calculation of the efficiency of investment n must be adopted at a level which minimizes E. Thus the formula 3 determines in fact the durability n of the plant as well. This is as it should be the durability being an economic rather than a technological parameter.

It should be noted that the rate of growth of output in the newly completed establishments a and the respective rate of growth of costs c – may differ for various classes of plant durability, i.e. for different values of n. In the absence of data on the subject as well as for the sake of simplicity we assumed uniform a and c namely 7 and 3 per cent for all durability classes.

Modification of the formula to account for the variability of output and costs during the lifetime of the plant

Let us consider again a flow of output yielded by plant of a durability of n years, where respective investment per unit of time grows at a rate a per annum. The formula obtained above for the stock of fixed capital in a given year is

$$M_n = \sum_{i=1}^{i=n} J\left(\frac{1}{1+a}\right)^{i-1},$$

where J stands for the rate of investment in that year.

We abandon now the assumption that output is constant throughout the lifetime of the plant. Let us divide the plant into classes according to the shape of time curves of output during their existence. We assume, moreover, that all the partial flows of investment corresponding to these classes show the same rate of growth. Thus, the above formula for the stock of fixed capital in a given year remains valid for each partial flow of investment. (Now J will be the investment in that year and M the stock of fixed capital in that year related to the partial investment flow.)

Let us now find the output generated by the partial investment flow in a given year. Let w_i stand for the ratio of the output of plant in the year i of its life to the value of its fixed capital. In a given year the output of the plant, completed $i-1$ years back is characteristic for the year i of their existence. Thus the output of the plant completed $i-1$ years back is determined by the expression

$$J\left(\frac{1}{1+a}\right)^{i-1} . w_i.$$

Consequently, the formula for the output generated by a partial flow of investment considered (characterized by a given distribution curve of output over the time of existence of the plant) is:

$$F_n = \sum_{i=1}^{=n} J\left(\frac{1}{1+a}\right)^{i-1} . w_i.$$

Now let us suppose that the same amount of the output F_n is obtained from the same flow of investment with a constant w. We then obtain:

$$\sum_{i=1}^{i=n} J\left(\frac{1}{1+a}\right)^{i-1} . w_i = \sum_{i=1}^{i=n} J\left(\frac{1}{1+a}\right)^{i-1} . w_{const.},$$

where $w_{const.}$ may be called the equivalent of the sequence w_i. It follows from this formula that

$$w_{const.} = \sum_{i=1}^{i=n} J \left(\frac{1}{1+a} \right)^{i-1} . w_i : J \frac{\{1-[1/(1+a)]^n\}(1+a)}{a}.$$

Now only one more step is necessary in order to reduce the case in which output varies in the course of the life-span of the plant to one with constant output. Let us replace every plant having a specified uneven output distribution by another plant involving the same investment outlay but with a constant output of the volume

$$P_{const.} = \sum_{i=1}^{i=n} P_i \left(\frac{1}{1+a} \right)^{n-i} : \frac{1-[1/(1+a)]^n(1+a)}{a}.$$

We now see that the imaginary substitute plant yields the same flow of output as the actual plant. In this way the last formula determines the volume of constant output as an equivalent of variable output. This formula is based on the assumption that the partial flows of investment corresponding to the different types of output distribution over time maintain a constant relative share in the total flow of investment, and thus it is merely an approximation to reality. (The assumption involved is analogous to adopting the same a for various durability classes of plant in the preceding section.)

A similar argument can be applied to costs varying in the course of the existence of the plant. We shall obtain for the equivalent of variable costs the following formula:

$$K_{const.} = \sum_{i=1}^{i=n} K_i \left(\frac{1}{1+c} \right)^{i-1} : \frac{\{1-[1/(1+a)]^n\}(1+c)}{c}.$$

We may now generalize the formula for the efficiency of investment in order to account for the variation of output and costs during the life-span of the plant by substituting $P_{const.}$ and $K_{const.}$ as determined by the above formulae for P and K. We then obtain:

$$E = \frac{J(1/T)(1+q_z n_z) + K_{const.} \ Y_n}{P_{const.} \ Z_n}. \qquad 4$$

This formula for the efficiency of investment accounts for the 'freeze' of capital in the course of construction, for the durability

M. Kalecki and M. Rakowski 261

of the plant being different from the standard one and for the variability of output and costs over time.

It should be emphasized that we regard the formulae arrived at here as no more than a better approximation to the complex economic reality than those now in use, rather than as a final solution of the problem.

References

KALECKI, M. (1959), 'O współczynniku zamrozenia' (On the coefficient of freezing), *Ekonomista*, no. 1.

RAKOWSKI, M. (1959), 'Maksymalizacja wzrostu gospodarczego a oprocentowanie nakladów' (Interest on investment outlays and maximization of economic growth), *Gospodarka planowa*, no. 10.

12 J. Robinson

Consumer's Sovereignty in a Planned Economy

Excerpt from *On Political Economy and Econometrics: Essays in Honour of Oskar Lange*, Warsaw, P.W.N., 1964, pp. 513–21.

Orthodox academic economic theory in the West is based upon the presumption that the system of prices that would obtain in ideal conditions of atomistic competition guarantees the rational use, for the benefit of society as a whole, of 'scarce means with alternative uses'. In its own capitalist setting there are formidable objections to this claim, which the orthodox theory has never succeeded in meeting. The fact that private property in the means of production, combined with rights of inheritance, produces a totally irrational distribution of purchasing power within society undermines the whole conception. There are also more technical objections. Something like atomistic competition does prevail in the markets for certain primary commodities. For these, both demand and supply are very inelastic in the short run, so that slight changes in market conditions bring about violent swings in prices, often exaggerated rather than restrained by speculation. And long-run movements in the terms of trade, affecting the livelihood of whole nations, are admitted by all but the most fanatical of *laissez-faire* economists to be a serious blemish in the market system. On the other hand, in manufacturing industry, nothing like ideal competition prevails. 'Administered prices', fixed by the seller, are the rule and quasi-monopolistic conditions are universal.

Nowadays, therefore, it is fashionable to argue that the true sphere of operation of the rational price system is in the planned economies. Where there is no income from property and everyone's earnings are what it is considered right that he should have, the major objection to the market system does not apply. The defective foresight which causes the vagaries of commodity markets and the monopoly power of manufacturers does not exist in a planned economy. There the market, it is argued, could be made to behave *as though* ideal competition prevailed.

In what follows this argument is examined, not from the point of view of trying to extract useful hints for practical planners, but rather from the point of view of its basic philosophy which was once a favourite theme of Oskar Lange's (1938).

I

In old-fashioned orthodox theory, the price that a buyer is willing to pay for a commodity measures its *marginal utility* to him. This notion has been so much refined by modern criticism that precious little is left of it. But there is a solid justification for the market as a method of distributing consumer goods in the fact that it regulates itself. The task of choosing what to buy is thrown onto the consumer, and he, or rather she, feels this not to be a burden but a pleasure and a privilege. Moreover the system needs no police. A black market cannot exist when every commodity is rationed by its price. No doubt there is great scope for educating taste; it is necessary to safeguard the interests of children; consumption of some commodities (motor cars, for instance) imposes external diseconomies on other consumers, and so forth. But, by and large, the freedom of the consumer to spend his money as he chooses may be accepted as the basis of the concept of a rational price system.

Given the volume of money incomes being earned, allowing for personal saving, the overall level of prices in the planned economy has to be such that the total value of goods and services sold to the public is equal to the total purchasing power being spent. Shortages appear when prices have been set too low, and accumulation of stocks when they have been set too high. Since the value of commodities sold is absorbing the purchasing power earned by the whole labour force, including those whose income is derived from administration, the armed forces etc., and from investment, the surplus received from the sale of commodities over their own cost of production is just what is required to pay those other incomes.

To enjoy the advantage of the self-regulating market system it is not sufficient to achieve this overall balance. It is also necessary that the pattern of prices within the total should be such that demand corresponds to supply in every market. This, no doubt, is easier said than done. But something approximating to it has been arrived at in the planned economies by means of differential rates of turnover tax. The principle is that prices should reflect scarcities in the manner depicted in the Walrasian general equilibrium system.

Let us accept this for the sake of argument and see what it implies.

The claim that is made for the imitation market system is at two levels. First, that it indicates the correct plan for production – the plan that ensures that the maximum benefit is enjoyed from given resources. Second, that it promotes efficiency by permitting the devolution of decisions. On both levels, it is argued, the best results will be achieved if individual enterprises are instructed to behave like capitalists in the text books, that is, to strive to maximize profits from moment to moment.

The first point to observe is that, for the system to achieve the results claimed for it, the enterprises must not be given freedom over the prices at which they sell. The drawbacks of endowing socialist enterprises with the powers of capitalist monopolies are obvious enough. (They have been experienced to some extent in Yugoslavia.) But competition also has drawbacks. There would be no point in introducing the hog cycle into a socialist economy. Walras himself admitted the instability of competition, though in a backforemost way. He makes his traders find the equilibrium pattern of prices by shouting – everyone declares his offers and demands before any actual dealing takes place. This certainly is a useful hint. The proper procedure is for the price-fixing authority on the one side to estimate demands, and on the other to enquire from the enterprises what quantities of various products they could supply at what prices, thus working out the short-period supply and demand curves for the various commodities. Then the appropriate prices must be given to the enterprises. In the text book competitive system, price is given to the individual seller and his business is to produce, with maximum efficiency, the quantity whose marginal cost is equal to that price. The whole beauty of the system is lost if the seller can manipulate the price.

But what determines costs? There is a very radical difference between capitalist costs and socialist costs. To a capitalist enterprise, wages are the main element in costs. A rise in the wage rate in terms of his own product is a rise in costs. 'The more there is of mine, the less there is of yours'. In a socialist economy, the wage is the medium through which each individual draws his share of the social product. Once full employment has been achieved, labour power is a scarce resource and labour-time, not wages, is the basic cost. It is necessary to reconcile the cost of labour-time which an enterprise must pay with the wage regarded as a social dividend which the worker receives. This must be done by finding out the demand curve for labour. The enterprises must be instructed to offer employment up to the point where the net addition to proceeds (selling prices being given) from employing an additional team of workers is not less than the additional cost of labour, allowing for other prime costs, which we will discuss in a moment.

In the planned economy investment is absorbing a large proportion of national income, and the general expenses of government, defence and social services are also collected from the proceeds of industry. Overall profit margins (the excess of selling value of goods sold to the public over their own wage bill) are therefore high. If labour were supplied to the enterprises at the wage actually paid to the worker, (assuming that full employment has been achieved) there would normally be a large excess of demand, on the above reckoning, over the supply available to the commodity sector. Therefore the enterprises must be charged a pay-roll tax. The level of the tax is such as to bring the demand for labour of the enterprises into line with the available supply. This ensures that labour is nowhere being used to make a lower contribution to the value of output if it could be transferred to another enterprise where it would make a large contribution – in orthodox language, the short-period marginal productivity of labour is everywhere equal, and is equal to the cost per man-hour to the individual enterprise of employing labour.

An important part of the costs of an individual enterprise are materials and power, and the most important function of the pricing system is to allocate supplies of scarce resources to the most needed uses. To fulfil the prescriptions of the orthodox system a pseudo market has to be organized at which suppliers declare the amounts of each commodity that they would make available at different prices (after the armed forces etc. have requisitioned their share) when following the rule that marginal costs must not exceed marginal proceeds. The fabricating enterprises put in their bids on the same principle. Notional prices are lowered and raised until a fit is obtained in each market, and actual transactions then proceed. By this means every material is steered to the point where its comparative advantage is greatest. The bids of the electrical industry for copper set a price at which aluminium is preferred for kitchen ware. Leather may be absolutely better than cloth for making suitcases, but is better by more for making shoes; and so forth.

The whole system of final and intermediate prices and the payroll tax have to be worked out by a system of simultaneous equations (in effect, the Walrasian general equilibrium system), put into operation, and corrected by experience from month to month.

When marginal costs are everywhere equal to prices, large differences appear in the excess of total proceeds over total costs for different enterprises depending on the one hand upon the productivity of the equipment that each possesses, and the scarcity relative to demand of the particular commodities that it is suited to producing, and on the other hand upon the efficiency with which it is operated. It is clearly undesirable that profits should be easier to make in one enterprise than another. Each should therefore be charged a rent calculated so as to absorb the whole surplus over costs – the quasi-rent – due to the natural advantages of the particular enterprise. Then, squeezed between fixed prices and fixed costs, the manager of the enterprise must strive to maximize his surplus profit at zero by operating with perfect efficiency.

This is certainly an austere ideal. We are not here concerned to enquire what approximation to it might be feasible in a planned economy. The point of the present argument is only that *this* is the orthodox prescription.

If individual enterprises are permitted to fix prices, the evils of imperfect competition would creep into the system. Trial-and-error competition sets up cycles. A system of prices proportional to *values*, that is, a system in which the whole surplus is collected by the payroll tax, would generate chronic shortages and surpluses, since the pattern of supply would be quite unrelated to the pattern of demand. A system in which enterprises are charged interest on the investment sunk in their equipment, instead of rent reflecting its earning power, would make surplus profits too easy to earn in some and too hard in others.

The advantages claimed for the market system could, in principle, be realized only if prices, reflecting scarcities relative to demand, are given to the producers, and costs are adjusted to them.

Now that the socialist economists are discussing the uses of an imitation market system as a means of decentralizing control, it is important to consider wherein the virtue of the market system is supposed to lie.

II

The foregoing concerns the allocation of *given* resources between alternative uses. The orthodox system is most at its ease in a stationary state. Its treatment of accumulation has never been very satisfactory.

There are two ways in which the Walrasian system can be interpreted. In one model, individuals own means of production and possess the knowledge appropriate to particular lines; they trade their products with each other – in short it is an artisan economy. There may be a general rate of interest formed by the supply and demand for present purchasing power against future purchasing power; the individual producer then invests in his own business – the blacksmith in a forge, the weaver in a loom – when his estimate of the rate of return exceeds the rate of interest. This model is clearly of no use for discussing the problems of modern industry.

The other interpretation of the Walrasian scheme makes all owners of means of production perfectly versatile, so that each invests in the type of equipment which promises the highest rate of return.

At any moment, supply-and-demand prices rule for the commodities being produced. The wage rate in terms of any commodity, say bread, is such that it pays the owners of stocks of productive equipment – let us call them machines for short – to employ all the available labour. Various kinds of machines are yielding various returns in excess of operating costs (quasi-rents). With the gross incomes being enjoyed and the prospective profit on investment (which we shall discuss in a moment) there is a certain gross amount of saving which individuals propose to do. Saving is devoted to buying machines to maintain and increase productive capacity.

How is the prospective rate of profit determined? As investment goes on, the pattern of prices will change and the quasi-rents of various machines will alter. If investment is guided only by current quasi-rents, mistakes will be made. To present the model as a guide to the efficient use of resources, the orthodox theory has to postulate correct expectations about future prices. Given expected future prices and wage rates, the future quasi-rents in terms of bread of each kind of machine can be calculated. The rate of return on investment is then the rate of discount which reduces the future quasi-rents to equality with the present cost of the investment in terms of bread.

What governs the present cost? There must be somewhere in the system machines which can produce machines (including themselves). At any moment there is a limited capacity for producing machines, which is being fully utilized. The relative prices of different kinds of machines must be such that each offers an equal quasi-rent per unit of machine-making capacity; the overall bread-price level of newly-produced machines is the total volume of saving, say per annum, in terms of bread, divided by the annual output of machines. The savers order the type of machines which promise the highest rate of profit. The rate of profit is the rate of discount that reduces the expected future quasi-rents per machine (which are supposed to be correctly foreseen) to equality with its present cost. Thus the price of machines, like all other prices, is settled by supply and demand; the rate of return on investment measures the scarcity of equipment relatively to the demand for it, the demand for it being the rate of saving that individuals, taken together, want to carry out.

Here is a serious weakness in the orthodox scheme. It is impossible to regard this rate of saving as representing the 'will of society' in a sense which gives it authority. The amount of saving must be supposed to be strongly influenced by the distribution of income and wealth between families, which in this model is completely arbitrary. Moreover savings decisions are made by mortal men whereas 'society' must conceive itself to be perpetual.

If these objections could be met, a worse remains. The model is intended to depict a process of 'deepening' the structure of capital. To take the simplest case, technical knowledge is given and the labour force is constant. Accumulation is improving equipment per man and raising output per head. The capital/output ratio in value terms is rising. Labour is continually being released to man more productive equipment by raising the bread-wage rate to a level that less productive equipment can no longer pay. As time goes by, the rate of return on further investment falls. The faster accumulation takes place, the faster the wage rate rises and the faster the rate of profit falls. It seems that the benefit to 'society' from saving is not properly reflected in the 'reward' to the savers. How then does 'society' secure that the optimum amount of saving takes place?

Conceding that the overall rate of saving must be a political decision, (represented by a 'social welfare function' which tells us no more than that the authorities prefer whatever plan they have decided to carry out) the orthodox argument falls back upon the position that, whatever rate of saving the planners decide upon, it is still true that the pattern of investment should follow the rule of maximizing the rate of return from year to year.

Is this a helpful rule? Even with up-to-date techniques of computation, it would clearly be impossible for a planner to work out the infinitude of conceivable paths of development and calculate which yields the highest rate of return. Starting from supplies available today, he must pick out one or two paths that seem sensible, and choose between them. The relative scarcities, reflected in current quasi-rents, would no doubt be useful data, but he cannot be automatically guided by the pattern of current profits. Future demands, as supplies are increased, will form an integrated pattern. He cannot foresee demand, for instance, for household gadgets unless he foresees a supply of domestic power. He cannot foresee the demand for sea-side hotels unless he foresees the length of holidays. There is no way in which he can declare the pattern of future prices and then allow the pattern of investment to work itself out on the basis of maximizing profits. The pattern of investment and the pattern of future prices have to be worked out in a single operation.

The reason why the orthodox argument fails to be useful is that it is founded on a contradiction. Atomistic competition and correct foresight are irremediably irreconcilable. Competition finds out the equilibrium position by a process of *tâtonnement*, that is, by trial and error. To find the equilibrium price of fresh eggs in the village market, it may work well enough. But where long-lived investments are involved, it is excessively wasteful. For investment, Walras' process of shouting offers and demands corresponds to working out plans on paper, and iterating calculations until a fit is achieved. Once the fit has been found, the plan must be put into operation as a whole. Each individual enterprise has to accept its part in the scheme. Errors have to be corrected on paper, not embodied in bricks and steel before they are found out. No doubt, in the best of plans, gross errors occur, but they cannot be avoided by simulating competition.

III

The orthodox theory claims to settle the question of the effectiveness of investment – that is the choice of technique for producing a given future output (say, hydro versus thermal power stations) in a very simple manner. We only need to know the future cost of labour in terms of the product and the rate of interest that measures the present scarcity of capital. Discounting future quasi-rents at that rate, we calculate which investment has the higher present value.

The association of the rate of interest with capitalist exploitation has made socialist planners shy of using it. And, as we have seen, the rate of return which emerges from the Walrasian model has no particular authority. Yet the notion of a 'cost of waiting' has a commonsense meaning in a planned economy. When output is growing, there is a technical superiority of present over future resources, because present resources can be invested to increase future productivity. Thus the growth rate of the economy itself measures the cost of waiting. Any one investment, to justify itself, must show a rate of return at least as good as the average. When industrial output is going to maintain, over the life-time of the investment, a rate of growth of, say, ten per cent per annum, then an additional cost today, for instance for the hydro rather than the thermal installation, must show a saving on future running costs of at least ten per cent per annum on the initial outlay if it is to be justified.

On top of this there may be also a political 'cost of waiting' if the authorities prefer to offer the public a smaller rise in the standard of life in the near future rather than a greater one later on, for fear that they may grow tired of waiting meanwhile. On the other hand engineers have a bias in favour of capital intensive techniques, and argue for a low enough rate of interest to justify them.

The orthodox theory is on strong ground in claiming that the concept of a rate of interest simplifies the calculation of the effectiveness of investment, but it does not settle the question of what the rate of interest ought to be.

IV

The orthodox model is working towards a horizon at which the 'deepening' process will have been completed. Accumulation will then be required only for 'widening' the capital structure – that is, providing equipment, at the level already attained, for a growing labour force or implementing the potential growth of output per head due to technical progress. No one kind of product will be more scarce than any other.

A proposition which has lately been added to the orthodox canon[1] states that the optimum conditions obtain when the rate of profit on capital is equal to the rate of growth of output, which entails that consumption is equal to the wage bill.

The argument is as follows. In conditions of long-period competitive equilibrium, the individual enterprise carries investment per man employed to the point where the marginal productivity of capital is equal to the rate of profit. The marginal product from equipping an addition to the effective labour force at the average level is the addition to output that it makes possible. Thus the marginal productivity of 'widening' investment is identical with the growth rate. So long as the rate of profit exceeds the growth rate, 'deepening' investment increases future consumption. The

1. See Robinson (1962).

maximum maintainable rate of growth of national income is attained when the marginal productivities of 'widening' and 'deepening' are equal, that is, when the rate of profit is equal to the rate of growth.

Does this hold any moral for a planned economy in some ultimate state of economic bliss? It never seemed reasonable to think of goods being given away free under communism. Even under communism, current production must be carried on, and when I consume commodities I am consuming my neighbours' labour time. Surely the consumer should pay for the labour that goes into each product, so that his own labour time (his earnings) exchanges at a fair rate with everyone else's? It seems reasonable also that the consumers of any commodity should pay for the up-keep and expansion of the equipment required to produce it. This would be achieved if all prices were set at such a level as to yield the same rate of profit on all investments. But the surplus collected from consumers in the prices of commodities does not pay only for investment. It is required also to cover the over-heads of government and social services (let us hope that by the time communism has been reached defence will no longer be a large item). There does not seem to be any logic in charging these costs *pro rata* to capital invested. It would seem appropriate to recover them from a pay-roll tax, which would enter into all prices in proportion to prime costs.

But this is day-dreaming. Meanwhile the problem of pricing under scarcity remains to be solved.

V

If the foregoing argument is correct, proposals to relieve the burden on centralized planning by giving autonomy to the individual enterprise in respect to prices, the product mix or investment, are misconceived. Yet some kind of devolution is evidently necessary. Overall investment plans must continue to be made centrally to secure a fit, but as the standard of life rises the rigidity of central planning in detail becomes more and more tiresome to planners and consumers alike.

The new mathematical school in USSR is arguing for reforms, but they are still thinking in terms of costs rather than of demand. The true moral to be drawn from capitalist experience is that production will never be responsive to consumer needs as long as the initiative lies with the producer. Even within capitalism consumers are beginning to organize to defend themselves. In a planned economy the best hope seems to be to develop a class of functionaries, playing the role of wholesale dealers, whose career and self-respect depend upon satisfying the consumer. They could keep in touch with demand through the shops; market research, which in the capitalist world is directed to finding out how to bamboozle the housewife, could be directed to discovering what she really needs; design and quality could be imposed upon manufacturing enterprises and the product mix settled by placing orders in such a way as to hold a balance between economies of scale and variety of tastes.

No-one who has lived in the capitalist world is deceived by the pretence that the market system ensures consumer's sovereignty. It is up to the socialist economies to find some way of giving it reality.

Reference

LANGE, O. (1938), *On the Economic Theory of Socialism*, McGraw-Hill, 1964. (See Reading 4 of this volume).

ROBINSON, J. (1962), 'A neo-neoclassical theorem', *Review of Economic Studies*, June.

13 G. Garvy

The Monetary System and the Payments Flow

Excerpts from *Money, Banking and Credit in Eastern Europe*,
Federal Reserve Bank of New York, 1966.

Financial characteristics of the centrally planned economy

All the communist countries of Eastern Europe are now attempting, in various degrees, to make use of the market process. Many of the changes are being introduced only gradually, however, and in most countries details are still to be worked out for some of the most significant changes. In the meantime, the basic features of centrally planned economies remain intact. Production targets, formulated mainly in physical terms, are set by the central government and embodied in specific directives, usually cast in the form of output plans. Designated governmental agencies specify for each enterprise, or group of enterprises, the kinds and sources of inputs and the destination of outputs. Since all basic planning is in real magnitudes ('material balances'), the role of money is mainly to provide a common denominator (*numéraire*) for aggregation and projection. The allocation of resources is determined by the central plan and not through the price system. All prices are set by authority, and wage rates and total payroll costs of individual enterprises are strictly controlled. Consumer prices and transfer prices among producers are seldom changed, because stable prices facilitate global planning and an orderly distribution and redistribution of the national product. Administrative decisions, and not market adjustments, are relied upon to correct disequilibria and deviations from plans. Until experiments with more flexible policies were begun in recent years, individual enterprises in the government-owned sector of the economy (which, in each country, accounts for all but a small percentage of total output outside agriculture) had little scope for deciding between production alternatives or for making investment decisions.

The central role of the budget

All financial flows in the Eastern European countries, whether related to the movement of goods or to the flow of investment, are influenced by output plans and by direct controls over funds spent. They are not market determined and, indeed, there are no credit or capital markets. Instead the budget of the national government assumes the key role in the distribution of the national product. All major macroeconomic decisions – such as the division of current output between investment and consumption – are embodied in the government budget. In particular, the financial counterpart of the flow of real resources into investment is for the most part channeled through the budget. The national budget also fulfills an important allocative function with regard to investment flows (between industry and agriculture, among industries and regions), which in the free market economies is performed largely through the market process.

The budget is thus the most important funnel for all payments flows and the most important component of overall financial planning. Receipts of the state-owned enterprises in excess of expenditures for direct costs (mainly labor and materials) are siphoned off into the budget, either through taxes or by the transfer of profits (except for a relatively small part to be invested or spent for collective consumption by the enterprises themselves). About half of the national income of each country flows through the budget, a much larger proportion than in the United States and the other leading industrial countries of the West. This higher proportion results primarily from two facts: first, the channeling through the budget of the bulk of all investment (in working as well as fixed capital); and, second, the financing of a very large part of expenditures of all lower units of government through transfers from the national budget. Moreover, the bulk of 'collective consumption' – which includes not only free educational, health, and other services, but also subsidies for housing, transportation, and the like – is budget financed.

Financing of investment in the government sector of the economy involves essentially transfers from the accounts of enterprises to the budget (and vice versa). Voluntary savings provide a very minor though growing counterpart of real investment. The, in effect, forced sale of government bonds to the population, resorted to in various communist countries in the first postwar years (in the Soviet Union until 1957–58), must be regarded as a measure for preserving monetary equilibrium by reducing consumption, rather than as a normal means of financing investment.

The separation of payments flows

A considerable part of the activity of the banking system centers on the administration of a two-circuit mechanism – cash and 'noncash'. Currency is used for virtually all payments between the government (including the state-owned enterprises) and the population (as wage earners but also as entrepreneurs, to the extent that farming and some other activities remain in private hands). Practically all consumer expenditures are made in currency. The flow of purchasing power to consumers is planned to match the available supply of goods and services, plus an estimated increase in cash balances (supported by an increase in currency in circulation). Savings accounts (and, in some cases, bonds issued by savings banks or by the government) and hoarding of currency are the only means open to the population for accumulating financial assets. In contrast, all payments among enterprises, organizations, and the government (except very small and strictly limited amounts) involve transfers on the books of the banking system; this noncash circuit is best thought of as the counterpart of check circulation in Western countries. The relationship between the two circuits, which correspond to separate markets for consumer goods and producer (including raw material and intermediary) goods, will be discussed below (pp. 293–305).

Separation of the two circuits not only facilitates control but also makes it easier to detect disequilibria, bottlenecks, and various shortfalls in the execution of economic plans. Because of the separation of the payments stream into two watertight compartments, and the considerable differences between the functions of balances in the two sectors, the concept of the total money supply has very limited analytical significance in the countries of Eastern Europe.

Equilibrium through planning

Maintenance of equilibrium conditions and achievement of growth objectives are supposed to result from proper overall planning of material resources, and not through influencing, indirectly, aggregate pecuniary demand and its structure or the cost and availability of money and capital. From its very origin, Soviet financial planning has been 'derivative' – based on material balances, in which specific kinds of physical resources are allocated to achieve growth under conditions of overall equilibrium. Monetary flows are planned as the counterpart of physical flows, and adjusted to changes in such flows. Equilibrium between supply and monetary demand for consumer goods and services is to be attained by production, price, and wage decisions taken by the planning authorities. Equilibrium in the cash circuit is achieved when wage and other payments to the population equal the monetary value of the consumer goods and services that are to be produced by the economy at established prices which, ideally, remain stable for relatively long periods of time. Adjustments needed to maintain such an equilibrium are taken by the planning, not by the monetary, authorities.

Planning for growth under conditions of overall equilibrium of monetary demand and supply takes the form of an interlocking system of financial plans. In effect, these plans are projections, in the form of balances, of sources and uses of funds in the various sectors of the economy. They vary in their makeup – some flows are on a gross, others on a net, basis and a few are drawn up in stock terms. Some are, in effect, detailed operating plans while others are more in the nature of broad guidelines for the use of policy-making bodies. There are also considerable differences among countries in the number and articulation of such plans and in the extent to which the plans represent merely internal working documents or approach the status of binding operational directives. Moreover, the role of financial planning itself has been undergoing important changes in recent years.

Whatever the official status of the monetary plans, actual performance measured against plan figures provides a day-to-day check on the working of the economy – indeed the only overall check. Monetary flows in the socialized sector, recorded through the banking system (by entries in the appropriate accounts), reveal deviations from planned real flows and thus mirror disequilibria and bottlenecks in the real processes. Money thus performs an important signal function, but it is not relied on to any significant degree as an adjuster. Remedial action normally comes through direct intervention by the authorities in charge of production and distribution ('the economic organs') and through fiscal and pricing policies and other tools intended to change output levels and patterns directly. Much of what appears to be monetary action is rather the exercise of administrative functions by the banking system in support of policies formulated elsewhere in the planning structure.

The control of individual enterprises is shared among national, regional, and local authorities. As a general rule, enterprises producing basic materials, capital goods, or consumption goods for the national market are subordinated to a ministry. The other enterprises, which tend to be smaller, are responsible to regional political entities (federated republics in the Soviet Union) or to municipalities (which typically have jurisdiction over such enterprises as local retail and service establishments, bakeries, utilities, or movie theatres). Several enterprises of national significance, or even all units in the same industry, are frequently joined for administrative purposes into organizations variously called trusts, combines, groups, firms, aggregations, associations, and the like. (For the sake of consistency, these will hereafter be uniformly referred to as associations; they are normally subordinated to a ministry in charge of a given group of industries.)

The roles of money and credit

Because of the basic reliance on planning in terms of real flows, and the central importance of the national budget for financial planning, the functions of money and credit in Eastern Europe are radically different from the roles they play in free market economies. Ownership of money does not give an absolute command over resources. The individual can acquire only consumer goods and strictly limited categories of property for personal use. Small service establishments, artisans, and independent farmers also can acquire producer goods – and this is of some importance in countries like East Germany and Poland; but these nonsocialized sectors are not significant (with the major exception of agriculture in Poland). In the state sector, money may be used only in conformity with the plan; credit gives command over resources only if acquisition of the resources is foreseen in the plan, while plan allocation of resources carries with it an almost automatic claim on credit. The role of monetary flows is to implement the planners' intentions, not to invoke response or to correct movement away from equilibrium ('neutral money'). The power of money to influence real processes is severely limited by direct administrative controls. Attempts to use monetary incentives in order to guide economic activity have been made in recent years, but so far on a limited scale only.

The countries of Eastern Europe know no credit-granting institutions other than banks. To a very limited extent, banks have been used since the mid-1950s to finance certain minor kinds of fixed investment, but the main role of credit under the standard system is to provide the bulk of the financing of inventories at the various levels of production and distribution. Consumer credit and financing of cooperative and individual home building have become important only in recent years. Where a significant part of agriculture remains in private hands, notably in Poland, some efforts have been made since the mid-1950s to provide credit to farmers, both for seasonal needs and for improving technology. Except in East Germany, Czechoslovakia, and Poland, practically no credit is available to private enterprise in the other sectors of the economy. Changes of a rather marginal nature in credit policy and techniques, intended to provide somewhat greater flexibility, were made in the Soviet Union after the death of Stalin in 1954; these were also copied in the other countries, although in some cases in a modified form, and some changes were introduced for which there was no Soviet example. Until very recent years, however, such divergences involved chiefly techniques and details, rather than a fundamental reappraisal of the potentialities of monetary and credit policy.

The aggregate volume of credit is determined almost automatically by the production and distribution goals set in real terms. The proper amount of total working capital and the extent to which it consists of the enterprises' own resources (designated as 'own funds') are determined by the central authorities for each individual industry. Thus changes in the volume of credit are, for the most part, the counterpart of changes in the volume of inventories, unless planning authorities decide to change the relative share of enterprise funds and bank credit in the carrying of inventories. Under the standard system, the granting of credit is almost automatic, once the borrower's output plan has been approved, and the mechanics of credit granting is geared to rigid rules. Changes in the cost and availability of credit are not relied on as the means of achieving changes in resource use, although in recent years differentiation in interest rates has been increasingly used to achieve greater efficiency and to favor socially desirable activities. The prevailing official view is that the essential function of the credit system is the redistribution of cash balances (temporarily redundant enterprise balances, budget surpluses, and consumer savings) rather than credit creation.

During the first twenty-five years after the credit reforms of 1930–32, the credit policy of the Soviet Union was concerned exclusively with providing the payments counterpart of the movement of real goods through the production and distribution process. The other countries originally copied the Soviet credit system to the smallest details. In very recent years, however, at least some of the countries have begun to explore the possibility of adapting credit administration techniques as instruments of active credit policy. [. . .]

Liquidity position of enterprises

Since the ability of enterprises to acquire goods depends, theoretically at least, on the planners' intent and not primarily on liquidity, the liquidity position of the enterprise sector is ostensibly of no concern to credit policy. In effect, however, administrative and financial controls have not proved sufficient to prevent 'unplanned' spending: enterprises have frequently made use of their financial resources to support their operations, as dramatically evidenced in several instances of inflationary outbursts – especially in 1950–53 – in all the smaller communist countries with the exception of East Germany. Thus, while the monetary system has no way of influencing the liquidity of the socialized sector on a day-to-day basis, some countries have at times resorted to the device of temporarily sterilizing (blocking) enterprise balances or imposing limitations on their use.

The individual enterprise, which under the standard system has very limited latitude in managing its working capital, is rarely confronted with liquidity problems in the same sense as firms in capitalist countries. Its liquidity position has no direct bearing on its fixed investment plans, since these are, with negligible exceptions, implemented by financing from budgetary resources. Loans are made automatically on bills of lading to cover the standard collection period, and usually provision is made for easy access to bank credit in order to finance unforeseen expenditures, such as bulges in inventories of raw materials due to deliveries ahead of or beyond schedule. At the same time, considerable emphasis is placed on 'improving the payments discipline', since failure to pay on time is tantamount to extending interunit credit; it disrupts the circular flow of capital and creates payments difficulties all down the line.

While the management of an enterprise has usually little difficulty in temporarily replenishing working funds through bank loans, its ability to use its own bank balance is strictly circumscribed. In communist countries the absolute order to pay is unknown; all payments must be documented as consistent with the applicable plan, and the purpose of the payment is normally verifiable from the underlying documents. Interenterprise payments are usually made not by check but on the basis of drafts supported by documents related to the shipment of goods, and collection of payments for shipments (or services rendered) requires time-consuming movement of documents. Claims arising from production and distribution are nonnegotiable and nonassignable: they can give rise only to deposit transfers (settlements) between the accounts of the actual buyer and seller.

A shortage of funds normally results in difficulties of one sort or another, but the accumulation of free funds (excess liquidity in Western terms) confers little advantage, since it does not in itself entitle the enterprise to purchase additional resources. It may actually lead to a loss of working capital (if the superior economic authority directs the enterprise to relinquish the excess to other enterprises), or failure to obtain an additional allocation ('replenishment') of working capital from the budget next year, or even a permanent reduction of allotted working capital. Policy makers in communist economies have an interest in keeping the enterprises' own working funds at a minimum, so that extension of credit would give the bank a greater lever to exert tighter controls over each enterprise.

Indeed, the total volume of credit does not have the same significance that it has in the Western countries. The dividing line between credit and working capital owned by the individual enterprise is fluid and not of great significance in itself. The choice between more 'own' capital and more credit hinges on overall policy considerations, embodied in industrywide 'norms' (prescribed standard ratios). Since all capital in the state enterprise sector is owned by the government and is merely assigned to individual enterprises, a working-capital shortage in any given enterprise can be remedied either by granting it more credit or by adding to its capital (through budgetary resources or through transfers from other enterprises administered by the same ministry or from other 'higher echelon' organizations in the economic administration). In principle, all state enterprises operate in part with borrowed funds, mainly because it is desired to increase control by the banking authorities, but the precise share of loans in working funds varies.

The role of the banking system

Even before he took power, Lenin envisaged the banking system as becoming the backbone of the socialist state's administrative apparatus. Nationalization of private banking and establishment of a government monopoly of all foreign exchange transactions were among the first economic measures taken by the Bolshevik government in 1917. In the other Eastern European countries, foreign exchange transactions were virtually a government monopoly at the time the communists obtained a dominant position, and nationalization of banks and other financial institutions was uniformly one of the first actions of the new governments. Centralization of bank credit appeared to be a logical concomitant of centralized planning and management of production and distribution.

The particular form of banking organization developed

originally in the Soviet Union combines in the State Bank most of the attributes of a central bank with those functions of commercial banking that are relevant in the communist economy, and also with a wide range of activities related specifically to the characteristics of such economies. The term 'monobank' fits well this type of banking institution. The monobank is supplemented by a small number of banks that serve special functions, including an Investment Bank, which is a key institution for channeling funds into fixed capital.

In specific terms, the monobank is the *bank of issue* and is responsible for the regulation of note circulation. It manages the gold and foreign exchange reserves, in close cooperation with (and in some cases under the direction of) the Ministry of Finance and the Ministry of Foreign Trade (which in all countries of Eastern Europe is responsible for administering the foreign trade monopoly). In most of the countries the financing of foreign trade, and even of related domestic activities, has in recent years been shifted to special foreign trade banks.

The monobank (along with the other banks, to the limited extent that they extend short-term credit) is the sole *source of short-term credit*, as the extension of direct interenterprise ('commercial') credit is forbidden. The bank is not the ultimate but the only lender. Since control of credit is exercised directly, the monobank is not concerned with the same problems (such as controlling the reserves or liquidity of independent commercial banks) or activities (such as discounting and open market operations) as central banks in Western countries. As there are no financial markets or instruments (except savings bonds held by individuals), authorities do not have to worry about the prices of financial assets.

The monobank services the *currency needs* of the entire economy, including the savings banks and all specialized banks, where these exist as separate entities. Its offices act as *agents for specialized banks* in localities where these are not represented.

Since all payments within the socialized sector are transfers on its books, the monobank is the one and all-encompassing *settlements and clearing center* of the country. It keeps the accounts of the national government and of all subordinate government units, and performs all the usual *fiscal agency functions* carried out by central banks in Western countries (e.g. the collection and disbursement of revenue to support regular government activities, the issue and redemption of public loans). Of the proceeds deposited at the monobank from the sale of goods by the state enterprises, a part is paid out in cash for wages and the remaining part is credited to various accounts through book transfers. Thus it functions as a *social accounting center*, which not only keeps track of payments flows but, in many cases, also allocates single payments among several special-purpose accounts.

Because payments flows are planned and tied to plan fulfillment, all such monobank operations as cash withdrawals, book transfers, and credit extensions involve an *audit function* to check conformity of payment to underlying authorization. This important activity – essential to what is called 'control by the rouble' (or the forint, or the koruna), which is a basic feature of centrally planned economies – entails more than financial supervision; indeed, it makes the monobank a key part of the policy and administrative apparatus of the communist state.

In view of its manifold functions, it is logical that the monobank is an active participant in all phases of economic planning. It is also a major, and frequently the main, channel through which any failures in the meshing of gears come to the attention of the authorities. But the monobank raises the flag without cracking the whip; when the signals it transmits require corrective action, this is normally taken through policy measures that emanate from the higher authorities of the state.

The difference between the monobank and both the central and the commercial banks of capitalist countries is reflected in the structure of the balance sheet. The assets side of the monobank's balance sheet consists mainly of loans to the various segments of the economy (possibly including a small amount of housing loans to individuals), in addition to gold and foreign exchange; it contains no government or private securities. Among the monobank's liabilities (in addition to capital accounts and note liabilities) are the free balances of its clients – the counterpart of demand deposits in capitalist countries. These balances are owned mainly by economic or governmental units and, to a lesser extent, by cooperative farms and nonprofit organizations. The only counterpart of the interbank balances held by banks in Western countries is the uncommitted deposits of specialized banks. There are no time deposits and only a negligible amount of deposits of individuals.

The monobank's activities have some similarities to those of central banks in underdeveloped countries, with their rudimentary or nonexistent money and capital markets, their reliance on government for the bulk of capital formation, the relatively large volume of lending either by the central bank directly or through development banks, and largely fixed or stable rates of interest. Differences between Eastern Europe and the West in regard to the functions of money and credit and the central bank are considerable and basic.

Sources of bank funds

No State Bank of any country of Eastern Europe currently publishes data on the liabilities side of its balance sheet. It is known, however, that funds available for lending are acquired each year from a combination of the following sources (disregarding any resources of foreign origin): cumulative budget surpluses of previous years (a main means of achieving equilibrium in the economy), an increase in capital resources (from profits or transfers from the budget), an increase in note circulation, funds held at the State Bank by the specialized banks, reserves of social insurance funds (where they exist as separate entities, as in Czechoslovakia), deposits of savings banks (particularly where, as in the Soviet Union, they have no lending business of their own), and an increase in balances of enterprises and organizations. The last of these, being strictly controlled and kept at a minimum, is likely to be of greater significance from a seasonal than from a longer run point of view. In the Soviet Union, for instance, such balances at the beginning of 1965 stood at 12.1 billion roubles which, in relation to the value of industrial output, is considerably below the ratio between the level of commercial bank balances maintained by United States corporations and the value of the corporate product.

Even though the banking literature of the communist countries keeps repeating that the State Bank can make loans only within the limits of resources at its disposal, and though considerable day-to-day efforts are made to attract ('mobilize') additional resources (for instance, by inducing farm cooperatives to keep their free funds with banks), the implied analogy with commercial banks in capitalist countries is misleading. The State Bank cannot lose funds to any other bank, since it accounts for 95 per cent or more of total credit and is the depository of the uncommitted funds of all other banks. Issue of additional currency may be, and almost certainly will be, the result of any additional lending, but this merely represents a shift in the composition of the liabilities that match the loans added to the assets side of the balance sheet. The real, indeed the only, limit to the extension of bank credit in communist countries – where bank liabilities are not subject to reserve requirements and there is full administrative control of foreign payments – is determined by macroeconomic decisions made by the political and planning authorities and embodied in the financial plans.

The bank and its clientele

The relationship between the monobank and its clientele also bears little resemblance to the corresponding relationship in capitalist countries. Rather than being an agent of the depositor, the monobank, when dealing with the individual enterprise, is, in fact, the representative of the state; the population at large has no direct contact with it. It protects the interests of the state by debiting from the depositor's account – in most cases, automatically – the various payments due to the Treasury. If necessary, it extends credit to meet such payments. More generally, criteria that the bank applies in relations with its clientele are tied to the borrower's execution of the economic plan, to which the meeting of the borrower's financial obligations to the bank is subordinated. Each enterprise, unit of government, or nonprofit (voluntary) organization has to bank with the single office in whose territory it is located. This arrangement obviously provides no incentive for the management and personnel of any unit of the banking system to improve service in order to retain or attract depositors.

Until the emergence of new trends in recent years, the bank and its customers were merely involved in a web of impersonal accounting relationships, embracing set, uniform, and rigid rules, few alternatives, a minimum of flexibility, and supervision that reached into the minute details of an enterprise's activities and amounted in effect to a continuous and detailed audit of physical and financial performance. The monobank used no other criterion for measuring performance than the degree of success with which an enterprise discharged its current financial obligations (maintained a sufficient balance to pay bills and loans when due) and avoided exceeding norms – most importantly, the inventory norms – imposed from the outside by planning authorities and various economic administrations, including ministries. (See Campbell, 1963, pp. 205 et seq.)

Monetary policy in a planned economy

From the foregoing brief summary it is clear that the functions of monetary policy in planned economies are very different from those it serves in the West. In the communist countries, as elsewhere, the basic objective of economic policy is to achieve optimum growth rates without exposing the existing price structure to pressures caused by imbalances between the flow of consumer purchasing power and the availability of consumer goods. And the underlying analysis of capabilities – in terms of available real resources – and of the required changes in money supply, credit, and financial flows resulted in procedures not much different from those used in making macroeconomic projections in Western countries. But in formulating and implementing monetary policies that will serve their objectives, the two types of economies differ completely, reflecting their fundamental differences in capital ownership, economic organization, and political and social philosophy.

In Western countries the formulation of monetary policy is a continuous process, responding flexibly to changes in the performance of the market economy. In communist countries, monetary policy is embodied in all-embracing financial plans, which carry final authority and are changed only at fixed intervals. Although one can identify the nature of credit and note issue policies pursued by a communist country, and show what policies it follows with regard to encouraging personal saving, providing financing for small-scale capital improvements, or managing foreign exchange reserves, it is difficult to tie these separate aspects into something that would add up to a socialist monetary policy. But in all such matters the banking system acts merely as a vehicle for the execution of broader government decisions as embodied in the detailed plans; monetary action is not geared to the market but is determined by administrative processes centered on the planned allocation of resources. The familiar tools of monetary policy available to Western central banks are irrelevant. In communist countries, monetary policy is concerned primarily with assuring the efficiency of currency circulation and of the payments mechanism and with facilitating the economic performance of enterprises, while fiscal policy is heavily relied upon to assure balance between aggregate demand and supply.

In fact, one would look in vain in the writings of Soviet economists, who so far have been setting the tone in the other countries of Eastern Europe as well, for an explicit discussion of monetary policy. Typically, Soviet textbooks and treatises merely discuss the various functions of credit in the socialist economy. The more sophisticated treatment makes a distinction between the 'functions' and the 'role' of credit, reserving the first term for the place of credit in the socialist economy and equating 'role' with the results achieved in accelerating growth and output. (See for example Shenger, 1961, pp. 63–4.) Economic literature in Eastern Europe deals with the practical problems of controlling monetary circulation, crediting production and trade, and financing capital investment, usually under separate headings, but it does not discuss monetary policy, as such, or its relationship to fiscal policy, even though in the communist countries the two are closely integrated and the relationship between the monobank and the Ministry of Finance is at least as close as between central bank and government in Western countries. Similarly, banking officials, in their published speeches and articles, typically focus on how the State Bank can best implement the economic plan or party decisions. Such statements clearly reflect the implementary nature of the monobank's activities and characteristically treat the monetary aspects of those activities (credit, currency circulation) on the same footing as routine operations (mutual offsets) or control functions (control over payroll disbursements).[1]

Even though the monobank plays essentially the role of an implementing agency, it has significant functions in the central administration's efforts to influence aggregate demand and stimulate growth. It contributes – to an extent that varies from country to country – to the determination of realistic plan targets and of the proper magnitudes that will 'correctly' implement them, as well as serving indispensably in furthering the proper execution of the various financial plans. The monobank's role in economic administration is enhanced by an organizational advantage: in contrast to the various ministries, organized on an industry principle, and to regional economic bodies, it has a close and continuous contact, not only with specific branches or areas, but with the entire economy.

Nevertheless, the fact remains that, when the level and distribution of spending power do not conform with the underlying plan, the means used to correct the disequilibria are not changes in the cost and availability of credit but administrative improvisation by the monobank – unless the matter is so serious that higher echelon government or party authorities step in with a change in the ground rules. The monobank is an adjuster, not a steerer; its role – to borrow Robert V. Roosa's terminology, coined in a different context – is defensive rather than dynamic.

Communist countries have no effective means of controlling

1. In the authoritative Soviet two-volume *Dictionary of Finance and Credit* (issued by the official publishing house specializing in financial literature), there is no entry for 'monetary policy'. 'Credit policy' is defined as 'a system of measures in the area of credit, designed to secure the economic interests of the ruling class'. There is no definition for a socialist economy, but a short review of the tasks of credit policy is prefaced by the statement that 'In the Soviet Union credit policy corresponds to the tasks that the government places before the country in each phase of the construction of socialism and communism' (vol. I, pp. 584–5). 'Credit restrictions' (p. 585) are described as 'limitations or reductions in the volume of credit, which are put into effect by capitalist banks and the bourgeois state', and correspondingly, 'credit expansion' (p. 591) is 'enlargement of credit, put into effect by capitalist banks and the bourgeois state, which exceeds the growth of production, stimulates overproduction and the coming about of economic crises'. There is no reference to a possible role of either process in a socialist economy.

the excess liquidity of the population sector and its threat to price stability, except through the harsh and dramatic measures of currency conversions and upward price adjustments (and in some cases, until the mid-1950s, through forced loans placed with the population).[2] Thus a primary objective of financial planning and action is to prevent excess liquidity of consumers from coming into existence and in general to avoid inflation, both overt and repressed (though the word 'inflation' is banned from the vocabulary of Soviet economists, at least in relation to their own economy). Nevertheless, inflationary pressures have recurrently arisen in all the countries of Eastern Europe. To combat inflationary tendencies, to remove their causes, and to re-create conditions favorable to maintenance of price stability, centrally planned economies rely on a combination of fiscal, price, wage, foreign trade, and monetary and credit measures, and also on administrative shifts in the allocation of resources (and, if necessary, changes in planned targets).[3]

The nature of the monobank's role in monetary policy has been clearly stated in an interview given by Dr O. Pohl, General Director of the State Bank of Czechoslovakia: 'Of decisive importance for the expansion of an active financial policy is a structurally sound and well-balanced plan. Once the material resources have been incorrectly employed, the bank will be too late with whatever measures it could take.' Increased bank participation in the preparation and drawing-up of the plan is desirable, he said, 'to enable the bank to step in with its own knowledge and demands when there is still time to influence the

2. The experience of currency conversion, common to all these countries in the first postwar years, left few fond memories, though the 1947 conversion in the Soviet Union, and some others, did produce a more favorable ratio of exchange for small savings and for certain groups of account holders. See Ames (1954).

3. Even a cursory review of the Eastern European countries' efforts to neutralize the inflationary overhang of World War Two and to combat the subsequent succession of inflationary threats would exceed the limits of the study. Fortunately, adequate accounts of these developments are readily available. See Montias (1964, pp. 216–50); also Holzman (1960). For an (unorthodox) communist view of this problem, see Oyrzanowski (1962, pp. 323–58), and the several papers by Oyrzanowski and other Polish authors cited by Michael Kaser in his comments on Montias (1964, pp. 276–83).

anticipated employment of material means, in other words to strengthen the preventive character of the bank's role'.[4] After the plan is accepted, the monobank's efforts are directed toward keeping the monetary variables in line with the projections that relate changes in credit and currency circulation to real targets. Within the framework of the plan, credit policy can help bring about a more efficient use of the resources than the plan provides, and thus contribute to lowering costs. But the monobank will automatically validate any of the plan's misjudgments and short-comings that are binding for it. And although it is expected to prevent spending in excess of stipulated amounts – particularly for wage disbursements and inventory building – it can do little to bring inadequate spending to target levels.

Toward greater reliance on 'economic levers'

With the new policies that began to emerge in the post-Stalin era which became generally accepted throughout Eastern Europe only by 1965, the role of the banking system has begun to change. In general, the new developments involve a downgrading of physical indicators and an elevation of profitability to a position as an indicator of success – in other words, a differentiation between good and poor performers, a more liberal treatment of the former, increased stress on financial performance, as compared with physical output, and greater reliance on initiative and on material incentives. Although the new policies that have been taking shape in recent years give greater latitude to the local bank official, they by no means change his position as agent of the state: the difference lies in a shift from the state's exclusive reliance on administrative controls to a system that makes increasing room for 'steering by self-regulation', in which 'economic levers' are assigned an active role.

The degrees to which the individual countries have at this writing moved away from the Soviet prototype vary greatly. It is clear that much greater variety in institutional arrangements and policies is developing as each country's specific conditions and experience, as well as the differing views on the way in which a communist economy can make use of the market mechanism and dispense with detailed administrative controls, are gradually

4. *Rudé Právo* (Prague), 20 May, 1964.

being embodied in new banking legislation and regulations. It appears that any further moves in individual countries toward greater reliance on the impersonal mechanism of the market for achieving a more rational and more effective allocation of resources and greater efficiency in their use will be accompanied quite generally by an increased role assigned to financial criteria (including profits) and incentives. Credit policy is likely to play a greater and, in some respects, different role, losing much of its purely implementary character. In this process the bank official will become less concerned with the interpretation of regulations and gauging plan performance and more with evaluating the profitability of alternative uses of credit.

Monetary and credit plans

Although the basic planning in the communist countries is in real terms, output goals must be translated into monetary terms. The cash, credit, and investment financing needed to implement a given output plan must be spelled out and meshed. Thus the national monetary plans – on which the activities of the State Bank and of all other banks are based – are the counterparts of economic plans articulated in physical magnitudes.[5]

All plans discussed in this chapter are tied together in an overall financial plan, usually prepared at the Ministry of Finance or by the central planning authority, which shows intersector financial flows, particularly the sources of investment funds and in some cases the use of credit in the economy. As a rule the overall plan takes the form of a sources-and-uses-of-funds statement, prepared on an annual basis and for the country as a whole. Its purpose is to make certain that projected uses and available resources will balance; its main component parts are the national budget and the credit and cash plans of the State Bank. As a sample, the articulation of the Financial Plan of Czechoslovakia is shown in Table 1.

The government budget, in addition to determining the volume and distribution of centrally channelled investment funds, indicates the amount of resources allocated to the banking system for extending medium- and long-term loans and the amount of surpluses

5. For additional discussion of the history of monetary plans in the Soviet Union, see Garvy (1964).

Table 1 The Financial Plan (Czechoslovakia)

Resources	Uses
Government-owned enterprises: Profits	Government-owned enterprises: Investments and capital maintenance
Depreciation allowances	Housing construction (part included in the national plan)
Other revenues	Other expenditures
Decrease in working capital	Increase in working capital
Profits and depreciation allowances of financial and insurance institutions	Noninvestment government expenditures (such as health and social welfare, defense, and administration)
Turnover tax	
Other taxes and fees	
Social insurance receipts	
Other government revenues	
Resources of special budgetary organizations	Noninvestment needs of special budgetary organizations
Decrease in domestic inventories	Increase in domestic inventories
Decrease in credits to agricultural and other cooperatives	Increase in credits to agricultural and other cooperatives
Consumer savings	Expenditures of the population exceeding the plan
Increase in banking and commercial indebtedness to foreign countries	Decrease in banking and commercial indebtedness to foreign countries
	Increase in credits granted abroad
Balance-of-payments deficit	Balance-of-payments surplus
	Reserves
Other resources	Other needs
Total resources	**Total uses**
Deficiency of resources	Excess of resources

Source: *Basic Questions of the Financial Economy of the Czechoslovak Socialist Republic*, Prague, 1965. In the interest of greater clarity, the items have been rearranged and in some cases their designation has been translated into Western terms.

expected to accumulate at the State Bank. The plans of the monetary and banking system itself – the credit and cash plans – are prepared by the State Bank and are designed to accommodate the economy's needs for currency and credit while preserving price stability. Two of the principal activities of the State Bank – extension of credit and management of currency circulation – are based on these plans, which are tantamount to internal operating documents. They guide the day-to-day activities of the banking system and provide the formal framework for current reporting on its activities. This comprehensive and current reporting, in turn, permits the monitoring of the actual performance of the economy in relation to the projected path. Although they are interrelated, the banking plans are sufficiently different in form, time horizon, method of preparation, and territorial detail to warrant separate discussion.

The short-term Credit Plan

The Credit Plan,[6] an important component of the overall economic plan of each communist country, determines the increase in short- and medium-term credit to be made available to the economy during the period of the plan. It is prepared by the State Bank and is essentially a sources-and-uses-of-funds statement cast in terms of outstanding balances projected for the end of the period. Basically, the Credit Plan is derived by combining the projected credit needs of all enterprises with the amounts allocated for extending credit to collective farms, to individuals, and where applicable to independent farmers and private entrepreneurs. Short-term credits to the construction industry, extended by the Investment Bank, and credits for exports, extended by the Foreign Trade Bank, are usually included in it, though for operational purposes separate plans for these specialized banks are also prepared. Marginal changes during the period of the plan are projected for each sector of the economy (industry, trade, agriculture) and by purpose (such as seasonal needs, inventories, advances on collection float). As an example, the structure of the Credit Plan used in the Soviet Union is shown in

6. In contrast to the plan for long-term credit, described in the following section, that for short-term credit is usually referred to briefly as 'the Credit Plan'.

Table 2. It follows strictly administrative lines (reflecting the successive addition of new 'objects of crediting'), with no attempt at a functional or analytical presentation.

Table 2 The short-term Credit Plan of the State Bank (USSR)

Sources of funds	Uses of funds
Capital, reserves, and profits	Loans secured by inventories and for seasonal needs
Government balances (all levels)	Loans for new technology
Balances of economic units and collection float	Loans for increasing output of consumer goods
Balances of nonprofit organizations	Loans against drafts in the process of collection
Balances of credit institutions[7]	Loans to bridge payments gaps
Currency in circulation	Loans for temporary needs
Other	Loans for the payment of wages
	Reserve for allocation by head office
	Other[8]
Total	Total

Source: M. B. Bogachevskii, *Finansy i kredit v SSSR* (Finances and Credit in the USSR), Moscow, 1964, p. 271.

Outsiders' knowledge of the plan itself is limited to its structure (stubs and column headings), since neither its projections nor its actuals are published. Only scant information is available on the relative contributions of the various sources of funds – the budget, changes in bank capital and reserves, deposit balances of enterprises, net changes in currency in circulation, and so on. On the uses of funds, however, most countries publish actual figures, at least on an annual basis, usually by purpose and main industry categories and in some cases by territorial subdivisions. Thus it is possible to analyse at least the broad changes in the volume and structure of credit in use. Indeed, these data represent the most significant body of monetary information regularly published by the countries of Eastern Europe.

7. Savings and specialized banks.
8. Bank buildings and other property, currency in vaults and in transit, foreign exchange, precious metals.

Before the recent trend toward decentralization, which allows the branches of the State Bank greater participation in credit planning, the process of planning changes in credit volume involved little more than centralizing the credit requests of the various enterprises and setting proper criteria for checking their conformity with established (but not necessarily immutable) crediting norms. Credit demands were presented to the State Bank on a consolidated basis – usually quarterly, except for agriculture – by the ministries or administrations in charge of each branch of industry. The Credit Plan was an almost automatic by-product of the collation of these claims by industry and purpose, with a certain amount of scaling-down of the original requests. In the Soviet Union, about half of all short-term credit is still centrally planned at the head office on the basis of these claims presented by ministries or economic administrations, but the percentage is apparently considerably lower in Poland and Czechoslovakia, where the State Bank's credit planning has been decentralized. In general, the planning of inventory (including seasonal) loans is now left to the monobank's branches, while the amounts earmarked for settlement credits and for various needs that cannot be foreseen in advance continue to be planned centrally, with specific quotas ('limits') for the various major purposes distributed to individual regional and local offices.

To the extent that resources for lending are derived from budget surpluses and from the increase in currency circulation, their use can be planned only nationally. Such resources allocated from the main office are supplemented in each territorial and local branch by balances maintained by the enterprises and lower level governmental units whose accounts these offices carry.

The Credit Plan is broken down into territorial plans, extending to the lowest administrative unit, which combine credit allocations planned centrally with those made by the local or regional offices. The articulation of Credit Plans by purpose, which originally comprised only two categories (financing of inventories and collection items), has grown with the introduction of new 'objects of crediting'. Further changes in the format of the plans have occurred from time to time as a result of major changes in the organization of the administration of the economy. And, since the introduction in the mid-1950s of medium-term loans to finance improvements in technology, the Credit Plan has been restructured in most countries to show separately the amounts provided for medium-term lending.

The method of preparing the Credit Plan differs, although not significantly, from country to country. In Bulgaria, Poland, and Rumania, as in the Soviet Union, plans are prepared quarterly (in Rumania, they are further broken down by months); in Czechoslovakia, East Germany, and Hungary, plans are constructed annually and subsequently broken down by quarters. In addition, longer term Credit Plans are prepared in Czechoslovakia (five years), Rumania (six years), and East Germany (seven years). The need for quarterly Credit Plans arises in part from the seasonal character of production and in part to provide a basis for checking the performance of individual enterprises. Also, unforeseen divergences from planned output schedules and inventory goals may require corrective measures, including alteration of plans. For example, an overfulfillment of planned targets in a given consumer goods industry may result in increased deliveries of such goods to wholesale organizations, which then need more credit to carry them than had been anticipated.

The Credit Plan must be approved by a higher authority, which in most countries, including the USSR, is the Council of Ministers. It then becomes a binding government 'directive' in the areas of short-term credit and currency circulation. The whole evaluation of the role played by such a plan hinges on the significance of this directive for the actual operations of the banking system. Available evidence suggests that the Credit Plan is in reality little more than a set of projections consistent with the material plans and capable of providing guidelines for the credit activities of the banking system. The 'planned' totals are, in effect, permissible limits rather than targets to be achieved. The fact that they are more frequently achieved and exceeded than 'underfulfilled' reflects general inflationary tendencies and the desire to keep large inventories as a protection against unforeseen but recurrent disruptions and slowdowns in the circular flow of goods.

The long-term Credit Plan

In addition to the plan for short-term (including medium-term) credit, the State Bank prepares a separate plan for its long-term lending. Since such plans involve the financing of fixed investment, with most projects requiring several years for completion, they are prepared on an annual basis only. Like the plans for short-term credit, they are, in effect, sources-and-uses-of-funds projections, but instead of showing outstanding balances they indicate gross flows – the amounts to be made available during the year under the various headings; thus no integration of the two plans is possible. The structure of the Soviet long-term credit plan is shown in Table 3.

Table 3 The long-term Credit Plan (USSR)

Sources of funds	Uses of funds
Loan repayments:	Loans granted:
Collective farms[9]	Collective farms[9]
Farm population	Farm population
Individuals[10]	Individuals[10]
Consumer cooperatives	Consumer cooperatives
Municipal enterprises	Municipal enterprises
Budgetary resources:	Repayment of temporary Treasury
For enlarging the long-term	loans
credit fund	
Temporary loans from the	
Treasury[11]	
Subsidies of Union republics[12]	

Sources: M. M. Usoskin, *Organizatsiia i planirovanie kredita* (Organization and Planning of Credit), Moscow, 1961, p. 408; and M. B. Bogachevskii, *Finansy i kredit v SSSR* (Finances and Credit in the USSR), Moscow, 1964, p. 337.

Long-term credit plans include only repayable loans (not only for productive but also for nonproductive investment, such as housing and municipal services), although in some cases, subsidies to meet part of the cost of the project to be financed are also channelled through the plan. In addition to repayments, the sources of funds shown in the plan normally include budgetary

9. Including construction enterprises servicing collective farms.
10. Loans for home construction in non-urban areas.
11. To meet seasonal peaks.
12. Provided for meeting part of the cost of houses built to accommodate internal migrants.

resources – articulated by earmarked purpose, such as financing of agriculture, home building, and so on. Where separate Investment Banks exist, or where other specialized banks extend a certain amount of long-term credit, their activities of this kind may (as in the Soviet Union) or may not be consolidated in the overall plan prepared by the State Bank. Again, the plans are not published, but historical data on long-term lending are available for most countries. Until the partial shift from grant to loan financing in industry was initiated in the early sixties, financing of investment in agriculture, particularly by farm cooperatives, represented the bulk of long-term credit granted in the communist countries.

Balance of money incomes and expenditures of the population

Planning of currency circulation involves determination of the additional amounts to be put into (or retired from) circulation each year without disturbing monetary equilibrium, and also detailed projections of seasonal and geographic variations of currency needs. Quarterly plans for gross currency receipts and payments were developed in the Soviet Union as early as 1930, but until the 1947 currency reform they do not seem to have been successfully enforced. Actually, these were years of price increases of inflationary proportions, and increases in currency in circulation exceeded the planned percentages by large margins during the 1930s. It was only toward the end of that decade, with the more rigid enforcement of wage and other controls, that Gosbank planning and control of currency flows became a significant tool of economic policy.

The 'Balance of Money Incomes and Expenditures of the Population' (subsequently referred to as the Balance) is the starting point in preparing the Cash Plan, and it also serves the broader purpose of aiding in planning the production and distribution of consumer goods and services. It consists of a two-part sources-and-uses-of-funds statement: payments flows between the population and the combined socialized sector (Sector A, consisting of economic and administrative units) are distinguished from transactions within the population (Sector B). Its preparation starts as a trial comparison of anticipated disposable income with the projected supply of consumer goods and services,

Table 4 Balance of Money Incomes and Expenditures
of the Population (USSR)

Money incomes	*Money expenditures*
A. Receipts from government and cooperative enterprises and nonprofit organizations:	A. Payments to government and cooperative enterprises, nonprofit organizations, and savings:
Wages and salaries	Purchases of goods
Money income of collective farms	Payments for services and other expenditures
Individuals' receipts from sales of agricultural products[13]	Compulsory and voluntary payments (taxes, contributions, insurance premiums membership dues)
Pensions and similar payments	
Stipends (to students, etc.)	
Receipts from the financial system[14]	Savings (net increase in savings bank balances, purchases of 3 per cent government savings bonds)
Other income	
Personal money transfers[15]	Personal money transfers[15]
Subtotal for A	*Subtotal for A*
B. Receipts from sales of goods and services to the population:	B. Payments for purchases of goods and services from the population:
Sales of farm products through collective farm outlets	Purchases of farm products from collective farm outlets
Sales of household and other goods and services	Purchases of household and other goods and services and other expenditures
Subtotal for B	*Subtotal for B*
Total incomes (A + B)	**Total expenditure (A + B)**
Excess of expenditures over receipts	Excess of receipts over expenditures

Source: M. B. Bogachevskii, *Finansy i kredit v SSSR* (Finances and Credit in the USSR), Moscow, 1964, p. 285.

13. Sales made to the socialized sector from the private output of collective farm members and individual farmers.

14. Interest on savings deposits, lottery prizes, insurance payments, loans for housing construction.

15. Largely money orders and letters of credit; included only in balances for individual territories, such as republics and regions.

and it ends up as a formal quarterly plan approved by the Council of Ministers or some other high-level authority. It is not a complete statement of the consumer account, since payments in kind (and the imputed value of free services) are not included. Sector A serves as the basis for preparation of the Cash Plan, because transactions in Sector B merely increase the velocity of the currency that is put into circulation through transactions between the socialized sector and the population; only a very small part of Sector B transactions enters into the Cash Plan. The Balance is usually prepared by the national Planning Office. Various sources are used in its preparation, ranging from actuals of the Cash Plan in the preceding period to sample surveys of consumer expenditures. The form of the Balance used in the Soviet Union is shown in Table 4.

There is no doubt that the Balance meets important analytical needs, in part because in the process of its construction the size and origin of prospective disequilibria are revealed. Indeed, the permissible 'noninflationary' increase in circulation is determined within an implicit analytical framework that is not unfamiliar to Western economists. Measures to make the two sides of the account balance may involve changes in production, distribution, wages, or prices. Such measures may aim, depending on conditions, at increasing the volume of available resources or reducing their prospective uses, or both, and are taken largely by authorities outside the State Bank; the accounts and the monetary plans of the State Bank merely register the monetary effects of actions initiated elsewhere.

The Cash Plan

The Cash Plan, which is the basic operating plan of the State Bank (and hence is broken down to the successive administrative levels), is essentially an abbreviated sources-and-uses-of-funds statement of the consumer sector, derived from the Balance, primarily from its A section. For all practical purposes, the Balance may be regarded as the analytical framework, and the Cash Plan as the operating document, for the State Bank's major efforts to preserve monetary balance. The plan, which is prepared quarterly, serves as the basis for all bank activities involving the issue of currency and also for the elaborate controls over the disbursements of currency. This explains the great emphasis placed on strict adherence to the Cash Plan figures on all administrative levels. The form of the Cash Plan as used in the Soviet Union is given in Table 5.

Table 5 The Cash Plan of the State Bank (USSR)

Deposits	Withdrawals
Retail sales receipts	For wage and other labor income payments
Receipts from railroad, water, and air transportation	For payments for agricultural products and raw materials
Taxes and contributions	From accounts of collective farms
Rents and municipal services	For individual housing construction, consumer and pawnshop loans
Receipts from local transportation	By post offices
Receipts for the accounts of collective farms	By savings banks
Post office receipts	For pension allowances, stipends, and insurance payments
Savings bank receipts	Advances for official travel and for cash disbursements of economic units
Receipts of amusement enterprises	
Receipts from personal service establishments	
Receipts from housing cooperatives	
Other receipts	
Total	**Total**
Excess of withdrawals over deposits (currency put into circulation)	Excess of deposits over withdrawals (withdrawal of currency from circulation)

Source: M. B. Bogachevskii, *Finansy i kredit v SSSR* (Finances and Credit in the USSR), Moscow, 1964, p. 290.

On the assumption of stable velocity for each of the main categories of consumers, the rise in consumer disposable income that would result from a planned growth in national product yields an estimate of the required 'noninflationary' increase in currency in circulation. This estimate determines, in turn, what adjustments are required in the Credit Plan into which it enters as a source of funds. The proper annual change in the amount of currency in circulation is one of the 'proportionalities' that are supposed to underlie planning in communist countries and to assure the consistency of the various monetary plans among themselves and with physical plans.

Official sources estimate that in the Soviet Union about 90 per cent of the money income of the population finds its counterpart in currency withdrawn from banks, and that conversely the same percentage of consumer expenditures eventuates in currency receipts by bank offices, since trade and service establishments (with very small exceptions) immediately bank all their receipts. The figure is probably much the same in the other countries. Wages account for about four-fifths of the outgo side of the Cash Plan, and thus the latter ties in closely with the wages fund plan, another key element in all communist planning. In the Soviet Union, the Planning Office has been responsible since 1959 for establishing ceilings on wage and salary payments in each republic, and the Gosbank must fit payments within these limits into its cash plans all down the line to the lowest office.

Indeed, the formulation of the Cash Plan requires cooperation of the State Bank with planning organizations and several ministries. Unlike the Credit Plan, however, the preparation of the Cash Plan begins at the local-office level, even though much of the basic information is supplied from the central office. Individual enterprises and government units usually submit their own cash plans – supported by a wide range of factual and analytical data, including actuals for past periods – to the State Bank office with which they hold their accounts. In preparing the cash plan for a territorial division, the data obtained by the local offices are combined with information supplied by the regional bank office. The data obtained locally pertain mostly to projected changes, from current actuals, while the central authorities pass down information on increased needs to be expected from the erection of new factories and from the introduction of new programs, such as changes in farm procurement procedures and prices, or new social benefits. Projects submitted by local offices are reviewed by the supervising offices, and a process of successive reviews, adjustments, and consolidations results in the national plan; its formal structure has undergone only minor changes over the years. The Cash Plan includes the transactions (on a net basis) of the specialized and savings banks and the postal system.

The national Cash Plan is ultimately broken down into detailed plans for each banking office. These plans make provision for issuance of additional currency in specific periods or, as the case may be, for retirement of excessive amounts (and their retention in local vaults or transfer to regional offices). Since the discontinuance in some countries of central government review and approval of quarterly (as contrasted with annual) economic plans, the quarterly Cash Plan (with monthly or even ten-day-period distributions of totals) has become a main instrument for controlling the day-to-day performance of the economy, especially with regard to the consumer sector.

The preparation of the Cash Plan, in particular its territorial breakdown, has encountered many difficulties, notably in the Soviet Union. They are rooted not only in insufficiency of basic information, but also in the fact that in some areas the amount of expenditures may considerably exceed income payments (or vice versa) – as a result of regional differences in spending habits and in the use of consumer credit, tendencies to shop in distant places for goods not available locally, growing travel, changes in turnover velocity, and so on. The difficulties of preparing cash plans for relatively small areas are compounded when farmers and farm cooperatives are given comparative freedom in disposing of their output and can thus sell it in markets or shops outside the given territory. Considerable study is being given, particularly in the Soviet Union, to the problem of interregional currency flows.

References

AMES, E. (1954), 'Soviet Bloc currency conversions', *American Economic Review*, June.
CAMPBELL, R. W. (1963), *Accounting in Soviet Planning and Management*, Harvard University Press.

GARVY, G. (1964), 'The role of the state bank in Soviet planning', in J. Degras and A. Nove (eds.), *Soviet Planning: Essays in Honour of Naum Jasny*, Basil Blackwell, Oxford.

HOLZMAN, F. (1960), 'Soviet inflationary pressures, 1928–50: causes and cures', *Quarterly Journal of Economics*, May.

MONTIAS, J. M. (1964), 'Inflation and growth: the experience of Eastern Europe', in W. Baer and I. Kerstenetzky (eds.), *Inflation and Growth in Latin America*, Richard D. Irvin.

OYRZANOWSKI, B. (1962), 'Problems of inflation under socialism', in D. C. Hague (ed.), *Inflation: Proceedings of a Conference Held by the International Economic Association*, St Martins Press, New York.

SHENGER, I. E. (1961), *Ocherki sovetskogo kredita* (Essays on Soviet Credit), Moscow.

Part Four
Economic Reforms

The Soviet economic model, with emphasis on accumulation and growth and with a centralized allocation of resources, allowed the Soviet economy to achieve survival in a hostile environment, victory in war and fast economic growth. The economic drawbacks of this model (we are not dealing here with the political and other drawbacks) derived mainly from the emphasis on gross production and the use of physical indicators of plan fulfilment as 'success indicators' of the operation of enterprises. The trouble with this system was not so much the distortion in the allocation of resources for the production of alternative groups of commodities or for catering for alternative needs, but rather the lack of pressure on enterprises to provide a satisfactory assortment of commodities; the biases introduced by physical indicators as to the weight, area or volume of the commodities produced; the concealment of productive potential by enterprises; the waste of intermediate products. These drawbacks, combined with a reduction of the emphasis on growth, led to the gradual emergence in the socialist economies of an approach to the choice of final output and of techniques with a considerable role for profit and profit rates. Implementation of the new rules has been relying – more than in the past – on material incentives and bonus schemes for managers and workers of state enterprises, rather than on centralized direction.

The debate on this kind of planning change is very much associated with the name of Liberman (one of whose early articles is included here), but many other economists and industrial managers have contributed critiques and proposals. The official reception of the new principles is represented by excerpts from Kosygin's famous speech (September 1965). The other socialist countries of Eastern Europe – where similar proposals had already been put forward in the 1950s – soon followed suit. Nove's essay is a comparative study of Soviet and Hungarian developments. In some countries the emphasis on profit and profit rates was taken to its ultimate conclusions and actual interest rates and discounted cash flow methods replaced the earlier Soviet-type rules for investment choice (this is discussed in Nuti's paper on the Czech reforms). These changes have been regarded by observers from the right and left as a move towards capitalism. However, no accumulation of private wealth out of profits in the form of productive capital is allowed. This seems to rule out – at least for the time being – the hypothesis of convergence of economic systems (also, there still remain other alternatives, see Part Six). On the whole, the current reforms seem to bring these countries closer to the textbook model of socialist economies than to the capitalist model.

14 E. G. Liberman

The Plan, Profits and Bonuses

Excerpt from E. G. Liberman, 'The Plan, profit and bonuses', *Pravda*, 9 September 1962.

It is necessary to find a sufficiently simple and at the same time well-grounded solution to one of the most important problems set forth in the Party Program: the formation of a system for planning and assessing the work of enterprises so that they have a vital interest in higher plan assignments, in the introduction of new technology and in improving the quality of output – in a word, in achieving the greatest production efficiency.

In our view, it is possible to accomplish this if the enterprises are given plans only for volume of output according to assortment of products and for delivery schedules. These must be drawn up with the maximum consideration for the direct ties between suppliers and consumers.

All other indices should be given only to the economic councils; they should not be apportioned among the enterprises.

On the basis of the volume and assortment assignments they receive, the enterprises themselves should draw up the final plan, covering labor productivity and number of workers, wages, production costs, accumulations, capital investments and new technology.

How is it possible to entrust the enterprises with the drafting of plans if all their calculations are, as a rule, far lower than their true potentials?

It can be done if the enterprises have the greatest possible moral and material interest in making full use of reserves not only in plan fulfillment but also in the very compilation of plans. To this end, planning norms of profitability must be worked out for each branch of industry and must be firmly established for an extended period. It would be most expedient to confirm these norms through a centralized procedure in the form of scales fixing the amounts of incentive payments to collectives of enterprises in accordance with the level of profitability achieved (in the form of profits expressed as percentages of production capital).

Here is an example of an incentive scale worked out for machine-building enterprises on the basis of an analysis of the operation of 25 enterprises over a five-year period:

Table 1 Sample Scale of Incentive Payments for Enterprises

Profitability (Profit balance in % of fixed and working capital)	*Incentive payment:*	
	(a) in kopeks per rouble of capital.	*(b) supplementary, in % of profit exceeding lower limit of grouping.*
0·01 to 5·0	0·0	42·0
5·1 to 10·0	2·1	18·0
10·1 to 20·0	3·0	9·0
20·1 to 30·0	3·9	5·0
30·1 to 45·0	4·4	3·3
45·1 to 60·0	4·9	2·7
More than 60·0	5·3	2·0*

* But not more than 5·5 kopeks per rouble of capital.

Let me show through an example how this scale would be used. Let us suppose that the net profits of an enterprise for one year came to 7,500,000 roubles and the average annual figures for fixed and working capital amounted to 50,000,000 roubles. This means that the enterprise has a profitability of 15 per cent. In this case, it is proposed that the enterprise receive three kopeks for each rouble of capital, which would come to 1,500,000 roubles. Additionally, the enterprise would receive 9 per cent of the amount of profit above the lower limit of its profit grouping – i.e. above 5,050,000 roubles, or 10·1 per cent of the value of capital. In this case the 9 per cent would be computed on 2,450,000 roubles and would amount to 221,000 roubles. Thus the enterprise would receive a total of 1,721,000 roubles.

The rates of the table, of course, can be increased or decreased. The important thing here is the principle, not the figures.

In the first place, this principle means that the higher the profitability, the more the incentive provided. For example, if profitability increases from 5·1 per cent to 61 per cent, i.e. 12 times, the incentive payments to the enterprise increase from 2·1 kopeks to 5·3 kopeks, i.e. 2·5 times. This guarantees a powerful material stimulus for the enterprise to increase productivity. At the same time, the amount of income for the state would increase relatively much faster – from three kopeks to 54·7 kopeks per rouble of capital, or 18 times. This guarantees a still more rapid increase in public wealth and at the same time provides insurance against extremely high deductions in favor of the enterprises. There is no danger whatever to budget revenues. On the contrary, there is reason to expect a substantial increase in state revenue under the influence of a powerful material interest on the part of enterprises in increasing profits generally.

In the second place, the principle means that the enterprises would be granted incentives on the basis of a share in the generated income: the higher the profitability plan drawn up by the enterprise itself, the greater the incentives. If the plan for profitability is not fulfilled, the enterprise would receive an incentive payment, based on the same scale, in accordance with profitability realized. If the profitability plan is over-fulfilled, the enterprise would receive an incentive based on the same scale but at a rate midway between plan and actual profitability. Let us say that the enterprise plans for a profitability of 10 per cent but achieves a profitability of 15 per cent. It would then receive an incentive payment based on a profitability of 12·5 per cent, i.e. the figure midway between planned and actual profitability. This means that it will be an extreme disadvantage for enterprises to draw up plans that are too low. At the same time, the system retains a stimulus to over-fulfill plans. Of course, when the volume of output, the assortment and delivery schedules are not met, the enterprise would be deprived of the right to bonuses.

On this basis it is possible to simplify radically and at the same time to improve low-level planning. In fact, an enterprise would receive only one assignment for output in the proper assortment and, in addition, would proceed in its plans from a set table of incentive payments for profitability.

In order to achieve a high level of profitability, an enterprise must strive to place the fullest load on equipment and capacity when working out plans under our conditions and at plan prices (after all, profits will be computed as a percentage of capital!). This means it will be in the enterprises' interests to increase the number of shifts and the load on existing equipment, to stop asking for excess capital investments and machine tools and creating unneeded reserves. While all these surpluses now serve the enterprises almost as a free reserve, under the new system they would 'drain the pockets' by cutting down the size of incentive payments. Consequently, the 'struggle' waged by an enterprise to obtain lower plan figures would disappear. After all, such plan figures would never give the enterprise a sufficiently high level of profitability.

Also, the enterprise would strive to reduce production costs as much as possible, to be thrifty and to avoid artificial increases in norms for the expenditure of materials, fuel, tools and power. Reduction of expenditures would lead directly to increased profitability regardless of what norms manage to 'creep' into the plan or orders. Therefore, profitability expressed as a percentage of fixed and working capital of the enterprise is an objective criterion. It does not depend on what kind of plan the enterprise has tried to get for itself.

The last and main point is that the enterprise will strive for the maximum increase in labor productivity. They will stop requesting and hiring surplus manpower. These surpluses reduce profitability and consequently the incentive funds.

The incentive fund is formed in accordance with the level of profitability achieved and must be the single and sole source of all types of bonuses. It is important to tie individual and collective material incentives together in one single system. Let the enterprises have somewhat more freedom in using 'their' part of the profits!

One might naturally ask if the centralized basis of our planning would be retained and strengthened under this system.

There is every reason to assert that the proposed system would relieve centralized planning from petty tutelage over enterprises and from costly efforts to influence production through administrative measures rather than economic ones. The enterprise alone knows and can discover its reserves best. But in order to do this, they should not have to fear that through their own good work they will put themselves in a difficult position in the following year. All the basic levers of centralized planning – prices, finances, budget, accounting, large capital investments – and finally all the value, labor and major natural indices of rates and proportions in the sphere of production, distribution and consumption will be determined entirely at the center.

Their fulfillment will be assured and guaranteed because obligatory annual control figures on all important indices will be presented to the economic councils (and to the executive committees of local Soviets). The economic council would no longer be just an intermediate agency (as it often still is, unfortunately) but a center or hub at which all the lines of planning converge. Generalized state assignments for the economic region as a whole would be sent to it from above. From below the economic council would receive the plans prepared by the enterprises themselves, which would take account of the obligatory assignments for the quantity and assortment of goods. Since enterprises, when compiling their plans, will have a vital interest in providing maximum output with a minimum of current and capital expenditures, it is possible to say with reasonable confidence that the sum of the plans for the enterprises in the economic council will suffice to fulfill and even overfulfill the assignments from the center.

The enterprises will not 'meet with fixed bayonets' the economic council's proposals concerning the improvement of certain indices, because the basis of incentives will not be altered at all. The scale for the deductions will remain exactly the same. If the plan is improved upon, the scale will only promise the enterprise a higher incentive payment. As things are now, any change in the plan (and there are scores every year!) evokes demands by the enterprises that all the interrelated indices be revised.

Many economists assume that enterprises can be spurred to uncover reserves by improvement of the accounting base, a centralized system of technical norms, and so forth. There is no arguing the point that accounts and norms are necessary. But these should be left up to the enterprises themselves. This is necessary so that the enterprises will have a material interest in the progressiveness of these norms.

Thus the proposed system proceeds from the principle: what is profitable for society must be profitable for each enterprise. And conversely, what is unprofitable for society must be extremely unprofitable for the collective of any enterprise.

Some economists say that profit should not be made too conspicuous, that this is supposedly a capitalist index. This is not so! Our profit has nothing in common with capitalist profit. Where we are concerned, the essence of such indices as profit, prices and money is something else entirely, and they successfully serve the cause of communist construction. Our profits, where planned prices for the products of labor exist and clear revenue is used for the benefit of society as a whole, is the result and at the same time the measure (in monetary terms) of the actual effectiveness of labor expenditures.

Fears exist that the enterprises will start to make only profitable output and to abandon unprofitable production. But in the first place, the enterprise would be deprived of all incentive payments if the assignment for a given assortment of goods is violated. In the second place, it is a very bad thing that some of our types of output are highly profitable because of shortcomings in price formulation while others are losing propositions. It follows from the decisions of the 22nd Party Congress that the task of price formulation is to render the complete assortment of goods profitable.

People fear also that the enterprises will start to raise the prices of new products artificially. But right now, this is one of the most difficult things to control from the center or from the economic council. After all, the consumer is rather indifferent to the suppliers' calculations; the consumers need their deliveries at any price, as long as the price has been approved at some point. The system we propose would change this situation. Any increase in prices for the goods delivered would reduce the profits of the consumer. This means that they would be extremely demanding about checks on the prices set by the suppliers. This would help the economic councils and the state planning committees in carrying out effective, not formal, control over price formulation.

At present, profitability is reduced if the enterprises are mastering many new products and a great deal of new technology. For this reason, we have worked out a scale of supplements to and reductions in incentive payments in accordance with the proportion of new products in the plan. The incentive payments will be somewhat reduced for the output of items long established in production and raised substantially for the introduction of new products.

Besides this, the very process of price formulation must be flexible. Prices for new products that represent more efficiency in production or consumption should be set to begin with so that the manufacturer can cover his additional expenditures. The consumer would not suffer from this at all but, on the contrary, would reap benefits for himself and for the national economy. In this way profitability incentives might become a flexible weapon in the struggle for rapid introduction of new technology and for increased quality (durability, reliability) of products. The present incentive system for inducing enterprises to reduce production costs and to increase output above the plan or above the figure for the previous years is a direct impediment to increasing product quality or mastering new products.

In quest of a solution to this, economists look for good new 'indices'. There is no disputing that some indices need correction. But even 'ideally' conceived indices are not worth anything in themselves. This is a matter not of indices but of the system of relations between the enterprises and the national economy and of methods for planning, evaluating and providing incentives for production collectives. We already have the example of a new index provided for the clothing industry to replace the gross value of output index. This is the index of 'normative value of processing'. It was meant to prompt the clothing factories to produce clothing from cheap textiles rather than expensive ones. What has come of it? The result has been that the factories now willingly make old-line articles from cheap textiles, for which the 'normative value of processing' has become advantageous, but are quite reluctant to make new, fashionable articles from more expensive textiles. And the population wants these very things.

Therefore, it follows that any indices will be distorted when they are imposed on the enterprises from above by the method of apportionment.

Instead of doing this, we must make it possible for the enterprises to compute for themselves the optimum combination of indices, with the final result being the best products, ones the consumers really need and that can be produced with the greatest profitability. Without this 'freedom of economic maneuvering' it is impossible to increase sharply the efficiency of production. Without it, we can talk as much as we like about increasing the rights of enterprises, but we shall not accomplish this.

Therefore the current plan must be freed from the function of a standard yardstick for determining the degree of incentive, and at the same time there must be an increase in the importance of the plan as a production regulator for ensuring production growth and increased production efficiency.

Far be it from us, of course, to think that the proposed method is some sort of panacea, that by itself it will remove the shortcomings. Clearly the organizing, educational and controlling job done by the Party and economic apparatus will remain a decisive force. But this force will grow many times if it is supported from below by a firm stake in the success of the cause, and not for the sake of 'indices' but in the name of true production efficiency. Then the apparatus of the administration will decrease sharply.

Let us note that the proposed procedure forces the enterprises to put out only products that are capable of being sold and of paying their way. Further, the enterprises will calculate the efficiency of new technology with some care and will stop thoughtlessly ordering any and all kinds of new equipment at state expense.

It is now common practice to assume that any evaluation of the enterprises' work and any incentive for them must proceed from plan fulfillment as the most trustworthy yardstick. Why is this so? Because the plan creates supposedly equal conditions for enterprises, takes into account different natural conditions, different degrees of mechanization and other 'individual' circumstances. In actuality, the plans of enterprises are now set according to the so-called 'record basis', i.e. proceeding from the level attained. What this creates is completely unequal conditions, privileged for those who work poorly and strenuous for those enterprises that really uncover and use their reserves. Why strive for good work in these conditions? Is it not simpler to try to obtain a 'good' plan? It is time to amend this system!

Is it not clear that truly 'equal conditions' can be created if there is the single standard of profitability for enterprises finding themselves in roughly the same natural and technical conditions? It is less dangerous to ignore a few differences in these objective conditions than to level off the quality of economic guidance. By such leveling, we are preserving backward methods of production. Let the enterprises themselves, having the production program from the center and the long-term standard of profitability to go by, show what they are capable of doing in competition for the best results. It is right that we have no rivalry, but this in no way means that we have no competition for the best methods of leadership. On the contrary, such competition must receive full scope here.

And so, what specifically is proposed to improve the situation?

1. To establish that the plans of enterprises, after concurrence on and confirmation of the volume and assortment program, are composed entirely by the enterprises themselves.

2. To guarantee conscientiousness toward state interests and a stake in the maximum efficiency of production on the part of enterprises, to establish a single fund for all types of material incentive depending on profitability (from profits calculated in percentage of production funds).

3. To confirm centrally, as standards for long-range activity, incentive scales depending on profitability for various branches and groups of enterprises having approximately the same natural and technical conditions.

4. To improve centralized planning by carrying obligatory assignments (control figures) only as far as the economic councils (executive committees, departments). To eliminate the practice on the part of the economic councils of appointing assignments among enterprises according to 'the level attained'. To instruct the economic councils to check, evaluate and improve, on the basis of economic analysis, the plans independently worked out

by the enterprises, without thereby changing the scale of profitability as a basis for the enterprises' incentive payments.

5. To work out a procedure for using single incentive funds accumulated out of profits of enterprises, keeping in mind the expansion of the enterprises' rights in the expenditure of funds for their collective and personal incentive payments requirements.

6. To establish a principle and procedure of flexible formulation of prices for new manufactures, taking into account that the more effective manufactures must be profitable both for the producer and for the consumer, that is, for the national economy as a whole.

From the editors of *Pravda*: The materials published in *Pravda* on questions of perfecting economic management and planning are arousing great interest on the part of the public. Important and basic questions are raised in today's article by Doctor of Economics Ye. Liberman. The editors of *Pravda*, attaching great significance to these questions, invite economics scholars and officials of industry and of planning and economic agencies to express their opinions regarding the author's specific proposals.

15 A. N. Kosygin

On Improving Industrial Management

Excerpt from a Report to the CPSU Central Committee,
25 September 1965.

In order to expand the economic independence of individual enterprises it is proposed to reduce the number of indices which are assigned from above. At the same time those indices that are retained in the plan should be aimed at raising production efficiency.

As seen from experience, the index of over-all volume of output does not stimulate the enterprise to produce goods which are really needed by the national economy and the public, and in many cases tends to limit any improvement in the assortment of goods produced and their quality. Not infrequently our enterprises are producing low-quality goods which the consumer does not want and which therefore remain unsold.

Instead of using an over-all volume of production index, it is proposed that the plans for enterprises should incorporate assignments for the volume of goods actually sold. Enterprises will then have to pay greater attention to the quality of goods they produce in order to be able to fulfil their assignment for marketed produce. An enterprise that produces low-quality articles will experience difficulties in disposing of its goods and, consequently, will not be able to fulfil its plan. Under the existing system of evaluating the activities of an enterprise on the basis of over-all volume of output, such an enterprise would have been considered to have fulfilled its plan.

It is not sufficient to appraise the work done by an enterprise only on the basis of the volume of goods sold. The national economy requires definite items of production for satisfying social needs. For this reason assignments for the more vital assortments of goods must be retained in the system of planned indices.

When economic ties between enterprises are well organized and the contract system is well developed, then it will be possible to reduce steadily the assortment of goods whose production would have to be assigned by the state plan, and to substitute for it a group, or enlarged list of commodities.

The assignment for goods sold is aimed at establishing closer ties between production and consumption, and in order to orientate the enterprise towards raising efficiency it would appear better to use the profit index, the index of cost accounting. The size of obtained profits characterizes, to a considerable extent, the contribution made by an enterprise to the over-all national profit which is used for the expansion of production and the raising of the people's wellbeing.

It goes without saying that profit assignments do not tend to weaken the importance of the need to lower production costs but, quite to the contrary, raise it. One of the most important tasks of economic managers is to lower production costs. The production costs index should command special attention in the technical, production and financial plan of the enterprise.

The state is interested in constantly increasing accumulations not only by means of lowering the cost of production of each item of production, but also as a result of increasing the quantity of goods produced, of expanding and modernizing the range of manufactured goods and raising their quality. Profit reflects all these aspects of the production activities of an enterprise in a much more complete way than the cost of production index. What is important in this case is to take into account not only the amount and increment of profit obtained, but also the level of cost accounting that has been reached, i.e. the amount of profit per rouble of fixed assets.

Substantial changes are also envisaged in the planning of work at enterprise level.

At present the enterprises receive four labour indices from above – the productivity of labour, number of workers, level of average wages and the size of the wages fund. From now on it is proposed to hand down only one of the above-listed indices – the wages fund. This, of course, doesn't mean that the other indices have lost their significance. The indices of labour productivity, the number of workers employed and of average wages remain, as before, important elements in the national economic plan and the production plan of the enterprise itself. But is it really necessary to hand down all these assignments to an enterprise from above? We have discovered from experience that such a system of planning puts the initiative of the enterprises into leg-irons in the search for ways of increasing labour productivity.

There have been proposals that the wages fund of an enterprise also need not be assigned from above. But to discard the planning of the wages fund would be premature. The necessary balance between the quantity of consumer goods manufactured and the population's purchasing power must be guaranteed in the national economy. And the population's purchasing power is determined in large measure by the wages fund.

In the future, when we are able to considerably expand the production of consumer goods and accumulate the necessary reserves of these goods then it will be possible to abolish the system of pre-determining the wages fund for the enterprises. It is planned to do this, first of all, in the branches producing consumer goods.

Thus, an enterprise will have the following indices passed down from above:

1. The volume of goods to be sold.
2. The main assortment of goods.
3. Its wages fund.
4. Its rate of profits and level of cost accounting.
5. Its payments into the state budget and allocations from the state budget.

Besides those indices they will also be directed as to:

1. The volume of centralized capital investments and the putting into operation of production capacities and fixed assets.
2. The main assignments for introducing new technology.
3. The indices of material and technical supplies.

All other indices of economic activity will be planned by the enterprise independently, without endorsement from a higher organization. This will relieve the enterprises from excessive control and will permit them to adopt the most economic decisions in the light of actual conditions of production.

While expanding the economic independence of the enterprises, the state will continue to conduct a unified policy in the sphere of technical progress, capital investment, labour remuneration, prices and financing, and will secure the compilation of accounts and statistical returns according to a unified system.

One of the main tasks facing the planning and economic organizations is to improve the quality of goods in conformity with the demands of consumers and modern technical standards.

The plans must incorporate the most important indices relating to technical standards and the quality of goods, and all the financial, manpower and material resources necessary to secure them.

It is necessary to raise the role of State Standards as an effective means of raising the quality of output. The State Standards must be raised constantly in the light of the latest achievements of science and engineering. A system of state certification of the quality of goods should be introduced.

The normal economic activity of an enterprise is frequently upset by the fact that the plans assigned to it from above are not substantiated by the necessary technical and economic calculations, and that different sections of the plan are not inter-correlated. Up to now sufficient concern was not given to working out the technical and economic norms which are necessary in planning and in economic management. Assignments are frequently changed, which tends to disrupt the work of an enterprise and lowers the production efficiency. One of the main tasks in improving the planning system is to work out stable plans for enterprises, compiled on the basis of scientifically worked-out norms and technical-economic calculations which take into account the peculiarities of different branches of industry and groups of enterprises.

The raising of scientific standards of planning presents our professional economists with the job of analysing modern processes of the technical and economic development of the country and of defining the trends and prospects that are emerging. Special attention should be allotted to the increasing of economic effectiveness of new machinery and equipment, to re-adjustments in the patterns both of production and consumption, and to the exploration of economic inter-relationships, the comprehensive development of regional economies and the territorial division of labour throughout the country.

In the obtaining conditions, when the raising of the technical standards of production and its efficiency has been moved to the forefront as the most important task, the planned management of the economic activity of enterprises cannot be restricted to annual plans. Due importance has not been ascribed to long-term plans. Many enterprises did not take the trouble to compile them at all, and those that did usually failed to correlate them with the plans for the development of the national economy. Another major drawback in the existing system of long-term planning is that the assignments included in such long-term plans and in particular, the target figures for the Seven-Year Plan, were not broken down into annual figures.

Such a state of affairs leads to a situation where enterprises do not know in advance what prospects are in store for their own work and thus cannot organize their production in advance, nor establish long-term ties with suppliers and consumers.

It is proposed to establish the five-year plan as a basic planning form, including the annual distribution of the more important assignments, so that the enterprises may implement their production and economic activities on the basis of the plan.

Not enough attention has been paid recently in national-economic plans to measures directed at increasing production efficiency in relation to different branches of industry, which is a violation of the management by branch principle in industry. In industrial management and in compiling national-economic plans the problem now is to increase the significance of each branch of industrial production, and to guarantee the correct combination of planning by branches and planning at Republic and economic region level.

In this connection we must mention the tasks facing the USSR State Planning Committee. The Committee must concentrate on the securing of correct balances and interrelationships within the national economy, on raising efficiency levels in social production, on working out means for an accelerated growth of the national income and for raising the people's wellbeing. Of special importance, in this respect, will be a more profound and thorough working out of national-economic balance-sheets, in particular of the national income and of its utilization, of the man-power supply and its utilization both in the country as a whole and in separate areas, the balance between money incomes and expenditures of the population, the sources and distribution of financial resources, and supply and utilization of the more important material balances.

On increasing economic stimuli for enterprises and strengthening the cost-accounting system

Improvement of the forms and methods of planning will make it possible to tackle the problem of strengthening and developing the system of cost accounting in a new way. Lenin stressed that each enterprise must work on the basis of its rentability, i.e. it should completely cover its expenditures from its income and should make a profit.

The enterprises operating on the cost-accounting system and their managers must bear full responsibility for the economic results of the work they do. Lenin's ideas on the cost-accounting system must become firmly entrenched in our economic activities. In the consistent implementation and further development of the idea of cost accounting we see the way to the solution of many of the current problems of communist construction at the present stage.

What must be done in order to strengthen and develop cost accounting in the new conditions?

Firstly, conditions must be created under which the enterprises will be able to solve their problems of improving production independently, and that they will be interested in utilizing to the utmost the fixed assets assigned to them for increasing output and the amount of profit they receive. It is therefore necessary to leave to the enterprises more of the profits which they derive, so that they will be able to develop production, improve their techniques, materially encourage their workers and improve the labour and living conditions of the industrial and office workers on their staff. The proportion of its profits to be left to the enterprise should be in direct proportion to the effectiveness with which it utilizes the fixed assets assigned to it, the increase in volume of the goods it sells, the improvements in the quality of its goods, and to the increased cost accounting of the enterprise.

At the same time financial grants made by the state to enterprises for capital investment must be restricted and the credit system expanded.

Secondly, it is necessary to strengthen the cost-accounting system in inter-enterprise relations and to guarantee that enterprises adhere strictly to consignment deliveries as stated in concluded contracts, and to increase their material responsibility for discharging their obligations.

Thirdly, on the basis of the cost-accounting system, it is necessary to provide material incentives for the entire collective and every shop and section of the enterprise to make them interested in fulfilling not only their own individual assignments but also in improving the over-all results of the enterprise. In doing this, incentives must be organized so that enterprises will be interested in working out and fulfilling higher planned assignments, and in the better utilization of internal resources.

In short, it is necessary to orientate all the activities of the enterprise towards seeking out means of improving the economy of production, of increasing its own incomes and thereby increasing the over-all national income.

Under the existing system, capital investments are almost exclusively allocated according to the central plan, and in the main are devoted to the construction of new enterprises. In many cases operating enterprises do not have the necessary means at their disposal and thus cannot replace obsolete equipment quickly enough. The result is a tendency towards slowing down the growth of labour productivity, the improvement in the quality of the goods produced and an increase in the cost-accounting production.

It is proposed that at every enterprise there should be established a production development fund which would be formed from deductions from its profits. Such funds will also be supplemented by part of the depreciation fund which is intended for the complete replacement of fixed assets. At present this part of the depreciation fund is used wholly for centralized financing of capital construction, and enterprises cannot use these means at their own discretion.

When these measures are implemented, the size of the production development fund – which the enterprises will be free to use for technical improvements in production – will comprise a much larger sum than is the case nowadays. This can be seen from the following data.

In 1964, expenditures from enterprises' funds for the introduction of new techniques and development of production totalled – in industry – 120,000,000 roubles, and 600,000,000 roubles of bank credits were spent for the same purpose; the total figure was therefore 720,000,000 roubles. Under the new conditions the development funds will be equal to approximately 4,000 million roubles in 1967, including 2,700 million roubles of the depreciation fund.

The strengthening of the cost-accounting system and the economic stimulation of production depends on the basis on which the state grants means to the enterprise, and on the way in which enterprises transfer part of their income to the state budget.

The financing of capital investment is at present made gratis from the state budget. Enterprise managers show little concern as to the cost of the reconstruction of the enterprise or how effective the additional capital investment will be, because their enterprises are not obliged to refund the sums granted them. Hence we need a system such as will induce our economic managers to be more concerned as to how to use investment funds in the most effective manner, so that new installations and workshops will be built with a minimum of capital investment, will be put into operation in good time and their designed capacities will be utilized as quickly as possible.

One way of tackling this problem is to switch from the free allocation of means for capital construction to long-term crediting of the enterprises. It is suggested that the credit system will, first of all, be introduced for capital investments in already operating enterprises. As for new construction work, it appears that it might be expedient to introduce long-term credit for those construction sites where expenditures might be re-fundable in a comparatively short period of time.

Of great importance in making production more efficient is the correct and economical use of the working capital allocated to an enterprise. At present, any deficiency in working capital is refunded to the enterprise from the state budget. We cannot, therefore, speak of a genuine cost-accounting system if the enterprise does not, essentially speaking, bear any economic responsibility for the utilization of the working capital allocated to it. It is proposed to abolish the practice of providing free supplements to the working capital of enterprises from the state budget and instead, where necessary, to grant them credits for these purposes. Such a system will encourage enterprises to use the working capital allocated to them more thriftily.

A change in the system by which the enterprises make payments to the state budget from their incomes is also envisaged.

At present the size of the deductions made from the profits of the enterprises in favour of the state budget does not depend on the value of the fixed assets assigned to them. That is one of the reasons why enterprises attempt to obtain more money from the state for capital investments, and for supplementing their working capital, without taking the necessary measures for their rational use. It sometimes happens that an enterprise purchases equipment for which it has no need, merely in order to have spent the means allocated to it.

As has already been said, the rentability of fixed assets has recently declined in a number of branches of industry. It is most important, therefore, to interest enterprises in increasing their output and raising not only the sum total of their profits but also the size of these profits divided by the value of the fixed assets assigned to them. To do that it is necessary to introduce deductions in favour of the state budget from the profits of enterprises in proportion to the value of the fixed assets and working capital allocated to them, with these deductions being considered as payments for fixed assets.

The norms for payments for fixed assets and working capital will be established for a prolonged period of time – several years – so that a normally functioning enterprise will have profits left, after making its payments, for setting up incentive funds of its own and for covering its planned expenses. Those enterprises which make better use of their fixed assets and working capital will retain more profits for setting up incentive funds, which will provide the necessary material encouragement for the better use of state money allocated to the enterprise.

New machines, newly-installed equipment, and shops and enterprises just put into operation, cannot in every case produce their maximum effect immediately, and enterprises might experience certain financial difficulties in this connexion. Therefore it is proposed that payments for assets be made only after the end of the planned period envisaged for the full utilization of capacities.

It should be stressed that these payments are not proposed as additional contributions to the state budget over and above the payments which the enterprises are making now; the idea is to divert a considerable portion of the payments to the state budget through new channels. Looked at in perspective, payments for assets will become the most important part of the state's income, and the importance of other payments, including the turnover tax, will be correspondingly reduced.

It is also planned to introduce cost accounting on a broader scale into inter-enterprise relations. At present the economic responsibility of an enterprise in its dealings with other enterprises is most inadequate. Contracting has not as yet acquired the importance it deserves in relations between enterprises.

It is proposed to increase an enterprise or organization's material responsibility in cases of non-fulfilment of contract obligations for deliveries of goods so that, as a rule, the guilty party will make good any losses incurred. Also increased is the responsibility of rail, water, road and other transport organizations for delays in moving goods from enterprises and retarding their delivery to the customer. It is also necessary that design organizations should be responsible for errors they make in projects, technical drawings and designs, where these errors lead to material losses and additional expenditures during the building of a project or while production is being organized.

The introduction of the goods-realized index makes the position of the producing enterprises and the formation of their assets dependent on payments by customers. It goes without saying that every enterprise must itself bear full responsibility for making payments and for clearing accounts with suppliers on time. A cost-accounting relationship between enterprises demands that payment discipline be tightened. Simultaneously the role of state credit in economic turnover must be intensified with the aim of guaranteeing unhindered clearance of accounts between suppliers and their clients.

On measures to stimulate the material interests of workers in improving the work of enterprises

At present, the material incentives provided for producing collectives and for individual workers to make them interested in improving the over-all results of their enterprise's work are quite inadequate. Enterprises possess very limited opportunities for raising the remuneration of industrial and office workers from the sources of income created by the enterprise itself.

About 50 per cent of industrial enterprises do not possess funds created from their own profits, and in those cases where enterprises do possess them, these funds are very small and sums paid out from them for encouraging workers are insignificant. Nearly every kind of bonus and other stimulus is being paid out not from profits but from the wages fund. The achievements of the enterprise in increasing profits and profitability of production do not have any direct effect on the wages of the staff of the enterprise.

It is necessary to change this system in order to give the workers a greater material interest. It is necessary to introduce a system under which the enterprise's opportunities for increasing the remuneration of its workers would be determined, above all, by the growth of production, improved quality, increased profits and greater profitability of production. The basic wages and salaries of factory and office workers will continue to be raised by central impetus as before. At the same time the enterprises must have at their disposal – in addition to the wages fund – their own source for stimulating the workers to individual achievements and to high over-all results for their enterprises.

This source must be a part of the profit obtained by the enterprise. Out of this profit the enterprise will not only pay bonuses to the factory and office workers for high labour achievements in the course of the year, but also a lump sum at the end of the year. In doing this the length of uninterrupted service of the individual at the enterprise will be taken into account, which will have a positive influence on the stabilization of manpower.

Under the existing system of material incentives, the enterprises are not interested in providing for the utmost utilization of their internal resources in their plans, because the entire appraisal of the enterprise's work and the system of material incentives for the workers is mainly based on stimulation towards overfulfilment of the plan. Such a system encourages enterprises to strive for lower plan assignments in terms of volume of production, growth in labour productivity, and lowering costs of production, and for higher assignments in terms of the wages fund, the number of workers, capital investments and material funds, so that it will be easier for them to overfulfil the plan. This makes it more difficult to compile realistic plans. How is this system to be changed?

A fund for the material stimulation of the workers will be set up at each enterprise from the profits obtained by the enterprise. Allocations made to the material stimulation fund should be made according to stable norms, established for a number of years and in such a manner as to ensure that the volume of the material incentive funds are dependent on an increase in the volume of goods sold or in profit and on the level of profitability envisaged by the plan. The sums for stimulating overfulfilment of the plan will be relatively less than the sums paid for achievement of the planned indices. This will tend to induce enterprises to find reserves in sufficient time and to agree to larger planned assignments.

The material stimulation fund will also increase, depending on the share taken up by new goods and on additional income derived by the enterprise from additions made to the prices of its goods because of their higher quality. The enterprises will be interested in mastering the production of new models as quickly as possible and in improving their quality.

Because the pattern of production, the cost of production and the ratio between profit and wages are not the same in different branches, a differentiation is suggested in the norms for deductions made to the stimulation funds according to the branch of industry and perhaps even according to separate groups of enterprises with due account to the wages fund.

A fund for financing social and cultural undertakings and for housing construction must also be set up at enterprises. The means from this fund will go for new housing (over and above the central resources allocated for this purpose), for building and the upkeep of pre-school children's institutions, Young Pioneer camps, rest-homes, sanatoriums and for other socio-cultural needs.

Consequently, the better an enterprise functions the more opportunities it will have not only for raising wages but also for improving the living conditions of its workers and for cultural and health-protection undertakings.

The proposed changes in the methods of planning and economic stimulation are not based on theoretical conclusions alone but also on the results of practical experience which we have already obtained.

In 1964 and 1965, new methods of planning and economic stimulation were introduced in a number of enterprises of the garment, footwear and textile industries. The work of those enterprises was evaluated on the basis of the fulfilment of the plan for goods sold and of the profit obtained.

Recently a new system of bonus payments to managers, engineers, technicians and office workers was introduced at enterprises in a number of industrial branches, aimed at raising the workers' interest in the growth of production and the quality of the goods. The first results which we have at our disposal already confirm the correctness of the road chosen. I would like to dwell in greater detail on one practical experiment involving the use of the new system. I shall speak about road-transport enterprises.

There are some major shortcomings to be observed in the work of road-transport enterprises. About half of all journeys are performed by empty lorries. The plans, of course, envisage annual assignments to reduce empty runs, to diminish maintenance costs, to increase loads carried by lorries, etc. In practice, however, they yield little result. The road-transport organizations cite a host of arguments to prove the impossibility of fulfilling the planned quotas assigned to them.

Five months ago the Council of Ministers of the USSR delegated the Labour and Wages Committee, together with the Moscow and Leningrad City Soviets, to introduce the new system of planning and economic stimulation in some road-transport organizations. The system was introduced in three Moscow and two Leningrad organizations. They were major organizations with different specialities – servicing construction, the trade network, industry, and inter-urban transport.

The economic independence of those organizations was expanded: they had a reduced number of planned indices assigned from above; they were granted major rights as regards the use of any profit above the planned level, and savings in the wages fund, for the material stimulation of their workers, for improvement of socio-cultural conditions and for developing their own production base.

The Presidium of the Council of Ministers of the USSR recently examined the first results of their work and heard the reports of the directors of two of the Moscow road-transport organizations. Already the first results of their work have shown that the introduction of the new system of planning and material stimulation yields a considerable effect. Being in receipt of major rights and opportunities, the collectives found ways to improve their work and to carry more cargo, above all by reducing empty runs. They expanded the circle of enterprises and organizations which they were servicing, considerably increased the quality of the services they offered, interested their clients in cutting down the time required for loading and unloading operations, improved the organization of repairs and maintenance, sold off superfluous lorries and equipment and discontinued the employment of redundant staff members.

The new system of planning and economic stimulation increased the workers' interest in the results of their work. In the course of four months of work under the new conditions (May–August, 1965) empty runs were reduced by 15 per cent, and the freight turnover jumped 34 per cent as a result. Labour productivity went up by 31 per cent and profits more than doubled, making it possible to raise the workers' wages. The profit for the five organizations over and above the planned level totalled 969,000 roubles in four months. As before, they transferred 40 per cent of profits to the state budget, and the balance – over 550,000 roubles – was used for improving the production base, accumulating reserves, for socio-cultural requirements and for the material stimulation of the workers.

Of course, one can hardly expect the work of all road-transport organizations to improve as easily as this. Nevertheless, the results of the experiment speak for themselves. We cannot fail to see in them new factors which will yield important effects in other branches of the national economy, too.

The transition to new forms and methods of economic stimulation of industrial production demands the improvement of the system of price formation. Prices must increasingly reflect expenditures of socially necessary labour, and must cover production and turnover outlays and secure the profits of each normally functioning enterprise.

The existing neglect of economic levers in planning and managing the national economy, and the weakening of the system of cost accounting, are to a great extent connected with the considerable shortcomings in the system of price formation. If prices are not substantiated, then economic calculations lose their dependability which in turn encourages the adopting of subjectivist decisions.

At present, when wholesale prices are determined for industrial goods, it is becoming absolutely necessary to substantiate scientifically the calculated level of profitability in the branches of industry. Normally functioning enterprises must obtain their profits from the realization of their produce at wholesale prices; in this way they must derive an opportunity to set up stimulation funds and to dispose of the necessary means for expanding their activities, for paying for their fixed assets and for making other transfers to the state budget.

Price must also play a major role in tackling the problems connected with the raising of the quality of goods, and improving the length of service and durability of goods. Thus, when prices are determined for new improved models, they must reflect the additional expenditures made by the manufacturers and the economic effect which the customers will get from using better quality goods. In such a situation, manufacturers will be more interested in improving their produce and it will be economically more advantageous for consumers to purchase such goods.

In the course of preparing for this Plenary Meeting, the Presidium of the CPSU Central Committee and the Council of Ministers of the USSR have decided to set up a State Committee for Prices attached to the USSR State Planning Committee. This Committee is entrusted with working out and presenting, by 1 January 1966, proposals relating to the main trends in the evaluation of wholesale prices for industrial goods, basing its decisions on the need to bring prices as near as possible to levels of expenditure of socially necessary labour. These prices must guarantee the implementation of the planned measures for the improvement of planning and the economic stimulation of the enterprises.

Improvements in the system of price formation and in the methods of determining wholesale prices will help in improving the economic organization of the work of industry, in finding additional reserves and in securing systematic and constant reduction in the cost of production. There can be no question but that retail prices can be reconsidered only with the aim of reducing them.

Experience shows that the task of establishing wholesale price levels for all the kinds of goods, and the preparations of new price lists for all branches of industry, take considerable time. It will probably be possible to introduce the new prices in 1967–8.

At the same time, the State Planning Committee, the Ministry of Finance and the Committee for Prices will have to introduce – for those branches of industry where the transition to new forms of economic stimulation will take place at an earlier date – the necessary amendments to operating prices in order to eliminate unjustified differences in profits derived from goods made by those branches.

Such is the general outline of the main proposals for improving planning and the stimulation of industrial production. The proposed system of planning and stimulation is also applicable, in its main features, to construction work, railway transport and certain other branches of national economy. But it must not be extended to those branches mechanically, without taking into account their specific economic features and the tasks facing them. Work in this direction will be carried on gradually.

16 A. Nove

Economic Reforms in the USSR and Hungary, a Study in Contrasts

From A. Nove, 'Economic reforms in the USSR and Hungary, a study in contrasts', in J. Chapman and Shun Msi-chou (eds.), *The Economics of the Communist World*, forthcoming.

Background to change

The centralized or 'Stalin' model of planning, devised in the USSR, was adopted in Hungary as in other countries of the Soviet sphere, in the period in which they all, regardless of size, traditions and resource endowment, copied all things Soviet. In all these countries this model is being questioned and, to varying degrees, changed. No longer is there any compulsion to copy the Soviet way of doing things in all its detail, and so no two countries are alike in the pace and shape of their reforms. The USSR and Hungary are chosen here as examples, in the one case because its size and key position makes it an essential object of study, Hungary because it has gone furthest (Yugoslavia apart) in the direction indicated by the reforming philosophy. It is also significant that the USSR is among the more 'conservative' countries in its sphere in its approach to change.

It is necessary to begin any discussion of the causes of reform by a brief analysis of the purpose and logic of the 'Stalin' system and the changing circumstances within which it was operating in the Soviet Union.

These can be analysed as follows:

The origin of the 'Stalin' system in organizing the 'revolution from above'. Central control was maximized not just to please the power-hungry leadership, but to change society. If one is seeking rapid structural changes, then market forms expressing the pattern of demand of the *existing* society are not merely irrelevant but a danger. Economists who argue in favour of objective criteria become 'objective' allies of those political forces opposed to the great leap forward. This helps to explain how so many eminent economists of the twenties were in prison in the thirties.

The 'revolution from above' had the objective of extremely rapidly creating a heavy-industrial base. It involved sacrifices, the priority of key sectors of industrial materials, fuel and equipment, the neglect of the needs of agriculture and of citizens, and all this by methods reminiscent of a war economy (the parallel is Oscar Lange's). In a war economy, the centre imposes its choices and ignores the market's because, in relation to the war, relative priorities are incommensurate. This is why, say in Britain or Germany, private car manufacturers were not allowed to compete for the available metal, and materials were allocated administratively, at fixed prices.

It was a time of 'extensive' investment, with a large reserve of underemployed peasant labour. New industries were being created. Such problems as training factory labour, and building great new industrial complexes, seemed much more important than 'efficiency', or replacing machines by better machines. New industrial models could in any case be purchased or copied from abroad. What could not be copied from abroad was development economics. There was *no* development economics, until after the last war. And even today there is endless argument about the nature of 'development strategy' and its connexion with static efficiency criteria.

Times were changing. Fundamental structural change was no longer a major objective. There was no more 'revolution from above'. The economy had grown much more mature, sophisticated, complex. It was increasingly hard to control it from the centre in the old way. The labour situation became tighter; it is true that to this day over 30 per cent of the labour force is in agriculture, but many of these are old, female, unskilled. In many parts of the USSR there developed a shortage of urban labour. After Stalin's death the iron priorities of the despot were substantially modified. More attention was paid to agriculture, housing, consumers' goods and services. Various controls over people were relaxed: amnesties emptied the mass of the forced labour camps, workers were allowed to leave their jobs without permission. All these factors created strains, representing a growing contradiction between structure and the forces of production. They became the subject of widespread discussion in the USSR in 1956 if not earlier.

Possibly the end of the Stalin terror, i.e. the immediate consequences of Stalin's death, facilitated the process of change by making discussion of the various problems possible. But of course the problems were already there.

The various factors making for reform, briefly referred to above, require some more detailed examination.

One such factor was and is *growing complexity*. This meant in practice that a great many orders which ought to have been issued were not in fact issued, for lack of time and information. It is a characteristic of the traditional Soviet system of planning that 'the plan' is the sole criterion for decision-making. This follows from the logic of substituting deliberate allocation of resources by the authorities (representing the needs and priorities of 'society') for the automatically-functioning economic forces. Prices, the 'law of value', play no allocation role, at least not in the process of deciding *what* to produce. The planning organs have the duty of collecting information about needs, from enterprises for producers' goods, from state retail stores about consumers' goods. This information is combined with instructions from the highest political organs about investment policies, growth targets, priorities. In the end, the planners must 'translate' all this into *plan-instructions*, covering every enterprise's output, delivery, inputs, labour, cost, finance, investment and other plans. The fulfilment of these plans becomes the highest duty of all intermediate and lower echelons of the system.

But the scale of the necessary decision-making process is far too great. Several consequences followed:

1. Detailed and balanced plans could only in fact be made for key priority sectors. The rest made do with what was left.

2. The 'Centre' had to be divided, for purposes of administering and planning the economy, into ministries and departments, each of which developed strong interests of its own. This in practice meant a sort of 'polycentric centralism' or 'pluralistic

monolithism'. No realistic picture of the Soviet economic system can be obtained if one speaks of 'the centre'. In fact the various ministries, etc., are *competitors* for resources, especially investment resources.

3. Plans reached enterprises from different units of the planning hierarchy. Thus supply and production, finance and investment, labour and costs, were planned by different offices. This created inconsistencies. The reconciliation of these and other inconsistencies necessitated frequent changes of plan.

4. Plans had to be aggregated, to be manageable. Thus, ton-kilometres, square metres, millions of roubles, represented totals of dissimilar goods, and the product mix was distorted by the attempt to fulfil plans so expressed. These aggregate totals were *not* arrived at by adding together the elements of which they were composed, but rather by adding a percentage to past plans or past performance, this being the so-called ratchet principle, or planning '*po dogtignotomu urovnyu*' as the Russians say. Hence the familiar distortions: making goods heavy to fulfil plans in tons, choosing dearer variants to fulfil them in roubles, poorer quality to fulfil cost reduction plans, and so on.

5. This contradicted the desire of the authorities to achieve a closer relationship between consumer demand and production. Stocks of unsold goods increased, queues for goods in short supply did not decrease.

6. The inconsistencies of plans, and especially between the supply plan and the production plan, and also frequent changes in plans during the year, encouraged hoarding of materials, and also an understatement of production potential, to keep a reserve in hand, just in case. These actions led to unnecessary losses, and also distorted the flow of information upon which plans are based.

Innovation suffered from lack of any built-in incentive to innovate. Grossman once spoke of 'routine, inertia and pressure'. The traditional system gave no reward for risk-taking, gave good bonuses to those who went on doing and making whatever they did before, only more so. Pressure, orders from above, did lead to technical progress in many sectors, yet lack of incentives for change has caused loss. The lack of direct influence of user-enterprises on their suppliers in the matter of the product mix, mentioned already, also damages technical progress. In many instances modern productive equipment is not supplied, because aggregate plans for machinery are more easily fulfilled by making obsolete machines.

All the above factors were a relevant part of the background to the reform. They are long-term in the sense that they provide no explanation as to the *date* of any actual reform measure. They raise questions, problems, difficulties, with which Stalin's successors had somehow to grapple. The evolution of the economy and of society put these matters on the agenda. But this need not necessarily mean that anything is actually done. There are, as we shall see, obstacles to change: inertia, vested interest, habit, ideology (or is 'ideology' a form in which inertia, vested interest, etc., is expressed?). After all the existence of inefficiency is not in itself proof of ineffectiveness. The western war economies were in many respects inefficient, but, as already pointed out, they were tolerated, the inefficiency being a *necessary* cost of concentrating resources for war. In the case of Russia we must also mention *national-historical* tradition, a factor which distinguishes it from most other countries and which deserves a paragraph to itself.

The role of the state in Russian economic development, and in Russian society, has been noted by many historians. Its obverse has been the relative weakness of spontaneous social-economic forces. Of course, the overwhelming role of the state contributed to this weakness, while being in large part explained by it. To keep up with the more developed West, or to catch up when the gap became too great for safety, Russian monarchs organized society to serve the state, and serfdom as an institution arose as part of this process, as a means of supporting the Tsar's civil and military servants. Stalin was, at least in this sense, the successor of the modernizing Tsars, and his actions found some response in the historical subconsciousness of many of the people. This tradition in Russia, its absence in other countries helps to explain the contrast between the attitudes and policies of the Soviet Union and those of their European allies.

All this does not answer the questions: why did reforms get

adopted when they did? Why were they so widely discussed and still widely argued about? Perhaps the following reasons are among the most important:

1. Stalin's death and the abandonment of mass terror led to the voicing of criticism which was previously suppressed, and this had a gradual effect on official thinking.

2. The attempt by Stalin's successors to satisfy many wants at the same time led to overstrain, and contributed not only to dangerous disequilibria but also to a sharp *decline in growth rates*, especially after 1958. This made the authorities particularly receptive to new ideas.

3. The failure of the *sovnarkhoz* (regionalization) experiment of 1957–64, the agricultural troubles of the last Khrushchev years, the administrative confusions which accompanied them, led to a widespread realization that something new is needed. The 'something new' had evidently to provide greater managerial autonomy, based on criteria other than those of fulfilling plans sent down from above.

4. The experience and experiments in other eastern countries were having some influence in Russia.

5. The rapid development of computer and mathematical techniques, attractive possibilities of their use in planning, presented new problems and opportunities. Such influential senior scholars as the Academician Nemchinov played a significant part in convincing the leadership that something ought to be done.

Hungary goes ahead

Hungarian experience was very different. The 'Stalin' model was adopted only in 1948–50. It served no urgently-felt Hungarian national needs, it had no basis in Hungarian traditions but was a copy of an alien model. Hungary was a small country with a heavy reliance on foreign trade. Because of lack of raw materials and fuel within its borders, the attempt to create a native heavy industry increased Hungary's propensity to import. In this instance at least, as in some other of the smaller communist countries, a policy which might appear to have been autarkic in intent had the opposite result. Furthermore, a high rate of forced saving plus an attempt to force the peasantry into collectives led to increased discontent, and for these as well as more purely political reasons there was an outburst against the regime in 1956. The Kadar government has ever since acted with diplomacy and caution ('it achieved peaceful coexistence with its own people', a critical Hungarian once said to me). There was no longer, after 1956, any overriding necessity to copy Russia, and, as we shall see, the invasion of Czechoslovakia, did not mean any halt in economic experimentation in Hungary. Therefore there was a tendency to search for a solution which, while leaving the communist government in supreme political control, reflected the position of Hungary as a small country, dependent on foreign trade, with recent memories of a market economy and, even among party members, a widespread disbelief in the efficacy and desirability of centralization.

The reforms in all the countries of Eastern Europe were, in varying ways, seeking a new balance between central planning and decentralized market (or 'commodity-money') mechanism. No one really imagined that basic investment decisions, affecting the whole shape and proportions of the economy, could be left to the market in a country in which the state owns the instruments of production and in which there is no stock exchange and so only a limited kind of capital market could be conceived. No one really doubted that the product mix – e.g. of cloth, farm implements, hats, dyestuffs, shoes – should accord with the requirements of the users; since these could not be determined by the central planners, there would have to be more direct links between customer and supplier. Prices would therefore have to act as information-carriers, and profit would then have to act as an important part of managerial incentives, to make it worth their while to satisfy demand. Be it noted that the proposed changes would not introduce incentives where previously there were none: the 'Stalin' model included substantial bonus payments to managers, but they were paid for plan fulfilment, i.e. obeying orders from above. They provided no inducement for the managers to take any decision of their own, except to such as would enable them to say (or claim) that the orders received had been obeyed. All the reformers were agreed as to the necessity of a closer link between prices, profits and resource allocation, i.e.

the introduction of some elements of a 'socialist market'. But opinions differed widely as to the proper balance between market and plan.

To make reforms a reality, it would plainly be necessary to dismantle all or most of the current production and supply planning procedures. These go together. Obviously, so long as the allocation of inputs by administrative supply organs continued, each productive unit would have to be told what to produce, since one firm's input is another firm's output. The supply system involves designating customers and suppliers, and so eliminate competition. Real reform requires the elimination of supply planning.

This the Hungarians have done. Their reform document surprised most observers by the far-reaching new principles which it embodied. Competition was praised. When, because of economies of scale, a monopoly within Hungary was none the less inevitable, the proposals provided for a combination of price control and competition from abroad. Various categories of prices were envisaged: wholly free, partly free (subject to maxima, or maxima and minima) and fixed. But even the fixed prices took on a different meaning in the context of the abandonment of 'administered' production and supply decisions: the authorities would be compelled to amend those prices which failed to stimulate the required output or activity, since the new 'rules of the game' excluded direct administrative orders. It was explicitly recognized that prices must reflect *supply and demand and scarcity*. The state was to retain its power over strategic investment decisions, it could and would influence development by economic means, by making and altering the rules by which management was to live, and also by appointing the managers themselves and dismissing them. It was not proposed to adopt the Yugoslav 'workers' self-management' model. None the less a substantial operational autonomy was to be granted to enterprises (in some cases to associations of enterprises). This was to extend even into the field of foreign trade.

As we shall see, other reforms – including the Soviet reform decree of 1965 – promised action which was not taken. So the readers of the Hungarian proposals could have been excused if they greeted them with polite scepticism. Yet the scepticism proved very largely baseless. The Hungarian 'model' has been radically altered. With few exceptions, the administrative allocation of materials and the planning from above of enterprise output have been abandoned. The exceptions, which are described in a valuable book on the reform, are transitional in character and so few that, they 'do not hinder the free unfolding of our (new) system of economic control, since central interference affects only a small fraction of the global social product'.

Enterprises draw up their own plans, independently, based on demand. They are free to choose their inputs. With a few exceptions, they are free to buy foreign goods and to sell to foreign customers, and the exceptions relate in the main to bilateral commitments to the USSR and similar 'traditional' centrally planned economies. Competition, including competition from foreign suppliers, is positively welcomed, as a way of avoiding predictable monopolistic distortion. To avoid the use of unrealistic exchange rates, a series of conversion coefficients ('foreign trade price multipliers') have been established, reflecting the cost of acquiring the given currency, prices in 'socialist' trade being higher. Thus the effective rouble–dollar cross rate is nowhere near the official $1 = 0.90$ roubles; the dollar is subject to a surcharge of 100 per cent, the rouble of 20 per cent. This has the net effect, after complex adjustments, of making a rate of 40 forints = 1 rouble, 60 forints = \$1. This could be regarded as an unofficial devaluation of the rouble with respect to the dollar, or alternatively as a form of COMECON preference rate (in that it makes imports from convertible-currency countries dearer). There are also customs duties, which, unlike the situation under Stalinist-type centralized planning, do actually affect behaviour. This is not the place for any detailed exposition of the Hungarian trade system of today. There are many complications, some of them transitional. Thus most firms conduct their foreign dealings through the specialized 'foreign-trade corporations', and the state licenses those enterprises which are authorized to deal direct. However, the fact remains that enterprises buy and sell across borders, whether directly or through intermediaries, and can sometimes choose, at a given exchange-rate, whether to buy from the West, from the East or from a home producer. A major problem is the persistence of bilateral trade and payments agreements, with non-convertibility, with other COMECON countries, which is inconsistent with the logic of the Hungarian reform. Therefore there is Hungarian pressure for convertibility within COMECON, and necessarily also for the establishment of 'genuine prices', 'genuine markets', linked with world-market prices. Ausch, the author of a vigorous statement of the Hungarian position is well aware that this process of adjustment is complicated in 'countries where the system of obligatory plan directives will be maintained'.

The whole reform rests on a new approach to the role of prices. The Marxist formulation about 'socially necessary labour' is retained – for instance in Istvan Friss's contributions both to the already-quoted reform symposium and (in Russian) in *Voprosy ekonomiki*, but the content of these words has been transformed, very much on the lines advocated by the more radical school of Soviet reformers. As a first approximation, or as an 'ideal price', to use the words of Csikos-Nagy, prices were computed based on prime cost (the Russian *sebestoimost*) plus a surcharge of 12 per cent on wage costs and 10 per cent on value of capital. The resultant figures were then modified in the light of public policy (e.g. higher for drink, lower for staple foodstuffs), and also – which is most important – to achieve demand-and-supply equilibrium and to establish a logical relationship with prices in foreign trade (via the 'foreign-trade price multiplier'). Indirect taxes levied on goods were greatly diminished. It may be of interest to reproduce a table showing the impact of this on the budget, comparing 1968 with a classical 'Stalinist' budget, that of 1956:

Above all: 'We have reached the conclusion that an approximation of the market price system is the most expedient. Evidently we have to do here with a matter that develops on the basis of the economic plans made by the state'. But, once again, the point is the adoption in micro-economic reality of the *market*, and also of *competition*.

Price controls exist on a variety of goods. As already indicated, prices are of several kinds. Some, such as coal, electricity, oil, most farm products, are still fixed prices. Many are subject to ceiling prices (i.e. no increase greater than a given amount is permitted), some have maxima and minima. Others are wholly free.

Table 1 Revenues of the State Budget (Per Cent)

State revenues	1956	1968
Charge on assets	—	21
Wage tax and social insurance allowances	10	16
Taxes on profits and incomes	19	33
Production tax and rents	—	2
Centralized amortization	6	5
Total of direct taxes	35	77
Turnover tax	53	7
Customs duties and import taxes	—	4
Total indirect taxes	53	11
Other revenues	12	12
Total of revenues	100	100

The latter category is by no means insignificant. It includes, for instance, 60 per cent of wood and paper materials, 55 per cent of chemical products, 90 per cent of the wholesale prices of textiles and clothing, 100 per cent of wood and paper manufactures, 65 per cent of the products of the engineering industry. Controls are somewhat tighter on retail prices; only 23 per cent of retail turnover is wholly free of price control. There seems to be a trend towards gradual relaxation of some of these controls. The latest information suggests that Hungary has found a way of combating the persistent tendency towards excess demand, which still bedevils the Soviet and the other centralized economies. Fears of a sharp rise in the general price level have proved groundless so far.

The state owns the enterprises, appoints managers, possesses reserve powers to issue orders. However, the basic 'rules of the game' are that the state planners influence micro-economic life mainly (though not solely) through economic and not administrative regulators. These express the intentions of the plan, and so the Hungarians claim with justice that theirs is still a planned economy. This is particularly so in respect of the investment plan. Here we have both 'individual large projects approved by the government' and the earmarking of sums for particular economic sectors. Thus, although an estimated 40 per cent of all investments are to be decentralized, in the sense of being decided at enterprise-management level, the government, acting either directly or through the banking system, is able to influence growth in the direction indicated by its own long-term plans.

What of incentives for management and employees? These are related to profits and are paid out of profits. As already indicated, the enterprise pays into the budget a capital charge and a levy based on its wages bill. There is a tax on profits – this, as shown on page 345 above, is in fact the largest single source of budget revenues. This tax is levied at different rates according to the uses to which profits are to be put. In respect of profits used to supplement incomes this tax is sharply progressive, in order to avoid excessive income differentials (more of this problem in a moment). Profits after tax are divided between three funds: income-supplementation, investment and reserves.

Managers and their immediate deputies may receive profit shares up to a maximum of 80 per cent of their basic salaries. For intermediate-grade staff the maximum is 50 per cent, and for all other workers it is 15 per cent. It is estimated that this last group includes '87–95 per cent' of all employees. If there is a loss, then managers and intermediate-grade staffs receive 75 and 85 per cent respectively of their basic salaries. The workers must be paid in full. (The above bonus percentages were found to be excessively differentiated and have been modified.)

It may be seen that the management has a very strong interest indeed in making profits. However, voices have been raised to draw attention to the widening of income differentials, and questioning the social acceptability of this. The successful manager of a profitable firm plainly gains much more than his workers. The management and workers of a profitable enterprise gain as against the less profitable, though the difference may be due to fixed price or to other circumstances outside their control. There being still no effective capital market, what is to prevent the successful and profit-making firms from continuing to make high profits, without either bothering or being able to raise capital to increase output? Yet the whole social-economic purpose of profits is to stimulate a response. What of the possibility of a vicious-circle effect: the successful attract the better management and workers, thus ensuring that the below-average firm goes from bad to worse? There is no effective provision for bankruptcy nor for takeovers. Finally, might firms in search of profits so reduce their labour force as to threaten unemployment? Job security is much prized.

I mention these difficulties because they do exist, and because no reform is costless and painless. There may be discontent among the masses, and some of the discontent could express itself in political-ideological forms. However, the essential fact is that in Hungary there has been *a real change of model*. Perhaps wishing to avoid the fate of their northern neighbours, the Hungarian leadership, in full control over organs of mass communication, tended to underplay the newness of the model. It is, of course, still rather soon to pronounce upon its effectiveness, or on its influence on changes still to come in other countries of Eastern Europe.

Some Soviet-Hungarian contrasts

In March 1969 the literary journal *Novyi mir* published an account of a visit to Hungary by a certain P. Volin. His reaction, as he wishes to convey it, was one of naïve surprise. What, managers are *not* told what to produce? They are allowed to make and sell what the customers wish? They are free to choose their own suppliers? They can buy what they like, even foreign-made commodities? Ministries *really* do not interfere? Suppose the wrong goods are made? 'Suppose the enterprise decides to make not what is needed, but what is simpler and easier to make? Suppose, to take a very simple example . . . , a factory decides to stop making cups and increase the output of plates, although the state needs cups. Can it then issue instructions?'

The Hungarian replies: 'The state actually needs neither cups nor plates. The people need crockery. People buy it in shops. The shops can buy plates or cups from several enterprises. They can also import them from abroad. Therefore the people will not be left without cups'. There must be competition, of course. Some will then win, others lose. 'The market must be a real market and not a pseudo one. Otherwise we will have to return to administrative methods of control. And a real market requires competition'.

The tone of Volin's article suggests that he had great sympathy with what the Hungarians were doing, that he wished that things had also changed in the USSR.

However, change in the USSR is slow. The essential fact is that *no real change of model is yet contemplated*, or, if it has been contemplated, the authorities have changed their minds. There has been a reform, it is true, but of the old system and within the old system.

Let us illustrate this proposition with a series of quotations (page 349).

Thus the Soviet official view is hostile to the underlying concept of market socialism and is not prepared to recognize the logic of 'active', information-carrying prices. Much necessarily follows from this, as we shall see.

Soviet controversies and the new official ideology

Many Soviet reformers advocated something very different from this. A whole paper could readily be devoted to the many schools which contended, and to some extent still contend. Some go so far as to cause other, even quite radical, reformers to label them as 'free market dogmatists' (the words belong to A. Birman). Birman himself would like to see the abolition of most or all of the system of material allocation, the basing of most enterprise plans on contracts with their customers, through trading relations. Liberman achieved world-wide fame through emphasizing the key role of profits, with the slogan 'What is good for society must be profitable for the enterprise', on the pages of *Pravda*. The virtues of supply-and-demand-balancing prices, the logic of socialist market relations, their conformity with a properly-understood Marxian economic theory, were extolled by Novozhilov in Leningrad, Petrakov in Moscow. The last two have also been engaged in advocating the widespread use of mathematics, of programming techniques. Kantorovich urged the adoption of the so-called 'O.O.O.s', the Russian initial letters for 'objectively determined valuations', i.e. the use of prices derived from a mathematical plan-programme. The director of the Central Economic-Mathematical Institute (TsEMI), Fedorenko, wrote and spoke extensively about the 'theory of optimal planning'.

Fedorenko rejected accusations of 'bourgeois marginalism'. True, his theory uses marginal concepts. However, the fact that

Hungary

Enterprises should be free to decide 'what and how much they want to produce and market . . . from what enterprises and in what quantities' they purchase inputs.

Prices 'should balance supply and demand.' 'The value judgments of the market should express themselves in prices.'

'Competition between enterprises . . . will stimulate efficiency.'

'An active role . . . for the market.'

'Freedom to choose between domestic and imported goods . . . or whether to sell goods in domestic or foreign markets.'

USSR

'Right-wing opportunists . . . argue for "market socialism" and for competition between enterprises. This has nothing to do with Leninist principles of socialist management.'

'Some argue . . . that the customer should find his own supplier, and supplier his customer. This must be rejected, as it implies the absolutization of the law of the market and of supply and demand, the development of competition between suppliers and an underestimation of the role of the centre.'

It is wrong 'to abandon the practice of (planning by) compulsory quantitative indicators.'

'Market prices are, in our view, alien to our economy and contradict the task of centralized planning. It is . . . incorrect to imagine that prices should balance supply and demand. The balance between demand and supply . . . is the concern of the planning organs.'

'It is impossible to agree to proposals to permit (enterprises and associations) to operate on international markets other than through the Ministry of Foreign Trade.'

such concepts are misused by 'bourgeois apologists' give no ground for 'accusing of "marginalism"' those experts who work out the means of achieving optimal results in a socialist society. . .'. Fedorenko then outlined a methodology as follows: 'The central planning organ, guided by the experience gained in constructing an objective consumption function for society, and some other preliminary considerations, values the utility of various goods and the possibility of reproducing them, in relation to the availability of productive resources at that given moment. It sends down these valuations to lower production units (sectors, enterprises). These, having obtained guideline prices for resources and for their output, draft a local plan for developing production. In doing so they endeavour to maximize the local criterion, for instance profits. Having drafted its own plan variant (on the basis of prices sent down from above and the local optimality criterion), the production units send it up to the central planning organ'. The centre aggregates these plans, discovers some surpluses and deficits in relation to availability and needs, and sends down a different set of prices. On this new basis the 'locals' draft another plan. By this iterative method, which the use of computers makes possible, one can arrive at a balanced plan with rational prices, on which the search for profits will stimulate an approach to the optimum. But this cannot possibly cover all the millions of items of which a fully disaggregated plan is composed. So the detailed product mix will be a matter for enterprises to decide along with their customers. Detailed prices would also often be decided without central control, 'in the process of this special kind of "socialist competition"'. The behaviour of consumers in the market would be a vital source of information about demand. 'In this way the commodity-money mechanism plays in a socialist society the role of a regulator, with feedback effects not only in the sphere of production but also of consumption'. Further, 'since these prices balance supply and demand, they play the economic function of a "market" or commodity-money mechanism. . . . Concretely this means that prices are based on *social utility*. . . . The marginal social utility of any commodity (production resource) is inversely related to the quantity available . . .'

It is worth noticing that a multi-level iterative planning process has been much discussed in Hungary, especially in the work of Kornai and Liptak.

Fedorenko was looking forward to a synthesis between plan and market, with consumers, management and planners alike responding to prices at which supply and demand balance. He envisaged a micro-economic market. He would doubtless have agreed with another reformer, who asserted that without a market *valuation* the planners could not know whether their plans are correct. The 'objective function' is based on demand. Indeed, what other objective function can there be? To assert that the party leaders' preferences could serve as the criterion of optimality is open to one devastating objection: how are even the party leaders themselves to know that they are right? They too need a criterion. They may prefer a high growth rate, or modern weapons, or a reduced consumption of vodka. But a disaggregated plan for production and investment consists in the main of items which the leadership cannot logically 'prefer'. Either one is concerned with consumer satisfaction, or with the best means to achieve given ends (e.g. plastics versus metals, or machine X versus machine Y). By this I do not mean that non-economic preferences are irrational. Obviously regional or strategic policy considerations enter into decision-making. However, it remains necessary to distinguish and identify the nearest practicable approximation to an *economic* optimum, and this cannot usefully be so defined as to open the door wide to political arbitrariness. Even the politicians will not thank their economic advisers for depriving them of a criterion for decision-making, which is the consequence of basing plans on the preferences of politicians!

Some western critics imagined that the mathematical school would be 'centralizers'. This is not the case, and for at least one good reason: a fully disaggregated central plan would have to include literally millions of separately identifiable commodities, produced by hundreds of thousands of enterprises of all sizes, involving millions of production-and-supply links through time and requiring a quite impracticable volume of information. Furthermore, most of this information – e.g. as to the detailed product mix – itself arises out of market relations. So the bulk of Soviet mathematical economists support the 'socialist market' solution.

There have always been some who opposed this whole approach, as they also opposed Liberman's proposals and Kantorovich's theories. However, the opposition has seemed much stronger of late, possibly because 'market socialism' has been associated with the Czech heresy of Ota Sik, and the bulk of official opinion seems to have hardened in a conservative mould. We shall see that this attitude has halted the reform process with relatively little accomplished.

Here are some examples of the now dominant counter-arguments.

'This concept of "market socialism" occupies a special place amid various anti-Marxist theories of socialism. It is adopted by right-wing revisionists, as an integral part of the general conception of "democratic" or "human" socialism, and is also used in the imperialists' policy of "building bridges" and "quiet counter-revolution"'. Furthermore 'the functioning of the market mechanism causes deep inequalities in incomes between enterprises and sectors and between different categories of working people'. Finally, 'as may be seen, contrary to the conceptions of many bourgeois economists, the central questions of economic reform are not concerned with weakening but with strengthening the centralized basis of planning . . .'

The same issue of the same journal contains an attack on the mathematicians: 'the bridge between mathematics and economics is not built, and indeed the inter-relationship between the two disciplines has not been defined'. Then in a later issue the well-known statistician A. Boyarski joins in the offensive. Of course he advocates the use of mathematical methods. However, Fedorenko's whole construct is attacked for being based on subjective marginal utility theory. Prices cease to reflect value, marginal social utility is substituted. Boyarski cites Marx against the view that different goods ('meat, wool, wine') have the common property of utility; no, their only common property is that they are the products of labour. In any case, the Fedorenko model cannot be applied in real life, and amounts only to promises for the future. A simple numerical example is used to criticize the proposition that marginal pricing – or 'objectively determined valuations' – would lead to optimal utilization of scarce materials, in this case oil and gas, and his conclusion is: 'the question of who is to continue to use oil and who is to go over to gas is best decided at the planning centre'.

In the same issue as Boyarski, the economist A. Vikentyev takes a similar line on a non-mathematical level. He accuses various writers of wrongly understanding the economic reform adopted in 1965 as the replacement of administrative by economic methods. 'Of course this is not the essence of the (party) decisions. . . . The reform does not reject administrative methods which, based on the utilization of the economic laws of socialism, are the necessary condition of the development of the national economy'. The author attacks the identification of centralization with arbitrariness. If the centre's plan-instructions are correct, then they are 'economic' and not arbitrary. Indeed he goes so far as to say the following: 'Soviet planning and administration taken as a whole successfully fulfilled their tasks principally because they were on a sound scientific base. Therefore planning taken as a whole *was always optimal*'. Vikentyev even rejects the critique of centralized methods made by Kronrod, himself a moderate who has criticized Kantorovich and other reformers.

Vikentyev has a long record of dogmatic conformism behind him and his ideas are not worth a minute's time, save in one respect: even a year ago such nonsense would not be published. Today it is merely an extreme statement of the position of the counter-reformers. His general position is consistent with the quotations made from *Pravda* and from Sitnin on page 349, above, and also with another *Pravda* attack, by the influential I. Kuzminov, on 'new models of socialism'.

Even stronger and in a sense more authoritative attack came in an editorial in the November 1969 issue of *Planovoe khozyaistvo*, signed by one of the senior deputy-chairmen of Gosplan, A. Bachurin, significantly and prominently in black print. He denies Fedorenko's concept of the criterion of optimality. He agrees that such a criterion is required, 'and not only to facilitate the use of computational techniques . . . but whatever this criterion may be, it cannot be indifferent to the concrete aims of the plan'. Fedorenko and his colleagues are accused of making 'the methods of a market economy into the motive force of development'. He is further accused of proposing prices that balance supply and demand yet 'an increase in prices consciously limits the possibility of the satisfaction of the needs of society, instead of making every effort to satisfy them by expanding production'. Fedorenko's definition of the purpose of production under socialism is declared to be inferior to that of Stalin, who did give due emphasis to the aim not only of consumption but also of expanding production. Fedorenko and some other economists contradict the labour theory of value, 'following Marshall, Böhm-Bawerk, Keynes and other bourgeois economists'. He goes on: 'our economists should surely know that the new and eminent bourgeois mathematical economists – Tinbergen, Koopmans, Danzig, Neumann, Klein and others – unanimously denounce Marxist economic theory and in particular the labour theory of value and the theory of surplus value. Their apologetic conception and numerous models of economic processes are based on the theory of marginal utility and the scarcity of resources. And when these ideologists of capitalism note with pleasure that in the Soviet Union, in connection with the widespread use of mathematical methods, some economists shift from the labour theory of value on to a position close to the marginal utility theory, this cannot but cause legitimate concern'.

The reformers, whether mathematical or no, have been repulsed. True, the computer and mathematics are being and will be used *in the process of planning*. True also, changes have been made in various aspects of the 'traditional' system, and these we will be describing in a moment. However, the old system, whether of ideas or of organizational-economic substance, has survived without fundamental change.

The reform that never was

The September 1965 reforms appeared, on the surface, to usher in a period of fundamental changes. Certainly this was the opinion of a number of Soviet economists at the time. 'All our reforms so far consisted in changing labels on the doors of the same officials; now it is going to be different', declared one economist. He was wrong.

Yet apparently there were indeed some changes. Let us recapitulate them:

1. The abolition of the regional *Sovnarkhozy*, the restoration of

economic ministries, the reconcentration of planning function in Gosplan, with material supplies organized by *Gossnab* (the State Committee on Supplies).

2. The reduction in the number of compulsory indicators planned from above. The following are still so planned:
(a) Value of sales (*realizatsiya*)
(b) 'The basic nomenclature of output'
(c) The wages fund total
(d) Profits in roubles
(e) Profitability as a percentage of capital
(f) Payments to and out of the state budget
(g) Centralized investments and new capacity
(h) 'Basic tasks in the introduction of new technique'
(i) Material supply.
Among the many abandoned indicators are the value of gross output and the cost reduction plan.

3. The computation of profits as a percentage of capital was accompanied by the (gradual) introduction of a capital charge, a percentage of the capital of the enterprise payable annually into the state budget. New price lists, based on cost plus a percentage on capital, came into operation in July 1967; these greatly diminished the number of loss-making enterprises.

4. A larger proportion of investments would henceforth be financed by returnable interest-bearing credits.

5. It was intended gradually to expand wholesale trade in producers' goods, thereby partly replacing their administrative allocation.

6. There was a total recasting of managerial incentives. These were now to be paid out of profits. There are three funds financing respectively personal material incentives (for labour and management), amenities and decentralized investments. The computation of the three incentive funds were and are exceedingly complex. They are a function of the following elements:
(a) Planned profits, profit rate (*rentabel'nost'*) and sales (*realizatsiya*), usually a combination of *two* of these.
(b) The size of the wages fund, or, in the case of payments into the investment fund, the value of capital.

(c) The 'norm' applicable to the given enterprise or sector. (Thus in one case a 1 per cent planned increase in profits might result in a payment of 0·3 per cent of the wages fund into the material incentives fund, while in another the figure could be 0·2 per cent or 0·5 per cent, and so on).

(d) All the above calculations are modified if the enterprise's results are above or below the plan. (Achievements in excess of plan are subject to a reduced 'norm' of payment into the incentive funds, so as to discourage concealment of productive potential.)

(e) There are preconditions: thus the enterprise must fulfill all or most of the compulsory plan indicators listed above, and since 1968 must also ensure that its total payments to labour (including any bonuses out of profits) do not exceed the rise in labour productivity.

In the Shchekinsk chemical combine, a new idea is being tried out: that of letting the employees share the economies in wages due to a reduction in the labour force. (This is exceptional so far.)

The incentive schemes are barely comprehensible and often contradictory. Thus, to take but one example, an economy in wages could have the effect of *reducing* the incentive fund, since this is computed not as a percentage of the (increased) profits but of the (reduced) wages fund. The sales indicator, which is in roubles and is gross, in the sense of including the value of purchased inputs, is frequently inconsistent with the profits indicator. Since the main object is to fulfil planned increases in sales and profits it has become 'rational' to avoid too rapid an increase, to keep some in hand for subsequent years. In any case, as more and more enterprises were transferred to 'the new system', old ministerial habits reasserted themselves. Plans are altered arbitrarily, even retrospectively, by the ministry, instructions are issued on matters which are supposed to be within the competence of enterprise management, and so on. Protests have frequently appeared in the press about the arbitrary disruption of long-established supply links by ministries, striving for 'ministerial self-sufficiency' or to ensure priority in supplies for 'their' enterprises, duplicating or contradicting in the process the supply network of Gossnab.

These deficiencies or contradictions must be seen as *the consequences of non-reform*. Prices do not reflect demand or scarcities save by coincidence. The price recomputations of 1967 were still based on cost-plus, though it is now cost plus an amount which includes a rate of return on capital. The capital charge cannot in practice have much effect on demand for capital from below, in so far as it is included in prices. In just the same way, higher prices for inputs have little effect on demand for them, or even at times the opposite effect to that which was intended, so long as the higher-priced inputs are included in costings and in the official price. (The resultant increase in total value of output and sales 'improves' plan performance in roubles.) Such prices as these are useless as indicators of economic behaviour. They do not transmit information. Nor are they really intended to do so. The power to allocate resources and to take production decisions remains with the central authorities, and is shaped between the revived industrial ministries, Gosplan and *Gossnab*, under the general supervision of the higher party organs. Chronic excess demand, and particularly for investment goods, provides the rationale for administrative allocation based on priorities. Indeed, with existing prices the profit motive cannot operate rationally. There is no connection between profit and need, only between profit and (planned) cost. It is interesting to note that current doctrine regards an increase in profits due to a change in the product mix or in inputs as somehow illegitimate. Profits should be 'cleansed' of such elements before being considered as indicators of efficiency. Yet this means that both the product mix and the inputs of the enterprise are laid down in a plan initiated or approved at ministerial or *glavk* level. It logically follows that the supply plans made in one or other of the central bodies cover the major part of industrial output, and that both its production and its delivery to designated customers must form part of obligatory plan-orders from above. This is the essence of the old system. It survives today.

The system has an inner logic which defies gradual change. Thus the elimination of some item from central production, allocation or investment plans usually has two consequences; the necessary inputs cease to be available, because they are fully committed to *planned* outputs or investments; and the desired goods may not be produced at all, since no effective market links exist to replace the 'traditional' obligatory plan-order.

The 'traditional' system, let it be re-emphasized, was based on central administrative assessment of need, upon which basis instructions were issued and plans formulated. In Hungary a new basis has been found. In the USSR the older pattern remains with little change.

Experiments continue in an effort to improve the system. Indeed, it may be cogently argued that it works better on the 'ministerial' basis than it did under the *Sovnarkhozy*. There is, after all, no acute crisis, output continues to rise, living standards are improving slowly. The present conservative-minded leadership reacts adversely to radical ideas in any field.

It is at present attracted to the idea of basing industrial administration on intermediate bodies, the *industrial associations* (*ob'edineniya*). These have spread in many industries, and are amalgamations of enterprises in the same sector and/or area, under the general authority of an economic ministry. Sometimes the constituent enterprises have been virtually eliminated as autonomous bodies, being relegated to a status similar to that of the workshop (*tsakh*) within an enterprise. Sometimes they retain their separate identity. There are experiments in turning ministerial *glavk* into a species of industrial association, and indeed of putting them and whole ministries on to commercial accounting.

Some western critics regard the move towards industrial association as 'anti-liberal', as yet another move to restrict managerial autonomy and market relations. This appears to me to be only part of the truth. The Soviet industrial enterprise is usually one factory. Western experience suggests that in many sectors the large corporation, which includes many factories, is the most efficient managerial unit. In so far as the Soviet rulers are seeking a Soviet equivalent of Dupont, General Electric and Krupp, they can hardly be criticized for conservative resistance to necessary change. However, the industrial association is also doubtless seen by the 'conservatives' as an alternative to markets, competition and similar new-fangled notions.

The point concerning the corporation is only one of many which some of the more naïve would-be reformers are inclined to overlook. Perhaps they visualize a market model of the textbook kind, and compare the Soviet economy with it. Yet the problems of economies of scale and of externalities cannot be handled within the confines of a model in which they are assumed out of existence. This criticism can be directed equally at the constructs of Fedorenko and of Liberman. Though the former is much more sophisticated than the latter, both envisage a system within which the profitability of the parts adds up to – or is in conformity with – the profitability of the entire economy. Yet this has never been achieved within the confines of the western corporation. Its very existence is due in large part to the 'internalization of externalization', to the fact that profitability is more clearly appreciated at the headquarters of DuPont than in each of the units of which the corporation is composed. Nor can one assert that only political resistance stands in the way of adopting the mathematicians' advice. Some critics of the various mathematical models have a sound basis for their caution as to the applicability of these models to real life. We have only to look at some of the best-known western growth models. At best they explain, or forecast, the behaviour of semi-autonomous economic forces. They are not and cannot be a substitute for either operational administrative centralization or for devolution of micro-economic decision-making to management acting within a market.

There are other unsolved questions: the link between incentives based on profits and a non-existent capital market; the emergence of uncontrolled and perhaps undeserved income inequalities; possible danger of unemployment; the cost of competition – and it has a cost; the problem of bankruptcy, and so on.

None the less despite very real objective difficulties, it must surely be accepted that the major obstacle to change lies in a combination of inertia, habit and self-interest. The party and state bureaucracies are accustomed to work in 'traditional' ways, to interfere to enforce priorities. Not least of these to this day are directly military priorities, connected with the cost of the arms and space race. To this some would add ideology, the Marxist–Leninist stress on deliberate planning as against the 'anarchic' market. Others argue that the opponents of reform clothe their practical objections in ideological garb, selecting their quotations from Lenin from the period up to 1920, while such reformers as Lisichkin cite the Lenin of NEP in support of their 'market' ideas. Whether due to interest, habit or ideology, or all three, the fact remains that opposition is strong among members of the political machine, and recent Czech events have strengthened the hand of the conservatives, as we have seen. One of the principal contrasts with Hungarian experience is that in Hungary the 'traditional' system had only been in operation for a few years, whereas few in the USSR can remember living under any other than a centrally planned economy. To these factors must be added the much greater dependence of Hungary upon foreign trade, and her much lesser concern with arms and space expenditures. Also the Hungarian communist leadership is far less determined upon, or confident in its right to impose, tight party control over the operations of the country's economy.

Conclusion

When I was in the Soviet Union in 1967, and remarked upon the slow progress in implementing even the modest reform measures of 1965, I was several times told by my Soviet colleagues: 'change must be gradual, but we are on the way. Come back in two years and you will hardly recognize the system'. I came back in 1969 and it was all very familiar. These same economists were much more cautious in forecasting change, and less confident about the adoption of major reform measures. The more radical voices seldom find their way into the press, the 'conservatives' seem to be in control. The contrast with Hungary is striking. It is interesting to note that the Hungarian 'new model' is tolerated, even cautiously described in the Soviet press – as in the articles by Friss and by Volin – and much discussed privately by staff and students, as I heard for myself in Moscow University. Yet the Czech proposals of 1968, the ideas of Ota Sik, are denounced as heretical. The explanations of this apparent contradiction are purely political: the Hungarian leadership, in full control of the organs of mass communication, has been careful not to claim the discovery of a 'new model', to play on muted strings. There has been no association in Hungary between economic reform and political liberalization, no doctrine of 'socialism with a human face', a doctrine which implies the existence of socialism with an inhuman face.

The question arises: what next in the USSR? The more progressive and original minds in the Soviet economics profession have been arguing for years that the 'traditional' system is inefficient, that it has outlived its usefulness, that it stands in the way of the effective utilization and rational expansion of productive forces. It continues to serve as a means of enforcing priorities, it operates adequately in some sectors of heavy industry which are relatively easy to plan in the old way (steel, electricity, coal, cement, and similar relatively homogeneous commodities). The familiar chronic diseases are still causing trouble: over-taut planning, lack of balance between production and supply plans, between the investment plan and the output of building materials and equipment, resistance to innovation, and to technical progress at the lower echelons, the distortion of local initiative by the need to simulate plan fulfilment, and so on. The need for change is urgent, even though, as already pointed out, there is no urgent crisis, no demoralization and stagnation such as affected Czechoslovakia in and after 1962 and provided such a powerful impetus to new ideas in that country.

Crystal-gazing is an imperfect science. Conservatism is strong, and not only in Russia! The adaptation of all established structures to change is a painful and slow business. Even to change the organization and methods of a university is no simple job, as all of us must readily agree from our own experience. Resistance to change is very strong in the political organs of the USSR, and could be overcome, in my view, by a combination of two circumstances. Firstly, a clear realization that the present economic system is responsible for continued relative backwardness in the competition with the West; at present the leaders seem to think that its admitted inadequacies can be corrected by minor procedural and organizational changes. Secondly, a firm leader or group of leaders must not only be committed to reform, but have the power and will to enforce their views on the party and state machine. No such leader or leaders seem to exist today, and certainly Brezhnev has neither the power nor the will to do the job.

Change towards greater reliance on market elements will come. The old way has been outgrown. But in the immediate future there is no sign of any major changes in either theory or practice. Many of us have underestimated the conservatism of the 'establishment' and the strength of inertia. Some hold that any major reform requires prior changes in the political structure, affecting particularly the power of the Communist party. Others point out that one could conceive of a greater reliance on managerial autonomy and rational calculation without there being any move towards a relaxation of political controls. There is no time or space to pursue this argument here, it is only one of several question-marks which cloud our vision of the future.

References

BIRMAN, A. (1968), *Novyi mir*, no. 12.

KORNAI, J., and LIPTAK, T. (1962), 'A mathematical investigation of some economic effects of profit-sharing in Socialist firms', *Econometrica*, vol. 30.

LISICHKIN, G. (1966), *Plan i rynok*, Moscow.

NOVE, A. (1969), 'History, hierarchy and nationalities', *Soviet Studies*, July.

SIK, O. (1967), *Planning and the Market Under Socialism*, New York and Prague: PASP.

VOLIN, P. (1969), *Novyi mir*, no. 3.

17 D. M. Nuti

Investment Reforms in Czechoslovakia

From D. M. Nuti, 'Investment reforms in Czechoslovakia',
Soviet Studies, 1970, vol. 21, no. 3.

In 1967 in Czechoslovakia two official documents introduced new
regulations for the choice of investment projects by state enterprises.[1] These regulations were based on the same kind of discounted cash flow methods described in business textbooks (see
for example Merrett and Sykes, 1963; 1966) and recommended
by government agencies in Western countries (see for example
HMSO, 1965); they replaced the Soviet-type investment rules
issued by the Státní Plánovací Komise (1961). In this article we
shall give a summary of the old and new investment rules and
discuss the extent of the changes and their implications for
socialist economic planning.

The old investment rules

Before 1967, the investment criteria used in Czechoslovakia were
based, as in the Soviet Union, on the concept of 'recoupment
period'. Given a target for expansion of output capacity expressed in physical terms, whenever alternative methods of
production were available, the 'recoupment period' of a project
was defined as the number of years over which the additional investment expenditure associated with the project, with respect to
the immediately less investment-intensive project, was 'recouped'
by means of lower current operating costs (including amortization). Given two alternative projects characterized by investment
costs I_1 and I_2 and operating costs V_1 and V_2 (inclusive of
amortization), such that $I_1 < I_2$ and $V_2 < V_1$, the 'coefficient of
economic effectiveness of additional investment' k is defined
(Státní Plánovací Komise, 1961, p. 17) as

1. See Státní Komise pro Techniku-Státní Banka Československá (1967);
Státní Komise pro Techniku (1967).

$$k = \frac{V_1 - V_2}{I_2 - I_1}, \qquad\qquad 1$$

i.e. as the inverse of the recoupment period of the more invest-ment-intensive project 2. The coefficient of effectiveness of a project was then compared with the *normative* coefficient of effectiveness k_n, fixed for the industry by the Planning Com-mission and, in the simple case of no gestation, the project was selected (Státní Plánovací Komise, 1961, p. 18) for which

$$V + k_n I = \text{minimum}, \qquad\qquad 2$$

i.e. the recoupment period was closest to but lower than the 'standard' recoupment period for the industry.

The loss of potential output N due to the 'freezing' of invest-ment resources during the period of gestation was estimated as

$$N = \sum_{j=1}^{t} I_j \left[\frac{(1 + k_u)^{t-j+1}}{H} - 1 \right], \qquad\qquad 3$$

where I_j is investment expenditure in the jth year of the t-years-long construction period, $j = 1, \ldots, t$; k_u is the rate at which in-vestment expenditures are compounded during the construction period (the rate was equal to the average of the normative co-efficients in different industries, i.e. $0 \cdot 15$); and H is 'a coefficient expressing the uniformity of investment outlays during the year' (for $k_u = 0 \cdot 15$, $H = 1 \cdot 071$). These investment regulations could be synthesized by the rule

$$C + \left(\frac{1}{T} + \frac{1}{n} \right) \sum_{j=1}^{t} I_j \left[\frac{(1 + k_u)^{t-j+1}}{H} \right] = \text{minimum}, \qquad\qquad 4$$

where C is the current operating cost (wages and materials) of the project, T is the standard recoupment period for the industry (7–10 years in power, ferrous metallurgy, construction; 6–8 years in fuel and non-ferrous metallurgy; 5–8 years in chemicals; 4–6 years in food, consumer goods and engineering; $k_n = 1/T$), and n is the expected lifetime of the plant for the purpose of amortiz-ation. (See Kočtúch, 1963; Komárek and Řiha, 1964; Ferfecký, 1965.)

Similar rules were used in other socialist countries, like Poland and Hungary, (see Komisia Planowania Przy Radzie Ministrów, 1962; Országos Tervhivatal-Pénzügyminisztérium-Epitésügyi Minisztérium, 1963) and were all derived from the Soviet

Metodiki (1960 and 1962).[2] While the Polish and Hungarian instructions had been partly modified, with the introduction of uniform instead of diversified standard recoupment periods and other modifications,[3] the Czechoslovak instructions were practically identical with those of the Soviet Union.[4]

In addition to the basic rule stated above, five other indexes in the field of investments connected with international trade were taken into account (Státní Plánovací Komise, 1961, part 4, pp. 49–53). These were: 1. The yearly gross and net currency earnings; 2. The ratio between the value of yearly output at international prices obtainable at the Czech border and the value of yearly output at internal wholesale prices; 3. The ratio between the value of yearly output at international prices obtainable at the Czech border and the yearly operating costs; 4. The ratio between the net currency earnings and the sum of labour costs *plus* transport and other costs of international trade; 5. The 'index of dependence on foreign currency', i.e. the ratio between the value of imported (or exportable) materials contained in exported commodities, and the value of exported commodities (at Czech border prices).

The drawbacks of the old rules

The most interesting feature of these rules was the introduction of a kind of shadow interest rate, under the guise of the normative coefficients of investment effectiveness k_ns and the coefficient k_u, which were meant to induce firms to economize investment funds although these were granted free of charge from the state budget. These shadow rates, however, had a limited scope of application and had a number of drawbacks.

2. See Akademiya nauk SSSR (1960); Gosplan i AN SSSR (1962).

3. In the Polish case, extensive modifications were introduced to allow for the comparison of investment projects characterized by different gestation periods, lifetime, and time pattern of costs and output. These modifications embodied *in toto* the suggestions put forward in an article by Kalecki and Rakowski(1959).

4. Both included straight line amortization in operating costs, had diversified recoupment periods that were longer for heavy than for light industries, with only two minor differences, namely the use of the inverse of the *average* rather than the *sectoral* standard recoupment period to compound investment outlays within the gestation period, and the introduction of the corrective coefficient H.

There was a peculiar asymmetry between the application of k_n and that of k_u. To make comparable investment expenditure at different dates during the construction period the shadow rate k_u was compounded and, by means of the coefficient H, allowance was made even for the fact that investment outlays do not all take place at the beginning of a year. For the determination of the shadow capital charge (k_n plus straight line depreciation), however, no compounding was taken into account. It would have seemed more reasonable to use compound interest throughout.

Different shadow rates were used in different sectors (and, within each sector, for different purposes, unless $k_u = k_n$). If the shadow interest rate were to be used to choose between production of different products, a diversified pattern of shadow rates could have been justified if it reflected a deliberate strategy of sectoral priorities. But since shadow rates were used to select the production technique of given output targets, the adoption of different rates could have led to straightforward inefficiency.

It is clear that the values of the coefficients k_ns and k_u must satisfy a number of macroeconomic equilibrium conditions. Given the current and planned prices of production goods, the level and structure of wage rates and the set of targets for the expansion of productive capacity in all sectors, the values of k_u and the k_ns must be such that the value and composition of investment and current inputs demanded by firms undertaking new projects should be equal to the value and composition of investment and production goods available during the same period. At the same time, the jobs provided by the construction and operation of new plants must be consistent with the maintenance of full employment of labour. In these circumstances, one would expect the value of the coefficients to be determined every period (and possibly for some periods ahead) by some process of iteration between firms stating the input requirements associated with their output targets at alternative levels of prices and coefficients and the centre fixing the initial targets and prices and revising them after checking the internal consistency of firms' requirements, till an overall balance is reached. Although this role of the coefficients was clearly understood in Czech literature, (see for example Šrein, 1967) no satisfactory explanation was provided for the way they were actually determined, why they should differ in different sectors and why they should remain constant in time. Like all the other prices, these coefficients have proved too rigid for use as operational parameters. If these coefficients have had practical impact in actual technical choice, equilibrium must have been reached, as far as one can see, by adjusting output targets and/or aggregate investment decisions to the pre-selected value of the coefficients, rather than the other way round.

The investment rules were directed to enterprises and had to be observed, at least for investment projects directly included in the national plan, but the level and structure of incentives for decision-makers was geared to indexes (e.g. gross output, degree of fulfilment of plan, etc.) other than the indexes on the basis of which investment decisions should have been taken. In principle it should be possible to induce managers to take shadow prices into account for the purpose of decision-making, by means of schemes including such prices among the variables on which incentive payments depend. (See Nuti, 1966.) In the Czech case, however, managers seem to have had no incentive (and possibly some disincentive) to consider the shadow capital charge implicit in the basic investment rule, or the other indexes listed in the *Směrnice*.

The five indexes related to international trade are not 'rules' but simply ways of summarizing information which might be relevant for a decision. They express the preoccupations of the planners of an open economy but do not provide direct guidance for investment choice and should be best regarded as auxiliary indicators which reduce the area of arbitrariness ('voluntarism') in economic decisions.

Investment reforms: the new rules

The *Podmínky* establish a procedure for investment choice for all projects directly planned from the centre and all those over 1·5 million crowns planned by the enterprises ('investors'). The selection procedure is organized at branch level, or at the central office of the investors, in collaboration with the State Bank. Investors submit the technical specifications of projects and the additional information required for their assessment. The decision is taken by the Bank and the 'national authorities of economic management', and the *Podmínky* give a long list of general criteria and five synthetic indexes of various aspects of projects. The general criteria are rather vague and open to wide interpretation. They include: the basic aims of the state plan; planned development of branches and areas; credit regulations; information on supply conditions for the whole period of construction; the state and utilization of fixed assets, the period of construction and its influence on the effectiveness of a project; the introduction of technical progress; the consistency of the planned development with the findings of market research, the requirements of regional development, etc. The indexes of effectiveness are given here in the same order as they appear in the appendix (*Příloha*) to the *Podmínky*, but it is stressed that the order does not indicate relative importance.

The first four indexes are required for the assessment of all investment projects:

1. The ratio between the value of yearly output of the project evaluated at international prices (corrected for differences in quality, and taken at the Czech border, i.e. allowing for insurance, transport and other costs) and converted into crowns at a shadow rate of exchange (called 'coefficient of equalization of the internal reproduction price' or VRCV for *koeficient vnitřního reprodukčního cenového vyrovnání*), and the value of yearly output calculated at internal wholesale prices; this is calculated both at current and expected future prices.

2. The index of investment activity, i.e. the ratio between the value of yearly output of the project, evaluated at international prices and converted to internal prices at a shadow exchange rate (VRCV), and the total investment outlay at internal prices.

3. The index of productivity of investment outlays. This is the sum of gross profits earned by the project after completion, discounted at a given discount rate (12 per cent in 1967), divided by the number of years of operation of the project and expressed as a fraction of total investment outlays. These are given by the cost of investment at completion, computed as the sum of investment outlays during the construction period, cumulated up to the period of completion at the same rate used to discount profits. Two alternative versions of this index are given, according to whether or not the sum of discounted increases (decreases) in

circulating capital is added to (subtracted from) actual investment outlays. The first index is given as

$$V\phi_d = \frac{\sum_{m=1}^{n} HZ_m \, v^m}{n \left[\sum_{j=1}^{t} JP_j \, r^{t-j} + \sum_{m=1}^{n} OP_m \, v^m \right]} \qquad 5$$

and the second as

$$V\phi_d = \frac{\sum_{m=1}^{n} HZ_m \, v^m}{n \sum_{j=1}^{t} IP_j \, r^{t-j}} \qquad 6$$

where j indicates individual years of the construction period going from 1 to t, the year of completion; m indicates individual years of the period of operation of the completed plant, going from 1 to n; HZ_m is gross profit (*hrubý zisk*) in the mth year of operation; IP_j is investment outlay (*investiční prostředky*) in the jth year of the construction period (JP_j in the first index – *jednorázové prostředky*[5]); $v = 1/(1+p)$; $r = 1+p$; p is the discount rate; OP_m is the change in circulating capital in the already existing plants, due to the investment project.

4. The pay-off period of investment outlays. This is the period over which the sum of undiscounted profits, net of interest charges and some other compulsory payments and allowances but gross of amortization, covers the *total* cost of investment. This period is taken into account when all investment outlays are financed by credit.

The other two indexes mentioned in the *Podmínky* are required to assess investment projects requiring more than 5 million crowns for their construction or for their yearly operating costs, for projects directed to import substitution and to export promotion and for centrally planned investment projects. These indexes are:

5. The index of the currency evaluation of production. This is the ratio between the value of yearly output at international prices (taken not at the Czech border but at the factory, i.e.

---

5. There appears to be a slight difference between the two definitions of investment expenditure, which can be ignored here.

adjusted allowing for the costs of foreign trade agencies, customs duties, subsidies, etc.) and the yearly production costs expressed in currency crowns (*devizoví kčs.*).

6. The index of the currency evaluation of investment. This is the ratio between the value of yearly output at international prices (as above) minus yearly production costs expressed in currency crowns and the investment expenditure expressed also in currency crowns.

Each index is designed to evaluate a particular aspect of an investment project and 'the final judgement rests upon the appraisal of all analytical indexes taking into account the different importance that must be attached to them in the actual case in particular economic situations'.[6]

Additional variants of these indexes, with minor modifications, are presented in two other documents of the *Státní Komise pro Techniku*, containing also more detailed explanations and the actual forms to be filled in by investors. These are the *Zásady* already mentioned[7] and a set of recommendations, *Doporučené Zásady* (1967) on the evaluation of investment projects from the viewpoint of international trade. Of the indexes presented in these documents, the most interesting is the *internal rate of return* (VVP or *vnitřní výnosové procento*). Section 3 of the *Zásady* is entitled 'a method for the evaluation of the economic effectiveness of investment on the basis of assessing the global development of the economy of the enterprise by calculating the internal rate of return'. This rate is obtained by solving the equation

$$K'_n v^n + \sum_{i=1}^{n} (CZ_i + Od_i + OP'_i)v^i - K_o - \sum_{i=1}^{n} (K_i + NI_i)v^i = O \qquad 7$$

for v, where $v = 1/(1+p)$ and p is the internal rate of return; K'_n is the residual value of the assets of the enterprise at the end of the period n; CZ_i is net profit in the ith year; Od_i is the depreciation allowance (*odpisy základních prostředků*) in the ith year; OP'_i is the increase (or decrease) in the amount of circulating capital in the ith year; K_o is the value of the assets of the enterprise at the beginning of the period; K_i is investment expenditure in the ith year; NI_i represents outlays in the ith year, which do

6. *Příloha k Podmínkám*, p. 11.
7. See footnote 1.

not increase the value of the assets of the enterprise (e.g. outlays on 'unrealized projects').

This is the first time that, in the actual practice of socialist countries, the internal rate of return is introduced as a criterion for actual investment choice.

Another interesting aspect of the reforms, finally, is the institution of competitions (*konkurs*) organized by the Bank, Ministries and other central bodies, 'to stimulate the interest of investors to project and realize investments especially needed and efficient'.[8]

The investment reforms: a critique

The changes introduced by the *Podmínky* are quite far-reaching. The indexes related to international trade are almost unchanged and still rather crude, in spite of remarkable advances in the theory of international trade planning, (see for example Piaszczynski and Trzeciakowski, 1962; Kronsjö, 1964; Augostinovics, 1966) but the basic investment rule of Soviet origin is totally abandoned and the new approach is substantially identical to that of enterprises in the capitalist economies.

First, the notion of the pay-off period of *total* investment replaces the more limited traditional notion of the recoupment period of the *additional* investment associated with alternative projects. This is a fundamental difference in that the traditional criterion was meant to discriminate among alternative technical ways of achieving a *given target*, whereas the new criterion is presumably meant to discriminate *among alternative targets* (otherwise there would be no point in introducing this new concept at all).

Secondly, the practice of discounting – previously confined to the addition of investment outlays occurring at different dates – is now extended with the introduction of discounted cash flow methods to the whole process of investment choice. The criterion of internal rate of return is introduced explicitly (see equation 7); the present value criterion is implicit in the indexes defined in

8. Státní Komise Pro Techniku-Státní Banka Československá (1967, p. 8). It is not clear whether the 'Konkurs' should consist simply in the award of prizes to deserving enterprises, or take a role similar to that of the Yugoslav 'investment auctions' (see Neuberger, 1959).

equations **5** and **6**. If we indicate with P the present value of an investment project, and with I the investment cost of the project at completion date, we can express the index V_{ϕ_a} as

$$V\phi_a = \frac{P+I}{n\,I} \qquad\qquad\qquad 8$$

(the present value of a project is equal to the sum of discounted profits minus the cost of investment, so we can substitute $P+I$ for the sum of discounted profits), while the difference between equations **5** and **6** is in the kinds of costs included among investment costs. The capitalist rule that $P \geqslant O$ can therefore be expressed in the form $V_{\phi_a} \geqslant 1/n$. As a test to reject unprofitable projects both indexes would give the same result, but as indexes for *ranking* alternative projects V_{ϕ_a} would not necessarily give the same result as P. It looks as if the attempt at developing socialist investment criteria has led to the invention of a curious hybrid between discounted cash flow methods and the pay-off criterion.

Thirdly, the introduction of the new rules is reinforced by changes in the schemes of incentive payments, which are now geared to the amount of current profits obtained by enterprises,[9] which would obviously induce state managers to use pay-off and discounted cash flow criteria. The competition for investment projects indicated in the *Podmínky* seems also designed to enforce the new rules.

The practice of investing up to the point where the total investment outlays are recouped by current profits within a given number of years could be justified as the rational behaviour of a capitalist enterprise operating in conditions of imperfect competition and subject to uncertainty about technical progress which might undermine the semi-monopolistic position of the enterprise. Even within the capitalist context this practice has been widely criticized as being conducive to biases in the technical choice (see Harcourt, 1967) and for the rather crude treatment of time which is implicit in the use of the pay-off period. (See Merrett and Sykes, 1963; 1969 and HMSO, 1965.) This critique might not be relevant when the firm is operating in a capitalist economy,

9. See 'General guidelines for enterprise operation, valid from 1 January 1967', in *New Trends in the Czechoslovak Economy*, booklet no. 6, September 1966

but certainly applies to the use of this criterion in a socialist economy, especially if we expect such an economy to simulate the functioning of a competitive system.

The introduction of discounted cash flow methods does not present these kinds of problems, but has unfortunately other disadvantages. First of all, it is debatable whether one should apply a unique interest rate to investment choice in different sectors. If the interest rate is used only to choose the technical form of investment, as in the traditional rules, then there is a case for a uniform rate; but if, as in the new rules, the sector of production is chosen *as well* as the technical form of investment, the argument in favour of a uniform rate does not apply any longer. There is no reason why the pattern of interest rates should not be diversified, in different sectors, to reflect the pattern of priorities assigned to the sectors in the national plan.

Secondly, if discounted cash flow methods are used in technical choice, the prices at which the calculations are performed can only be reliable if the internal rate of return of investment projects at those prices is equal to the interest rate, that is if the present value of the projects is equal to zero. If the present value is positive, i.e. if the internal rate of return differs from the interest rate, this might mean one of three things: that there is imperfect competition; that there are scarce factors like land, or access to natural resources, or perhaps managerial abilities, which are not priced as their scarcity requires, so that unpaid-for rents are included in the present value of the project; or that prices expected by firms are different from the prices which will prevail in reality. In one way or another, if prices are such that they yield a positive present value, they cannot be taken to indicate alternatives in a reliable way and the discounted cash flow methods might recommend courses of action which, from a macroeconomic point of view, are defective either in the choice of the product, or the technical method of production, or both.

The use of discounted cash flow methods of the kind introduced in the new Czech regulations can only be acceptable if it is considered as a *single stage* of a process of iteration directed to checking the internal consistency both of the quantities produced by all investment projects under examination and of the prices which would prevail if all those projects were actually implemented. This process of iteration could start with all firms sending in to the central offices of the State Bank the investment projects which they would wish to undertake in view of the level of the interest rate announced by the bank and the expected prevailing prices of all inputs and outputs. The second stage could consist in the centre putting together all the quantities of all inputs and outputs of all the investment projects, and checking whether all inputs would be available and outputs could be sold at the expected prices. If the internal consistency of quantities of inputs and outputs and their prices is not reached at the first round, the centre could either change the parameter which is directly under its control, namely the interest rate, or rectify the expectations of firms. On the basis of these signals issued by the centre firms would start a second round of calculations; they would revise their investment projects, which would then be submitted again to the centre and so on until the desired consistency is reached.

The new Czech investment rules contain certain provisions for the central control and checking of the internal consistency of projects, but there is no mention of such an iteration process, and the provisions are actually rather loose. Although it is stated that the central authorities will exercise a control over the sources of supply and on the sales outlays of the investment projects submitted by firms, it is difficult to visualize how the decentralization of investment decisions introduced by the reforms could be consistent with the maintenance of central control over the overall level and sectoral allocation of national investment. It appears from the recent economic experience of Czechoslovakia that the teeth of these regulations have been drawn for, in practice, state firms are capable of undertaking the projects they like, simply by reinvesting their profits, without having to borrow from the bank and, therefore, without being subject to most of the new investment regulations. If, however, the new rules have to be taken at all seriously, it can be said that they were going to bring Czechoslovakia very much into line with the Yugoslavian model of economic planning. This implies the loss of the main advantage of socialist economic planning, namely the control by the state of the overall rate of capital accumulation and growth. Decentralization of investment decisions to a similar extent has brought, in Yugoslavia, inflationary processes, regional unbalances in the process of development and, in general, a loss of control by the planning authorities over the direction of the development of the economy.[10] To maintain central control over the macro-economic processes of investment and growth the decentralization of investment decisions must be coupled to a process of iterative flows of information from the enterprises to the centre and back, until the consistency of enterprises' decisions with the central plan is checked and guaranteed.

It would be inaccurate to say that the Czech economic reforms were leading to some kind of capitalist model of a mixed economy. The letter of the official documents issued in the field of investment, however, shows that the new Czech economic system was certainly bound to lose control over accumulation and growth – the main advantages of socialist planning. Had the economic discussion been allowed to continue, undoubtedly some more precise form of central control over investment would have been devised.

10. Discussing the scope of centralization and decentralization in a socialist economy, Brus states explicitly that the domain of decentralization in a socialist economy cannot be extended to the process of investment (Brus, 1961). It has been stressed by Dobb that one of the main points about socialist planning is the removal of what Koopmans calls 'secondary uncertainty', namely uncertainty about the overall direction of development of the economy, which is the outcome of a large number of individual decisions (especially investment decisions) independently taken (Dobb, 1937; 1969 Part II, ch. 1).

References

Akademiya Nauk SSSR (1960), *Tipovaya metodika opredeleniya ekonomicheskoi effektivnosti kapital' nykh vlozhenii i novoi tekhniki v narodnom khozyaistve SSSR* (Standard methodology for determining the economic effectiveness of capital investment and new technology), Moscow.

Augostinovics, M. (1966), 'Linear inquiries into foreign trade' (a paper submitted at the conference of the IEA), Nice.

Brus, W. (1961), *Ogólne problemy funkcjonowania gospodarki socjalistycznej* (General problems of the functioning of a socialist economy), Warsaw.

Dobb, M. H. (1937), 'The question of economic law in a socialist economy', *Political Economy and Socialism*, London.

Dobb, M. H. (1969), *Welfare Economics and the Economics of Socialism*, Cambridge University Press.

Doporučené Zásady Propočtu Ekonomické Efektivnosti Investic Z
Hlediska Působení Světovych Cen a Mezinárodni Dělby Práce
(Principles recommended for the calculation of the economic
effectiveness of investment from the point of view of the influence of
international prices and the international division of labour),
c.j. 34987 – II/42/66, Prague.

FERFECKY, O. (1965), 'Methodology of industrial project evaluation in
Czechoslovakia', United Nations Inter-Regional Symposium on
Industrial Project Evaluation, Prague.

Gosplan i AN SSSR (1962), *Metodika opredeleniya ekonomicheskoi
effektivnosti vnedreniya novoi tekhniki, mekhanizatsii i avtomatizatsii
proizvodstvennykh protsessov v promyshlennosti* (Methodology for
determining the economic effectiveness of the introduction of new
technology, mechanization and automation of productive processes in
industry), Moscow.

HARCOURT, G. C. (1967), 'Investment decision criteria, capital intensity
and the choice of techniques', *Czechoslovak Economic Papers*, no. 9.

HMSO (1965), National Economic Development Council, *Investment
Appraisal* and *Investment in Machine Tools*, London.

KALECKI, M., and RAKOWSKI, M. (1959), 'Uogólnienie wzoru
ekonomicznej efektywności inwestycji' (A generalized formula of the
effectiveness of investment), see Reading 11 in this volume.

KOCTÚCH, H. (1963), 'The recoupment period: a Czechoslovak view',
Soviet Studies, vol. 15, no. 2.

KOMAREK, L., and ŘIHA, L. (1964), 'Problems in measuring the
effectiveness of investments under socialism', *Czechoslovak Economic
Papers*, no. 3, Prague.

Komisia Planowania Przy Radzie Ministró (1962), *Instrukcja Ogólna w
sprawie metodyki badán ekonomicznej efektiwności inwestycji* (General
instructions on the methodology for determining the economic
effectiveness of investment), Warsaw.

KRONSJÖ, T. (1964), 'Iterative price and quantity determination for
short-run production and foreign trade planning', Regional Science
Association, *Papers*.

MERRETT, A. J., and SYKES, A. (1963), *The Finance and Analysis of
Capital Projects*, London.

MERRETT, A. J., and SYKES, A. (1966), *Capital Budgeting and Company
Finance*, Longman.

NUTI, D. M. (1966), 'Material incentive schemes and the choice of
techniques in Soviet industry', *Australian Economic Papers*, December.

NEUBERGER, E. (1959), 'The Yugoslav investment auctions', *Quarterly
Journal of Economics*.

Országos Tervhivatal-Pénzügy-Minisztérium-Épitésügyi Minisztérium
(National Planning Board-Ministry of Finance, Ministry of Building)
(1963), *Beruhazasi Kodex* (Investment Code), Budapest.

PIASZCZYNSKI, W., and TRZECIAKOWSKI, W. (1962), 'Efficiency prices and economic calculation in foreign trade', Regional Science Association, *Papers*.

ŠREIN, Z. (1967), 'Investment decision criteria and the recoupment period', *Czechoslovak Economic Papers*, no. 9.

Státní Plánovací Komise (1961), *Směrnice o určování efektivnosti investic a nové techniky v národním hospodářství ČSSR* (Directives for the assessment of the economic effectiveness of investment and new techniques in the national economy of the CSSR), 10 April.

Státní Komise Pro Techniku – Státní Banka Československá (1967), *Podmínky pro provádění výběrového řízení investic* (Conditions for the procedure of investment choice), 6 April.

Státní Komise Pro Techniku (1967), *Zásady hednoceni ekonomické efektivnosti investic* (Criteria for the determination of the effectiveness of investment), Č.j. 16653/42/67, May.

18 V. V. Novozhilov

Problems of Planned Pricing and the Reform of Industrial Management

V. V. Novozhilov, 'The problems of planned pricing and the reform of industrial management', *Ekonomika i Matematicheskiye Metody*, vol. 2, no. 3, (1966), pp. 327–39.

The problem is to provide personal incentives –V. I. Lenin

The reform of industrial management represents a reconstruction not only of the organs but also of the *methods* of management. Economic methods are being expanded, administrative directives are contracting. The economic independence of the main production link – the enterprise – is being correspondingly increased. At the same time the central planning authority is being strengthened. Branch management is being restored on a new basis (CPSU-Resolution, 1965; Kosygin, 1965). Naturally such a deep-going reform of economic management is a very complex task. The reconstruction of the methods of management is more complicated than the reorganization of the organs of management. It is easy to extend the rights of the enterprise. It is difficult, however, as a result of this extension to reconcile the interests of the enterprise employees with those of the economy. For this purpose an involved system of measures is required. The democratization of the administration of a socialist economy presupposes the strengthening and perfecting of the centralized direction of the national economy (CPSU Programme, 1961).[1] Therefore, the democratization of its management is the last link in the tendency to develop a system of managing a socialist economy. It develops on the basis of the optimization of planning and price setting, economic accounting, and distribution according to work done (Novozhilov, 1965b, p. 648). The optimization of planning is the leading link in the chain. This is dictated

1. 'On the improvement of industrial management, perfection of planning and increased economic stimulation of industrial production', (1965). Plenum of the CC of CPSU – Resolution. *Pravda*, 30 September 1965.

(Editor's note: this refers to the abolition of the regional economic councils – *sovnarkhozy* – and the restoration of industrial ministries.)

by the primacy of production. This is also confirmed by the theory of duality in mathematical programmes.

At the present moment the planning of prices is the main bottle-neck in the organization of the socialist economy.

Methods of optimal planning, used partly in planning production are still not utilized in pricing. In an era of strict centralization of economic administration, the problem of reconciling economic accounting with the plan and local with general advantage was not one which pricing had to resolve. The possibility of continuing unprofitable production was even considered an advantage of socialism over capitalism. In the first stages of socialist reconstruction of the economy this was correct. As a result there came into being a system of prices and economic accounting which differs markedly from a system based on optimal planning. The existing price system also diverges from the law of value (optimal prices reflect the law of value when it is used most precisely in planning).

According to the law of value that only labour expenditure creates value, the product of which corresponds to social needs in all respects both in quantity and in quality. If the product does not correspond with demand whether in quality or quantity, then part of the expenditure incurred creates no value. Present prices frequently do not take these requirements into account. They are mainly based on expenditure, as if any expenditure of labour creates value.

Another rule of the law of value states that all socially necessary methods of production of the given commodity must be profitable. If, therefore, costs of production differ in different factories and all these factories are essential to satisfy demand, the price must cover the highest level of necessary costs. Pricing practice does not satisfy this requirement of the law of value either. Prices are based on average branch costs. This method does not only give rise to enterprises making planned losses but, what is more important, deprives economic practice of criteria on the basis of which it would have been possible to separate justified from unjustified costs.

Finally optimal prices include an effectiveness norm for the use of material resources of production. Correspondingly, economic accounting under optimal planning includes payment for the use of productive funds, current assets, capital investment and natural wealth. Until the 1965 reform, prices were based on the assumption of the free use of material resources. We will show below that this divergence of pricing practice from the mathematical theory of planning is also a deviation from the law of value.

Existing prices include much less information than is required both by the law of value and by the theory of optimal planning. Prices neither tell enterprises *the nature and the quality* of things to be produced nor the socially necessary *limit to expenditure* in production. The lack of a price for the use of material resources means that prices do not give information as to *how* productive funds, working assets and natural wealth should be employed and the minimum level of profitability for their utilization.

The result is that the use of the law of value in our economics is more apparent than real, more in form than in content. In these conditions it is only natural that 'economic accounting in the factory is largely formal' (Kosygin, 1965), administrative methods predominate over economic and 'the work of the enterprise is regulated by a large number of plan indicators which limit the independence and initiative of the collective of an enterprise and reduce their responsibility for improving production' (Kosygin, 1965). In fact, if prices do not give information necessary for an economic decision then the information which is lacking has to be given in the form of an administrative order. Since information contained in prices often differs from plan-directives, these directives have to be enforced with sanctions. Threats, however, as many centuries of administrative experience show, are a less effective stimulus to production than economic or moral interest. The advantage of incentives is the greater when the results of labour depend on the creative initiative of the individual. Therefore, it is only natural that the deficiency of purely administrative methods of management of our economy should be increasingly felt in connection with the growing role of technical progress and the organization of production in the development of the economy.

In the complex system of our present day economy it is very difficult to achieve the personal interest of each worker in the results of his labour. The interconnection between costs and results of different production has now become so complex that measurement of the results of labour not only of each worker but of each enterprise has become a very difficult task. It is much more difficult than the problem which arose on the transition to NEP, when Lenin wrote (1921) that 'every important branch of the national economy must be based on personal incentive'. NEP was a temporary and partial return to capitalist relations and methods whereas the 1965 economic reform is a big step *forward* along the road to *communism*. It corresponds to the fundamental law of development of the system of management of a socialist economy – a two-sided development of democratic centralism (Kosygin, 1965, p. 88). To advance is always harder than to retreat.

Nonetheless, there are now possibilities for progress in the organization of our economy, which could not even be dreamt of in the time of NEP. New mathematical methods of optimal planning have been devised. The basis for a theory of management of complicated systems (cybernetics) has been laid. A rapid electronic computational technique – has been invented and has already reached a high level. These new scientific and technical means allow great success to be achieved in reconciling economic accounting with the plan and the interests of the enterprise with that of the national economy. Therefore the reform which has been introduced can become an important step on the road to the gradual conversion of the plan-directive into the plan-economic law, i.e. into a directive the best fulfilment of which coincides with the personal interests of all those involved. For this, however, it is first of all necessary to overcome the worst bottleneck in the organization of our economy – i.e. to reconstruct the price system.

We see that the existing practice of price formation differs from prices in optimal planning in the very principles of price determination. This cannot be said of the planning of production. Methods of optimal planning, although imperfect, are being used in the planning of production and transport. In price formation, however, methods of optimal planning have not yet received general recognition. Speaking concretely, some Soviet economists only permit the application of optimal plan valuations in local and not national-economic planning problems (Boyarski,

1961). These views support existing practice in price formation.

A gap has opened between the principles of planning production and the planning of prices. This gap has caused disorganization to our economy. The production plan gave enterprises one task while the planning of prices provided another. Economic accounting often contradicted the plan objectives. As a result the planning apparatus laboured with an unnecessary workload in order to remove this self-caused blockage. It is difficult to calculate the loss caused to our national economy by incorrect price formation. 'If the worker spoils an article the loss is obvious and easy to calculate. It is much more difficult to estimate loss through bad organization of a workshop or plant, though they may be much greater than losses through spoilt goods. Economists, however, face the greatest difficulties when trying to observe and measure losses from incorrect methods of calculating costs and results, although these losses may come to many milliards of roubles' (Novozhilov, 1959). Mistakes in principles and methods of pricing are the source of many errors in practical calculations. Therefore erroneous principles of pricing lead to systematic underestimation or overstatement of costs and results, and therefore to inefficient decisions. This, however, is not all. The principles of price formation which have developed in our country also cause other losses, which cannot be measured – from excessive centralization of enterprise management. As a result of lack of conformity between the plan, the enterprise and economic accounting there occurs an unavoidable centralization of decision-making on such problems as those for which the planning centre cannot have sufficient or timely information, with present levels of accounting and computing techniques.

It is clear from this that there is in the theory of planned price formation an enormous productive force, which is direct, of widespread effect and which is more accessible to socialism than to capitalism.

On the dual expression of socially necessary labour expenditure

'Prices must reflect, to an increasing degree, socially necessary labour expenditure and ensure payment for the costs of production and exchange and a certain level of profit for every normally operating enterprise.' (CPSU, 1961, p.90)

Since the existing price system gives insufficient economic information, it is essential to increase the information content of prices. It is precisely this task in respect of price formation which has been put by the CPSU programme. Socially necessary labour expenditure is a magnitude with a surprising wealth of content. From one point of view it expresses that expenditure of labour necessary under *conditions of production*, and from another the labour expenditure which society considers necessary *in conditions of consumption*, taking into account not only the given product but also its substitutes. Equality of expenditure necessary in conditions of production with that required under consumption signifies that the production of the given product corresponds to social needs and is being produced efficiently, i.e. the labour expended on it corresponds to socially necessary norms.

However, the problem of approximating prices to socially necessary expenditures on labour is made much more complex, when prices tend not towards value but towards its modification, because of the controversial nature both of its methods and of the principles of definition. It is accepted that socially necessary expenditure is expressed only in average labour-time required for the production of a commodity under socially normal conditions. This expression of SNLE (socially necessary labour expenditure) is sufficient if the difference between individual labour expenditures is accidental (determined by the individual workers' qualities). It is insufficient however, if those differences are not accidental, as for example, when determined by conditions of the application of labour – by differences in technique and natural resources. In this case prices must not only contain norms of labour utilization but also norms for the utilization of the limited conditions of its application.

Differences in expenditure caused by differences in the effectiveness in use of the means of production are not accidental but necessary.

If, for whatever reason, it is socially necessary in the production of a commodity to use producer goods which differ in their effectiveness, then costs incurred under below-average conditions are socially necessary, as well as costs under average conditions or better.

In this case *average* SNLE does not give the information needed for choice between means of production; it is essential to know the *marginal* (highest) magnitude of SNLE – prices do not tend to value but to its modification.

Let us move from general considerations to our practice. Experience demonstrates the necessity of reflecting capital intensity and differential rent in prices. The gratuitous use of productive capital and natural resources is clearly linked to wasteful practices. Mathematical models of optimal planning prove that prices which reconcile economic accounting with the plan must include payment for material resources utilized. This means that the optimum price represents modified value. The generally accepted conception of socially necessary labour expenditure, however, relates only to that worker's time which forms the substance of value. *With such a concept of socially necessary expenditure*, the conformity of *economic accounting with the plan* (*by including capital intensities, differential rent and inter-commodity substitution etc. in prices*) *appears irreconcilable with the approximation of prices to socially necessary labour expenditure*. For it would appear that the undoubtedly progressive new beginnings in our practice *do not bring* prices *nearer* to but *further* from that socially necessary labour expenditure which forms the substance of value. In these conditions, the progressive tendencies in pricing practice are either disputed (by some economists) or lead to an eclectic theory of planned price formation. Indeed, if it is considered that only value is determined by socially necessary expenditure, then it must be concluded that optimal prices are not determined only by socially necessary labour expenditure but also by capital intensity, intercommodity substitution and other factors. This conception is inconsistent and therefore impractical. It is impractical because no model of planned pricing can be made from it. The formulae for calculating the separate factors in price formation have no connection with each other, and the estimated magnitudes are artificial or random.

According to the law of labour value, proportionality and economy in production are necessarily connected with a labour exchange equivalent. If it is considered that socially necessary labour expenditure is expressed only in average SNLE, then exchange in prices which are modified values is not equivalent exchange. In fact, prices are not only proportional to socially necessary labour expenditure in those cases when pricing is made proportional to value but also when pricing is done through the formation of a connected (modified) form of value. Prices are always proportional to socially necessary labour expenditure, but the expenditure is not the same as that which forms the substance of value. Price is always derived from value but only under certain historical conditions are these derivatives equal to value. The value of a commodity unit is determined by the average socially necessary labour expenditure, while *price* is determined by *incremental* (marginal) expenditure of socially necessary labour. Price reflects the *increment* in the expenditure of social labour necessary for an increase in production of the given commodity. This is because under decentralized decision making on the production of each commodity it is not the whole production of each commodity but its relatively small growth which is under consideration. When deciding the economic practicality of increasing production of any commodity it is necessary to ascertain not the average total of expenditure per unit of commodity but the marginal magnitude, i.e. expenditure on a relatively small increase in production. If, therefore, average socially necessary expenditure on a commodity is equal to ten roubles per unit and marginal expenditure of social labour is equal to eight roubles per unit, then a price, at average expenditure, of ten roubles per unit will distort calculations on effectiveness of additional production of this commodity and show an illusory economy on production (for example, on expenditure equal to nine roubles per unit) while really overpaying (to the extent of one rouble per unit). Another example: let the marginal socially necessary expenditure equal twenty roubles per unit while the average is ten roubles per unit. At the same time the given commodity can be replaced by another on which the marginal expenditure equals fifteen roubles per unit. If the price of a commodity is equal to average socially necessary expenditure (ten roubles per unit), then the production of a substitute of equivalent use-value at fifteen roubles will be at a loss. In fact, however, the substitute in this case is of great benefit to the national economy as its production will lead to considerable real economies instead of imaginary excess expenditure.

It is clear from this simple discussion that the argument as to which costs should be used as a basis for planning prices – industrial-average or marginal (differential) – is of tremendous practical importance. Incorrect solution of this problem causes losses incomparably greater than those caused in technology or through economic miscalculation (as in choosing the construction site of a plant). The mistake in the *principle* of price formation is the cause of huge miscalculations. These are very difficult to correct, firstly because they are not easily noticed (they are hidden by an appearance of correct economic calculation), and secondly because they are stimulated by the economic accounting at enterprise level. The greater and more consistent is the extent of economic accounting the more miscalculations are caused by the mistake of price formation.

The determination of prices on the basis of marginal costs is sometimes disputed on the grounds that goods will be more expensive than when using average costs. This objection shows just how difficult it is to notice mistakes caused by incorrect price formation. The real cost of goods does not depend on prices but on the level of costs. For society as a whole commodities cannot become cheaper through decreeing low prices if these prices will lead to tremendous miscalculations – and therefore to unnecessary expenditure. On the contrary, nominal cheapness will become expensiveness.

Another objection to marginal cost price determination is that producers, as a result, are encouraged to use outmoded technology. Marginal costs, however, themselves change in accordance with technical progress. The latter systematically, year by year, reduces the marginal costs of reproduction through the assimilation of new technique and the elimination of old instruments of labour. Marx long ago showed that prices should be equal to marginal costs while their level is continuously declining, provided that differences in efficiency of the equipment in use survive.

Engels wrote in a letter to Marx on 7 January 1851 (Marx and Engels, *Selected Correspondence*, p. 151):

'The law of rent, as laid down by Ricardo in its simplest form, apart from its elaboration, does not assume the diminishing fertility of the soil but (*in spite of the fact that the general fertility of the soil increases as society develops*) only presupposes *different* degrees of fertility of different pieces of land, or different results from the successive investment of capital in the same land.'

This point of view is even more important today than when Marx lived as technical progress is more rapid than a hundred years ago. It is of fundamental importance for the analysis of the law of value as a whole and not only as an explanation for the prices of agricultural products. This is because it is *technical progress itself which causes* differences in the effectiveness of tools in use. This applies not only to agriculture but also to industry. The appearance of new, more efficient means of production now occurs in many industries, in such a short space of time that it is economically impossible to remove from service the previously produced means of production. Therefore, tools of different efficiency function simultaneously. This difference is less marked in view of the decline in value of the old means of production (through obsolescence). But the scale of obsolescence of machinery shows the variety of the difference in the effectiveness of technology being simultaneously employed. As a result, Marx's model, which explains price formation in agriculture under conditions when soil fertility is increasing, can be used to explain the role of marginal costs under conditions of technical progress. (Marx and Engels, *Collected Works*, p. 211).

Nonetheless, as is usual, there is a certain drop of wisdom in the essentially incorrect opposition to marginal cost pricing. There is an implied warning against basing prices on the *actual* marginal cost. Prices will tend to optimal solutions only when they are based on marginal costs in the *optimal plan*, i.e. on marginal SNLE.

The definition of prices by socially necessary labour expenditure corresponds to the statement in the CPSU programme that prices must 'ensure the replacement of costs of production and a certain level of profit for each normally operating enterprise.' The basing of prices on average socially necessary cost is connected with the planned losses of many of those enterprises which operate in below-average technical and natural conditions although they are socially necessary for the satisfaction of needs.

The main principles of the optimal planning of production and prices are included in the literature of the September (1965)

Plenum of the CC of the CPSU: 'On the improvement of industrial management, the perfection of planning and the further economic stimulation of industrial production.' To this is related: the demand for optimum national economic plans, the increased role of profitability as an indicator of effectiveness of production, payment for the use of productive and circulating capital, the approximation of prices to socially necessary labour cost, the inclusion of the quality of production in the calculation of price, etc. (Kosygin, 1965). Payment for the use of productive and circulating capital assumes the inclusion of profit in plan prices in some relation to capital investment and productive capital and not in proportion to cost. This signifies that price formation must gravitate towards a modification of value.

The idea that modified value can express socially necessary labour expenditure does not yet enjoy widespread usage. Yet, it not only derives from Marx's value theory, but is indicated by him.

Marx noted that with a proportional division of social labour: 'products of different groups are sold according to value (in their further development in their prices of production) or even according to prices which are modified values, corresponding to prices of production, defined by general laws.' (Marx and Engels, *Collected Works*, p. 185.)

This remark of Marx has not attracted sufficient attention. Nonetheless it has great significance. It means that *modified value* 'defined by general laws' *also expresses socially necessary labour cost just as value does*. Under commodity production proportionality in the social division of labour is only possible upon exchange of socially necessary labour equivalents.

Obviously not all modified value reflects socially necessary labour. For example, until now our prices have been constructed on a formula of 'average value'. It is a modification of value in which profit enters price as a proportion of cost. However, such average values do not express the exact labour expenditure connected with the production of the given product: it varies not only from average labour expenditure on the production of the goods (value), but also from the increment of labour expenditure on the final social product. Only that modification of value reflects socially necessary labour expenditure which is proportional to this increment, assuming proportionality of production with consumption.

What then are those general laws which determine the formation of modified value, the existence of which Marx refers to in the above citation?

The mathematical model of the national economy helps to answer this question. It shows that prices based on the law of value are partial derivatives of the value of the final social product, dependent on the quantity of the given product (Novozhilov, 1965a). In the absence of any resource constraints these partial derivatives are in direct proportion to value. When there are constraints on material resources then prices are proportional to a value modified to take account of these constraints. When the level of development of the forces of production is low and there is a slow rate of growth, similar modes and means of production predominate. Then socially necessary labour expenditure approximates to average expenditure and prices are proportional to values. When there is a high level and rate of growth of the productive forces then in each unit of production not only the best but also less effective means of production are utilized. Then, socially necessary expenditure is not determined by an average quantity expended on the production of the given goods but by the increment of labour expended on the whole final social product, required for the production of the given goods.

The scarcity of the best resources (machines, installations, natural resources) leads to the necessity for social norms for the permitted margin of effectiveness of their use. This is vividly demonstrated in the mathematical models of the optimal plan: with constraints on resources for the construction of the plan auxiliary multipliers are essential (Lagrange–Kantorovich). These multipliers permit conformity of profitability with national economic effectiveness, and between cost accounting and the optimal plan. In cost accounting they take the form of payment for productive and circulating capital, capital investment and natural resources.

What labour cost, then, reflects optimal modified value?

It expresses two increments formed by the production of a unit of the commodity:

1. The increment of labour cost to the entire final social product (i.e. that production, which goes to make up the national income).

2. The increment of national income (as a total of prices of the final product).

In the optimal plan these two increments are equal for each commodity. The equality signifies the production is proportional to consumption: i.e. on each commodity there is expended as much labour as the society requires, i.e. SNLE.

Nonetheless this feature of optimal modified value is not complete. The optimal plan is the best plan, which corresponds most exactly to the economic laws of socialism. It achieves on the one hand a minimum expenditure of labour on the final social product and on the other the maximum national income possible within the given labour expenditure.

Expenditure is minimized by a corresponding selection of planned and draft variants, and national income maximized by the best relationship of production to requirements.[2]

In this way the above two increments, which are proportional to modified value, relate to the minimum labour expenditure on the needed final social product and to the maximum national income possible within the given resources. Therefore, we determine to what degree costs correspond to the average minimum labour expenditure, by comparing individual costs of production (calculated to include payment for resources) with the optimum price (equal to optimum modification in value). By comparing the sale price of a commodity with the optimum price we determine to what degree the produced commodity corresponds to social requirements in quality and quantity. It follows that the optimum price (modified value) serves as a criterion for separating necessary from excess expenditure in each production unit. These qualities of the optimum modification of value also indicate that it expresses differential socially necessary labour expenditure with the best planning of the national economy.

2. In the case of a disproportion between consumption and production the excess labour expended creates no value. Therefore the given labour creates more national income the closer production corresponds to requirements.

The connection between the planning of prices and the planning of production

While expanding the economic independence of the enterprise, the Party and Soviet Government will continue to conduct a unified policy in the planning of the main trends in the development of production, technical progress, capital investment, prices, labour expenditure and finance. (Plenum of CC of CPSU-Resolution, 1965)

In spite of the remarkable amount of information contained in prices, it is still insufficient for the purpose of planning the economy. Even with the best planning, when prices exactly reflect differential socially necessary labour expenditure, they do not give guidance on a number of very important economic issues. They tell us nothing about the quantity which can be produced with given costs, or the quantity which could be bought at a given price at a given time. They also provide no information on the future costs or on future demand.

Finally, for the calculation of expenditure by sectors and regions, the national economy as a whole requires either overall indices of expenditure on the production of the given product (or group of them) or average expenditure and the amounts produced. Optimum prices cannot serve for this purpose, since they are proportionate to marginal socially necessary labour expenditure.

Thus, the information content of prices is achieved at the cost of narrowing to the margin that part of the economy to which it refers, i.e. to extremely small increments in the output of one product. Information, however, is obtained from these increments (extremely small relative to the whole economy), on the following:

1. On the expenditure of social labour including all direct and feedback relationships between expenditure on the reproduction of the given commodity and other commodities;
2. On the result – i.e. the increment of the national income which results from the availability of the given commodity for use.

This information is sufficient for decentralized fulfilment of the plan on the basis of economic independence and for small corrections in the plan. It is, however, insufficient for important changes in the plan and also for plan formulation for a number of years in the future. This limitation of information expressed in prices in time and scale (small plan changes), is especially felt in the solving of questions affecting an important part of the economy, and capital construction.

Therefore, even with optimum price formation, enterprises must receive from the economic administration such economic information as prices cannot give, but which is necessary for planning their economic unit, however small it may be in relation to the national economy. The nature of the information can only be defined after a detailed and concrete analysis of the problem. For the present this information need be noted only in the most general terms: the quantity of goods to be produced, the rates of payment for resources over a number of years (norms of effectiveness for capital investment and for the capital assets of the enterprise, rate of differential rent), wage and salary rates, and planned prices of basic products over a number of years. This information must be obtained in the course of long-term planning of the economy.

The defects of optimum prices for long-term planning of the economy, are clear from their definition as differential SNLE. In fact in drawing up plans of the development of the national economy it is impossible to be guided by current differential SNLE, while future differential SNLE are still unknown and can only be computed in the process of completion of the new plan. In order to work out a long term plan of development of the economy, minimizing total expenditure of labour on the final product, data on the full labour cost of the most important products and the principal means of their production are essential. At the same time it is essential to have the indicators of total capital requirements of these products according to various production methods, and demand for the most important natural resources. In the very near future similar calculations should be directed to the planning of optimal paths of technical progress and the determination of rates of efficiency of capital investment. This rate must be fixed so as to achieve the maximum general effect of capital investment while maintaining equilibrium between the growth in jobs and the number of workers. *The pricing plan for the most important commodities must be worked out simultaneously with the production plan.* The planning of prices must be coordinated with the planning of production at all levels. It was the degree of separation of production and price planning which maintained the defects in our practice of price formation. This situation contradicts the law of value and is not in conformity with the mathematical theory of optimal planning.

According to the law of value, the proportionality and the economical nature of commodity production are linked to the labour equivalence of exchange. When the equivalence of exchange is violated, disproportions are introduced into production and less productive economic forms are employed instead of more productive. Mathematical programming looks at plan and prices as two sides of the same coin.

The need for a connection between price and plan refers not only to planning methods but also to the administrative system. The territorial system of industrial management (through *Sovnarkhozy*) was not suitable for rational price formation. It is only through the sectoral system of planning that it is possible to determine differential SNLE by different products as well as the differential efficiency of use of these products by the consumers.

The main method of determination of optimal prices and an optimal plan is by bringing closer together the differential income of the national economy for the given product with the differential cost of its production. The differential income of the national economy for each commodity is expressed in its demand price. The demand price is the *maximum* price at which all the commodity on offer can be cleared in the course of average (normal) time in the market. In the optimal plan the demand price is calculated so that all consumers distribute their expenditure in relation to the utility of the products being acquired. The demand price expresses that labour which society considers necessary (maximum permitted) to be spent on additional units of the given commodity, including, in this, its quality (useful properties) in comparison with other commodities of a similar purpose, prices of other commodities and the size of incomes.

Differential expenditure or costs can be called the supply price, understanding by that the *minimum* price covering the cost of production of the given commodity by the various methods of production used, provided that all producers utilize the most effective means of production available to them.

The main way of equilibrating demand price with supply price consists in the regulation of supply; through production, import and export, and inventories. The control of these components of supply should be directed to the support of a stable equilibrium of supply and demand.

In these circumstances prices are determined by the *differential expenditure of production in the most progressive conditions of the application of labour*. The reduction in the costs of production caused by technical progress reduces profitability and the valuation of the old equipment (obsolescence). *The equilibration of demand with supply by acting on the demand price is only necessary when all measures to regulate supply in order to maintain equilibrium prove insufficient*. Such are cases of obsolescence of commodities (by going out of fashion, technically outdated) and cases of insufficient production of commodities the expansion of which requires a considerable amount of time, etc.

Optimization of a sectoral plan and plan prices is performed by compiling such iterative variants of the plan which bring demand and supply prices closer together.

In that case, where differential expenditure can be calculated for *each* separate *product*, the optimal plan and prices are determined by equating demand and supply prices for *each product*.

In the case of the *complex* production of several products in the same technological process, optimization is achieved by equilibrating the *overall total* of supply prices of the set of products with the sum of their demand prices, weighted by the quantity of each product.

Supply and demand balances are drawn up by aggregated groups of commodities (at the higher levels of planning) as well as by separate commodities. The disaggregation of planned prices is naturally connected with the disaggregation of production plans.

Under modern conditions the best approximation of economic management to its optimal model will apparently give the economically autonomous planning system suggested by Academician Nemchinov. This system can be used for the joint planning of prices and production. For this system the enterprises have to give the planning organs suggestions about the conditions under which they are prepared to fulfil this or that planning order for the delivery of output (with details of the product mix, quality, period, prices). The economic and planning organs must distribute their orders only to those enterprises which will propose the best conditions for their fulfilment.

We have already written about the iterations essential for the compiling of a long term plan which combines economic independence with the plan (Novozhilov, 1965b).

The economic accounting (autonomous) system of planning does not guarantee the achievement of the optimum. The compilation of a plan and its prices under such a system will, by its properties, the more approach the optimal plan and its prices the more reliable is the economic information and the closer the iterative process converges. Under this system of planning:

1. All planning tasks will be supplied with means of production.

2. Only those production variants will enter the plan which require less expenditure than rejected variants.

3. Enterprise economic accounting will be reconciled with the production plan and with prices in the process of plan formulation.

Conclusion

The September (1965) Plenum of the Central Committee of the Communist Party of the Soviet Union and the decisions of the Twenty-third Congress of the party provided the start of a profound transformation of industrial management. Its implementation can only be gradual. The price system which was formed in the era of rigid centralization is not compatible with the expansion of enterprise rights. Price has less economic information than necessary for the independent solution of economic problems by the enterprise. Therefore the approximation of prices to socially necessary labour time is the main task in the reconstruction of price formation. A lot depends on it fulfilment. Therefore, the theory of planned price formation acquires exceptional importance. Generally, a mistake in the determination of the price of a separate commodity causes many miscalculations. A mistake, moreover, in the principles of planned price formation leads to enormous errors and waste. Nonetheless until recently neither the methods nor the principles of planned price formation have served as the subject of acute disagreement. Actual price formation differed metrically (in its principles) from the law of value and theory of optimal planning.

Of late the views of Soviet economists have drawn closer together on problems of price formation. The introduction of payment for the use of productive funds, circulating capital and capital investment decided in practice a number of arguments. The discussion, however, on price formation only converges on a number of general problems – mainly the structure of price.

The most difficult task, however, is in front of us: methods of price formation have to be evolved which would supply a sufficiently close connection between plan prices and the production plan of each commodity.

In our opinion the solution is to be sought in the development of the system advanced by the late Nemchinov (1965) and correctly called the economic accounting (*Khozvaschyomy*) system of planning.

References

BOYARSKI, A. Ya. (1961), 'K voprosu o primenenii matematiki v ekonimike', *Voprosy Ekonomiki*, no. 2.

KOSYGIN, A. N. (1965), 'On the improvement of industrial management, perfection of planning and increased economic stimulation of industrial production'. Plenum of CC of CPSU, from *Pravda*, 30 September, see Reading 15 in this volume.

LENIN, V. I., *Collected Works*, 4th ed., vol. 33, Moscow.

MARX, K., and ENGELS, F., *Marx–Engels: Selected Correspondence*, p. 62, Moscow.

MARX, K., and ENGELS, F., *Collected Works*, 2nd edn., Moscow.

NEMCHINOV, V. S. (1965), Sotsialisticheskoye Khozyaistvovaniye i planirovaniye proizvodstva, *Kommunist*, vol. 5.

NOVOZHILOV, V. V. (1959), 'Izmereniye zatrat i ikh rezultatov v sotsialistecheskom khozyaistve', in V. S. Nemchinov (ed.), *Primeneniye Matematiki v ekonomicheskikh issledovanniyakh*, Sotsekgiz.

NOVOZHILOV, V. V. (1965a), 'Zakon stoimosti i planovoye tsenoobrazovaniye, Problemy primeneniye matematiki v sotsialisticheskoi ekonomike, Trs. *Leningr. inzh. Ekonom. in-ta im. P. Togliatti no. 53.* Izd-vo, LGU.

Novozhilov, V. V. (1965b), 'Zakonomernostirazvitiya sistemy upravleniya sotsialisticheskim khozyaistvom', *Ekonomika i Matematecheskiye Metody*, vol. 1, no. 5, p. 648.

Plenum of the Central Committee, CPSU (1965), 'On the improvement of industrial management, perfection of planning and increased economic stimulation of industrial production'.

CPSU Programme (1961), Goslitizdat, Moscow.

Part Five
Mathematical Techniques and Socialist Planning

During the Stalinist period, the use of mathematical techniques in economics was regarded as a bourgeois deviation, and in spite of the early start of Russian mathematical economics (with Dmitriev's *Ekonomicheskie Ocherki*, 1898) and the brilliant contributions in the Soviet literature of the 1920s (see Reading 7), later developments remained dead letters until the mid-1950s. It then became apparent that mathematical techniques had an important contribution to make to socialist planning and the earlier veto was removed with the aid of skilful quotations from Marxist sources and of the pioneering work of a few economists (Lange, Kantorovich, Novozhilov, Nemchinov). Some of their most significant contributions are reproduced here (Kantorovich, Nemchinov, Novozhilov). Their approach leads to the open recognition of the usefulness of notions such as interest, rent, profit, and its development is closely linked with the process of economic reform. It is interesting to see their preoccupation for couching the new techniques in traditional Marxian terminology (especially the labour theory of value, which was certainly not developed to tackle planning problems). This makes the texts less readable to the non-initiated Western reader, but they are representative of the 'style' of economic discussions in socialist literature.

At the microeconomic level mathematics provides useful algorithms for the efficient realization of everyday production tasks in fields such as transport, allocation of sectoral output targets among different plants, metal-cutting, and many other forms of rationalization of production processes.

At the macro-level the operational significance of these models is less clear. In the view of some authors (e.g. Lange, Reading 19), the computer can replace the market and assist in the preparation of the overall economic plans (Professor Wiles calls this the replacement of 'perfect competition' by 'perfect computation'). Others have expressed considerable doubts about the feasibility and desirability of this approach. Veinshtein's essay is a good example of these perplexities. The most interesting development on this front is Kornai's approach to 'multi-level' planning, which attempts to formulate a central plan by mathematical methods, decentralizing the preparation and the computation of sectoral plans to the lower levels (Reading 22). Another important feature of Kornai's paper, based on the Hungarian experience, is the suggestion that mathematical methods should be used not to *replace* but to *improve* plans drawn by more traditional methods.

19 O. Lange

The Computer and the Market

Excerpt from C. Feinstein (ed.), *Capitalism, Socialism and Economic Growth*, Cambridge, 1967, pp. 158–61.

I

Not quite thirty years ago I published an essay *On the Economic Theory of Socialism* (Lange, 1936). Pareto and Barone had shown that the conditions of economic equilibrium in a socialist economy could be expressed by a system of simultaneous equations. The prices resulting from these equations furnish a basis for rational economic accounting under socialism (only the static equilibrium aspect of the accounting problem was under consideration at that time). At a later date Hayek and Robbins maintained that the Pareto–Barone equations were of no practical consequence. The solution of a system of thousands or more simultaneous equations was in practice impossible and, consequently, the practical problem of economic accounting under socialism remained unsolvable.

In my essay I refuted the Hayek–Robbins argument by showing how a market mechanism could be established in a socialist economy which would lead to the solution of the simultaneous equations by means of an empirical procedure of trial and error. Starting with an arbitrary set of prices, the price is raised whenever demand exceeds supply and lowered whenever the opposite is the case. Through such a process of *tâtonnements*, first described by Walras, the final equilibrium prices are gradually reached. These are the prices satisfying the system of simultaneous equations. It was assumed without question that the *tâtonnement* process in fact converges to the system of equilibrium prices.

Were I to rewrite my essay today my task would be much simpler. My answer to Hayek and Robbins would be: so what's the trouble? Let us put the simultaneous equations on an electronic computer and we shall obtain the solution in less than a second. The market process with its cumbersome *tâtonnements* appears old-fashioned. Indeed, it may be considered as a computing device of the pre-electronic age.

II

The market mechanism and trial and error procedure proposed in my essay really played the role of a computing device for solving a system of simultaneous equations. The solution was found by a process of iteration which was assumed to be convergent. The iterations were based on a feedback principle operating so as to gradually eliminate deviations from equilibrium. It was envisaged that the process would operate like a servo-mechanism, which, through feedback action, automatically eliminates disturbances. (See Steindl, 1964, pp. 552–4 in particular.)

The same process can be implemented by an electronic analog machine which simulates the iteration process implied in the *tâtonnements* of the market mechanism. Such an electronic analog (servo-mechanism) simulates the working of the market. This statement, however, may be reversed: the market simulates the electronic analog computer. In other words, the market may be considered as a computer *sui generis* which serves to solve a system of simultaneous equations. It operates like an analog machine: a servo-mechanism based on the feedback principle. The market may be considered as one of the oldest historical devices for solving simultaneous equations. The interesting thing is that the solving mechanism operates not via a physical but via a social process. It turns out that the social processes as well may serve as a basis for the operation of feedback devices leading to the solution of equations by iteration.

III

Managers of socialist economies today have two instruments of economic accounting. One is the electronic computer (digital or analog), the other is the market. In capitalist countries too, the electronic computer is to a certain extent used as an instrument of economic accounting. Experience shows that for a very large number of problems linear approximation suffices; hence the wide-spread use of linear programming techniques. In a socialist economy such techniques have an even wider scope for application: they can be applied to the national economy as a whole.

It may be interesting to compare the relative merits of the market and of the computer in a socialist economy. The computer has the undoubted advantage of much greater speed. The market is a cumbersome and slow-working servo-mechanism. Its iteration process operates with considerable time-lags and oscillations and may not be convergent at all. This is shown by cobweb cycles, inventory and other reinvestment cycles as well as by the general business cycle. Thus the Walrasian *tâtonnements* are full of unpleasant fluctuations and may also prove to be divergent. In this respect the electronic computer shows an unchallenged superiority. It works with enormous speed, does not produce fluctuations in real economic processes and the convergence of its iterations is assured by its very construction.

Another disadvantage of the market as a servo-mechanism is that its iterations cause income effects. Any change in prices causes gains and losses to various groups of people. To the management of a socialist economy this creates various social problems connected with these gains and losses. Furthermore, it may mobilize conservative resistance to the iteration process involved in the use of the market as a servo-mechanism.

IV

All this, however, does not mean that the market has not its relative merits. First of all, even the most powerful electronic computers have a limited capacity. There may be (and there are) economic processes so complex in terms of the number of commodities and the type of equations involved that no computer can tackle them. Or it may be too costly to construct computers of such large capacity. In such cases nothing remains but to use the old-fashioned market servo-mechanism which has a much broader working capacity.

Secondly, the market is institutionally embodied in the present socialist economy. In all socialist countries (with the exception of certain periods when rationing was used) consumers' goods are distributed to the population by means of the market. Here, the market is an existing social institution and it is useless to apply an alternative accounting device. The electronic computer can be applied for purposes of prognostication but the computed forecasts have later to be confirmed by the actual working of the market.

An important limitation of the market is that it treats the accounting problem only in static terms, i.e. as an equilibrium problem. It does not provide a sufficient foundation for the solution of growth and development problems. In particular, it does not provide an adequate basis for long-term economic planning. For planning economic development long-term investments have to be taken out of the market mechanism and based on judgement of developmental economic policy. This is because present prices reflect present data, whereas investment changes data by creating new incomes, new technical conditions of production and frequently also by creating new wants (the creation of a television industry creates the demand for television sets, not the other way round). In other words, investment changes the conditions of supply and demand which determine equilibrium prices. This holds for capitalism as well as for socialism.

For the reasons indicated, planning of long-term economic development as a rule is based on overall considerations of economic policy rather than upon calculations based on current prices. However, the theory and practice of mathematical (linear and non-linear) programming makes it possible to introduce strict economic accounting into this process. After setting up an objective function (for instance, maximizing the increase of national income over a certain period) and certain constraints, future shadow prices can be calculated. These shadow prices serve as an instrument of economic accounting in long-term development plans. Actual market equilibrium prices do not suffice here, knowledge of the programmed future shadow prices is needed.

Mathematical programming turns out to be an essential instrument of *optimal* long-term economic planning. In so far as this involves the solution of large numbers of equations and inequalities the electronic computer is indispensable. Mathematical programming assisted by electronic computers becomes the fundamental instrument of long-term economic planning, as well as of solving dynamic economic problems of a more limited scope. Here, the electronic computer does not replace the market. It fulfils a function which the market never was able to perform.

References

LANGE, O. (1936), 'On the economic theory of socialism', *Review of Economic Studies*, London. Reprinted in O. Lange and F. M. Taylor, *On the Economic Theory of Socialism*, edited by B. E. Lippincott, Minneapolis, 1938, see Reading 4 of this volume.

STEINDL, J. (1964), 'Servo-mechanisms and controllers in economic theory and policy', in *On Political Economy and Econometrics, Essays in Honour of Oskar Lange*, Warsaw.

20 V. Nemchinov

Basic Elements of a Model of Planned Price Formation

From V. Nemchinov, 'Basic elements of a model of planned price formation', *Voprosy Ekonomiki*, no. 12, 1963, pp. 105–21.

Conception of prices

The only objective basis for the formation of the general level of prices is value. Value is created in the process of productive work by men in conditions of social division of labour. The members of the socialist society, and its production and consumption units, and also production and territorial complexes, exchange the results of their labour with each other. It is necessary that the principle of equivalent exchange be observed.

Value only receives its ultimate quantitative expression at the level of the national economy. Together with the formation of value there takes place a process of differentiation and individualization of value. At the same time as value is being differentiated it is split up into its component parts. In the process of the interaction of social and individual value, necessary and surplus labour are isolated and also the component elements of value $(c+v+s)$ are distinguished. The differentiation and individualization of value are effected in the shape of a process of transformation of the form of value. In the process of transformation value acquires a form which allows the process of the individualization of value to proceed unimpeded, that is, the process of reduction of social value to individual value. At the same time this is also the process of realization of value. Over the national economy as a whole the amount of value which can be realized is only as much as has been created. Therefore the total realized value is equal to (or less than) total created value. Marx more than once pointed out the formation in certain definite conditions of unrealized value.

In the process of transformation of the form of value, which is inseparably linked with the differentiation and individualization of value, the national economic coefficients of profitability of the fixed and working capital employed, and also the rent valuation of utilized natural resources are determined. The system of labour payment, the system of coefficients of profitability of fixed and working capital, the system of rent valuations of natural resources permit the unimpeded transition from the national economic value level to individual value, always within the limits of created and realized value.

Simultaneously with the process of transformation of the form of value on the basis of the interaction of labour and use value there also takes place a process of differentiation and individualization of social value and likewise the formation of the divergence of prices from value, which is closely connected with the influence of the law of supply and demand and also with the consumer qualities of products of labour which have taken the form of commodities. Use value is a bearer of value and in this capacity it particularly influences prices, causing them to diverge from value. The divergences of prices are limited: they always take place not only within the total value of commodities, but also within the total of substitutable commodities which can satisfy the given social requirement.

Within such a total of substitutable commodities the divergences of prices from value always have a tendency to cancel each other out and the total of prices which show such divergences always tends to equal the total of values. When examining this process of gravitation of prices towards value one should work from the general to the particular. Comparison of prices and value should be begun with such general totals of commodities as total commodity production, consumption, accumulation and replacement.

Within consumption, prices of individual commodities diverge from value, but their total always tends to equal the total of values. Divergences of prices occur primarily under the influence of the consumer's evaluation of each commodity group as revealed by preferences displayed in purchase or consumption. The consumer's evaluation is connected with the degree of satisfaction of a given requirement, its degree of urgency (essentiality) and with the elasticity of demand.

In the process of the divergence of prices from value each

aggregated group of commodities in its turn is broken down into detail, whereupon the most detailed designations of commodities all receive their evaluation, reflecting consumer properties of the commodities.

Within the aggregated commodity group the total of prices within the more detailed groups tends to equal the value of the whole aggregated group multiplied by the group coefficient of proportional divergence of prices. At each successive level of detail of commodity nomenclature the coefficient of proportional divergence is supplemented by a new multiplier, but prices will always remain linked to value. The total of prices does not go beyond the limits of the value created in production and tends to remain proportional to value.

The initial model of production and social division of labour

In the process of formation of value and prices we can distinguish a number of different contours of successive mathematical and economic description of different stages of the processes of formation of value and prices. Both these processes occur objectively in actual economic reality and they are only imitated in mathematical form.

The first contour describes the process of formation of the material or physical structure of social production and the social division of labour.

In the construction of a model of social production and of the social division of labour, particular attention is paid to the most rational choice of the nomenclature of commodities and products. This nomenclature reproduces the list of the major key commodities and products distinguished in the compilation of current and long term plans. From this list the 'basic backbone' of the model of commodity prices is constructed, consisting of products and commodities which are strategically important for the planned economy. The commodity nomenclature includes 800–1000 commodity items. It comprises the basic necessities of life which make up the basis of the family budget, the main kinds of agricultural and mineral raw materials, the basic kinds of energy and fuel, industrial raw materials and semi-finished goods and the principal kinds of equipment and construction units. The list of commodities and products is given in terms of the basic consumer properties of the commodities (fuel in conventional fuel units, motors and turbines in conventional horse-power units, mineral raw materials in terms of metal content, fertilizers in terms of assimilable substances, feed in terms of feed units, metal goods in normative hours of work, and so on).

The main aim of the commodity nomenclature of the basic model of production and social division of labour is to distinguish the basic kinds of consumer values as bearers of value and thus to ensure in the future the possibility of determining the value level of commodity prices. The commodity-product nomenclature includes not only the basic commodities and products, but also groups called 'other products of the sector' (there are 80–90 of these sectoral groups). 'Other products of the sector' are given in constant fixed prices. The Soviet statistical system of national economic and local primary accounting allows this to be done. On the basis of such a commodity nomenclature a model of social production and social division of labour is constructed. This model of social production is formulated in two ways: as an overall material balance (in physical and monetary units) and as an intersectoral balance of production and distribution of products (in monetary units).

The overall material balance which is a model of the material structure of social production consists of two blocks, formulated as two product-sector matrices: intermediate products (A) and final products (B). The model of social division of labour includes these two blocks and is supplemented by a third block (C) reflecting expenditures of labour (by categories of workers – engineering-technical workers, junior white collar personnel and workers by wage rate-groups). This block is given in units of working time and the expenditures of working time are calculated including not only direct but also indirect expenditures of labour in auxiliary workshops and on general factory work. Indirect labour expenditures are allocated among products and commodities in accordance with factory practice for allocating overhead and indirect costs between commodities and products. The total expenditures of labour time by columns give the role vector 'expenditure of labour'. The third block is arranged under the first two blocks. Blocks A and B form the overall material balance. In the roles of the first block of intermediate products the general commodity-product nomenclature is specified (with import commodity groups divided into non-competing imports), and in the columns there are pure sectors of production grouped by kinds of commodities produced but not by enterprises.

Thus, the first block (A) reflects the distribution of products and commodities by the sectors producing them (rows) and consuming them (columns) at the same time. In the rows of the second block (B) the corresponding positions of the whole commodity-product nomenclature are distinguished, and in the columns, the social funds (gross accumulation fund, consumption fund, external relations fund). Between the first and second blocks a column 'losses and retirals' is provided. The gross accumulation fund in the second block is in its turn sub-divided into capital repair, renewal of fixed capital (replacement), capital investment and growth of working capital. In addition the productive and non-productive spheres are distinguished for each of these sub-groups. In the block of final products the consumption fund distinguishes the consumption of families of workers in the sphere of material production and also consumption of other groups of the population and the operating expenses of social, cultural and administrative institutions. If we have in view both a model of social production and a model of the social division of labour the first and second blocks are given in three units of measurement (in physical units, in units of working time, by labour intensity, and in current prices) and the third block (expenditures of labour) is given in two units of measurement (working time and labour pay in money).

The model of social production in current prices is supplemented (in comparison with the overall material balance) by a fourth block which shows in money terms the so-called 'conventional net income' (block D). The columns of block D have the same nomenclature of pure sectors of production and the rows indicate amortization deductions, kinds of labour pay (basic and supplementary earnings, social insurance charges, *kolkhoznik* labour pay in money, other money incomes of the population, and the social consumption fund) and kinds of net income of society (profit, turnover tax, rent). The combination of the first and second blocks describes the structure of production, consumption and the division of the social product in three units of measurement. The combination of the first block (in monetary units) and block D shows the value structure of social production and permits the three basic value elements of production to be distinguished, namely: material costs (first block plus the amortization deductions row of block D), labour pay, and value of surplus product.

The model of the social product in monetary units is supplemented in addition by a fifth block – 'fixed and working capital'. The rows of the fifth block contain a more aggregated physical nomenclature of capital and the columns show the corresponding nomenclature of sectors of production, i.e. of sectors corresponding to the aggregates composed of the pure sectors of production. As a result the combination of the first, second and third blocks measured in units of complete and direct expenditures of working time form a model of the social division of labour as the basis of the further mathematical description of the process of formation of social value.

It is assumed that the planned model of the social product reflects the optimal plan determined on the basis of the corresponding economic criterion. It is also assumed that in the selection of the optimal variant of the plan both economic and economic-mathematical criteria are used. In accordance with general economic criteria, the production plan, for example, must meet the general directives of the controlling organs, the condition of achievement of the maximum results with minimum expenditures, and the law of economy of social labour. Consequently it must ensure the minimum losses of labour in the choice of both the regional location of production and the technological methods of production and also provide rational means for the fulfilment of the plan. Thus it is assumed that the plan which provides for the physical structure of production is based on selection of technological methods by evaluating them not only from the point of view of whether they correspond to the requirements of technical progress, but also from the point of view of correspondence to the mathematical criteria of the optimal plan, for example to the optimal vector of intensity of technological methods of production and intensity of substitutable products.

The process of formation of value

The initial basic model of production and social division of labour allows us to describe mathematically, and thus to a certain extent to imitate, the complicated process of formation of social (labour and exchange) value. The first contour of this mathematical description consists in the determination, on the basis of the absolute magnitudes of the initial model, of the corresponding parameters and coefficients of the model of planned price formation. At the first contour stage of building the model of planned prices, the matrix of technological expenditure coefficients (from the first block of the initial model), the matrix of labour intensity and labour pay (from the third block), the matrix of capital coefficients and coefficients of consumption (from the second block) and the matrix of capital intensity (from the fifth block) are determined.

Let the physical volume of output of production be x_i for the rows and x_j for the columns and the expenditure of the ith product of labour in the production of the jth product be x_{ij}. Then the technological coefficients of expenditure will equal

$$a_{ij} = \frac{x_{ij}}{x_j}.$$

For imported objects of labour they will be

$$\tilde{a}_{mj} = \frac{\bar{x}_{mj} \cdot \tilde{p}_m}{x_j},$$

where $\tilde{p}_m$ is the import currency coefficient which converts foreign into domestic currency.

Let T_{lj} be the working time of the lth category of workers in the production of the jth product. Then the coefficients of labour intensity will be

$$t_j = \sum_t T_{lj} : x_j,$$

and also $$t_{lj} = \frac{T_{lj}}{x_j}$$

(for the lth category of workers).

Let F_{kj} be the fixed capital of the kth sort employed in the production of the jth product and F_{oj} be the working capital. Then the coefficients of capital intensity are

$$\hat{f}_{kj} = \frac{\hat{F}_{kj}}{x_j} \quad \text{and} \quad f_{oj} = \frac{F_{oj}}{x_j}.$$

The second element of the mathematical description of planned price formation reproduces the process of formation of value. The building of the model comprises three stages: the determination of the full expenditures of labour, the determination of the socially necessary expenditures of labour and the determination of value.

For the determination of the full expenditures of labour the matrix of technological coefficients (including import coefficients and the coefficient of amortization deductions), and the vector of labour intensity in units of working time, and in units of simple labour, are used. The matrix of coefficients and the vector of labour intensity are determined in the process of the plan calculations involved in the first contour. But, in addition, the coefficients of labour intensity per rouble of amortization deductions, and the coefficients of labour intensity per rouble expended on the import of commodities, have to be determined. The second block of the initial model showed the composition of expenditures on capital repair and replacement, and the commodity structure of exports, and both of these are given both in physical units of measurement and in current prices. Labour intensity per rouble of amortization deductions is determined by means of dividing the money expenditure on capital repair and replacement by the labour expenditure on it. By comparing similarly the value of the column vector 'export' in two units of measurement (in domestic currency monetary units and in labour intensity) we obtain labour intensity per rouble of exports. In valuing exports in domestic currency monetary units the import current coefficient, which enables us to convert the foreign currency received for exports into domestic currency, has already been taken into consideration. In view of this, and the fact that the aim of exports is to provide the currency to pay for imports of commodities, we equate labour intensity per rouble of imports to labour intensity per rouble of exports. As a result the matrix of technological coefficients of the first block is supplemented by two row vectors expressed in units of labour intensity, namely the vector of amortization coefficients and the vector of import coefficients.

We determine full labour intensity on the basis of this supplementary matrix using the following iteration equation of Dmitriev–Leontief:[1]

$$\tau_j = \sum_i a_{ij}\tau_j + t_j, \quad \text{where } i = 1, 2, \ldots, n; j = 1, 2, \ldots, n.$$

In the symbols of matrix algebra we have

$$t(E-A)^{-1} = \tau.$$

Here a_{ij} are the technological coefficients of outlay (and also amortization and import), t_j is the row of the coefficient of labour intensity, τ_i is the transposed row of full coefficients of labour intensity, τ_j is the sector row of the coefficient of full labour intensity, $(E-A)^{-1}$ is an inverse matrix. A is the matrix of coefficients (a_{ij}), E is a unit matrix, t is the vector of labour intensity, and τ is the vector of full labour intensity.

The full expenditure of labour in units of simple labour can be determined similarly, for this it is necessary to apply the inverse matrix separately to each vector of labour intensity of the different categories of workers. The coefficients of full labour intensity obtained are multiplied by the tariff coefficients or by special coefficients which reflect the relationship of total family and social expenditures on the training of personnel of various specialities and skills. Summing these products we obtain the row vector of full expenditures of labour measured in units of simple labour τ_j. After this we pass on to the determination of the socially necessary expenditures of labour, bearing in mind that in economic reality expenditures of live labour may be broken down into necessary and surplus labour and surplus labour begins to be distributed, in conditions of equivalent exchange, in proportion to necessary labour.

For the purpose of building a model of this economic process coefficients of consumption of the necessities of life by the families of those working in the sphere of material production need to be preliminarily determined. In the second block of the model the material composition of the consumption fund of the families of those working in the sphere of material production is

1. See Dmitriev (1904, pp. 7–8). For the identity of the results obtained from Dmitriev's equation (1904) and Leontief (1938), see Zauberman (1962) and also the collection *Primenenie Matematiki i Elekronnoi Tekhnike v Planirovani* (1961, pp. 28–31).

distinguished separately. On the basis of budget survey data and the plan for raising the material and cultural standard of living of the workers, we construct a matrix for the consumption fund of the families of those working in the sphere of material production in the form (Q_{ij}), where Q_{ij} is the volume of products and commodities of the ith kind consumed by the families of those working in the sphere of material production employed in the production of the jth product. Now let T_j be the quantity of working time expended in the production of the jth product and T'_j be the quantity of simple labour expended in the production of the same product. Then the coefficients of consumption per unit of labour (which will be necessary for determining the volume of expenditures of necessary labour) equal:

$$h_{ij} = \frac{Q_{ij}}{T_j}; \quad h'_{ij} = \frac{Q_{ij}}{\tau'_j}.$$

On the basis of the coefficients of full labour intensity (τ_j), and the coefficients of full expenditures of simple labour (τ'_j) we construct a model of the social division of labour, not in units of labour intensity (as was done in the basic model of the social division of labour) but in units of full labour intensity and units of full expenditures of simple labour. For this we transpose the row vectors of coefficients of full labour intensity and coefficients of full expenditures of simple labour and multiply each row of the first block of the model of social production (x_{ij}) by the corresponding component of the transposed coefficients. Here we proceed on the assumption that the value of a commodity in units of full expenditures of labour is determined only by the technological conditions of production and that these values do not vary with the sector in which the particular commodities are consumed. As a result, we obtain a model of the social division of labour in units of full labour intensity $(x_{ij} \tau_i)$ and in units of simple labour $(x_{ij} \tau'_i)$. Similarly we obtain a matrix of magnitudes $(a_{ij} \tau_i)$ and a matrix of magnitudes $(a_{ij} \tau'_i)$.

By multiplying from the right the matrix of coefficients h_{ij} by the diagonal matrix of coefficients of expenditures of simple labour (τ'_i), we obtain a matrix of magnitudes $(h_{ij} \tau'_i)$, which are valued in units of simple labour, and express the volume of necessities of life consumed by those working in the sphere of material production in the process of reproduction of labour power. The sum of these magnitudes is equal to necessary labour.

Under conditions of the social division of labour there occurs exchange of commodities for commodities and exchange of expenditures of labour power for the necessities of life. In this exchange the expenditures of living labour may be broken down into expenditures of necessary labour and expenditures of surplus labour.

In the exchange of expenditures of labour power for the necessities of life, the quantity of necessities of life of the ith kind consumed by the families of those working on production of the jth product (Q_{ij}) will be evaluated by the ratio of the full expenditures of simple labour on the production of the ith product (τ'_i) to the labour intensity in units of simple labour of the production of the jth product (t'_j). Calculated per unit of output (x_j) we will have magnitudes of the type $h_{ij} \cdot \tau_i$. This valuation allows us to take into account the ratio of the full expenditures of labour (τ_i) and the labour intensity of the necessities of life consumed (t_j).

In reality in the exchange of the necessities of life ($Q_{ij} \tau_i$) for expenditures of labour power ($x_j \cdot t_j = T_j$) we have the following relationship

$$\frac{Q_{ij}}{x_j} \times \frac{\tau_i}{t_j}.$$

In the exchange of necessities of life for expenditures of labour power the surplus labour is separated from the necessary labour since the productivity of labour is higher than the expenditures of labour on the necessities of life which are essential for the reproduction of the labour power. The ratio of these magnitudes also permits us to determine the coefficient of surplus labour (e_o), which is equal to the ratio of the material composition of the national income Y_i to the material composition of the consumption fund of families of those working in the sphere of material production, that is

$$e_o = \frac{\sum\limits_i Y_i \tau'_i}{\sum\limits_i \sum\limits_j Q_{ij} \tau'_i}$$

In conditions of the social division of labour the whole process of exchange of commodities for commodities and exchange of expenditures of labour power for necessities of life in the form of commodities can be described and reproduced mathematically on the basis of the following iteration formulae[2]

$$\sum_i a_{ij}\tau'_i + e_o \sum_i h_{ij}\tau'_i = \tau_j.$$

In the course of the iteration the coefficient e_o changes as the ratio

$$e_o = \frac{\sum_i Y_i\tau_i}{\sum_j \sum_i Q_{ij}\tau_i}$$

changes. The iteration process is concluded when this coefficient ceases to change. In the symbols of matrix algebra the iteration equation takes the form

$$\left(E - A - \frac{1}{e_o}H\right)^{-1}\tau = 0,$$

where H is the matrix of coefficients h_{ij}. The result we obtain is the vector of full expenditures of simple labour per unit of output under the condition that surplus labour is distributed in proportion to necessary labour. This is also the socially necessary expenditure of labour since, firstly, they are mutually coordinated (iterated); secondly, correspond to the plan providing for the optimal physical structure of social production; thirdly, correspond to the principle of equivalent exchange under which surplus labour is proportional to necessary labour.

In the transition from socially necessary expenditures of labour (τ_i) to social value (ω_i) the coefficient of surplus labour (e_o) must not only be iterated but also dynamically optimized. For each particular future period, for example five years, the optimal coefficient of surplus labour (e^*_o) must correspond to the optimal development of the given economic system in time. For this a special dynamic model of the social division of labour must be constructed, reflecting the growth of labour productivity by

2. A similar procedure is used by Morishima, Seton and Johansen 1961). They use it to determine value from prices, that is, the inverse of our problem.

sectors and having an optimal vector of sector coefficients which define the ratio of necessary and surplus labour. But the problems of constructing such a dynamic model are beyond the scope of the present article. Here it is only necessary to point out that the choice of the extreme magnitude (in the form of a saddle point) of the optimal coefficient can be made if we have for each year of the future period basic plan models of production and the social division of labour, or if the economic development beginning from the initial year is subject to a condition such that, for example, the maximum approach to the set material and cultural standard of living of the workers with the least full expenditures of simple labour per unit of gross output should be achieved in the last year of the period. We denote the optimal socially necessary expenditures of simple labour by τ^*_j. Value is proportional to the optimal socially necessary expenditures of simple labour with a coefficient of proportionality equal to the monetary scale of value (Ω_o); this scale is equal to the ratio of the two measures of the physical volume of national income (Y_i), that valued in current prices ($\Sigma\, Y_i\, P_i$) to that valued in units of socially necessary expenditures of simple labour ($\Sigma\, Y_i\, \tau^*_i$). Consequently,

$$\Omega_o = \frac{\Sigma\, Y_i\, P_i}{\Sigma\, Y_i\, \tau^*_i},$$

and value (ω_i), proportional to the optimal socially necessary expenditures of labour, will equal: $\omega_i = \Omega_o\, \tau^*_i$.

The process of transformation of the form of value

The aim of the third element of the calculations in the planning of prices is the mathematical description of the process of transformation of the form of value. In this process the magnitude of value does not change, but only its form.

The change of the form of value and the creation of the transformed form of value are objectively necessary so that the process of realization of value can proceed freely. Social value is realized at the individual level of the separate production-consumption cells of society (families, enterprises, production and territorial complexes).

In its primary form social value cannot be individualized, i.e.

it cannot be reduced to individual value. For this, social value must be broken down into its component elements (transferred value, value of paid labour, and value of surplus product).

The appearance of money in the process of the social division of labour leads to the change in the form of value, for the process of creation and realization of the latter begins to proceed not in direct labour but in monetary form. The further development of commodity production leads to the pay of labour taking the form of wages, the wearing out of fixed capital taking the form of amortization deductions, expenditures of intermediate products taking the form of material costs, surplus value taking the form of profit, rent, turnover tax, etc.

The process of reduction of social value to individual value, reflecting the process of realization of value, can only take place in the transformed form of value. Therefore it is necessary to describe mathematically the process of formation of the component elements of value into which social value is broken down in the process of its realization. Wages and labour pay in general are isolated. On the basis of the matrix of technological co-efficients (A) full payments out of the wages fund can be determined by the formula $W^* = W(E-A)^{-1}$, where E is a unit matrix, $(E-A)^{-1}$ is the inverse matrix of technological co-efficients, W is the vector of wages per unit of product, and W^* is the vector of full payments from the wages fund.

Under socialism, apart from individual labour pay, depending on quantity and quality of work, a social form of labour pay arises which includes payments made from the social consumption fund (education, health, cheap housing and communal services, free factory meals, social insurance and so on). Although the social consumption fund is distributed without payment, society as a whole incurs great expenditures of labour and material resources. The expenditures on this social fund require reproduction. In the determination of value these expenditures must be added to wages either directly (on the basis of direct accounting data or data from special surveys) or indirectly, that is in proportion to the fund of individual labour pay. Then the vector W will define all payments and distributions both from the individual and from the social consumption fund. The vector of full payments from the wages fund is also determined taking the social consumption fund into account. The vector of full payments for amortization deductions $(d^*{}_j)$ is determined similarly.

If for each product separately we deduct from the social value (ω_j) the full payments from the wages fund $(W^*{}_j)$ and the full amortization deductions $(d^*{}_j)$ we obtain the net income of society, that is, the value of surplus product:

$$\pi_j = \omega_j - W^*{}_j - d^*{}_j.$$

If the net income of society, equal to the value of surplus product, is related to the productive and natural resources employed, then we obtain an indicator of the profitability of the use of these resources. In conditions of socialism productive resources have a monetary form in the shape of balance sheet value of fixed and working capital. However, natural resources (land, minerals, forests, water) do not have such a value. Therefore it is first necessary to determine indicators of the overall profitability of the use of productive resources including both forms of net income (profits and differential rent).

In determining the coefficients of profitability of the use of resources it is important to avoid repeated duplication of profitability. It is necessary to take special measures so that the profitability of resources is not duplicated in material expenditures. At each stage of production only the profitability of those resources which have been borrowed at the given stage of the production process should be calculated. The volume of transferred value of surplus product also should not depend on the number of stages into which production is divided. This duplication can be avoided if the coefficients of profitability are determined in relation to full capital utilization. Thus, if $\hat{f}_{kj}$ is the capital intensity of production of the jth product in the kth physical kind of fixed capital and $\hat{f}_{oj}$ is the capital intensity of production of the jth product in the oth physical kind of working capital then the vector of full capital intensity will equal: for fixed capital

$$\varphi_K = \hat{\varphi}_K (E - A)^{-1},$$

and for working capital

$$\psi_o = f_o (E - A)^{-1}.$$

Then the overall capital intensity (for all physical kinds of capital) will be represented accordingly by the vectors φ and ψ. We will denote the components of these vectors for production of the jth product by φ_{kj} and ψ_{oj}. Altogether they form the matrix of coefficients of full capital intensity in fixed and working capital in terms of their physical composition by the sectors of production in which they are employed.

In determining the coefficients of overall profitability of fixed capital of the kth kind (a_k) and of working capital of the oth kind (β_o) the following must be taken into account:

1. For each sector – net income equal to the value of surplus product (π_j);

2. For each physical kind of capital its reproduction value and its turnover period (which reflects its value by the degree of use in production). Let the annual capital investment in fixed capital equal its growth $\Delta \hat{F}_k$, and let the growth of the physical elements of working capital be similarly ΔF_o.

Then their coefficients of reproduction will equal:

$$(1+\hat{r}_k) \text{ and } (1+r_o), \text{ where } \hat{r}_k = \frac{\Delta \hat{F}_k}{\hat{F}_k}, \text{ and } r_o = \frac{\Delta F_o}{F_o}.$$

Let the turnover period of capital (more accurately, the degree of utilization in production) equal for fixed capital m_k and for working capital m_o. Then the coefficients of overall profitability of capital can be determined from the system of equations:

$$\pi_j = \sum_k a_k \varphi_{kj}(1+\hat{r}_k)^m k + \sum \beta_o \psi_{oj}(1+r_o)^m o.$$

These equations are formed for each sector of production separately and the coefficients of general profitability of the particular kind of capital (a_k and β_o) are determined from them. The magnitudes π_j (net income of the jth sector) were already determined at the stage of the second contour of the mathematical description of the process of formation of value. The matrix of parameters φ_{kj} and ψ_{oj} is obtained on the basis of the coefficient of capital intensity of the initial plan model of the social product and the turnover periods of capital are established according to data from technical examinations.

It must be particularly emphasized that in these equations coefficients of profitability of capital consist of two factors, namely for fixed capital a_k and $(1+\hat{r}_k)^{m_k}$, and for working capital β_o and $(1+r_o)^{m_o}$. Thus it is important that the factors $(1+\hat{r}_k)^{m_k}$ and $(1+r_o)^{m_o}$ in these equations are known magnitudes, as they are determined from the coefficients of capital intensity of the initial basic model, namely: $\Delta \hat{F}_k$ and ΔF from the data of the second block, and $\hat{F}_k$ and F_o from the data of the fifth block. In our equations the reproduction periods of capital are also viewed as known magnitudes (they are determined by data from technical economic examination). The coefficients a_k and β_o are obtained on the basis of the solution of the above system of equations. Both factors contained in the coefficient of profitability of capital of the given physical kind are independent of what sector of production the capital is employed in. In this sense they are the same for the whole economy.

National economic accounting practice usually provides a more aggregated nomenclature for fixed and working capital than for sectors of production.

In order that the number of equations be equal to the number of unknowns we form more highly aggregated sectors of production corresponding to the nomenclature for capital. Our object is to determine the average coefficients of profitability of fixed and working capital separately for the jth sector. The coefficients a_k and β_o, determined for the different forms of capital, only play an auxiliary part in the establishment of these average sector coefficients. Although the coefficients $(a_k; \beta_o)$ only change for different forms of capital the average sectoral coefficients of profitability $(\bar{\varphi}_j$ and $\bar{\psi}_j)^3$ change for different sectors of production since they depend on the sectoral structure, the physical composition of the capital employed in them and also on the turnover period of capital (on its degree of utilization in production) and on its coefficient of reproduction. This quality of the sectoral coefficients of profitability of capital permits us when necessary to disaggregate the coefficients of profitability right down to the individual enterprise on the basis of the physical structure of the capital employed in it.

3. In calculating the average sectoral coefficients of profitability of capital not only capital intensity but also the coefficients of reproduction of capital and its turnover period must be taken into account a, weights, that is, the magnitudes $\hat{F}_k(1+\hat{r}_k)^{m_k}$ and $F_o(1+r_o)^{m_o}$.

It should be noted that in a number of countries accelerated amortization is practised, which does not correspond to the periods of service of fixed capital. In this case amortization deductions include a part of the net income of society. In such a case it is economically correct to determine the gross profitability of fixed capital inclusive of amortization deductions rather than the general profitability. Then in the preceding system of equations we will have on the left-hand side the total value of surplus product and amortization equal to $\pi_j + a^*_j$, and on the right-hand side gross (not general) coefficients of profitability of fixed capital (a'_k). Then by deducting the average normal amortization coefficient for the sector from the average sectoral gross profitability of capital of the jth sector (a_j) we obtain the average sectoral general coefficient of profitability corrected with respect to amortization deductions.

However, in reducing the capital profitability coefficients to the level of the separate production territorial complex and individual enterprises we need to calculate not the general (and still less the gross) coefficients of capital profitability but rather the net norms of profitability from which the profitability of natural resources has already been deducted. For this, differential rent must be determined, which must also be calculated once only in the production turnover process (at the stage of the extractive sectors of production).

For the determination of differential rent for each sector of production zonal coefficients of resource intensity are necessary (for the forms of natural resources used in production). Their magnitudes are determined as the inverse of the indicators of output of production per unit of natural resources. For agricultural production one hectare of arable land is used as a unit of resources (for livestock and sheep breeding on pasture one hectare of agricultural land, for irrigated cotton growing one hectare of irrigated land). For mineral extractive sectors one cubic metre of mineral ore extracted can serve as the unit of resources and so on.

Differential rent can be determined by mathematical programming methods by the use of solution factors of the shadow price and objectively determined valuations type. In the determination of differential rent the extractive sector of production concerned is sub-divided into S zones. In each zone the corresponding categories of natural resources used in the given sector of production are distinguished according to their productivity. Then the matrix of coefficients of productivity of a unit of natural resources (z_{rs}) is determined. These coefficients are the inverse of the coefficients of resource intensity. Thereafter the matrix of zonal individual-group values is determined (λ_{rs}). By zonal individual-group values is understood the transformed form of value determined separately for each particular zone and for each group of lands or group of sources of useful minerals. For each of these groups the following parameters are determined; the vector of technological expenditure coefficients (a^{rs}_{r})$_j$ the average labour pay per unit of output w^{rs}, the average capital intensity of the unit of production in fixed capital $\hat{f}^{rs}$ and in working capital f^{rs}; the coefficients of capital intensity are determined as average weighted magnitudes on the basis of the physical composition of capital (for each group of lands or each source of minerals) within each zone. As a result the zonal individual-group value is determined according to the following formula of transformed value:

$$\lambda^j_{rs} = \sum_i a^{rs}_{ij} \omega_i + w^{rs}_j + \overline{\varphi}^{rs}_j + f^{rs}_j + \psi_j f^{rs}_j.$$

Here a^{rs}_{ij} are the technological expenditure coefficients for expenditure of the ith means of production in production of the jth product in the Sth zone using the rth resources; $\hat{f}^{rs}_j$ and f^{rs}_j are the capital intensity of fixed and working capital in production of the jth product; w^{rs}_j is the labour pay per unit of production under similar conditions; ω_i is the social value of intermediate products of the ith kind used; $\overline{\psi}_j$ is the average coefficient of gross profitability of fixed capital (including amortization); $\overline{\psi}_j$ is the average coefficient of profitability of working capital. In measuring differential rent the estimated zonal value c_s of a unit of production produced in the best natural conditions is determined by equating the zonal valuation c_j to the maximum zonal individual-group value, i.e. λ^o_{rs}. Then for the remaining categories of the given natural resource the saving is determined (η_{rs}), reduced to the level of the zonal value of a unit of the particular kind of production on the basis of the equation

$$\frac{\omega_s}{c_s}(\lambda^o_{rs} - \lambda_{rs}) = \eta_{rs}.$$

This will also be the differential rent from a unit of production which is formed in the conditions of the Sth zone and the rth category of resources.

The differential rent from a unit of natural resources is equal to

$$R_{rs} = z_{rs}\,\eta_{rs}.$$

The total amount of differential rent for the production of each product depends on the volume of commodity production of the Sth region obtained with the use in the Sth zone of the rth category of natural resources (N_{rs}). Delivery of the production of extractive sectors for further industrial processing and for construction purposes is considered to be commodity production. Enterprises of the extractive sectors are considered independent even if they do not have an independent financial balance sheet. Differential rent per unit of gross output of production of a given extractive sector (ζ_j) will equal:

$$\zeta_j = \sum N_{rs}\,\eta_{rs} : x_j,$$

where x_j is the gross output of the jth product.

Now the capital profitability norms can be determined, i.e. the net coefficients of profitability (a'_k and β'_o), by the same means as the gross and general coefficients of capital profitability were determined. Only in this case net income per unit of production (π_j) must be reduced by differential rent. Consequently

$$\pi_j - \zeta_j = \sum_k a'_k\,\varphi_{kj}(1+r)^m{}_k + \sum_o \beta'_{rs}\,\psi_{oj}\,(1+r)^m{}_o.$$

Then the average sectoral norm of profitability of fixed capital in production of a unit of the jth product will equal

$$\hat{\xi}_j = \sum_k a'_k\,\varphi_{kj}(1+r)^m{}_k \,/\, \sum_k \varphi'_{kj}.$$

Average profitability of working capital (ξ_j) is established earlier in a determination of total profitability. Consequently the full formula for determining the transformed form of value now takes the following form:

$$\omega_j = \sum_i a_{ij}\,\omega_j + W_j + (d_j + \hat{\xi}_j)\hat{f}_j + \xi_j f_i + P_j,$$

where ω_j is the value of a unit of the jth product, ω_i is the value of a unit of the ith object of labour (fuel, raw materials and so on), a_{ij} are the technological expenditure coefficients (for objects of labour), W_j is wages per unit of the jth product, d_j are the average sectoral amortization deductions per unit of fixed capital, $\hat{\xi}_j$ is the profitability norm of fixed capital, $\hat{f}_j$ is the capital intensity per unit of the jth product, ξ_j is the profitability norm of working capital, f_j is the capital intensity in working capital, and P_j is the rate of rent per unit of production.

In the method set out above value can be determined at any level (country, union republic, *sovnarkhoz*, sector or enterprise). Consequently individual value can also be determined in this form. It must also be emphasized that in the model examined above sectoral transformed form of value is equal in magnitude to sectoral social value. In our model the form of value is only modified to ensure that the process of realization of value and also the process of interaction of social and individual value continue uninterrupted, both in the reduction of social value to individual value and inversely in the conversion of individual value to social value.

At the present time it is imperative to plan not only direct cost but also value for sectors and enterprises. Direct cost (C) is a part of value, and equals:

$$C_j = \sum a_{ij}\,\omega_j + W_j + d_j \hat{f}_j.$$

The process of divergence of retail prices from value

The fourth element of the mathematical description of the process of planned price formation reproduces the objective process of divergence of prices from value under the influence of supply and demand and also under the influence of the relationships which arise in reality between the productive forces of society and its capacity for consumption.

Supply and demand operate primarily on retail prices, for which it is specially important to ensure equilibrium between the effective demand of the population and the total amount of commodities on the market. In planning prices and commodity turnover this equilibrium is usually checked on the basis of the balance of money incomes of the population and of retail commodity turnover. The balancing is based on the following equality:

$$\sum_i \lambda_i\, Q_i = W_o + D_k + S_r + D_r + Y_o - N - O_y + \Phi_o,$$

where

Q_i is the volume of market consumption by the population of commodities of the ith kind;

λ_i is the retail price of commodities;

W_o is the wages fund;

D_k is the total sum of money incomes of *kolkhozniki*;

S_r is the total sum of pensions and stipendiums;

D_r is other money incomes of the population;

Y_o is the value of non-commodity services for which payment is made;

N is the savings of the population;

O_y is market demand by social institutions for free supply of certain categories of the population (the army, hospitals), and

Φ_o is market demand from the social consumption fund.

If the equilibrium of the money incomes of the population and the retail commodity turnover is broken, then it must be re-established either by increasing the total amount of commodities on the market or, if this is impossible, by the divergence of the prices of certain commodities from their value. In planning such divergences the elasticity of demand with respect to price and family income, which is determined from family budget data, must be taken into account. The elasticity of quantitative demand (Q_i) for the ith commodity at price (λ_i) is determined by the following formula:

$$E_{ii} = \frac{\Delta \ln Q_i}{\Delta \ln \lambda_i} = \frac{\lambda_i}{Q_i} \times \frac{\Delta Q_i}{\Delta \lambda_i}.$$

The future elasticity of demand for the ith commodity with respect to the price of another kth commodity (E_{ik}) and the elasticity of demand with respect to family income (S) are determined analogously.

From determining the elasticity of demand (assuming that $\Delta \lambda_i = \lambda'_i - \lambda_i$; $\Delta Q_i = Q'_o - Q_i$) we can establish the following relationship between the state of demand and prices:

$$\left(1 - \frac{\lambda'_i}{\lambda_i}\right) = \frac{1}{E_i}\left(1 - \frac{Q'_i}{Q_i}\right).$$

On this basis we can determine a new system of commodity

prices (λ'_i) which meet the requirements of the new state of demand (Q'_i) on the basis of the following equation:

$$\lambda'_i = \lambda^o_i \left[\frac{1}{E_{ii}} \left(\frac{Q'_i}{Q^o_i} - 1 \right) + 1 \right]$$

where λ^o_i and Q^o_i are magnitudes relating to the system of budget data for which the coefficient of elasticity of demand is determined.

The equilibration of prices and demand at the family budget level, of course, is different from that at the level of the national economy. This discrepancy is the basic reason for the divergence of retail prices from value. Establishing on the basis of the amount of commodities on the market the degree of satisfaction of the demand for commodities Q'_i which is possible in fact, and working on the basis of the magnitudes determined by the budget data $(E_{ii}, Q^o_i$ and $\lambda^o_i)$ we can determine the level of prices (λ'_j) which correspond to the amount of these products available on the market. The difference between these prices and the value of the commodities will also reflect the divergence of prices from value $(\Delta_i = \lambda_j - \omega_i)$. To determine the divergences of prices from value in which the future elasticity and elasticity of demand with respect to family income are taken into account, the following formula in particular can be used

$$\Delta_j = P'_j - \omega_j = P^o_j \pi_i \left(\frac{Q'_i}{Q_i} \right)^{\xi_{ij}} \left(\frac{S'}{S_o} \right)^{\xi_j} - \omega_j,$$

where ξ_{ij} and ξ_j are the inverse of the coefficients of elasticity and π_i is a symbol of the future products of two numerical characteristics of the budget equilibrium conditions of demand and family incomes.

The optimal structure of production of consumer goods can be determined from the condition

$$\sum x_i \Delta^2_i = \text{minimum},$$

where x_i are weights.

The system of retail prices plays an enormous role in the economy of the country and as a result the basis of divergences of retail prices from the value must be in every way as well-founded as possible. Retail prices depend not only on elasticity of demand, but on the measure of satisfaction and the measure of urgency of different requirements, which are satisfied by particular commodities. The measure of satisfaction and the measure of urgency of a requirement govern, in particular, the overall consumer valuations of commodities.

The magnitude of the measure of satisfaction and the measure of urgency of requirement can be determined by the following ratios: the measure of satisfaction of requirements

$$\mu_i = \frac{N_i}{N^o{}_i},$$

the measure of urgency of a requirement

$$\eta_i = \frac{N^o{}_i \, \omega_i}{D_o},$$

where $N^o{}_i$ is the consumption norm corresponding to satisfaction (for this future consumption norms are usually accepted), N_i is the actual norm of consumption, ω_i is the value of a unit of the product, and D_o is the average money income per consumer unit.

For the consumer valuation of a unit of the ith commodity it is convenient to take the value of the exponential function from the magnitude of the corresponding measure:

$$U(\mu_i) = emi^{-1}; \qquad U(\eta) = e^{1-ni}.$$

On the basis of the consumer valuation of each kind of commodities included in the balance of money incomes and retail trade turnover we determine the weighted average value of the consumer valuations, and then the ratio of individual commodity valuations to the average magnitude. Let

$$K_i(\mu) = \frac{U(\mu_i)}{\overline{U}(\mu)} \quad \text{and} \quad K_j(\eta) = \frac{U(\eta_i)}{\overline{U}(\eta_i)}.$$

Assuming that retail prices correspond to value only on the average for the total amount of consumer commodities on the market and that for separate commodity groups retail prices are only proportional to value we obtain

$$P_i = K_i(\eta) \times \omega_i \quad \text{and} \quad P'_i = K_i(\mu) \times \omega_i.$$

In the planning of retail prices, apart from the objective data indicated, it is essential to pay attention to many other considerations which are relevant to price policy. In particular, the incentive and redistributive function of price must be taken into account. The overall total of prices of the commodities in retail trade turnover always tends to equal the total of their values. In order that retail price should not be divorced from wholesale prices the divergences of retail prices from value should, in our opinion, be covered from a special fund for the regulation of retail prices, from which divergences of retail prices below value should be financed and which would be replenished from divergences of prices above value.

The process of divergence and individualization of wholesale prices

The following, the fifth element of the model of planned price formation comprises the basis of the divergences of wholesale prices from value. Wholesale prices cannot be detached from the value base. Usually wholesale prices must be equal to retail prices minus the margin for the retail trade network.

The independent divergences of wholesale prices from value depend on the relationship of the quantity of commodities actually produced (X_i) and that socially necessary from the point of view of society's requirement for them (Z_i). The coefficient of proportional divergence of wholesale prices from value depends on the measure of satisfaction of society's consumer strength, determined from the equation:

$$\eta^o{}_i = \frac{Z_i}{X_i}.$$

It is equal to:

$$K^o(\eta) = e^{1-\eta^i}.$$

Then wholesale prices will equal:

$$P^o{}_i = K^o{}_i(\eta)\omega_i.$$

Apart from the indicated divergences of prices from value it is also important in building a model of wholesale prices to reflect in the wholesale price of concrete commodities the process of individualization of value, which consists of the transition from aggregated commodity positions to concrete commodities, that is, to a nomenclature which takes account of different kinds of commodities and their grade, mark, article, type, size, and so on.

In the planning of wholesale prices the main task is to reflect in price the qualities in use of the output produced (that is, to establish the relationship of prices for different commodities according to their mark, grade, type, model, style, size and so on). The fact is that the value level of prices, like the divergences of prices from value too, are capable of determination only for aggregated commodity groups (aggregates). The planning of wholesale (as well as retail) prices is closely associated with the compilation of price lists which take into account the consumer qualities of commodities in full accordance with the existing system of state standards (technical instructions, types, norms).

The nature of the individualization of the value level of wholesale and retail prices is one and the same since the individualization of both wholesale and retail prices takes place equally under the influence of use value reflected in consumer valuations of commodities. This individualization of the value level of wholesale and retail prices is reflected in price lists. For commodities on the wholesale market it is also important to take into account the temporary scarcity of certain commodities and the unmarketable character of others. But it is convenient to use other methods to take account of this aspect of commodity turnover, for example, changing the normal deduction of profits into the enterprise fund according to the temporary scarcity of commodities or whether they are old stock.

Let us illustrate the process of individualization of planned prices. The individualization of prices for fuel reflects their consumer qualities as fuels (calorific value, ash content, moisture and so on), for machines and lathes, the production capacity and the saving obtained by the user in the process of employing the machines, and the individualization of prices for food commodities reflects their content of various nutrients.

Let there be an mth aggregate of products (for which value is determined) which includes the total of the ith kind of concrete products amounting to a quantity Q_i^m. Let each concrete kind of food commodity contain k nutrient elements in quantities E_{kj}, and let the content of these nutrient elements in the normal daily ration equal $\widecheck{E}_k$. Then the content of k nutrient elements for a weight unit in shares of the daily food ration of the commodity will equal:

$$\xi_{kj} = \frac{E_{kj}}{\widecheck{E}_k}, \quad \text{that is } E_{kj} = \xi_{kj} \widecheck{E}_k.$$

For the particular collection of actual commodities corresponding to the nutrient elements we are taking into account we construct the matrix of magnitudes $\xi_{kj} \widecheck{E}_k$. Let c_j denote the normative or planned direct cost of the concrete commodities and ω_m the value of their mth aggregate (with those weight coefficients which are laid down in the basic plan of the model of the social product). In these conditions with the individualization of wholesale prices (that is with the determination of the divergences of concrete prices from the value of a unit of their aggregate) it is essential to determine the unknown consumer valuations of the individual commodities (γ_k) and the normal profitability of their aggregates (r_m), established as percentages of direct cost (where the prices used in the calculation of direct cost already correspond to the value level).

We find the magnitudes γ_k by solving the following extreme problem:

$$\sum \widecheck{E}_k \gamma_k = maximum.$$

Under the conditions:

$$\widecheck{E}_k \geqslant O; E_{kj} \geqslant O; \tag{1}$$

$$\sum_k \xi_{kj} \widecheck{E}_k \gamma_k \leqslant C_j. \tag{2}$$

According to the second condition the scale of consumer valuations (γ_k) is chosen at the level of planned direct cost (c_j). Then the price of a concrete commodity (λ_j) included in the mth aggregate is determined by solution of the following system of equations:

$$P_i(m) = \sum_k \xi_{kj} \widecheck{E}_k \gamma_k (1 + r_m).$$

under the condition:

$$\sum_m Q_j{}^{(m)} \lambda_j{}^{(m)} = \sum_m Q_j{}^{(m)} \omega_m.$$

The last condition ensures the equality of the total of commodity prices with the total of values for each separate aggregate of commodities and products distinguished in special positions in the initial basic plan model of the social product and the social division of labour (for example, the product group vegetables, starch foods, groats, vegetable oil, fats, dairy and other meat products).

The value and prices of grain, fodder and feed, different fuels, textiles, machines, equipment and so on can be individualized in a similar way. In each case the basis is the particular system of valuations of consumer properties of the commodities taken from the system of state standards and also on a system of indices indicating user convenience and possible economy in the sphere of consumption of material values and monetary resources.

In addition, for agricultural procurement prices, it is important to have a system of insurance payments guaranteeing the insured level of revenue per hectare of land and thus ensuring a minimum guaranteed pay for the labour of *kolkhozniki*. The necessity of such a supplementary insurance system is caused by variations in the level of yield as a result of meteorological causes (particularly for grain). Procurement prices, as we know, are based on multi-year average yields, on normal labour productivity and on social value in normal conditions. The system of insurance is required to take account of the actual variations in different years in the value and productivity of labour which do not depend on agricultural producers.

The sixth and last contour of calculations in the planning of prices is thus connected with the current work of the compilation of price lists. In this it is assumed that the value level of prices for the basic leading commodities which form the 'backbone' of prices is already provided. At this stage, consequently, a supplementary system of calculations is envisaged connected with the current calculation of direct cost. In this the calculation of direct cost on the basis of the use of the transformed form of value can also be supplemented by the determination of individual value for all the productive units of society.

The time has come when each enterprise in the course of its operations should determine not only direct cost but also individualized value on the basis of such social normatives as the coefficient of profitability of fixed and working capital, and taking account of the differential rent for all the natural resources it employs. In a socialist society economic results cannot be determined on the basis of direct cost alone, which represents only a part of value. The economically profitable operation of an enterprise or the unprofitableness of certain enterprises should be determined on the basis of current accounting of individual value, by comparing this with zonal, sectoral and social value. In addition, periodical checking of the correspondence of wholesale and retail prices to the value level is essential. In any case such a check needs to be made each time during the compilation of the next plan for the future development of the national economy.

References

DMITRIEV, V. K. (1904), *Ekonomicheskiye Ocherki*, Moscow.
JOHANSEN, L. (1961), A note on 'Aggregation in Leontief matrices and the labour theory of value', *Econometrica*, no. 2, April.
MORISHIMA, M., SETON, F. (1961), 'Aggregation in Leontief matrices and the labour theory of value', *Econometrica*, no. 2.
ZAUBERMAN, A. (1962), 'A few remarks on a discovery in Soviet economics', *Bulletin of the Oxford Institute of Statistics*, November.
Primenenie Matematiki i Elekronno Tekhnike v Planirovani, Moscow (1961).

21 L. V. Kantorovich

Mathematical Formulation of the Problem of Optimal Planning

Excerpts from L. V. Kantorovich, *The Best Use of Economic Resources*, Moscow, 1959. Pergamon Press, 1955, pp. 262–301.

The problem of programme allocation

The general formulation of this problem (see Kantorovich, 1939) is as follows:

n different products (kinds of operations) in a given assortment are to be produced by means of m production units (factories, machines, machine-tools). The assortment consists of $k_1, k_2, \ldots, k_n$ units of products of types (1), (2),..., (n) respectively. The productivity of each unit in each product is known: if the ith unit ($i = 1, 2, \ldots, m$) is assigned to the production of the jth product ($j = 1, 2, \ldots, n$), then a_{ij} units of this product are produced per unit of time. It is required to distribute the work among the production units in such a way that in a unit of time the maximum number of complete sets of products is produced.

If we denote by h_{ij} ($i = 1, \ldots, m; j = 1, \ldots, n$) the fraction of the working time of the ith production unit spent on the production of the jth product, then the search for the optimal plan reduces to the following purely mathematical problem.

Problem A

Given the non-negative numbers

$$\{a_{ij}\} \quad (i = 1, \ldots, m; j = 1, \ldots, n), \qquad k_j > 0 \quad (j = 1, \ldots, n),$$

with $\max_{1 \le i \le m} a_{ij} > 0 \quad (j = 1, \ldots, n)$

(each product may be produced by at least one of the production units), find the set of numbers (the plan) $\pi = \{h_{ij}\}$ ($i = 1, \ldots, m; j = 1, \ldots, n$) satisfying the following conditions:

1. $h_{ij} \geqq 0$ ($i = 1, \ldots, m; j = 1, \ldots, n$) (the fraction of working time expended by a production unit for the processing of a given product is a non-negative number);

2. $\sum_{j=1}^{n} h_{ij} \leq 1$ $(i = 1, \ldots, m)$

(the total working time of each production unit is limited by the planned calendar time);

3. The quantity

$$\mu(\pi) = \min_{1 \leq j \leq n} \frac{x^{\pi}_{j}}{k_j}, \qquad\qquad 1$$

where $\quad x^{\pi}_{j} = \sum_{i=1}^{m} a_{ij} h_{ij}$ $(j = 1, \ldots, n)$, $\qquad\qquad 2$

takes its maximum possible value (the numbers x^{π}_{j} express total output of the various products if the work is performed according to plan π, and the quantity $\mu(\pi)$ shows the scale of production under this plan, the number of complete assorted sets produced per unit of time).

A plan π, which satisfies conditions 1–3, is said to be *optimal*, and a plan satisfying conditions 1 and 2 *feasible*.

First of all we note that in Problem A an optimal plan always exists.

In fact, let $\pi_v = \{h^v_{ij}\}$ $(v = 1, 2, \ldots)$ be a sequence of feasible plans such that $\mu(\pi_v) \to \mu = \sup \mu(\pi)$, where the exact upper limit (sup) is taken for all feasible plans π. Without loss of generality, we may obviously assume that the sequence converges to the limit

$$\lim_{v \to \infty} h^v_{ij} = h_{ij} \quad (i = 1, \ldots, m; j = 1, \ldots, n)$$

(such convergence exists always for some subsequence). Then the plan $\pi = \{h_{ij}\}$ is optimal.

Now we may formulate a proposition in general form about a characteristic property of an optimal plan – the existence of objectively determined valuations for all kinds of products.

Theorem 1

To determine whether a feasible plan is optimal it is necessary and sufficient that multipliers $c_1, c_2, \ldots, c_n$ (valuations for all kinds of products) exist such that

(a) $c_j \geq 0$ $(j = 1, \ldots, n)$, $\max_{1 \leq j \leq n} c_j > 0$

(these valuations are non-negative, with at least one of the products having a positive valuation);

(b) $c_j a_{ij} = \max\limits_{1 \leqq t \leqq n} c_t a_{it} = d_i,$ only if $h_{ij} \neq 0$

(each production unit is used for the preparation of only those products for which its productivity valuation is maximum; the numbers d_i may be taken as valuation of the productive power of the production units);

(c) $c_j = 0,$ if $x^\pi{}_j > k_j \mu(\pi)$

(for those products which are produced in excess, the valuations are equal to 0);

(d) $\sum\limits_{j=1}^{n} h_{ij} = 1,$ if $d_i \neq 0$

(production units with positive valuations of productive power are fully used).

Indeed, if for a given feasible plan $\pi = \{h_{ij}\}$ such multipliers exist, then for any other feasible plan $\pi' = \{h_{ij}\}$, we have, from **1, 2** and conditions **1, 2** (a–d):

$$\left(\sum_j c_j k_j \right) \mu(\pi') \leqq \sum_j c_j x^{\pi'}{}_j = \sum_j c_j \sum_i a_{ij} h_{ij} = \sum_i \sum_j (c_j a_{ij}) h'{}_{ij}$$

$$\leqq \sum_i d_i \sum_j h'{}_{ij} \leqq \sum_i d_i = \sum_i d_i \sum_j h_{ij} = \sum_j \sum_i (c_j a_{ij}) h_{ij}$$

$$= \sum_j c_j \sum_i a_{ij} h_{ij} = \sum_j c_j x^\pi{}_j = \sum_j c_j [k_j \mu(\pi)] = \left(\sum_j c_j k_j \right) \mu(\pi),$$

which leads to the inequality $\mu(\pi') \leqq \mu(\pi)$. In view of the arbitrary choice of a feasible plan π', this inequality shows that the given plan π is optimal, and the first part of the theorem has been proved. The second proposition, that for every optimal plan there is a set of multipliers which satisfy conditions (a–d), will be proved below where a more general problem will be considered.

Note 1

If all the numbers $a_{ij} > 0$ (all kinds of product may be produced by every production unit), then for every optimal plan $\pi = \{h_{ij}\}$, and the multipliers corresponding to it according to Theorem 1, the following conditions are satisfied:

$2'.$ $\sum\limits_{j=1}^{n} h_{ij} = 1$ $(i = 1,\ldots, m)$

(all production units are fully utilized);

$$3'. \quad \frac{x^{\pi_1}}{k_1} = \frac{x^{\pi_2}}{k_2} = \ldots = \frac{x^{\pi_n}}{k_n} = \mu(\pi)$$

(the given assortment of products is maintained);

(a') $c_j > 0 \quad (j = 1,\ldots,n)$

(all products have positive valuations).

Indeed in this case all the numbers $d_i > 0$; and then from (d) we have 2'. Further, for all j we have $h_{ij} \neq 0$, for some i (each product is produced on some one production unit); therefore, (b) implies (a'). From (a') and (b) we obtain 3'.

Consequently, in the case considered (when all $a_{ij} > 0$) it is necessary and sufficient for the optimality of a feasible plan π that it satisfies conditions 2', 3', and that there exists a system of positive multipliers which satisfy condition (b).

Note 2

In the general case (when some $a_{ij} = 0$) it is also possible to limit the consideration to so-called *assortment* plans, which satisfy conditions 1, 2' and 3', since each feasible plan π is an assortment plan π' with the same scale of production, $\mu(\pi') = \mu(\pi)$ (for obtaining such a plan it is sufficient to reduce certain h_{ij}, which correspond to those products which are produced in excess, $x^{\pi_j} > k_j \mu(\pi)$, and to increase other h_{ij}, corresponding to $a_{ij} = 0$).

Note 3

Let all costs of production be sums of expenses, which are proportional to the volumes of outputs of each product, and of the outlays on work performed by the production units which are independent of the type of products produced by them; then, for an optimal assortment plan, the costs of some one assortment set of products are minimal. For any feasible plan π' these costs comprise

$$\frac{1}{\mu(\pi')} \left(\sum_j p_j x^{\pi'}_j + \sum_i r_i \right) \geqq \sum_j p_j k_j + \frac{1}{\mu(\pi')} \sum_i r_i$$

$$\geqq \sum_j p_j k_j + \frac{1}{\mu(\pi)} \sum_i r_i, \qquad 3$$

where p_j are the costs for producing a unit output of product (j) $(j = 1,\ldots,n)$; r_i $(i = 1,\ldots,m)$ are the operating expenses of the production unit; $\mu(\pi)$ is the scale of production under an optimal plan; and the inequalities **3** become equations if, and only if, π' is an optimal assortment plan.

Note 4

Problem A may always be reduced to the case where $k_1 = k_2 = \ldots = k_n = 1$ (all products are required in equal quantities). In fact, if, for every product (j), we take a new unit of measurement equal to k_j old units, the problem becomes one in which

$$a'_{ij} = \frac{a_{ij}}{k_j} \quad (i = 1, \ldots, m; j = 1, \ldots, n), \qquad k'_j = 1 \quad (j = 1, \ldots, n).$$

The *case of output of multiple products*. Suppose now that for every production unit (i) ($i = 1, \ldots, m$) there are r_i methods of working; and when working according to method s, $a^s_{i1}, a^s_{i2}, \ldots, a^s_{in}$ units of the respective products are made by the production unit (i). In this case the following more general problem arises, which was also considered in Kantorovich (1939).

Problem B

Given the non-negative numbers

a^s_{ij} $(i = 1, \ldots, m; s = 1, \ldots, r_i; j = 1, \ldots, n)$,

$$k_j > 0 \ (j = 1, \ldots, n),$$

for which $\max\limits_{i, s} a^s_{ij} > 0$,

it is required to determine the set of numbers (the plan)

$\pi = \{h_{is}\}$ $(i = 1, \ldots, m; s = 1, \ldots, r_i)$

from the conditions

1. $h_{is} \geq 0$ $(i = 1, \ldots, m; s = 1, \ldots, r_i)$;

2. $\sum\limits_{s=1}^{r_i} h_{is} \leq 1$ $(i = 1, \ldots, m)$;

3. the quantity $\mu(\pi) = \min\limits_{1 \leq j \leq n} \dfrac{x^\pi_j}{k_j}$,

so that $x^\pi_j = \sum\limits_{l=1}^{m} \sum\limits_{s=1}^{r_i} a^s_{ij} h_{is}$ $(j = 1, \ldots, n)$,

takes the largest possible value.

As above, a plan π which satisfies conditions 1–3 is said to be *optimal*, and one satisfying conditions 1 and 2 *feasible*.

It is not difficult to see that for this problem too an optimal plan always exists. The following theorem characterizes the optimal plan.

Theorem 2

For a feasible plan π to be optimal it is necessary that multipliers $c_1, c_2, \ldots, c_n$ (valuations for all kinds of products) exist such that

(a) $c_j \geqq 0 \quad (j = 1, \ldots, n), \qquad \max_{1 \leqq j \leqq n} c_j > 0;$

(b) $\sum_{j=1}^{n} c_j a^s{}_{ij} = \max_{1 \leqq t \leqq ri} \sum_{j=1}^{n} c_j a^t{}_{ij} = d_i, \quad \text{if} \quad h_{is} \neq 0;$

(c) $c_j = 0, \quad \text{if} \quad x^\pi_j > k_j \mu(\pi);$

(d) $\sum_{s=1}^{ri} h_{is} = 1, \quad \text{if} \quad d_i \neq 0.$

We do not supply a proof of this theorem here since it will be obtained below as a consequence of the more general Theorem 3.

We note that Problem B may be interpreted in a way different from that above.

There are m kinds of composite raw materials, which are available in given proportions, $p_1:p_2:\ldots:p_m$. r_i technical methods exist for the treatment of raw material of type (i), $(i = 1, \ldots, m)$; when working according to method (s) $(s = 1, \ldots, r_i)$ the composite set $a^s{}_{i1}, a^s{}_{i2}, \ldots, a^s{}_{in}$ of units of products are obtained from the p_i units of this raw material. The required assorted set of products consists of $k_1, k_2, \ldots, k_n$ units of products of type $(1), (2), \ldots, (n)$. We are looking for a plan $\pi = \{h_{is}\}$ (the numbers h_{is} in this case show what part of the raw material of type (i) is treated by method (s)) for which a maximum number of assortment sets of products is obtained from one composite set of raw material, which consists of $p_1, p_2, \ldots, p_m$ units of raw material of type $(1), (2), \ldots, (m)$, or, what amounts to the same thing, the minimum quantity of composite sets of raw materials that must be used for one assorted set of products.

This kind of problem occurs regularly in various sectors of industry (treatment of metals, wood-processing, chemical, oil refining, non-ferrous metallurgy, etc.). As a characteristic example of such problems we may take the rational cutting out of industrial materials (sheet metal, profile rollings, pipes, wood and so on). See Kantorovich, 1939, Kantorovich—Zalgaller, 1951; Zalgaller, 1956.

In the special case when

$$r_i = n \quad (i = 1,..., m), \quad a^s{}_{ij} = \begin{cases} a_{ij} & \text{for} \quad s = j, \\ 0 & \text{for} \quad s \neq j \end{cases}$$

(for every technical method only one product is obtained from a raw material), Problem B evidently coincides with Problem A. In another special case, when $m = 1$ (there is only one type of raw material), we have the following problem.

Problem C

Given the non-negative numbers

$$\{a^s{}_j\} \quad (s = 1,..., r,; j = 1,..., n) \quad k_j > 0 \quad (j = 1,..., n),$$

for which $\max\limits_{1 \leq s \leq r} a^s{}_j > 0 \quad (j = 1,..., n)$,

it is required to determine the vector (plan) $\pi = (h_1,..., h_r)$ from the conditions

1. $h_s \geq 0 \quad (s = 1,..., r)$;

2. $\sum\limits_{s=1}^{r} h_s = 1$;

3. the quantity $\mu(\pi) = \min\limits_{1 \leq j \leq n} \dfrac{x^\pi{}_j}{k_j}$,

where $x^\pi{}_j = \sum\limits_{s=1}^{r} a^s{}_j h_s \quad (j = 1,..., n)$,

takes the largest possible value.

In analysing this problem we shall pause to consider some details. We shall take, for example, the auxiliary problem C', in which the surpluses (as compared with the required assortment), $h_{r+1},..., h_{r+n}$, of each product appear as unknowns, as well as the levels of application of the various methods, $h_1,..., h_r$: in an optimal plan it may turn out to be necessary to provide for the possibility of such surpluses.

Problem C'

With the data of Problem C, to find the vector $\bar{\pi} = (h_1,..., h_r, h_{r+1},..., h_{r+n})$ from the conditions

1. $h_s \geqq 0 \quad (s = 1, \ldots, r+n);$

2. $\sum_{s=1}^{r} h_s = 1;$

3. the equations $\dfrac{x\bar{\pi}_1}{k_1} = \dfrac{x\bar{\pi}_2}{k_2} = \ldots = \dfrac{x\bar{\pi}_n}{k_n},$ **4**

hold, where $\quad x\bar{\pi}_j = \displaystyle\sum_{s=1}^{r} a^s{}_j h_s - h_{r+j} \quad (j = 1, \ldots, n);$

4. the quantity $\mu(\bar{\pi})$, equal to the common value of the ratios 4, is a maximum.

The required vector is said to be *optimal*, a vector $\bar{\pi}$ which satisfies conditions 1 and 2 is called *feasible*, and one which satisfies conditions 1–3 is called an *assortment* vector.

It is not difficult to see that Problems C and C′ are equivalent. Indeed, a plan $\pi = (h_1, h_2, \ldots, h_r)$ is optimal in Problem C clearly if, and only if, the vector $\bar{\pi} = (h_1, \ldots, h_r, h_{r+1}, \ldots, h_{r+n})$, whose first r components coincide with the corresponding components of the vector π, and the remaining components are defined by the equations

$$h_{r+j} = x\pi_j - k_j\, \mu(\pi) \quad (j = 1, \ldots, n),$$

is optimal in Problem C′; then $\mu(\bar{\pi}) = \mu(\pi)$.

To make clear the geometrical meaning of Problem C′, we shall consider an n-dimensional space R_n, whose elements $x = (x_1, x_2, \ldots, x_n)$ we shall call points or vectors, without elaborating these concepts. To each permissible vector we relate the point

$$x(\bar{\pi}) = (x\bar{\pi}_1, x\bar{\pi}_2, \ldots, x\bar{\pi}_n) = \sum_{s=1}^{r} h_s\, a^s + \sum_{j=1}^{n} h_{r+j}\, e^j \in R_n, \qquad \textbf{5}$$

where $a^s = (a^s{}_1, a^s{}_2, \ldots, a^s{}_n)$ are points characterizing the available technical methods, and

$$e^j = (\overbrace{0, \ldots, 0}^{j-1}, -1, 0, \ldots, 0)$$

are unit vectors along the respective co-ordinate axes.

It may easily be seen that the points **5**, corresponding to all possible feasible vectors $\bar{\pi}$, fill the convex closed polyhedron M, which is spanned by the points a^s ($s = 1, \ldots, r$) and the negative orthant. Assortment vectors $\bar{\pi}$ (and only these), given by **4**, correspond to points $x(\bar{\pi})$ situated on the axis[1]

$$Y = \{y \mid y = \lambda z, \ -\infty < \lambda < +\infty\},$$

where $z = (k_1, k_2, ..., k_n)$ is a vector characterizing the necessary assortment of products. With this notation the quantity $\mu(\bar{\pi})$ (the scale of production) coincides with the corresponding value of λ.

Hence it is clear that optimal feasible vectors are those, and only those, which correspond to the extreme point of intersection of the y-axis with the polyhedron M, i.e. the point $y^* = \lambda^* z$, where

$$\lambda^* = \max_{\lambda z \in M} \lambda.$$

Figure 1 shows the polyhedron M, the y-axis and the point y^*, which correspond to the following numerical data:

$n = 2$, $r = 5$, $a^1 = (1; 6)$, $a^2 = (4; 5)$, $a^3 = (5; 4)$, $a^4 = (8; 3)$, $a^5 = (11; 0)$, $z = (3; 2)$.

The point y^* is evidently on the boundary of the polyhedron M. Therefore (according to a well-known theorem in n-dimensional geometry) there exists a supporting hyperplane, H, of the polyhedron M, which passes through the point y^* (see, for example,

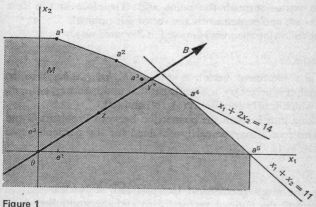

Figure 1

1. This notation indicates that Y consists of points y, represented by the form $y = \lambda z$, where λ is any real number.

A. B. Aleksandrov, *Convex Polyhedra*, 1950). Let the equation of this hyperplane be

$$(c, x) = c_1 x_1 + c_2 x_2 + \ldots + c_n x_n = d, \qquad 6$$

where[2] $\max_{x \in M} (c, x) = (c, y^*) = d$.

It is not difficult to check that the coefficients of the variable co-ordinates in equation **6** satisfy condition (a) (see p. 438).

Let $\bar{\pi} = (h_1, h_2, \ldots, h_{r+n})$ be an optimum vector; then

$$d = (c, y^*) = \left(c, \sum_{s=1}^{r} h_s a^s + \sum_{j=1}^{n} h_{r+j} e^j \right) = \sum_{s=1}^{r} h_s (c, a^s)$$

$$+ \sum_{j=1}^{n} h_{r+j} (c, e^j) \leqq \max_{1 \leqq s \leqq r} (c, a^s) \sum_{s=1}^{r} h_s - \sum_{j=1}^{n} h_{r+j} c_j \leqq d,$$

whence we have

(b′) $\sum c_j a^s{}_j = (c, a^s) = \max_{1 \leqq t \leqq r} (c, a^t) = \max_{1 \leqq t \leqq r} \sum c_j a^t{}_j = d,$

$$\text{if} \quad h_s > 0,$$

(c′) $c_j = 0$, if $h_{r+j} > 0$.

Conversely, if conditions (b′) and (c′) are satisfied for a given assortment vector $\bar{\pi}$ and for certain numbers $c_1, c_2, \ldots, c_n$, then equation **6** defines a supporting hyperplane of the polyhedron M, which passes through the point $x(\bar{\pi})$. Therefore in this case $x(\bar{\pi}) = y^*$, and consequently the vector $\bar{\pi}$ is optimal.

The following theorem is proved in the same way.

Theorem 2

For an assortment vector $\pi = (h_1, \ldots, h_r, h_{r+1}, \ldots, h_{r+n})$ to be optimal, it is necessary and sufficient that multipliers $c_1, c_2, \ldots, c_n$, exist which satisfy conditions (a), (b′) and (c′).

Taking into account the connection between Problems C and C′, Theorem 2 may be easily obtained for the particular case when $m = 1$.

Note 5

From the given geometrical interpretation it is clear that in Problem C the optimal vector (plan) and the multipliers (o.d.

2. If this is not so, then it may be brought into this form by changing the sign of all coefficients in equation **6**.

valuations) corresponding to it always exist but, generally speaking, are not uniquely determined. In fact, if the point y^* permits various representations of the form **5**, there exists more than one optimal plan; if, however, the point y^* lies on the face of a polyhedron M of dimensions less than $n-1$, then the vectors as well are not uniquely determined (it is possible to draw various supporting hyperplanes of M through the point y^*). However, multipliers which correspond to one of the optimal plans correspond to all others.

The basic problem of industrial planning[3]

We direct our attention now to the more general problem studied in Chapter II. (Not included here.)

We consider production where there are N ingredients (different types of industrial factors, raw materials, intermediate and final products). There are r permissible technical methods (methods of organizing production). Each of these methods is characterized by a vector

$$a^s = (a^s_1, a^s_2, ..., a^s_N) \quad (s = 1, ..., r),$$

whose components indicate the volume of output of the respective ingredients per unit level of the particular method (negative components denote use of inputs). A plan for the organization of production is determined by the choice of a vector $\pi = (h_1, h_2..., h_r)$ with non-negative components which indicate the level of application of the respective methods. For a plan $\pi = (h_1, h_2, ..., h_r)$, the various elements are produced in quantities

$$x^{\pi}_i = \sum_{s=1}^{r} a^s_i h_s \quad (i = 1, ..., N) \qquad 7$$

(elements, for which $x^{\tau}_i < 0$, are used in quantities $\mid x^{\pi}_i \mid$).

In addition to technical methods, it is necessary in compiling an industrial plan to take into account also the resources available and the assortment of products required. These additional conditions may be stated in various ways. Here we consider one of the possible ways of stating them; however, the basic result that in an optimal plan there exists a system of o.d. valuations for all elements holds for any natural statement of these conditions (see Note 7, p. 446).

3. See Kantorovich (1957).

For some elements (certain final products) it may be necessary to achieve maximum output with the required assortment, while for others, there are limits of the kind, $x^{\pi}_i \geqq b_i$, where b_i are given real numbers. (The positive b'_i correspond to final products required in definite quantities; for the intermediate products, which do not have to be completely exhausted in the plan, the respective b'_i are equal to zero; negative b'_i correspond to factors of production and various types of raw materials of which not more may be used than the resources available, i.e. $|b_i|$.) In this case we pass on to the following problem.

Problem D

Given the real numbers

$a^s_i \quad (i = 1,..., N; s = 1,..., r), \quad b_i(i = 1,..., m),$
$k_j > 0 \quad (j = 1,..., n; n = N - m)$

it is required to determine the vector (plan) $\pi = (h_1, h_2,..., h_r)$ from the conditions

1. $h_s \geqq 0 \quad (s = 1,..., r)$;

2. $x^{\pi}_i \geqq b_i \quad (i = 1,..., m)$;

3. the quantity $\quad \mu(\pi) = \min_{1 \leqq j \leqq n} \dfrac{x^{\pi}_{m+j}}{k_j}$

to attain its maximum value (here and in the above conditions, the quantities x^{π}_i are defined by 7).

A plan π, which satisfies conditions 1 and 2 is called *feasible*, and one which satisfies conditions 1–3 *optimal*.

This problem may be looked at as a mathematical model of current (short-term) planning of which the previous problems are clearly special cases. For example, in Problem B there are m factors of production, n final products and

$$r = \sum_{i=1}^{m} r_i$$

technical methods, by each of which one unit of the respective factor (use of a plant, factory or machine) is used up and a certain set of products is produced; the resources of each factor are here equal to 1, and therefore $b_i = -1 \quad (i = 1,..., m)$. The problems considered below also lead to Problem D. Hence the latter is called the basic problem of production planning.

The following theorems give the properties of an optimal plan and conditions for its existence.

Theorem 3

For a feasible plan $\pi = (h_1, h_2, \ldots, h_r)$ to be optimal it is necessary that multipliers $c_1, c_2, \ldots, c_N$ (o.d. valuations for all elements) exist such that

(a) $c_i \geq 0$ $(i = 1, \ldots, N)$, $\max\limits_{1 \leq j \leq n} c_{m+j} > 0$

(these valuations are non-negative, at least one of the products included in the assortment set having a positive valuation);

(b) $\sum\limits_{i=1}^{N} c_i \, a^s{}_i \leq 0$ $(s = 1, \ldots, r)$

(for every technical method the valuation of the product cannot exceed the total valuation of the ingredients used up);

(c) $\sum\limits_{i=1}^{N} c_i \, a^s{}_i = 0$, if $h_s > 0$

(for the methods used, the valuation of the products is equal to the valuation of the elements used up, the principle of profitability is observed);

(d) $c_i = 0$, if $x^{\pi}{}_i > b_i$ $(1 \leq i \leq m)$

or $x^{\pi}{}_i > k_{i-m} \, \mu(\pi)$ $(m+1 \leq i \leq N)$

(for factors of production which do not limit production and for products produced in excess, the respective valuations are equal to zero).

Theorem 4

For the existence of an optimal plan it is necessary and sufficient that the following conditions be fulfilled.

(α) a feasible plan π exists;

(β) no plan π (satisfying condition 1) exists for which

$x^{\pi}{}_i \geq 0$ $(i = 1, \ldots, m)$; $x^{\pi}{}_{m+j} > 0$ $(j = 1, \ldots, n)$.

Note 6

Condition (β), indicating that no plan exists in which certain elements are produced (in positive quantities) without any kind of outlay, is clearly always satisfied in practical problems.

Condition (a), generally speaking, may not be satisfied. Violation of this condition indicates that, with the resources available at a given production base, even the first m elements cannot be produced in the necessary quantities. However, if all the numbers $b_i \leqq 0$, condition (a) is necessarily satisfied.

Note 7

Theorem 3 refers to Problem D, in which the available resources and required assortment of products were taken into account in a definite fashion. However, for any reasonable definition of optimality, plan π is clearly not optimal, if there exists a plan π' according to which all elements are produced in greater quantities (or where the available resources are used in smaller quantities), i.e.

$$x^{\pi}_i < x'^{\pi}_i \quad (i = 1, \ldots, N).$$

This property is indeed sufficient to ensure that an optimal plan is associated with a certain system of non-negative valuations, which satisfy conditions (b) and (c).

Note 8

In the general case, valuations of all the ingredients are necessary in order to characterize an optimal plan in Problem D. However, if each technical method involves only one of the first m elements (or one of the last n elements), then an optimal plan may be specified in terms of the valuations of only the last n elements (first m elements). We have met such a situation in Problems A, B and C.

Note 9

Practical interest is provided by the case when the application of certain technical methods in Problem D is limited, when the only permissible plans are plans, $\pi = (h_1, h_2, \ldots, h_r)$, in which

$$h_s \leqq q_s \quad (s = 1, \ldots, r_1; \; r_1 \leqq r),$$

where the q_s are given positive numbers. This case may be reduced formally to the basic one quite easily (it is sufficient to introduce the limitations on technical methods as additional resources). However, the problem may be treated also without such a reduction. In doing this though, it is true that in Theorem 3, which specifies an optimal plan, the inequality

$$\sum_{i=1}^{N} c_i a^s_i \leqq 0$$

must be assumed for those of the limited methods which are being fully used ($h_s = q_s$).

Note 10

In foreign literature, the special case of Problem D, in which $n = 1$, (see Koopmans, 1951; Kuhn Tucker, 1956) is usually considered as the fundamental problem of linear planning. The following problem will serve to illustrate this case.

Problem E

Let there be m kinds of raw material in amounts of $b_1, b_2, ..., b_m$ units. From this raw material, r different products can be produced. The price of one unit of product (s), ($s = 1, ..., r$), is a_s, and $a^s_1, a^s_2, ..., a^s_m$ units of the respective kind of raw material are spent on it. It is required to select a quantity of products of various kinds in such a way that, as a set, they may be manufactured from the available raw material and so that their total value is a maximum. In other words, a vector (or plan) $\pi = (h_1, h_2, ..., h_r)$ is to be found from the conditions:

1. $h_s \geqq 0 \quad (s = 1, ..., r)$;

2. $\sum_{s=1}^{r} a^s_i h_s \leqq b_i \quad (i = 1, ..., m)$,

3. the quantity $\mu(\pi) = \sum_{s=1}^{r} a_s h_s$ to be maximized.

In order to make clear the geometrical meaning of Problem D, and to prove the theorems given above, we shall consider the points in N-dimensional space R_N

$$a^s = (a^s_1, a^s_2, ..., a_N^s) \quad (s \neq 1, ..., r);$$

$$e = (\underbrace{0, ..., 0}_{i-1}, -1, 0, ..., 0) \quad (i = 1, ..., N):$$

$$y^0 = (b_1, ..., b_m, 0, ..., 0);$$

$$z = (0, ..., 0, k_1, ..., k_n).$$

Let[4]

$$K = \left(x \,|\, x = \sum_{s=1}^{r} h_s \, a^s + \sum_{i=1}^{N} h_{r+i} \, e^i; \ h_s \geqq 0, \ s = 1,...,r+N \right)$$

be a convex polyhedral cone, with vertex at the origin of co-ordinates, which is spanned by the points a_s ($s = 1,...,r$) and e_i ($i = 1,..., N$), and let

$$Y = \{y \,|\, y = y^0 + \lambda z; \ -\infty < \lambda < +\infty\}$$

be a line through the points y^0, $y^0 + z$, directed towards the side of increasing λ.

For every feasible plan $\pi = (h_1, h_2,..., h_r)$ the point

$$y^0 + \mu(\pi)z = \sum_{s=1}^{r} h_s \, a^s + \sum_{i=1}^{N} h_{r+i} \, e^i, \qquad\qquad \textbf{8}$$

where

$$h_{r+i} = x^{\pi_i} - b_i \quad (i = 1,...,m), \qquad\qquad \textbf{9}$$
$$h_{r+m+j} = x^{\pi_{m+j}} - k_j \, \mu(\pi) \quad (j = 1,...,n)$$

clearly belongs to the cone K. Conversely, if the point $y^0 + \lambda z \, \epsilon \, K$, there exists a feasible plan π for which the quantity $\mu(\pi) \geqq \lambda$.

Hence it is clear that Problem D amounts essentially to the study of the intersection of the axis y with the cone K. If this intersection is empty, or contains the point $y^0 + \lambda z$, no matter how large λ is, then in this problem no optimal plan exists.

If, however, $Y \cap K \neq \wedge$ ($\wedge$ denotes the empty set) and if

$$\lambda^* = \sup_{y^0 + \lambda z \, \epsilon \, K} \lambda < +\infty,$$

then optimal plans exist; these optimal plans comprise only those feasible plans π, for which the point **8** coincides with the extreme point of intersection of the line y and the cone K, i.e. with the point $y^* = y^0 + \lambda^* z$.

Through the point y^* it is possible to draw a supporting hyper-plane H to the cone K which does not contain points of the line y other than y^*. Let the equation of this hyperplane be

$$(c, x) = c_1 x_1 + c_2 x_2 + ... + c_N x_N = 0, \qquad\qquad \textbf{10}$$

where $\max_{x \,\epsilon\, K} (c, x) = (c, y^*) = 0$.

4. This expression indicates that K is a set of points x, belonging to the space R_N, which can be represented in the given form, where $h_s \geqq 0$ are arbitrary non-negative numbers.

Then, as may easily be shown, the numbers $c_1, c_2, \ldots, c_N$ (co-efficients of the variables in equation **10**, satisfy conditions (a) and (b) of Theorem 3, and conditions (c) and (d) of this theorem are also satisfied for every optimal plan (i.e. for any plan such that $y^0 + \mu(\pi)z = y^*$).

On the other hand, if for a given feasible plan π there are multipliers $c_1, c_2, \ldots, c_N$, which satisfy conditions (a)–(d), then the hyperplane H, determined by **10**, is a supporting hyperplane of the cone K and intersects the line y at the point $y^0 + \mu(\pi)z$. Hence it follows that $y^0 + \mu(\pi)z = y^*$, and, consequently, that the plan π is optimal.

Thus Theorem 3 has been proved, and from it follow, in particular, Theorems 1 and 2, which were given above without complete proof.

As we have seen, for the existence of an optimal plan, it is necessary and sufficient that the conditions

$$Y \cap K \neq V,$$

$$\lambda^* = \sup_{y^0 + \lambda z \,\epsilon\, K} \lambda < +\infty.$$

are fulfilled. The latter, as may be easily checked, is equivalent to the conditions of Theorem 4.

By means of the above geometrical interpretation it is also easy to prove Note 7 which is of fundamental importance.

Relation to Leontief's input-output matrices

We shall pause to consider a particular problem in production planning.

Let there be n products and one factor of production (labour). The technical methods are such that only one product is produced by each of them, while other products and the factor of production are fully used. The supply of the factor of production is limited. It is assumed that there exists a plan by which all products are produced in positive quantities (only the factor of production is consumed). In this case:

1. The optimal plan problem (plan D) is soluble for any set of products (i.e. for any numbers $k_j \ldots 0$, $j = 1, \ldots, n$).

2. The collection of technical methods which are used in the optimal plan, and the values of the multipliers (o.d. valuations)

are independent of the resources of the factor of production available and of the required set of products.

In the case here considered the technical methods are characterized by the vectors

$$a^{js} = (a_0^{js}, a^{js}_1, \ldots, a_n^{js}) \quad (j = 1, \ldots, n; \ s = 1, \ldots, r_j),$$

where $a_0^{js} < 0$, $a_j^{js} > 0$, $a_l^{js} \leqq 0$, if $l \neq j$.

The plan is determined in terms of a matrix

$$\pi = \|h_{js}\| \quad (j = 1, \ldots, n; \ s = 1, \ldots, r_j)$$

whose elements indicate the level of application of the various methods. An optimal plan is sought from the conditions

1. $h_{js} \geqq 0 \quad (j = 1, \ldots, n; \ s = 1, \ldots, r_j)$;

2. $x^\pi_0 = \sum\limits_{j,\,s} a^{js}_0 h_{j,} \geqq b_0$

($-b_0$ denotes the available supply of the factor of production);

3. the quantity $\mu(\pi) = \min\limits_{1 \leqq l \leqq n} \dfrac{x^\pi_l}{k_l}$, where $x^\pi_l = \sum\limits_{j,\,s} a^{js}_l h_{js}$

($l = 1, \ldots, n$), is a maximum (the numbers k_l characterize the required assortment of products).

For every product (v) $(v = 1, \ldots, n)$ we consider a plan $\pi^v = \|h^o_{js}\|$ (satisfying condition 1), for which the input of the factor of production does not exceed one unit $(x^{\pi^v}_0 \geqq -1)$, and for which the products are produced in non-negative amounts $(x^{\pi^v}_l \geqslant 0, \ l = 1, \ldots, n)$, the product (v) being produced in maximum quantity $(x^{\pi^v}_v = \max)$. We assert, that for plan π^v

$$x^{\pi^v}_0 = -1, \quad x^{\pi^v}_l = 0, \quad \text{if} \quad l \neq v.$$

In fact, if $x^{\pi^v}_0 > -1$, the volume of production of product (v) may be increased by including partially a plan for which all products are produced in positive quantities; if, however, for a certain $l_0 \neq v$, $x^{\pi^v}_{l_0} > 0$, then it is also possible to include the above plan at the cost of reducing one of the numbers $h^v_{l_0 s}$.

It is not difficult to verify that, whatever the numbers $k_j > 0$ $(j = 1, \ldots, n)$, the quantities

$$c_0, \quad c_1 = \frac{c_0}{x^{\pi^1}_1}, \quad c_2 = \frac{c_0}{x^{\pi^2}_2}, \quad \ldots, \quad c_n = \frac{c_0}{x^{\pi^n}_n},$$

where c_0 is an arbitrary positive number, represent a system of o.d. valuations, and the plan $\pi = \|h_{js}\|$, in which

$$h_{js} = \frac{-b_0 \sum\limits_{v=1}^{n} c_v k_v h^v_{js}}{\sum\limits_{v=1}^{n} c_v k_v} \quad (j = 1, \ldots, n; s = 1, \ldots, r_j),$$

is optimal. From this proposition, 1 and 2 follow.

We note the important special case when, for every product (j) $(j = 1, \ldots, n)$, there is only one process of production, which is characterized by the vector

$$a^j = (a^j{}_0, a^j{}_1, \ldots, a^j{}_n); \quad a^j{}_0 < 0, \quad a^j{}_j > 0, \quad a^j{}_l \leqq 0, \quad \text{if} \quad l \neq j.$$

Here an optimal plan clearly uses all methods. Therefore the appropriate system of valuations may be found from the simultaneous equations [5]

$$\sum_{l=0}^{n} a^j{}_l c_l = 0 \quad (j = 1, \ldots, n);$$

more exactly; from these simultaneous equations the valuations for all products may be expressed in terms of c_0 (the valuation of one unit of labour).

This last case corresponds to Leontief's open production model, [6] which is frequently used in economic analysis. It has to be pointed out, however, that this model is only a very rough approximation to the real conditions of production which determine the current production plan. In fact:

1. In real problems it is necessary to take into account also many factors other than labour which are available in limited quantities, in particular useful natural sources and especially certain production capacities. Moreover, since there are usually several categories of labour, this too must not be treated as a single factor.

2. Output of multiple products not included in the above scheme constantly occurs.

3. In the actual conditions of modern production there are a great many methods for manufacturing a particular product, and

5. Clearly these equations can be solved immediately.

6. For Leontief's model, see, for example, Koopmans (1951), and also the last article in the collection edited by Kuhn and Tucker (1956).

the application of the various methods used brings out in particular the limitations mentioned in 1.

Leontief's model appears useful for compiling matrices of intersector relations in which the coefficients a_i^j are the costs of a product of the given type in terms of the inputs of products of other sectors. Although constructing such matrices of relations and obtaining total expenditures from them is of special interest this approach may not be considered sufficiently satisfactory for calculating valuations of products. Indeed, instead of actual methods of production, broad averages are used here and the results obtained depend essentially on the methods chosen for aggregation. Therefore there is no justification for thinking that the valuations of products obtained in this way will give realizable equivalent relations, and thus these valuations may not be directly used in the analysis of economic planning. Their basic shortcoming is that they do not take into account the limitations mentioned in 1 and the limitations on the indirect expenditures associated with them.

The transport problem

In the simplest case this problem consists of the following.

Problem F[7]

Let there be m points connected by a railway system consisting of r sections. Along the section (s) $(s = 1,..., r)$ of the network goods may be conveyed from point i_s to point j_s; the costs for conveying one unit of the goods (for example, one wagon) are a_s (in particular, the quantity a_s may be taken as equal to the distance between the points i_s and j_s). At each point (i) $(i = 1,..., m)$ there is a given demand b_i for a single kind of product (for points of demand $b_i > 0$, for points of production $b_i < 0$, for other points $b_i = 0$), and

$$\sum_{i=1}^{m} b_i = 0$$

7. Special methods of solving Problem F have been considered in Tolstoi (1939); a mathematical analysis and general methods for solving this problem and also certain more general problems connected with transport planning (in particular Problem G which will be considered below) have been given in Kantorovich (1942); Kantorovich–Gavurin (1949), and later in Koopmans (1951).

(the total amounts of production and demand are equal). The transport plan is determined by the choice of a vector $\pi = (h_1, h_2, \ldots, h_r)$, whose components indicate the volume of transport in each section of the system. The problem is to find an optimal plan, which satisfies the conditions

1. $h_s \geq 0 \quad (s = 1, \ldots, r)$;

2. $\displaystyle\sum_{j_s=i} h_s - \sum_{i_s=i} h_s = b_i \quad (i = 1, \ldots, m)$

(each point obtains the required net quantity of the product):

3. the quantity

$$z = \sum_{s=1}^{r} a_s h_s$$

is to be a minimum (the total cost of transport is to be minimized; for example, wagon-kilometres are to be a minimum).

It is not difficult to see that the given problem is a particular case of the basic problem of production planning. In fact, one may suppose that in this case there are $(m+1)$ elements; the first m of these are the goods considered, situated at the various points, and the last one corresponds to the transport costs. The feasible technical methods are characterized by the vectors

$$a^s = (a^s{}_1, a^s{}_2, \ldots, a^s{}_{m+1}) \quad (s = 1, \ldots, r),$$

where $a^s{}_{m+1} = -a_s$, $a^s{}_i = 1$ for $i = j_s$, $a^s{}_i = -1$ for $i = i_s$, and $a^s{}_i = 0$ for the other i.

On the basis of Theorem 4 one may easily conclude that an optimal plan in this problem always exists. The plan is characterized by Theorem 3, which here reduces to the following.

Theorem 5

For a plan $\pi = (h_1, h_2, \ldots, h_r)$ (satisfying conditions 1 and 2) to be optimal it is necessary and sufficient that there exist numbers $c_1, c_2, \ldots, c_m$, such that

(a) $c_{j_s} - c_{i_s} \leq a_s \quad (s = 1, \ldots, r)$;

(b) $c_{j_s} - c_{i_s} = a_s$, if $h_s \neq 0$.

The numbers c_t appearing in Theorem 5 are called potentials of the various points. The difference of potential shows by how much more expensive a unit of the given product is at one point than at another.

When planning transport in practice it is sometimes necessary to take into further account the limited carrying capacity of the various sections of line. This leads to a more general problem.

Problem G

According to the conditions of Problem F, feasible plans are only those plans, $\pi = (h_1,\ldots, h_r)$, for which the condition

$2'.\ h_s \leq q_s \quad (s = 1,\ldots,r)$

is observed (the numbers q_s characterize the carrying capacity of the various lines).

In the present case, the following proposition, which also follows from Theorem 2, characterizes the optimal plan.

Theorem 6

For a plan $\pi = (h_1, h_2,\ldots, h_r)$ (satisfying conditions 1, 2 and $2'$) to be optimal it is necessary and sufficient that numbers $c_1, c_2,\ldots, c_m, d_1, d_2,\ldots, d_r$, exist such that

(a) $c_{js} - c_{is} \leq a_s + d_s \quad (s = 1,\ldots,r)$;

(b) $c_{js} - c_{is} = a_s + d_s$, if $h_s > 0$;

(c) $d_s \geq 0$, while $d_s = 0$, if $h_s < q_s$.

Note 12

The numbers d_s are the rents (hire valuations) for the various sections of line, calculated per unit of load (for example, one wagon).

Dynamic problem

By means of the basic production planning problem considered above the more general problem may be analysed, i.e. that of drawing up a production plan for a certain period of time divided into a series of intervals, $t = 1, 2,\ldots, T$ (problem of long-term planning).

One and the same product (or factor), produced (or used) in various periods of time, is treated here as a different element. Therefore the available technical methods are characterized now by means of the matrices

$$a^s = \|a^s_{it}\| \quad (i = 1,\ldots, N; \ t = 1,\ldots, T; \ s = 1,\ldots, r),$$

whose elements show the amounts of the various products and factors produced in different intervals of time (negative elements denote inputs). Included among the methods may be also those which refer to one period of time (methods which appeared in the compilation of the current plan). Technical progress in these methods may be taken into account by means of converting the inputs for their application at later periods and by stating the period from which the particular improved method is used, and so on. Clearly, this kind of initial data is of a prognostic nature and is inevitably quite approximate. Together with other factors, it is convenient to introduce, as special elements, some particular productive capacities. Among the latter are reproducible factors, and the possibility of their production is envisaged.

The concept of an optimal plan may be introduced in various ways; for example, with given resources for the first period (certain resources, say the natural ones, may be given for all periods) and with a given demand for final products (for each period of time) it is required to make up a plan in which balances are maintained, and the accumulation of final output of a specified composition (or of definite productive capacity) up to the end of the planning period is a maximum. However, for any natural definition of being optimal, a plan $\pi = (h_1, h_2,\ldots, h_r)$ is not optimal, if there exists a plan $\pi' = (h'_1, h'_2,\ldots, h'_r)$ in which all the elements are produced in greater quantities,

$$x^\pi_{it} = \sum_{s=1}^{r} a^s_{it} h_s < \sum_{s=1}^{r} a^s_{it} h'_s = x^{\pi'}_{it}$$

$$(i = 1,\ldots, N; \ t = 1,\ldots, T).$$

This property turns out to be sufficient for the optimal plan π to be associated with a system of multipliers $\{c_{it}\}$ $(i = 1,\ldots, N; \ t = 1,\ldots, T)$ (of valuations for all products and factors over the whole period) such that

(a) $c_{it} \geqq 0$ $(i = 1,...,N; t = 1,...,T)$, and not all $c_{it} = 0$;

(b) $\sum_{i,t} c_{it} a^s_{it} \leqq 0$ $(s = 1,...,r)$;

(c) $\sum_{i,t} c_{it} a^s_{it} = 0$, if $h_. > 0$.

The multipliers (valuations) may naturally be normalized. For instance if

$$c_{it} = \lambda_t c'_{it} \quad (i = 1,...,N; t = 1,...,T),$$

the valuations c'_{it} may be chosen to satisfy the conditions

$$c'_{i_1 t} + c'_{i_2 t} + ... + c'_{i_n t} = 1 \quad (t = 1,...,T),$$

or the valuations of a certain stated set of products in each interval of time are equal to 1. In carrying this out, the left-hand sides of the inequalities and equations in conditions (b) and (c) are replaced by the following

$$\sum_{t=1}^{T} \lambda_t \sum_{i=1}^{N} c'_{it} a^s_{it} \quad (s = 1,...,r),$$

i.e. in evaluating a technical method for production and expenditure belonging to different intervals of time, the valuations must be converted to a single interval by means of multipliers λ_t.

The ratio λ_t/λ_τ is (for a given unit) a conversion coefficient for inputs in period t to period τ. In particular the quantity

$$\left(\frac{\lambda_t}{\lambda_{t+1}} - 1 \right) = \frac{\lambda_t - \lambda_{t+1}}{\lambda_{t+1}}$$

gives the normal efficiency of capital investment in the transition from period t to the following one.

The quantities c_{it} characterize the dynamics of valuations; they are valuations of inputs and outputs which have been converted to a single instant of time. The quantities c'_{it} characterize the relative dynamics of valuations. Correspondingly, there are two methods for calculating the efficiency of certain capital investment (of a new method of production, calculated for a long period): namely, if inputs and outputs during the years of the capital investment are characterized by the matrix $\|\bar{a}_{it}\|$, then the question of the usefulness of its application is solved by determining whether the sum

$$\sum_{i,t} c_{it}\, \bar{a}_{it} = \sum_{t} \lambda_t \sum_{i} c'_{it}\, \bar{a}_{it}$$

is positive or not. The first expression is calculated directly according to the dynamics of valuations, and the second is calculated according to the relative dynamics followed by a conversion of inputs in each period to one particular period.

The calculation is simplified if the relative valuations do not change with time. Then it is sufficient to know the valuations at the initial time c'_{il} and the conversion coefficients λ_t; to evaluate a process it is sufficient to apply the second of the expressions given above with c'_{il} replaced by c'_{it}.

Properties of valuations. Variation of a plan

In the analysis of the basic production planning problem its geometrical meaning was elucidated. In particular, it was shown that o.d. valuations are given by the coefficients of the variables in the equation of the hyperplane H, which is a supporting hyperplane of the cone K, and which passes through the boundary point y^* of the intersection of the line y with this cone. Hence, first of all it is clear that o.d. valuations are completely realistic, that is, they are related to the situation (available technical methods, volumes of resources, assortment task) and change when the situation changes. Indeed, during such changes, the cone of plans K and the assortment axis y change, and with them also the supporting hyperplane H.

However, if we exclude special cases, when the point y^* which corresponds to the optimal plan lies on the boundary of the cone K of dimensions less than $N-1$, then, for small changes in the assortment task and in the resources, the extreme point y^* remains on the same boundary; therefore o.d. valuations are not changed. For other small changes (in the methods) the cone K changes somewhat; this leads to small changes in the o.d. valuations.

Thus o.d. valuations possess a certain stability with respect to changes in the situation.

By changing from the point $y^* = (x^*_1, x^*_2, \ldots, x^*_N)$ to the neighbouring point $\bar{y}^* = (x^*_1 + \Delta x_1,\ x^*_2 + \Delta x_2, \ldots,\ x^*_N + \Delta x_N)$ on the same supporting hyperplane, we arrive at an optimal plan corresponding to different resources and to a different assortment task. During this change, as has been noted, o.d. valuations $c_1, c_2, \ldots, c_N$, do not alter: therefore

$$\sum_{i=1}^{N} c_i x^*_i = \sum_{i=1}^{N} c_i(x^*_i + \Delta x_i) = 0,$$

hence $\sum_{i=1}^{N} c_i \Delta x_i = 0.$ 11

The last relation is called, naturally enough, the equation of variation of a plan; it specifies the condition for an equivalent substitution of some kinds of product and factors of production by others which must be satisfied in moving from a given optimum plan to a slightly altered optimal plan and which, generally speaking, is sufficient for the realization of the latter. In particular one unit of ingredient (i_1) may be replaced by c_{i1}/c_{i2} units of ingredient (i_2). When using other valuations (different from o.d. valuations), such a substitution is generally speaking impossible. Hence it is clear that relations, defined by o.d. valuations, between products and factors of different kinds are completely realistic.

The above properties of o.d. valuations, and also the equation of variation, lead to many applications of these valuations in various problems of adjustments in plans and of obtaining separate partial solutions.

Note 14

We have pointed out that the solution to the problem of efficiency of some new method, characterized by the vector $\bar{a} = (\bar{a}_1, \bar{a}_2, \ldots, \bar{a}_N)$, is determined according to whether the sum

$$\sum_{i=1}^{N} c_i \bar{a}_i$$

is positive or not. However, this refers only to the case when the method may be applied at any level. Methods of production commonly occur, which may be used only at a given level (indivisible methods or investments). In evaluating such a method, the necessary condition for its application

$$\sum_{i} c_i \bar{a}_i \geqq 0$$

is retained; this condition, however, may not be sufficient, since inclusion of this method in the plan may require variations which are greater than the feasible ones. Hence, in order to solve this problem it may be necessary to reconsider the plan with the inclusion of the new method, and to compare the products and inputs of the plan thus obtained with the original plan.

Rents and hire valuation

The analysis of the basic problem of industrial planning carried out above has shown that in the application of methods for optimal planning to concrete problems it turns out to be convenient to take into account other forms of output besides those usually considered in economic analysis. Among inputs may be included, for example, the use of more fertile ground, the use of production floor-space, the rent for a definite time of scarce equipment (apart from its wear), the rent of circulating resources, and so on. If these factors are available in limited amounts and are fully used, they receive positive valuations. Hence their omission from economic calculations often leads to incorrect solutions. Many examples of this kind have been introduced in the main text of the book.

Thus, in order to obtain correct solutions in an economic calculation, it is necessary to take into account rents (for the use of more favourable natural conditions) and hire valuations (for the rent of scarce equipment). Numerical values for these quantities are determined together with the other o.d. valuations.

The significance of mathematical models and their application in economic analysis

With the passage of time mathematical methods have been gaining more significance and a wider use. Whereas previously their basic field of application was in natural science and technology, nowadays they are finding appreciable application in other fields of science and human activity. Characteristic examples are the application of mathematical methods in philology (in connection with machine translation) and in military matters (operational research).

A highly important and natural field for the use of mathematical methods is provided by economics (analysis of economic planning), which by its very nature has a decidedly quantitative character.

Mathematical symbolism and methods occupy an important place in the economic researches of Marx, and in the economic and statistical works of Lenin which deal with the economic analysis of capitalism. These methods must receive special emphasis in the economic problems of a socialist society. The task of Marxist economic science is to review the social nature of capitalist society and to study its general laws and its tendencies of development and of decline. In socialist society economic science must serve as a tool for finding concrete solutions to problems of national economic development. Economic laws in a socialist society have an objective character but they are realized under the conditions of a planned economy to a large extent by means of deliberate solution. Therefore, the successful application of the laws in the interest of society depends on how completely and deeply we master them.[8] Hence it is clear that Marxist analysis of economic problems in socialist society and of the mechanism of the operation of its laws must be as accurate, detailed and specific as possible. One naturally expects that in this kind of analysis mathematics will be especially useful. In view of the complication and interdependence of economic problems in modern production one cannot expect that it will be possible to succeed in the quantitative analysis of these problems with the most simple mathematical means. Here undoubtedly the latest achievements of modern mathematics will be required.

Nevertheless, until recent times mathematical analysis was not only rarely used in economic problems, but it was even necessary to contend with definite objections to its use. Such objections cannot be accepted as justifiable.

The lack of appreciation of the possibility of applying quantitative mathematical methods in the analysis of economic

8. As an illustration of the various ways in which objective laws may be realized, we recall two classical problems of the calculus of variation: the problem of the catenary and the brachystochrone (the curve of steepest descent). A heavy thread sags in a catenary independently of whether the person holding its ends knows the solution to the relevant problem or not. How close a curve of descent is to a brachystochrone depends on the extent to which the constructor of the curve has mastered the laws of the calculus of variations.

phenomena because of their specific character is in our view a survival of notions about the unobjective character of the economic laws of socialism.

Equally unjustified is the prejudice against mathematical methods because of their partial use by bourgeois economic schools. Clearly, the precedents of the incorrect use of mathematics for purposes different from ours cannot prevent Soviet scientists from using mathematical methods in economic problems in a way which is correct and of advantage in the building of communism.

Mathematical analysis is not applicable directly to problems of reality. Usually, by means of abstractions, a mathematical model of the phenomenon considered is constructed, and this model may be treated mathematically. Such a model naturally does not include all its aspects but only some of the more important ones chosen for particular consideration. Hence the solutions and conclusions obtained as a result of the analysis are applicable to the real problem only to a certain degree of approximation. Often the succeeding qualitative analysis assists one in knowing in which direction the model should be made more accurate so that it may better reflect the real problem.

At the same time, if a model exists its mathematical analysis may be used not only for obtaining certain quantitative data, but also to reveal new conformities with laws, to analyse causal relationships and dependencies, and to predict new phenomena (examples of this kind in natural science are provided by the discovery of Neptune, and the theoretical prediction of certain phenomena occurring in supersonic speeds and in atomic physics).

Of prime significance for the effectiveness and applicability of a particular model is the correctness of the initial premises used in its construction; it is also necessary that the important factors are in fact included and that the lesser ones are discarded. Thus, certain models of capitalist economies introduced by bourgeois economists turn out to be necessarily fallacious, since in their construction the authors have ignored the existence of unemployment and similar phenomena which are always inherent in their social structure. Naturally, the conclusions drawn from these premises do not merit the least credence.

L. V. Kantorovich 463

Consequently, in applying mathematical analysis and in constructing mathematical models for the study of economic problems in a socialist society, it is necessary that the initial premises should be in agreement with the basic principles of the Marxist method of economic analysis, namely dialectical thought, the objective character of research, social analysis of the relations of production, pre-eminence of production and recognition of labour as the sole source of value.

The fundamental criteria for estimating the significance and correctness of such research, as for the truth of any knowledge in general, must be the Leninist criterion of practice. In other words, the greatest importance for its evaluation must lie in the agreement of the results obtained with reality and in their ability to explain and influence the phenomena of our economic reality, so that they may help in the development of more effective measures and solutions.

Socialist society as a whole, and in its various departments, is by its nature capable of securing a more complete and rational use of productive resources for the better satisfaction of the needs of society. Therefore, for each sector of socialist production and for socialist society as a whole, an optimal plan has a concrete reality, and the consistency of such a plan with economic laws corresponds to the real economic conformities with the laws of socialist society (similar to the way in which mechanical motion is governed by the extremal variational principles of mechanics). From this it is clear that in the quantitative mathematical analysis of the planned economy in a socialist society the basic approach must be research into extremal mathematical problems.[9]

In the conditions of socialist society, a critical problem is that of raising the level of production. In the study of this problem and of the economics of socialist society it is known to be correct to separate the problem of production from the problem of distri-

9. In capitalist society the existence of unemployment, crises and systematic under-utilization of production capacities shows that the use of the maximum principle for studying its economics as a whole is inadmissible. Hence the attempts on the part of the economists-apologists for capitalism (for example, Pareto) to study the economic laws of capitalism, starting from the mathematical conditions for a maximum, are faulty in their method.

bution. Independent consideration of the problem of the optimum organization of production is permissible since in socialist economy without crises and with public socialist ownership of the means of production in its two forms goods cannot be produced according to the requirements of society and then remain unused. In view of this we must accept the models of production planning (the fundamental problem and the dynamic model), which we have considered, as fully justified, and the same applies to the corresponding problems of current and long-term planning in which the object is to obtain the maximum level of production of the necessary composition from given resources or equivalently, to obtain the fast increase of output.[10] The results of analysing these schemes confirm that the requirement for a given plan of production to be optimal enables one to obtain rather substantive conclusions together with its important quantitative characteristics.[11]

One must not be surprised at the circumstance that, besides the qualitative difference in principle in the laws of socialist and capitalistic society and in the meaning of the fundamental economic categories, manifest formal analogies are to be found in various quantitative indicators and relations – for example, in normal efficiency and normal profit, normal valuations and the price of production. Lenin drew attention to this possibility when he noted that 'the unity of nature is displayed in the "strikingly analogous" differential equations relating to various fields of phenomena'. (See Lenin, *Collected Works*, vol. 14, p. 276.)

As we have noticed, the models under study must find application both in problems of national economic planning and in more special problems of the various units of socialist production and of particular planning problems.

10. In capitalism the use of such models for the general analysis of economics is impossible. There the economics of a country as a whole cannot follow a single plan, let alone a maximal one. In a capitalist economy, not only are the interests of society continually subordinated to those of the capitalist corporations, but instead of true requirements they follow short-term conditions of demand which altogether misrepresent these requirements.

11. In a figurative sense we may say that the problem of efficiency would be solved, if a supporting hyperplane to the cone of all economic plans were found.

The analysis of these schemes leads also to a certain system of objectively determined valuations.[12]

Socialist economy is concerned with obtaining scientifically based magnitudes of costs for various types of products. It is essential to know these magnitudes for solving problems of labour distribution and of replacing one product, or certain inputs, by others. Such a manifestation of value relations in socialist society is fundamental.

The choice of one solution or another as a separate economic problem makes no basic change to the general plan but is related only to one of its variations. Hence o.d. valuations that correspond to conditions of production in an optimal plan and permit us, as we have seen, to make a correct comparison of the results of different variations of a plan, are well adapted for determining the economic effect of the choice of specific economic solutions. This is a result of the fact that o.d. valuations correspond to the magnitude of the costs of (average) labour, which is necessary for producing this output under the given conditions. The fact that in so doing it is necessary to take into account the inputs of factors which determine the conditions for the application and economy of labour and that these factors also have o.d. valuations (rent, hire valuations of equipment) is connected simply with the necessity to calculate labour costs correctly, with allowance for the national economic conditions of its use; it is connected with the need to obtain not only partial labour costs in any production unit, but full labour costs.

Such a complete calculation also ensures that the level of costs of a given product characterizes not only the costs of varying the volume of its output, but turns out as a rule to be universal for all (rational) methods used for producing it on all units and hence coincides with the global (average) level of costs.[13]

12. It must be emphasized that analysis of a model is a necessary stage in studying an object even though the model does not represent the object completely. For example, in construction engineering the calculation for a building does not include all the beams, tie-rods and girders; however, without mastering the methods for calculating these elements it is impossible to make correct calculations for the building as a whole.

13. Ignoring indirect expenditure leads to misrepresentation of the real cost relations which may be compared with that obtained in, say, problems of mechanics, if forces of reaction, inertia, and friction were excluded from

It is important to note the realism of the above statement of the optimal planning problem. It is determined by the fact that the system of o.d. valuations, which is constructed together with the optimal plan, provides a means for solving a number of problems which are necessary for the practical realization of a plan: for example, the possibility of changing the plan (while keeping it optimal) according to changes in the situation, the possibility of obtaining indicators for evaluating the work of the separate production units and for stimulating the carrying out of the optimal plan, and so on.

It should be emphasized, however, that the models of production planning which have been considered are only approximations to the real problem. To make these studies more accurate it would be necessary to consider the assumption of linearity, which is not entirely justified, and to allow for the stochastic (problematical) nature of some initial data; finally, one should remember to allow for certain non-economic factors. However, the introduction of these considerations into the calculations cannot change the basic conclusions; hence it is of the greatest importance to follow those paths of the analysis of economic planning which the basic model provides.

In considering these models, of course, a number of important problems have been altogether ignored, for example, how to make adjustments to the composition of the final products in the sector of private demand on the basis of demand studies, problems of allocation, in particular the wage structure, and so on. All these problems require special study which does not come within the scope of this book; but it is to be assumed that here too mathematical methods and models would find their appropriate place.

The above area of problems as a whole requires a great deal of further research, which will probably introduce appreciable corrections to the propositions given in this book, and will lead to the treatment of many essential problems which have not been touched upon here.

However, there is no doubt that mathematical analysis will help towards a better understanding of the quantitative aspects of

consideration (or taken into account only qualitatively), and only 'visible' active forces were retained.

the economic laws which govern a socialist society and will produce a more complete discovery of the advantages of this highly perfected social structure. This will assist in a more complete realization of the possibilities of the socialist method of production in the national economy as a whole and in all its sectors.

References

KANTOROVICH, L. V. (1939), *Mathematical Methods for Organizing and Planning Industry* (Mathematicheskiye metody organizatsiyii planirovaniya proizvodstva) Leningrad State University Press.

KANTOROVICH, L. V. (1942), 'On the movement of masses', *Dokl. Akad. Nauk*, SSSR 37, nos. 7–8.

KANTOROVICH, L. V., and GAVURIN, M. K. (1949), 'The use of mathematical methods in analysing problems of goods transport', in the collection *Problems of Increasing Transport Efficiency* (Problemy povysheniya effektivnosti raboty transporta), Academy of Sciences Press.

KANTOROVICH, L. V., and ZALGALLER, V. A. (1951), *Calculation of Rational Cutting-out of Industrial Materials* (Raschet ratsional'nogo raskroya promyshlennykh materialov), Lenizdat.

KANTOROVICH, L. V. (1957), 'Methods for analysing certain extremal problems in production planning', *Dokl. Akad. Nauk* SSSR 115, 3. The basic results of this paper were reported at a scientific session at Leningrad State University, 12 May 1941.

KOOPMANS, T. C. (ed.) (1951), *Activity Analysis of Production and Allocation*, Wiley.

KUHN, H. W., and TUCKER, A. W. (eds.) (1956), 'Linear inequalities and related systems', *Ann. Math. Studies*, 38. Princeton.

LENIN, V. I. *Collected, Works*, Russian Edition, Moscow.

TOLSTOI, A. (1939), 'Methods for eliminating irrationalities from transport planning', *Sotsialisticheskii Transport*, no. 9.

ZALGALLER, V. A. (1956), *A New Development in the Composition of Log Sawing Consignments* (Novoye v sostavlenii postavov dlya raspilovki breven), Central Scientific Research Laboratory 'Sevzaples', Leningrad.

22 A. L. Veinshtein

Notes on Optimal Planning

Extract from A. L. Veinshtein, 'Notes on optimal planning', taken from the symposium *Ekonomiko–Matematicheskiye Metody*, 1966, Moscow.

Let us now take the basic problem of planning, the construction of an optimal plan for the whole economy of the country. We do not belong to those mathematical economists who consider that this plan cannot be obtained as the solution to some mathematical optimization problem with an enormous number of variables and constraints.[1]

It seems to us that it is possible to formulate the 'objective function' for the economy and try to optimize it, be it the maximization of national income, maximization of consumption for a period of time, the minimization of labour expenditure or the maximization of leisure, etc. The criteria of optimality, however, must be given externally, corresponding to the aims which the given social formation puts itself. If we accept that a single optimizing criterion exists for the whole national economy and is given to us, or let us select one of many possible criteria, then the problem of the *practical* possibilities of constructing an optimal national economic plan on the basis of the chosen criterion must be specially considered.

When we move from maintaining the principles of the possibility of constructing an optimal national economic plan to an attempt at numerical solutions of this problem, the picture changes. Let us assume that we have the given initial data and have constructed a corresponding objective function. A huge number of variables, and interrelations of various kinds con-

1. Some authors consider that the mathematical problem of optimization cannot be put in the perspective planning of the national economy as the significance of the objective function in this case does not tend mathematically to some limit – maximum or minimum – depending on the conditions of the problem. (See for instance Gerchuk, 1965.)

necting them to one another, place before us a barrier unsurmountable at the present time.

The researcher would have to consider, in this case, a limitless number of elements of the national economy: various types of raw materials, fuel, auxiliary supplies, final products of different grades, brands, size categories,[2] different natural resources, labour power, different means of production and transport – changes in the norms of these components in the course of the plan period, etc. Further, it is necessary to take note of the variety of interrelations among all the sections of the national economy and all the economic branches. Many of these interconnections, including some which are very important, have a non-linear character. It is essential to take into account that with an increase in the scale and complexity of planning the number and complexity of the interrelations increases to a much higher degree than the ingredients being introduced. As a result, it is practically impossible to compile an optimal national economic plan, as the solution to an extremal problem, over the course of the next one or two five year plans. Furthermore, we have to solve even separate large parts of this plan and isolated large-scale problems, for the solution of which mathematical methods are employed, by simplification and division into parts and ignore several important interconnections, extraordinarily complicating their formulation and solution.

Several economists suggest constructing the optimal plan of the national economy in separate large parts, beginning, for instance, with an optimal plan for railway transport.[3] Let us assume that we have formulated the problem of constructing an optimal plan for railway transport. For this, the total expenditure on the run of loaded and empty wagons would be a minimum. Then, the number of variables will be calculated in thousands of millions and the number of constraints in millions, assuming that there is a network of the number of departing and arriving loads set for

2. The planning schedule of material – technical supply – alone has at the present time 60–100 thousand entries.

3. Such for instance was Khachaturov's (1965) suggestion at the 'round table' conference, organized by the editorial board of the journal *Soviet Union*, in the spring of 1964.

each station and that the constraints are being observed on the traffic capacity of each station, the volume and composition of the rolling stock and the conditions of transport of loads in wagons of different types, i.e. the compilation of such a plan will be impossible. The simplification and consolidation of the initial data to permit solving the task under techniques of the present time, or even of the very near future, can lead to such a distortion of reality that its solution turns out to be practically useless.

This is not the end of the difficulties, since the optimal plan must form a compound part of the total national economic plan. Therefore the overall problem set out must include the inter-relation of the projected freight flow with all other problems of planning. The plan for the transport and employment of the rolling stock on the railways must be coordinated with the work of other types of transport, primarily water. In perspective planning, the optimal freight flow plan depends on the size and direction of capital investment, on the reconstruction and new building of railway transport and on the expansion of the traffic capacity of individual stations.

Finally, expenditure on transport does not always change in proportion to the size of the transport operation, which makes the mathematical solution of this problem by the methods of linear programming very much more difficult. In this respect, the corresponding curves can have a different character for different intervals of change in the argument (transport). The constraints to which the extremal economic problems and objective functions must conform cannot be exactly expressed in linear formulae. We have already touched on this aspect above in discussing the task of the optimal location of an enterprise. It is of relevance to stress here that Kantorovich (1959) also acknowledges that 'there are cases where non-linearity is basic and has furthermore a non-convex character' (p. 336), and uses as an example railway transport in the given region. Thus, even in constructing an optimal plan of railway transport we encounter extraordinarily great difficulties of a mathematical and computational order.

Turning to the construction of a plan of the national economy,

Kantorovich's prerequisite is unlikely to be accepted, to the effect that such a plan can be represented linearly as an aggregation of means applied with varying 'intensities'. The national economy is by nature, apparently, a non-linear system. Therefore, in constructing a non-linear plan it is impossible, in general, to employ only linear functions. It can lead to such a marked distortion of economic relations that the optimality of the result obtained will be highly doubtful.

The construction of an optimal national economic plan has to be formulated as a dynamic problem over a long period of time. It is not, however, possible to take fully into account a change in the factors which determine the plan in advance. Their sizes cannot be determined. They are accidental, with this or that probability assigned to them. The introduction of probabilities, elements and prerequisites complicates the solution of extremal problems to an extraordinary degree. The compilation of optimal national economic plans is converted into a problem of stochastic programming.

We conclude that in spite of the great achievements of mathematical science and computing technique in the sphere of the numerical solution of complicated extremal problems with a large number of variables and constraints linking these variables, we still do not have either a finished mathematical apparatus or the technical possibility of solving large complex problems which are obtained on translating the large problems of optimal planning into mathematical language. The obtaining of an optimal national economic plan *in the very near future* is still less hopeful. Its indicators would constitute a solution to the extremal problem. We are, in practice, still very far from achieving the possibility of constructing such a plan, although it is theoretically possible mathematically.

Our conclusions sound pessimistic only when we compare the existing possibilities with the ideal position, towards which we have to strive, let us say, with the discovery of a *genuine* optimum of the objective function for the whole national economy. The picture changes considerably when we approach the problem being investigated from another point of view, that of comparing the results of the application of programming methods with those which we observe at the present time without it.

The planning of individual sections of the national economy has, until the present, been based on an analysis of a few or a very limited number of plan variants. Therefore the contemplated or actually operating plans were much further from the optimal than those obtained as a result of applying linear programming methods. The situation is the same in the construction of a national economic plan. The latter is the result of considering a totally insignificant number in comparison with the innumerable multitude of possible plan variants. It is based on a very high aggregation of indications and on groups of elements of the plan. Therefore our plans are, in many cases, not only not optimal but not even balanced in all their parts. This is of importance not only in the sector of production and demand of articles of consumption but also in the sector of means of production, where the elements of supply and demand should have been determined.[4] By comparison with the existing situation the application of linear programming and mathematical methods in general provides, as we have already indicated, a fully real result. This will expand to the extent of the elaboration of partial models, as a result of the development and perfecting of the mathematical apparatus for their solution and for their approximation to the optimum of the solutions obtained.

Another very important circumstance must be set against the pessimistic conclusion – the huge gain in time, when utilizing mathematical variants for the compilation of the plan. This is so because it is only by mathematizing the process that it is possible to employ computers and reach fantastic speeds in calculating the plan (the computer requires hours and minutes instead of weeks and days). The rapidity of computation also makes it possible to conduct optimal operational – literally daily – planning of individual parts of the national economy effectively which would be impossible in most cases without the computer.

Starting from the arguments outlined, we do not have to be

4. The press provides us daily with many examples of such a lack of co-ordination. Thus in the newspaper *Izvestia* (1964) the contemporary picture of the planning of production is very colourfully described with the passing of orders for output being made in sets, and the stream of rejections of consumers' orders for articles which were, not long before this, in short supply (reduction gears and taps).

confused at the fact that in the next few years we will not obtain a perfectly optimal plan for the whole national economy. Instead, by consciously making simplifications and generalizations we will, in the meanwhile, achieve sufficiently satisfactory results at the first stage of the construction of a crude mathematical model of the national economic plan. As follows from the argument, the methods of linear programming are totally inadequate for this purpose. They must be supplemented with other forms of mathematical programming. The methods of linear programming have their own boundaries, even if sufficiently wide, but they are not the omnipotent mind of Laplace.

Nonetheless if it were not for the discovery of linear programming methods there would not have been the next stage of elaboration of other forms of mathematical programming, which constitute the further development of linear programming and can be coordinated with it in the solution of complicated economic problems. We must be very grateful to the discoverers for the reliable instrument which they found for the basic penetration of the laws in the economy, as well as to their followers who are laying the further paths of its development, which are far from being strewn with roses.

References

GERCHUK, Y. P. (1965), 'Granitsy primeneniya lineinogo programmirovaniya', *Ekonomika*.

Izvestia (1964), 'Another speed', 28 September, no. 272.

KANTOROVICH, L. V. (1959), *The Best Use of Economic Resources*, Moscow; English edition, London, 1965 (see Reading 21 of this volume).

KHACHATUROV, T. S. (1965), 'Ekonomisty i matematiki za kruzlym stolom', *Ekonomika*, Moscow.

23 J. Kornai

Mathematical Programming as a Tool of Socialist Economic Planning

Paper presented at the First World Congress of the Econometric Society, Rome, 9–14 September 1965.

The Hungarian economy-wide programming project

Some eighteen months ago (in 1963) a team of several hundred economists, practical planners, engineers and mathematicians started with the practical implementation of an economy-wide mathematical programming project.[1] The work was expected to be concluded in 1966.

As regards its mathematical form, our programming model is of the standard linear type; in this respect it is without any special interest. What does probably lend an interest to our work is the model's unusual environment. As a matter of fact, this is – at least to my knowledge – the first time that a relatively detailed model embracing the entire domain of the national economy and including the five-year plan's principal targets would be employed in a socialist country with a centrally planned economy. Although responsibility for the model lies with the scientists, close relations are being maintained with the leaders of the economy. The work is carried out not in remote and quiet university and research institute surroundings but at the National Planning Board itself as well as in the economic ministries.

This, of course, does not mean that Hungary's next five-year plan will be based on the program obtained by means of the mathematical model. *The official program*, based on methods that had been employed over several decades (to be called in the sequel the *traditional* methods), is being drawn up independently

1. Commissioned by the National Planning Board, the research team is working under the direction of the author. The project is guided by the Computing Centre of the Hungarian Academy of Sciences and the Scientific Section of the National Planning Board, with another fourteen scientific institutions participating.

of our work. Our relations with the traditional methods and the official plans display a peculiar duality. On the one hand, we are relying on their data. On the other hand, we are competing with them, endeavouring as we do to prove the superiority of mathematical planning over the traditional non-mathematical methods.

Let me now proceed to the brief description of the model.

The national model is composed of *forty sector models*. We define a sector as a productive and foreign-trading unit responsible for a definite range of products or services and obliged to supply to the rest of the national economy the products or services in question.

The individual sectors are generally responsible for several – six to ten, in some cases fifteen to twenty – product groups, aggregates composed of a variety of concrete products. In the following, the product aggregates will be called *products*. Our economy-wide model contains a total of some 400 products.

The variables are divided into two main groups: *capital transformation variables* and *operation variables*.

The capital transformation variables represent the economic activities which result in transforming a certain part of the capital stock, of the production and turnover fund, and of the country's stock of foreign assets and liabilities from a definite state in 1966 into a definite state in 1970.

The common purpose of all capital transformation variables is to create capacities and possibilities for the economic operation in 1970. Let us give a few examples also of the operation variables.

1. The production of a definite product in 1970.

2. The export and import of definite products in 1970 in definite market relations.

3. The collection of interest accrued on credits granted abroad and the payment of interest on foreign debts in 1970.

Summing up: *the program obtained by means of the model constitutes a complex investment, technical development, production, international financial, export and import plan.*

Our model contains a great number of constraints. The first main group of the constraints limits the capital transformation activities, particularly under three aspects:

Firstly, from the side of the initial state: e.g. the activities to preserve the initial state are limited by the stocks existing in 1966.

Secondly, from the side of the terminal state: e.g. the additional capacity which can be created by means of the technical reconstruction of an old plant is technically given.

Thirdly, from the side of the inputs required for the transformation: investment resources are limited. Within these, and in accordance with the conventions of traditional planning the quotas of machinery available for investment purposes are separately limited for domestically produced machines, those imported from socialist countries, and those imported from capitalist countries; a separate limit is set to the construction quota; and so on.

Another main group of constraints limits the 1970 activities, primarily under the following aspects:

1. Technological relations between the raw materials, semi-finished and finished products.

2. The obligation to satisfy final domestic demand. The non-productive requirements of the population and the public institutions are taken as given.

3. Foreign trade constraints. The upper bounds representing the marketing possibilities in exports; export obligations undertaken under international agreements as lower bounds; balances of payments and trade; and so on.

4. The constraints of labor available.

5. The scarce natural resources.

Finally the third main group of constraints includes those regulating the relationship between capital transformation variables on the one hand and operation variables on the other.

The sector models are not autonomous but related to one another by numerous links. From this point of view the constraints of the sector models may be classed into two main groups, namely *intrasectoral* and *intersectoral* constraints.

The intrasectoral constraints regulate the 'internal affairs' of the sector. They include those of the technological equations which describe the flow of products within the sector; the constraints of the sector's initial capital stock, initial capacities, etc.; the individual export marketing constraints relating to the sector's products.

The intersectoral constraints, on the other hand, regulate the sector's 'external affairs'. They include all equations which describe the flow of products between the individual sectors (e.g. electric energy constitutes the output of the electric-energy sector and an input for all other sectors – the balance of electric energy must therefore be considered an intersectoral constraint for all sectors). The same applies to the allocation of the resources which are being drawn upon by several sectors (e.g. the gross investment quota, the wage fund, etc.).

Let us introduce the following notation:

A_i = matrix of the coefficients figuring in the intersectoral constraints of the ith sector. (In our model $i = 1, 2,..., 40$, but for the sake of a more general formulation we will speak of n sectors.)

B_i = matrix of the coefficients figuring in the intrasectoral constraints of the ith sector

u_i = vector of the intersectoral constraint constants of the ith sector

b_0 = vector of the macroeconomic bounds of the intersectoral constraints

b_i = vector of the intrasectoral constraint constants of the ith sector

c_i = vector of the objective function coefficients of the ith sector

x_i = the program of the ith sector, including slack variables

x = $x_1, x_2,..., x_n$ = the national program

x_i^{off} = the official program of the ith sector as worked out on the basis of traditional methods

x^{off} = The official program

The calculations are carried out in two phases. In the first phase, each individual sector carries out its own programming project separately; in the second phase the sector models are linked up and combined into a single large-scale economy-wide model.

First phase

First of all, we will determine the intersectoral constraint vector u_i conform to the official sector program x_i^{off}

$$u_i = A_i x_i^{\text{off}}. \qquad\qquad 1$$

When constructing the model it should be made sure that the official program satisfies also the intrasectoral constraints

$$b_i = B_i x_i^{\text{off}}. \qquad\qquad 2$$

Should, in exceptional cases, this condition not be fulfilled, we will proceed to correct the official program and will in the sequel consider this corrected program, which satisfies condition 2, as x_i^{off}.

Now we will proceed by means of the electronic computer, to determine program x_i^*, which means the solution of the following linear programming problem:

$$
\begin{cases}
\text{(a)} & A_i x_i = u_i \\
\text{(b)} & B_i x_i = b_i \\
\text{(c)} & x_i = 0 \\
\text{(d)} & c_i x_i \to \text{max!}
\end{cases}
\qquad\qquad 3
$$

We would like to avoid the term 'optimal' for the program x_i obtained as a solution of problem 3, since the optimality of this program is rather relative. It will depend to a considerable extent, among others, on the intersectoral constraint vector u_i. We prefer to call it the *dominant* sector program, because it generally dominates the official sector program x_i^{off}; both x_i^* and x_i^{off} satisfy the conditions 3(a) to 3(c), and at the same time the dominant program is considerably better than the official one from the point of view of the objective function 3(d).[2] In the sector-level calculations carried out so far we have generally maximized the net surplus of the balance of external trade as expressed in terms of dollars. This objective function showed 5 to 15 per cent savings in the dominant sector programs as against the official sector programs.

By the end of the first phase there will be already at least two national programs available, namely

$$x^{\text{off}} = x_1^{\text{off}}, x_2^{\text{off}}, \dots, x_n^{\text{off}},$$

2. For the sake of simplicity, we will disregard the theoretically not entirely impossible case where $x_i^* = x^{\text{off}}$. In our actual practice up to now this has not yet occurred.

the official program of the national economy, and

$$\bar{x} = x_1, x_2, \ldots, x_n,$$

the conjunction of the dominant sector programs obtained as a result of the calculations carried out in the first phase, as the solution of problems **3**. Let $\bar{x}$ be called in the following the national program of the first *approximation*.

Second phase

Here, the sector models are combined into a single large-scale national model. We consider the following linear programming problem:

$$
\begin{cases}
\text{(a)} \ A_1 x_1 + A_2 x_2 + \ldots + A_n x_n = b_0 \\
\qquad B_1 x_1 \qquad\qquad\qquad\quad = b_1 \\
\qquad\qquad\quad B_2 x_2 \qquad\qquad\quad = b_2 \\
\text{(b)} \qquad\qquad\qquad \ldots \\
\qquad\qquad\qquad\qquad B_n x_n = b_n \\
\text{(c)} \ x_1 = 0, x_2 = 0, \ldots x_n = 0 \\
\text{(d)} \ c_1 x_1 + c_2 x_2 \to \max!
\end{cases}
\qquad 4
$$

In relation to our computation-technical possibilities the dimensions of problem **4** are very large; it contains, in fact, several thousand variables.

The constraint vector of the intersectoral constraints – b_0 – can be determined, in a manner analogous to calculation **1**, as follows:

$$b_0 = \sum_{i=1}^{n} A_i x_i^{\text{off}} = \sum_{i=1}^{n} u_i. \qquad 5$$

The following statements can now be made about the two national programs already known:

Firstly, both the official national program x^{off} and the national program of the first approximation x are feasible, i.e. they satisfy the conditions **4**(a) to **4**(c).

Secondly, the national program of the first approximation $\bar{x}$ dominates the official national program: according to objective function **4**(d) it is more advantageous than the latter.

In the second phase of the calculations the aim is to find a program which is more advantageous according to the objective function **4**(d) than the one of the first approximation, i.e. which dominates the official program to an even greater extent.

In the two phases of the calculation we are gradually 'drifting away' from the official program. In the first phase vector u_i, the official intersectoral distribution of the intersectoral constraints as derived from the official sector program in accordance with equation **1**, was still considered binding. In the second phase this restriction is already removed (i.e. $A_i x_i$ may be greater or smaller than u_i, as the case may be). It is now only the constraint b_0 relating to the national economy as a whole that is derived from the official program in accordance with equation **5**, while for the distribution of the constraints b_0 among the sectors our mathematical model is left free scope. The calculations will be based on various alternative objective functions: in the first experimental programming project, the net surplus of the country's balance of external trade (in dollar terms) will be maximized.

The given state of computing techniques in this country does not allow a direct solution of the large-scale economy-wide programming problem by means of some usually employed algorithm (as, for instance, the simplex method). Instead, we will have to employ one of the so-called *decomposition methods*, making use of the block-diagonal arrangement of the matrices B_i.

After theoretical investigations in several directions and practical checking calculations we have come to the decision to carry out our first experimental computations on the basis of the *Dantzig–Wolfe* method. (See Dantzig and Wolfe, 1961.) As with the other decomposition methods, this is a rather lengthy procedure. It has, however, the great advantage that it brings about a monotone improvement in the value of the objective function. Thus, we will obtain a workable result even in the case that we are compelled to stop the iteration before attaining an optimum. Another method had been worked out originally for the purpose of the economy-wide planning problem by mathematician Th. Liptak and the present author. (See Kornai and Liptak, 1965.) The method in question is based on the same theoretical interpretation of the problem and utilizes the so called method of fictitious play. The principal advantage of this latter method of fictitious play consists in the fact that here the dimensions of the model will practically not be limited by the computer's *storage capacity*. The intersectoral part of the problem will, as a matter of fact, require no 'regular' linear programming but only the carrying out of a set of considerably simpler operations (such as the calculation of arithmetic means, etc.). However, the method is not monotonic: while it approaches the optimum the value of the objective function is strongly fluctuating. It is precisely the monotonic character of the convergence that we consider the principal advantage of the Dantzig–Wolfe method. Moreover, the Dantzig–Wolfe method affords a possibility to profit at the beginning of the economy-wide calculations from the programs worked out in the first phase of sector-level programming, already in the first step of the iteration.

The economy-wide planning carried out on the basis of decomposition methods was termed *two-level* planning. (The term had been originally introduced to designate the algorithm using fictitious play; but in our opinion its generalization is wholly justified.) The work of planning is being carried out on two 'levels': partly within the sectors themselves and partly at the National Planning Board, the central government agency responsible for and supervising the sectors. On both levels, a certain amount of initial information will be available. Moreover, in the course of the planning process, information will flow between the two levels. The information 'output' of the Planning Board's calculations will constitute the information 'input' of the sector-level calculations and conversely. From what has been said it will be already clear that decomposition in our case means more than simply a mathematical and computation-technical 'trick' to solve a large-scale problem more smartly. We have here two-level planning in the true sense of the word: the sector models actually represent existing institutions with a certain degree of independence whose planning work is being co-ordinated by the centre, the National Planning Board.

On the basis of the traditional planning methods it will take two to three years to draw up a five-year plan. During that period several complete plan proposals may be drawn up *one after the other*, based always on the latest information and on the latest instructions received from the governing political bodies. But never so far have several complete plan variants been submitted *at the same time as alternatives* to the decision-makers in Hungary. And it is here that the significance of mathematical programming lies, in the fact that by means of sensitivity tests and parametric programming it lends itself for drawing up side by side a whole range of complete national plan variants.

It is on purpose that we are avoiding here the term of determining an 'optimal' plan. Our program could be 'optimal' in the general sense of the term only if there existed a 'welfare function' which would express in itself the interests of society.

In our experience, the political body which performs the task of central administration in the socialist economy will not be able to give a numerical definition in *advance* of its own 'preferences'. Mathematical programming, on the other hand, lends itself for generating a whole range of complete and efficient national programs which will reflect a variety of economic consequences which the alternative economic policies would entail. The leading political bodies will have to study intensively the complete national plan variants representing the alternative economic policies in order to be able to reach a well-founded decision. The program variant adopted in the end may then be described as *the program that will efficiently further the economic policy laid down by the decision-making political body*. The definition may be less attractive than the term 'optimal program' – but it is more realistic and expresses more accurately the relationship between economic policy and planning in the actual practice of the socialist planned economy.

The debates on the role of mathematical planning

While work on the first experimental national model is in full swing, extensive discussions are now taking place in Hungary between the representatives of top management, the economic planners and the theoretical economists over the questions relating to the 'mechanism' of the economy. Mechanism is meant here as a broad collective term including the entire system of planning, economic management and the institutional forms of the economy. To mention but a few of the questions under discussion: which of the economic indicators should be drawn into the orbit of planning and which should be left out? What should be the role of directives in economic management? (Or, in the terminology of the French planners: to what extent should planning be imperative and to what extent indicative in character?) What should the price system be like?

Now, in the course of these discussions there arose also the question, what should be the role of planning based on mathematical methods in the national economy? From the wide variety of views, let me mention but two characteristic ones.

One opinion could be summed up in its crudest form as follows: 'The allocation of resources and with it price formation should be left to the mechanism of the market. Centralized economic planning did in the past not prove sufficiently rational – it should, therefore, be restrained within narrow bounds or even abandoned altogether. Nor can the introduction of mathematical methods alter these negative features of planning. The models of mathematical economics are unrealistic and cannot be considered anything but an interesting intellectual pastime entirely out of contact with the actual functioning of the economy.'

It will be worthwhile to point out that such views are not unequivocally associated with some political attitude. I have heard them voiced in Budapest by socialists and in London by persons who were certainly nothing of the kind.

In my opinion, such views are behind the times and anachronistic. They are both overrating the perfection of the market mechanism and underestimating the achievements of modern science. When in the 1930s the concept of socialism was discussed by Western economists, Professor Hayek could still raise the argument against Barone's mathematical model of the socialist economy that in actual practice it would be impossible to solve the enormous number of equations involved by means of mathematical tools. (See Hayek, 1935.) The three decades that have since passed witnessed significant changes. Sufficient to mention only four closely interrelated achievements: firstly, the extensive spread of punched-card machines, of the modern methods of data processing and storing; secondly, the appearance of high-capacity electronic computers and the incredibly rapid growth of their efficiency; thirdly, the elaboration and steady improvement of numerical methods and algorithms suited to solving large equations systems; and finally, the application of decomposition methods enabling the combination and joint solution of mathematical models composed of large equation systems. These achievements went a long way towards extending the sphere of decisions where mathematical models may play a part, i.e. the sphere of strictly rational, exact planning.

The other opinion could be summarized as follows:

'The highly centralized system of economic administration as developed up to now under socialism should be maintained together with the central planning of partial economic processes down to the most minute detail and with the central fixing of all prices – but all this should be from now on carried out by means of mathematical programming. A country-wide network of computing centres should be set up, linked with one another, and the whole economy should then be subjected to detailed planning based on mathematical models.'

If the former view can be characterized as a naïve nineteenth century notion, a naïvely optimistic belief in the market mechanism – the latter view is certainly a naïve twentieth century notion, a naïvely optimistic belief in the computer. Its representatives include mathematicians who have never directly experienced the infinitely intricate character of economic reality, or practical economists whose knowledge of mathematical methods, operations research and programming derives from promotional literature, and who are not aware of the fact that this discipline is still more or less in its infancy. Only those who are themselves engaged in the practical application of mathematical planning methods will know how far such models are from perfection. Immense efforts will be required even in the construction and solution of an equation system where only 400 product aggregates are involved, with but one or two technological variants to each, and where a few thousand relationships within the economy are only taken into consideration. Even in a small country like Hungary the Price Control Board will in the course of a general price adjustment fix the price of several hundred thousand products. The number of plan figures and indices set by the National Planning Board and the economic ministries in the course of drawing up a five-year plan is estimated to run to seven digits (no one has actually counted them so far). And yet, these examples refer only to the mass of figures to be handled at some given date – in connection with a general price adjustment scheme or with the drawing up of a five-year plan. Actually, the economy is in continuous movement: all external conditions are continually changing and decisions will, accordingly, have to be made continually. One cannot know what the twenty-first century might bring – but *for the time being* it would still be illusory to believe that every decision could be 'mathematized'.

In my opinion a modern economy – and especially a socialist economy – can dispense neither with planning nor with the market mechanism. What is needed is, however, not the 'happy mean' of the two, not their 'convex combination' with 50 per cent of market mechanism and 50 per cent of planning, both in half-developed, half-disintegrated form. Both should function in their fully developed form. In the human organism certain functions are controlled by the autonomous nervous system, others by the central nervous system. It would give rise to grave difficulties if the control of, let us say, breathing or the temperature of the body were to devolve on the central nervous system; this would absorb our mental capacities and it is by no means certain that the control would be reliable. On the other hand, an activity of a higher order – e.g. the composition of an economic treatise – cannot be left to the autonomous nervous system.

In the economic organism it is primarily the market that will perform the role of the autonomous nervous system whereas planning performs that of the central nervous system. Neither can replace the other, and it must be endeavoured to keep both intact and in working order. Without pretending to completeness or to systematization of general validity, I will list a few criteria of the division of labour between the two 'nervous systems'.

One viewpoint is that of sovereignty over the economy. Theory tends to deal with pure types; it would describe the case of unlimited consumers' sovereignty when, due to the operation of the market mechanism the allocation of resources is in full conformity with consumer preferences, and confront it with the case of the unlimited sovereignty of a central authority when, due to the plan, the allocation of resources conforms to the preferences of the political decision-makers. However, none of the pure cases does actually prevail in the socialist economy. Consumer preferences will assert themselves over a wide sphere of decisions (and, together with a great number of Hungarian economists, I am of the opinion that they ought to assert themselves over an even wider sphere, with less friction and shorter time lags). But the prevalence of consumer preferences is not unlimited, nor is it desirable to be so. It is but reasonable that certain economic decisions of fundamental importance should be made centrally and in accordance with the interests of society as a whole. Now, in the former sphere it is the market that should prevail, and in the latter sphere it is planning – if possible, planning based on exact mathematical methods. As pointed out above when describing the national economic programming project now carried out in Hungary, the purpose of the sensitivity tests performed by means of the model is exactly to present to the central decision-makers with full clarity the problem of choice and the whole system of consequences of the possible alternatives of economic policy.

The participants in the mechanism debate in Hungary are more or less unanimous in the view that it is primarily in the long-term decisions, in the investment plans that deliberate social resolutions should be made to prevail. There are several arguments in favour of this view. It would be wrong to leave to atomistic individual resolutions the decisions which will affect later generations and the future of the whole society: what part of output is invested; how to allocate investments to the various sectors of the national economy, etc. Beyond the political and moral considerations involved, there is also the requirement of the efficient utilization of information to confirm this view. The complex of individual and isolated entrepreneurial decisions made on the basis of the momentary market situation and of momentarily valid prices, cannot result in reliable resolutions. The decisions based on the survey of the national economy as a whole and on the simultaneous consideration of the development of all sectors, will be much more reliable. The mathematical model described in the first part of this paper clearly demonstrates the dependence of the efficiency of a single investment variable of a single sector on all the model's other variables and its links with them through the whole enormous equation system.

As generally known, in a planless market it is the capital market that constitutes the least perfectly functioning part, that with the highest degree of friction and the greatest amount of false information. In my opinion, while the market mechanism should be left to assert itself in the daily flow of commodities, the allocation of investment resources (or, at least, of their major part) should be based on mathematical planning. The capital market should be simulated on the electronic computer in such undistorted form and with such perfection as will never be reached by the real capital market. The meaning of 'two-level planning' is just that the sectors are competing with one another for the capital 'put up to auction' by the central authority.

The role of mathematical planning consists in *preparing* rational economic decisions; that of the market is to *check subsequently* the rationality both of the decisions themselves and of their execution. The market will thus signal whether the plan was acceptable to the operative units within the economy; whether the estimates were realistic; whether disequilibria were manifesting themselves in divergence from the originally balanced plan, and so forth. We are able to survey only a few of the problems to which the appearance of mathematical planning methods in the socialist economy has given rise. My remarks can naturally not pretend to having given a satisfactory theoretical solution of these problems – they may, however, have been suited to call forth a debate.

References

DANTZIG, G. B., and WOLFE P. (1961), 'The decomposition algorithm for linear programs', *Econometrics*, no. 29, pp. 767–78.

HAYEK, F. A. (ed.) (1935), *Collectivist Economic Planning*, Routledge & Kegan Paul, see Reading 3 of this volume.

KORNAI, J., and LIPTAK, T. (1965), 'Two level planning', *Econometrics*, no. 33, pp. 141–69.

Part Six
The Chinese Model

The traditional discussion of socialist planning has taken place in terms of the efficient allocation of *given* resources. One of the distinctive features of the Chinese model is the idea that human response to objective conditions is as important as the actual objective conditions of an economy and the reliance on the mobilization of hidden economic potential rather than on the economic management of given resources. Other important aspects of the Chinese model – the encouragement of local initiative, the use of moral incentives, the use of material incentives only in a collective and not an individual form, the role of agriculture, the importance attached to education and social consciousness – make it an important alternative to the model developed through the experience of Soviet and East-European socialist countries. Gray's essay provides a preliminary discussion of the specific features of the Chinese model.

24 Jack Gray

The Chinese Model: Some Characteristics of Maoist
Policies for Social Change and Economic Growth

J. Gray, 'The Chinese model: some characteristics of Maoist policies for
social change and economic growth', *L'Est*, Milan, 1971, no. 2.

An outline for discussion

Our understanding of the Chinese model is still very inadequate.
Until 1958, it was assumed that the aims, methods, and problems
(both economic and political) of the Chinese People's Republic
were closely parallel to those of the Soviet Union, and China's
divergence from the orthodox Soviet model was not anticipated
by many observers. The close political and ideological alliance
of China with the Soviet bloc indeed led the Chinese to disguise
even the fundamental divergences represented by the Great Leap
Forward and the Communes by appeals to Soviet precedents. It
was only in the course of the subsequent Sino-Soviet dispute that
the Chinese felt free to point to the essential contrasts between
their own policies and those current in the Soviet Union; and
even then, some colour of orthodoxy is still given to Chinese
actions by refusal to accept Krushchev's unqualified condemnation of Stalin.

Since 1958, we have accepted that the Maoist wing in China
offers a pattern of development which is significantly different
from the orthodox model, and also in sharp contrast at many
points with the policies which have emerged in Russia and
Eastern Europe since the Twentieth Congress of the CPSU. The
tendency, however, has been to dismiss these divergences as
unrealistic aspirations, pursued in the teeth of ineluctable objective facts, at the expense of sound pragmatic policy; with the
paradoxical result that the Soviet system, so often condemned by
western liberals, has become to the same liberals, in the context
of discussion of China, the realistic and sensible norm from which
China's voluntaristic, utopian leaders have departed.

Three lines of research are necessary in order to appreciate the real significance of China's vast and fascinating experiments in social engineering. The first is the historical study of the Chinese economy; and no aspect of China's recent past has been so grossly neglected in the West as this, although Japanese scholars have paid great attention to it. Some pioneering work is now going on in the United States, and, in Europe, by Dr Mark Elvin of the University of Glasgow; but a very considerable effort of research is necessary before we will be able to judge, on the basis of a firm knowledge of pre-existing local economic relationships and potentialities, Maoist plans for an economy based largely upon local economic initiative.

The second necessary line of research is into the economic theories of the Maoist wing in China, and the experience which has led to the formulation of these theories. Here again, very little work has been done.

The third line of research is into the results of the application of these policies, a most difficult subject in which little progress has been made. The most obvious problem here is the lack of global statistics from China since 1958, but there are more fundamental problems. Firstly, neither the Maoist nor the so-called Liu-ist line has been consistently applied for long enough to show clear results; and secondly, we tend very often to ask the wrong questions, based upon false assumptions, as to what is most significant. We tend to be obsessed with national and sectoral totals when the diversification of products, even at the expense in the short term of total growth, may at present be more important in China. We are obsessed with average performance in the Chinese economy when, given the very short time of operation and the very localized application of the Maoist model so far, it is not the average performance but the best performance which is interesting. We are reluctant to face the inconvenient fact that in an economy which is based largely upon local enterprise we must look first at local developments, however poor, unsystematic, and inaccessible the documentation of local affairs may be. We try to judge the Chinese economic model in terms of the arithmetical apportionment of fixed resources, when the whole model is explicitly concerned with the calling forth of latent resources. Finally, we neglect China's enormous investment in the educational aspects of economic development and social change, simply because this investment is not amenable to measurement.

Perhaps the great obstacle to understanding of the Chinese model, however, is the form in which Chinese economic analysis is expressed. We must appreciate the methodology of Maoism before we can appreciate its economic applications.

Maoist analysis

Maoism is both an ideology and a method of social analysis. Both aspects of Maoism are relevant to Chinese economic policies; but the ideological aspect can only be fully understood by detailed investigation of what it means in actual application; and the first step to such an investigation must be to study Maoism as a methodology.

A full study of Maoist methods of analysis is not the subject of this paper; but certain points must be made here, in summary fashion at least:

1. Maoism is concerned with the investigation of dynamic relationships. Its purpose is to anticipate, to stimulate, and to control complex social changes over time. So much could be said in theory of any form of Marxist analysis, but there is ample evidence that within the general Marxist framework, and subject to certain particular preconceptions, one fundamental aim of Maoism is to secure from Party, government personnel and citizens much more empirical investigation and pragmatic action than is normally expected in other communist countries.

2. The dynamic relationships which Maoism studies are of course described in the Hegelian language of contradictions, although in fact the variety of relationships so described is so great as almost to drain the word 'contradiction' of any true meaning.

3. Within this language of contradiction, there is in Maoism a very significant stress upon the idea of the unity of opposites, and also a strenuous insistence upon two important ideas: firstly, that contradictions will continue indefinitely to be thrown up in the processes of social development; and secondly, that contradictions must be transcended in a new synthesis, and not merely palliated by compromise. The motive force of politics is continuing contradiction; the function of politics is a continuous

effort to synthesize. It is a concept which, language apart, is not exclusively Marxist.

4. Within its Marxist framework, Maoism depends upon a particular theory of knowledge, understanding of which is vital to the understanding of Chinese policies and political style. This theory of knowledge is described in orthodox Marxist terms of the relationship between theory and practice. As expressed in Mao's philosophical essays, it seems to lack originality and point; but as expressed in his actual advice and instructions to cadres, military commanders, and others responsible for the making of public decisions, it emerges with force and pungency. While philosophical originality can scarcely be claimed for it, it is highly personal and it is unique in its practical implications. Mao's theory of knowledge emphasizes that (a) all knowledge comes from experience, (b) this knowledge is ineffective until generalized in theory, (c) such theory is never more than hypothesis subject to inductive verification, (d) the most effective form of verification is pragmatic – the truth is what works, (e) the process of experience – generalization – verification by experience – improved generalization – is continuous and unending, (f) accepting that the aim of Marxists is not to explain the world but to change it, the verifying experience consists of action aimed at change; pragmatism is thus limited by the aims of change, which are in the last analysis value judgments; and this is the only major limitation which appears to be set to Mao's consistent and vigorous pragmatism.

5. It is in its intimate relationship with Mao's theory of mass-line politics that the real significance of this theory of knowledge appears. The two are mutually dependent. The first stage in the acquisition of knowledge in relation to social change is to identify mass demands; then to articulate these in terms of policy; then to verify them by experimental implementation of policy, in which the judgement of the masses is critical; then to articulate the results in terms of improved or changed policies; and this process is continuous and unending. The whole process is expressed of course as a complex of contradictions and their solutions. The one *a priori* assumption involved is that the masses share the Maoist value system upon which the whole process is postulated;

but there is constant emphasis upon the need to relate action to the actual state of consciousness of the masses, which at any one time is partial and imperfect – as is, though normally at a higher level, the consciousness of their leaders.

It would perhaps be too much to expect that any ruling group would apply this consistent theory consistently. The point in this description is not to suggest that things in China always go in this way, but that they are meant to, and that social action is therefore posited in terms of such expectations.

It may be asked why this theory is relevant to economics; it seems a long way from the detached contemplation of the functioning of economic laws. We have already suggested, however, that the Chinese economic model is concerned not with the apportionment of given resources, but with the calling forth of unused resources, both material and human; and to such a model, both Mao's theory of knowledge and his theory of mass-line investigation and action are relevant in the highest degree. Indeed Mao's economic policies are the most obvious, and the most vital, application of both aspects of his thought.

If there is any substance in Maoist analysis, then the Maoist model should have a coherent and satisfying history of problems posed and problems solved, of new problems emerging and new solutions, a history of widening experience, of changing relationships and of increasing success in the solution of problems. Maoism has no such smooth history; but it has a history of a kind, to which we must now turn.

The history of the Maoist model

Some elements of Maoist economic ideas emerged in the period of the Kiangsi Soviet; but the experience of the border regions was of much greater significance in their development. The present author has attempted elsewhere to sum up the consequences of this experience for economic attitudes in Communist China: in a wartime, scattered, siege economy lacking capital, there arose a number of preconceptions which favoured labour-intensive development in cooperative forms, a certain indifference to costs, autarkic assumptions, and willingness to depend upon local initiative as well as central planning. Institutionally, the most interesting result of the border region experience (and one to which Ch'en Po-ta gave decisive significance in an analysis of Mao's ideas published on the eve of the Commune experiment) was the use of surplus rural labour through the mutual aid teams, which adumbrated the possibility of a gradualist approach to the collectivization of agriculture.

The period 1955–56, during which China was following the Soviet model of centralized material-balance planning, produced ideas which represent the second phase of development of the Maoist economic model. Two documents are important for this period: the *High Tide of Socialism in the Chinese Countryside* in which Mao put forward the ideas which were to be fully developed in the Great Leap Forward and the Communes, especially those ideas centred upon the mechanization and industrialization of the countryside, starting from the use of surplus labour and proceeding via an intermediate technology; and the *Ten Great Relationships* in which he expressed his views of the relationship between such things as consumption and accumulation, industry and agriculture, etc., views which are fundamental to his dynamic vision of the Chinese economy, seeing these contradictions as sources of mutual stimulus rather than as mere simple competition for given resources.

The condemnation of Stalin at the Twentieth Congress and the malaise in the Communist movement which followed and culminated in the Hungarian rising, a malaise echoed in minor ways within China, both posed new problems and provided (in the end) a new freedom to experiment. In his speech on *How to Handle Contradictions Among the People*, Mao gave his interpretation of the political problems of the socialist states. This speech became the main text for the changes which soon followed, when in 1958 the Great Leap Forward and the Commune movement were launched. But to understand these major departures from orthodoxy, all three of these sources must be related: *How to Handle Contradictions* described and interpreted the conflicts of interest in Chinese socialist society; the *Ten Great Relationships* provided an economic theory on the basis of which these contradictions among the people could be transcended; and the *High Tide of Socialism* suggested the practical policies which could put the economic theory into operation. It is interesting and significant that these documents appeared chronologically in precisely the reverse of the order suggested here. The practical possibilities were expressed first; the pattern of economic relationships second; and the theoretical statement of social conflict appeared last.

The subsequent events of 1958 are not represented in Maoist writing as an application of theory from above, however much weight the ideas and influence of Mao himself are given. On the contrary, they are represented as a consequence of a mass movement, 'guided but free'. The current Chinese historical explanation of the events of 1958 is that the rectification campaign of 1957 gave the masses an opportunity to express their condemnation both of bureaucratism in the Party, and of the 'rightists' who had offered inappropriate social-democratic solutions to the problem of bureaucratism; and with the knowledge gained from, and the confidence engendered by, the rectification movement and the anti-rightist struggle, the masses swept on to create their own mass-line alternative to both bureaucratism *and* bourgeois parliamentarianism, in the Great Leap institutionalized in the Communes. Whatever the precise relationship of spontaneity and popular enthusiasm on the one hand, and planning and political pressure on the other, there is no doubt that the rationale of the Great Leap period (ignoring for the moment the haste and crudity of application) expressed very fully the economic ideas which Mao had been developing in the preceding three years.

The latest stage of development, still rather obscure, is represented by the Great Proletarian Cultural Revolution, during which the attack on Liu Shao-ch'i and his associates was carried on very much in terms of an emphatic defence of the Commune idea and the Great Leap view of economic development, and there are now signs that if the Maoist victory is consolidated, policies representing a development of, and perhaps a refinement of, the ideas of 1958 will be restored, as the use of the Ta Chai Production Brigade and the Ta Ch'ing Oilfield as examples strongly suggests.

The Ten Great Relationships

This is a speech said to have been made by Mao Tse-tung in April 1956 at the end of two months discussion of economic problems by the Politburo. A text said to be based on notes taken at the meeting was published in the course of the Cultural Revolution; its publishers claimed that Mao had authorized publication, but was not himself satisfied with the ideas expressed and sought comment from party committees at all levels. The relationships are listed as follows between:

1. Industry and agriculture and between heavy and light industries
2. Coastal and inland industries
3. Economic and defence construction
4. The state and the productive units and individual producers
5. The centre and the regions
6. Han and other nationalities
7. The Party and others
8. Revolution and counter-revolution
9. Right and wrong
10. China and other countries.

Five of these relationships are economic or have direct economic implications (1–5), and it is these which concern us. They do not, however, exhaust the relationships with which Mao's economic comments have dealt. Franz Schurman suggested others between:

1. Select and simultaneous development
2. Long term planning and short term planning
3. Large scale industry and medium and small scale industry
4. Production and consumption
5. Production and accumulation
6. Accumulation and consumption
7. Capital-intensive and labour-intensive
8. Centralism and democracy
9. Centralization and decentralization
10. Material incentives and ideology
11. Individual rewards and collective rewards
12. Wages and distribution.

Let us look at the most important of these relationships as Mao and his supporters see them.

Intersectoral relationships: *industry and agriculture, heavy industry and light industry*. In the *Ten Great Relationships* Mao.

while first insisting that heavy industries are 'the centre of gravity' (an emphasis never changed although formulated in different metaphors from time to time, to indicate changing relationships with other sectors), goes on to emphasize that stress upon heavy industry can be excessive. 'We have not repeated the mistakes of some socialist countries which attached excessive importance to heavy industries at the expense of light industries and agriculture . . . unlike the market situation in some countries immediately after the revolution, goods in our markets have been more plentiful . . . (and) their prices are stable. This is not to say that no problems remain. There *are* problems – e.g. greater attention to light industries and agriculture than before, and adequate readjustment of the rates of investment . . . to give a comparatively greater weight to investment in light industries and agriculture.'

Will this change shift the centre of gravity? It will not be shifted. . . . The result will be a more extensive and better development of heavy industries, of the production of the means of production.

The more the output of daily necessities, the more the accumulation of capital . . . light industries and agriculture can accumulate more capital and faster. . . . If you really want heavy industries badly, you should invest more in light industries. . .

As to agriculture, the experience of some socialist countries has proved that bad management could fail to raise production even after collectivization. . . . They put too heavy a tax burden on the peasants, and they lowered agricultural prices in terms of industrial prices. . . .

The relationship between the state and productive units and individual producers. In the course of this section, Mao carries his argument about agricultural taxes and prices further.

Our method of accumulating state capital is through taxation, not through the manipulation of the price mechanism. In our country, exchange between industrial and agricultural goods must follow a policy of minimizing the differential between (industrial and agricultural) labour. . . . Our policies with regard to industrial goods are a low rate of profit, greater sales, and stable prices. . . .

As to the peasants, we have always maintained good relations with them. However, on the question of grain we have made a mistake. In 1954 output dropped because of floods, but we bought 70 million more catties of grain. . . . The peasants became disgruntled. . . . And we discovered our mistake. So in 1955 we bought 70 million catties less (*sic*) and arranged the 'Three Stabilizations'. . . . The disgruntled ones calmed down. . .

Any inadequacy, any neglect of the peasants' welfare, will result in a failure of the collective economy. . . . Unless under severe conditions of natural disaster, we must as far as agricultural production allows see to it that the peasant's income is higher than that of the previous year.

Relationships with the Centre. Perhaps the most critical of such relationships in China was not between the central government or ministries and the regions, but the industrial relationship between the developed centres of industry on the coast, and the relatively underdeveloped hinterland. Mao, typically, repudiates the simple either/or view of this situation, and sees the continued development of coastal industry as a condition of successful industrial development elsewhere:

We are in favour of developing our inland industries. The question is whether we are sincere or not. If you are sincere, not just pretending to be so, *you must make fuller use of the coastal industries and build more coastal industries, especially light ones*. . . . Our long term plan shows that we need 400,000 more technical cadres. These can be trained among the workers and technical cadres in the coastal industries. . .

The coastal industries have a high technical standard. . . . Their development can lead to a higher technical standard and better quality goods in all industries throughout the country.

On the question of central administrative control, Mao has this to say:

Judging by the present situation . . . it is necessary to expand the power of the regions. It is detrimental to socialist construction if regional power is too small. . . . At present there are dozens of hands interfering with local administration, making things difficult for the region. . . . *We must promote a consultative style of work with the regions*. . . . Everything must go through the process of consultation with the regions before an order is issued. . .

For the development of regional enthusiasm, *each region must have its individuality congenial to its local conditions, which is at the same time conducive to the interests of the totality*. . . . The provinces and municipalities have quite a few views concerning the departments of the Centre, and these should be expressed. Likewise, regions, countries, districts, and villages have their views. . . . to which the provinces and municipalities should listen. . . . All things have their common and their individual characters . . . *every productive unit or individual must have its initiative and its individual character which are coordinated with the common character.* . . . It would be bad if we centralized everything . . . (and) left the productive units with no initiative at all. . . .

Mao's speech was brief and laconic, but the germs of his economic theories are obvious here. If one had to sum up in a single phrase the impression which the *Ten Great Relationships* makes upon the reader, as far as its economic content is concerned, one might say that Mao rejects simple, static, arithmetical, either/or views of the economy, and perceives that economic relationships both sectoral and geographical are sufficiently complex to demand (a) simultaneous development through (b) the encouragement of local initiative (c) in market conditions which preserve a sufficiently high level of material incentives even if these (d) operate mainly through enterprises and collectives rather than through individuals. These ideas were fully developed in the literature of the period of the Great Leap Forward.

The high tide of socialism in the Chinese countryside

This collection of descriptions of cooperative and collective farms, whose themes included the illustration of Mao's argument that collectivization could and should precede the mechanization of agriculture in China, was published in late 1955. It is of particular interest in that it develops, though mainly by implication, Mao's view of the process of agricultural and rural development starting from the use of surplus rural labour to replace scarce capital.

Nurkse's classical statement of 'The Saving Potential Concealed in Rural Underemployment' was published in 1958 – the year of the Chinese Communes. But Mao had already begun to act on assumptions similar to those of Nurkse in 1955. Nurkse's argument may be summarized as follows:

The 'unproductive' surplus labourers on the land are sustained by the productive labourers. . . . If the productive peasants were to send their useless dependants . . . to work on capital projects and if they continued to feed them there, then their virtual saving would become effective saving. . . . There is in principle no necessity for either group of people to tighten their belts. . . . Some economists maintain that disguised unemployment on the land is only a seasonal phenomenon. . . . This is undoubtedly true in some countries. . . . (Even so) the question of making productive use of it still arises.

The labour-intensive construction of the border regions had impressed Mao with the possibilities of substituting labour for capital, and the cooperative use of labour for agricultural construction played a key part in persuading Chinese peasants of the advantages of cooperative farming between 1951 and 1956.

The problems involved were pointed out by Nurkse as well as the opportunities. As well as the seasonal nature of much rural unemployment, he pointed to three sources of leakage which could prevent the use of surplus labour from being self-financing: the peasants who remain on the farms may eat more when their dependants are absent; the construction workers may consume more when working harder than is usual for the season concerned; and some investment in simple tools will be needed.

The Maoist technique for the use of surplus labour gets over most of the disadvantages. First, the labour is normally employed locally, so that the construction force lives and eats at home; if not, it takes its rations with it. Second, because it is employed locally, this labour remains available for farming at the busy seasons. Third, the association of middle peasants with poor peasants in the cooperatives ensures the availability of simple tools, some animal power, and some savings to invest. Fourth, construction is so phased as to eliminate a significant gestation period – work done in the winter is designed to increase income from the subsequent harvest. The early cooperative farms in China, as described in the *High Tide*, were in a sense community development units pledged to an agreed year by year plan of development based on the use of middle-peasant resources to put surplus labour to work.

The idea of exploiting 'disguised unemployment' has been much disputed by economists. The crux of the disputes is the question, essentially, of how one measures 'disguised unemployment'. Myrdal in *Asian Drama* points out that the attempt to measure disguised unemployment is futile except in the context of a given set of proposed policies; and that existing working habits and leisure preferences may falsify assumptions derived elsewhere. Mao parallels Myrdal's thinking here when he refutes those in China who are pessimistic about the possibilities of the use of surplus labour, by proposing to employ this labour in the context of systematic mutually-agreed plans and in the perspective of new hopes and possibilities.

In reply to those who insisted that collectivization was irrelevant and even harmful in conditions of labour surplus, he replied:

In the past it was widely believed that the Agricultural Producers' Co-operatives would intensify the problem of surplus labour. Actual conditions have disproved this. If some APCs still have a surplus, this is because they have not yet broadened the scale and content of their production or used their labour in a sufficiently intensive way. This process is only in its infancy, and will go on indefinitely; agricultural production will be multiplied beyond what at present can be imagined. Industrial development will be even further beyond our power to imagine; and science, culture, education, public health, etc. will all have a comparable development.

An examination of the production plans of the APCs described in the *High Tide* shows the first stages of the process which Mao anticipated. It is clear that any successful use of surplus labour in agricultural construction or in successful development of auxiliary occupations would quickly cut down the labour surplus by creating new demands for routine labour – reclamation would increase the cultivated area, and irrigation and subsequent multiple cropping would sharply increase the demand for labour. An effort to farm the existing arable more intensively could absorb much labour power at the same time. Thus successful labour-intensive operations were expected quickly to produce a labour shortage and a demand for simple labour-saving machinery. At the same time, properly handled, the increased income accruing to the cooperative from its use of surplus labour could provide the capital for such simple forms of semi-mechanization. This in turn could release labour for further construction, but with greater mechanical help. Both the demand for the means of procuring new tools and machines would spiral; and this to Mao was the natural, economical, and proper course for agricultural mechanization and the diversification and development of the rural economy. This was, too, an essential stimulus for the development of heavy industry, always provided heavy industry was geared to serving agriculture's real needs. At the same time, rural economic diversification would increase the supply of consumer goods and provide its own incentives for development, which would again be eventually reflected in demands made upon heavy industry.

This last point brings us, via the *Ten Great Relationships*, to another significant aspect of Mao's economic thinking. In considering the question of capital formation, he does not think in terms merely of the *supply* of capital, but of the *demand* side of the problem: that capital cannot be effectively mobilized unless an effective demand for its products exists. This is another theme very familiar in western literature on the developing economies, but much less obvious in Communist economic writing. Hence his paradox that the quickest way to develop heavy industry fully is to give adequate scope for the development of light industry and of agriculture – which are the consumers of producers' goods.

How to handle contradictions among the people

The Hungarian rising and other similar events in 1956 in China and in the Communist bloc led Mao to think systematically about the political aspects of the processes of social change and economic development which China had undertaken. The signs of serious discontent with Communist regimes were too great to ignore; they had to be explained and the discontent dealt with. Mao rationalized these discontents in terms of a theory of contradictions among the people in a socialist state, including contradictions between the people and the administration. The contradiction with which he was most concerned was one upon which he had already touched in the *Ten Great Relationships*: that between the State, the productive unit (primarily the collective), and the individual. He clearly thought primarily of the peasant majority in this respect. The individual peasant is pulled between the desire to increase his personal income, and the desire of the collective to maximize its accumulation; the collective is pulled between the desire to maximize its own income and the desire of the state to maximize capital formation. Mao expressed the belief that the interests of individual, collective, and state were in the last analysis the same; hence the contradiction was not antagonistic. What made it difficult to solve was that bureaucratic organization and decision-making obscured the realities from the people.

His solution was to minimize bureaucratic responsibilities – to limit taxation and procurement in order to leave most of the profits of increased production in the hands of the collectives so that they could take responsibility themselves for the development of local industry. The land tax was in fact raised slightly (about 4·75 per cent) in 1958, and procurement norms were reduced to chaos by the agricultural disasters of 1959–61. But whether or not Mao's policy was ever applied, and to whatever extent, it is clear that this financial concession (combined with measures to raise peasant incomes relative to workers' incomes) was intended as the basis of the development of local small-scale industry and of agricultural construction during the Great Leap Forward.

The Maoist model in the Great Leap Forward

In the literature of the Great Leap Forward, Maoist economic ideas were elaborated at considerable length, although they were never (so far as the present author is aware) brought together into a single systematic argument. What follows is an attempt to outline what that single systematic argument might have been.

A systematization of Maoist economics

1. The major premise of Maoist economics is that economic laws express not only objective conditions, but human response to these conditions.

2. The quality of human response to economic circumstances can be improved by education and experience.

3. Economic analysis can be meaningful only if it takes place in relation to defined aims.

4. If the human response is to be effective these aims must represent the aspirations of the majority.

5. Given these conditions, constraints represented by the scarcity

of resources will seldom be so tight as to leave no room for effective manoeuvre towards economic growth.

6. To call forth the necessary responses at a low level of income, of security, and of accumulation, requires *both* an increase of personal income year by year *and* the encouragement of savings through education in the possibilities of modern technology and large-scale social organization, education which must in this case be largely through participation.

7. In so far as the human response is dependent upon historical conditioning, social and psychological obstacles can be a major factor in inhibiting economic growth: 'cultural revolution' in one form or another is a necessary part of the economic process. Superstructural means must be used to change the social and intellectual climate in relation to newly emerging economic possibilities.

8. As far as institutions are concerned, it follows that centralized economic decision-making can play only a limited and imperfect role in stimulating economic growth.

9. Given an appropriate social and intellectual climate and the provision of adequate incentives, local communities can respond to discover local resources and exploit them for economic development and for the provision of local social overheads. Many of these resources are beyond the capacity of the central government to identify, mobilize, and employ: natural resources because they may be too scattered; savings because they may not even exist until brought into existence by the will of the local community, in response to a shared view of new possibilities; labour because it too may not exist except in terms of an agreed plan of development which offers both a more rational use of labour and the incentives for intensified work.

10. At Chinese economic levels, local development must almost always lean heavily in the first stages upon labour-intensive operations. If these are to be self-financing, and if they are to result in effective savings for further development, a collective organization is necessary. The necessary freedom of economic decision is given therefore not to individuals but to communities and collectives.

11. Given an effective degree of positive human response in the necessary minimum conditions of freedom, economic development does not depend upon the arithmetical apportionment of known resources, but upon the calling forth of latent resources. This immediately transforms the relationships among economic sectors and geographical areas, and yields the possibility of dynamic mutual stimulus in place of competition.

12. In these circumstances, the role of planning is not to aim at equilibrium, but to exploit and control the stimulating imbalances which emerge from the exploitation of new resources in free conditions.

13. On this view of economic growth, simultaneous as opposed to select development is not only possible but necessary.

14. As local small-scale development must play such a major role in economic growth, planners and economists must turn their attention to providing the necessary conditions for local growth, changing the relationships among sectors, providing the necessary modern backbone for an intermediate technology, providing a cadre of technical advisers, skilled workers, and literate administrators, and generally bringing the resources of the developed cities into as close and effective a relationship with local communities as is possible.

15. In an economy geared to local development, the choice of techniques becomes a vital problem which must be solved by each community (with such expert advice as is available) in terms of its own local resources and conditions including the availability of resources, labour and capital, taking transport conditions into consideration, and reflecting the community's own sense of its present needs and capacities.

16. The economic demands of the state remain an important charge upon collective incomes, but these demands must be so limited as to leave in the hands of the collectives and communities the means for self-development. Taxation, procurement, and price policies must stimulate and not inhibit local development.

We are now in a position to look at this concept of economic development in terms of discussions of actual policies, as represented by the Great Leap Forward and the Commune Movement of 1958.

The actual pressing problems which faced Chinese planners and policy-makers in 1958 (the first year, officially, of the second five-year plan) were as follows:

1. The very rapid pace of industrial growth, as compared with the slower growth of agriculture, made it obvious that the brisk pace of industrial development could not be maintained without a rapid expansion of agricultural supplies.

2. The size and rate of growth of the population caused problems of feeding and employing an ever larger population, and threatened to minimize both accumulation and increasing *per capita* consumption.

3. Committed to a policy of low agricultural taxes, moderate procurement, and prices favouring agriculture, the main area which gave room for manoeuvre was that represented by grain-deficient villages, whose needs drastically reduced the food surplus available for industrialization. Policy therefore aimed in the first place at raising grain-deficient areas to a state of self-sufficiency.

4. Rising incomes meant a rise in purchasing power and a demand for more consumer goods; but there were limits to the availability of both capital and raw materials for these. It was hoped that local industry using local resources (often substitute materials) and savings could fill the gap between supplies of consumers' goods and rising purchasing power, prevent inflation, and increase the flow of goods necessary to maintain incentives. This was especially critical in 1958 as a rise in peasant incomes, relative to town incomes, had been decided upon. State investment as opposed to local investment in light industries was actually cut relative to investment in heavy industry and agriculture, for lack of raw materials.

In all these respects, it was local and rural development which was necessary. Mao Tse-tung's interest in such development, though it led to theory which went far beyond the mere negative solution of these problems, undoubtedly began from a consideration of them. They were not new, but had been the subject of concern, study, and experiment since 1953.

There is one other side of the period 1957–58 to which attention must be drawn: its political aspect. The 'rightists' had criticized not only the Communist Party's monopoly of political power, but their policies and the results of their policies. In this respect, these critics had generally taken an orthodox position with rather pessimistic implications. The launching of the Great Leap and the Commune Movement was very much a reply to such critics, who clearly had support for their views among the techno-crats and the planners. At the same time, the left-wing critics had attacked the party/state hierarchy as forming an obstacle to rapid change and to the direct and effective expression of mass aspirations. The events of 1958 were a reply to these left-wing critics also.

A full economic analysis of the Great Leap has never been made. Current western opinions concerning it are based on little except the criticisms made of it by the more conservative wing of the Chinese party after the Lushan Plenum, and upon the more extreme statements and actions of the time. It is true that haste and naïveté prejudiced the implementation of policy; and that, ironically, the willingness of cadres to take centrally-issued recommendations literally, regardless of local conditions, often made nonsense of a movement which was explicitly supposed to take advantage of these local conditions. But the results of the Great Leap were not negligible; and even if it was ill-done, it was not necessarily ill-conceived.

The crux of the Great Leap was not the backyard blast furnace run by uninstructed peasants. The crux of policy was precisely to bring China's newly acquired industrial strength and technical sophistication to the assistance of the local communities for the development of agriculture and the diversification of the rural economy, with the aims which our brief outline of Mao's econ-omic ideas has suggested. The new provincial steelworks and other provincial industrial establishments were given autonomy, and encouraged to develop appropriate branches in the special administrative districts, at which level the technical capacities of modern industry could be brought into contact with *hsien*-level small-scale enterprise using surplus and off-season agricultural labour on a short-term contract system, which would introduce large masses of peasants to modern technology.

Nor was the Leap based at first upon extravagantly long working hours; it was strongly emphasized that its basis was the more rational use of labour, not longer hours or harder work. The intolerable hours and the military discipline, and all the rather sham heroics which went with them, developed later, and had no warrant in the theory of the movement.

It is with discipline and Party direction that one now associates the Leap; but along with this in many places went a real degree of economic autonomy and freedom of collective enterprise, with substantial opportunities for increased incomes through intercommunal trade and contract handicraft production ancillary to factory production.

In agriculture itself, there were two aims. The first was to replace dependence upon large expensive virgin-land schemes of reclamation with a campaign of small-scale local reclamation and extension of irrigation. The second was to set fully in motion the process of development from labour-surplus operations into a phase of semi-mechanization, based upon simple, versatile power units – usually a coal–gas engine or a small generator using a local source of power. The eventual results in both cases were substantial.

The Great Leap, however, did not have a long enough run to prove or disprove the value of the ideas which underlay it. Bad weather and bad organization produced a threat of chaos and disaster on a nationwide scale. Mao's ideas still remain to be tested; the Cultural Revolution was clearly a prelude to further (if more cautious) experiments on the same lines; and the immediate future may well see, as has been frequently indicated by Mao's supporters during the last three years, a 'new high tide of socialism' (the revitalization of the communes), a new 'great leap' (already said to be under way in some provinces), and an attempt at the final destruction of the 'three great differences' – between town and country, industry and agriculture, and mental and manual labour – whose disappearance is regarded as signifying the achievement of Maoist economic aims.

Further Reading

In English: for translations, dates refer to the English publication.

The socialist economy (Marxist literature)

N. Bukharin, E. Preobrazhensky, *The ABC of Communism*, London, 1922.

H. M. Christman (ed.), *Communism in Action – A Documentary History*, New York, 1969.

V. I. Lenin, *State and Revolution*, Moscow.

V. I. Lenin, *Question of the Socialist Organisation of the Economy– Selected papers*, Moscow.

K. Marx, *Critique to the Gotha Programme* English translation, Moscow, 1891.

The socialist economy (Western literature)

H. D. Dickinson, *Economics of Socialism*, Oxford, 1939.

M. H. Dobb, *On Economic Theory and Socialism – Collected Papers*, McGraw-Hill, 1955.

M. H. Dobb, *On Welfare Economics and the Economic Theory of Socialism*, Cambridge University Press, 1969.

R. Hall, *The Economic System in a Socialist State*, London, 1937.

F. A. von Hayek (ed.), *Collectivist Economic Planning*, London, 1935.

B. N. Ward, *The Socialist Economy, a Study of Organizational alternatives*, New York, 1967.

P. J. D. Wiles, *The Political Economy of Communism*, Blackwell, 1962.

J. G. Zielinski, *On the Theory of Socialist Planning*, Oxford University Press, 1968.

The Soviet economy

A. M. Baykov, *The Development of the Soviet Economic System*, Cambridge, 1948.

M. Bornstein, and D. R. Fusfeld, *The Soviet Economy – a Book of Readings*, 1970.

E. H. Carr, *The Bolshevik Revolution*, vol. 2, Penguin, 1952.

E. H. Carr, *Socialism in One Country*, 1924–26, vol. 1, London, 1958.

E. H. Carr, R. Davies, *Foundations of a Planned Economy*, 1926–29, London, 1959.

M. H. Dobb, *Soviet Economic Development since 1917*, Routledge & Kegan Paul, 1966.

F. D. Holzman (ed.), *Readings in the Soviet Economy*, 1962.

M. Kaser, *Soviet Economics* Oxford University Press, 1970.

A. Nove, *The Soviet Economy*, Allen & Unwin, 1970.

A. Nove, *An Economic History of the USSR*, Allen Lane the Penguin Press, 1968.

US Congress, Joint Economic Committee, *New Directions in the Soviet Economy*, Washington, 1966.

US Congress, Joint Economic Committee, *Soviet Economic Performance, 1966–7*, Washington, 1968.

Other socialist economies

Boorstein, *The Social and Economic Transformation of Cuba*, New York, 1968.

J. Horvat, *An Essay on Yugoslav Society*, New York, 1969.

M. Kaser, *Economic Development for Eastern Europe*, Macmillan, 1968.

J. M. Montias, *Central Planning in Poland*, Yale University Press, 1962.

J. M. Montias, *Economic Development in Communist Rumania*, MIT. Press 1968.

United Nations–Economic Commission for Europe, *Economic Survey of Europe 1965, Part II, Incomes in Postwar Europe*, Geneva, 1967.

US Congress, Joint Economic Committee, *Mainland China in the World Economy*, Washington, 1967.

Economic Reforms

M. H. Dobb, *Socialist Planning: Some Problems*, London, 1970.

G. R. Feiwel, *New Currents in Soviet-Type Economies: a Reader*, Scranton and London, 1968.

I. Friss (ed.), *Reform of the Economic Mechanism in Hungary*, Budapest, 1969.

M. Ellman, *Economic Reform in the Soviet Union*, PEP, 1969.

M. Ellman, *Soviet Planning Today*, Cambridge, 1971.

J. Kornai, *Overcentralisation in Economic Administration*, London, 1959.

O. Šik, *Plan and Market Under Socialism*, IASP, New York, 1967.

J. Wilczynski, *The Economics of Socialism*, London, 1970.

J. Wilczynski, *Socialist Economic Development and Reforms*, London, 1972.

Accumulation and economic growth

M. H. Dobb, *An Essay on Economic Growth and Planning*, Routledge & Kegan Paul, 1960.

A. Erlich, *The Soviet Industrialisation Debate, 1924–28*, Cambridge (Mass.), 1961.

M. Kalecki, *Selected Essays on the Economic Growth of the Socialist and the Mixed Economy*, Cambridge, 1972.

E. Preobrazhensky, *The New Economics*, Oxford University Press, 1965.

N. Spulber (ed.), *Foundations of Soviet Strategy for Economic Growth*, Indiana, 1964.

Planning techniques

Ames, *Soviet Economic Processes*, Homewood, 1965.

R. W. Davies, *The Development of the Soviet Budgetary System*, Cambridge University Press, 1958.

G. Garvy, *Money Banking and Credit in Eastern Europe*, New York, 1966.

G. Grossman (ed.), *Value and Plan*, California University Press, 1960.

G. Grossman (ed.), *Money and Plan*, California University Press, 1968.

F. D. Holzman, *Soviet Taxation*, Oxford University Press, 1955.

A. Nove, A. Zauberman (eds), *Problems of Economic Theory and Practice in Poland, Studies in the Theory of Reproduction and Prices*, Warsaw, 1964.

M. Rakowski (ed.), *Investment Efficiency*, Pergamon 1964.

Mathematical methods

J. P. Hardt, *et al.*, *Mathematics and Computers in Soviet Planning*, Yale University Press, 1967.

J. Kornai, *Mathematical Planning and Structural Decisions*, Amsterdam, 1967.

L. V. Kantorovich, *The Best Use of Economic Resources*, Pergamon, 1965.

V. V. Novozhilov, *Problems of Cost-Benefit Analysis in Optimal Planning*, New York, 1970.

K. Porwit, *Central Planning – Evaluation of Variants*, Pergamon, 1967.

A. Zauberman, *Aspects of Planometrics*, Yale, 1967.

Special areas

J. S. Berliner, *Factory and Manager in the USSR*, Cambridge (Mass.), 1957.

M. J. Broekmeyer (ed.), *Yugoslav Workers' Self Management*, Amsterdam, 1970.

D. Granick, *Management of the Industrial Firm in the USSR*, 1954.

D. Granick, *Soviet Metal-Fabricating and Economic Development*, University of Wisconsin Press, 1967.

P. Hanson, *The Soviet Consumer*, Macmillan, 1968.

M. McAuley, *Labour Disputes in Soviet Russia*, Oxford University Press, 1969.

E. Strauss, *Soviet Agriculture in Perspective*, Allen & Unwin, 1969.

International trade

A. A. Brown, E. Neuberger (eds), *International Trade and Central Planning, an Analysis of Economic Interactions*, University of California Press 1968.

M. Kaser, *Comecon*, Oxford University Press, 1967.

T. Kiss, *Economic Cooperation Among Socialist Countries*, New York, 1968.

H. Kohler, *Economic Integration in the Soviet Bloc*, Praeger, 1965.

J. Wilczynski, *The Economics and Politics of East–West Trade*, Macmillan, 1969.

P. J. D. Wiles, *Communist International Economics*, Blackwell, 1967.

Periodicals (in English)

ABSEES–Soviet and East European Abstracts
Czechoslovak Economic Papers
Current Digest of Soviet Press
Eastern European Economics
Economic Bulletin for Europe
Economic Survey of Europe
Economics of Planning

Jahrbuch der Wirtschaft Osteuropas (Yearbook of East-European Economics, in English and German).

Management Science and Operations Research in the USSR and Eastern Europe

Mathematical Studies in Economics and Statistics in the USSR and Eastern Europe

Problems of Communism

Problems of Economics

Slavic Studies

Soviet and East European Foreign Trade

Soviet Studies

Acknowledgements

Permission to reproduce the following readings in this volume is acknowledged to the following sources:

2 Routledge & Kegan Paul
3 Routledge & Kegan Paul
4 *The Review of Economic Studies*
5 *The Economic Journal* and Professor M. H. Dobb
6 The Clarendon Press
7 Oxford University Press
8 Macmillan Co.
9 Mrs A. Kalecki
10 American Economic Association and Dr J. M. Montias
11 Polish Scientific Publishers
12 Polish Scientific Publishers
13 Federal Reserve Bank of New York
14 The American Association for the Advancement of Slavic Studies
16 Professor Alec Nove
17 Soviet Studies
19 Cambridge University Press
21 Pergamon Press Ltd
23 Artisjus and J. Kornai
24 *L'Est* and Mr J. Grey

Author Index

Abramovitz, M., 160
Aleksandrov, A. B., 444
Ames, E., 291
Augustinovics, M., 371
Ausch, S., 239, 240, 344

Bachurin, A., 353
Balassa, B., 239
Barone, E., 11, 52, 68, 101, 401, 484
Bauer, O., 85, 86, 87
Bauer, R., 240
Belkin, V., 229, 240
Birman, A., 348
Bogachevskii, M. B., 296, 299, 301, 303
Böhm-Bawerk, E., 10, 83, 354
Boyarski, A., 352, 353, 381–2
Bródy, A., 229, 239
Brus, W., 13, 173, 177, 206, 375
Bukharin, N. I., 11, 12, 13, 32–40, 88
Burchardt, F., 151

Campbell, R. W., 246, 288
Cassel, G., 94, 160
Červený, A., 229, 239, 246
Chenery, H. B., 234
Cole, G. D. H., 97

Dantzig, G. B., 354, 481–2
Devons, E., 243–4
Dickinson, H. D., 104, 122
Dmitriev, V. K., 414
Dobb, M. H., 12, 113, 120, 375
Domar, E., 13, 149, 161
Dorp, E. C. van, 121

Duhring, E. K., 24

Efimov, A. N., 239, 240
Eidel'man, M. R., 226, 244
Elvin, M., 492
Engels, F., 10, 19–24, 82, 385, 386, 387, 388
Erlich, E., 161
Eucken, W., 247
Evans, W. D., 230, 234

Fedorenko, N. P., 348, 351, 352, 353, 354, 359
Fedorowicz, Z., 191
Feinstein, C., 401
Fel'dman, G. A., 13, 149–54, 157, 158, 159, 161, 162, 168, 170
Fisher, I., 169
Friss, I., 344, 360

Gal'perin, N., 243, 244
Garvy, G., 14, 275, 293
Gerchuk, Y. P., 469
Granick, D., 223, 244
Gray, J., 491
Grossman, G., 223, 234–5, 338

Hall, R. L., 113, 116
Harcourt, G. C., 10, 373
Harrod, R. F., 169
Hatt, S., 245
Hawtrey, R. G., 118
Hayek, F. A. von, 10, 52, 75, 97, 101, 103, 152, 160, 401, 484
Hejsek, J., 244
Hensel, K. P., 247

Herer, W., 203
Hicks, J. R., 152
Hirsch, H., 223, 247
Holzman, F., 291
Hutchison, T. W., 126

Ignatov, B., 152
Inkeles, A., 240

Johansen, L., 415

Kalecki, M., 13, 14, 121, 174, 175, 192–3, 196, 200, 202, 205, 213, 252, 254, 365
Kantorovich, L. V., 15, 348, 352, 353, 389, 435, 471, 472
Kaplan, N. M., 161, 233
Karpiński, A., 245
Karpov, P., 224, 243, 245
Kaser, M. C., 227, 291
Kautsky, K., 10
Keynes, J. M., 150, 153, 157, 158, 354
Khachaturov, T. S., 470
Khan, R. F., 123
Kluckhorn, C., 240
Knyziak, Z., 174
Koctúch, H., 364
Koldomasov, I. I., 227
Komárek, L., 360
Koopmans, T. C., 354, 375
Kornai, J., 15, 351, 473, 479
Kosygin, A. N., 10, 14, 319, 378, 380, 381, 388
Kovalevskii, N. A., 153
Križan, M., 245
Kronrod, J., 353
Kronsjö, T., 367
Krzekovska, E., 229
Kucharski, M., 191
Kuzminov, 353
Kuznets, S., 151

Lange, O., 12, 15, 92, 113, 114, 116, 120–28, 201, 205, 263, 264, 336, 339
Laplace, P. S., 474
Laski, K., 13, 173, 177
Lenin, V. I., 11, 12, 25–31, 86–9, 283, 324, 359, 378, 381, 462, 464, 465
Leontief, W., 157, 414, 453, 454
Lerner, A. P., 95, 101, 113, 114, 116, 117–18, 128
Liberman, E. G., 14, 309, 318, 348, 352, 359
Liptak, T., 351, 481
Lisichkin, G., 359
Lisikiewicz, J. J., 174
Lissowski, W., 173
Lorine, H. S., 223
Lowe, A., 151, 160
Lutz, F., 161
Lutz, V., 161
Luxemburg, R., 10

Mahalanobis, P. C., 154
Malinvaud, E., 231
Mao Tse-tung, 491–510
Marshall, A., 103, 169, 354
Marx, K., 10, 19–24, 25, 65, 82–4, 109, 131, 145, 150–54, 352, 386, 387, 388, 462, 464
Merrett, A. J., 363, 372
Millikan, M., 161
Minc, B., 182
Mises, L. von, 12, 75, 85–6
Mlynarski, F., 191
Montias, J. M., 13, 223, 291
Morgenstern, O., 231
Morishma, M., 417
Myrdal, G., 502–3

Nemchinov, V. S., 15, 340, 394, 396, 406
Neuberger, E., 371

Neumann, J. von, 354
Neurath, O., 79, 89
Nove, A., 14, 252, 335
Novozhilov, V. V., 15, 348, 378, 382, 395
Nurkse, R., 151, 501
Nuti, D. M., 14, 363, 367

Orthaber, A., 237
Oyrzanowski, B., 191, 291

Pajestka, J., 173, 184
Pareto, V., 72, 107, 401
Parker, R. H., 10
Petrakov, N., 348
Piaszczynski, W., 371
Pigou, A. C., 96, 114, 126, 152
Piklikiewicz, H., 238
Pohl, O., 291
Polaczek, S., 182
Porwit, K., 205, 229, 231, 236, 239
Preobrazhensky, E., 11, 12, 13, 32–40, 130, 135, 150

Rakowski, M., 14, 205, 252, 253, 365
Riabushkin, T. V., 238–9
Ricardo, D., 386
Riha, L., 364
Robbins, L., 10, 12, 16, 103, 401
Robinson, E. A. G., 173
Robinson, J., 14, 150, 158, 263
Rolów, A., 241
Roosa, R. V., 290

Sadowski, W., 178, 205
Samuelson, P. A., 169
Savkin, A., 243
Schöhen, H., 229

Schurman, F., 498
Seton, F., 417
Shenger, I. E., 289
Sik, O., 352, 360
Sitnin, N., 353
Šrein, Z., 366
Stalin, J., 11, 13, 40–51
Stefánski, S., 244
Steindl, J., 402
Sulmicki, P., 182, 191, 205
Sweezy, P. M., 10, 150, 153
Sykes, A., 363, 372
Szybisz, B., 229

Tadra, O., 242
Taussig, F. W., 104
Taylor, F. M., 92, 102
Tinbergen, J., 354
Trotsky, L., 10, 12
Trzeciakowski, W., 205, 371
Tsuru, S., 150

Usoskin, M. M., 299

Vácha, J., 229, 239
van Dorp, E. C. see Dorp, E. C. van
Veinshtein, A. L., 15, 469
Vikentyev, A., 353
Volin, P., 347–8, 360
Von Hayek, F. A. see Hayek, E.C. von
von Mises, L. see Mises, L. von

Walras, L., 265, 267, 268, 271, 401, 403
Watanabe, T., 234
Webb, B., 109
Webb, S., 109
Whitehead, A. N., 201
Whitin, T., 231

Wicksell, K., 101, 115
Wolfe, P., 481–2

Zalewski, K., 244, 245

Zassenhaus, H., 109
Zauberman, A., 252, 412
Zieńkowski, L., 229
Zurkowski, J., 236, 239

Subject Index

ABC of Communism, 11, 32–40
Accounting prices, 102–4, 113
  applicability, 105–9
  balanced by taxes and social
      dividends, 123
  and capital, 120
  and investment, 118
Accounting rule, 98
Aggregation of coefficients, 230–31
Agricultural Producers'
    Cooperatives, China, 503
Agriculture
  land values, 386–7
  procurement prices, 433
  production, 189
Anti-Dühring, 24

Balances commodity, 238–48
  obstacles to, 242–6
  perspective balances, 225
  technological norms in, 242,
      248
Banks
  and credit, 279–81, 283
  credit loans, 137–9, 282
  Gosbank, 300
  and government policy, 289–92
  monobank, 284–8
  nationalization, 30–31, 85–6, 87,
      283
  redistribution of national
      income, 138–9
  sources of funds, 286–7
Budgets, 276–7, 293–5

Capital
  and accounting prices, 120
  accumulation, 94, 130–48
  equilibrium price of, 119
  goods, 151–2
  interest rate, 100–101
  issue of paper money, 135–6
  and prices, 54–5
  production, 52–74
  saturation, 120
  and saving, 58–9, 67–70
  state loans, 134–5
  taxation, 134
  trade exchange, 140–44
Cash Plan, 302–5
Central Planning Boards, 12
  and accounting prices, 105–9
  and capital accumulation, 101
  and consumers, 94
  marginal costs, 95–7, 114
  parametric function of prices,
      101–2, 106
  and prices, 96–9, 103
  and production, 105–6
  scale of preferences, 105, 108,
      109
  trial and error economics, 104–6
China
  communes, 491, 496–7, 501
  compared with the Soviet Union,
      491
  history, 495
  Maoist analysis, 493–5
  rural socialism, 501–4
  use of surplus labour, 502–3
  see also Great Leap Forward
Cobb-Douglas function, 173–4
Collectivism, 45, 56–7, 341
COMECON countries, 343–4

Commodities
  exchange, 81
  production, 43–6, 213
Commodity–money mechanism, 341
Communes, 88–9
  China, 491, 496–7, 501
Communism
  and administration, 36–7
  and industrialization, 25–6, 35
  and labour, 25
  Lenin's theory of, 26–7
  Marx's theory of, 25
  and production, 28–9
  and property, 19–21
  and revolution, 29
Communist Manifesto 1873, 19–21
Communist Party of the Soviet
    Union, 378, 383, 387
Computers
  and economic equilibrium, 401
  and the market, 402–5
  see also Programming models
Consumption
  and economic growth, 179–86
  growth, 162–8
  and investment, 180
  planning, 263–74
    payroll tax, 266–8
    price-fixing, 265
    savings, 268–70
    self-regulating market, 264–5
Cost-accounting system, 324–8
Credit
  and banks, 279–81, 283
  loans, 137–9, 282
  for capital investment, 326–7
  and monetary systems, 279–81,
    283
  monobank, 284–8
  State Banks, 295–305
  Soviet Union, 137–9
Credit Plan

  long-term, 298–300
  short-term, 295–8
Czechoslovakia
  financial plan, 294
  incentive payments, 355, 356–7
  investment, 363–76
    reforms, 367–71
  Planning Board, 244–5
  Planning Commission, 224, 232,
    238

Dantzig-Wolfe method, 481–2
Discounted cash flow methods,
    372–3
Discount function, 168–70
Distribution, 34–6, 75, 76

Economic growth
  and consumption, 179–86
    investment, 180, 215
  and foreign trade, 202–4
  in gross national income, 173–4
  Hungary and Soviet Union
    compared, 347–9, 357
  and non-investment factors,
    186–9
  and technical progress, 192–
    200
    consumption, 196–9
  variability of growth rate, 178–9
*Economics of the Transition
    Period*, 11
Employment-multiplier, 119
Equilibrium
  and computers, 401–3
  objective, 93, 97–9
  and parametric function of
    prices, 101–2
  and planning, 278–9
  subjective, 93–7
Equivalence
  between goods and services, 57,
    60

Extrapolation, 231

Foreign trade price multipliers, 343–4
Funded products, 225

Gauss–Seidel method, 233
Glavki, 225, 372
Gosbank, 300, 304
Gosplan, 226–7
  growth model, 13, 149–53
Gossnab, 370
Gotha Programme 1891, 22–4
Great Leap Forward, 491, 496–7, 501
  Maoist model, 505–10

Hungary
  economic growth, 340–47
    compared with the Soviet Union, 347–9, 360
  industrial management, 346–7
  National Planning Board, 47, 482, 485
  Price Control Board, 485
  price-fixing, 342, 344
  programming models, 475–88
  State Budget, 345
  trade, 343

Incentives, 310–14, 325
  workers', 329–32
Income distribution, 93
  and investment, 159–62, 216
Industrial management, 319–34
  Hungary, 346–7
  labour indices, 320–21
  production costs index, 320
  production standards, 322–3
  profit assignments, 320
  quality of produce, 319, 322
  reform, 378
    State standards, 322
    workers' incentives, 329–32
Industrial structure
  and national income, 218–22
Industry
  demand determined, 217
  and price policy, 144–7
  scale of output, 95–6
Inflation, 190–91
Input–output analysis, 228–38
  aggregation, 230–31
  extrapolation, 231
  Leontief matrices, 228, 230, 451–4
  more efficient routing, 232–8
Interest rate
  and amount of capital, 100
  as a control, 115
Investment
  and accounting prices, 118
  centrally planned, 126, 128
  coefficients, 366–7
  and consumption, 180–86
  efficiency, 252–62, 271–2
    freeze of outlays, 254–6, 364
    plant durability, 256–9
    plant output and cost, 259–62
  and employment, 123
  growth, 154–9, 215
  and income, 159–62, 216
  indices, 368–71
  and industrial profits, 119
  rate, 115–6, 175–7
  recoupment period, 363–5, 373
  and saving, 120
Iteration process, 232–8, 374

Khleboprodukt, 140
Kulaks, 134

Labour
  Communist view of, 25
  costs, 382–5, 389

Labour—*continued*
  indices, 320–21
  Marx's view, 22–4
  organization and control, 26–7
  and output, 117
  productive, 24
  social division of, 408–11
  socially necessary labour
    expenditure, 382–5, 387–8
  supply, 220
  surplus labour, 502–503
Leontief matrices, 228, 230,
    451–4

Mao Tse-tung
  analysis, 493–5
  rural socialism, 501–4
  surplus labour, 502–4
  Ten great relationships, 496–501
  see also Great Leap Forward
Marginal costs, 95–7, 114
  and marginal proceeds, 267
  and prices, 115, 384–6
'Market socialism', 351–2
Marxism
  laws of science, 40
  and marginal costs, 386–7
  and mathematical symbolism,
    462
  socially necessary labour, 344
  value theory, 15, 65
Mathematical models *see*
    Programming models
Ministry of Production, *see*
    Production, Ministry of
Monetary policy
  currency circulation, 300–
    302
  and financial plans, 288–300
Monetary systems, 37–40
  and credit, 279–81, 283
  liquidity, 281–3
Monobank, 284–8

National Coal Trust, 95
Nationalization of banks, 30–31
New Economic Policy, Soviet
    Union, 11, 12, 381

Objectively determined valu-
    ations, 466–7
Optimal planning theory, 348–53
  dynamic problem, 456–9
  economic analysis, 461–8
  industrial planning, 445–51
  input–output matrices, 451–3
  mathematical models, 389–90
  mathematical variants, 473
  national economy, 469–74
  and price systems, 381–2
  programme allocation, 435–45
  and rail transport, 470–71
  and resources, 380–81, 384
  and transport, 454–6
  valuations, 459–61
Output, 94–6
  planning, 309–17
    and Economic Councils, 313
    and incentives, 310–14

Paper money, 135–6
Planning
  and equilibrium, 278–9
  output, 309–17
    and incentives, 310–14
  perspective plan, 213–22
    growth rate, 214
  production plans, 323
  see also Optimal planning
Planning Commissions, 224, 232,
    238
  Czechoslovakia, 360
  Poland, 14, 231, 236
  Soviet Union, 226
Plant
  construction, 118
  durability, 256–9